The KENNEDYS

Mary Loretta
Kennedy
b. *6 Aug. 1892*
d. *18 Nov. 1972*

m. *12 Oct. 1927*

George William
Connelly
b. *10 June 1898*
d. *29 Aug. 1971*

Margaret Louise
Kennedy
b. *22 Oct. 1898*
d. *14 Nov. 1974*

m. *14 June 1924*

Charles Joseph
Burke
b. *23 Aug. 1899*
d. *5 Apr. 1967*

Robert Francis
Kennedy
b. *20 Nov. 1925*
d. *6 June 1968*

m. *17 June 1950*

Ethel Skakel
b. *11 Apr. 1928*

Jean Ann
Kennedy
b. *20 Feb. 1928*

m. *19 May 1956*

Stephen E.
Smith
b. *24 Sept. 1927*

Edward Moore
Kennedy
b. *22 Feb. 1932*

m. *29 Nov. 1958*

Virginia Joan
Bennett
b. *9 Sept. 1936*

Stephen Edward
Smith, Jr.
b. *28 June 1957*

William Kennedy
Smith
b. *4 Sept. 1960*

Amanda Mary
Smith
b. *30 Apr. 1967*
(adopted)

Kym Maria
Smith
b. *29 Nov. 1972*
(adopted)

Kara Anne
Kennedy
b. *27 Feb. 1960*

Edward Moore
Kennedy, Jr.
b. *26 Sept. 1961*

Patrick Joseph
Kennedy
b. *14 July 1967*

Robert Francis
Kennedy, Jr.
b. *17 Jan. 1954*

m. *3 Apr. 1982*

Emily Ruth
Black
b. *15 Oct. 1957*

David Anthony
Kennedy
b. *15 June 1955*
d. *25 Aug. 1984*

Mary Courtney
Kennedy
b. *9 Sept. 1956*

m. *14 June 1980*

Jeffrey Ruhe
b. *21 Feb. 1952*

Michael
Le Moyne
Kennedy
b. *27 Feb. 1958*

m. *14 Mar. 1981*

Victoria Gifford
b. *20 Feb. 1957*

Mary Kerry
Kennedy
b. *8 Sept. 1959*

Matthew Maxwell
Taylor Kennedy
b. *11 Jan. 1965*

Rory Elizabeth
Katherine
Kennedy
b. *12 Dec. 1968*

Christopher
George
Kennedy
b. *4 July 1963*

Douglas Harriman
Kennedy
b. *24 Mar. 1967*

Robert Francis
Kennedy, III
b. *2 Sept. 1984*

Michael
Le Moyne
Kennedy, Jr.
b. *9 Jan. 1980*

Kyle Frances
Kennedy
b. *6 July 1984*

The KENNEDYS

A WORLD ALMANAC BOOK

The KENNEDYS

A Chronological History
1823–Present

HARVEY RACHLIN

WORLD ALMANAC
AN IMPRINT OF PHAROS BOOKS • A SCRIPPS HOWARD COMPANY
NEW YORK

First published in 1986

Distributed in the United States by
Ballantine Books, a division of Random House, Inc.
and in Canada by Random House of Canada, Ltd.
Library of Congress Catalog Card Number: 86-50159
Pharos Books ISBN: 0-88687-261-8
Ballantine Books ISBN: 0-345-33729-8

Printed in the United States of America
World Almanac
An Imprint of Pharos Books
A Scripps Howard Company

200 Park Avenue
New York, NY 10166-0206

10 9 8 7 6 5 4 3 2 1

For Marla

PREFACE

January 6, 1986, marked the one hundredth anniversary of the Kennedy family's official service in politics. Patrick Joseph Kennedy, the founding father of what is arguably America's most remarkable political dynasty, entered public office on January 6, 1886, as a state representative of Massachusetts. Today his grandson, Edward M. Kennedy (who never saw his grandfather, as he was born after Patrick's death) continues the family's dedication to public service as a United States senator from Massachusetts. Members of the so-called new generation of Kennedys have already begun to pursue political office.

The ultimate destiny of the Kennedys of Ireland, Massachusetts, and America can only be revealed by time. But as the family continues to flourish through marriage, and as its younger members discover their heritage and tradition, it is more than probable that the ideals and visions of the now-ledgendary members of the family will continue to be fulfilled.

So much has been written about the Kennedys that we may well wonder what more there is to know about them. What else can be said? Yet there are always new facts to uncover, and for the Kennedy scholar or historian these may hold undisclosed significance. This book contains many such facts. It also presents the family history in a new chronological perspective. Finally, in a larger sense this book is also a celebration of the Kennedys' one hundred-plus years in public office as well as a commemoration of the family and its kin.

Many books about the Kennedys are intent on destroying or dispelling what their authors perceive as "myths" that have grown up about the family, propagated both internally and externally. Such purposes cloud our right to learn objectively about the family's contribution to American life. (Who cares that Joe Kennedy may have carried on a secret love affair? Or that Jack Kennedy may have had concealed adenoid disease?) What we should seek to understand is why the Kennedys have been, and remain, one of the focuses of our attention for so many generations. More than most in American political life, the Kennedys are inextricably linked to our culture and our heritage. It is this author's intention to present the facts accurately and comprehensively, which in themselves attest to the significant role of this unequivocally monumental family in the history of our republic.

ACKNOWLEDGMENTS

Part of the fascination in researching, writing, and publishing a work such as this is the people an author encounters during each stage of the process. Before beginning this project I could only hope that those I would meet might be patient and helpful. Happily, I was fortunate enough to find so many who encompassed those qualities, and more.

My first acknowledgment must be given to Beverly Jane Loo, my editor, to whom I owe a great debt, and without whom this work could not have come to fruition. Beverly's insight and recommendations gave my chronicle new depth; she reshaped a cumbersome manuscript and offered guidance that went far beyond the call of editorial duty to help create the final book.

Others at Pharos Books whom I would like to thank are publisher David Hendin and editor-in-chief Hana Lane for their support; Nancy Bumpus Eato, the talented art director; and Jo-Anne Volkers, editorial assistant, whose nimble fingers input thousands of words (and changes) into the Atex system.

Very special thanks go to the editors Cheryl Kupper and Nat LaMar for their fine sense of scholarship, language, and editorial style.

I also wish to thank my agent, Lynn Seligman.

There are two saints in Boston masquerading under the guise of human beings: Robert F. Hanan and John R. Cronin. Bob Hanan is chief of research of the Boston City Council, and his research skills and generosity are unearthly. He spent countless hours digging for information, particularly on the public service records of Patrick Kennedy and John "Honey Fitz" Fitzgerald. His research resulted in hundreds of pages of facts, which he pulled together and sent to me.

John R. Cronin, chief librarian of the *Boston Herald,* welcomed this complete stranger into the newspaper's archives, permitting unrestricted access to the paper's extensive files on the Kennedys and Fitzgeralds. Without Mr. Cronin's generous cooperation much of the information—especially on the very early years—would have been difficult to reconstruct. Enough cannot be said about the magnanimity of John R. Cronin.

Others of the *Herald* archive family who gave so much of their time are Rosella Kukjian, Rosann C. Tuttavilla, and Betsy Warrior.

For the historical information about Ireland, I am indebted to Professor Maurice R. O'Connell of the history department of Fordham University. Dr. O'Connell not only gave of his time but also searched out the information about the Kennedy farm in Dunganstown, Ireland, the details of which were provided by Dr. O'Connell's colleagues, Dr. Kevin Whelan, of the National Library of Ireland, and James Sutton, chairman of the New Rose Historical Society. Betty O'Connell also generously assisted in the gathering of these little-known facts about the Kennedy ancestors.

Invaluable assistance was provided by the outstanding staff of the John Fitzgerald Kennedy Library. Documents, papers, and other materials were supplied quickly and with courtesy. I would particularly like to single out the following individuals: Henry J. Gwiazda, the Robert F. Kennedy archivist who diligently researched and answered endless questions; Ronald E. Whealan, head librarian; Joan Carey, research librarian; Michael Desmond, research assistant; Allan B. Goodrich, supervisor of audiovisual archives, including the *Kennedy Family Collection*; James N. Cedrone, audiovisual archivist who, like Mr. Goodrich, was so very helpful in guiding me through thousands of Kennedy photographs; and Megan Floyd Desnoyers, supervisory archivist, who answered my many questions and shared with me the amusing queries she has received about the Kennedys, such as what JFK's favorite drinks were (daquiris and Heineken beer), his favorite song ("Greensleeves"), poem ("Ulysses" by Tennyson), and the watch he wore (Lord Elgin).

For the genealogical information, I owe a great debt to Robert A. Kane, chief historian of Brockton, who supplied the facts about the Hickeys; to Edward W. Hanson and Gary Boyd Roberts of the New England Historic Genealogical Society, for information about the Kennedys; and to Leona Kugler, who researched the genealogies of the Fitzgeralds and Hannons for me.

Brian P. Oherty, park ranger at the John F. Kennedy national Historic Site in Brookline, supplied many details on the Kennedy's Beals Street home.

Special thanks goes to the Shelter Rock Public Library of Albertson, New York—in particular to Lorraine Katz, who kindly arranged for interlibrary loans of needed materials. Likewise gratitude is extended to the staff of the Levittown Public Library, especially to Prescott Harmon and Glorida Scherer, who generously assisted me, and to the Manhasset (L.I.) Public library.

Grateful acknowledgment goes as well to: Dr. Robert S. Conte, Greenbrier Hotel; Lee Sylvester, Choate Rosemary Hall; William F. Ohinney, Dexter School; Donald J. Orth, U.S. Board on Geographical Names; Dr. Philip Melanson, Southern Massachusetts University; Kathryn Allamong Jacob, United States Senate Historical Office; Marion Conley, Dorchester High School; Teresa L. Jackson, Cedarwood Publishing Co.; Sister Catherine Baxter, Newton (Mass.) County Day School; Maureen Murphy, Hofstra University; Sheila H. Manley, Convent of the Sacred Heart; Laurie Joslin and Thomas Rodman, John F. Kennedy National Historic Site.

My family, especially my parents, Philip and Maizie, were incredibly encouraging and understanding throughout the ordeal of writing this book. And I will always be grateful to Maria Sivak Goldwert, for her ardent support, patience, and dedication, and for continually being available to lend a sympathetic ear to my vocalizations of frustration.

Last, but not least, I extend my gratitude to my research assistant, Michael Cervoni, and to my typist, Margret Dyke.

SOURCES

The following materials were consulted for the research of this book.

Vital data (births, marriages, and deaths): Edward L. Galvin, "The Kennedys in Massachusetts" in *The Irish in New England* (Boston: New England Historic Genealogical Society, 1985); Fitzgerald family Bibles and records of John F. Kennedy Library; records of the Archives Division of the Commonwealth of Massachusetts (where Fitzgerald family Bible dates differed from those in records of the Commonwealth of Massachusetts, the latter were used).

Results of primaries and elections of Patrick Kennedy and John Fitzgerald Kennedy, and their public service records: Municipal Register of Boston and other city documents.

Information pertaining to schools and colleges, including dates of term commencements and graduations, yearbook captions, speeches, and faculty: school records of each of the schools mentioned.

Boston Latin School: yearbooks, newspapers and documents in the Boston Public Library.

Joe Jr. and John F. Kennedy's prep school yearbook captions: *The Brief*, Choate Rosemary Hall.

Second- and third-grade courses of John F. Kennedy: 1924–1925 catalog of the Nobles and Greenough Lower School.

Kennedy homes: records of the Town of Barnstable, Massachusetts, Assessor's Office; Westchester County (N.Y.).

Activities of John Fitzgerald as Boston mayor; motion-picture career of Joseph P. Kennedy; Securities and change Commission activities of Joseph P. Kennedy; work of Joseph P. Kennedy as ambassador, and family activities during these years; congressional and senatorial activities of John F. Kennedy; subcommittee and senatorial activities of Robert F. Kennedy; senatorial activities of Edward M. Kennedy; Robert F. Kennedy's funeral; *Boston Advertiser; Boston American; Boston Herald; Boston Herald-American; Boston Herald-Traveler; Boston Post; Boston Record; Boston Record-American; Boston Transcript; Boston Traveler; Facts on File; New York Times; Newsday; Washington Evening Star; Washington Post; Washington Star; Associated Press* dispatches; *United Press International* dispatches.

Military service records of Joe Jr., John, and Robert Kennedy: Department of the Navy, Naval Military Personnel Command Office, National Personnel Records Center; of Edward M. Kennedy: Department of the Army, Office of the Adjutant General, U.S. Army Reserve components Personnel and Administration Center; PT-109 chronicle: Department of the Navy, Naval Historical Center, and John Hersey, "Survival," *The New Yorker*, June 17, 1944; final plane mission of Joe Jr.: Navy Office of Information, Internal Records Division.

Rose Fitzgerald's "debut": *Boston Advertiser*, January 2, 1911.

Joseph P. Kennedy–Rose Fitzgerald wedding: *Boston Globe*, January 14, 1914.

Kathleen Kennedy's wedding: *Boston Record, Boston Globe.*

Robert F. Kennedy–Ethel Skakel wedding: news release of John C. Dowd, Inc.

John F. Kennedy–Jacqueline Bouvier wedding: *New York Party News, Boston Globe*, and press release of John C. Dowd, Inc.

John Fitzgerald's death: *Boston Globe; Boston Post.*

Patricia Kennedy Lawford–Peter Lawford divorce; documents of County of Gooding, State of Idaho.

Location of Lord Hartington's death: Lynne McTaggart, *Kathleen Kennedy: Her Life and Times* (New York: The Dial Press, 1983).

Baptism and confirmation dates: records of the churches where they occurred.

John F. Fitzgerald and the Boston Customshouse: National Archives.

John F. Fitzgerald–Peter Tague controversy: *Congressional Record of the House*, October 23, 1914, debate pages 7381–7401.

Joseph Kennedy and Yellow Cab Company: *Fortune,* September 1937.

Joseph Kennedy's speech at Oglethorpe University: *Atlanta Constitution.*

John, Robert, and Edward Kennedy's primary and/or election results: *Guide to U.S. Elections: Presidential Elections since 1789* (third edition); Congressional quarterly.

John F. Kennedy's presidential activities (January 21, 1961–November 21, 1963): presidential appointment books of the John F. Kennedy Library.

John F. Kennedy's presidential speeches and writings: *Public Papers of the President, 1961–1963.*

John F. Kennedy's assassination, and prior activities of Lee Harvey Oswald: *The Warren Report; Report of the Select Committee on Assassinations,* U.S. House of Representatives (Bantam Books, Inc.).

Robert F. Kennedy's mountain climb: documents of the Yukon Department of Advanced Education and Manpower; articles in the *White House Star.*

Robert F. Kennedy's assassination: *Time,* June 14, 1968; *Newsweek,* June 17, 1968; newspapers stated above.

Edward Kennedy's Chappaquiddick incident and aftermath: John Barron, "Chappaquiddick, The Still Unanswered Questions," *Reader's Digest,* February 1984; *Facts on File* articles.

1960 Democratic party nomination of John F. Kennedy: *Official Proceedings of the Democratic National Convention, 1960.*

Robert F. Kennedy's senatorial activities: chronology prepared by the staff of the John F. Kennedy Library.

Charles M. Hickey information: Robert Kane and his article "The Mayors of Brockton," printed in the Brockton *Enterprises–Times.*

Kennedy–Nixon debates; transcript in *Freedom of Communications,* Vol.3.

"PT-109" lyrics: by permission of Cedarwood Publishing Company, a division of Musiplex Group, Inc.

Chart positions of phonograph recordings on the Kennedys: *The Billboard Book of Top 40 Hits,* Joel Whitburn, and information supplied by Record Research Co.

Inaugurations of U.S. presidents: *Presidential Elections Since 1789,* Second Edition (Congressional Quarterly, Inc.), whose source was Joseph Nathan Kane, *Facts About the Presidents* (revised edition, 1976).

Publication dates of books; *Catalog of Copyright Entries.*

Kennedy School of Government: *Official Register of Harvard University,* Vol. LXV, No. 10.

Official Proceedings of the (1960) Democratic National Convention, 1960.

The Handbook of the 1984 Democratic National Convention.

There are hundreds of books on the Kennedys available to readers, many fine ones among them. Those that were indispensable in my research were the following:

Johnny, We Hardly Knew Ye by Kenneth P. O'Donnell and David Powers with Joe McCarthy (Little, Brown, 1972); *Times to Remember* by Rose Kennedy (Doubleday, 1974); *Kathleen Kennedy: Her Life and Times* by Lynne McTaggart (Dial, 1983); *The Lost Prince Young Joe, the Forgotten Kennedy* by Hank Searls (World Publishing, 1969); *The Kennedys: Dynasty and Disaster 1848–1984* by John H. Davis (McGraw-Hill, 1984); *The Kennedys: An American Drama* by Peter Collier and David Horowitz (Summit, 1984); *A Hero for Our Time: An Intimate Story of the Kennedy Years* by Ralph G. Martin (Macmillan, 1983); *Robert Kennedy and His Times* by Arthur M. Schlesinger, Jr. (Houghton Mifflin, 1978); *To Seek a Newer World* by Robert F. Kennedy (Doubleday, 1967); *John Fitzgerald Kennedy... As We Remember Him,* edited by Goddard Lieberson (Atheneum, 1965); *Joseph P. Kennedy: A Life and Times* by David Koskoff (Prentice-Hall, 1974); *John F. Kennedy, Man of the Sea* by Tazewell Shepard, Jr. (William Morrow, 1965); *Edward Kennedy and the Camelot Legacy* by James MacGregor Burns (W.W. Norton, 1976).

CONTENTS

The KENNEDYS

Patrick Joseph Kennedy, aged 22, c. 1880.

ONE

THE EARLY YEARS

1800 · 1914

IRELAND
1823-1849

Historical Background

Celtic tribes from Europe invaded the British Isles in the fourth century B.C., and their Gaelic culture and literature had spread throughout England, Ireland, Scotland, and Wales by the fifth century A.D. By the end of that century, St. Patrick had converted Ireland to Christianity. The Normans occupied Ireland in the twelfth century, but were unable to conquer the whole country. Finally, in the mid-sixteenth century, the English determined to bring all of Ireland under their rule. They were able to accomplish this only gradually, however, and then only by exerting brutal force over strong resistance. The wars of conquest culminated in the Battle of Kinsdale in 1603.

1603

CORK, IRELAND. With the defeat of the last remnants of the Gaelic army under the command of Hugh O'Neill by the forces of Queen Elizabeth I, the English win the Battle of Kinsdale.

1642

ENGLAND. Civil war breaks out in England between Parliament and King Charles I. The King is comparatively tolerant of different religions while Parliament is aggressively anti-Catholic, and the Irish Catholics take up arms in support of the King.

1649

DUBLIN. Having executed Charles I (by beheading on 30 January), Oliver Cromwell arrives in Dublin as lord lieutenant and commander-in-chief. His purpose here is to promote English colonization and to maintain "freedom of conscience" and "justice." Cromwell's tolerance extends only to Protestants, however, and although he stays in Ireland for only nine months, the brutality of his forces and their repression and slaughter of Irish Catholics leave a lasting bitterness that continues into the twentieth century.

1650-1660

CONNAUGHT. The estates of nearly all the Irish Catholics are confiscated and given to English Protestants. By way of partial compensation, some of the dispossessed are granted small estates in the province of Connaught in the west of Ireland. This gives rise to the legend "To hell or Connaught."

1660

LONDON. With Cromwell dead of natural causes on September 3, 1658, the House of Stuart is restored with the accession of King Charles II to the English throne.

1685

LONDON. Charles II dies and is succeeded by his younger brother, James II, a convert to Catholicism.

1688

LONDON. Largely as a result of his determination to restore the Roman Catholic church in England, King James II is deposed. His Protestant son-in-law, William of Orange, succeeds James, who flees to Catholic France in the hope of raising an army.

Joseph Patrick Kennedy, c. 1888.

Kennedy Family Collection. Photographer unknown.

Kennedy Family Collection. Photographer unknown.

Agnes and Rose Fitzgerald, c. 1894.

1689
IRELAND. James II lands in Ireland with a French army. Irish Catholics flock to his support.

1690
DUBLIN. The Battle of the Boyne, fought some 30 miles north of Dublin on the banks of the river Boyne, seals the fate of James II, whose army is defeated by that of William of Orange. James flees to France, but Irish Catholics under the command of Patrick Sarsfield, continue the fight.

1691
LIMERICK, IRELAND. The Treaty of Limerick is signed on October 3, ending a siege by the Williamite army. The terms of the treaty guarantee Catholic freedom in Ireland, but the exclusively Protestant Irish Parliament later repudiates the essential parts of the treaty and instead institutes harsh penal laws against all Catholics. Limerick becomes known in history as "the city of the violated treaty."

1791
BELFAST, IRELAND. Influenced by the French Revolution, the Society of United Irishmen is founded by Wolfe Tone. It is a movement comprised largely of dissident middle-class Protestants—mostly Presbyterians—who, despite their Protestantism, suffer under English Protestant rule. The English government prosecutes the leaders of the Society, and its members are forced underground.

Kennedy Family Collection. Photographer unknown.

Loretta, Mrs. P. J. Kennedy, Joseph Patrick, c. 1895-6.

The Kennedy farm covers 24 acres of moderately good land. It lies halfway up the 900-foot *Slieve Coillte*, or Wooded Hill, on its southeast slope, giving the farm good morning and midday sun. The house has three rooms and a thatched roof. It is near an estuary, where the Kennedys probably engage in "snap-net fishing" to supplement their diet. With a farm of this size and quality, the Kennedys are above the poverty line, and they probably earn additional money as coopers by making barrels, wood casks, and tubs.

In this year, a son is born to Mary Johanna and Patrick Kennedy on their farm. The boy is named Patrick after his father. Patrick has two older brothers, John (born 1809), and James (born 1815), as well as a sister (her birthdate is unrecorded). As a young man, Patrick will emigrate to Boston, where he will become a cooper and will marry Bridget Murphy (born 1821), a girl who also grows up in County Wexford (although he does not know her there). The world will one day know Patrick's great-grandson as John Fitzgerald Kennedy.

1823-1824
DUBLIN. The Catholic Association is founded by Daniel O'Connell, a leading barrister and long-time agitator for Catholic rights within the law. The Association has a huge membership of common people, each of whom contributes a penny a month, and is supported by all Catholic Irish. The Association's aim is to achieve Catholic emancipation, that is, the right of Catholics to enter government and sit in Parliament. The poor man thus enters politics for the first time in Irish history.

1798
COUNTY WEXFORD, IRELAND. The Catholic peasantry is goaded into rebellion by repressive government forces. In early summer, the Catholics in South Leinster, including County Wexford, take up arms against government troops. Poorly led and badly disciplined, some members of this ragged Catholic army brutalize Protestant civilians. The English retaliate by smashing the Irish rebels in a bloodbath. (Members of the Kennedy family are in all likelihood involved in this rebellion, although the extent of their involvement is unknown.)

1823
NEW ROSS, COUNTY WEXFORD, IRELAND. The Kennedy farm, 5 miles south of New Ross, is part of the townland of Dunganstown. The area is deeply traditional, and most people, probably including the Kennedys, speak Gaelic.

1826
COUNTY WATERFORD, IRELAND. Across the estuary from Dunganstown, an historic election takes place in County Waterford. Henry Villiers-Stuart, a Protestant aristocrat, stands for Catholic emancipation against another Protestant aristocrat, Lord George Beresford, whose family has been in political control of County Waterford for generations. For the first time in Irish history, tenant voters rebel against their landlords and elect Villiers-Stuart. The Irish Catholics have won their first great victory since the seventeenth century.

1828
COUNTY CLARE, IRELAND. Daniel O'Connell is elected for County Clare as a Catholic candidate who refuses to take his seat until the required oath against the Catholic church is abolished. Supported by a vast majority, O'Connell becomes the focal point of the Irish rebellion.

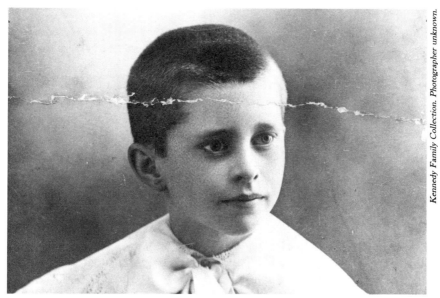

Kennedy Family Collection. Photographer unknown.

Joseph Patrick Kennedy, c. 1896.

1829
LONDON, ENGLAND. Fearing civil war, the Duke of Wellington, now prime minister, threatens to resign unless George IV assents to the Catholic Emancipation Act. The King, greatly dependent upon Wellington, agrees. Because Protestants still own nearly all of the land and make up the vast majority of its administrators, the Irish Catholic victory does not have any immediate significance; it does, however, set the stage for later success.

1841
IRELAND. In this first year of reliable census-taking in Ireland, the population is 8,500,000. It has been increasing rapidly, and the food supply cannot keep up with the demand. To provide for their families, farmers have been forced to subdivide their farms. The standard of living is so low that a majority of the people can afford to subsist only on potatoes.

Fortunately for the Kennedy family, their 24 acres allow them to grow corn and potatoes and keep a few cows. They can also supplement their income by working as coopers. Thus the Kennedys are only somewhat affected by the poverty that forces others to emigrate.

1845-1848
IRELAND. A potato blight of unknown origin spreads throughout the land. Due to overpopulation, un-deremployment, and English neglect, the standard of living in Ireland is extremely low, and most of its people rely on potatoes for sustenance. Half the crop fails in 1845; in 1846, the entire crop succumbs to the blight. In 1847, the ground is receptive to a healthy crop, but so few potatoes are left to sow that there is almost no yield. The crop sown in 1848 again fails, bringing to a million the number of Irish who die of partial starvation or of typhus and relapsing fever that is spread by lice. The situation creates such a sense of hopelessness that a vast exodus from Ireland begins; some emigrate to England, but most go to America. The famine will not be over until 1849, when a new crop is successfully sown and harvested.

1849
COUNTY WEXFORD, IRELAND. Patrick Kennedy, 26, decides to emigrate to Boston. Legend to the contrary, he is not driven out of Ireland by starvation. The Kennedys are relatively well-off, but the horrors of the Great Famine leave young men like Patrick with little confidence in Ireland's future. Patrick knows second-hand of the brutalities of 1798, and, like many other Irish, he feels a deep loyalty to the Roman Catholic church, a strong dislike of Protestantism, and a hatred of English rule.

Young Patrick believes that America offers economic opportunity and political freedom. He has just enough money to travel in a seaworthy ship and to pay for room and board in America until he can find a job.

BOSTON
1849-1884

4 March 1849
WASHINGTON, D.C. Zachary Taylor is inaugurated as the twelfth president of the United States. Millard Fillmore is sworn in as vice-president.

26 September 1849
BOSTON. Only recently arrived in America, Bridget Murphy, 28, and Patrick Kennedy, 26, are married at the Cathedral of the Holy Cross. The bride is the daughter of Richard and Mary Murphy; the groom is the son of Patrick and Mary Kennedy. (Bridget and Patrick Kennedy are the paternal grandparents of Joseph P. Kennedy.)

9 July 1850
WASHINGTON, D.C. After serving only sixteen months as president of the United States, Zachary Taylor dies of an illness.

10 July 1850
WASHINGTON, D.C. Millard Fillmore takes the oath of office and becomes the thirteenth president of the United States.

6 August 1851
BOSTON. A daughter, Mary L., is born to Bridget (Murphy) and Patrick Kennedy. Born on Meridian Street in East Boston, she is the couple's first child.

27 November 1852
BOSTON. A daughter, Joanna L., is born to Bridget (Murphy) and Patrick Kennedy. Their second child and second daughter, she too is born on Meridian Street in East Boston.

4 March 1853
WASHINGTON, D.C. Franklin Pierce is inaugurated as the fourteenth president of the United States. William R. King becomes vice-president.

21 October 1853
OTTAWA, ILLINOIS. The first of seven debates between Abraham Lincoln and Stephen A. Douglas, candidates for the Senate seat from Illinois, is held. Lincoln will lose the election but his eloquent denunciations of slavery will make him known across America.

4 January 1854
BOSTON. A son, John, is born to Bridget (Murphy) and Patrick Kennedy. He is the family's third child and first son.

12 February 1854
BOSTON. Mary Ann Fitzgerald, 19, and Michael Hannon, 21, are married by the Rev. H. O'Neill. The bride is the daughter of Edward and Mary (Linnenan) Fitzgerald; the groom is the son of John and Ellen (Noonan) Hannon. The couple are immigrants from Ireland. (Mary Ann and Michael Hannon are the maternal grandparents of Rose Fitzgerald Kennedy.)

19 January 1855
WEST ACTON, MASSACHUSETTS. A son, John, is born to Mary Ann (Fitzgerald) and Michael Hannon. He is the couple's first child.

Acton, which is subdivided into west, south, east, and north sections, is a township almost 25 miles northeast of Boston that was spun off from Concord in 1735.

18 July 1855
BOSTON. A daughter, Margaret M., is born to Bridget (Murphy) and Patrick Kennedy. She is their fourth child and third daughter, and she is born on Eutaw Street in East Boston.

24 September 1855
BOSTON. Patrick and Bridget Kennedy lose their firstborn son, John, at the age of 1 year, 8 months, and 10 days. He succumbs to cholera and infantum.

30 December 1856
SOUTH ACTON, MASSACHUSETTS. A second child, Ellen Augusta, is born to Mary Ann (Fitzgerald) and Michael Hannon.

5 March 1857
WASHINGTON, D.C. James Buchanan takes the oath of office and becomes the fifteenth president of the United States. John Cabell Breckinridge of Kentucky is sworn in as vice-president.

15 November 1857
BOSTON. Irish immigrants Rosanna Cox, 22, and Thomas Fitzgerald, 27, are married by the Rev. George H. Haskin. The bride is the daughter of Philip and Mary Cox, and the groom is the son of Michael and Ellen (Wilmouth) Fitzgerald. The groom is a peddler. (Rosanna and Thomas Fitzgerald will become the parents of John "Honey Fitz" Fitzgerald, the father of Rose Fitzgerald Kennedy.)

John Fitzgerald Kennedy Library. Photographer unknown.

John Francis ("Honey Fitz") Fitzgerald, left.
Patrick Joseph Kennedy, right. Date unknown.

6 December 1857

BOSTON. A daughter, Mary Augusta, is born to Margaret Martha (Field) and James F. Hickey, both immigrants from Ireland. She is their first child. The baby is born at 60 East Orange Street. (The Hickeys are the maternal grandparents of Joseph P. Kennedy.)

14 January 1858

BOSTON. A son, Patrick Joseph, is born to Bridget (Murphy) and Patrick Kennedy. He is their fourth child and eldest surviving son. The baby is born at 44 Liverpool Street in East Boston.

15 September 1858

BOSTON. A son, Michael, is born at 30 Ferry Street to Rosanna (Cox) and Thomas Fitzgerald. He is their first son.

22 November 1858

BOSTON. After ten years in the United States, Patrick Kennedy, a cooper, or barrel maker, dies of consumption at the age of 35. He leaves his wife Bridget, 36, his daughters Mary, 7, Joanna, 5, and Margaret 3, and a son Patrick Joseph, 10 months. (Patrick Kennedy's death

certificate from the Commonwealth of Massachusetts gives the cause of death as consumption, but family records indicate that he died of cholera.)

8 April 1859

SOUTH ACTON, MASSACHUSETTS. A son, Edmond Fitz, is born to Mary Ann (Fitzgerald) and Michael Hannon. He is their third child and second son.

2 December 1859

BOSTON. A second son, James F., is born to Rosanna (Cox) and Thomas Fitzgerald.

11 August 1860

BOSTON. Michael Fitzgerald dies at the age of 1 year and 11 months. His parents, Rosanna (Cox) and Thomas Fitzgerald, and his brother James, 8 months, survive him.

22 October 1860

SOUTH ACTON, MASSACHUSETTS. Mary Ann Hannon bears a fourth child, Michael, the third son of the family.

Agnes, Tom and Rose Fitzgerald, c. 1899

Kennedy Family Collection. Photographer unknown.

Joseph Patrick, Margaret and Loretta Kennedy, c. late 1880's.

6 November 1860

THE UNITED STATES. Republican candidate Abraham Lincoln defeats Senator Stephen A. Douglas, John Bell, and John C. Breckinridge in the election for the presidency of the United States. Lincoln is intensely disliked in the South, and receives hardly any votes there. The distribution of votes throughout the rest of the nation, however, gives him enough electoral college votes to win easily. Lincoln had served four terms as an Illinois state legislator and one term as a representative to Congress.

4 March 1861

WASHINGTON, D.C. Abraham Lincoln, 52, is sworn in as the sixteenth president of the United States before a crowd of over 25,000. Threats on his life have occasioned tight security. Senator Hannibal Hamlin of Maine takes the oath of office as vice-president. The United States has a population of over 32 million.

12 April 1861

FORT SUMTER, SOUTH CAROLINA. Differences between North and South erupt into a direct and violent confrontation. The Confederate attack on the Federal fort at Sumter signals the beginning of the Civil War.

17 April 1861

BOSTON. A second son, James F., is born to Margaret Martha (Field) and James F. Hickey. He is their third child. The baby is born at 60 East Orange Street.

7 August 1861

BOSTON. A son, Thomas, is born to Rosanna (Cox) and Thomas Fitzgerald. He is their second surviving son of three born.

27 October 1861

SOUTH ACTON, MASSACHUSETTS. John Hannon dies at the age of 6. His parents, a sister, and two brothers survive him.

1 January 1863

WASHINGTON, D.C. President Lincoln issues the Emancipation Proclamation, which decrees that all slaves in areas rebelling against the Union are free.

Kennedy Family Collection. Photographer unknown.

Joseph Patrick Kennedy, c. 1900.

11 February 1863
BOSTON. A son, John Francis, later nicknamed "Honey Fitz," is born to Rosanna (Cox) and Thomas Fitzgerald. He is their third surviving son of four born. The baby is born at 30 Ferry Street in the North End. (John Francis Fitzgerald will become the mayor of Boston in 1905.)

26 October 1863
SOUTH ACTON, MASSACHUSETTS. A son, James H., is born to Mary Ann (Fitzgerald) and Michael Hannon. He is the family's fifth child and third surviving son.

19 November 1863
GETTYSBURG, PENNSYLVANIA. A ceremony is held to dedicate a national cemetery at a field where the Union and Confederate armies suffered heavy battle casualties in July of 1863. Following a speech by former Senator Edward Everett of Illinois, President Lincoln delivers an address beginning with the words "Four score and seven years ago, our fathers brought forth on this continent a new nation conceived in liberty and dedicated to the proposition that all men are created equal...."

13 May 1864
BOSTON. A son, Michael, is born to Rosanna (Cox) and Thomas Fitzgerald. He is their fourth surviving son of five born.

4 March 1865
WASHINGTON, D.C. Abraham Lincoln, 56, is sworn in for a second term as president of the United States. Andrew Johnson, who had served as a Tennessee legislator, governor, U.S. representative, and U.S. senator, becomes vice-president.

26 March 1865
SOUTH ACTON, MASSACHUSETTS. Mary Ann (Fitzgerald) and Michael Hannon's second son, Edmond Fitz Hannon, dies less than two weeks before his sixth birthday. (Their first son, John, had died four years earlier at the same age.)

9 April 1865
THE UNITED STATES. Confederate commander-in-chief Robert E. Lee surrenders to General Ulysses S. Grant of the Union Army at the Appomattox Court House in Virginia, and the Civil War comes to an end. The four-year battle between South and North has been the bloodiest in the nation's history, taking the lives of over half a million people.

14 April 1865
WASHINGTON, D.C. While watching a performance of the English comedy *Our American Cousin* at Ford's Theater, President Lincoln is shot in the back of the head by John Wilkes Booth, a prominent actor. Booth flees, and the President is carried to a nearby house where doctors try to save him.

15 April 1865
WASHINGTON, D.C. President Lincoln succumbs to his gunshot wound and dies this morning. Andrew Johnson is sworn in as the seventeenth president of the United States.

26 April 1865
BOWLING GREEN, VIRGINIA. Soldiers surrounding the barn where John Wilkes Booth, the assassin of President Abraham Lincoln, is hiding order Booth to surrender. He refuses, and they set fire to the barn. A shot rings out. Booth is felled, and dies a short while later.

4 May 1865
SPRINGFIELD, ILLINOIS. The late president Abraham Lincoln is interred at Oak Ridge Cemetery.

10 October 1865

BOSTON. A son, William S., is born to Rosanna (Cox) and Thomas Fitzgerald. He is their fifth surviving son of six born.

31 October 1865

SOUTH ACTON, MASSACHUSETTS. A daughter, Mary Josephine, is born to Mary Ann (Fitzgerald) and Michael Hannon. She is their second daughter and fourth surviving child.

9 January 1866

BOSTON. A third son, John A., is born at 41 Seneca Street to Margaret Martha (Field) and James Hickey. He is the family's fourth child.

1 March 1867

BOSTON. A son, Edward, is born to Rosanna (Cox) and Thomas Fitzgerald. He is their sixth surviving son of seven born.

Margaret and Loretta Kennedy, c. 1900.

Kennedy Family Collection. Conlin, Boston.

10 September 1867

SOUTH ACTON, MASSACHUSETTS. A daughter, Emily Gertrude, is born to Mary Ann and Michael Hannon. She is their fifth surviving child and third daughter.

9 April 1868

BOSTON. A daughter, Catherine Frances, is born at 41 Seneca Street to Margaret Martha (Field) and James F. Hickey. She is their fifth child and second daughter.

10 May 1868

BOSTON. A son, Joseph Andrew, is born to Rosanna (Cox) and Thomas Fitzgerald, their seventh surviving son of eight born.

4 March 1869

WASHINGTON, D.C. Civil War general Ulysses Simpson Grant is inaugurated as the eighteenth president of the United States. Schuyler Colfax becomes vice-president.

17 December 1869

SOUTH ACTON, MASSACHUSETTS. A daughter, Elizabeth, is born to Mary Ann (Fitzgerald) and Michael Hannon. She is their sixth surviving child of eight and the fourth daughter.

8 January 1870

BOSTON. A daughter, Ellen Rosanna, is born to Rosanna (Cox) and Thomas Fitzgerald. She is the first daughter, after eight boys, seven of whom survive.

20 March 1870

BOSTON. A daughter, Margaret Martha, is born to Margaret Martha (Field) and James F. Hickey; their sixth child and third daughter. The baby is born on Oneida Street.

13 August 1870

BOSTON. Ellen Rosanna Fitzgerald, a blue baby, dies of cyanosis at the age of 7 months.

10 February 1871

BOSTON. A son, George Fred, is born to Rosanna (Cox) and Thomas Fitzgerald. He is the eighth surviving child of ten born.

22 September 1872

BOSTON. Joanna L. Kennedy, 19, is married to Humphrey Charles Mahoney, 24. The bride is the daughter of Bridget Murphy and the sister of Mary L.,

Margaret M., and Patrick Joseph Kennedy. The groom is a clerk.

4 March 1873
WASHINGTON, D.C. President Ulysses S. Grant begins his second term of office. The new vice-president is Henry Wilson.

9 December 1873
ACTON, MASSACHUSETTS. Elizabeth Hannon falls through the ice on a pond and drowns eight days before her fourth birthday. Her parents, Mary Ann (Fitzgerald) and Michael Hannon, and five brothers and sisters survive her.

24 October 1875
BOSTON. A son, Henry S., is born to Rosanna (Cox) and Thomas Fitzgerald. He is the ninth surviving child of eleven born.

17 November 1875
BOSTON. Ellen (Wilmouth) Fitzgerald, the mother of Thomas Fitzgerald and the paternal grandmother of John Francis Fitzgerald, dies at 78 of pulmonary tuberculosis, called *patisis*. Born in Ireland in 1797, she lived at 465 Hanover Street.

The Fitzgerald Family. Standing, l. to r., Agnes, Thomas, John Francis, Jr., Rose. Seated, l. to r., Mrs. Fitzgerald, Frederick, "Honey Fitz," Eunice, c. 1906.

Boston Herald.

Kennedy Family Collection. Photographer unknown.

Rose, "Honey Fitz," Agnes, c. 1907.

4 March 1877
WASHINGTON, D.C. Former Ohio governor Rutherford B. Hayes takes the oath of office, becoming the nineteenth president of the United States. William A. Wheeler is sworn in as vice-president.

14 March 1877
SOUTH ACTON, MASSACHUSETTS. A son, John Edward, is born to Mary Ann (Fitzgerald) and Michael Hannon. He is their sixth surviving child of nine born, and the fifth son.

28 November 1877
ACTON, MASSACHUSETTS. Ellen (Noonan) Hannon, maternal grandmother of Mary Josephine Hannon, dies at 84 of general debility.

11 January 1879
BOSTON. A daughter, Mary Ellen, is born to Rosanna (Cox) and Thomas Fitzgerald. She is the tenth surviving child of twelve born, and the only surviving daughter.

15 January 1879
BOSTON. Mary Ellen Fitzgerald, born four days earlier, dies, the third infant death in the family. Her parents and nine brothers survive her.

10 March 1879
BOSTON. Rosanna (Cox) Fitzgerald dies of cerebral apoplexy at the age of 45. She leaves her husband Thomas and nine sons. She lived at 465 Hanover Street.

1 September 1879
BOSTON. Having attended Eliot Grammar School and English High, John Francis Fitzgerald, 16, enters the Boston Latin School, in an "out-of-course" class. Founded 23 April 1633, Boston Latin, on Bedford Street, is the oldest public school in the country.

4 March 1881
WASHINGTON, D.C. James A. Garfield is inaugurated as the twentieth president of the United States. Chester A. Arthur is sworn in as vice-president.

2 July 1881
WASHINGTON, D.C.   As he waits in the station for a train taking him to a college reunion, President Garfield is shot twice and wounded by a disgruntled aspirant to a diplomatic post. Charles J. Guiteau had asked Garfield to appoint him ambassador to Austria, but the President made another choice. Despite a plea of insanity, Guiteau is later found guilty of murder and hanged.

19 September 1881
ELBERON, NEW JERSEY.   After eleven and a half weeks of fighting for his life, James A. Garfield becomes the second American president to die of an assassin's wounds.

20 September 1881
NEW YORK.   Following the death of James Garfield, Chester A. Arthur is sworn in as president at his home.

21 October 1881
BOSTON.   Michael S. Hannon dies of congestion of the lungs on the day before his twenty-first birthday. His parents and five brothers and sisters survive.

Still single, Hannon lived on Clark Street, in Acton, and worked as a bartender.

21 February 1882
BOSTON.   Margaret M. Kennedy, 26, marries John Thomas Caulfield, 20, a waiter. The bride is the daughter of Bridget (Murphy) and Patrick Kennedy, and the sister of Mary L. Kennedy, Joanna (Kennedy) Mahoney, and Patrick Joseph Kennedy.

1 May 1882
BOSTON.   Annual liquor licenses for taverns in the city of Boston are renewed for the year. Patrick Joseph Kennedy, 24, of 25 Border Street, runs a lager bar at 2 Elow Street in East Boston.

4 September 1882
BOSTON.   John Francis Fitzgerald repeats class 2, his junior year, at the Boston Latin School.

1 January 1883
BOSTON.   Mary L. Kennedy, 31, the eldest daughter of Bridget and Patrick, marries Lawrence M. Kane, a 24-year-old laborer. A native of County Wexford, the county where the bride's parents had been brought up, Kane had emigrated to the United States six years earlier.

1 May 1884
BOSTON.   Patrick Joseph Kennedy and John J. Quigley, partners in successful Kennedy & Quigley saloons at 81 Border Street and 2 Elbow Street, renew their commercial liquor licenses for the year. Quigley, also a water inspector at City Hall, resides at 76 Havre Street in East Boston.

30 June 1884
BOSTON.   John Francis Fitzgerald, 21, completes class 1, his senior year, and graduates from the Boston Latin School. The school had moved to the corner of Dartmouth Street and Warren Avenue in 1881.

25 September 1884
CAMBRIDGE.   John Francis Fitzgerald, 21, enters his first year at Harvard Medical School.

4 March 1885
WASHINGTON, D.C.   Grover Cleveland, 47, is inaugurated as the twenty-second president of the United States. Thomas A. Hendricks is sworn in as vice-president.

19 May 1885
BOSTON.   Thomas Fitzgerald, 55, dies of pneumonia. He leaves nine sons: James, 25; Thomas, 24; John, 22; Michael, 21; William, 19; Edward, 18; Joseph, 17; George, 14; and Henry, 9. A farmer and grocer, Fitzgerald lived at 465 Hanover Street at the time of his death.

FIRST POLITICS
1885-1914

3 November 1885
BOSTON.   Making his political debut, Patrick Joseph Kennedy, 27, is elected to the Massachusetts House of Representatives from Ward 2, East Boston (Second Suffolk House District).

Kennedy Family Collection. Photographer unknown.

Agnes, center, and Rose, right, enroute to Ireland aboard the S.S. Cyniric, July 1908.

6 January 1886
BOSTON.   Eight days before his twenty-eighth birthday, Patrick Joseph Kennedy begins his official duties as a state representative in the One Hundred Seventh General Court of the Commonwealth of Massachusetts. During this session, he serves on the Committee on Cities. The legislator lives at 25 Border Street, East Boston.

2 June 1886
WASHINGTON, D.C.   Frances Folsom, 21, becomes the youngest-ever First Lady when she marries Grover Cleveland at the White House.

2 November 1886
BOSTON.   Patrick Joseph Kennedy is re-elected to a second term in the Massachusetts House of Representatives from Ward 2, East Boston (Second Suffolk House District).

23 November 1886
BOSTON.   John Francis Fitzgerald, 23, is appointed Clerk, Class A, in the office of the Collector of the Boston Custom House. He had dropped out of Harvard Medical School to care for his younger brothers following his father's death.

28 November 1886
BOSTON.   John Francis Fitzgerald takes the oath of office as a Custom House clerk.

5 January 1887
BOSTON.   Patrick Joseph Kennedy begins his second term as a state representative in the One Hundred Eighth General Court of the Commonwealth of Massachusetts.

1 May 1887
BOSTON.   Commercial liquor licenses are again renewed for Kennedy & Quigley, a saloon at 81 Border Street, and two Cotter & Kennedy saloons at 12 Washington and 110 Union Streets. Patrick Joseph Kennedy, who still resides at 25 Border Street, is a partner in each of the three saloons.

Joseph Patrick Kennedy, far left. c. 1908.

8 November 1887

BOSTON.   Patrick Joseph Kennedy is re-elected to a third term in the Massachusetts House of Representatives from Ward 2, East Boston (Second Suffolk House District).

23 November 1887

BOSTON.   Mary Augusta Hickey, 29, marries Patrick Joseph Kennedy, also 29. The Rev. M. Clark officiates at the 9 A.M. wedding at the Church of the Sacred Heart. The bride is the daughter of Margaret (Field) and James Hickey, and the groom is the son of Bridget (Murphy) and the late Patrick Kennedy. The wedding guests received printed invitations.

4 January 1888

BOSTON.   Patrick Joseph Kennedy begins his third term as a state representative in the One Hundred Ninth General Court of the Commonwealth of Massachusetts.

6 September 1888

BOSTON.   A son, Joseph Patrick, is born to Mary Augusta (Hickey) and Patrick Joseph Kennedy. The baby, their first child, is born at 151 Meridian Street in East Boston.

6 November 1888

BOSTON.   Patrick Joseph Kennedy is re-elected to a fourth term in the Massachusetts House of Representatives from Ward 2, East Boston (Second Suffolk House District).

20 December 1888

BOSTON.   Bridget Murphy Kennedy, 67, dies of a cerebral hemorrhage at her home at 25 Border Street. She leaves three daughters, Mary Kane, Joanna Mahoney, and Margaret Caulfield, and a son, Patrick Joseph, whose own son, Joseph Patrick, had been born just over three months ago. Bridget Murphy Kennedy ran a notions shop in Boston.

2 January 1889
BOSTON.   Patrick Joseph Kennedy begins his fourth term as a state representative from Ward 2, East Boston, in the One Hundred Tenth General Court of the Commonwealth of Massachusetts. During this session, he serves on the Committee on Street Railways.

4 March 1889
WASHINGTON, D.C.   Benjamin Harrison, whose great-grandfather signed the Declaration of Independence, takes the oath of office as the twenty-third president of the United States. Levi Morton becomes the vice-president.

20 April 1889
SOUTH ACTON, MASSACHUSETTS.   James H. Hannon dies at the age of 25. He leaves his parents, three sisters, and a brother.

Kennedy Family Collection. Photographer unknown.

"Honey Fitz," and Rose in Ireland, August 1908.

Rose Fitzgerald in Ireland, August 1908.

Kennedy Family Collection. Photographer unknown.

1 May 1889
BOSTON.   Legislator Patrick Joseph Kennedy and his partner Charles R. Quigley renew their commercial liquor license for Kennedy & Quigley, a saloon at 81 Border Street. Kennedy and his family still live at 151 Meridian Street in East Boston.

18 September 1889
CONCORD, MASSACHUSETTS.   Mary Josephine Hannon, 23, and John Francis Fitzgerald, 26, are married at St. Bernard's Church by the Rev. John A. Grove. The bride, a native of South Acton, is a tailoress, and the groom is a customs clerk.

5 November 1889
BOSTON.   Patrick Joseph Kennedy is re-elected to a fifth term in the Massachusetts House of Representatives from Ward 2, East Boston (Second Suffolk House District).

1 January 1890
BOSTON.   Patrick Joseph Kennedy begins his fifth term as a state representative from Ward 2, East Boston, in the One Hundred Eleventh General Court of the

Commonwealth of Massachusetts. During this session, he serves on the Committee on Street Railways.

22 July 1890
BOSTON. A daughter, Rose Elizabeth, is born to Mary (Hannon) and John Francis Fitzgerald. She is the couple's first child. The baby is born at 4 Garden Court Street in the North End, up the street from the Paul Revere House.

31 December 1890
BOSTON. A state representative since 1886, Patrick Joseph Kennedy steps down from office at the end of his current term.

11 March 1891
BOSTON. A son, Francis Benedict, is born to Mary (Hickey) and Patrick Joseph Kennedy. Born at 151 Meridian Street in East Boston, he is their second child and second son.

15 June 1891
BOSTON. After filing a letter of notice on 16 May, John Francis Fitzgerald resigns from his employment at the Boston Custom House.

3 November 1891
BOSTON. Patrick Joseph Kennedy is elected to the Massachusetts State Senate from the Fourth Suffolk Senatorial District. The election results are Kennedy, 3,422 votes; Elliot, 142 votes; Prince, 1,234 votes. Of the 6,450 registered voters in the district, 4,798 men (74.39%) voted.

15 December 1891
BOSTON. John Francis Fitzgerald wins election to the Common Council, Ward 6.

4 January 1892
BOSTON. John Francis Fitzgerald, 28, of 4 Garden Court Street, begins his official duties as a councilman from Ward 6. During this session, he serves as a common council member on the committees of the City Council, City Messenger Department, Ferry Department, Legislative Matters, Grade Crossings (Causeway and Travers streets), East Boston Tunnel, and the committees to Attend the World's Fair and on the Celebration of Columbus Day.

6 January 1892
BOSTON. Patrick Joseph Kennedy, 33, begins his first term as a state senator from the Fourth Suffolk

Kennedy Family Collection. Photographer unknown.

Agnes Fitzgerald and friend in Ireland, August 1908.

Senatorial District. During this session, he serves on the Committee on the State House and the Committee on Street Railways.

5 May 1892
BOSTON. The Board of Aldermen confirms Patrick Joseph Kennedy's appointment by Mayor Patrick A. Collins as the city's Wire Commissioner. Kennedy's responsibilities include supervision, placement, and maintenance of underground and overhead wires, cables, and conductors and the abatement of any electrical dangers.

14 June 1892
BOSTON. Francis Benedict Kennedy, dies of diphtheria at the age of 1 year and 3 months. His parents, Patrick and Mary, and his brother, Joseph P. Kennedy, survive him.

BOSTON. Organized by a special legislative act taking effect today, the Columbia Trust Company becomes a corporation. The incorporators are Patrick Joseph Kennedy and sixteen others: Horace B. Butler, John Morrison, Frank C. Wood, William Waters, Jr., Benjamin J. Sullivan, J. Henry Stevenson, Edwin Rice, Albert

F. Low, Charles A. Kelly, Benjamin F. Campbell, Richard F. Keough, John H. Townsend, Frank E. Dimick, Charles T. Witt, John Morrison, and James Townsend. The corporation has the "authority to establish and maintain a safe deposit, loan and trust company in the city of Boston."

21-23 June 1892
CHICAGO. Patrick Joseph Kennedy is a delegate from the Commonwealth of Massachusetts to the Democratic National Convention. Grover Cleveland and Adlai E. Stevenson win the party's nomination for president and vice-president.

6 August 1892
BOSTON. A daughter, Mary Loretta, is born to Mary (Hickey) and Patrick Joseph Kennedy. She is their second surviving child of three born and their first daughter. The baby is born at 151 Meridian Street in East-Boston.

8 November 1892
BOSTON. Patrick Joseph Kennedy is elected to a second term in the Massachusetts State Senate from the Fourth Suffolk Senatorial District. Receiving 4,025 votes, he defeats his opponent, Louis A. Greyer, who totals 1,871 votes. Of the 7,847 men registered to vote in the district, 4,896 (75.14%) voted.

John Francis Fitzgerald is elected a state senator from the Third Suffolk District. The district includes wards 6, 7, and 8 of Boston and Ward 3 of Cambridge. The election results are: Fitzgerald (Democrat), 4,288 votes; Atwood (Republican), 1,040 votes; McGahey (Independent Democrat), 1,601 votes.

Rose, seated center, and Agnes, right, and friends aboard the S.S. Cyniric in July, 1908.

Kennedy Family Collection. Photographer unknown.

Kennedy Family Collection. Photographer unknown.

Unidentified friend, Rose, Sir Thomas Lipton, Agnes, and "Honey Fitz" in England, 1909.

10 November 1892

BOSTON. A daughter, Mary Agnes, is born to Mary (Hannon) and John Francis Fitzgerald. She is their second child and second daughter. The baby is born at 4 Garden Court Street in the North End.

4 January 1893

BOSTON. Patrick Joseph Kennedy begins his second term as state senator from the fourth Suffolk Senatorial District. During this session he serves as chairman of the Committee on the State House and on the Committee on Street Railways and the Committee on Water Supply.

John Francis Fitzgerald begins his first term as state senator from the Third Suffolk District. During this session, he serves as chairman of the Committee on Engrossed Bills, and on the Committee on the Election Laws and the Committee on Liquor Law.

This is the only term that both Patrick Joseph Kennedy and John Francis Fitzgerald serve simultaneously as state senators.

4 March 1893

WASHINGTON, D.C. Grover Cleveland becomes the first president of the United States to serve two nonconsecutive terms when he is sworn in today. Adlai E. Stevenson becomes the vice-president.

12 May 1893

BOSTON. Thomas Fitzgerald, Jr., 31, dies of chronic rheumatic heart disease. He was the brother of State Senator John Francis Fitzgerald and uncle of Rose Elizabeth Fitzgerald, now 2.

7 November 1893

BOSTON. John Francis Fitzgerald is re-elected State Senator from the Third Suffolk District. The election results are as follows: Fitzgerald (Democrat), 4,719; Blackman (Republican), 1,414; Cullen, 1.

3 January 1894

BOSTON. John Francis Fitzgerald begins serving his

second term as state senator from the Third Suffolk District. During this session, he serves on the committees on Rules, Liquor Laws, Taxation, and Transit.

14 April 1894

NEW YORK.   The first public exhibition of a motion picture, or kinetoscope, takes place here.

6 November 1894

BOSTON.   John Francis Fitzgerald is elected to the U.S. House of Representatives from the Ninth Congressional District, which encompasses wards 1, 2, 3, 6, 7, 8, 12, 16, 17, and 18, precincts 2, 3, 4, 6, of Ward 19 in the city of Boston, and the town of Winthrop in Suffolk County. The election results are: Fitzgerald (Democrat), 11,459 votes; Jesse M. Gove (Republican), 9,545; Patrick F. O'Neill (Socialist Labor), 511; all others, 5. Congressman-elect Fitzgerald is from Ward 6 in the North End. He will take office in December of 1895.

Joseph P. Kennedy, c. 1911.

Kennedy Family Collection. Photographer unknown.

Kennedy Family Collection. Photographer unknown.

Rose Kennedy, in Boston, June, 1911.

23 March 1895

BOSTON.   The Columbia Trust Company, organized in June of 1892, by Patrick Joseph Kennedy and fifteen others, begins business operations with capital of $130,300 and a surplus of $50,000. Its address is 20 Meridian Street in East Boston.

19 April 1895

BOSTON.   A son, Thomas Acton, is born to Mary (Hannon) and John Francis Fitzgerald. He is their third child and first son. The baby is born at 4 Garden Court Street in the North End.

1 May 1895

BOSTON.   Commercial liquor licenses in the city are again renewed for the year. Patrick Joseph Kennedy is a partner in Kennedy & Quigley, which now has saloons at three locations, 81 Border Street, 12 Washington Street, and 165 Webster Avenue.

John Fitzgerald Kennedy Library. Photographer unknown.

President Taft, "Honey Fitz," c. 1909.

3 November 1896

BOSTON. John Francis Fitzgerald is re-elected to a second term in the U.S. House of Representatives from the Ninth Congressional District (wards 1, 2, 3, 6, 7, 8, 9, and 10 in Boston and Winthrop). The election results are: Fitzgerald (Democrat), 13,979 votes; Walter Lincoln Sears (Republican), 7,819; John A. Ryan (Democratic Silver), 3,238; Hammond T. Fletcher (Republican-Independent), 503; all others, 5.

4 March 1897

WASHINGTON, D.C. Former Ohio governor William McKinley is inaugurated as the twenty-fifth president of the United States. Garret A. Hobart becomes vice-president.

15 March 1897

WASHINGTON, D.C. The first session of the Fifty-fifth Congress, of which John Francis Fitzgerald is a second-term member, convenes. The Fifty-fifth Congress began on 4 March 1897 and will end on 3 March 1899. The two senators from Massachusetts are George F. Hoar and Henry Cabot Lodge, both Republicans.

Joseph P. Kennedy in East Boston, c. 1911.

Kennedy Family Collection. Photographer unknown.

2 December 1895

WASHINGTON, D.C. The first session of the Fifty-fourth Congress, of which John Francis Fitzgerald is a member, convenes. The Fifty-fourth Congress opened on 4 March 1895 and will end on 3 March 1897. The two senators from Massachusetts are George F. Hoar and Henry Cabot Lodge, both Republicans.

Fitzgerald had been elected to his Congressional seat on 6 November 1894, but it was not unusual for officials to begin serving more than a year after their election. This practice proved unfeasible—an official could die in the interim, for example—and was changed by the Twentieth Amendment to the Constitution in 1933.

7-11 July 1896

CHICAGO. Patrick Joseph Kennedy is a delegate from the state of Massachusetts to the Democratic National Convention. William J. Bryan receives the party's nomination for president; Arthur Sewall is nominated for vice-president.

Kennedy Family Collection. Photographer unknown.

Back row: "Honey Fitz," Eunice, friend, Rose, Agnes.
Front row: Mrs. John F. Fitzgerald (second from left) and friends, c. 1910.

7 December 1897
CONCORD JUNCTION, MASSACHUSETTS.
A son, John Francis, Jr., is born to Mary (Hannon) and John Francis Fitzgerald. He is their fourth child and second son.

22 October 1898
BOSTON.   A daughter, Margaret Louise, is born to Mary (Hickey) and Patrick Joseph Kennedy. She is their third surviving child of four and the second daughter. She is born at 165 Webster Place in East Boston.

8 November 1898
BOSTON.   John Francis Fitzgerald is reelected to a third term in the U.S. House of Representatives from the Ninth Congressional District, which now encompasses wards 1, 2, 3, 6, 7, 8, 13 in Boston and Winthrop. The election results are: Fitzgerald (Democrat), 10,303 votes; Franz K. Krebs, Jr., (Republican), 5,450; James A. Gallivan (Democrat-Independent), 5,000; Florentine K. Bradman (by nomination papers) (Republican Citizens), 412.

4 December 1899
WASHINGTON, D.C.   The first session of the Fifty-sixth Congress convenes. It is Fitzgerald's third term as a representative. The Fifty-sixth Congress began on 4 March 1899 and will end on 3 March 1901. The senators from Massachusetts are still the Republicans George F. Hoar and Henry Cabot Lodge.

12 December 1899
BOSTON.   William S. Fitzgerald dies of kidney disease at the age of 34. He was the brother of John Francis Fitzgerald and uncle of Rose Elizabeth Fitzgerald, 9.

21 December 1899
BOSTON.   Mayor Josiah Quincy appoints Patrick Joseph Kennedy Election Commissioner to fill the vacancy created when the Hon. Joseph J. Corbett resigned on 24 October 1899. The interim position had been held by John H. Donovan, a member of the Board of Assessors. There are four election commissioners, and Kennedy is secretary of the board. His annual salary as Election Commissioner is $3,500. His term ends on 30 April 1902.

Kennedy Family Collection. Photographer unknown.

Rose and friend, c. 1912.

26 January 1900
CONCORD JUNCTION, MASSACHUSETTS.
Michael Hannon, a laborer during his lifetime, dies of pneumonia at the age of 67. The father of Mary (Hannon) Fitzgerald, he was the maternal grandfather of Rose Elizabeth Fitzgerald, 9.

4-6 July 1900
KANSAS CITY, MISSOURI. For the third time, Patrick Joseph Kennedy is a delegate from the Commonwealth of Massachusetts to the Democratic National Convention. William J. Bryan and Adlai E. Stevenson win the party's nomination for president and vice-president.

22 November 1900
BOSTON. James Hickey, 64, dies of chronic nephritis at his home at 144 Saratoga Street. Born at Conkilty Bay, County Cork, Ireland, he had been an engineer. He leaves his wife and six children, among them Mary (Hickey) Kennedy, the mother of Joseph P. Kennedy, 12. He is to be buried at the Holy Cross Cemetery in Malden.

1900-1901 [?]
BOSTON. John Francis Fitzgerald establishes a real estate business, with offices at Room 9, 30 Pemberton Square.

3 March 1901
WASHINGTON, D.C. The Fifty-sixth Congress adjourns, and Representative John Francis Fitzgerald of Massachusetts's Ninth Congressional District steps down as a congressman.

4 March 1901
WASHINGTON, D.C. William McKinley begins his second term as president of the United States. Theodore Roosevelt is his vice-president.

6 September 1901
BUFFALO, NEW YORK. President McKinley attends the Pan-American Exposition, where he greets visi-

Margaret, Mr. & Mrs. P. J. Kennedy and Loretta.
Date unknown.

Kennedy Family Collection. Photographer unknown.

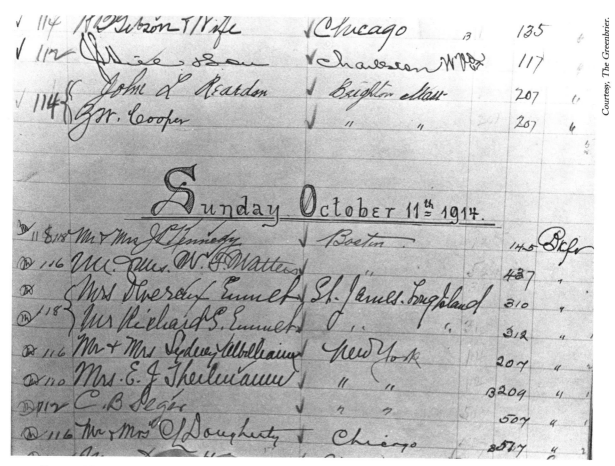

Courtesy, The Greenbrier.

Rose and Joseph P. Kennedy register for the first time as Mr. and Mrs. J. P. Kennedy at The Greenbrier hotel, on their honeymoon, 3 days after their marriage, October 7, 1914.

tors at one of the exhibitions. Leon F. Czolgosz, an anarchist obsessed with murdering a world leader, moves close to President McKinley and shoots him.

11 September 1901

BOSTON.   Joseph P. Kennedy enters class 6 (the seventh grade) at the Boston Latin School on the corner of Dartmouth Street and Warren Avenue. He had previously attended the parochial Assumption and the Xaverian schools.

14 September 1901

BUFFALO, NEW YORK.   Eight days after being wounded by an assassin's bullets, President William McKinley dies. Vice-President Theodore Roosevelt is sworn in as president. At 42, he becomes the youngest man ever to hold the office.

1901-1902 [?]

BOSTON.   John Francis Fitzgerald continues as publisher of the *Republic,* a weekly newspaper with offices at 15 School Street. Fitzgerald resides at 8 Unity Street in the North End.

28 April 1902

BOSTON.   Patrick Joseph Kennedy of 165 Webster Street is again appointed Commissioner of Wires by Mayor Patrick A. Collins. The position, subject to confirmation by the Board of Aldermen, fills a vacancy through 30 April 1903 caused by the resignation of William H. Lott.

5 May 1902

BOSTON.   Patrick Joseph Kennedy is unanimously confirmed by the Board of Aldermen as Commissioner of Wires and begins his duties. The position pays $5,000 an-

Kennedy Family Collection. Photographer unknown.

Rose and Joseph P. Kennedy on holiday in Poland Springs, Maine, January, 1915.

nually, and its term ends in 1903. The office is located at 11 Wareham Street.

8 June 1902
BOSTON. Patrick Joseph Kennedy of 163 Webster Street is again appointed Commissioner of Wires by Mayor Patrick A. Collins for a term of three years at an annual salary of $5,000. The appointment is subject to confirmation by the Board of Aldermen.

1 May 1903
BOSTON. Patrick Joseph Kennedy of 163 Webster Street begins serving his new three-year term as Commissioner of Wires.

4 May 1903
BOSTON. By unanimous vote, the Board of Aldermen retroactively confirm Mayor Collins's appointment of Patrick Joseph Kennedy as Commissioner of Wires for the three-year term that began 1 May 1903.

17 December 1903
KITTY HAWK, NORTH CAROLINA. Orville and Wilbur Wright make the first successful flights of a power-driven airplane. On one of the four flights, Wilbur Wright remains airborne for nearly a minute.

1 July 1904
CONCORD JUNCTION, MASSACHUSETTS. Mary Ann (Fitzgerald) Hannon dies of anemia at the age of 70. She was the mother of Mary Josephine (Hannon) Fitzgerald and the maternal grandmother of Rose Elizabeth Fitzgerald, now 13.

14 September 1904
BOSTON. Transferring from Concord High School, where she had attended the ninth and tenth grades, Rose Fitzgerald, 14, enters the eleventh grade at Dorchester High School. The school is located on Talbot Avenue in Codman Square, Dorchester. Built in 1901, the building is the third structure to serve as Dorchester High. The Fitzgerald family lives on Welles Avenue, a few blocks away from the school.

3 December 1904

BOSTON.   A son, Frederick Hannon, is born to Mary (Hannon) and John Francis Fitzgerald. He is their sixth child and third son.

17 February 1905

BOSTON.   While serving as Commissioner of Wires, Patrick Kennedy also becomes acting Fire Commissioner.

4 March 1905

WASHINGTON, D.C.   President Theodore Roosevelt begins his second term of office. Charles W. Fairbanks is his vice-president.

20 March 1905

BOSTON.   After thirty-one days as acting Fire Commissioner, Patrick Joseph Kennedy steps down from this job.

30 June 1905

BOSTON.   The school year ends at Dorchester High, where Rose Fitzgerald has completed the eleventh grade. Her marks for the years are: algebra I, A; French,

Rose Kennedy with Joseph P., Jr., 1916.

Kennedy Family Collection. Alfred Brown, Boston.

Joseph Patrick Kennedy, Jr., 1916.

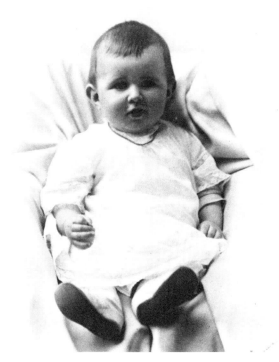

Kennedy Family collection. Alfred Brown, Boston.

A; Latin, A; English, B; physics, B; and physical education, A.

14 September 1905

BOSTON.   Mayor Patrick A. Collins dies in office. Daniel Wheltson, the chairman of the Board of Aldermen, succeeds him as acting mayor.

12 December 1905

BOSTON.   Following a hard-fought campaign, perhaps the toughest in the city's history, former congressman and state senator John Francis Fitzgerald is elected mayor of Boston. Winning by a margin of 8,143 votes, the Democratic candidate polls a total of 44,171. Other candidates and their vote totals are: Louis A. Frothingham (Republican), 36,028 votes; Henry S. Dewey (People's), 11,603; George S. Hall (Socialist), 712; James A. Watson (Municipal Ownership Citizens'), 457; all others, 14 votes. The total vote for all candidates is 92,990.

In numerous speeches, Fitzgerald had declared that he was not controlled by the so-called ward bosses (who included Martin Lomasney and Patrick Kennedy), and had promised a "bigger, better, busier Boston!" The term of office is two years, and the position pays $10,000 annually. Mayor-elect Fitzgerald will take office in January.

1 January 1906

BOSTON. John Francis Fitzgerald, also known as "Honey Fitz" ("Honey" for his lively personality and endearing charm), is inaugurated as the city's thirty-fifth mayor. "Honey Fitz" is 42 years and 11 months old, and the first child of Irish immigrants to serve as mayor of Boston. He and his family live at 39 Welles Avenue, Dorchester.

The induction ceremony takes place in the Common Council Chamber of City Hall on School Street at a joint session of the Board of Aldermen and the Common Council. The meeting begins at 10 A.M. on New Year's Day, as required by rules mandating such a convention, on the first Monday of January.

Mayor-elect Fitzgerald enters the chamber at 10:43 A.M., and an invocation is delivered by the Reverend Denis J. O'Farrell, chaplain of the day. At approximately 10:50 A.M., Massachusetts Supreme Judicial Court Chief Justice Marcus P. Knowlton administers the oath of office to Fitzgerald, who in turn swears in Aldermen-elect and Common Councilors-elect. At 11:15 A.M. he begins his inaugural address, speaking until 11:42 A.M.

30 April 1906

BOSTON. Mayor John "Honey Fitz" Fitzgerald reappoints Patrick Joseph Kennedy as Commissioner of Wires for a term ending 30 April 1909. The annual salary for the post is $5,000.

7 May 1906

BOSTON. The Board of Aldermen confirms Mayor Fitzgerald's 30 April appointment of Patrick Joseph Kennedy as Commissioner of Wires for a three-year term.

23 June 1906

BOSTON. Rose Fitzgerald graduates from Dorchester High School at its fifty-fourth annual exhibition, or graduation exercises. The program, consisting of music, speeches, and the presentation of the diplomas, starts at 7:30 P.M. Musical selections include "The Beautiful Blue Danube," "Sail Forth Into the Sea of Life," "Sail On, Nor Fear," "The Moonlight Boat Ride," and "The Fairy Revel." Mayor Fitzgerald awards the diplomas to the graduates. His daughter Rose is one of nine honor-roll students who are candidates for the "first diplomas." The program closes with a patriotic song, "To Thee, O Country."

29 June 1906

BOSTON. Classes end for the school year at Dorchester High where Rose graduated last week. Her grades for the twelfth year were: Latin, A; French, A; ge-

"Honey Fitz," Mrs. John Fitzgerald, Joseph P. Kennedy, Palm Beach, 1915.

Kennedy Family Collection. Photographer unknown.

ometry, A-; English, A-; German, A-; history, A; and physical education, B. Rose will stay on at Dorchester High for the next term, a "postgraduate" year.

22 June 1907

BOSTON. Rose Fitzgerald, 16, graduates from her "postgraduate" year at Dorchester High School.

Such a school term, sometimes referred to as the "thirteenth year" of high school, is taken by students who have received their diplomas but who do not wish or are not ready to go to work or to college during the coming school year. Instead, they take additional courses. An honor-roll student during her postgraduate year, Rose's grades were: English, A; French, A; Latin, B; German, B; algebra II, B; and chemistry, B. Rose receives this second diploma with her class of ninety-five boys and girls from her father, the mayor of Boston.

12 September 1906

BOSTON. Joseph P. Kennedy repeats class 2, his junior year, at the Boston Latin School, because of poor grades.

16 September 1907

BOSTON. Rose Fitzgerald, 17, enters the Convent of the Sacred Heart at 264 Commonwealth Avenue. Her tuition is $100 per term, and with other expenses, including "extra" fees for courses in German, embroidery, and painting, the total cost of her schooling for the year will be $396.96. The mother superior of the convent is Mother Katherine Cantwell.

September 1907

BOSTON. The *Latin School Register,* the monthly newspaper of the Boston Latin School, lists the results of the class elections and states that "J. P. Kennedy has been elected Class President of the First Class" (Volume 27, No. 1, page 14). Kennedy is also listed as captain of Company B of the school's military drill team (page 16).

14 November 1907

BOSTON. In the city's primary, "Honey Fitz"-Fitzgerald defeats John A. Coulthurst to win the Democratic nomination for mayor. The results are as follows: Fitzgerald, 21,848 votes; Coulthurst, 425; all others, 372.

Joseph P. Kennedy, Sr. with Joe, Jr., Brookline, 1917.

Rose Kennedy with Joe, Jr., Nantasket, 1916.

10 December 1907

BOSTON. In the aftermath of a scandal concerning graft among city officials, the incumbent Democratic mayor John "Honey Fitz" Fitzgerald loses his re-election bid. Republican George A. Hibbard, receiving 38,112 votes, is the new mayor-elect. Fitzgerald, with 35,935 votes, is narrowly defeated. A third candidate, John A. Coulthurst, running on the Non-Partisan and Independence League tickets, receives 15,811 votes. Mayor-elect Hubbard has served in the Massachusetts legislature and has been Postmaster of Boston.

8 June 1908

BOSTON. Mayor George A. Hibbard appoints James E. Cole to be Commissioner of Wires, filling the vacancy caused by the resignation of Patrick Joseph Kennedy.

17 June 1908

BOSTON. The academic year ends at the Convent of the Sacred Heart where Rose Fitzgerald has been a student since September, 1907.

Kennedy Family Collection. Bachrach, Boston.

Rose with Joe, Jr., 1917.

Manhattanville College), located at 133rd Street and Convent Avenue in the Morningside Heights section of Manhattan. (The school was founded on 3 August 1841 on Houston Street in Manhattan.) In February of 1847 it moved to Jacob Lorillard's property in the village of Manhattanville in Morningside Heights. Created to provide young women with a liberal arts education in the Catholic tradition, the academy is a post-high-school institution not currently chartered to grant undergraduate degrees.

11 January 1910
BOSTON. In an election marked by the arousal of unprecedented public emotion, John "Honey Fitz" Fitzgerald regains the mayoral office by defeating James J. Storrow, a banker, by a slim margin. The election results are: Fitzgerald, 47,177; James J. Storrow, 45,775; Mayor George A. Hibbard, 1,814; Nathaniel Taylor, 613; all others, 14. Using a slogan Manhood Against Money, "Honey Fitz's" campaign has revolved around an attempt to exonerate himself from charges of graft made during his previous administration.

20 January 1910
BOSTON. A recount of the vote in which "Honey Fitz" defeated James M. Storrow for mayor by a narrow margin upholds Fitzgerald's victory.

7 February 1910
BOSTON. In an induction ceremony at Faneuil Hall, John Francis Fitzgerald is sworn in as mayor, taking the oath of office from Chief Justice Knowlton. Fitzgerald takes office under a new city charter that, for the first time in the city's history, provides for a four-year term of office with a recall possible at the end of two years.

Mayor Fitzgerald outlines the policy of his new administration in an inaugural speech to an audience that includes many prominent people. He says he plans to improve the rapid transit system and the protection of public health.

15 April 1910
NEW YORK. A delegation of some 150 members of the Massachusetts Real Estate Exchange, led by Mayor John "Honey Fitz" Fitzgerald, arrives for a two-day inspection of city docks, subways, and buildings. The visitors want to make similar improvements in Boston's municipal and private facilities.

At a dinner held at the Hotel Ambassador in honor of the visitors later in the day, Mayor Fitzgerald scores a big hit, telling stories and singing "Sweet Adeline" among other songs.

20 June 1908
BOSTON. Joseph P. Kennedy, 19, graduates from the Boston Latin School. He has just completed class 1, his senior year. The headmaster of the school is Arthur Fiske.

[?] September 1908
VALLE, HOLLAND. Rose Fitzgerald, 18, enters Blumenthal Academy of the Sacred Heart for the 1908-1909 school year.

1 October 1908
CAMBRIDGE, MASSACHUSETTS. Joseph P. Kennedy begins his college career as a freshman at Harvard College. He is the first of the Kennedys in America to attend an Ivy League college.

4 March 1909
WASHINGTON, D.C. William Howard Taft takes the oath of office as president of the United States. James S. Sherman is his vice-president.

[?] September 1909
NEW YORK. Rose Fitzgerald, 19, enters the Academy of the Sacred Heart (later to become

June 1910

NEW YORK. Rose Fitzgerald graduates from the Academy of the Sacred Heart.

8 September 1910

BOSTON. Before a crowd of 25,000 spectators, Mayor Fitzgerald takes his first ride in an airplane. The Farmon biplane is piloted by Claude Graham-White, an English aviator and engineer. Watching and waving in the audience is President William Howard Taft.

4 November 1910

BOSTON. The Examining Committee of the Boston Public Library is appointed for the 1910-1911 year. The committee is an impartial review board of the library, its functions and services, and is required by a city ordinance. Rose Fitzgerald is named to a subcommittee, the Children's Department and Work With Schools. The chairman of the Examining Committee is Josiah H. Benton, president of the board of trustees of the Boston Public Library.

Joseph P. Kennedy, Sr. holding Joe, Jr., Brookline, 1917.

Kennedy Family Collection. Photographer unknown.

Kennedy Family Collection. Photographer unknown.

Grandfather "Honey Fitz" taking Joe, Jr. for a dip, Nantasket, 1916.

18 November 1910

BOSTON. A number of women defy Mayor Fitzgerald's edict that hats may not be worn during concerts. At tonight's Boston Symphony concert at Symphony Hall, they keep their hats on.

2 January 1911

BOSTON. Twenty-year-old Rose Fitzgerald makes her debut in Boston society at a coming-out party held at her family home at 39 Welles Avenue in Dorchester. Some 425 guests, including many prominent politicians, celebrate the occasion in the large house, which has been decorated with roses and other flowers. Among the crowd is an inconspicuous 22-year-old named Joseph P. Kennedy.

5 June 1911

BOSTON. Margaret (Field) Hickey, 75, dies of cancer of the omentum (part of the peritoneum) at her home at 144 Saratoga Street. The mother of Mary (Hickey) Kennedy, she was Joseph P. Kennedy's maternal grandmother.

Kennedy Family Collection. Alfred Brown. Boston.

John Fitzgerald Kennedy, 1918.

17 June 1911
BOSTON. Members of the Boston Chamber of Commerce and their families leave for a two-month tour of Europe. Rose Fitzgerald accompanies her father.

31 July 1911
BUDAPEST, HUNGARY. In her diary, Rose Fitzgerald records the events of her summer trip:

"Houses of Parliament—Chamber of Commerce—museum—nothing important—drive through park—saw city, house of Gladys Vanderbilt—statue of 'anonymous' monk reading a manuscript. Trip in the Blue Danube. *Waltzed the Blue Danube on the Blue Danube.* Dinner on top of the mountain—wonderful view—gypsy orchestra—cymbals—only fair! Coffee house after dinner party."

20 August 1911

BOSTON.   An account of Rose Fitzgerald's impressions of Europe appears in *The Boston American* following her return from a Chamber of Commerce tour with her father and her sister Agnes. She declares, "We had a most delightful trip, and I enjoyed every minute of it, but I still think America is the best home."

14 September 1911

BOSTON.   Classes begin at the New England Conservatory of Music where Rose Fitzgerald is registered as a special student. The school is located at Huntington Avenue and Gainsborough Street, and her instructor is Alfred DeVoto.

7 January 1912

BOSTON.   Concerned that the city's youth is being attracted to tawdry halls to dance the Turkey Trot, the Grizzly Bear, and other popular steps, Mayor Fitzgerald proposes that schoolhouses be opened for nightly entertainment. There, he declares, boys and girls could enjoy

Young John Fitzgerald Kennedy playing in Nantasket, c. 1918.

Kennedy Family Collection. Photographer unknown.

clean recreation safe from the improper influences of the city's cheap dance halls.

19 June 1912

BOSTON.   The school year ends at the New England Conservatory of Music where Rose Fitzgerald has been studying the piano.

20 June 1912

CAMBRIDGE, MASSACHUSETTS.   Joseph P. Kennedy, 23, graduates from Harvard College with a bachelor of arts degree. His yearbook caption reads:

> Home address, 159 Locust Street, Winthrop, Massachusetts. In college four years as undergraduate. Freshman baseball team; University baseball team, 1911. Institute of 1770, D.K.E., Delta Upsilon, Hasty Pudding Club, St. Paul's Catholic Club, Boston Latin Club. Kennedy had been awarded a varsity "H" for the 1911 baseball season by the Harvard Athletic Association.

20 June-2 July 1912

BALTIMORE, MARYLAND.   Mayor John "Honey Fitz" Fitzgerald is chairman of the Massachusetts delegation to the Democratic National Convention. Woodrow Wilson and Thomas R. Marshall win the party's nomination for president and vice-president. Fitzgerald's daughter, Rose, accompanies him on the trip.

12 September 1912

BOSTON.   Joseph P. Kennedy is hired as a staff examiner for the Massachusetts Commissioner of Banks. He will serve under Commissioner Augustus L. Thorndike.

Rose Fitzgerald continues her piano studies at the New England Conservatory of Music.

5 November 1912

BROCKTON, MASSACHUSETTS.   Charles M. Hickey, an uncle of Joseph P. Kennedy, runs as a Democrat for state representative from the Ninth Plymouth District and loses to Edward N. Dahlborg of the Progressive Party, who receives 985 votes. Hickey comes in second with 712 votes, followed by Stewart B. McLeod, a Republican, with 656 votes, and the Socialist Party candidate, Olander Benson, with 411 votes.

3 December 1912

BROCKTON, MASSACHUSETTS.   Undaunted by his recent defeat, Charles Hickey is elected mayor of Brockton for the municipal year 1913 by a narrow margin. The election results are: Hickey (Democrat), 3,293 votes; Harry C. Howard (Republican), 3,265; Dr.

Kennedy Family Collection. Photographer unknown.

Three generations: Joe, Sr., Joe, Jr., P. J. Kennedy, Nantasket, 1917.

Charles S. Bragdon (Progressive), 2,809; and Joseph D. Poitras (Socialist), 997. The victory of Hickey and other Democrats enables the party to dominate Brockton politics for the first time since the city was incorporated in 1881.

5 December 1912
PHILADELPHIA. In a speech before the National Housing Association, Mayor Fitzgerald scores the wealthy citizens of the country for their apathy toward the abject conditions of the poor. However, he predicts reform of the income tax law that will improve the plight of the impoverished.

9 December 1912
BROCKTON, MASSACHUSETTS. A recount of the city's mayoralty election upholds Charles M. Hickey's victory over Mayor Harry C. Howard. The recount, however, cuts down his original plurality of twenty-eight votes to twelve. With the recount, the official results of the mayoral election are: Hickey, 3,285; Howard, 3,273; Bragdon, 2,806; Poitras, 1,014.

6 January 1913
BROCKTON, MASSACHUSETTS. Charles M. Hickey is inaugurated as mayor. At the ceremony he says: "Public office is an honor as well as a trust. We should prove ourselves worthy of that honor as well as faithful to that trust."

3 February 1913
BOSTON. Inaugural exercises of the new Boston City Council are held at City Hall. John "Honey Fitz" Fitzgerald, entering the fourth year of his term, delivers his final annual message as mayor.

4 March 1913
WASHINGTON, D.C. Woodrow Wilson is inaugurated as the twenty-eighth president of the United States. Thomas R. Marshall is sworn in as vice-president.

10 April 1913
BOSTON. Tossing the ball from the pitcher's mound, Mayor Fitzgerald opens the baseball season for the world champion Boston Red Sox. The Red Sox lose to the Philadelphia Athletics, 10-9.

John Fitzgerald Kennedy Library. Photographer unknown.

Joseph P. Kennedy holding Joe, Jr., left and John, right, c. 1917

21 April 1913
BOSTON. Mayor Fitzgerald blames society dances for the abuses that occur in public dance halls. He tells a committee that hotel ballrooms should not be exempt from a regulation that dance halls close at 12 A.M.

15 May 1913
NEW YORK. Returning from the Panama Canal, Mayor Fitzgerald, his daughter Rose, and members of the Boston Chamber of Commerce arrive aboard the *Metopan,* a vessel owned by the United Fruit Company. Fitzgerald reports that the Canal is nearly complete and that potential business with South American republics could be enormous.

June 1913
BOSTON. As the school year ends, Rose Fitzgerald completes her piano studies at the New England Conservatory of Music.

11 October 1913
BOSTON. An order issued by Mayor Fitzgerald prohibits Tango-dancing, as well as a number of other new steps in public dance halls. The halls must also bar youths under 17 unaccompanied by a parent or guardian, and they must set prescribed curfews. Noncompliance with the mandate means revocation of the dance hall's license.

14 November 1913
BOSTON. Joseph P. Kennedy resigns as assistant bank examiner for the Commonwealth of Massachusetts.

29 November 1913
BOSTON. Mayor John "Honey Fitz" Fitzgerald announces that he will run for re-election for a third term. Although he had earlier agreed not to run, he changed his mind after his old political enemy James Michael Curley announced his candidacy.

John Fitzgerald Kennedy Library. Photographer unknown.

Mary Hannon Fitzgerald, left, and her daughter, Rose. Date unknown.

2 December 1913

BROCKTON, MASSACHUSETTS. Harry C. Howard, a Republican, defeats incumbent Charles M. Hickey in the election for mayor. The election results are: Howard (Republican), 4,019 votes; Hickey (Democrat), 3,947; Penney (Progressive), 1,843; Kelley (Socialist), 532.

17 December 1913

BOSTON. Mayor Fitzgerald announces that he will not run for re-election. "Honey Fitz" attributes his withdrawal from the upcoming race for mayor to his weakened physical condition. He had collapsed during an investigating tour two weeks before, and his physicians have ordered him not to run.

23 December 1913

WASHINGTON, D.C. President Wilson signs legislation creating the Federal Reserve System, a centralized banking system with a seven-person supervisory board in Washington and branches in each of twelve districts throughout the United States. The Federal Reserve Act took control of banking practices and the issuance of money out of private hands and made it a matter of government policy for the first time.

26 December 1913

BOSTON. Following an absence of three weeks after his collapse, Mayor Fitzgerald returns to work at City Hall.

2 January 1914

BROCKTON, MASSACHUSETTS. This is the last day of Mayor Hickey's term as mayor.

9 January 1914

BOSTON. Speaking before a hearing of the Committee on Reserve Bank Organization, which is to recommend locations for centers of regional federal reserve districts, Boston's Mayor John F. Fitzgerald blames

New York bankers for the dilemma of the railroad system in New England and urges that Boston be chosen as the site of a regional bank.

13 January 1914

BOSTON. James Michael Curley, who had previously served on the Boston Board of Aldermen, becomes the new mayor. With 43,262 votes, he edges out Thomas J. Kenny, who receives 37,522 votes.

20 January 1914

BOSTON. Following a successful fight to prevent a takeover of the faltering Columbia Trust Company, Joseph P. Kennedy, 25, is elected its president. The First Ward National Bank had threatened to buy out the East Boston bank, which had been organized in 1892 by Patrick Joseph Kennedy and others. Many of the stockholders were amenable to the takeover, but Patrick Kennedy was not. Seeing an opportunity both to save the bank and to further his career in banking—he had some experience already as a state bank examiner—young

Mrs. John F. Fitzgerald and her daughter, Rose Kennedy, Palm Beach, 1915.

Kennedy Family Collection. Jack Sussman, Los Angeles.

Sisters Agnes Fitzgerald and Rose Kennedy, 1923.

Kennedy Family Collection. Photographer unknown.

Kennedy sought control of the institution by borrowing money from various sources: his father, relatives, and associates such as Eugene Thayer, president of the Merchant's National Bank, and Henry J. O'Meara, his partner in a joint real estate venture. Joseph Kennedy succeeded in raising some $45,000, and, after a proxy fight, acquired a majority of the bank's stock. Subsequently, First Ward dropped its takeover attempt. His election today by the board of directors may make him the youngest bank president in the United States.

24 January 1914

BOSTON. Joseph P. Kennedy, of 144 Saratoga Street, is appointed a director of the Collateral Loan Company by Mayor Fitzgerald for a term ending in December of 1914.

Rose Kennedy, P. J. Kennedy, and Rosemary Kennedy in Nantasket, c. 1921.

Kennedy Family Collection. Photographer unknown.

P. J. Kennedy, top left and Joseph P. Kennedy, top right; Bottom, Rosemary, left and Kathleen Kennedy, right, in Nantasket, c. 1921.

The Collateral Loan Company had been created in 1859 as the Pawners' Bank to lend money on articles offered by owners. The Pawners' Bank lent up to 80 percent of value and gave owners up to a year to redeem their items while paying the loan at ½ percent interest per month. Unredeemed articles were auctioned, the proceeds going to a "profit-and-loss fund." At the end of a year, any profits of the bank were distributed to the needy for winter fuel in January, February, and March. The legislation provided that seven directors of the agency be selected annually, one chosen by the mayor, another by the governor, and five by the incorporators. On 21 February 1876, the name of Pawners' Bank had been changed by law to the more sophisticated Collateral Loan Company.

2 February 1914

BOSTON. John Francis Fitzgerald's second term as mayor ends, and James M. Curley is inaugurated. The former mayor becomes chairman of the Chamber of Commerce's Foreign Trade Committee.

18 February 1914

NEW YORK. Meeting with a group of businessmen, former mayor John F. Fitzgerald discusses ways to develop trade relations with South American countries. With the opening of the Panama Canal imminent, he predicts that business in South America will play an important role in the future commercial development of the United States.

Rose Fitzgerald Kennedy, October 1914.

TWO

THE FOUNDING OF A DYNASTY

1914 · 1946

JOE AND ROSE
1914-1928

1 June 1914

BOSTON. The engagement of Rose Elizabeth Fitzgerald to Joseph Patrick Kennedy is announced.

16 July 1914

SOUTHAMPTON, ENGLAND. Aboard the *Erin* off the coast of Southampton, Sir Thomas Lipton, the tea magnate, responds to a letter recently received from his friend John "Honey Fitz" Fitzgerald: "My dear Fitzgerald: Your kind letter of the 6th to hand. I note that Rose is getting married. Her fiance is a very lucky chap. He is getting a girl that is one of the best and cleverest that ever breathed...."

28 June 1914

SARAJEVO, SERBIA. A Serbian nationalist shoots and kills the Archduke Franz Ferdinand of Austria as his carriage moves through the streets of this Bosnian city. Russia, along with her allies England and France, lines up behind Serbia; Germany supports Austria–Hungary. Following the incident, armed troops mass along several European borders.

28 July 1914

EUROPE. After decades of tension among the great nations of Europe, the assassination of the Austrian Archduke topples the uneasy peace, and World War I erupts.

20 August 1914

BROOKLINE, MASSACHUSETTS. Soon to be married to Rose Fitzgerald, Joseph P. Kennedy buys a nine-room, two-and-a-half-story frame house at 83 Beals Street, in the Boston suburb of Brookline. The purchase price is $6,500, and he gives a down payment of $2,000 in borrowed money. The house is bought from Howard and Laura Kline in Joseph Kennedy's name. The young bank president will move into the house with his bride, Rose, when they return from their honeymoon.

Built between October 1, 1908, and April 1, 1909, the house is on a street named after James M. Beals of *The Boston Post*. Beals owned the tract of land on which it was built, and when he died, the new owner, Boston real estate dealer Benjamin B. Newhall, named the street after him. It is not totally developed, and no houses are yet built on either side of or across the street from the newly purchased Kennedy home.

(Norfolk County [Massachusetts] records indicate that under the terms of consideration, Joseph Kennedy took a $4,000 mortgage. These records make no reference to purchase price or down payment, but the $6,500 purchase price and $2,000 down payment are cited in many sources.)

7 October 1914

BOSTON. Rose Elizabeth Fitzgerald, 24, and Joseph Patrick Kennedy, 26, are married in the private chapel connected to the residence of William Cardinal O'Connell of 25 Granby Street. The Cardinal performs the wedding, which begins at 9 A.M., assisted by his secretary, the Rev. Dr. Charles J. Sullivan. The bride wears a white satin gown. The wedding party includes the bride and groom's immediate families and relatives, among them former Brockton Mayor Charles Hickey, the groom's uncle, as well as numerous friends. Rose's sister Agnes is the maid of honor; Joe's Harvard friend Joseph Donovan, class of 1911, is the best man. Following the ceremony, the wedding party travels by automobile to a breakfast reception at the Fitzgerald home at 39 Welles Avenue.

Five young Kennedys in Cohasset in 1924. Top to bottom: Joe, Jr., John, Rosemary, Kathleen, and Eunice.

Kennedy Family Collection. Photographer unknown.

Rosemary and John F. Kennedy, in Cohasset, 1924.

11 October 1914
WHITE SULPHUR SPRINGS, WEST VIRGINIA

Newlyweds Joseph and Rose Kennedy arrive by train at the Greenbrier Hotel for a two-week honeymoon. They check in at breakfast time and are given Room 145 on the first floor (immediately above the main lobby). The Greenbrier, which opened in October of 1913, is a six-story 250-room building on 7,000 acres of land. Activities include golf, horseback riding, tennis, swimming, exercise, mud baths, and mineral baths in sulphur water. There are afternoon teas and evening dances in the ballroom. The rate for a double room with twin beds ranges from $8 to $12 per day. Meals, which are extra, cost $1.50 for breakfast, $2.00 for lunch, and $2.50 for dinner.

43

15 October 1914

WASHINGTON, D.C. Congress passes the Clayton Act, which provides for greater federal regulation over monopolies and mergers.

29 October 1914

BOSTON. George Fred Fitzgerald, the brother of former mayor John "Honey Fitz" Fitzgerald and the uncle of newly married Rose (Fitzgerald) Kennedy, dies at 43 of exhaustion due to paralysis at McLean Hospital, where he had been a patient for fifteen months.

8 December 1914

BROCKTON, MASSACHUSETTS. Former Mayor Charles M. Hickey is defeated by Dr. John S. Burbank in the election for mayor. The election results are: Burbank (Republican), 5,218 votes; Hickey (Democrat), 4,431; LaCouture (Socialist), 510.

12 June 1915

SOUTH BEND, INDIANA. John Francis Fitzgerald receives an honorary Doctor of Laws degree from the University of Notre Dame at the school's commencement ceremony.

Kennedy Family Collection. Photographer unknown.

Joseph P. Kennedy and wife, Rose, in California, 1927.

Rose Kennedy and Agnes Fitzgerald, 1923.

Kennedy Family Collection. Photographer unknown.

25 July 1915

HULL, MASSACHUSETTS. A son, Joseph Patrick, Jr., is born to Rose (Fitzgerald) and Joseph P. Kennedy. The first child of the Brookline couple is delivered by Dr. Frederick L. Good of 20 Commonwealth Avenue, Boston, in a rented cottage on Atlantic Avenue in Nantasket.

The cottage, which the Kennedys have rented for the summer, is near the large Victorian-style Tudor mansion on Nantasket Avenue on Allerton Hill that Rose's parents use as a summer home. Originally the Indian name Nantasket described the whole area. It later came to designate the older end of the peninsula where the boats landed, and in about 1644 the entire area was given the name Hull.

26 September 1916

MASSACHUSETTS. John "Honey Fitz" Fitzgerald of Boston runs unopposed and wins the Democratic primary for the senatorial seat. Fitzgerald polls 64,551 votes, while "all others" receive 5. He faces the Republican candidate, Senator Henry Cabot Lodge, in the November election.

Rosemary, John, and Kathleen Kennedy in Brookline, May 1926.

15 October 1916

BOSTON. Following speculation that he would withdraw from the race for the U.S. Senate, *The Boston Globe* reports that Democratic candidate John "Honey Fitz" Fitzgerald is ready and willing to drop out of the race "if it is to the advantage of President Wilson and the Democratic ticket." He got into the race, he says, because Governor Walker and Sherman Whipple, the two most likely Democratic candidates, refused to run. Fitzgerald entered "rather than have Mr. [Henry Cabot] Lodge unopposed." Fitzgerald has bitterly criticized Senator Lodge. It is said that Fitzgerald's willingness to withdraw as a Democratic candidate is based on the fact that there might be "too many Irish names on the ticket."

7 November 1916

MASSACHUSETTS. Henry Cabot Lodge of Nahant defeats John "Honey Fitz" Fitzgerald by a plurality of nearly 33,000 votes to win the state election for the U.S. Senate. The results are: Lodge (Republican), 267,177 votes; Fitzgerald (Democrat), 234,238; William N. McDonald of Northampton (Socialist), 15,558; all others, 26.

[?] January 1917

QUINCY, MASSACHUSETTS. Joseph P. Kennedy is hired as the assistant general manager of the Fore

River Shipyard of the Bethlehem Steel Corporation. With World War I raging in Europe and the United States about to enter the war, Kennedy foresees both opportunity and challenge. He resigns as president of the Columbia Trust Company and begins his new $20,000-a-year position, in which he participates in the direction of over 30,000 men. Charles M. Schwab is chairman of the company.

4 March 1917

WASHINGTON, D.C. Woodrow Wilson and Thomas Marshall begin their second terms as president and vice-president.

2 April 1917

WASHINGTON, D.C. Following Germany's threat of unrestricted submarine warfare against all ships at sea, President Woodrow Wilson submits to mounting pressure and delivers his war message to Congress. The Senate adopts the war resolution on April 4, and with the concurrence of the House on April 6, the United States enters World War I.

Rose and Joseph P. Kennedy, 1927.

Joe, Jr., John, and Rosemary Kennedy in Nantasket, c. 1921.

29 May 1917

BROOKLINE, MASSACHUSETTS. A son, John Fitzgerald, is born to Rose (Fitzgerald), 26, and Joseph P. Kennedy, 28. He is born at 3 P.M. in the family home at 83 Beals Street in the master bedroom on the second floor. Named after his maternal grandfather, "Honey Fitz," the former mayor of Boston, John Fitzgerald Kennedy is the family's second child and second son. The baby is delivered by the family obstetrician, Dr. Frederick L. Good of Boston.

19 June 1917

BROOKLINE, MASSACHUSETTS. Twenty-one-day-old John Fitzgerald Kennedy is baptized by the Rev. Msgr. John T. Creagh at St. Aidan's Catholic Church, 158 Pleasant Street.

13 September 1918

BROOKLINE, MASSACHUSETTS. A daughter, Rosemary, is born to Rose (Fitzgerald) and Joseph P. Kennedy in the family home at 83 Beals Street. She is their third child and first daughter. Dr. Frederick L. Good delivers the baby. (Her birth certificate lists her name as Rose Marie.)

23 September 1918

BOSTON. A handbill, signed by Martin M. Lomasney, is promulgated from Ward 5 Democratic headquarters at 11-A Green Street, urging election of John "Honey Fitz" Fitzgerald in tomorrow's congressional primary.

If "Honey Fitz" is elected, the flyer says, the district will be represented by "a man of red blood, a man of vision, a tireless worker." "Honey Fitz's" opponent, Peter F. Tague, has in the past "betrayed the trust imposed in him" and voters are urged to "rebuke him sternly for his gross neglect of the interests of the plain people." Tague is "weak, spineless, ineffectual, neglectful, and powerless to accomplish," while "Honey Fitz" is "strong, courageous, able, energetic, and a powerful advocate in the cause of justice."

24 September 1918

MASSACHUSETTS. In the state primary held today, John "Honey Fitz" Fitzgerald defeats Congressman Peter F. Tague for the Democratic nomination in the Tenth Congressional District (Boston wards 1, 2, 3, 4, 5, 6) by a plurality of 50 votes. Fitzgerald receives 5,022 votes; Tague, 4,972; all others, 1.

November 1917

MOSCOW. The Bolshevik Revolution in Russia succeeds. The revolutionary forces depose Czar Alexander and assume power. Within months, the Bolshevik government will negotiate a peace treaty with Germany and drop out of the war.

5 November 1918

BOSTON. In a close race, Democrat John "Honey Fitz" Fitzgerald is elected U.S. Representative from the Tenth Congressional District. Receiving 7,227 votes, he defeats Peter F. Tague, who received 6,998 votes as an Independent and the Republican candidate Hammond T. Fletcher, who got 1,069 votes. Fitzgerald's son-in-law Joseph P. Kennedy served as a fund-raiser in his campaign.

11 November 1918

GERMANY. German representatives sign the Armistice, acknowledging the defeat of the Central Powers and ending World War I.

29 January 1919

WASHINGTON, D.C. The Eighteenth Amendment, which prohibits the manufacture, sale, and transportation of intoxicating liquor and the import or export of such liquor for beverage purposes, is ratified. Now the law of the land, prohibition is to take effect one year from this date.

19 May 1919

WASHINGTON, D.C. The first session of the Sixty-sixth Congress, of which John "Honey Fitz" Fitzgerald is a member, convenes. Fitzgerald's election is being protested. The congressional session began on 4 March 1919 and will end on 3 March 1921. The senators from Massachusetts are Henry Cabot Lodge (Republican) and David I. Walsh (Democrat).

23 October 1919

WASHINGTON, D.C. The House of Representatives meets to decide the contested election between Peter F. Tague and "Honey Fitz." Congressman-elect

Eunice, Rosemary, John, Joe, Jr., and Kathleen Kennedy in Cohasset, c. 1924.

Kennedy Family Collection. Photographer unknown.

The Kennedy family home on the corner of Naples and Abbottsford roads in Brookline, c. 1925.

Fitzgerald narrowly defeated Tague in both the Democratic primary of September 1918 and the election of November 1918. Tague, however, charged that Fitzgerald won by fraud in the primary and by "bribery, coercion, intimidation, bossism, and fraud" in the election. The House Committee on Elections has held hearings and has recommended ousting Fitzgerald.

At the end of the session, the House votes to adopt one of two resolutions: either to unseat Fitzgerald or to declare that neither candidate was properly elected and that Fitzgerald's seat be deemed vacant. By a yea-and-nay vote, it declares: "*Resolved,* That John F. Fitzgerald was not elected a Member of the House of Representatives from the Tenth Congressional district of the State of Massachusetts in this Congress and is not entitled to retain a seat herein," and "that Peter F. Tague was duly elected a member of the House of Representatives from the Tenth Congressional district of the State of Massachusetts in this Congress and is entitled to a seat herein."

1 January 1920
BOSTON.   Joseph P. Kennedy continues as a manager with the Boston branch of Hayden-Stone Company, investment bankers.

20 February 1920
BROOKLINE, MASSACHUSETTS.   A daughter, Kathleen, is born to Rose (Fitzgerald), 29, and Joseph P. Kennedy, 31. This fourth child and second daughter is born at home at 83 Beals Street and delivered by Dr.

Kennedy Family Collection. Photographer unknown.

Joe, Jr., left, and John F. Kennedy in Brookline, c. 1925.

Frederick L. Good of 95 Newbury Street, Boston. Joseph P. Kennedy is a business broker at this time.

16 March 1920
BROOKLINE, MASSACHUSETTS. To accommodate his growing family (four children and another on the way), Joseph Kennedy purchases, in Rose Kennedy's name, a large house at 51 Abbottsford Road. (In 1936 the address changed to 131 Naples Road, probably because the major entrance faces this street.) It is a 12-room corner house at the junction of Naples Road. At the time of the move, the ages of the children are: Joe Jr., 5; John, 3; Rosemary, 2; and Kathleen, 1. The Kennedys buy the house from Walter O. Hannigan for $16,000.

26 August 1920
WASHINGTON, D.C. The Nineteenth Amendment, stating that no citizen shall be denied the right to vote on account of sex, is ratified. Women can now vote in the United States of America.

18 September 1920
BOSTON. The Kennedy home at 83 Beals Street is purchased by close family friends, Edward and Mary H. Moore, in Mrs. Moore's name.

19 October 1920
BOSTON. Joseph Andrew Fitzgerald, 52, dies at Carney Hospital of aortic regurgitation. He was the brother of John Francis Fitzgerald and the uncle of Rose Kennedy.

4 March 1921
WASHINGTON, D.C. Warren G. Harding is inaugurated the twenth-ninth president of the United States. Calvin Coolidge is his vice-president.

10 July 1921
BROOKLINE, MASSACHUSETTS. A daughter, Eunice, is born to Rose (Fitzgerald), 30, and Joseph P. Kennedy, 32, in the family home at 51 Abbottsford Road. She is their fifth child and third daughter. Dr. Frederick L. Good of 64 Commonwealth Avenue delivers the baby.

Joseph P. Kennedy and sons Joe, Jr., left, and John, 1927.

Kennedy Family Collection. Royal Atelier, New York.

7 September 1921

[?]   Thomas Acton Fitzgerald marries Marion W. Reardon. The groom is the son of John Francis and Mary (Hannon) Fitzgerald and the brother of Rose Kennedy.

8 April 1922

BOSTON.   John "Honey Fitz" Fitzgerald, 61, announces that he will run for governor of Massachusetts in next fall's election.

12 September 1922

MASSACHUSETTS.   John "Honey Fitz" Fitzgerald carries nine of fourteen counties and wins the Democratic nomination for governor in the state primary by a wide margin. The election results are: Fitzgerald (Boston), 89,381 votes; Peter F. Sullivan (Worcester), 53,679; Joseph B. Ely (Westfield), 21,523; Eugene N. Foss (Boston), 13,576; all others, 0. Fitzgerald will be the Democratic candidate in the November gubernatorial election.

12 September 1922

BROOKLINE, MASSACHUSETTS.   The formal education of John F. Kennedy begins as he enters kindergarten at the Edward Devotion School at 345 Harvard Street.*

7 November 1922

MASSACHUSETTS.   Channing H. Cox is re-elected governor, defeating Democratic challenger John "Honey Fitz" Fitzgerald. Fitzgerald's son-in-law, Joseph P. Kennedy, assisted in the campaign. The election results are: Cox (Republican), 464,873; Fitzgerald (Democrat), 404,192; Walter S. Hutchins (Socialist), 9,205; John B. Lewis (Prohibition), 6,870; Henry Hess (Socialist Labor), 4,713; all others, 10.

20 May 1923

BOSTON.   Mary (Hickey) Kennedy, 65, dies of uremia at New England Baptist Hospital. She lived at 97 Washington Street in Winthrop. She leaves her husband,

---

* Records of the Edward Devotion School indicate that John Kennedy began kindergarten there on 11 October 1921. He would have been 4 years old then, and 5 when he started first grade at Devotion. In mapping out his education, this leaves one year unaccounted for. Records at the John F. Kennedy Library indicate that John began kindergarten at Edward Devotion in 1922 and first grade in 1923. Because this makes more sense, these years have been used in listing the first few years of his education. However, according to Edward Devotion records, John entered kindergarten on 11 October 1921 for nine weeks, first grade on 12 September 1922 for thirty weeks, and second grade on 11 September for 24 weeks.

Patrick Joseph, and three children, Joseph P., Loretta, and Margaret. Among her grandchildren are Joe Jr., 7; John, 5; Rosemary, 4; Kathleen, 3; and Eunice, 1.

2 August 1923

SAN FRANCISCO.   President Warren Harding's tour of the United States, with visits to Canada and Alaska, ends in tragedy when he suddenly falls ill and dies on the way back to Washington from Alaska. Harding served as president for two years and five months.

3 August 1923

WASHINGTON, D.C.   Following the death of President Harding, Vice-President Calvin Coolidge succeeds to the presidency.

[?] September 1923

BROOKLINE, MASSACHUSETTS.   John F. Kennedy, 6, begins first grade at the Edward Devotion School.

25 September 1923

BOSTON.   Eunice Fitzgerald, 23, dies of tuberculosis at her home at 39 Wells Avenue, Dorchester. The daughter of John and Mary Fitzgerald, she was the sister of Rose Kennedy, 33. Eunice had not married.

6 May 1924

BROOKLINE, MASSACHUSETTS.   A daughter, Patricia, is born to Rose (Fitzgerald), 33, and Joseph P. Kennedy, 35, in the family home at 51 Abbottsford Road. Their sixth child, she is their fourth daughter. The baby is delivered by the family physician, Dr. Frederick L. Good. Joseph Kennedy is in New York on business and is not present at the birth.

8 May 1924

NEW YORK.   After trying for weeks to halt the plunging stock price of the Yellow Cab Company, Joseph P. Kennedy succeeds in leveling off trading. Principals of the company had hired him to devise and carry out a strategy for keeping the company financially solvent after substantial trading by a Chicago brokerage firm was purportedly depressing the stock value.

29 May 1924

BROOKLINE, MASSACHUSETTS.   Patricia Kennedy, 23 days old, is baptized by the Rev. Msgr. John T. Creagh at St. Aidan's Catholic Church.

Eunice, Kathleen, and Rosemary Kennedy in Brookline, c. 1925.

Top row: Rosemary Kennedy, Rose Kennedy, Joseph P. Kennedy, Betsy Roosevelt, James Roosevelt, and Eunice Kennedy. Bottom row: Jean and Patricia Kennedy, 1934.

51

John Bouvier and daughter, Jacqueline, in August 1933.

29 September 1924

BROOKLINE, MASSACHUSETTS. John F. Kennedy, 7, enters the second grade (D class) at the Nobles and Greenough Lower School on the corner of St. Paul, Pleasant, and Freeman streets in Longwood, Massachusetts. The Nobles and Greenough Lower School (there is an Upper School in Dedham) was established in 1892 and incorporated in 1913. Miss Myra E. Fiske is the principal of the Lower School, and the tuition is $400 a year. The courses in the second grade are arithmetic, drawing, English, basket weaving, penmanship, phonics, reading, and spelling.

4 November 1924

MASSACHUSETTS. Democratic voters nominate John F. Fitzgerald, Jr., "Honey Fitz's" son and Rose Kennedy's brother, and William A. Gaston, both of Boston, as candidates for at-large membersip in the Electoral College. They lose, however, to at-large Republican candidates George A. Bacon of Longmeadow and Hester S. Fearing.

4 March 1925

WASHINGTON, D.C. President Calvin Coolidge takes the oath of office for the second time, and Charles G. Dawes becomes vice-president.

10 June 1925

BOSTON. Michael Fitzgerald, 61, dies at Homeopathic Hospital, 190 Eustic Street, of hypertrophy of the prostate. He was "Honey Fitz's" brother and Rose Kennedy's uncle.

28 September 1925

BROOKLINE, MASSACHUSETTS. John F. Kennedy, 8, enters the third grade at the Nobles and Greenough Lower School. The school catalog lists the "course of study" for the third year as arithmetic: *Atwood's Arithmetic,* Book III, *New Stone-Millis Arithmetic,* Book I, Part III; English: *Woodley's Foundation Lessons in English,* Book I, pp. 44-100; Reading: *Fables and Folk Stories, Merry Animal Tales, Fifty Famous Stories,* and other books of corresponding grade; geography: Frye's *First Book in Geography;* history: Wilson's *History Reader for Elementary Schools, and* Hubbard's *Little American History Plays;* spelling: Pearson & Suzzalo's *Essentials of Spelling,* Lower Grades, pp. 33-84; penmanship: muscular movement, medium slant; drawing: color, object and nature groups, design, lettering, action figures.

20 November 1925

BROOKLINE, MASSACHUSETTS. A son,

Robert, is born to Rose (Fitzgerald), 35, and Joseph P. Kennedy, 37, in the family home at 51 Abbottsford Road. He is their seventh child and third son. The baby is delivered by Dr. Frederick L. Good of 20 Commonwealth Avenue in Boston. (Robert Kennedy was not given the middle name Francis at birth. He took the name upon confirmation—see 1 May 1933.)

13 December 1925
BROOKLINE, MASSACHUSETTS. Thirty-day-old Robert Kennedy is baptized by the Rev. Msgr. John T. Creagh at St. Aidan's Catholic Church.

28 January 1926
BOSTON. A group of trustees, who are also parents of students who attend the Nobles and Greenough School, form the Dexter School as a corporation "to es-

John Fitzgerald Kennedy, c. 1932.

Rose and Joseph P. Kennedy in Bronxville, Christmas 1933.

tablish and maintain a school for boys which shall be devoted to educational purposes and shall never be operated for pecuniary profit...." Joseph P. Kennedy is listed as a trustee, with an address of 87 Mill Street, Boston.

7 February 1926
NEW YORK. Joseph P. Kennedy, 37, enters the motion picture production business by buying, with some associates, control of the Film Booking Offices (FBO), a British concern comprised of R-C Pictures Corporation, Film Booking Offices of America, and various subsidiaries. Kennedy and his associates purchased FBO from Lloyd's Bank, the Graham's Trading Company, and other English financial interests for a reported $10,000,000. He will later become chairman and president of FBO.

23 February 1926
REVERE, MASSACHUSETTS. Joanna (Kennedy) Mahoney dies at the age of 73. She was the sister of Patrick Joseph Kennedy and aunt of Joseph P. Kennedy. She leaves her husband, Humphrey, and her children, Frances, Henry, and Frederick.

53

7 May 1926

BOSTON.   Mary (Kennedy) Kane, 74, dies. She was the sister of Patrick Joseph Kennedy, aunt of Joseph P. Kennedy, and widow of Lawrence Kane, who died at age 46 on 19 July 1905. She leaves three children, Joseph, George, and Gertrude.

26 June 1926

BOSTON.   At a special meeting, the board of trustees of Dexter School confirms the purchase agreement of real estate—the Nobles and Greenough School in Brookline. Because of financial and other problems, the Nobles and Greenough School has sold its property to a group formed under the corporate name of Dexter School.

7 July 1926

WINTHROP, MASSACHUSETTS. James F. Hickey dies at the age of 65. A police captain and resident of 144 Saratoga Street, East Boston, he never married. The uncle of Joseph P. Kennedy, Hickey is to be buried in the Holy Cross Cemetery in Malden.

29 September 1926

BROOKLINE, MASSACHUSETTS. John F. Kennedy, 9, enters the fourth grade at Dexter School. The school catalog lists the "course of study" for the fourth year as: arithmetic: Atwood's *Arithmetic,* Book IV, pp. 170-263, Milne's *Arithmetic,* pp. 9-98; English: Woodley's *Foundation Lessons in English,* Book I, pp. 99-195, *Mother Tongue,* selected pages; geography: Frye's *New Geography,* Book I, pp. 1-142; history: Montgomery's *Beginner's American History,* Perry & Price's *American History,* First Book, pp. 1-202; reading: *Thirty More Famous Stories Retold, Stories of American Life and Adventure, Book of Legends,* and other books of corresponding grade; spelling: Pearson & Suzzallo's *Essentials of Spelling,* Middle Grades, pp. 1-32; penmanship: muscular movement, medium slant; drawing: color scales, drawing of plant forms and groups, decorative design, landscape, poster.

20 May 1927

ROOSEVELT FIELD, NEW YORK. Charles Lindbergh departs in the "Spirit of St. Louis" for the first nonstop transatlantic plane flight.

September 1927

BRONX, NEW YORK. By private railroad car, the Kennedy family—Joe Sr., Rose, Joe Jr., John, Rosemary, Kathleen, Eunice, Patricia, and Robert—moves from Brookline to a home at 5040 Independence Avenue on the corner of 252nd Street in the Riverdale section of the Bronx. Joseph P. Kennedy, now heavily involved in motion picture production, has greater business needs in New York. He also believes that his Irish Catholic family will never be able to climb the Yankee-dominated Boston social ladder, despite his great wealth.

27 September 1927

BRONX, NEW YORK.   John F. Kennedy, 10, enters the fifth grade at Riverdale Country School, a prestigious boarding and day school occupying twelve acres in Riverdale-on-Hudson. The school was founded in 1907 by its headmaster, Frank C. Hackett.

12 October 1927

WINTHROP, MASSACHUSETTS.   Mary Loretta Kennedy, 35, marries George William Connelly, 29. She is the daughter of Patrick Joseph Kennedy and Joseph P. Kennedy's sister.

Edward E. Moore, left, and Edward Moore Kennedy in Hyannis Port, c. 1934.

Kennedy Family Collection. Photographer unknown.

Kennedy Family Collection. Photographer unknown.

Bobby, Pat, and Eunice Kennedy in Bronxville, c. 1934.

23 November 1927
NEW YORK. *The Story of the Films,* edited by Joseph P. Kennedy, is published by A. W. Shaw Company. The 377-page book contains analyses of the industry by motion picture executives as told to students of the Harvard University Graduate School of Business Administration. Kennedy had invited the executives to speak at the school.

February 1928
NEW YORK. Joseph P. Kennedy is hired as a consultant to the motion picture production firm Pathé Exchange, Inc. (In one year he will be elected chairman of the Pathé board.)

20 February 1928
BOSTON. A daughter, Jean, is born to Rose (Fitzgerald), 37, and Joseph P. Kennedy, 39. This eighth child

and fifth daughter is born at St. Margaret's Hospital in Dorchester. Although the Kennedys are now residents of New York, Rose returns to the Boston area so that her long-time obstetrician, Dr. Frederick L. Good, can deliver the baby.

4 March 1928
BROOKLINE, MASSACHUSETTS. Jean Ann Kennedy, 13 days old, is baptized by the Rev. Msgr. John T. Creagh at St. Aidan's Catholic Church.

28 April 1928
DORCHESTER, MASSACHUSETTS. John F. Fitzgerald, Jr., marries Catherine O'Hearn at St. Ambrose's Church in Dorchester. The groom is "Honey Fitz's" son and Rose Kennedy's brother. The bride's father, the late Patrick O'Hearn, was building commissioner of Boston.

55

Kennedy Family Collection. Photographer unknown.

The Kennedy family in Palm Beach, c. 1934.
Top row: Joe, Jr., Joe, Sr., John, Eunice, and Rosemary.
Bottom row: Pat, Jean, Rose, Bobby, Teddy, unidentified friend.

16 May 1928
NEW YORK. E. F. Albee, president of the Keith-Albee-Orpheum Corporation, announces that Joseph P. Kennedy, in association with a financial group, has purchased a large portion of the company's common stock and will be involved in its management. Keith-Albee-Orpheum is a vaudeville theatrical circuit. Later in the year Kennedy is elected chairman, and remains in that position until 1930.

10 August 1928
NEW YORK. First National Pictures announces that Joseph P. Kennedy has been hired as a consultant in film production and distribution.

26 September 1926
BRONX, NEW YORK. John F. Kennedy, 11, enters the sixth grade at Riverdale Country School.

6 November 1928
COUNTY OF BARNSTABLE, MASSACHUSETTS

The purchase of two parcels of land in Hyannis Port by Joseph P. and Rose Kennedy is recorded in the county Registry of Deeds (Book 460, page 116). The property is on Marchant Avenue and was drawn by engineer Arthur L. Sparrow in 1928.

11 November 1928
BOSTON. Ellen (Hannon) Hefferan dies at the age of 71. She was the sister of Mary Fitzgerald and the aunt of Rose Kennedy. On 10 June 1885, she had married Maurice Hefferan, with whom she had four children: Ellen, Mary, Gertrude, and Grace.

4 March 1929
WASHINGTON, D.C. Herbert Hoover is sworn in as the thirty-first president of the United States. Charles Curtis becomes vice-president.

2 April 1929
REVERE, MASSACHUSETTS. Margaret (Kennedy) Caulfield, dies at the age of 73. She was the sister

of Patrick Joseph Kennedy and the aunt of Joseph P. Kennedy. She leaves her husband, John Thomas Caulfield, whom she married on 21 February 1882, and their children: Mary, Edith, Jeanette, and John.

4 May 1929
WESTCHESTER COUNTY, NEW YORK.   The purchase of a house at 294 Pondfield Road, Bronxville, a twelve-room colonial mansion on over six acres of land, in the name of Rose Kennedy is recorded at the Land Records Office in Deed Book 2938 (page 90).

18 May 1929
BOSTON.   Patrick Joseph Kennedy, 71, dies of carcinoma of the liver at Deaconess Hospital. He was a resident of 97 Washington Avenue in Winthrop. He leaves his son, Joseph P., and two daughters, Loretta Connelley and Margaret Burke. Among his grandchildren are Joe and Rose's children: Joe Jr., 13; John, 11; Rosemary, 10; Kathleen, 9; Eunice, 7; Patricia, 5; Robert, 3; and Jean, 1.

5 June 1929
NEW YORK.   Kathleen and Rosemary Kennedy complete grade 4, and Eunice, grade 2, at the Neighborhood School in the Bronx. All of the girls will transfer to different schools in the coming fall, and Rosemary will attend a special school in Pennsylvania.

25 September 1929
BRONX, NEW YORK.   Jack Kennedy, 12, enters the seventh grade at Riverdale Country School.

30 September 1929
WALLINGFORD, CONNECTICUT.   Classes begin at the Choate School, where 14-year-old Joseph P. Kennedy, Jr., a transfer student from Riverdale Country School, enters the third form (freshman year). His courses for the 1929-1930 school year are English 3, French 1, algebra 1, public speaking, sight singing, and intermediate Latin. Joe Jr.'s dormitory is Memorial House 2 under housemaster Ray Wentworth Tobey. The Choate School is a prestigious boys' preparatory school founded in 1896 by Judge William G. Choate. Mark Pitman was its first headmaster.

26 October 1929
[?]   Frederick Hannon Fitzgerald marries Rosalind Miller. The groom is "Honey Fitz's" son and Rose Kennedy's brother.

29 October 1929
NEW YORK.   As some 16,000,000 shares are sold at declining prices, the New York Stock Exchange fails. The day, known as "Black Tuesday," is the harbinger of the Great Depression. The Depression will last for three years, the worst the nation has ever known.

5 May 1930
BRONXVILLE, NEW YORK.   Kathleen Kennedy is confirmed by the Rt. Rev. John J. Dunn, auxiliary bishop of New York, at St. Joseph's Church on Kraft Avenue and Cedar Street. She takes as the confirmation name Agnes. Eunice Kennedy is also confirmed by the Rt. Rev. John J. Dunn and takes the confirmation name Marie.

7 May 1930
NEW YORK.   Joseph P. Kennedy resigns as president of Pathé Exchange, Inc., in order to pursue other corporate interests. Although this means he is leaving the motion picture business, he still retains an interest in a New England movie theater chain.

16 September 1930
MASSACHUSETTS.   Former Governor Joseph B. Ely of Westfield wins the Democratic nomination for governor. With 117,548 votes, he defeats both John J. Cummings and John "Honey Fitz" Fitzgerald, 67, who had withdrawn but whose name was nevertheless placed on the ballot. Fitzgerald polls 84,744 votes; Cummings 12,701. Fitzgerald concedes defeat from his bed at the Robert Breck Brigham Hospital where he is a patient.

24 September 1930
NEW MILFORD, CONNECTICUT.   The academic year begins at Canterbury School where John F. Kennedy, 13, is enrolled in the second form (eighth grade). He has transferred from Riverdale because his grades were poor and his parents felt he might do better at a boarding school. His courses for the 1930-1931 term are English, Latin, history, mathematics, and science. Away from home for the first time while attending school, he lives in Middle House dormitory. Canterbury is a Catholic preparatory school founded in 1915 by a group of Roman Catholic laymen and is the fist nonsecular academic institution John has been enrolled in.

29 September 1930
WALLINGFORD,   CONNECTICUT.   The school year begins at Choate, where Joseph P. Kennedy, Jr., 15, enters the fourth form (sophomore year). His courses for the 1930-1931 academic year are English 4, French 2, algebra 2, public speaking, and Latin (Caesar).

In Hyannis Port, c. 1934: Bobby, unidentified friend, Pat and another
unidentified friend. Jean is kneeling.

11 October 1930
MILFORD, MASSACHUSETTS. Thomas Acton
Fitzgerald, 35, "Honey Fitz's" eldest son and Rose
Kennedy's brother, is married to Margaret B. Fitzpatrick
at St. Raphael's Church by Fr. Charles F. Glennen.
Fitzgerald's first wife, Marion, died on 17 February
1925, and this is his second marriage.

30 March 1931
BOSTON. Emily Gertrude Hannon, 63, dies in
Dorchester. She was Mary Fitzgerald's sister and Rose
Kennedy's aunt.

2 May 1931
NEW MILFORD, CONNECTICUT. John F.
Kennedy officially withdraws from Canterbury School,
where he is an eighth grade student. Jack had suffered an
attack of appendicitis and had not returned to school after the Easter vacation. He will complete the academic
year with the aid of tutors.

BOSTON. Jack Kennedy's appendix is removed by
Dr. Verds of New Haven.

19 September 1931
WALLINGFORD, CONNECTICUT. Fourteen-
year-old John Kennedy begins the academic year at a
new boarding school, the Choate School, where he enters
the third form (freshman year). Jack's courses are English 3, French 1, algebra 1, and Latin 3. His roommate
in Choate House is Godfrey W. Kauffmann, and the
housemaster is Earl Blasmire ("Cappy") Leinbach. Joe
Jr., also a student at Choate, enters the fifth form (junior
year). Joe's courses for the 1931-1932 school term are
English 5, French 3, plane geometry, and Latin 5. Also a
resident of Choate House, his housemaster is Edward
Berry.

22 February 1932
BOSTON. A son, Edward Moore, is born to Rose
(Fitzgerald), 41, and Joseph P. Kennedy, 43, at St.
Margaret's Hospital in Dorchester. He is their ninth
child and fourth son. The baby is named after Edward
Moore, his father's personal aide and close friend. Jack,
14, is named as Edward's godfather. As she did with Jean,
Rose came to Boston from New York so that the baby
could be delivered by her regular obstetrician, Dr.
Frederick L. Good of 20 Commonwealth Avenue.

28 February 1932

BOSTON. Six-day-old Edward Kennedy is baptized at St. Peter's Church at 311 Bowdoin Street in Dorchester by the Rev. Leo O'Day. His brother, Jack, 14, is his godfather, and his sister, Rosemary, 13, is his godmother.

3 October 1932

WALLINGFORD, CONNECTICUT. The academic year begins at Choate, where Joe Jr. and Jack Kennedy are enrolled. Joe, in the sixth form (senior year) takes English 6, French 4, American history, public speaking, and physics; Jack, in the fourth form (sophomore year) takes English 4, French 2, algebra 2, and Latin (Caesar). In Hill House on the fourth floor, Joe's roommate is Jack Hopwood and his housemaster is F. D. Gurll. In East Cottage, Jack's roommate is K. LeMoyne Billings and his housemaster is Eugene F. Musser.

15 February 1933

MIAMI, FLORIDA. Giuseppe Zangara, an Italian immigrant, tries to shoot President-elect Franklin Delano Roosevelt. He misses and instead kills Anton Cermak, the mayor of Chicago.

4 March 1933

WASHINGTON, D.C. Former assistant secretary of the Navy and governor of New York Franklin Delano Roosevelt is inaugurated as the thirty-second president of the United States. John N. Garner is sworn in as vice-president.

6 March 1933

WASHINGTON, D.C. After thousands of American banks fail and their depositors panic, President Roosevelt orders all remaining banks closed until the Treasury Department can determine their viability.

Palm Beach, 1934. Top row: Rosemary, Pat, Eunice, Rose.
Center: Bobby, Joe, Sr., and Jean. Bottom: Teddy.

Kennedy Family Collection. Photographer unknown.

Top row: Eunice, Joseph, Sr., Rose, Kathleen, and John.
Bottom row: Jean, Teddy, Bobby and Pat, September, 1935.

9 March 1933

WASHINGTON, D.C. A special session of Congress is called by President Roosevelt to enact measures that he hopes will spur economic activity and end the Depression. The session, which lasts nearly one hundred days, marks the beginning of Roosevelt's New Deal.

1 May 1933

BRONXVILLE, NEW YORK. Robert Kennedy is confirmed by the Rt. Rev. John J. Dunn, auxiliary bishop of New York, at St. Joseph's Church at Kraft Avenue and Cedar Street. There are 137 students in his class. He takes the confirmation name Francis. Patricia Kennedy is also confirmed by the Rt. Rev. John J. Dunn and takes the confirmation name Ann.

10 June 1933

WALLINGFORD, CONNECTICUT. Joseph P. Kennedy, Jr., 17, graduates from the Choate School. His name is engraved on the Harvard Trophy as the senior who best combines scholarship and sportsmanship. He is the first Choate student to receive this honor. The Harvard football team had given the trophy to Choate two years earlier, and a similar trophy exists at Harvard. Joe's entry in the school yearbook *The Brief,* reads:

JOSEPH PATRICK KENNEDY, JR.
"Joe" "Ken"
294 Pondfield Road, Bronxville, N.Y.
Age: 17
Height: 5 ft. 11 in.
Weight: 165 lbs.

Number of years in school: 4
1929-30: League Football Team, League Hockey Team,
League Baseball Team
1930-31: League Football Team, League Hockey Team,
League Baseball Team
1931-32: Football Squad, Wrestling Squad, *Brief* Board
1932-33: Football Team, Wrestling Squad, Crew Squad,
Vice-President of the St. Andrew's Society, *Brief* Board,
Handbook Board

Harvard

30 June 1933

PALM BEACH, FLORIDA. Joseph P. Kennedy's purchase of a home at 1095 North Ocean Boulevard for $100,000 and of property adjacent to it for $15,000 is recorded in the Land and Records Office. The seven-bedroom oceanfront home will be used for family vacations. The home had been built ten years earlier by retail magnate Rodman Wanamaker.

21 September 1933

DARIEN, CONNECTICUT. Kathleen Kennedy, 13, begins the ninth grade at the Convent of the Sacred Heart in Noroton, Connecticut. The Convent of the Sacred Heart is a girls' boarding and a college preparatory school. It was founded and administered by the Religious of the Sacred Heart, a teaching order founded in France in 1800.

Kathleen and her sisters Eunice, Patricia, and Jean will, over the next several years, attend classes at convents of the Sacred Heart in different locations. All are run by the same order of nuns, and it is easy for students to transfer to different locations because the curriculum for each grade is exactly the same in each school in classes such as Latin, mathematics, science, literature, religion, psychology, and logic.

2 October 1933

WALLINGFORD, CONNECTICUT. The 1933-1934 school year begins at Choate, where John F. Kennedy, 16, enrolls in the fifth form (junior year). His courses are English 5, French 3, history A, and plane geometry. Jack's dormitory is West Wing, where K. LeMoyne Billings is his roommate for the second year, and John J. Maher is the housemaster.

9 October 1933

LONDON. The academic year begins at the London School of Economics and Political Science, where Joseph P. Kennedy, Jr., 18, is enrolled as a General Course student for the 1933-1934 session. (The General Course is equivalent to the junior year at an American college.) Joe's courses are in international relations and public ad-

ministration, and his tutor is Richard Greaves. In 1900 the London School of Economics became a recognized school of the University of London.

5 December 1933

THE UNITED STATES. The Twenty-first Amendment repeals the Eighteenth Amendment, which had prohibited the manufacture and sale of alcoholic bneverages. The manufacture, sale, transportation, and import and export of liquor are once again legal. Just a couple of months before this, Joseph Kennedy had secured American franchise rights to distribute various liquors made in Great Britain.

In September Kennedy, his wife, Rose, and James and Betsy Roosevelt had visited England, where Kennedy, along with President Franklin Roosevelt's eldest son, met with officials from Gordon's Dry Gin Company, Haig and Haig, and John Dewars and Son. Anticipating repeal of the Eighteenth Amendment (such a resolution had been passed by Congress in February), Kennedy has negotiated to distribute the products of these companies in the United States.

12 February 1934

BOSTON. John "Honey Fitz" Fitzgerald, 71, of 39 Welles Avenue, is appointed a member of the Boston Port Authority by Mayor Frederick W. Mansfield. Fitzgerald replaces the late Thomas J. A. Johnson. His five-year term will end in 1939.

The Boston Port Authority was had been formed in response to the city's decline in international maritime commerce in the face of competition from New York, Philadelphia, New Orleans, and other cities. In 1911, legislation established a directorship of the Port of Boston to further the welfare of the port, and in 1929 the Port Authority was established to promote the shipping trade. The statute provides for the mayor to name three members and for the governor of Massachusetts to name two. The agency has offices overlooking Boston Harbor from the sixteenth floor of the Custom House.

THE RISE OF JOSEPH P. KENNEDY
1934-1941

30 June 1934

WASHINGTON, D.C. President Franklin D. Roosevelt appoints five commissioners to the new Securities and Exchange Commission: Joseph P. Kennedy (Democrat), financier; George C. Mathews (Republican), a commissioner of the Federal Trade Commission (FTC); Robert E. Healy (Republican), chief counsel of the FTC; James M. Landis (Democrat), of the FTC; and Ferdinand Pecora (Democrat), a Senate Counsel.

An act of Congress in 1934 had established the Securities and Exchange Commission as a bipartisan agency of the federal government to protect the public from investing in unsafe securities and to regulate stock market prices. Because some of Kennedy's previous stock market practices have been considered unethical, his appointment immediately sparks controversy. Roosevelt's appointment of Kennedy to a five-year term—the other terms are for one, two, three and four year periods—is taken as a recommendation for chairman of the Commission. (President Roosevelt sent a memo to Ray Moley, former assistant secretary of state and now unofficial advisor to Roosevelt, regarding the chairmanship of the Securities and Exchange Commission: "I have no objection against telling Landis and Matthews that it is my best considered judgment that even if no decision is now arrived at as to the permanency of the chairmanship, the situation today calls for election of Kennedy as chairman.")

2 July 1934

WASHINGTON, D.C. The commissioners of the newly formed Securities and Exchange Commission (SEC) elect Joseph P. Kennedy its first chairman. Commissioner Ferdinand Pecora, however, had opposed the nomination. Pecora had conducted an investigation revealing that Kennedy had recently participated in the investment of a substantial amount of money in a large pool operation involving the stock of the Libbey-Owens-Ford Glass Company. Deemed to be against the public interest, corporate pools are now prohibited by law. Kennedy, James Landis, and Pecora meet in Landis' Federal Trade Commission office, and Pecora is won over. He backs Kennedy for the chairmanship. They then join the other members of the commission in George Mathews' office where they are sworn in at a ceremony. Following the oath-taking, the commissioners unanimously elect Kennedy the first chairman of the SEC for a one-year term (although his appointment as a commissioner is for five years). Kennedy's election as SEC chairman is his first major political job.

15 July 1934

WASHINGTON, D.C. The Senate Stock Market Investigating Committee releases a report harshly criticizing stock pools. Specifically cited is the pool of the Libby-Owens-Ford Glass Company, which realized a profit of $395,000 and in which it is reported that Joseph P. Kennedy was a participant. The report states that the company benefited from the popular misconception that it manufactured glass bottles and would therefore greatly profit from the repeal of prohibition, whereas in fact it did not make bottles and repeal would have no effect on its business. The report is the first of six committee investigations into questionable Wall Street activities.

19 July 1934

NANTUCKET, MASSACHUSETTS. After a year of study and travel abroad, Joseph P. Kennedy, Jr., arrives home on the *New York,* a ship of the Hamburg-American-North German Lloyd Line.

18 September 1934

NEW YORK. The commissioners of the Securities and Exchange Commission, led by Chairman Joseph P. Kennedy, begin a two-day inspection of the New York Stock Exchange. The exchange's president, Richard Whitney, and other officers guide the five SEC commissioners and John J. Burns, general counsel of the SEC, on a tour of the trading floor, the quotation departments, the bank departments, the Stock Clearing Corporation, the offices, and other departments and facilities. The commissioners and exchange officers discuss operations and problems. As of 1 October 1934, the SEC will fully regulate securities markets in the United States. Chairman Kennedy acknowledges the tremendous amount of work necessary in devising final rules and regulations for stock exchange operations and expresses hope that the SEC will have its work ready soon after the 1 October effective date.

24 September 1934

CAMBRIDGE, MASSACHUSETTS. Joseph P. Kennedy, Jr., 19, begins his freshman year at Harvard College. He is the second member of his family to attend Harvard, his father having graduated in the class of 1912.

In Palm Beach, c. 1934. Top: Pat. Center: Jean, Joe, Sr., Bobby. Bottom: Teddy.

1 October 1934

WALLINGFORD, CONNECTICUT. John F. Kennedy, 17, begins the 1934-1935 academic year at the Choate School, where he is in the sixth form (senior year). His courses are English 6, French 4, history CH, public speaking, and physics. Jack lives in West Wing with K. LeMoyne Billings, his roommate for the third year. The housemaster is again John J. Maher.

28 October 1934

WINTHROP, MASSACHUSETTS. Dr. John A. Hickey dies at the age of 68. Hickey had never married. The uncle of Joseph P. Kennedy, he was a physician who resided at 238 Shore Drive. He will be buried in the Holy Cross Cemetery in Malden.

1 November 1934

WASHINGTON, D.C. President Roosevelt confers with Securities and Exchange Commission chairman Joseph P. Kennedy on the federal budget, which had shown a deficit of over a billion dollars for the past four months (a record high for the year).

15 November 1934

BOSTON. Joseph Kennedy clarifies the role of the Securities and Ex hange Commission in a speech before the Boston Chamber of Commerce that is broadcast on nationwide radio. As a partner "of honest business" and a prosecutor "of dishonesty," the newly formed commission will encourage legitimate enterprise and eliminate those businesses involved in illegal activities. Kennedy addresses criticism that the SEC imposes stringent liability on corporate directors and that registration can be excessively long, expensive, and require impertinent information. Careful directors can avoid liability, he indicates. Registration delays are exaggerated, and modest registration expenses are calculated under a normal accounting formula. He further claims questionnaires requesting only relevant information were being drawn up. He warns the public of many fraudulent offerings and urges buyers to take special precautions before turning over their cash or securities to anyone. The initials SEC, he hopes, "will come to stand for 'Securities Ex-Crookedness.'"

16 January 1935

WASHINGTON, D.C. The Senate confirms the nomination of Joseph P. Kennedy as chairman of the Securities and Exchange Commission.

5 February 1935

LOCATION UNKNOWN. Frederick Hannon Fitzgerald dies at the age of 30. On 26 October 1929 he

had married Rosalind Miller. In addition to his wife he leaves his parents, his sisters, Rose Kennedy and Agnes Gargan, and his brothers, Thomas and John Jr.

19 March 1935

NEW YORK. In an address before members of the American Arbitration Association, SEC chairman Joseph P. Kennedy praises President Roosevelt's New Deal and describes how these policies will result in economic recovery,.

23 April 1935

BOSTON. Joseph P. Kennedy, class of 1908, delivers the keynote speech at the Boston Latin School's three hundredth anniversary dinner.

30 April 1935

BRONXVILLE, New York. Jean Kennedy is confirmed by the Rt. Rev. Stephen J. Donohue, auxiliary bishop of New York, at St. Joseph's Church. She takes the confirmation name Ann.

1 May 1935

WASHINGTON, D.C. President Roosevelt holds a White House conference on the national work-relief program. He urges its various managers to carry out operations as rapidly as possible. Those attending include Joseph P. Kennedy; Frank C. Walker, chairman of the Emergency Council; Secretary of the Treasury Henry Morgenthau, Jr.; and Secretary of the Interior Harold L. Ickes. Joseph P. Kennedy is affirmed as unofficial business adviser to the work-relief project.

8 June 1935

WALLINGFORD, CONNECTICUT. John F. Kennedy, 18, graduates from the Choate School. Of 110 students in his class, Jack Kennedy is voted "most likely to succeed" by his classmates. His entry in the school yearbook, *The Brief,* reads:

JOHN FITZGERALD KENNEDY
"Jack" "Ken"
294 Pondfield Road, Bronxville, N.Y.
Age: 17
Height: 5 ft. 11 in.
Weight: 155 lbs.
Number of years in School: 4
1931-32: League Football, League Basketball, League Baseball
1932-33: League Football, Second Baseball Squad, Blue Basketball Team, *Brief* Board
1933-34: Junior Football Team, Second Basketball Squad, *Brief* Board
1934-35: Business Manager of the *Brief,* Golf Squad

Kennedy Family Collection. Photographer unknown.

LeMoyne Billings and John F. Kennedy in Palm Beach, c. 1936.

19 June 1935
BROCKTON, MASSACHUSETTS.   Charles M. Hickey, 76, dies of pneumonia. The uncle of Joseph P. Kennedy and a former mayor of Brockton, Hickey had been president of a funeral home at the time of his death. He is survived by a daughter, Alice M. J. Collins; four sons, Frank, James, John, Charles F.; and one sister, Catherine Hickey. He had been married on 4 September 1884 to Hannah C. Murphy.

1 July 1935
WASHINGTON, D.C.   Joseph P. Kennedy, whose one-year term as chairman of the Securities and Exchange commission comes to a close, is re-elected chairman for a second one-year term.

23 July 1935
NEW YORK.   *Time* magazine publishes a cover story on SEC chairman Joseph P. Kennedy. Underneath his picture is the caption, "He makes it easy for the honest" (Volume XXVI, number 4). The cover boasts a circulation of "more than 500,000."

14 August 1935
WASHINGTON, D.C.   Congress passes the Social Security Act, which provides retirement benefits, unemployment insurance benefits, and financial assistance to the needy and the blind.

22 September 1935
WASHINGTON, D.C.   After fourteen months in office, Joseph P. Kennedy officially steps down as chairman of the Securities and Exchange Commission. Kennedy believes he has achieved his goals: the SEC is now one of the most successful of the New Deal reform agencies, and even Kennedy's opponents have admitted their mistake in criticizing his appointment. Later in that day James M. Landis is elected the commission's second chairman.

25 September 1935
NEW YORK.   Joseph, Rose, Jack, and Kathleen Kennedy leave by ship for England. The elder Kennedys will visit a number of countries in Europe; John will study in London, Kathleen in France.

NEW YORK. Eunice Kennedy, 14, enters the Convent of the Sacred Heart in Maplehurst in the Bronx, to begin the ninth grade. The convent has a day school and a five-day boarding school.

7 October 1935

LONDON. The academic year begins at the London School of Economics and Political Science (University of London), where John F. Kennedy is registered as a general course student for the 1935-1936 session. Jack's assigned supervisor is Professor K. B. Smellie.

24 October 1935

LONDON. The London School of Economics and Political Science issues instructions that the tuition fees of John F. Kennedy be refunded. He is withdrawing because of illness. According to records at LSE, it is unlikely that Kennedy attended any lectures.

26 October 1935

PRINCETON, NEW JERSEY. Having withdrawn from the London School of Economics and Political Science following an attack of jaundice, Jack Kennedy returns to the United States. Now he enters Princeton University, where classes began on 25 September. Registered as a freshman, Jack joins his Choate friends K. LeMoyne Billings and Ralph Horton, Jr. The three share a dorm room at Reunion Hall.

14 November 1935

WASHINGTON, D.C. Back after six weeks in Europe, Joseph P. Kennedy reports on monetary and other economic conditions in England, France, and elsewhere to President Roosevelt. Kennedy points out that foreign officials have confidence in Roosevelt's recovery programs and that the President enjoys a fine reputation abroad. Kennedy is an overnight guest at the White House.

5 December 1935

PRINCETON, NEW JERSEY. A recurrence of jaundice forces John F. Kennedy to leave Princeton.

12 December 1935

PRINCETON, NEW JERSEY. John F. Kennedy formally withdraws from Princeton University. No specific reason is officially given.

31 January 1936

NEW YORK. Joseph P. Kennedy explains his recapitalization plan to officers of RCA. In essence, the plan calls for borrowing $10 million at 2½% as working capital, retiring all outstanding Class A preferred stock for cash, and exchanging all shares of Class B preferred stock for a combination of securities of first preferred and common shares, with the preferred shares convertible into common stock.

1 May 1936

NEW YORK. The board of directors of Paramount Pictures, Inc., announces that it has retained Joseph P. Kennedy as a special consultant to improve the company's performance. He is to survey problems such as the rising cost of making motion pictures and recommend ways to cut costs and make production more profitable.

16 July 1936

NEW YORK. Joseph P. Kennedy's report on studio profitability to Paramount Pictures, Inc., is made public. The report cites problems such as unsuitable personnel and poor morale within the company and calls for drastic revision of management and for experienced theater executives to be added to the board of directors. Kennedy also suggests a compensation schedule of salary and bonus—a nominal fixed salary and a bonus for different increments of profit reached by a motion picture. Kennedy's report to the board of directors, for which he receives $50,000, is dated 12 June 1936.

21 August 1936

NEW YORK. *I'm for Roosevelt* by Joseph P. Kennedy is published by Reynal and Hitchcock. The 149-page book demonstrates that the programs and policies of President Roosevelt have helped to revitalize America's economy and defends the New Deal.

28 August 1936

NEW YORK. A letter concerning Jack Kennedy's college career is sent by Joseph P. Kennedy from his offices at 30 Rockefeller Plaza to the dean of freshmen at Harvard College, Delmar Leighton. Kennedy explains that Jack's illness forced him to withdraw from Princeton in December 1935, and that he spent the following months at Boston's Peter Bent Brigham Hospital, in the South, and in Arizona, but "is now in good condition." The elder Kennedy writes of his son's ambition to complete his education in three years and asks that a Harvard adviser meet with Jack to discuss this.

17 September 1936

BOSTON. Mary Agnes (Fitzgerald) Gargan dies at the age of 43 of chronic hypertensive cardiorenal disease

Keystone, Courtesy of Boston Herald.

The Kennedy family at the coronation of Pope Pius XII: Kathleen, Pat, Bobby, Jack, Rose, Joe, Sr., Teddy, Eunice, Jean, Rosemary (?).

at 22 May Street in West Roxbury. The daughter of John "Honey Fitz" and Mary Fitzgerald and the sister of Rose Kennedy, she leaves her husband, Joseph, whom she married on 29 April 1929, and children: Joseph Jr., 6; Mary Jo, 3; and Ann, 2.

23 September 1936
BOSTON. Agnes Gargan is buried at St. Joseph's Cemetery in West Roxbury.

23 September 1936
NEW YORK. Patricia Kennedy, 12, enters the Convent of the Sacred Heart in Maplehurst and begins the ninth grade.

28 September 1936
CAMBRIDGE, MASSACHUSETTS. John F. Kennedy enters Harvard University as a freshman. Attacks of jaundice had forced him to withdraw, the previ-

ous fall, first from the London School of Economics and then from Princeton University. In entering Harvard, 19-year-old Jack joins his brother Joe Jr., who is a junior there. Jack will be taking economics, history, and French.

30 September 1936
CAMBRIDGE, MASSACHUSETTS. Joseph P. Kennedy arrives from New York to visit Joe Jr., at Philips House, while his son recovers from an operation to repair football injuries.

5 October 1936
NEW YORK. Joseph P. Kennedy urges the re-election of President Roosevelt in a nationwide radio address over a Columbia Broadcasting System hookup. He says that "any substantial reversal of the New Deal economic policy...would retard rather than advance recovery."

Kennedy Family Collection. Photographer unknown.

Teddy, Jack, and Bobby in Palm Beach, c. 1937.

12 October 1936
NEW YORK. Joseph P. Kennedy releases a study and analysis of certain Paramount Pictures business affairs to the company's board of directors.

21 October 1936
NEW YORK In a radio address over WABC that is broadcast nationwide over the Columbia Broadcasting System, Joseph P. Kennedy urges American businessmen to re-elect President Roosevelt in next month's election.

24 October 1936
BOSTON. Speaking at a dinner of the Democratic Business Men's League of Massachusetts, Joseph P. Kennedy assails those who claim that President Roosevelt's actions are communistic and radical. The President, he says, has given the people a "Christian program of social justice."

31 October 1936
BOSTON. Joseph P. Kennedy makes a final campaign speech on President Roosevelt's behalf. In a radio address, Kennedy criticizes last-ditch Republican attempts to smear social security as "grossly unfair."

3 November 1936
THE UNITED STATES. Franklin Delano Roosevelt is re-elected by a landslide to a second term as president.

MASSACHUSETTS. John "Honey Fitz" Fitzgerald, 73, is chosen as the presidential elector from the Twelfth Congressional District. In Massachusetts, presidential electors are members of the Electoral College, which usually meets during the month after a presidential popular election. The outcome of the popular vote determines whether the Democratic or Republican electors will meet to vote. In the Commonwealth of Massachusetts, anyone chosen to participate in the Electoral College is entitled to the title Honorable for the rest of his or her life.

5 November 1936
HYDE PARK, NEW YORK. A luncheon is held at President Roosevelt's home in honor of the papal secretary, Eugenio Cardinal Pacelli. On a tour of the United States, Cardinal Pacelli journeys to Hyde Park from New York aboard a private train in a party that includes Joseph and Rose Kennedy and prelates Bishop Donahue

of New York, Bishop Spellman of Boston, and Vatican assistant Enrico Galleazzi. The train arrives at Poughkeepsie shortly after noon, and the visitors are taken in two White House cars to the President's home.

BRONXVILLE, NEW YORK. Later in the day, Cardinal Pacelli and his party visit the Kennedy home at 294 Pondfield Road. Many important citizens from the area come to meet the church dignitaries, and several of the Kennedy children are presented to them.

14 December 1936
BOSTON. With the other Massachusetts Democratic presidential electors, John "Honey Fitz" Fitzgerald meets at the State House to vote for presidential nominee Franklin D. Roosevelt. Under the Constitution, a congressman cannot serve as a presidential elector. Fitzgerald is a *former* congressman now serving as an elector.

20 January 1937
WASHINGTON, D.C. Franklin D. Roosevelt takes the oath of office and begins his second term as president.

24 March 1937
WASHINGTON, D.C. President Roosevelt nominates Joseph P. Kennedy for chairman of the United States Maritime Commission.

15 April 1937
WASHINGTON, D.C. The Senate confirms President Roosevelt's appointment of Joseph P. Kennedy as a member of the United States Maritime Commission.

Established by the Merchant Marine Act of 1936 as an independent government agency, the commission administers that statute as well as the Shipping Act of 1916, the Merchant Marine Act of 1920, and the Intercoastal Shipping Act of 1933. The Maritime Commission is responsible for developing and maintaining a Merchant Marine that is "sufficient to carry its domestic water borne export...and import foreign commerce...and capable of serving as a naval and military auxiliary in time of war or national emergency." The act provides for a five-member commission.

Bobby Kennedy in Palm Beach, c. 1934.

Kennedy Family Collection. Photographer unknown.

16 April 1937

WASHINGTON, D.C. President Roosevelt appoints Joseph P. Kennedy chairman of the Maritime Commission. Kennedy now faces the huge task of building an American Merchant Marine. The chairman's salary is $12,000 per year.

17 April 1937

WASHINGTON, D.C. Speaking at a convention of the American Society of Newspaper Editors, U.S. Maritime Commission Chairman Joseph P. Kennedy discusses his responsibilities and analyzes the trend toward centralization in government.

7 May 1937

CAMBRIDGE, MASSACHUSETTS. Spring term ends at Harvard College, where Jack Kennedy has completed his freshman year. This summer he will travel to Europe with his friend LeMoyne Billings.

27 September 1937

CAMBRIDGE, MASSACHUSETTS. Fall term begins at Harvard College, where John F. Kennedy, 20, is a sophomore. Jack will be taking government, history, fine arts, and English courses.

8 June 1937

DARIEN, CONNECTICUT. Kathleen Kennedy, 17, is graduated from the Convent of the Sacred Heart, Noroton. Kathleen had attended the school for the ninth and tenth grades, but left in June 1935 to spend the following school year abroad, returning to classes on 21 September 1936 and enrolling in the twelfth grade.

5 January 1938

WASHINGTON, D.C. President Roosevelt formally nominates Joseph P. Kennedy as ambassador to Great Britain. Robert W. Bingham, the present ambassador, suffers from malaria and has tendered his resignation. Senate confirmation and English government approval are needed for the appointment to become final. If approved, Kennedy will be the first person of Irish descent and the first Roman Catholic to serve as an American ambassador to predominantly Protestant Great Britain.

8 January 1938

LOS ANGELES. U.S. Maritime Commission chairman Joseph P. Kennedy arrives to study shipping conditions on the Pacific coast.

13 January 1938

WASHINGTON, D.C. The Senate confirms President Roosevelt's appointment of Joseph P. Kennedy as ambassador to Great Britain.

24 January 1938

BOSTON. At a ceremony held at the Mechanics Building, Joseph P. Kennedy officially opens the Greater Boston 1938 Community Fund Campaign.

25 January 1938

BOSTON. Suffering from severe abdominal pains, Rose Kennedy undergoes an appendectomy at St. Elizabeth's Hospital in Brighton. Dr. Frederick L. Good performs the operation, assisted by Dr. Joseph Doyle and Dr. Thomas White.

26 January 1938

WASHINGTON, D.C. Speaking before the Senate Commerce Committee, U.S. Maritime Commission Chairman Joseph P. Kennedy says that, despite union objections to the Commission interventions in labor disputes, he believes government arbitration and mediation is necessary for the shipbuilding industry and not harmful to labor.

11 February 1938

BOSTON. A testimonial luncheon is sponsored by the Boston Chamber of Commerce to celebrate the seventy-fifth birthday of "Honey Fitz" Fitzgerald. Over 750 merchants, bankers, and industrialists gather to honor the former mayor.

12 February 1938

BOSTON. An acrostic written by the "Kennedy Brothers, Joe and John" appears in today's edition of *The Boston Post.* This tribute in verse to their grandfather on his seventy-fifth birthday reads:

Jolly toward his fellow men,
Obstinate in his will to be,
Helpful where and when he can,
Novel plan of land and sea.

Fruitful seeds of liberty.

Fighting Fitz has pioneered,
Inimitable with wit and charity,
To virtues both his life reared,
Zealous for truth, beloved and feared,
Gracious champion of the melting pot,
Energetic now and when he appeared,
Resistless defender of Boston's lot
Alert in giving the helpless care
Lovable chief, the first to bear,
Deserving title, "Boston's Greatest Mayor."

Kennedy Family Collection. Photographer unknown.

Kathleen and Joseph P. Kennedy, Jr., in Ireland, 1937.

14 February 1938

BOSTON. Released from St. Elizabeth's Hospital four days earlier, Rose Kennedy leaves for New York. From there she will go to Palm Beach, Florida, to recover from her recent appendectomy.

17 February 1938

WASHINGTON, D.C. After ten months as chairman of the Maritime Commission, Joseph P. Kennedy submits his resignation to President Roosevelt. In his letter he reports that the shipping problem is far from solved and that the United States must take strenuous measures to preserve a fleet of present proportions in foreign or domestic trade.

18 February 1938

WASHINGTON, D.C. Associate Supreme Court Justice Stanley Reed swears in Joseph P. Kennedy as Ambassador Extraordinary and Plenipotentiary to the United Kingdom of Great Britain and Northern Ireland. President Roosevelt watches the ceremony and receives the new ambassador after a press conference. Roosevelt also accepts Kennedy's resignation as chairman of the Maritime Commission. In a letter he praises his accomplishments and states that his regret "is tempered by the fact that you are staying in the family and taking over a new assignment." Roosevelt appoints Rear Admiral Emory S. Land (Retired) as the new chairman of the Maritime Commission.

22 February 1938

HYDE PARK, NEW YORK. Prior to Joseph P. Kennedy's voyage to London, where he will take up duties as U.S. Ambassador to the Court of St. James, President Roosevelt confers with Kennedy at his home for several hours on the political and economic situation in Europe and outlines the objectives he wants the new ambassador to achieve.

February-March 1938

NEW YORK. Patricia Kennedy transfers from the Convent of the Sacred Heart in Maplehurst to the Convent of the Sacred Heart at Roehampton, England.

NEW YORK. Robert F. Kennedy withdraws from the Riverdale Country School in the Bronx in order to leave with his family for England.

1 March 1938

LONDON. The new ambassador to Great Britain Joseph P. Kennedy takes up residence at the American embassy at 14 Prince's Gate.

4 March 1938

LONDON. After a brief ride through the streets of London on horseback, Ambassador Joseph P. Kennedy makes an official call on Prime Minister Neville Chamberlain at 10 Downing Street. The American ambassador presents Chamberlain with President Roosevelt's view that the two countries should resist any threats made by Hitler and should strengthen their joint economies through more vigorous trade.

8 March 1938

LONDON. Before officially assuming the duties of ambassador to the Court of St. James, Joseph P. Kennedy presents his credentials to King George VI. Landaus from the palace with coachmen and footmen in formal attire bring Ambassador Kennedy and his staff to Buckingham Palace.

9 March 1938

NEW YORK. Rose Kennedy and five of her children,

Kathleen, Patricia, Robert, Jean, and Edward, embark on the *Washington* for England to take up residence in London. The other children, Joe Jr. and John, both students at Harvard, and Rosemary and Eunice, both at convent schools, will join the family later. At the pier to bid the voyagers farewell are a group of family and friends, including Rose's parents and Joe Jr. The actress Mary Pickford, also at the pier, interviews the departing family for a newspaper article.

17 March 1938

LONDON.   In white tie and tails, Ambassador Joseph P. Kennedy attends his first levee at St. James's Palace. It is an afternoon reception at which King George VI, in full dress military uniform, receives male guests only.

CAMBRIDGE, MASSACHUSETTS.   The results of the class-day committee election at Harvard are announced. Seven candidates have been selected from a pool of nine. Joe Kennedy, Jr. is elected to the committee, which will coordinate graduation ceremonies in June. Having received the most votes, he is also the committee's chairman.

23 March 1938

CAMBRIDGE, MASSACHUSETTS.   Explaining that he is receiving too much publicity over his membership in the cast of a Pi Eta Club show, Joe Kennedy, Jr., resigns from the troupe that is rehearsing a show called *Revolt in Reverse.* Joe denies reports that he is leaving because he had to appear in the show as a hula girl. He says that he was to have briefly portrayed a marine.

24 March 1938

LONDON.   Speaking before members of the American Club, Ambassador Kennedy claims that war will not break out in Europe before the end of 1938. This belief, he says, is based upon his discussions with British leaders.

29 March 1938

LONDON.   Several important British bankers attend a dinner given by Ambassador Kennedy at the American embassy to discuss England's economic plans for rearmament and for trade relations between the United States and Great Britain.

7 April 1938

LONDON.   Eighteen-year-old Kathleen Kennedy makes her debut in London society at a reception given at the Dartmouth House. She is to be presented next at the royal court.

9 April 1939

WINDSOR.   Ambassador and Mrs. Joseph P. Kennedy are weekend guests of King George and Queen Elizabeth at Windsor Castle.

10 April 1938

BOSTON.   Before 1,000 members of the YMCA at an annual communion breakfast, "Honey Fitz" Fitzgerald announces the establishment of a full annual scholarship sponsored by Rose Kennedy to aid a deserving graduate of any public or parochial grammar school in the greater Boston area. Rose has not specifically named a recipient, and Fitzgerald assigns the fund to Boston College High School, which he feels merits it most.

16 April 1938

DARIEN, CONNECTICUT.   Eunice Kennedy withdraws from the Convent of the Sacred Heart in Noroton, where she is enrolled in the eleventh grade. She will complete her secondary education at the Convent of the Sacred Heart, Roehampton, England.

20 April 1938

NEW YORK.   Rosemary Kennedy, a student at Marymount Convent in Tarrytown, New York, and Eunice Kennedy, a student at Sacred Heart Convent in Noroton, in Darien, Connecticut,* leave on the *Manhattan* to join the family in England. This is their first trip to the country where their father serves as United States ambassador.

29 April 1938

BROOKLINE, MASSACHUSETTS.   Before an audience of six hundred, Joseph Kennedy, Jr., debates John Doyle Elliott on the Townsend plan at the Town Hall. Elliott supports the plan and Kennedy speaks against it. No decision is given.

11 May 1938

LONDON.   Rose Kennedy and her daughters Rosemary and Kathleen are presented at court along with five other American women. The presentation creates a mild sensation both because it is the first under the new ambassador's policy of restricting presentations to permanent American residents in England (in the past, visiting American debutantes were presented at Court, and many ladies' noses are out of joint over the issue), and because Ambassador Kennedy, disregarding the custom of wearing knee breeches, wears white tie and tails. Mrs.

---

* Despite the Noroton in the school's name, it is actually in Darien.

Kennedy and Rosemary wear Molyneaux gowns; Kathleen wears a Chanel.

30 May 1938
LONDON. Ambassador Joseph P. Kennedy observes Memorial Day by attending services at the Collegiate Church of Saint Peter in Westminster Abbey.

2 June 1938
LONDON. Rosemary and Kathleen Kennedy make their London debut at a party given by their father. They dance with a number of eligible bachelors, including the Earl of Craven, Prince Frederick of Russia, Viscount Duncannon, David Rockefeller, and Baron von Flotow.

23 June 1938
CAMBRIDGE, MASSACHUSETTS. Joe Kennedy, Jr., 22, graduates from Harvard College with a Bachelor of Arts degree. Class day exercises begin at 2:00 P.M. His entry in the *Harvard Class Album,* Volume XLIX reads:

> In college four years. John Winthrop House. House Basketball (2-4); Football (1); Squad (2, 4); House Swimming (2-4); Rugby (1,2); Union Committee; Freshman Smoker Chairman; Student Council (3, 4); House Committee (3), Chairman (4), Pi Eta Theatricals (2, 3); St. Paul's Catholic Club (1-4). Hasty Pudding-Institute of 1770; Pi Eta; Iroquois Club. Junior Usher; *Album* Committee, Business Chairman; Class Day Committee, Chairman (4). Field of Concentration: Government. Intended Vocation: Business. Joe Jr. is listed as one of the *Album*'s five publishers.

25 June 1938
WASHINGTON, D.C. Ambassador Joseph P. Kennedy spends all day in conference with different American leaders and government officials. In the morning, he meets separately with Undersecretary of State Sumner Welles and Secretary of State Cordell Hull; in the afternoon, he discusses trade relations between America and England with directors of the Trade Agreements Division; in the evening, he discusses relations between the United States and Great Britain over dinner with President Roosevelt.

7 July 1938
DUBLIN. Ambassador Joseph P. Kennedy receives an honorary Doctor of Laws degree from the National University. The award is presented by Irish Prime Minister Eamon de Valera, who is also the chancellor of the school. Joe Kennedy, Jr., is presented at the ceremony.

8 July 1938
DUBLIN. The Irish government gives a banquet in honor of Ambassador Joseph P. Kennedy at Dublin Cas-

tle. Prime Minister Eamon de Valera welcomes the Ambassador, praising both Kennedy and the United States in a toast.

12 July 1938
WINCHESTER, ENGLAND. Ambassador Kennedy attends the unveiling of a window in honor of the late King George V at Westminster Cathedral. Following the dedication, Kennedy speaks briefly, praising the Intergovernmental Refugee Conference at Evian-les-Bains in eastern France, which, he says, reflects King George's ideals.

13 July 1938
LONDON. A dinner party is given at the American embassy by Ambassador and Mrs. Joseph P. Kennedy. Among the guests are the Finnish Minister and Mme. de Gripenberg, United States Treasurer and Mrs. William Julian, and Mr. and Mrs. Eddie Cantor.

22 July 1938
LONDON. Twenty-eight nuns from Barcelona are given refuge in England due to the efforts of Ambassador Joseph Kennedy. Since visiting his daughters—Patricia, Eunice, and Jean—at their school, the Convent of the Sacred Heart, Roehampton, Ambassador Kennedy has sought sanctuary for the Spanish Sacred Heart sisters. With the assistance of Prime Minister Neville Chamberlain, the cooperation of the Spanish government is obtained, and the nuns are brought to England aboard the British warship *Hero.* The sisters will take up residence at various Sacred Heart convents in England.

2 September 1938
ABERDEEN, SCOTLAND. Speaking at the dedication of a memorial for Samuel Seabury in Aberdeen Cathedral, Ambassador Joseph P. Kennedy assails governments that oppress citizens because of their religions. He also says that war, which looms ahead, could be avoided by "common sense" and "spiritual courage."

11 September 1938
LONDON. Following four days of conferences with high-ranking British ministers, both Prime Minister Neville Chamberlain and Foreign Secretary Viscount Halifax meet with Ambassador Kennedy to present the British government's position with regard to Germany's aggression and the threat of war.

18 September 1938
LONDON. With the outbreak of war a possibility, Ambassador and Mrs. Kennedy send their younger children to Ireland for their safety.

26 September 1938

CAMBRIDGE, MASSACHUSETTS. John F. Kennedy, 21, begins fall classes at Harvard. Now in his junior year, Jack's courses include economics, government, English, and history.

29 September 1938

MUNICH. Acting for England and France, Prime Minister Neville Chamberlain signs an agreement with Hitler that sidesteps armed conflict with Germany and, in effect, cedes Czechoslovakia to Nazi Germany.

6 October 1938

LONDON. Following a debate in the House of Commons in which Neville Chamberlain criticized political appeasement, Ambassador Kennedy calls on the Prime Minister at 10 Downing Street.

14 October 1938

LONDON. Ambassador Kennedy discusses the proposed partition of Palestine with British Foreign Secretary for Colonies and Dominions Malcolm MacDonald.

19 October 1938

LONDON. Speaking at a Navy League's annual Trafalgar Day dinner, Ambassador Joseph P. Kennedy says that democracies and dictatorships "have to live together in the same world" and that there is no sense in letting their "differences grow into unrelenting antagonisms." He also says that countries, including the United States, must end their frenetic buildup of armaments, as it may eventually result in "a major disaster."

27 October 1938

EDINBURGH, SCOTLAND. The City Council confers the Freedom of the City award on Ambassador Joseph P. Kennedy. Prime Minsiter Neville Chamberlain also receives the award.

13 November 1938

ESSEX, ENGLAND. At the country home of British Secretary for Colonies and Dominions Malcolm MacDonald, Ambassador Kennedy describes how urgent it is for England and the other countries of the Commonwealth to rescue German Jews from a crisis that worsens each day.

15 November 1938

LONDON. Prime Minister Neville Chamberlain studies a plan for rescuing and resettling German Jews that he had devised earlier with Ambassador Kennedy, British Foreign Secretary Viscount Halifax, and Dominions and Colonial Secretary Malcolm MacDonald. The proposal calls for huge financial contributions both from governments and from individual citizens of many countries, and for certain geographic areas to be developed for Jewish organizations.

17 November 1938

LONDON. Discussions are held this morning between Ambassador Kennedy and Malcolm MacDonald, British Secretary for Colonies and Dominions, on England's plans to help Jews in Germany find refuge from Nazi persecution. In the evening, Ambassador Kennedy discusses British refugee proposals with members of the Labor Party. Earlier that day in the House of Commons, Prime Minister Neville Chamberlain said that Tanganyika was being considered as a refuge for German Jews.

24 November 1938

LONDON. Addressing a Thanksgiving Day dinner of the American Society, Ambassador Joseph P. Kennedy discusses the need for democracies to recognize the rights of minorities and says that failure in this area can lead to "internal decay" and "perhaps to civil conflict."

5 December 1938

BOSTON. In an interview published in the *Boston American* John F. Kennedy reports that his parents hold no grudge against Sophie Tucker, who makes some quips about the Kennedys onstage in Cole Porter's new broadway musical, "Leave It to Me." "My mother and father have a swell sense of humor," Jack says. He adds that his mother has requested a script of the show.

16 December 1938

WASHINGTON, D.C. Having arrived in New York from England yesterday, Ambassador Joseph P. Kennedy meets with President Roosevelt to discuss the political situation in Europe.

9 January 1939

WASHINGTON, D.C. Joseph P. Kennedy and William C. Bullitt, the American ambassador to France, counsel President Roosevelt on the volatile political situation in Europe. Roosevelt is to deliver a national defense message within the next few days, and their advice will support his request for greater military aid.

10 January 1939

WASHINGTON, D.C. Ambassadors Kennedy and Bullitt testify before a secret joint executive hearing of the House and Senate Military Affairs Committee. They discuss the superior military strength of Germany, particularly its air force, and the effect that this military superiority has had on England and France. They also warn that Mussolini's demands could result in war.

7 February 1939
CAMBRIDGE, MASSACHUSETTS. John Kennedy is granted a leave of absence from Harvard for the spring semester to go abroad. He will sail for London in two weeks. At his father's suggestion, Jack will work at the American embassy in London. The Ambassador thinks this will give his son an opportunity to see if a career in international relations appeals to him. When he returns, Jack plans to double up on his studies and graduate from Harvard with his class.

16 February 1939
MADRID. The city is under fire by Nationalist troops. Joe Kennedy, Jr., arrives to observe the Spanish Civil War first-hand. The Spanish government has supplied him with a bus to travel in.

25 February 1939
LONDON. After an unofficial meeting between Arab and Jewish representatives about the problems of establishing an independent Arab and Jewish state in Palestine, two Jewish leaders, Rabbi Stephen Samuel Wise and Louis Lipsky, confer with Ambassador Joseph P. Kennedy. The Jewish delegation to the Palestinian conference is considering an appeal to President Roosevelt if the conference, promoted and mediated by the British government, takes a turn they consider unfavorable.

28 February 1939
LONDON. British Foreign Secretary Viscount Halifax confers with Ambassador Joseph P. Kennedy on the current status of the Palestinian Conference. Earlier in the day, Jewish delegates had told the British that their terms for the creation of an Arab state in Palestine were unacceptable.

8 March 1939
LONDON. The Palestinian Conference makes no progress toward a successful solution to the problem of independent Jewish and Arab states in Palestine. Egyptian Premier Aly Maher Pasha presents the Arab delegation's case in conference with Ambassador Kennedy.

11 March 1939
ROME. Ambassador and Mrs. Kennedy and eight of their children arrive late in the afternoon for the coronation of Pope Pius XII the following day. Joe Jr., the only child not to attend, is in Spain.

12 March 1939
ROME. Over three-quarters of a million people gather at Vatican City for the coronation of Pope Pius XII. Attending the ceremony as President Roosevelt's personal representative is Ambassador Joseph P. Kennedy. With him are his wife, Rose, and children John, Rosemary, Kathleen, Eunice, Patricia, Bobby, Jean, and Teddy. Elected upon the death of Pope Pius XI, the new pontiff is Eugenio Cardinal Pacelli, the former Vatican secretary of state, who had been a houseguest of the Kennedys in November, 1936.

13 March 1939
ROME. At Castle Gandolfo, the papal country villa, Pope Pius XII interrupts his morning conferences to receive Ambassador and Mrs. Kennedy and John, Rosemary, Kathleen, Patricia, Robert, Jean, and Edward. Breaking with Vatican protocol, the Pope greets them informally and engages in long conversations. The new Pontiff gives his first rosaries to the Kennedy children.

25 March 1939
PARIS. Rose Kennedy fills in as hostess at a dinner party given by William C. Bullitt, the U.S. ambassador to France, in honor of Albert Lebrun, president of the French Republic, and Mme. Lebrun.

29 March 1939
MADRID. Despite the possibility of open fighting between the Nationalists and Loyalists, Joe Kennedy, Jr., remains in Madrid. All Americans in official capacities have withdrawn.

3 April 1939
MADRID. After spending almost six weeks in the besieged city, Joe Jr. departs for London.

21 April 1939
EDINBURGH, SCOTLAND. In a ceremony at Usher Hall, Joseph P. Kennedy receives an honorary Doctor of Laws degree from Edinburgh University. Kennedy then signs the Burgess Rolls and receives the "freedom of the city."

9 April 1939
WINDSOR. Ambassador and Mrs. Joseph P. Kennedy are weekend guests of King George and Queen Elizabeth at Windsor Castle.

25 April 1939
BOSTON. Workmen raze the former Fitzgerald

home at 39 Welles Avenue in Dorchester. The family resided there while "Honey Fitz" was mayor of Boston, and, except for two years at school in Holland and in New York, it had been Rose Kennedy's home from her Dorchester High School days until her marriage.

4 May 1939

LONDON. Ambassador and Mrs. Joseph P. Kennedy give a farewell dinner party at the American embassy for the King and Queen of England, who are about to leave for a tour of Canada and the United States. Many royal guests attend, and all the Kennedy children are present. After dinner, Rose entertains Queen Elizabeth in her chambers, bringing in the other ladies for short, private conversations. Later, the Kennedys show the guests a popular motion picture.

13 May 1939

CHEQUERS, ENGLAND. Ambassador Joseph P. Kennedy is the weekend guest of Prime Minister Neville Chamberlain. Their agenda includes a discussion of Britain's proposals on the Palestine issue.

17 May 1939

MANCHESTER, ENGLAND. Joseph P. Kennedy receives an honorary Doctor of Laws degree from the University of Manchester.

17 May 1939

LONDON. Dr. Chaim Weizman, president of the World Zionist Organization and head of the Jewish Agency for Palestine, confers with Ambassador Joseph P. Kennedy after both Arabs and Jews reject the British government's White Paper. The Jewish delegation plans to appeal to the United States for support.

18 May 1939

LIVERPOOL, ENGLAND. Joseph P. Kennedy receives an honorary Doctor of Laws degree from Liverpool University.

24 June 1939

LONDON. Millions of Britons line the streets to watch King George VI and Queen Elizabeth ride in a procession to Guild Hall to a reception and luncheon following their return from Canada and the United States. Ambassador Joseph P. Kennedy, who facilitated many of the arrangements for the visit, sits with the royal couple at lunch.

4 July 1939

LONDON. In a speech before the American Society, Ambassador Joseph P. Kennedy praises the recent American trip of King George and Queen Elizabeth. They have won the hearts of American people, he says, and he reads letters to him that express great enthusiasm for the royal couple.

10 July 1939

LONDON. Ambassador and Mrs. Joseph P. Kennedy give a dinner at the American embassy in honor of Queen Mary. Among those present are Lord and Lady MacMillan, the Dowager Countess of Airlie, Lord and Lady Cavendish, Mr. and Mrs. William Randolph Hearst, and Mrs. Ogden Reed.

11 July 1939

LONDON. Ambassador and Mrs. Joseph P. Kennedy sponsor a celebration at the American embassy for American college athletes living in Great Britain. There is music, food, and entertainment.

31 July 1939

MADRID. Joe Jr. returns to Madrid with his sister Kathleen. The two are on a tour of Spain "eager" to see the war-torn sectors resulting from the Civil War.

1 September 1939

POLAND. German forces invade the country.

3 September 1939

LONDON. Neville Chamberlain announces that England is at war with Germany. Subsequently, New Zealand, Australia, and France also declare war against Germany.

THE ATLANTIC OCEAN. German submarines torpedo the liner *Athenia* as it sails near Ireland. More than one hundred people are killed.

5 September 1939

WASHINGTON, D.C. The United States declares its neutrality in the war that has broken out in Europe.

7 September 1939

GLASGOW, SCOTLAND. John F. Kennedy meets with American survivors of the *Athenia,* a British liner recently sunk in the North Atlantic by the Germans. Jack's father has sent him to obtain firsthand accounts of the attack and to reassure the survivors that an American ship will soon return them safely to the United States.

[?] September 1939

SOUTHAMPTON, ENGLAND. Rose Kennedy and her children, Joe Jr., Kathleen, Eunice, Patricia, Robert, Jean, and Teddy leave by ship for the safety of America. Ambassador Kennedy remains in England with his daughter Rosemary, who is at a convent school in Hantfordshire.

16 September 1939

NEW YORK. Eunice Kennedy, 18, enters Manhattanville College of the Sacred Heart at 133rd Street and Convent Avenue in Manhattan. Rose had attended the same school thirty years earlier, when it was known as the Academy of the Sacred Heart. (In 1917, the school had been chartered to confer Bachelor of Arts and graduate degrees.)

18 September 1939

BOSTON. John ("Honey Fitz") Fitzgerald and his wife celebrate their fiftieth wedding anniversary.

19 September 1939

CONCORD, NEW HAMPSHIRE. Robert F. Kennedy enters the second form (eighth grade) at St. Paul's School.

20 September 1939

FOYNES, IRELAND. John F. Kennedy leaves for New York aboard the *Dixie-Clipper*.

25 September 1939

CAMBRIDGE, MASSACHUSETTS. John F. Kennedy, 22, starts fall classes at Harvard, where he is a senior. He will continue to study government and economics. Joe Jr. enters his first year at Harvard Law School. Both brothers have spent the last several months in Europe, working, traveling, and witnessing the early events of the war.

2 October 1939

NEW YORK. After spending the last school year in England, where they attended the Convent of the Sacred Heart in Roehampton, Patricia Kennedy begins the eleventh grade and Jean Kennedy the seventh grade at the Convent of the Sacred Heart in Maplehurst.

6 October 1939

CONCORD, NEW HAMPSHIRE. Robert F. Kennedy withdraws from St. Paul's School. (The records do not say why.)

7 October 1939

BOSTON. Though separated by an ocean, Ambassador and Mrs. Kennedy exchange felicitations on their twenty-fifth wedding anniversary by telephone. From her parents' apartment at the Hotel Bellevue, Rose Kennedy speaks to her husband at the American embassy in London. Among the many cables and telegrams she receives is a message offering "sincerest congratulations" from King George and Queen Elizabeth of England.

CAMBRIDGE, MASSACHUSETTS. In the afternoon, Rose Kennedy, Joe Jr., Kathleen, and Bobby watch a Harvard football game.

[?] October 1939

PORTSMOUTH, RHODE ISLAND. Robert F. Kennedy is admitted to the second form (eighth grade) at Portsmouth Priory, a Catholic boarding school for boys on the shores of Narragansett Bay. It was founded in 1926 by the Rev. Dom Hugh Diman, O.S.B.

28 October 1939

BOSTON. "Honey Fitz" Fitzgerald calls on New England couples who have been married fifty years or more to form Golden Wedding Associations. These, he believes, will discourage divorce and sell the idea of long, happy unions to young married couples.

[?] November 1939

NEW YORK. Kathleen Kennedy enrolls as a freshman at Finch College.

13 November 1939

BOSTON. "Honey Fitz" Fitzgerald is reappointed a member of the Boston Port Authority for a new term. Amended legislation in 1938 provides for seven- instead of five-year terms.

WASHINGTON, D.C. Joseph P. Kennedy receives an honorary LL.D. degree in absentia from the Catholic University of America, which is celebrating its semicentennial.

8 December 1939

WASHINGTON, D.C. In the United States on one of his frequent trips, Ambassador Joseph P. Kennedy endorses President Roosevelt for re-election at a press conference. Kennedy later briefs the President on the war in Europe and submits a confidential report on developments abroad.

11 December 1939

BOSTON. Speaking before a dinner audience at the Church of the Assumption, Ambassador Kennedy declares that there is no reason for the United States to get involved in the war in Europe. If the country were to enter the war, he says, it would mean its demise.

14 February 1940

NEW YORK. *The New York Times* reports that despite his supporters' efforts to secure his nomination as the Democratic candidate for president, Ambassador Joseph P. Kennedy has said he will refuse. Kennedy is quoted as saying: "Appreciating as I must the great honor implied in this step, nevertheless I must with positiveness state that I am not a candidate....I cannot forget that I now occupy a most important government post which at this particular time involves matters so precious to the American people, that no consideration should permit my energies or interests to be diverted."

3 March 1940

BOSTON. Edward Fitzgerald, 73, dies of bronchopheumonia at Boston City Hospital. He had suffered from arteriosclerotic heart disease for many years. He lived at 41 Lyndhurst Street and was retired from the hotel business. Fitzgerald was the brother of John "Honey Fitz" Fitzgerald and the uncle of Rose Kennedy.

7 March 1940

BOSTON. A slate from the Ninth Congressional District is filed with the Secretary of State bearing the names of Joseph P. Kennedy, Jr., and Daniel H. Coakley as candidates for delegates to the Democratic National Convention. This slate is pledged to Postmaster-General James A. Farley.

15 March 1940

CAMBRIDGE, MASSACHUSETTS. For his course in international government, John Kennedy submits a thesis entitled "Appeasement at Munich (The Inevitable Results of the Slowness of the Conversion of the British Democracy from a Disarmament to a Rearmament Policy)." "This thesis," he begins, "is a study devoted to one phase of the most controversial subject in modern diplomacy—the agreement at Munich. In this thesis it is proposed to show that most of the critics have been firing at the wrong target. The Munich Pact itself should not be the object of criticism but rather the underlying factors such as the state of British opinion and the condition of Britain's armaments, which made surrender inevitable....To blame one man, such as Baldwin for the unpreparedness of British armaments is illogical and unfair, given the conditions of Democratic government."

20 March 1940

CAMBRIDGE, MASSACHUSETTS. The right of Joe Kennedy, Jr., to file nomination papers as a candidate for Ninth Congressional District delegate to the Democratic National Convention is attacked and defended during a hearing at the State Ballot Commission at the State House. Cambridge ward chairman John McDonald, who on 15 March 1940 filed an objection that the Harvard law student is not a registered voter of the Ninth District and is under 21, takes the offensive. Representing Joe Jr., John Brennan answers the charges, saying that Kennedy is over 21 and has not registered as a voter in Cambridge because he has not lived there long enough. After considering the testimony, the commission throws out McDonald's objection.

30 May 1940

LONDON. Ambassador Joseph P. Kennedy is a guest of King George VI at Buckingham Palace. Later, Kennedy attends Decoration Day services at St. Margaret's on the north side of Westminster Abbey, then lays a wreath at the Tomb of the Unknown Warrior, a monument erected in Westminster Abbey after World War I.

14 June 1940

PARIS. Paris falls to German forces.

20 June 1940

CAMBRIDGE, MASSACHUSETTS. John F. Kennedy, 23, graduates cum laude from Harvard College with a bachelor of science degree in political science. His senior thesis, "Appeasement at Munich," was awarded a magna cum laude.

Kennedy's yearbook caption reads:

Crimson (2-4); Chairman Smoker Committee (1); St. Paul's Catholic Club (1-4). Football (1), Junior Varsity (2); Swimming (1), Squad (2). Golf (1). House Hockey (3, 4); House Swimming (2), House Softball (4). Hasty Pudding-Institute of 1770, Spee Club. Permanent Class Committee. Field of Concentration: Government Intended Vocation: Law.

15 July 1940

CHICAGO. The Democratic National Convention opens. Joseph P. Kennedy, Jr., attends as a delegate from Massachusetts.

18 July 1940

CHICAGO. In a poll of the Massachusetts delegation, Joseph P. Kennedy, Jr., votes with a dissident group in favor of Postmaster-General James A. Farley as the nominee for president rather than for President Roosevelt, whom his father publicly supports.

John F. Kennedy in Palm Beach, 1937.

1 August 1940

NEW YORK. *Why England Slept,* by John F. Kennedy, 23, is published by Wilfred Funk, Inc., a new firm. Adapted from his Harvard senior thesis, "Appeasement at Munich," the book analyzes England's delay in building its military power against a rearming Germany. The 252-page work includes a foreword by Henry R. Luce, the publisher of *Time,* and sells for $2.

31 August 1940

ENGLAND. German planes continue to bomb British airfields. The Luftwaffe has made almost daily attacks for the past three weeks.

3 September 1940

LONDON. On the first anniversary of England's declaration of war against Germany, a commemoration service is held at Westminster Abbey. Among those attending are Prime Minister Winston Churchill and Ambassador Joseph P. Kennedy.

15 September 1940

WINDSOR, ENGLAND. Ambassador Joseph P. Kennedy is a weekend guest of the King and Queen at Windsor Castle.

25 September 1940

PALO ALTO, CALIFORNIA. John F. Kennedy begins to audit classes at Stanford University where he is registered on a permit-to-attend-classes basis for the autumn quarter. He is enrolled for graduate classes in business and political science but, as an auditor, he does not have a major, will not be graded, and is free to attend classes as he wishes. He lives at 624 Mayfield Avenue.

1 October 1940

ENGLAND. The German air assault on England continues. Over the last several weeks Nazi bombers have attacked London, damaging Buckingham Palace in some raids, as well as Southampton, Bristol, Yeovil, and other cities. At both the American embassy in London and at Windsor, Ambassador Kennedy has been nearby when several bombs have hit.

20 October 1940

WINDSOR, ENGLAND. Planning to return to America and resign his ambassadorship, Joseph P. Kennedy visits King George VI and Queen Elizabeth at Windsor Castle to say good-bye.

22 October 1940

LONDON. His formal resignation as ambassador imminent, Joseph P. Kennedy leaves England. Kennedy's outspoken opinion that the United States should stay out of the war in Europe has alienated many Britishers. Kennedy believes that Roosevelt has ignored his advice, and the President is said to be displeased with his ambassador. Kennedy leaves for Lisbon, where he will board a plane for the United States.

27 October 1940

WASHINGTON, D.C. Despite the friction between them, at a meeting at the White House President Roosevelt urges Ambassador Kennedy to endorse Roosevelt's re-election publicly.

29 October 1940

NEW YORK. To dispel rumors of a falling out with the President, Kennedy goes on nationwide radio to reiterate his views on the world situation. At the same time, he asks voters to support President Roosevelt for a third term.

5 November 1940

THE UNITED STATES. Franklin D. Roosevelt wins re-election to a third term as president.

MASSACHUSETTS. "Honey Fitz" Fitzgerald is chosen from the Eleventh Congressional District as one of seventeen Democratic presidential electors. The party-picked ticket received 1,076,522 votes statewide.

6 November 1940

WASHINGTON, D.C. Joseph P. Kennedy verbally tenders his resignation as ambassador to England to Roosevelt. Roosevelt asks him to continue as ambassador.

1 December 1940

WASHINGTON, D.C. Ambassador Joseph P. Kennedy again proffers his resignation. This time President Roosevelt accepts it.

2 December 1940

WASHINGTON, D.C. Joseph P. Kennedy submits his formal letter of resignation to Secretary of State Cordell Hull, effective 30 November 1940. Kennedy's official resignation comes after almost nineteen months of ambassadorial service.

16 December 1940

BOSTON. The Massachusetts Electoral College assembles to vote for presidential nominee Franklin D. Roosevelt. "Honey Fitz" Fitzgerald is a presidential elector.

17 December 1940

CAMBRIDGE, MASSACHUSETTS. A group of students dedicated to the purpose of keeping the United States out of war announces the formation of the *Harvard Committee Against Military Intervention in Europe.* Joe Kennedy, Jr., is a member. This committee opposes another student group demanding that the United States aid England in its war in Europe.

4 January 1941

PALO ALTO, CALIFORNIA. The winter quarter at Stanford University begins, but Jack Kennedy, who registered to audit classes the previous quarter, does not enroll. Apparently he stopped attending classes without officially withdrawing. This spring he will tour South America.

6 January 1941

BOSTON. At the Ford Hall Forum, Joe Kennedy, Jr., says he is against sending aid to America's European allies—even if it means their defeat by Germany. If the Nazis are victorious, he says, a barter trading system can be devised to maintain an economic status quo. Other speakers vehemently oppose his views.

20 January 1941

WASHINGTON, D.C. President Roosevelt begins his third term of office.

21 January 1941

WASHINGTON, D.C. Joseph P. Kennedy testifies at a House Foreign Affairs Committee hearing on the administration's proposed lend-lease bill. He advocates a program in which the United States would supply aid to England but would not enter the war. He says the United States should concentrate on rearmament.

26 January 1941

BOSTON. In response to a question at a meeting of the Foreign Policy Association, Joe Kennedy, Jr., says that the United States should not send a convoy of food and war supplies to England. The sinking of even one ship, he believes, could produce an emotional reaction strong enough to propel the United States into the war. Young Kennedy is absolutely opposed to this. In a discussion with Harvard professor Arthur N. Holcombe and Williams College president James Phinney Baxter III, Kennedy says the United States should refrain from aiding Britain by convoy even if it means that Germany would overtake England.

11 March 1941

WASHINGTON, D.C. President Franklin D. Roosevelt signs the Lend-Lease Act into law. The bill allows the President to sell or lend weapons and other war materials to any nation whose freedom is deemed vital to the security of the United States.

29 April 1941

BROOKLINE, MASSACHUSETTS. Before the brotherhood of Temple Ohabei Shalom, Joe Kennedy, Jr., and Harvard instructor William S. McCauley debate the questions of whether Germany could invade the United States and whether the United States should send convoys of supplies to aid England. Kennedy urges that the United States establish bases in Latin America. These bases, he argues, would prevent a German attack on America. McCauley argues that the Nazis could reach the United States by indirect routes. Kennedy also asserts that sending convoys to England will bring the United States into the war; McCauley favors such aid because without it England will be defeated by Germany. This would leave the United States and Nazi Germany as the only major world powers.

25 May 1941

ATLANTA, GEORGIA. Former Ambassador Joseph P. Kennedy delivers the commencement address to the graduating class of Oglethorpe University, where he also receives an honorary Doctor of Laws degree. In his speech, which is broadcast over Atlanta radio station WGST, Kennedy declares that the United States should not enter the war in Europe. Rather, its policy should be "to rearm as swiftly as possible, to give every aid to Great Britain, to stay out of the war." He says that the United States, thousands of miles away from Europe, is virtually unconquerable. "A direct attack on us would require an armada mightier than the power of man could create....We have barriers against attack that nothing could destroy."

30 May 1941

NEW YORK. Eunice Kennedy completes two years at Manhattanville College of the Sacred Heart. She will transfer to Stanford University.

Top to bottom: Teddy, Jack, Bobby, Palm Beach, c. 1936.

[?] June 1941

NEW YORK. The semester ends at Finch College, where Kathleen Kennedy completes her second and final year. This marks the end of her formal academic education.

1 June 1941

SOUTH BEND, INDIANA. Joseph P. Kennedy delivers the commencement address to the graduating class of the University of Notre Dame, and receives an honorary Doctor of Laws degree fromthe Rev. J. Hugh O'Donnell, president of the university. More than 6,000 attend the graduation.

10 June 1941

NEW YORK. Patricia Kennedy, 17, graduates from the Convent of the Sacred Heart in Maplehurst. (The school will move to Greenwich, Connecticut, in 1945.)

24 June 1941

BOSTON. Joe Kennedy, Jr., enlists in the United States Naval Reserve, Class V-5, as a Seaman Second Class at the Naval Aviation Cadet Selection Board. His enlistment number is 400 99 00.

27 June 1941

NEWPORT NEWS, VIRGINIA. Patricia Kennedy christens the *President Polk* at the Newport News Shipbuilding and Dry Dock Yards prior to its launching in the James River.

15 July 1941

SQUANTUM, MASSACHUSETTS. Seaman Second Class Joe Kennedy, Jr., reports for active duty at the naval air station. He will go through elimination flight training for the next three weeks at a base pay of $54 a month. If he qualifies, he will then transfer to the naval cadet course at Jacksonville, Florida. After completing his duty, he plans to continue his studies at Harvard Law School, where he is a senior.

7 August 1941
SQUANTUM, MASSACHUSETTS.   Joe Kennedy, Jr., completes his elimination flight-training course.

8 August 1941
SQUANTUM, MASSACHUSETTS.   Orders are given for the transfer of Joe Kennedy, Jr., to the Naval Air Station in Jacksonville, Florida.

23 September 1941
TORRESDALE, PENNSYLVANIA.   Jean Kennedy, 13, begins the ninth grade at the Convent of the Sacred Heart, Eden Hall.

ROSEMONT, PENNSYLVANIA.   Patricia Kennedy enters Rosemont College, a small Catholic liberal arts school for women in suburban Philadelphia.

8 October 1941
BOSTON.   John F. Kennedy is appointed an ensign in the U.S. Naval Reserve. His officer file number is 11607.

15 October 1941
BOSTON.   The enlistment of Joe Kennedy, Jr., is terminated so that he can accept an appointment as an aviation cadet in the U.S. Naval Reserve.

16 October 1941
JACKSONVILLE, FLORIDA.   Joe Kennedy, Jr., reports to the Naval Air Station for advanced flight training. He enters as a Naval Reserve aviation cadet. The pay is $105 per month.

26 October 1941
WASHINGTON, D.C.   John F. Kennedy reports for active duty in the U.S. Naval Reserve.

27 October 1941
WASHINGTON, D.C.   John F. Kennedy begins working on the *Daily Digest* in the office of the chief of Naval Operations of the Navy Department. The publication summarizes local and world events, and is circulated to Naval officers.

[?] November 1941
WASHINGTON, D.C.   Kathleen Kennedy joins the *Washington Times Herald* as a reporter. She writes a column called "Did You Happen to See...."

Ambassador Joseph P. Kennedy, second from right, England, March 1938.

THE WAR YEARS
1941-1945

7 December 1941
HONOLULU, HAWAII. The Japanese attack Pearl Harbor.

8 December 1941
WASHINGTON, D.C. The United States declares war on Japan.

11 December 1941
WASHINGTON, D.C. The United States declares war on Germany and Italy.

6 January 1942
PALO ALTO, CALIFORNIA. Eunice Kennedy begins the winter quarter at Stanford University as a transfer student from Manhattanville College of the Sacred Heart. Eunice will live in room 275 at Longunita Hall.

24 January 1942
CHARLESTON, SOUTH CAROLINA. John Kennedy reports to the commandant, Sixth Naval District. His assignment is to work on defense plans at the District Security Office.

26 March 1942
NEW YORK. Archbishop Francis J. Spellman announces that Pope Pius XII has awarded the Pro Pontifice et Ecclesia Cross to Rose Kennedy in recognition of her charitable service to the church.

10 April 1942
JACKSONVILLE, FLORIDA. Joe Kennedy, Jr., completes his flight training course and becomes a naval aviator.

5 May 1942
JACKSONVILLE, FLORIDA. With his father proudly watching, Joe Kennedy, Jr., receives his "wings" and a commission as ensign (to date from 3 April 1942) at graduation ceremonies at the naval air station. The former ambassador also gives a brief speech to the graduating class. In becoming an Eaglet, young Kennedy re-

signs as president of the novice flier's group, the Cadet Group.

3-6 June 1942
PACIFIC WAR THEATER. Air reconnaissance spots a Japanese fleet several hundred miles from Midway on 3 June, and Flying Fortresses are dispatched to attack it. In the following days, there is intensive fighting between Japanese and American naval forces. The Japanese suffer heavy casualties, and by 6 June the Japanese lose the Battle of Midway.

12 June 1942
NORFOLK, VIRGINIA. Joe Kennedy, Jr., reports for active duty. He will fly with the Transitron Training Squadron attached to the Atlantic Fleet.

27 July 1942
CHICAGO. John Kennedy reports to the U.S. Naval Reserve Midshipman School, Abbott Hall, Northwestern University, for officers' training.

7-8 August 1942
PACIFIC WAR THEATER. American forces land on Guadalcanal, one of a few strategic islands of the Solomons from which the Japanese operate. Fierce combat in the air, on water, and on land ensues.

15 September 1942
MASSACHUSETTS. John "Honey Fitz" Fitzgerald, 79, is defeated in the state primary for the Democratic nomination for U.S. senator by Representative Joseph E. Casey. He runs second to Casey in thirteen counties, including his own, Suffolk County. The results of the statewide election are as follows: Casey (of Clinton), 108,251 votes; John F. Fitzgerald (Boston), 80,456; Joseph Lee (Boston), 32,260; Daniel H. Coakley (Boston), 17,105; all others, 18; blanks, 31,528 (total votes cast, 269,618). Casey will run against Republican candidate Henry Cabot Lodge in the November election.

23 September 1942
MILTON, MASSACHUSETTS. Robert F. Kennedy, 16, begins form five, his junior year, at the Milton Academy. He has transferred here from Portsmouth Priory where he completed the second, third, and fourth forms. Milton Academy is a nonsectarian school that opened in 1807.

1 October 1942
PORTSMOUTH, RHODE ISLAND. John F. Kennedy reports to Motortorpedo Boat Squadron Train-

Kathleen, Rose, and Rosemary Kennedy are presented at the season's first court at Buckingham Palace.

Boston Herald.

ing Center for a PT training program. (The acronym PT stands for patrol torpedo boat, a light, maneuverable craft capable of launching torpedoes against enemy craft at sea.) He is also promoted to lieutenant, junior grade, for temporary service in the U.S. Naval Reserve.

8 November 1942
NORTH AFRICA. U.S. and British forces land at Casablanca, Oran, and Algiers in an attempt to overtake the German and Italian armies on the African continent.

3 December 1942
CHICAGO. At the University of Chicago, physicists conducting atomic research achieve the first nuclear chain reaction.

PORTSMOUTH, RHODE ISLAND. Lt. (j.g.) John F. Kennedy completes his PT training course. He is ordered to Motortorpedo Boat Squadron 4 for duty as commanding officer of Motor Torpedo Boat 101.

10 January 1943
SAN JUAN, PUERTO RICO. Joe Kennedy, Jr., joins Patrol Squadron 203 at the U.S. Naval Air Station for flying duty.

[?] February 1943
PORTSMOUTH, RHODE ISLAND. Lt. (j.g.) John F. Kennedy is ordered to active duty with Motortorpedo Boat Squadron 2 in the Solomon Islands.

85

Sport and General Press Agency, London.

Counterclockwise from center: Kathleen, Jack, Bobby, Teddy, and Joseph P. Kennedy, Sr. enjoying a soccer game. London, 1939.

11 February 1943

PORTSMOUTH, RHODE ISLAND. A naval "fitness report" of Lt. (j.g.) John F. Kennedy is written, and it is noted that he had been Commanding Officer of PT-101 for approximately one month.

11 April 1943

SOLOMON ISLANDS, SOUTH PACIFIC. Lt. (j.g.) John F. Kennedy reports to Motortorpedo Boat Squadron 2.

24 April 1943

PACIFIC WAR THEATER. Lt. (j.g.) John F. Kennedy becomes the commanding officer of USS PT-109, relieving the former commanding officer, Ensign Leonard J. Thom, USNR.

Three weeks earlier, a gunner on PT-109 shot down a Japanese bomber during an attack on Tulagi Harbor. (This particular motor torpedo boat, an 80-foot plywood vessel powered by three engines of 1,350 horsepower each, was built by the Electric Boat Company of Bayonne, New

Jersey, and delivered to the Naval Shipyard in Brooklyn on 10 July 1942.)

1 May 1943

SAN JUAN, PUERTO RICO.   Joe Kennedy, Jr., is promoted to lieutenant (junior grade) for temporary service in the U.S. Naval Reserve.

18 May 1943

PACIFIC WAR THEATER.   John F. Kennedy requests assignment to Patrol Torpedo Craft, according to Naval personnel file records.

John F. Kennedy in the South Pacific, c. 1943.

John Fitzgerald Kennedy Library. Photographer unknown.

29 May 1943

ATLANTA, GEORGIA.   At Oglethorpe University, Joseph P. Kennedy addresses some 200 guests, including members of the board of directors, graduating students, and invited friends of the school, in the college dining room. It is Kennedy's first public speech since his last address at the school two years earlier. Afterward, he receives the President's Medal, an award bestowed as "a personal expression of appreciation for educational, national and/or international service of exceptional merit," by the president of the university.

3 July 1943

LONDON.   Kathleen Kennedy, 23, arrives with a contingent of American Red Cross workers.

1 August 1943

PACIFIC WAR THEATER.   World War II rages on, and the Pacific theater continues to be the scene of intense, bitter fighting between Japanese and Allied forces. Each side has important bases on islands from which it launches attacks by ship or plane.

Japanese bombers raid the Rendova Harbor PT base on Lombardi Island in an attempt to destroy the boats there. The PT boats are customarily used to patrol various passageways, or "slots" of water, in the southwest Pacific, looking for Japanese destroyers carrying supplies or carrying out missions. This air raid is intended to clear the passageway for five Japanese warships scheduled to run from Bougainville in the north Solomon Islands, through Blackett Strait on the west side of Kolombangara Island, to Vila, an island in the south New Hebrides. The Japanese air raid damages only two boats, and the remaining PT boats are dispatched in anticipation of the incoming "Tokyo Express."

At 6:30 P.M. fifteen motor torpedo boats from the Rendova Harbor base depart to patrol the Blackett Strait. The boats are grouped in four divisions: B, A, R, and C. Division B's station is off of Vanga Vanga; Division A is off Gatere; Division R is east of Makati Island; and Division C is south of Ferguson Passage.

Division B consists of four PT boats under the direction of Lt. H. J. Brantingham in PT-159. The other boats and their captains are PT-157 (Lt. [j.g.] W. F. Liebenow); PT-162 (Lt. [j.g.] J. R. Lowrey); and PT-109 (Lt. [j.g.] Jack Kennedy). The division itself is split into two sections: PT-159 and PT-157; and PT-162 and PT-109. PTs 159 and 162 are equipped for interboat communication. PT-109 is ordered to stay close to the starboard quarter of PT-162, which is in communication with PT-159.

PT-109 carries a crew of 13. In addition to Lt. (j.g.)

John F. Kennedy, there are: Leonard J. Thom, Raymond Albert, Charles A. Harris, William Johnston, Andrew Jackson Kirksey, George Ross, Harold Marney, Edgar Mauer, John McGuire, Patrick H. McMahon, Raymond Starkey, and Gerald Zinser.

The PT boats reach their stations at 8:30 P.M. and patrol through the evening without incident.

2 August 1943

PACIFIC WAR THEATER. As the day begins, gunfire sounds from the direction of Kolombangara's southern shore. PT-159 spots what seems to be enemy landing craft. Making a strafing run to get into close range and being met with shell fire, PT-159 can respond with only a few torpedoes.

The other PTs, however, cannot determine if the gunfire is from the island itself or from a nearby vessel. PT-109 intercepts PT-162 and hears that the fire seemed to come from shore. Then a message is heard on the PT-109 radio: "I am being chased through Ferguson Passage! I have fired fish!" The Americans realize then that the enemy is attacking.

Requesting instructions from base, the PTs are ordered to return to their patrol stations. PT-109 leads the way back, with PT-162 and PT-159 following. When the boats reach a destination due east of Gizo Island, they head south. PT-109 begins its patrol on one engine at idling speed.

At about 2:30 A.M. , in Blackett Strait, with Lt. Kennedy at the wheel, a dark shape on the PT's starboard appears about 250 yards away. In the darkness, visibility is poor. The shape looming nearby at first seems to be another motor torpedo boat. As it approaches at high speed, however, it becomes clear that it is a Japanese destroyer. To fire at the enemy, PT-109 begins to turn to starboard, but within seconds, the *Amagiri,* traveling at 40-knot speed and without slowing or firing, rams the smaller boat, slicing it in half.

The hull of PT-109 remains afloat with Kennedy, Ross, Thom, Albert, Mauer, and McGuire clinging to it. In its wake, the destroyer carries burning gasoline some 60 feet. When the fire dies out a quarter-hour later and the danger passes, Lt. Kennedy and the five of the crew crawl aboard the hull.

Seven men are missing. Kennedy calls out, and a number of voices respond from the water. Harris, McMahon, and Starkey are some 300 feet away to the southwest; Zinser and Johnston are about the same distance away to the southeast. But no answers come from Andrew Kirksey and Harold Marney. They are gone.

Pat McMahon yells out that he is badly burned. The boat's engineer, he was below deck when the gas tanks exploded. Kennedy jumps into the sea to rescue him. Because of the currents, it takes over an hour for Kennedy to tow him to safety. Meanwhile, Ross and Thom have swum out to rescue Zinser and Johnston. Kennedy then strikes out for Harris and Starkey. Starkey, suffering from minor burns, is unable to swim. Kennedy exchanges his life jacket for Harris's water-logged Kopak life jacket, and together they tow Starkey in. After three hours, the eleven survivors are finally aboard the broken hull of PT-109. They are 4 miles north of Gizo Anchorage.

By dawn the hull is taking on water, and it becomes apparent that it will sink. The group decides to abandon the wreckage and make their way to land. Many of the islands nearby are believed to be occupied by Japanese. Situated about 3 miles away from the northeast reef of Gizo, the men pick an island located almost 4 miles southeast of Gizo, the closest one, they believe, that is uninhabited by the enemy.

The men set out at 2:00 P.M. Dressed only in his underwear, Kennedy tows the badly burned McMahon, who can neither swim nor kick in the water. With McMahon draped in a life preserver, Kennedy swims breaststroke through the water, pulling the wounded engineer by a strap gripped between his teeth. Those of the crew who are injured or unable to swim are tied to a float made from a board that had been part of PT-109's gun mount. The good swimmers among the remaining men push the float. After five hours, all the survivors of PT-109 reach land, Kennedy, and the wounded McMahon in tow, arriving first. The crew has with it only a half-dozen .45's, one .38, a few knives, and a flashlight.

Remembering that PT boats travel through Ferguson Passage on the way to their patrol areas, Kennedy decides to venture into the passage in hopes of summoning a passing boat. With a gun strapped around his neck and a lantern covered in a life preserver, he leaves around 6:30 P.M. He reaches a small island a half-mile to the southeast and pulls himself to his destination along the sharp reef. It takes Kennedy an hour and a half to reach Ferguson Passage. He marks time, treading water, ready to signal with the lantern. No boats come, but he sees aircraft flares, indicating that the PTs are operating in Gizo tonight, not in Blackett Strait. Kennedy makes his way back to the reef, but a strong current carries him back into Ferguson Passage. He starts the journey over again.

3 August 1943

PACIFIC WAR THEATER. Kennedy arrives bruised and feverish. Before he passes out, he describes his unsuccessful trip to the others. Ensign Ross decides to try it himself, and that evening he embarks on the same route. He reaches the west side of Ferguson Passage and waits for passing PTs, but none appear.

4 August 1943

PACIFIC WAR THEATER.   Their group's supply of meat and coconut milk almost depleted, Kennedy decides they must leave Bird Island, so called for its many feathered creatures. They must head for an island closer to Ferguson Passage. At 12 noon the men begin swimming, with Kennedy towing the injured McMahon and the rest making their way on an improvised float. They head for an islet west of Cross Island, arriving about three hours later, Kennedy and McMahon first. Pulled by a current, the others land on the island's eastern section. In the evening it grows too cold for anyone to swim into Ferguson Passage.

5 August 1943

PACIFIC WAR THEATER.   In the morning, the men see a New Zealand patrol boat making a strafing run by Cross Island, indicating that perhaps enemy troops are nearby. Kennedy and Ross nonetheless head for Cross Island, arriving there about 1:30 P.M. Not knowing whether there are enemy soldiers there, they furtively make their way across the island to the east side. On the beach there they find several bags of crackers and candy, left behind by the Japanese, and a small canoe. They try to attract the attention of two natives out in a canoe, but, frightened, the natives paddle away.

In the evening, Kennedy takes the abandoned canoe into Ferguson Passage to look for passing PT boats. By 9:00 P.M. none have come by, and he returns to Cross Island. Taking the candy and crackers with him, Kennedy heads back to his crew, leaving behind Ross, who will swim back the next day. Kennedy arrives about two and a half hours later, and the men heartily welcome the food. He finds there the two natives who had fled earlier. Ensign Thom has convinced them that the men are Americans, and the natives are friendly and helpful.

6 August 1943

PACIFIC WAR THEATER.   Early in the morning, Kennedy and the two natives canoe to Cross Island, picking up Ross on the way. The natives show the Americans a hidden two-man canoe. Kennedy finds a coconut and carves a brief message on it: "NAURO NATIVE KNOWS POSIT HE CAN PILOT 11 ALIVE NEED SMALL BOAT KENNEDY." He hands it to one of the natives with a note written the day before by Thom, instructing the man to take it to the coastwatcher on Wana Wana.

After sunset, Kennedy and Ross again venture out into Ferguson Passage, even though both are sick from lack of food and water and are suffering from infected coral cuts. A storm capsizes their canoe. In the crashing waves, the two men lose their grip on the craft, and the current carries them to the reef of the island where, hungry and hurting from bruises and infections, they sleep the night away.

7 August 1943

PACIFIC WAR THEATER.   In the morning, eight natives bring Kennedy and Ross food and a note instructing the senior officer to go with the natives to Wana Wana. First, Kennedy has the natives take him and Ross to the island where the rest of his crew are. The food is dropped off, and Ross remains. In the afternoon, Kennedy covers himself with ferns to hide from Japanese aircraft overhead and leaves with the natives. At 3 o'clock, they arrive at a designated point where they are met by an Australian coastwatcher. The coastwatcher makes arrangements for Kennedy to rendezvous with PT boats in Ferguson Passage at 10:30 P.M. At 11:15 P.M. , contact is made. Kennedy is met by PT-171 and PT-157. He is brought aboard PT-157, which is commanded by Lt. (j.g.) W. F. Liebenow, and he directs the boat to his waiting crew.

8 August 1943

PACIFIC WAR THEATER.   At about 5:30 A.M., the eleven surviving crew members of PT-109 are returned to Rendova Harbor, the motor torpedo base from which they set out one week earlier. Believing that the crew had been killed by the Japanese destroyer, the squadron had held a funeral mass for them during the week.

19 August 1943

HYANNIS PORT, MASSACHUSETTS.   Joseph P. Kennedy reveals to the *Boston Post* that he had withheld from his family a Navy Department telegram reporting his son missing in action. The elder Kennedy says faith led him to believe that his son was alive. Only after his son was rescued did he tell his wife and children about the telegram.

1 October 1943

PACIFIC WAR THEATER.   John F. Kennedy is promoted to lieutenant for temporary service in the U.S. Naval Reserve.

5 October 1943

BOSTON.   Robert Kennedy, 17, enlists as a Seaman

Apprentice in the United States Naval Reserve at the Naval Aviation Cadet Selection Board (NACSB) in Boston. His term of enlistment runs "during minority until 19 November 1946."

18 November 1943

LAMBU LAMBU, SOUTH PACIFIC. Lt. John F. Kennedy is directed by a physician to leave service from PT-59.

LOS ANGELES. At a Beverly Hills hospital, Lt. John Kennedy undergoes treatment for injuries sustained the previous August in the South Pacific.

11 February 1944

BOSTON. The eighty-first birthday of John Fitzgerald "Honey Fitz" is celebrated by hundreds of business and political leaders at a luncheon at the Parker House Hotel. Mayor Maurice J. Tobin presides at the ceremony, and Brigadier General Clarence H. Kells awards the octogenarian an achievement trophy. The former mayor and congressman shows his appreciation by singing his theme song, "Sweet Adeline." Harry Johnson, who wrote the lyrics, accompanies him. A special moment occurs when Lieutenant John F. Kennedy, who has recently returned from the South Pacific, joins the celebration and hugs his grandfather, to the frenzied cheers of the audience.

12 February 1944

BOSTON. A Lincoln's Birthday fund-raising rally is held in Copley Plaza before 1,000 persons. John F. Kennedy is a guest along with two of his PT-109 buddies, Bill Johnston and Pat McMahon. On behalf of the city, Mayor Tobin purchases $50,000 in war bonds from Kennedy; an equal amount is purchased on behalf of Joe Kennedy, who is not present.

13 February 1944

BOSTON. At an awards ceremony at Faneuil Hall, where Mayor Tobin is presenting prizes to school children who have won an essay contest on the topic of racial and religious discrimination, Lieutenant John F. Kennedy dramatically recounts an episode he observed in the South Pacific. He tells of a Japanese prisoner of war who pulls a hidden gun and shoots to death a Jewish chaplain just as the chaplain is giving the prisoner a glass of water. Kennedy urges racial and religious tolerance. "Every time an American voices expressions of anti-Semitism," he says, "he is fighting for our enemies."

1 March 1944

CAMBRIDGE, MASSACHUSETTS. Commencing active duty, Robert F. Kennedy, 18, reports to the Navy V-12 unit at Harvard University. The V-12 program is an officer-procurement program that permits men who do not yet have college degrees to obtain them and become officers in the U.S. Navy or Naval Reserve.

19 March 1944

MIAMI, FLORIDA. Lt. John F. Kennedy reports for duty at the Subchaser Training Center.

14 April 1944

PALO ALTO, CALIFORNIA. Eunice Mary Kennedy is awarded a Bachelor of Arts degree from the School of Social Sciences of Stanford University. She completed five quarters at Stanford after transferring from the College of the Sacred Heart in Manhattanville, New York, but still had some work to finish for her degree. She did this at Radcliffe College in Cambridge, Massachusetts, and transferred the work to Stanford to complete the degree requirements.

6 May 1944

LONDON. Kathleen Kennedy, 24, marries 26-year-old William John Robert Cavendish, Lord Hartington, heir to the Duchy of Devonshire, in a 10-minute civil ceremony at the Chelsea Registry Office just before noon. The groom, who comes from an aristocratic English family, is an officer in the Coldstream Guards. Six months earlier Lord Hartington had been defeated as a candidate for the West Derbyshire seat in Parliament. The wedding causes quite a stir because of the couple's different religions. Kathleen is Catholic; the Marquis of Hartington is Protestant. Of Kathleen's family, only her brother Joe attends the civil ceremony. A reception follows at the home of Viscountess Hambledon.

BOSTON. Only hours after her daughter Kathleen is married in London, Rose Kennedy, a devout Catholic, checks out of New England Baptist Hospital, where she had been a patient for two weeks. Police Commissioner Joseph Timilty takes her to Logan Airport, where she boards a plane for New York. At the airport she refuses to comment directly to reporters, but an official statement explains that she is "physically unfit" to comment on her daughter's wedding. While waiting in a room for the weather to clear for takeoff, Rose Kennedy buries her head in her hands.

7 May 1944

BOSTON.   "Honey Fitz" wires members of his party's congressional delegation that although he has "no intention" of seeking the Democratic nomination for the Senate, he is allowing his name to be used in filing before the primary deadline so that Republican governor Leverett Saltonstall does not run unopposed.

22 May 1944

BOSTON.   John "Honey Fitz" Fitzgerald withdraws from the race for the Democratic nomination for the U.S. Senate. At least a half-dozen other candidates have entered the race for the nomination.

27 May 1944

MILTON, MASSACHUSETTS.   Robert Kennedy, 18, graduates early from Milton Academy. (Early graduation was common during the war years.) He attended Milton in 1942-1943, Class II (eleventh grade), and 1943-1944, Class I (twelfth grade).

31 May 1944

MIAMI, FLORIDA.   Due to back injuries, John F. Kennedy leaves the Subchaser Training Center and enters the U.S. Naval Hospital in Chelsea, Massachusetts.

6 June 1944

NORMANDY, FRANCE.   The Allied forces launch their invasion of Europe with the landing of forces at several points along the Norman coast. From these beachheads, Allied troops will engage the German forces occupying France, Holland, and Belgium. The day is designated as "D-Day."

12 June 1944

CHELSEA, MASSACHUSETTS. Lt. John F. Kennedy of the U.S. Naval Reserve receives the Navy and Marine Corps Medal. Captain Frederick L. Conklin of the United States Navy presents the medal and a citation, signed by Secretary of the Navy James Forrestal "for the President," to the former PT officer at the U.S. Naval Hospital, where he is undergoing treatment for back injuries. The citation reads:

> For extremely heroic conduct as Commanding Officer of Motor Torpedo Boat 109 following the collision and sinking of that vessel in the Pacific War Area on August 1-2, 1943. Unmindful of personal danger, Lieutenant (then Lieutenant, Junior Grade) Kennedy unhesitatingly braved the difficulties and hazards of darkness to direct rescue operations, swimming many hours to secure aid and food after

he had succeeded in getting his crew ashore. His outstanding courage, endurance and leadership contributed to the saving of several lives and were in keeping with the highest traditions of the United States Naval Service.

17 June 1944

NEW YORK.   The *New Yorker* magazine publishes an article by John Hersey entitled "Survival," an account of the ramming of PT-109 by a Japanese destroyer in August, 1943, and the events that followed for Lt. (j.g.) John F. Kennedy and his crew. (Hersey is the husband of a former girlfriend of Kennedy's, Frances A. Cannon, of the well-known Cannon Mills family.)

1 July 1944

DUNKESWELL, DEVON, ENGLAND.   Joe Kennedy, Jr., is promoted to lieutenant for temporary service in the U.S. Naval Reserve.

18 July 1944

ENGLAND.   Joe Kennedy, Jr., is assigned and reports to Bombing Squadron 110.

August 1944

PLEASANTVILLE, NEW YORK. *Reader's Digest* reprints a condensed version of John Hersey's *New Yorker* article, "Survival," about Lt. John Kennedy and the PT-109 episode in the South Pacific. The appearance of the article in *Reader's Digest,* with its large national audience, brings the young man widespread attention.

12 August 1944

EUROPEAN THEATER.   Lt. Joseph P. Kennedy, Jr., has volunteered for a hazardous special assignment that is executed today. The mission, a joint effort of the Army and Navy, provides for a pilot and co-pilot to take up a "drone"—an unmanned robot plane that can be piloted by radio from another aircraft—into the air and keep it in flight until two "mother" planes achieve complete radio control over it. This drone is loaded with high explosives. The pilots will parachute out and be recovered on the ground while the mother planes guide the drone to a German V-2 rocket-launching site in Normandy, where it will crash and detonate upon impact. Neither bombers nor troops have been able to destroy the V-2 site, and a special aviation unit has decided to use these highly experimental pilotless planes as the means of attack.

The drone is a PB-44 Liberator bomber. The two control planes (the second, a substitute for the first should its control equipment fail), are twin-engine Vega Ventura bombers, which have come from the Naval Air Station at Traverse City, Michigan. The drone Liberator and the two control planes have been ferried to England and based at the Winfarthing (Fersfield) military base. Extensive flight tests and sample loadings have been made. It has been discovered that a drone must be manned initially because if a heavily loaded it cannot take off by remote control.

Lt. Joseph P. Kennedy, Jr., who has completed his tour of duty, is looking for a mission from which he will return a hero. When he hears of the special operation designed to destroy German rocket-launching sites, he is determined to be on it. He has flown over three dozen dangerous missions in the Bay of Biscay and has over a year's experience flying B-24s as a patrol plane commander. Kennedy volunteers—indeed campaigns—for the mission and finally gets it. Lt. Wilford ("Bud") J. Willy of Newark, New Jersey, is accepted as co-pilot.

A German rocket pen in Normandy, France, is selected as the site. On the August target date, the weather is favorable, and the mission gets the go-ahead.

At the zero-hour, 5:52 P.M. , Lt. Joseph P. Kennedy, Jr., USNR, and Lt. Willy, USN, take off in a PB-44 drone Liberator (code-named "Zoot-Suit Black") loaded with 21,170 pounds of TNT and other explosive materials from Fersfield Air Base in Winfarthing. Escorted by two mother planes, they attain an altitude of several thousand feet and open radio contact with the other planes. The flight proceeds according to schedule. But at 6:20 P.M. , as a mother plane guides the drone to the left one mile east of Blydhburgh, Suffolk, about 20 miles east of Beceles, the PB-44 drone Liberator bomber explodes at 2,000 feet and Lt. Kennedy, 29, and Lt. Willy, 35, are instantly killed.

17 August 1944
HYANNIS PORT, MASSACHUSETTS. Kathleen, Marchioness of Hartington, arrives from England to join her family in mourning at their home here.

2 September 1944
WASHINGTON, D.C. Joe Kennedy, Jr., is officially declared missing by the U.S. Naval Reserve.

10 September 1944
HEPPEN, BELGIUM. Lord William Hartington, 26, a captain in Britain's Coldstream Guards, is killed while leading his regiment in action. According to reports, his last words, "Come on you fellows, buck up," were uttered as a bullet cut him down. He leaves his wife, Kathleen (Kennedy), whom he had married four

months earlier; a brother, Lord Andrew Cavendish; two sisters, Ann and Elizabeth Cavendish; and his parents, the duke and duchess of Devonshire. His wife is in America with her family, mourning the death of her brother Joseph Kennedy, Jr.

[?] October 1944
CHELSEA, MASSACHUSETTS. Suffering from back injuries resulting from the PT-109 incident, John F. Kennedy enters the U.S. Naval Hospital.

1 November 1944
LEWISTON, MAINE. Robert F. Kennedy reports to the Navy V-12 unit at Bates College. He does not complete this program, and continues his service as an enlisted man.

6 November 1944
CAMBRIDGE, MASSACHUSETTS. Following in the footsteps of his father and his two older brothers, Robert F. Kennedy, 18, enters his freshman year at Harvard College.

7 November 1944
THE UNITED STATES. President Franklin D. Roosevelt is re-elected to an unprecedented fourth term.

MASSACHUSETTS. John "Honey Fitz" Fitzgerald is elected an at-large member of the Massachusetts Democratic Electoral College.

18 December 1944
BOSTON. The Massachusetts Electoral College assembles to vote for presidential nominee Franklin D. Roosevelt. John "Honey Fitz" Fitzgerald is a presidential elector.

20 January 1945
WASHINGTON, D.C. President Franklin D. Roosevelt is inaugurated a fourth time. Harry S. Truman is his vice-president.

2 February 1945
WASHINGTON, D.C. The Navy Department releases the names of nine servicemen from the New England area officially listed as dead. Among the casualties is Joseph P. Kennedy, Jr.

BOSTON. After suffering an attack of rheumatism at his home, John "Honey Fitz" Fitzgerald is rushed to St. Margaret's Hospital.

Kennedy Family Collection. Norman Parkinson, London.

Rose Kennedy in England, 1939.

4-11 February 1945
CRIMEA, USSR.   Franklin Delano Roosevelt, Winston Churchill, and Joseph Stalin confer at Yalta. Premier Stalin agrees that Russia will enter the war against Japan.

19 February 1945
IWO JIMA.   The U.S. Marines land on this small island to establish a base from which American planes can protect the land forces that will invade Japan.

1 March 1945
WASHINGTON, D.C.   John F. Kennedy is placed on the "retired" list of the U.S. Naval Reserve at the rank of lieutenant.

2 March 1945
WASHINGTON, D.C.   Senator David I. Walsh announces for the Navy that a destroyer will be commissioned in memory of Lieutenant Joseph P. Kennedy, Jr., and named in his honor.

21 March 1945
CLINTON, OKLAHOMA.   Lt. Wilford J. Willy, the copilot who died with Lt. Joseph P. Kennedy, Jr., on special assignment over England, receives the Navy Cross posthumously. At the Naval Air Station, Mrs. Willy accepts her husband's medal.

April 1945
CAMBRIDGE, MASSACHUSETTS.   *As We Remember Joe*, a memorial album of essays and recollections of the late Joseph Kennedy, Jr., by friends and family, is privately printed by the University Press (unrelated to any specific university press). The book was compiled by Joe's brother John, who also wrote part of it. The other contributors are Joseph P., Kathleen, and Ted Kennedy; Arthur Krock; Professor Harold J. Laski; Edward and Mary Moore; Joseph Timilty; Ensign Richard Flood; Arthur Mann; Lt. Timothy J. Reardon; Capt. Maurice S. Sheehy; Mrs. Alice Harrington; Robert Downes; Dr. Payson Wild, Jr.; Mrs. George H. dePinto; Frank More O'Ferrall; Commander James Reedy; and Ensign James Simpson. Also included are a letter from Joe Kennedy, Jr., to the 15 February 1939 issue of *Atlantic Magazine,* a condolence letter from Secretary of the Navy James Forrestal to Joseph P. Kennedy, and an excerpt from a poem by Maurice Baring.

11 April 1945
OKINAWA.   The Marines land here on this strategically located island occupied by Japan.

12 April 1945
WARM SPRINGS, GEORGIA.   While on vacation, President Franklin Roosevelt, 63, dies of a cerebral hemorrhage.
WASHINGTON, D.C.   In the early evening, Harry S. Truman is sworn in as president of the United States.

16 April 1945
BOSTON.   The will of the late Joe Kennedy, Jr., is filed for probate. His estate, which is estimated at $200,000, is bequeathed in its entirety to his father, who is also named as executor. The will is dated 18 March 1943.

A donation of $10,000, unrelated to the will, is given by Joseph P. Kennedy, Sr., to the Guild of St. Apolonis for the purpose of providing dental care to students attending parochial schools.

25 April-26 June 1945
SAN FRANCISCO.   A conference is held to establish and draw up a charter for a United Nations, a world-

Boston Herald.

Flashing the Kennedy smile: Teddy, sans a couple front teeth, and Joe, Jr.

wide organization devoted to working for peace. John F. Kennedy covers the conference as a journalist for the International News Service.

7 May 1945
EUROPEAN WAR THEATER. Germany surrenders to Allied representatives.

8 May 1945
WASHINGTON, D.C. President Harry Truman proclaims this Victory-in-Europe, or "V-E," Day. People around the world celebrate and offer prayers of thanks. A short nine months before, Joe Kennedy, Jr., and Lord William Hartington had been killed in separate missions against the Germans.

14 May 1945
NEW YORK. The Joseph P. Kennedy, Jr. Foundation is established to help children in need. Its major goal is to provide financial aid for organizations that care for children—orphanages, institutions for the mentally retarded, and hospitals and organizations affiliated with these institutions.

4 June 1945
ROSEMONT, PENNSYLVANIA. Patricia Kennedy, 21, graduates from Rosemont College with a Bachelor of Arts degree.

6 June 1945
DARIEN, CONNECTICUT. Jean Kennedy, 17, graduates from the Convent of the Sacred Heart in Noroton. She completed the eleventh and twelfth grades here after finishing the ninth and tenth grades at the Convent of the Sacred Heart, Eden Hall.

26 June 1945
SAN FRANCISCO. The charter for United Nations, a world organization dedicated to promoting international peace and economic and social cooperation among countries of the world, is signed by representatives from some four dozen nations.

27 June 1945
BOSTON. The Navy Cross is posthumously awarded to Joe Kennedy, Jr., in a ceremony at the First Naval District Headquarters. The award is presented to Rose Kennedy by Rear Admiral Felix T. Gygax, as her husband and children Patricia, Robert, Jean, and Teddy look on.

The citation accompanying the medal reads:

For extraordinary heroism and courage in aerial flight as pilot of a United States Navy Liberator bomber on August 12, 1944. Well knowing the extreme dangers involved and totally unconcerned for his own safety, Lieutenant Kennedy unhesitatingly volunteered to conduct an exceptionally hazardous and special operational mission. Intrepid and daring

Kennedy Family Collection. Photographer unknown.

Kathleen, Joe, Sr., Teddy, Rose, Pat, Jean, and Bobby, 16 March, 1938.

in his tactics and with unwavering confidence in the vital importance of his task, he willingly risked his life in the supreme measure of service and, by his great personal valor and fortitude in carrying out a perilous undertaking, sustained and enhanced the finest traditions of the United States Naval Service.

5 July 1945
LONDON. Hearst news correspondent John F. Kennedy covers the parliamentary elections here.

17 July-2 August 1945
POTSDAM, GERMANY. A conference of the Allied powers is held in this city outside Berlin. Germany had surrendered in May of 1945, but the war continues

in Asia. American, British, and Russian political leaders and chiefs of staff now meet to discuss how to deal with Japan and to study reconstruction and other problems of Europe. John F. Kennedy attends, reporting on the conference as a special correspondent for the International News Service. The young journalist also meets General Dwight D. Eisenhower.

26 July 1945
QUINCY, MASSACHUSETTS. The U.S.S. *Joseph P. Kennedy, Jr.*, a 2,200-ton destroyer commissioned by the Navy and named in honor of the dead war hero, is launched at the Bethlehem Steel Company's Fore River Shipyard. In two days, Joe would have been 30. The ceremony is attended by Joseph Sr., Rose, John, Patricia,

Ambassador and Mrs. Joseph P. Kennedy, March 1938.

Eunice, Robert, and Edward Kennedy, and by "Honey Fitz" and Mary Fitzgerald. Jean Kennedy, another sister and sponsor of the vessel, christens the ship by smashing a bottle of champagne across its bow.

6 August 1945

HIROSHIMA, JAPAN. The United States drops the first atomic bomb on Hiroshima, virtually destroying the city and killing more than 80,000 Japanese. Col. Paul Tibbets pilots the plane, named *Enola Gay* after his mother, that drops the bomb.

8 August 1945

NAGASAKI, JAPAN. The United States drops the second atomic bomb on Nagasaki, consequently killing 40,000 Japanese citizens. President Truman threatens Japan with further atomic destruction unless the country agrees to accept the terms of the Potsdam Declaration and also agrees to surrender unconditionally to the United States. Late in the evening, with the emperor in accord, the Japanese Supreme War Council accepts the terms of the declaration.

15 August 1945

JAPAN. A taped message by Emperor Hirohito is broadcast over radio to the Japanese people. Hirohito informs his subjects that Japan has surrendered to the Allied forces.

11 September 1945
BOSTON. A speech on the theme "England the Victor, Eire the Neutral, and Germany the Vanquished" is delivered by John F. Kennedy at a luncheon sponsored by the Boston Advertising Club at the Hotel Statler. While many feel that the United States should not cooperate with Germany, Jack urges that the government there is in no position to build a democracy and that "it is not desirable for us to leave any kind of political vacuum that Russia would be only too glad to fill."

12 September 1945
NEW YORK. Jean Kennedy, 17, enters Manhattanville College of the Sacred Heart. She graduated from the Convent of the Sacred Heart in Noroton, Connecticut, in June.

13 September 1945
LOWELL, MASSACHUSETTS. A $1,200 research scholarship in memory of Joseph Kennedy, Jr., is established at the Lowell Textile Institute by the deceased Navy lieutenant's father.

27 September 1945
WASHINGTON, D.C. The First Naval District announces that the Air Medal will be posthumously awarded to Joe Kennedy, Jr., for "numerous flights under extremely hazardous conditions."

4 October 1945
NEW YORK. At the Waldorf-Astoria Hotel, John F. Kennedy joins such prominent leaders as Bernard Baruch and Governor Thomas E. Dewey in speaking at a fund-raising dinner for the Alfred E. Smith Memorial Hospital. The 28-year-old Naval hero speaks of Al Smith as a source of inspiration for young people.

19 October 1945
BOSTON. Joseph P. Kennedy, chairman of a special commission to develop industry in Massachusetts, says at a business luncheon at the Hotel Statler that taxes will not be greatly reduced now or in the near future, even though the high tax rate is keeping new businesses out of the city.

23 October 1945
BOSTON. Addressing members of the Boston Credit Men's Association, Joseph P. Kennedy, chairman of Governor Tobin's special commission on Massachusetts commerce, tells the group that the resources of the state should be publicized to promote business.

24 October 1945
WASHINGTON, D.C. The Navy Department reveals details of the "hazardous special mission" in which Lt. Joseph P. Kennedy, Jr., USNR, and Lt. Wilford J. Willy, USN, were killed on 12 August 1944 over England. (Experimental radio-controlled bombers had been considered Top Secret, and the announcement is made with reluctance.)

29 October 1945
BOSTON. In a speech at the Parker House Hotel before the New England Newspaper Advertising Bureau, Joseph Kennedy urges editors and publishers to help prevent potential trouble in New England commerce by concerning themselves with conditions in their own communities.

November 1945
CHICAGO. Joseph P. Kennedy purchases the Merchandise Mart, then regarded as the world's largest office building. Constructed by Marshall Field and Company and opened one year after the stock market crash on 1 May 1930, the building covers an entire two-block area on the north bank of the Chicago River between Wells and Orleans Streets. Kennedy pays over $12.5 million for the Merchandise Mart.

8 November 1945
BOSTON. Speaking on the theme that enduring peace can be achieved only if leaders tell their people the truth, John F. Kennedy addresses members of the New England Transit Club at the Hotel Statler.

11 November 1945
BOSTON. John Kennedy speaks on the dangers of inflation that Ireland faces before members of the Eire Society of Boston at the Copley Plaza Hotel.

HYANNIS PORT, MASSACHUSETTS. Kathleen, Lady Hartington, arrives at her parents' home to spend everal months, including the Thanksgiving and Christmas holidays, with her family. She had arrived in New York two days earlier aboard the *Queen Mary* and attended the Army-Notre Dame football game before coming here.

7 December 1945
BOSTON. The youngest man ever to be elected for the position in the fifty-year history of the Veterans of Foreign Wars, John F. Kennedy, 28, is chosen general chairman of the group's 1946 national convention, to be held here next summer.

Joe Kennedy, Jr., far left, reports for duty at the Squantum Naval Air Base, July 1941.

With his father looking on, Robert F. Kennedy is sworn into The United States Navy.

14 January 1946

BOSTON. The stockholders of the Columbia Trust Company meet and vote to turn the corporation's stock over to the National Shawmut Bank. National Shawmut, under an agreement dated 4 January 1946, will assume deposit liabilities and will pay to the trust company a total of $557,400. The majority of Columbia's stock is owned by Joseph P. Kennedy and his family. For several years, the Columbia Trust Company has been the only commercial bank in East Boston. The previous week, Governor Maurice Tobin had announced that Kennedy would invest his proceeds from the sale in Massachusetts industry.

24 January 1946

BOSTON. The Veterans of Foreign Wars organize a Joseph P. Kennedy, Jr. Post at the Parker House in honor of the dead Naval hero. John F. Kennedy is elected commander by the more than fifty veterans present.

1 February 1946

BOSTON. Robert F. Kennedy reports for duty aboard the U.S.S. *Joseph P. Kennedy, Jr.*

4 February 1946

BOSTON. The U.S.S. *Joseph P. Kennedy, Jr.* leaves for the Caribbean for shakedown training.

16 February 1946

BOSTON. John F. Kennedy is inaugurated as commander of the Joseph P. Kennedy, Jr. Post, V.F.W.

18 March 1946

NEW YORK. An article entitled "The U.S. and the World" by Joseph P. Kennedy appears in *Life* magazine. The former ambassador offers a blueprint for the American political policy that should be implemented to prevent World War III.

15 April 1946

BOSTON. At the Seaman's Club, John F. Kennedy tells over one hundred fifty members of the city's chapter of Former Prisoners of War that veterans should assist each other in their return to civilian life.

At the christening of the *President Polk* in Newport News, Virginia, June 1941: Rosemary, Loretta (Kennedy) Connelly, Bobby, Pat, Jean, Teddy, and Rose. (The three men in the rear are unidentified.)

Kennedy Family Collection. Newport News Shipbuilding Company.

Senator John F. Kennedy with his wife and parents.

THREE

THE RISE
TO POLITICAL
POWER

1946 · 1961

CONGRESSMAN
1946-1953

25 April 1946
BOSTON. Making his debut into politics, John F. Kennedy announces his candidacy for the Democratic nomination to Congress from Massachusetts's Eleventh Congressional District. He seeks the seat held by Representative James Curley, who is not running for re-election. In his announcement, young Kennedy says, "Each passing day brings to light the increased need for prompt and intelligent action in public service.... Everyone who is able should do his utmost in these days of world and national progress to contribute his talents in keeping with his abilities and resources. It is with this feeling that I declare my candidacy for Congress." The Democratic primary will be held in June.

25 April 1946
NEW YORK. The former Kathleen Kennedy, Lady Hartington, leaves on the *Queen Mary* for Southampton to return to her home in London.

25 May 1946
[?]   Joseph Gargan dies. He is Rose Kennedy's brother-in-law, the widower of Rose's sister, Agnes (Fitzgerald) Gargan. He leaves his three children: Joseph, Mary Jo, and Ann.

29 May 1946
BOSTON. Robert F. Kennedy reports to the Personnel Separation Center of the U.S. Naval Reserve.

30 May 1946
BOSTON. Robert F. Kennedy is released from active duty and is discharged from the Naval Reserve; he reenlists on the same day as a seaman second class, U.S. Naval Reserve.

BOSTON and CAMBRIDGE, MASSACHUSETTS.
Congressional candidate John F. Kennedy addresses various veterans' groups at Memorial Day services in both cities on the theme that American can guarantee peace only by its strength. Until the U.N. can guarantee security, he declares, America needs a strong army and navy. He says that attempts at international disarmament have failed and that building the military is the only way to insure peace. "We can only pray that man's political skill can keep abreast of his scientific skill. If not, we may yet live to see World War III and Armageddon."

17 June 1946
WATERVILLE, MAINE. At the one hundred twenty-fifth graduation exercises at Colby College, former ambassador Joseph P. Kennedy delivers the commencement address. "With all of its defects the American system is the best yet devised," he says. "It has provided us with individual freedom and a higher standard of living than is to be found anywhere else in the world. Private enterprise and democracy go hand in hand: they will rise and fall together. If through unwise legislation or the imposition of intolerable burdens we destroy private enterprise, then all forms of activity will be regimented under government control. There is no alternative." Kennedy receives an honorary Doctor of Laws degree from the school.

18 June 1946
BOSTON. John F. Kennedy wins his first election, the Democratic nomination for Congress from the Eleventh Congressional District. Making a strong showing in all parts of the district, he defeats nine other candidates, polling 40.5 percent of the total vote. The Eleventh Congressional District consists of Boston wards 1, 2, 3, and 22; Cambridge; and Somerville wards 1, 2, and 3. The election results are: Kennedy (Boston), 22,183 votes; Michael J. Neville (Cambridge), 11,341; John F. Cotter (Boston), 6,677; Joseph Russo* (Boston), 5,661; Catherine E. Falvey (Somerville), 2,446; Joseph Lee (Boston), 1,848; Joseph Russo* (Boston), 799; Michael DeLuca (Boston), 536; Francis X. Rooney (Somerville), 521; Robert F. DiFruscio (Boston), 298; all others, 0; blanks, 2,444 (total vote cast, 54,754).

29 June 1946
HYANNIS, MASSACHUSETTS. A ceremony to dedicate an altar given by the Kennedy family in memory of the late Lt. Joseph P. Kennedy, Jr., is held at St. Francis Xavier Church.

12 August 1946
BOSTON. The Joseph P. Kennedy, Jr. Foundation presents its first grant, a gift of $600,000 to the Franciscan Missionaries of Mary to establish a convalescent home for children of poor families. The grant is made exactly two years after Lt. Kennedy's death. John

---

* Two different men named Joseph Russo ran in the primary.

Photographer unknown.

Mary Hannon Fitzgerald, Rose Kennedy, and "Honey Fitz," at the New York World's Fair, 31 May, 1939.

Kennedy presents the check at the home of Archbishop Cushing in Brighton as his parents and family look on.

17 September 1946

BOSTON. On the occasion of Boston's three hundred sixteenth birthday, former mayor John "Honey Fitz" Fitzgerald recalls the city's history over radio station WDHO. Although the area had been explored and settled several years prior to its official founding, 17 September 1630, the date when a court of Puritans ordered the settlement named after Boston in Lincolnshire, the town many had come from, is generally accepted as the town's date of origin.

18 September 1946

MILTON, MASSACHUSETTS. Edward M. Kennedy begins the ninth grade at Milton Academy.

28 September 1946

WALLINGFORD, CONNECTICUT. On the occasion of the fiftieth anniversary of his alma mater, the Choate School, congressional candidate John F. Kennedy attends a dinner celebration, where he gives a speech on public affairs.

25 October 1946

LONDON. Thieves break into the home of Kathleen, Lady Hartington, on Smith Square, Westminster. They steal jewelry valued at over $35,000 and some articles of personal importance.

31 October 1946

LONDON. In a newspaper advertisement, Lady Hartington appeals to thieves who robbed her home. She asks that they return only two small mementos that mean more to her than the gems: a gold pin with the pilot's wings of the U.S. Navy Air Force, given her by her brother Joe and inscribed "To K from J," and a pair of cuff links owned by her late husband. (There was no response to the ad.)

5 November 1946

BOSTON. John F. Kennedy is elected to his first political office, U.S. Representative from the Eleventh Congressional District of Massachusetts. He receives 71.9 percent of the popular vote, winning by a plurality of over 43,000. The election results are: Kennedy (Democrat), 69,093 votes; Lester W. Bowen (Republican), 26,007; Philip Greer (Prohibition), 1,036; blanks, 9,237 (total votes cast, 105,373). In January, Congressman-elect Kennedy will fill the seat vacated by former Boston mayor James M. Curley. The term of office is two years.

12 November 1946
BOSTON. John Kennedy files a report with the Massachusetts secretary of state stating that no money was spent or collected on his recent campaign. All candidates are mandated to file a statement on their campaign disbursements and receipts.

26 November 1946
WASHINGTON, D.C. The American Defense Service Medal, given for active service prior to 7 December 1941, and the World War II Victory Medal, given for active service during the war, are posthumously awarded to Joe Kennedy, Jr. Joe's father accepts the medals.

27 December 1946
WASHINGTON, D.C. The Air Medal with three Gold Stars and the Distinguished Flying Cross are posthumously awarded to Joseph P. Kennedy, Jr., U.S.N.R. The citations accompanying the medals are signed "for the President" by Secretary of the Navy James Forrestal. They commend the late aviator for "meritorious achievement" (Air Medal) and "heroism" (Flying Cross) "in aerial flight as pilot of a United States Naval Patrol bomber plane in anti-submarine operations in the Bay of Biscay and the western approaches to the United Kingdom from October 22, 1943 to June 16, 1944." The Air Medal is presented for Kennedy's completion of his tenth mission during this period, the Flying Cross for his twentieth mission.

3 January 1947
WASHINGTON, D.C. As the Eightieth Congress begins its first session, John F. Kennedy, 29, is sworn in and commences his first term of office as U.S. representative from the Eleventh Congressional District of Massachusetts. Representative Kennedy is a member of the House Committees on the District of Columbia and Education and Labor. The two Massachusetts senators are Leverett Saltonstall (Republican) and Henry Cabot Lodge, Jr. (Republican).

16 January 1947
WASHINGTON, D.C. The appointment of Eunice Kennedy as executive secretary of the National Conference on Prevention and Control of Juvenile Delinquency of the Department of Justice is announced.

19 January 1947
TULSA, OKLAHOMA. The U.S. Junior Chamber of Commerce announces the winners of the nation's "ten outstanding young men of the year" award. Congressman John F. Kennedy is among those named. (Nominees must be between the ages of 21 and 36.)

27 February 1947
WASHINGTON, D.C. Speaking before members of the Harvard Club, Representative John Kennedy says the American people have a right to be informed of the government's foreign policy. If they are going to be asked to make sacrifices, he declares, they must be told the reasons for them.

10 March 1947
CHICAGO. On the opening day of the National Public Housing Conference, Representative John Kennedy expresses support for a federal program to provide low-cost public housing; a spokesman for the National Association of Real Estate Boards calls for abolishing public housing in favor of low-cost private housing. Citing the two options available—federal loans to public agencies to build low-cost homes and financial guarantees to private investors for low-cost rental housing—Kennedy expresses doubt that a feasible plan for private capital could be devised.

13 March 1947
WASHINGTON, D.C. At a session of the Education and Labor Committee, Representative Kennedy asks that Harold Cristoffel and Robert Buse, officials of a Milwaukee United Auto Workers' Union local, who have denied they were Communists, be indicted for perjury. (Testimony of a former officer in the Communist party has contradicted their denial.)

1 April 1947
WASHINGTON, D.C. A rule, set on 5 March by House Doorkeeper Monroe Melletio, that all congressional page boys must now wear blue uniforms with white shirts becomes effective. Some younger congressmen, including the boyish-looking John Kennedy, have been confused with page boys by their fellow representatives.

10 April 1947
NEWTON, MASSACHUSETTS. Catherine Frances Hickey dies at the age of 79. She was Joseph P. Kennedy's aunt. Never married, Catherine Hickey lived with her niece Margaret Burke, at 22 Bernard Lane. She is to be buried in the Holy Cross Cemetery in Malden.

14 April 1947
WASHINGTON, D.C.   Congressman Kennedy signs a minority report opposing the Taft-Hartley Act, a measure designed to place curbs upon labor unions. He also files a commentary explaining why he is against it: "The testimony of the representatives of management and labor before the Labor Committee and reporting of this bill to the House by the Committee do not augur well for the future of America....Management has been selfish. Labor has been selfish. And the majority of this committee has succumbed completely to the old and deeply rooted antilabor prejudices which delayed for decades the development of a forthright and constructive labor policy in America...."

14 May 1947
BOSTON.   The National Shawmut Bank takes over the assets and deposit liabilities of the Columbia Trust Company. In January 1946, Shawmut agreed to assume the responsibilities of Columbia Trust for a payment of $557,400. Joseph P. Kennedy and his family own a majority of the stock.

5 June 1947
CAMBRIDGE, MASSACHUSETTS.   Voting by ballot, Harvard alumni elect Representative John F. Kennedy director-at-large of the school's alumni association. Kennedy was a member of the Harvard Class of 1940.

14 June 1947
BOSTON.   In a speech before to an audience of over 1,000 at the New England Zionist Region convention, Representative John F. Kennedy calls for a free Jewish state. "Today the United States has before it the solution of the Palestine problem," he says. "It is my conviction that a just solution requires the establishment of a free and democratic Jewish commonwealth in Palestine...."

8 July 1947
WASHINGTON, D.C.   Representative John F. Kennedy announces that he has declined to sign a petition asking President Truman to grant executive clemency to James Michael Curley, who is serving a jail term for mail fraud. The petition is being circulated by Democratic House whip John McCormack and has been signed by all other Massachusetts Democrats in Congress. Representative Kennedy, who succeeded Curley as Representative of Massachusetts' Eleventh Congressional District, says that he cannot sign such a petition when he has refused to help obtain pardons for nonpolitical prisoners.

16 July 1946
WASHINGTON, D.C.   Joseph P. Kennedy is named to the Commission on Organization of the Executive Branch of the Government. The commission was created by Congress on 7 July 1947 to study the organization and operating methods of various executive departments, bureaus, and independent agencies in order "to determine what changes therein are necessary or will be beneficial...to bring about greater economy and efficiency in the public service." It is also known as the Hoover Commission, after Herbert Hoover, its chairman.

BOSTON.   Robert F. Kennedy receives an honorable discharge from the United States Naval Reserve at the headquarters of the First Naval District.

31 July 1947
SPRINGFIELD, MASSACHUSETTS.   In a speech given at the Massachusetts Federation of Labor convention, Representative John F. Kennedy denounces the Taft-Hartley Act as weakening the American labor movement.

31 August 1947
BOSTON.   Representative John F. Kennedy leaves for a seven-week tour of Europe to study Communist involvement in labor unions and other conditions in various countries. He plans to travel to Ireland, England, France, and Italy. He is paying for the trip himself. Representative Charles J. Kersten of Wisconsin accompanies him.

23 September 1947
CORK, IRELAND.   Rose Kennedy and her daughter Patricia arrive here to visit Kathleen, Marchioness of Hartington, at Lismore Castle. They left New York on September 17 on the liner *America*.

11 October 1947
SOUTHAMPTON, ENGLAND.   Representative John F. Kennedy cuts short his European tour after being hospitalized for an attack of malaria. He leaves for New York on the *Queen Elizabeth*.

16 October 1947
BOSTON.   Carried into the New England Baptist Hospital on a stretcher, Congressman Kennedy is admitted for treatment of the malaria attack to which he succumbed several weeks ago in Europe. Having arrived in New York earlier in the day, he flew to Boston by chartered plane.

105

17 November 1947

WASHINGTON, D.C. Congressman John F. Kennedy introduces a bill in Congress proposing that a national cemetery be established in Massachusetts.

14 December 1947

BOSTON. Representative John F. Kennedy lashes out at the Taft-Hartley law at a Massachusetts CIO convention. He calls the legislation "a severe blow to those who believe in the importance of harmonious industrial relations."

16 December 1947

WASHINGTON, D.C. In an attempt to expedite congressional action on the Taft-Ellender-Wagner National Housing Bill, a government program addressing veterans' housing needs that has been sitting in Congress for a long time, Representative John F. Kennedy and co-sponsor Jacob Javits (Republican, New York) call for a national conference of veterans' groups to encourage passage of the bill.

15 January 1948

BOSTON. At a New England Printing and Publishing Week dinner held at the Copley Plaza Hotel, Representative John F. Kennedy calls for a plan under which congressional funds would subsidize lower airmail rates for printed matter. This would mean more economical shipment of American publications around the world.

8 February 1948

EAST CAMBRIDGE, MASSACHUSETTS. Speaking at a communion breakfast of the Holy Name Society of St. Francis of Assisi Church, Representative John F. Kennedy declares veterans are at fault for lack of congressional action on a federal housing bill. "One reason for the delay is a lack of interest on the part of veterans themselves," he says. "There's a lot of talk about housing, but veterans just don't take the necessary steps to do anything about it, despite all the talk. Veterans have not done the job of contacting their Congressmen. I certainly feel that public pressure would do the job." Legislation for veterans' housing had been written in 1945.

29 February 1948

WASHINGTON, D.C. Representative John F. Kennedy is named in an Associated Press poll of the nation's most eligible bachelors. The Congressman is 30, 6'1", has reddish-brown hair, and greenish-gray eyes. In an AP interview, Kennedy expresses hope that he will find a suitable mate this year. "There are still ten months left," he says, knocking wood.

15 February 1948

BOSTON. In an address to observers of Lithuania's thirtieth anniversaty of independence at South Boston High School, Representative Kennedy urges that thousands of Lithuanians in displaced-person camps in Europe be permitted into the United States. He supports passage of the Stratton Bill, which would allow them to enter this country.

13 May 1948

LONDON. In the late morning, Lady Kathleen Hartington leaves by plane for Cannes with Peter Fitzwilliam, a wealthy, 37-year-old British Lord. She is romantically involved with Earl Fitzwilliam, much to the consternation of her family and the few friends who know. She is Catholic and widowed; he is married. But she is in love with him, and after spending a couple of days on the Riviera, they plan to fly to Paris to meet with her father and convince him to accept Peter as her husband once he has obtained a divorce. (Joseph Kennedy is in Europe making an economic survey for the Marshall Plan.) Rose Kennedy has already voiced absolute disapproval.

For the trip to Cannes, Fitzwilliam charters a two-engine DeHavilland Dove from the Skyways Corporation of London. Captain Peter A. Townshend is the assigned pilot; his co-pilot is Radio Officer Arthur F. Freeman. Captain Townshend notes thunderstorms in southern France and plans to land in Paris, where he will evaluate weather conditions before deciding whether to continue.

PARIS. The chartered plane arrives at LeBourget Airport in the early afternoon. Lord Peter and Lady Hartington debark, returning in a couple of hours. Townshend is reluctant to fly because of bad weather reports. Fitzwilliam, however, is engaging, adamant, and persistent. He convinces the pilot to take off. At 3:30 P.M. (Greenwich Meridian time), the plane takes off with its passengers and crew for the French Riviera.

SOUTHERN FRANCE. High above the Cevennes Mountains, the plane is battered by raging thunderstorms. The two crewmen desperately try to keep it airborne, but to no avail. At about 6:15 P.M. (G.M.T) the plane starts its fall. It descends through a cloud, a wing breaks off, and it plunges into a rugged chasm at the base of LeCoran Mountain. All aboard are killed.

Hearing the roar of the plane's engine, a farmer looks up and sees the crash. He goes to investigate, searching for an hour in the rain and darkness before he finds the four lifeless bodies in the wreckage. Rushing to the local village, he informs the gendarmerie, who make their way to the crash site. The dead woman is lying on her back with a deep gash on the side of her face; the male passenger is cradled under his seat; the two crewmen lie crushed below the instrument panel. The police search the bodies for identification and find that the two passengers both have titles.

The bodies are taken by oxcart to the local village and then to Privas, about 10 miles away, where they are placed in the town hall. Three local gendarmes stand guard. U.S. embassy officials at Marseilles are notified as news of the crash begins to travel around the world.

14 May 1948
BOSTON. In a copyrighted story, the *Boston Globe* reports the circumstance under which Joseph Kennedy learns of his daughter Kathleen's death. A reporter for the *Globe,* Joseph F. Dineen, Jr., knows that the former ambassador has read the story of Lady Hartington's death in the plane crash in France as it came over the teletype. He calls Kennedy's room at the Hotel George Cinq in Paris to ask if Kennedy has heard the news. Boston Police Commissioner Joseph Timilty, Kennedy's longtime friend, picks up the phone and says Kennedy is sleeping. When informed of the young woman's death, Timilty says, "That's terrible. We had no idea of it here. It's the first news of it we had. I'll have to break the news to Kennedy." After awakening the sleeping Kennedy, Timilty returns to the phone and tells the reporter: "I just broke the news to the Ambassador. He was speechless when I told him. It was a terrible shock to him. When I awakened him and told him, he couldn't utter a word."

PARIS. Later in the day, Joseph Kennedy receives condolences from Queen Elizabeth.

PRIVAS, FRANCE. U.S. Embassy officials from Marseilles gather at the temporary mortuary in the town hall where the local gendarmerie stands guard.

14 May 1948
PALESTINE. The United Nations partitions Palestine into separate Jewish and Arab territories. Israel is established as an independent state, with Chaim Weizmann as its first president.

15 May 1948
ISRAEL. Several Arab countries defy the United Nations mandate, refuse to recognize the new Jewish state, and attack Israel.

17 May 1948
PARIS. Lady Kathleen Hartington lies in state at the Church of St. Philippe du Roule. Her body has been brought here at her father's request.

18 May 1948
HYANNIS PORT, MASSACHUSETTS. A memorial High Mass is held for Lady Kathleen Hartington at St. Francis Xavier Church. Rose Kennedy attends with her children John, Patricia, Eunice, Jean, and Teddy, and her brother, Henry Fitzgerald. Too ill to travel from Boston, Rose's parents do not attend. Her son Robert is in Europe.

PARIS. Joseph P. Kennedy accompanies his daughter's body on the plane to London.

20 May 1948
LONDON. In the morning, a requiem mass is celebrated by the Rev. Francis G. Devas, S.J., for Lady Kathleen Hartington at the Immaculate Conception Church on Farm Street. The casket containing Kathleen's body lies on a catafalque before of the altar. Hundreds of mourners, including Randolph Churchill, Anthony Eden, John Jacob Astor, Ambassador Lewis Douglas, and Sir John Anderson, attend the service. Joseph Kennedy sits next to the duke and duchess of Devonshire, the parents of the late Lord Hartington.

DERBYSHIRE, ENGLAND. Arriving by train in the afternoon, the body of Lady Kathleen Hartington is buried next to the grave of her husband, the marquis of Hartington, in the Cavendish family plot at Chatsworth. Joseph Kennedy, who had traveled on the same train, attends the burial and leaves immediately afterward.

10 June 1948
CAMBRIDGE, MASSACHUSETTS. Robert F. Kennedy, 22, graduates from Harvard University. (Following graduation, he joins the *Boston Post* as a correspondent and is sent to Palestine to cover the Arab-Israeli Conflict.)

24 June 1948
NEW YORK. John F. Kennedy leaves by ship for England to settle his sister Kathleen's estate.

20 July 1948
BOSTON. John F. Kennedy files nomination papers with the secretary of state for a second term of office as representative from the Eleventh Congressional District.

Leading Massachusetts Democrats have tried to draft Kennedy as a candidate for governor.

2 August 1948
WASHINGTON, D.C. Threatened with deportation, a group of Latvians recently arrived in Boston gain a temporary delay in the proceedings against them when Representative John F. Kennedy files a bill supporting their case.

14 September 1948
BOSTON. John F. Kennedy, running unopposed, wins the Democratic primary for representative from the Eleventh Congressional District of Massachusetts. He receives 31,362 votes; 19,022 are blanks.

16 September 1948
CHARLOTTESVILLE, VIRGINIA. Robert F. Kennedy begins his law studies at the Department of Law of the University of Virginia.

2 November 1948
THE UNITED STATES. Democrat Harry S. Truman is elected president for his first full term, with Senator Alben Barkley as his vice-president. In a surprising show of strength, they defeat not only their Republican challengers Thomas E. Dewey, the governor of New York, and Earl Warren, the governor of California, but also the candidates of two Democratic factions, J. Strom Thurmond, who ran as a "Dixiecrat," and Henry Wallace, who ran on the Progressive ticket.

BOSTON. John F. Kennedy is re-elected to a second term in the U.S. House of Representatives from the Eleventh Congressional District of Massachusetts. The election results are: Kennedy (Democrat), 106,366 votes; all others, 2; blanks, 28,357.

MASSACHUSETTS. John "Honey Fitz" Fitzgerald is chosen as an at-large member of the Massachusetts Democratic Electoral College in the state election.

1 November 1948
BOSTON. Eighty-five-year-old John "Honey Fitz" Fitzgerald is reportedly upset when Governor Robert Bradford does not reappoint him commissioner of the Port Authority of Boston, an unpaid position the ex-mayor has held for several years.

17 November 1948
BOSTON. John "Honey Fitz" Fitzgerald, whose commission at the Boston Port Authority was recently discontinued by Governor Robert Bradford, loses his appeal to stay on. The executive board of the Boston Port Authority upholds Governor Bradford's selection of Alexander Macomber to succeed the former Boston mayor.

2 December 1948
LONDON. The will of Lady Kathleen Hartington is filed for probate. She leaves an estate of approximately $50,000.

7 December 1948
BOSTON. Citing their wish to have the benefit of Fitzgerald's years of experience, the commissioners of the Boston Port Authority unanimously elect "Honey Fitz" as their special consultant.

13 December 1948
BOSTON. The Electoral College assembles to vote for presidential nominee Harry S. Truman. John "Honey Fitz" Fitzgerald is a presidential elector.

3 January 1949
WASHINGTON, D.C. As the Eighty-first Congress opens, John F. Kennedy, 31, begins his second term of office as a representative of the Eleventh Congressional District of Massachusetts. Throughout this congressional session, Representative Kennedy is a member of the District of Columbia Committee and the Education and Labor Committee. The two senators from Massachusetts are Leverett Saltonstall and Henry Cabot Lodge, Jr.

12 January 1949
WALLINGFORD, CONNECTICUT. Congressman John F. Kennedy returns to his alma mater, the Choate School, to address the Current History Club on the legislation facing the Eighty-first Congress during 1949.

20 January 1949
WASHINGTON, D.C. Harry S. Truman takes the oath of office as president of the United States for the second time. Alben W. Barkley becomes his vice-president.

30 January 1949
SALEM, MASSACHUSETTS. In a speech, Representative Kennedy blames President Truman and U.S. military leaders and diplomats for the troublesome question of continuing United States support for Chiang Kai-shek and the Nationalist Chinese, who are losing their battle with the Chinese Communist forces.

7 February 1949
BOSTON. At a dinner of the Brighton Women's

Club held at the Kenmore Hotel, Representative John F. Kennedy speaks of the bravery of the cardinal primate of Hungary, Archbishop Joseph Mindszenty, who is to be tried the next day on espionage charges by the Communist regime. "The thoughts and prayers of everyone here are in a small prison cell in Hungary which holds Cardinal Mindszenty," he says.

11 February 1949
BOSTON. A dinner in honor of the eighty-sixth birthday of John "Honey Fitz" Fitzgerald is held at the Engineers' Club. Governor Paul Dever lauds the special consultant to the city's Port Authority as an "outstanding citizen of all New England!" The octogenarian expresses his appreciation by singing his old theme song, "Sweet Adeline."

1 March 1949
WASHINGTON, D.C. The Hoover Commission ends, and Joseph P. Kennedy winds up his duties as a commissioner.

7 June 1949
BOSTON. At the Boston Opera House, Representative John F. Kennedy delivers the commencement address to the twenty-seventh graduating class of Emmanuel College.

NEW YORK. Jean Kennedy, 21, graduates with a Bachelor of Arts degree in English from the Manhattanville College of the Sacred Heart. She minored in history and was a member of the Dramatic Club and the tennis and hockey squads.

1 July 1949
JEFFERSON, WISCONSIN. Rosemary Kennedy, who is mentally retarded, enters St. Coletta School, an institution dedicated to providing education and care for the handicapped.

16 July 1949
WASHINGTON, D.C. A 1,200-plus-page State Department compilation of messages obtained from caches of Nazi documents reveals that Ambassador Herbert Von Dirksen of Germany informed Adolf Hitler that Joseph P. Kennedy was anti-Semitic. Following a meeting with Kennedy, Von Dirksen cabled the Führer on 13 June 1938 that the American ambassador had said that "it was not so much the fact that we wanted to get rid of the Jews that was harmful to us, but rather the loud clamor with which we accompanied this purpose." According to the German ambassador, Kennedy thought the Nazis were doing "great things" for Germany.

17 July 1949
HYANNIS PORT, MASSACHUSETTS. In an Associated Press interview, Joseph Kennedy responds to the previous day's disclosure characterizing him as anti-Semitic as "complete poppycock."

12 August 1949
BOSTON. Announcement is made that the Joseph P. Kennedy, Jr. Foundation has donated $440,000 to various charities.

17 September 1949
CHARLOTTESVILLE, VIRGINIA. Robert F. Kennedy begins the semester as a second-year law student at the University of Virginia.

26 October 1949
BOSTON. Representative John F. Kennedy shares the speaker's platform with Indiana state legislator Philip H. Wilkie at the fiftieth-anniversary dinner of the Massachusetts Civic League at the Harvard Club. (Wilkie's father, the late Wendell Wilkie, had been the unsuccessful Republican candidate for president against Roosevelt in 1940.) Young Wilkie declares that the Republicans need a new program. In the last election, he says, the people had voted for the ideas of a party, not the candidates. Kennedy says that reform is needed in Congress, "not just a physical face-lifting" but "real independence and actual political freedom to enable it to respond quickly and effectively to the will of the American people."

8 November 1949
MEDFORD, MASSACHUSETTS. Visiting his Harvard friend Torby Macdonald, assistant football coach at Medford High School, Congressman Kennedy is invited to work out with the team. He does so incognito—and goes unrecognized. Afterward he complains of muscle aches.

4 December 1949
NEWTON, MASSACHUSETTS. At a meeting of the Newton Lodge of Elks, Representative John F. Kennedy praises the group for their fine "civic and public spirit."

7 January 1950
GREENWICH, CONNECTICUT. During a party at the Lake Avenue home of George and Ann (Bran-

nack) Skakel, the engagement of their daughter Ethel to Robert F. Kennedy is announced. Ethel, born 11 April 1928 in Chicago, had been the roommate of Bobby's sister Jean, at Manhattanville College in Purchase, New York.

29 January 1950

SOUTH BEND, INDIANA. At mid-year graduation ceremonies of the University of Notre Dame, Representative John F. Kennedy delivers a commencement address and receives an honorary Doctor of Laws degree from the school's president, the Rev. John J. Cavanaugh. He is the youngest recipient of the award in the school's history. (His grandfather, John Francis Fitzgerald, had received the same honorary degree in 1915.)

In his address, Kennedy says that "the basic purpose of every Catholic college is to prepare young men and women for eternal residence in the City of God. But Catholic colleges likewise realize that they have a fundamental duty to prepare their students for life in the City of Man." "With the decisions of government becoming more important in our lives with the issue of war and peace hanging in the balance," the "major challenge" confronting college graduates this year, he says, is in some degree "to answer the call to service."

6 March 1950

NEW YORK. Eleanor Roosevelt expresses disapproval of a bill sponsored by Congressman John F. Kennedy that would earmark educational funds for use by religious schools.

7 March 1950

WASHINGTON, D.C. After being approved by the Senate, a $300-million-dollar educational aid bill, sponsored by John F. Kennedy, that would provide funds for busing parochial students to school is rejected by the House Labor Committee.

8 March 1950

NEW YORK. *The Surrender of King Leopold,* by Joseph P. Kennedy and James M. Landis, is published by the Joseph P. Kennedy, Jr. Foundation.

2 June 1950

RIVERDALE-ON-HUDSON, NEW YORK. Graduation exercises are held for the forty boys of the Riverdale Country School Class of 1950. In the outdoor amphitheater of the school, Representative John F. Kennedy delivers the commencement address. He speaks of the need for young "men and women of integrity and

courage in public service" and of how the talents of high school graduates "can contribute materially to efficient and worthwhile government." Kennedy had been a student at Riverdale for the fifth, sixth, and seventh grades, from September of 1927 through June of 1930.

10 June 1950

HYANNIS PORT, MASSACHUSETTS. A pre-wedding party is given for Ethel Skakel and Robert Kennedy at the Hyannis Port Golf Club by the brothers and sisters of the groom-to-be.

MILTON, MASSACHUSETTS. Edward Kennedy, 18, graduates from Milton Academy. At graduation exercises in the Robert Saltonstall Gymnasium, his father, Joseph P. Kennedy delivers the commencement address. Ted Kennedy attended Milton Academy from 1946 until 1950 for the ninth, tenth, eleventh, and twelfth grades.

12 June 1950

CHARLOTTESVILLE, VIRGINIA. Robert F. Kennedy completes his second year in the Department of Law at the University of Virginia. (The University's law school was then known as the Department of Law.)

17 June 1950

GREENWICH, CONNECTICUT. Ethel Skakel, 22, becomes the bride of Robert F. Kennedy, 24, in St. Mary's Church. The nuptial mass is celebrated by the Rev. Terrence L. Connolly, S.J., at 11:30 A.M. An apostolic blessing is received from Pope Pius XII. Ethel wears a white satin gown with a fitted bodice embroidered with seed pearls, and having a bateau neckline and a deep lace bertha. Ann Skakel, the bride's sister, is the maid of honor, and John F. Kennedy, brother of the groom, is the best man. Following the wedding, a reception is held at the home of the bride's parents, where tenor Morton Downey sings. Later in the day, the couple leave for a honeymoon in Hawaii.

25 June 1950

SOUTH KOREA. North Korean Communist forces invade South Korea, and the Korean War begins.

27 June 1950

WASHINGTON, D.C. President Truman orders American military support for the South Koreans.

7 September 1950

NEW YORK. Francis Cardinal Spellman announces

Joseph P. Kennedy's donation of 2.5 million dollars for the construction of a home for neglected children in the Bronx at 1170 Stillwell Avenue. The contribution is given to the archdiocese on behalf of Kennedy's son, Joe Jr., who died in World War II.

16 September 1950
CHARLOTTESVILLE, VIRGINIA. Robert F. Kennedy begins his third and final year at the University of Virginia Department of Law.

19 September 1950
BOSTON. John F. Kennedy wins the Democratic primary for U.S. Representative from the Eleventh Congressional District of Massachusetts. The election results are: John F. Kennedy, 38,322 votes; Frank Bevilacqua, 4,237; Philip J. Diehl, 854; Charles DiSessa, 1,327; Paul S. Martelluci, 936; Andrew Zona, 365; blanks, 10,912 (total votes cast, 56,953).

29 September 1950
CAMBRIDGE, MASSACHUSETTS. Edward M. Kennedy, 18, enrolls as a freshman at Harvard College.

2 October 1950
BOSTON. Following a long illness, John Francis "Honey Fitz" Fitzgerald, 87, dies of a coronary thrombosis due to arteriosclerosis in his apartment at the Hotel Bellevue, 81 Beacon Street. His wife, Mary, his sons John and Thomas and their wives, and a nurse are at his bedside when he expires at 11:55 P.M. His daughter, Rose Kennedy, is in Paris.

3 October 1950
BOSTON. John Francis Fitzgerald's body lies in state at the home of his son Thomas at 3 Arundel Park, Dorchester. Outside a police detail stands guard, and at the arched entrance to the living room two firemen stand at attention. Many messages of condolence are received, including the following from President Harry S. Truman: "I have sorrow and offer you and all who mourn with you this assurance of deepest sympathy."

5 October 1950
BOSTON. A procession carrying the body of John "Honey Fitz" Fitzgerald moves down Washington Street. It is headed by two hundred firemen, and 1,500 people line the streets. At 10:00 A.M. , a High Requiem Mass is sung at the Cathedral of the Holy Cross, with Archbishop Richard J. Cushing officiating. The church is filled with 3,500 mourners. Unable to obtain plane trans-

portation from Paris in time, Rose is unable to join the family at the funeral. Fitzgerald's widow, Mary, is ill and also unable to attend.

Among the honorary pallbearers are Governor Paul A. Dever, ex-Governor Joseph B. Ely, Senator Henry Cabot Lodge, Jr., and Senator Leverett Saltonstall, Mayor Hynes, and all the living Boston ex-mayors: James Curley, Malcolm Nichols, Daniel A. Whelton, Frederick W. Mansfield, and Maurice J. Tobin (now secretary of labor). The pallbearers include Edward E. Moore, Congressman John W. McCormack, Police Commissioner Thomas F. Sullivan, and Judge Michael Kennedy. Others in attendance include Speaker of the House of Representatives Thomas P. O'Neill, Fire Commissioner Michael T. Kelleher, Congressman Foster Furcolo, and Chief Justice of the Superior Court John P. Higgins.

WEST ROXBURY, MASSACHUSETTS. In the afternoon, the body of John Francis Fitzgerald is interred at St. Joseph's Cemetery.

1 November 1950
WASHINGTON, D.C. An attempt is made to assassinate President Harry S. Truman at Blair House, his temporary home while the White House is being renovated. Two Puerto Rican nationalists storm the residence and after an exchange of gunfire with the President's guards, one of the Puerto Ricans and one of the Secret Service agents are killed. President Truman is unharmed.

7 November 1950
BOSTON. Representative John F. Kennedy of Massachusetts's Eleventh Congressional District is re-elected to a third term. He defeats the Republican candidate by a margin of nearly 5 to 1. The election results are: Kennedy (Democrat), 87,699 votes; Vincent J. Celeste of Boston (Republican), 18,302; Martha E. Greer of Boston (Prohibition), 582; blanks, 10,123 (total votes cast, 116,706).

8 December 1950
BOSTON. John "Honey Fitz" Fitzgerald leaves an estate of $76,000, according to his will filed in Suffolk probate court on this date. The will provides for the estate to be divided between Mary Fitzgerald and her two sons, John, Jr., and Tom, with some $2,000 going to a number of public institutions. The late mayor's daughter, Rose Kennedy, is named executrix. Rose is left no part of the estate, "for reasons," wrote the late Fitzgerald, "best known to myself."

Kennedy Family Collection. Photographer unknown.

Eunice and Joe, Sr., at Hyannis Port, 1940.

12 December 1950

CHARLOTTESVILLE, VIRGINIA. Joseph P. Kennedy delivers an address at the University of Virginia School of Law, in which he criticizes U.S. foreign policy and the United Nations. He declares that the United States should withdraw its military forces from Europe, Korea, and Asia, and build up defenses in the Western hemisphere. He describes the United Nations as ineffective, saying "the veto power alone makes it a hopeless instrumentality for world peace."

3 January 1951

WASHINGTON, D.C. The Eighty-second Congress opens its first session as John F. Kennedy, 33, begins his third term as a member of the House of Representatives. Throughout the session that convenes on this date, Representative Kennedy is a member of the House Committees on the District of Columbia and Education and the District of Columbia and Labor. The two senators from Massachusetts are Leverett Saltonstall and Henry Cabot Lodge, Jr.

8 January 1951

WASHINGTON, D.C. Representative John F. Kennedy leaves for Western Europe to study rearmament and defense installations in various countries and to confer with political leaders. His month-long tour includes Italy, Yugoslavia, Spain, and Germany.

10 January 1951

LONDON. Representative John F. Kennedy begins a three-day study of England's rearmament program. He is assisted by his father, who is also in England.

19 January 1951

WASHINGTON, D.C. A bill written by John F. Kennedy for the purpose of improving working conditions for longshoremen is introduced in the House of Representatives.

25 January 1951

BELGRADE, YUGOSLAVIA. Premier Marshal Tito discusses the threat to peace in Europe posed by the Soviet Union in an interview with Congressman John F. Kennedy.

30 January 1951

ROME. At Vatican City, John F. Kennedy has a private audience with Pope Pius XII. The young congressman had attended the pontiff's coronation in 1939.

6 February 1951

NEW YORK. On a national broadcast over the Mutual Radio Network, Representative John F. Kennedy reports on his tour of Western Europe. Based on his discussions with a number of leaders, he says the Atlantic Pact nations face the threat of Communist expansion. "The plain and brutal fact is that Europe is not making sacrifices commensurate with the danger that threatens to engulf her people," he says. Kennedy concludes that this will be a dangerous year for peace.

8 February 1951

BOSTON. The Crosscup-Pishop Post of the American Legion gives a dinner in honor of John F. Kennedy at the Hotel Bradford. In an address to the audience of almost eight hundred, Kennedy urges that the United States bring West Germany into the Atlantic Pact because, he believes, it will probably be the strongest nation in Europe in a few years.

18 February 1951

BEVERLY, MASSACHUSETTS. At a dinner given by the Jewish War Veterans of America, held at the Jewish Community Center, John F. Kennedy predicts a critical period ahead for world peace. He says that Russia, whose military strength is superior to Western Europe's, will have to attack within eighteen months if it intends to expand there.

21 February 1951

MALDEN, MASSACHUSETTS. Before a mixed religious audience, B'nai Brith's Louis B. Brandeis Lodge awards a citation to Representative John F. Kennedy for "outstanding contributions to the principle of brotherhood."

22 February 1951

WASHINGTON, D.C. Testifying at a session of the Senate Foreign Relations and Armed Services committees, Representative John F. Kennedy proposes that there should be one American soldier for every six from other nations in the army of the North Atlantic Treaty Organization (NATO) in order to defend Western Europe against an attack by Russia. "We must demonstrate to the Europeans," he says, "that we are determined to hold the line and more important, to encourage the Europeans to develop their own forces."

4 March 1951

BOSTON. At a communion breakfast at Emmanuel College, Representative John F. Kennedy says more European troops in the NATO army are necessary for adequate defense against Russia and its satellites. Otherwise, he says, the ratio of American troops to European forces will be inadequate, and the United States "will be left holding the bag."

10 March 1951

BOSTON. Representative John F. Kennedy praises the Irish at a dinner of the Ladies' Auxiliary of the Ancient Order of Hibernians. The three personality traits common to the Irish are, he says, "love of family, love of country, and love of God."

15 MARCH 1951

BOSTON. At the annual dinner of the South Boston Citizens' Association in the Hotel Vendome, Congressman John F. Kennedy says that the loyalty of the Irish for family, God, and country have become embedded in the American national character and that the country should be grateful to them.

1 April 1951

HAVERHILL, MASSACHUSETTS. Addressing 150 members of B'nai Brith at Temple Emmanuel, Representative John F. Kennedy says that if Atlantic Pact troops were withdrawn from Western Europe, the Soviet Union would invade and overtake the continent.

9 April 1951

WASHINGTON, D.C. Addressing colleagues in the House of Representatives, Representative John F. Kennedy says the Italian Peace Treaty of February 1947, prohibits Italy from building up the military power necessary to defend itself from Soviet oppression. He asks that the United States renounce the treaty, which is, he says, dangerous to the entire world.

14 April 1951

BOSTON. In a speech delivered to 1,200 students attending an annual conference of the New England Region of the National Federation of College Students at Boston College, John Kennedy warns that communism is spreading from Russia to other areas, and that the United States must assist Europe in fighting Soviet aggression.

21 April 1951

BOSTON. In a speech before members of the Massachusetts Association of Taxpayers Federation at the Hotel Statler, John Kennedy asserts that a defense setup similar to that provided by the North Atlantic Pact is necessary in the Mid-East. The volatile nature of the oil-rich area, he says, makes a "comprehensive regional defense arrangement" advisable.

5 May 1951

BOSTON. Joseph P. Kennedy offers to give securities to the city to cover its expenses in awarding the Patrick J. Kennedy Medal of Honor to firemen who display heroism in the line of duty. (His father, Patrick J. Kennedy, had served as fire commissioner briefly in 1905.) Mayor John B. Hynes says the city would accept the donation.

9 May 1951

WASHINGTON, D.C. Charging that the millions of dollars' worth of supplies that American exporters are sending each year to Hong Kong find their way into Communist China, Representative John F. Kennedy introduces a bill in Congress that would prohibit the shipment of strategic war materials to Hong Kong. The bill also provides for cutting off U.S. aid to any foreign country exporting war materials to Communist China or Hong Kong.

29 May 1951

NEW YORK. John Kennedy confers with General Douglas MacArthur. General MacArthur tells Kennedy that combat methods presently being used against the Communist Chinese in Korea can only bring indecisive results.

30 May 1951

BOSTON. In a pair of Memorial Day speeches, Representative John F. Kennedy warns that civilization is on the verge of a third world war. He calls for the United States to rebuild its strength during the time gained while the United Nations troops fight in Korea. These addresses are made before the Boston Lodge of Elks at Mt. Hope Cemetery in Dorchester and the Michael J. Perkins Post of the American Legion at the New Calvary Cemetery in Mattapan.

31 May 1951

BOSTON. An honorary doctoral degree in oratory is presented by Dr. Delbert Staley of Staley College to Representative John F. Kennedy. Kennedy then delivers the commencement address to the school's fifty-first graduating class at ceremonies held at Copley Plaza.

11 June 1951

CHARLOTTESVILLE, VIRGINIA. Robert F. Kennedy graduates from the Department of Law at the University of Virginia with a Bachelor of Laws degree.

12 June 1951

CAMBRIDGE, MASSACHUSETTS. The spring semester ends at Harvard College. Edward M. Kennedy will not return for his second year. During the semester just past, a friend of Kennedy's was caught taking Ted's Spanish exam in his place, and both boys have been suspended.

25 June 1951

FORT DEVINS, MASSACHUSETTS. Edward M. Kennedy takes his physical and enlists in the United States Army. His number is RA 11 233 980.

4 July 1951

GREENWICH, CONNECTICUT. A daughter, Kathleen Hartington, is born to Ethel Skakel and Robert Kennedy. She is the couple's first child and the first grandchild of Rose and Joe Kennedy. The baby is named in memory of Robert Kennedy's late sister, Lady Kathleen Hartington.

5 July 1951

FORT DIX, NEW JERSEY. Edward M. Kennedy reports for basic training in the Thirty-ninth Infantry of the Ninth Infantry Division.

Joe Kennedy, Jr., in Ireland, 1937.

Kennedy Family Collection. Photographer unknown.

6 August 1951

WORCESTER, MASSACHUSETTS. In a speech given at the annual convention of the Massachusetts Federation of Labor, John F. Kennedy blames inflation on the Defense Production Acts, Congress, and President Harry Truman.

20 August 1951

WASHINGTON, D.C. In the wake of a West Point cheating scandal, Representative John F. Kennedy introduces a bill asking Congress to commission a study for the purpose of devising new criteria for admitting students to the country's military schools.

22 September 1951

BOSTON. In an address before members of the Massachusetts Italian Peace Treaty Committee, Representative John F. Kennedy calls for a new peace agreement with Italy that would provide for the buildup of Western military defenses.

2 October 1951

NEW YORK. From Idlewild Airport, Representative John F. Kennedy leaves on a tour of Europe, the Near East, and the Far East to study political, military, and economic conditions in various countries. He is paying for the trip out of his own funds. He is accompanied by his brother Robert and his sister Patricia.

4 October 1951

PARIS. Representative John F. Kennedy confers with General Dwight D. Eisenhower on defense installations in Europe.

11 October 1951

TEHRAN, IRAN. After conferring with officials of the Iranian government, Congressman Kennedy says that economic aid from the United States is necessary to prevent that Mid-Eastern nation from falling under Communist influence.

13 October 1951

NEW DELHI, INDIA. Prime Minister Jawaharlal Nehru discusses the country's food shortage at a luncheon meeting with Representative John F. Kennedy. Both Robert and Patricia Kennedy are present.

16 October 1951

KARACHI, PAKISTAN. In the midst of Pakistan's disputes with India, Premier Liaquat Ali Khan is assassinated. Representative John F. Kennedy, who had just interviewed the Premier, is the last American to see him alive.

19 October 1951

SAIGON, VIETNAM. Representative John F. Kennedy arrives with his entourage.

25 October 1951

SINGAPORE. John F. Kennedy commences a tour of the island's industry.

8 November 1951

TOKYO. A recurrence of malaria forces Congressman Kennedy to cut short his fact-finding tour and return to the United States.

10 November 1951

FORT HOLABIRD, MARYLAND. Edward M. Kennedy is assigned to the Counter Intelligence Corps Center here as a military police student.

17 November 1951

EAST WOBURN, MASSACHUSETTS. In a speech to members of the Goodyear Parent Teachers Association at the Goodyear School, Representative John F. Kennedy says that the peoples of Indochina and India are hostile to the United States and deem it an imperialistic nation.

18 November 1951

BOSTON. The Fraternal Order of Eagles initiates John F. Kennedy into membership in induction ceremonies at the Hyde Park Municipal Auditorium.

19 November 1951

BOSTON. Addressing the Boston Chamber of Commerce at the Hotel Bradford, John F. Kennedy criticizes the various aspects of American foreign policy. He characterizes American diplomats as "unconscious of the fact that their role is not tennis and cocktails but the interpretation to a foreign country of the meaning of American

life." Kennedy also calls the Voice of America radio program ineffectual, saying that a revision of foreign policy in the Middle East and Far East is necessary.

21 November 1951

BOSTON. Robert F. Kennedy is admitted to the bar of the Commonwealth of Massachusetts.

WASHINGTON, D.C. On the same date, Robert F. Kennedy is appointed an attorney adviser in the Criminal Division of the Department of Justice. It is his first job for the federal government.

2 December 1951

CAMBRIDGE, MASSACHUSETTS. Speaking at the Lodge of Elks memorial services, John F. Kennedy says that the United States is years behind Russia in the production of planes.

7 December 1951

BOSTON. At a convention of the Massachusetts CIO held at the Copley Plaza Hotel, John F. Kennedy declares that tax money from New England is being appropriated by the federal government to build up other areas of the country, thereby putting the region's competitive position at risk.

13 December 1951

NEW YORK. At the Lt. Joseph P. Kennedy, Jr. Home for Underprivileged Children in the Bronx, Francis Cardinal Spellman announces that Pope Pius XII has bestowed the title of papal countess upon Rose Kennedy. The Cardinal presents Rose with a papal document executed by the Vatican secretary of state, conferring the title. The award comes as a surprise to Mrs. Kennedy, who is visiting the children's home with her husband and daughter Patricia. Cardinal Spellman says the title is presented to Rose Kennedy "for her exemplary life and for her many charities in this country and all parts of the world."

18 December 1951

WEST CONCORD, MASSACHUSETTS. John Edward Hannon dies at the age of 74 after a fall while at work on board the *Nova Scotia*. He was the brother of Mary Josephine (Hannon) Fitzgerald and uncle of Rose (Fitzgerald) Kennedy. On 26 December 1912, he married Leonore Hurley. They had two children, Geraldine Mary (born 12 March 1914) and John Edward (born 18 January 1916).

Kennedy Family Collection. Swaebe, London.

Joe, Jr., and Kathleen in London, 1943.

7 January 1952
CAMP GORDON, GEORGIA. Military police trainee Edward M. Kennedy is transferred to the Provost Marshal General's School.

14 January 1952
CAMP GORDON, GEORGIA. Edward M. Kennedy is assigned to the Military Police Replacement Training Center.

18 January 1952
LYNN, MASSACHUSETTS. A Distinguished Service Award Key is presented to Representative John F. Kennedy in recognition of his being selected the "outstanding young man in the state" by the Massachusetts Junior Chamber of Commerce. The presentation is made at a banquet at the Hotel Edison.

19 January 1952
BOSTON. In a radio address, John Kennedy declares that the Marshall Plan has been ineffective. The American aid that it provides to Western Europe, he says, has not improved the standard of living of the common people due to wasteful expenditures in administering the plan.

30 January 1952
BOSTON. At a CIO convention, Congressman Kennedy tells over 550 delegates that aid to distressed areas of New England may be forthcoming. He says that the federal government now has the authority to place defense contracts in regions where labor costs may be higher but where worker surpluses exist. Also addressing the delegates is Roy Wilkins president of the National Association for the Advancement of Colored People (NAACP).

117

Kennedy Family Collection. Associated Newspapers, London.

Lord Hartington and Kathleen, 1944.

7 February 1952
BOSTON. John F. Kennedy speaks about his recent visit to Israel and his meeting with Prime Minister David Ben Gurion to members of the Brotherhood of the Beth El Jewish Center in Dorchester.

13 February 1952
BOSTON. John F. Kennedy is named the recipient of the Italian government's highest honor, the Star of Solidarity, First Order. The young congressman receives this tribute in recognition of his untiring efforts on behalf of the Italian government and his acts of good will toward Italian-Americans. (Kennedy had requested aid for Italy and had asked the United States to renounce the Italian Peace Treaty.) He is the first member of Congress ever to receive the award, which a representative of the Italian government will present formally at a later date.

28 February 1952
WASHINGTON, D.C. A letter of appointment names Robert F. Kennedy special assistant to the attorney general of the Criminal Division, Department of Justice, for assignment to Brooklyn, New York.

2 April 1952
WASHINGTON, D.C. Two amendments proposed by Representative John F. Kennedy for funding a New England water-power study are rejected by the House of Representatives.

7 April 1952

CAMP KILMER, NEW JERSEY. Edward M. Kennedy is transferred to the 1277th Area Service Unit. Having completed his military police training, he is sent as a replacement and awaits assignment.

24 April 1952

BOSTON. Representative John F. Kennedy declares his candidacy for the United States Senate. The three-term congressman will seek the seat now held by Republican incumbent Henry Cabot Lodge, Jr. Lodge is a Republican liberal who, like Kennedy, has a family heritage of public and political service. (In 1916, the grandfathers of both Kennedy and Lodge had battled for the same Senate seat, which Lodge won.)

18 May 1952

WORCESTER, MASSACHUSETTS. John F. Kennedy opens his senatorial campaign with an address at the Hotel Sheraton. An audience of over four thousand enthusiastic women cheers and applauds frequently as he stands on stage on the crutches that he needs due to a recent accident. Afterward, the crowd leaves the main ballroom to attend a tea hosted by Rose, Eunice, and Patricia Kennedy in the adjacent parlors.

4 June 1952

Paris. Edward M. Kennedy is assigned as military policeman to the Five Hundred Twentieth Military Police Service Company, with the rank of private first-class.

6 June 1952

NEW YORK. Robert F. Kennedy resigns from the Criminal Division of the Department of Justice. As special assistant to the U.S. attorney general in Brooklyn, he had been working on a racketeering case before a federal grand jury.

7 June 1952

BOSTON. Robert F. Kennedy begins serving as campaign manager in his brother John's bid for the Democratic nomination for senator from Massachusetts.

22 June 1952

FALL RIVER, MASSACHUSETTS. In a campaign speech before 1,000 women at the Hotel Mellen, senatorial candidate John F. Kennedy says that if elected, he will provide the aggressive leadership the state needs. A tea follows, hosted by members of his family.

23 June 1952

BOSTON. Calling him "one of the finest young men to come into public life in the last twenty years," Mayor John B. Hynes pays tribute to John F. Kennedy and endorses him for Senate candidacy before more than five hundred supporters at the Parker House Hotel.

25 June 1952

WASHINGTON, D.C. Addressing the House of Representatives, John F. Kennedy warns that large imports of fish fillets are crippling New England's fishing industry and asks Congress to study the problem.

26 June 1952

BROCKTON, MASSACHUSETTS. Rose Kennedy hosts a reception at the Walk-Over Club on behalf of her son John, who is running for candidate for the U.S. Senate. Robert Kennedy reads a telegram from the congressman expressing regrets that he is unable to attend the function due to political duties in Washington. An overflow crowd crams into the club to greet the Kennedys and join them at tea.

1 July 1952

WASHINGTON, D.C. John F. Kennedy is chosen the handsomest member of Congress by reporters from *Capitol News.*

2 July 1952

WASHINGTON, D.C. Visiting a school run by CBS to coach political candidates, Congressman John F. Kennedy receives expert advice on how to communicate effectively with viewers over television. He is taught to shift his attention to the different cameras so that it will appear that he is talking directly to the viewer when the cameras change.

16 September 1952

MASSACHUSETTS. John F. Kennedy, running unopposed on the ballot, wins the Democratic primary for senator from Massachusetts. The election results are: Kennedy, 394,138; all others, 4; blanks, 123,469 (total votes cast, 517,611). In November, Kennedy will face incumbent Henry Cabot Lodge, Jr., who captures the Republican nomination unopposed.

24 September 1952

BOSTON. A son, Joseph Patrick II, is born to Ethel (Skakel) and Robert Kennedy. Their second child and first son is born at St. Elizabeth's Hospital in Brighton. He is named after his paternal grandfather and late uncle. (Had Joe Kennedy, Jr., left a namesake son, that child would have been Joseph P. Kennedy III; however, because Bobby's son is Joe Jr.'s nephew and not his direct issue, he is properly designated Joseph P. Kennedy II.)

John F. Kennedy served as a lieutenant in the United States Navy during World War II.

1 October 1952

CAMBRIDGE, MASSACHUSETTS. Almost six thousand women pack the Commander Hotel to hear Senate candidate John Kennedy deliver a campaign speech and greet him at tea afterward. Thirteen thousand female residents of the city had been invited.

18 October 1952

WASHINGTON, D.C. Representative John F. Kennedy announces that he has received a letter from Kohei Hanami, the commander of the Japanese warship that had knifed PT-109 in half in August 1943. The former commander of the *Amagiri* recounts his naval career in

World War II and tells how his destroyer came to ram PT-109. He writes, "I am firmly convinced that a person who practices tolerance to a former enemy like you, if elected to high office in your country, would no doubt contribute not only to the promotion of genuine friendship between Japan and the United States, but also to the establishment of the universal peace."

20 October 1952
[?]   A letter in which Eleanor Roosevelt endorses John F. Kennedy for senator is made public. "You have been a tower of strength to oppressed minorities throughout the world," the former First Lady writes.

27 October 1952
BOSTON.   The Iupa Romana Award, which is given by the city of Rome to individuals who contribute to its welfare, is presented by New York's mayor Vincent R. Impelliteri to John F. Kennedy at John Hancock Hall.

4 November 1952
THE UNITED STATES.   Republican candidates Dwight D. Eisenhower and Richard M. Nixon are elected president and vice-president. They defeat Democratic candidates Governor Adlai E. Stevenson and Senator John Sparkman.

MASSACHUSETTS.   John F. Kennedy defeats three-term Republican incumbent Henry Cabot Lodge, Jr., in the race for senator from Massachusetts. Winning by a plurality of over 70,000 votes, Kennedy becomes only the third Democrat ever elected to a Senate seat from the state. The election results are: Kennedy (Democrat), 1,211,984; Lodge (Republican), 1,141,247; Thelma Ingersoll (Socialist Labor), 4,683; Mark R. Shaw (Prohibition), 2,508; all others, 3; blanks, 64,123 (total ballots, 2,424,548). Kennedy's victory comes in the face of an overwhelming win in Massachusetts for Eisenhower and the Republicans. His six-year term begins in January.

5 November 1952
BOSTON.   Just after 7:30 A.M., the telephone rings in John Kennedy's campaign headquarters. Robert Kennedy answers and repeats aloud the concession message from Henry Cabot Lodge being read to him over the phone: "I extend my congratulations and express my hope that you [John Kennedy] will derive from your term in the Senate all the satisfaction that comes from courageous and sincere efforts in public service."

SENATOR
1953-1961

3 January 1953
WASHINGTON, D.C. As the Eighty-third Congress opens, John F. Kennedy, 35, is sworn in and begins his first term as United States senator from Massachusetts. Senator Kennedy serves on the Government Operations and Labor and Public Welfare committees. Leverett Saltonstall, a Republican, is the other senator from Massachusetts.

12 January 1953
WASHINGTON, D.C.   Senator John F. Kennedy is appointed a member of the Committee on Government Operations, to which the Senate Permanent Subcommittee on Investigations, headed by Senator Joseph R. McCarthy (Republican, Wisconsin), will report.

14 January 1953
WASHINGTON, D.C.   Staff positions for the Senate Permanent Subcommittee on Investigations, which will study and report on subversive activities affecting the U.S. government, are announced. Senator Joseph McCarthy, a friend of Joseph P. Kennedy, heads the committee. Roy Cohn, 25, is named chief counsel; Robert Kennedy, 27, is appointed assistant counsel.

20 January 1953
WASHINGTON, D.C.   Dwight D. Eisenhower is inaugurated as the thirty-fourth president of the United States. Richard M. Nixon is sworn in as vice-president.

29 January 1953
WASHINGTON, D.C.   In the Senate John F. Kennedy cosponsors a reintroduction of the Ives-Humphrey bill, which provides for the protection of civil rights in employment.

7 February 1953
WASHINGTON, D.C.   Senator Kennedy announces that he will keep his official office in the room he used as a representative—Room 1702 in the Federal Office Building.

10 February 1953
BOSTON.   In an address given at an annual dinner of the Brighton Women's Club at the Hotel Kenmore, Senator John F. Kennedy shares some of his observations

about his new office. He emphasizes the important role Massachusetts plays in national affairs.

14 February 1953
NEW YORK. Senator John F. Kennedy attends the Eastern States Jackson-Jefferson Day Dinner at the Waldorf-Astoria Hotel, where he is the highest office holder in the Massachusetts group. Adlai E. Stevenson is the honoree at the $100-per-plate banquet.

17 February 1953
PARIS. The French government posthumously awards the Legion of Honor (Chevalier) to Joseph P. Kennedy, Jr.

1 March 1953
BOSTON. Senator John F. Kennedy is the main speaker at a Bonds of the Israeli Government dinner at the Hotel Somerset. The comedian Jack Benny entertains at the function.

3 March 1953
WASHINGTON, D.C. Interviewed on a radio program sponsored by the *Boston Post*, Senator Kennedy calls upon the United States to act independently from England and quickly reach an agreement with Iran. If the United States does not act, he fears, the Middle Eastern country will suffer financial ruin and will be unable to supply oil. The show is aired to Boston over local stations.

5 March 1953
FORT DEVENS, MASSACHUSETTS. Pfc Edward M. Kennedy reports to the Personnel Separation Center.

7 March 1953
WASHINGTON, D.C. Senator John F. Kennedy files a statement with the Senate Interior Committee requesting Congress to continue federal government ownership of off-shore oil resources and to use of these revenues for national defense and education. He declares these resources should not be given to "a few states whose claim is based only on geographical accident."

15 March 1953
[?] Announcement is made of the engagement of Eunice Kennedy to Robert Sargent Shriver, Jr. Born on 9 November 1915 in Westminster, Maryland, Shriver is a 1938 graduate of Yale University with a law degree from Yale Law School. He has worked for a New York law firm, *Newsweek* magazine, and, since 1948, for Joseph P. Kennedy's Merchandise Mart.

17 March 1953
BOSTON. At the pre-opening of the Israel Exposition, sponsored by the Bonds for the Israeli Government (BIG) at the Hotel Bradford, Senator John F. Kennedy says that an economically strong Israel is necessary to prevent the spread of communism in the Middle East.

27 March 1953
FORT DEVENS, MASSACHUSETTS. Edward M. Kennedy is released from active military service with the rank of private, first class.

28 March 1953
ST. LOUIS, MISSOURI. Edward M. Kennedy re-enlists in the Army Reserve and is assigned to the 1019th Control Group at the U.S. Army Reserve Components and Administration Center. Although released from active duty, he still has more than six years remaining to complete his military obligation.

12 April 1953
DEDHAM, MASSACHUSETTS. Speaking at a communion breakfast of St. Mary's Holy Name Society at Dedham High School, Senator John F. Kennedy declares that the most important challenge facing the United States is the thwarting of communism.

24 April 1953
BRIDGEPORT, CONNECTICUT. Speaking at the local Democratic Jefferson-Jackson Day dinner, Senator John F. Kennedy accuses some high-ranking Republican officials of failing to inform the public of the actual dangers presented by the Soviet Union.

26 April 1953
PAWTUCKET, RHODE ISLAND. Senator John F. Kennedy warns of the Soviet Union's superior military strength at a Jefferson-Jackson Day dinner at the Rhodes Ballroom.

14 May 1953
WASHINGTON, D.C. At a press conference, Senator John F. Kennedy announces that within the next few days he will begin a series of speeches outlining a legislative program designed to correct the industrial and economic problems of New England.

15 May 1953
BOSTON. Senator John F. Kennedy is the guest of honor at the annual dinner-dance of the Lt. Joseph P. Kennedy, Jr. Post, Veterans of Foreign Wars, at John Hancock Hall. Addressing an audience of 500, he warns against reductions in American military forces.

18 May 1953

WASHINGTON, D.C. On the floor of the Senate at 5:30 P.M. , Senator John F. Kennedy begins the first of three speeches on the economic problems of New England and the federal actions that can alleviate them. He announces that his program will include forty legislative recommendations and that, while they aim to revive the declining industry of New England, will also benefit the rest of the country.

Discussing industrial expansion and diversification in this first speech, Kennedy introduces legislative steps that call for the establishment of regional industrial development corporations, greater assistance from the Reconstruction Finance Corporation and Small Defense Plants Administration, expansion of retraining programs, and tax-amortization incentives. This is his maiden speech before the United States Senate.

20 May 1953

WASHINGTON, D.C. Senator John F. Kennedy delivers the second of three major speeches on New England's economic woes and the part Congress can play in their solution. Outlining some means of preventing further decline and industrial dislocation in the region, Kennedy presents a program providing for a minimum hourly wage, revision of the Taft-Hartley Act to enable "equalization of unionization" in the different regions of the country, the establishment in all states of minimum unemployment benefits, and the elimination of unfair labor practices, wage policies, and discrimination.

In a televised hearing before members of the Senate Permanent Subcommittee on Investigations, Assistant Counsel Robert F. Kennedy reports on vessels of Allied nations being used for trade with Red China. Robert Kennedy also cites the increase in British exports to Communist China.

23 May 1953

NEW YORK. Eunice Kennedy, 31, is married in the morning to Robert Sargent Shriver, Jr., 37, at St. Patrick's Cathedral. Francis Cardinal Spellman officiates at the nuptial mass. Pope Pius XII sends papal blessings.

The church is banked with flowers and lit only by candles for the 11 A.M. ceremony. The bride, given in marriage by her father, wears a white Christian Dior gown with a fitted bodice.

Guests at the wedding include former Massachusetts governor Paul A. Dever, Associate Justice of the Supreme Court William O. Douglas, Margaret Truman, former postmaster general James A. Farley, and Senator Joseph R. McCarthy. The bridegroom's brother, T. Herbert Shriver II, is the best man. A luncheon reception at the Waldorf-Astoria Hotel follows the wedding.

25 May 1953

WASHINGTON, D.C. In the last of three major speeches on the business decline in New England and actions for revitalization there, Senator John F. Kennedy proposes several means of curing economic hardship, including a reinsurance program for state unemployment benefits to safeguard these systems in times of economic distress, federally funded unemployment benefits for laid-off workers who have exhausted state assistance, a national agricultural program that would benefit all areas of the economy, and tax incentives to induce employers to increase their hiring.

8 June 1953

PURCHASE, NEW YORK. Rose Kennedy receives an honorary degree from her alma mater, Manhattanville College, which had moved to Purchase in 1950. She is cited for her collaboration with her husband "in the mighty and magnificent program of giving" that perpetuates the memory of their late son, Joe Jr., and helps thousands of needy and suffering children. "In all phases of her life," the citation continues, "a convinced and fervent Catholicism has been the source of her strength, as well as an inspiration to those within and those without the Church."

12 June 1953

WASHINGTON, D.C. In a letter to Senator William Langer, the chairman of the judiciary committee that is holding hearings on amendments to the Refugee Relief Act of 1953, Senator John F. Kennedy proposes that quotas on refugees who may enter the country be substantially increased. Citing the recent earthquakes as well as overpopulation in Greece and the overpopulation and unemployment crises in Italy, Kennedy urges that the quotas for these two countries in particular be augmented.

13 June 1953

NEW YORK. "The Senate's Gay Young Bachelor," a profile of the wealthy and unmarried 36-year-old Massachusetts politician, John F. Kennedy, appears in the *Saturday Evening Post*. In his article, Paul F. Healy says that the Senator lives up to his role as one of the most eligible bachelors in the country "when he drives his long convertible, hatless and with the car's top down in Washington, or accidentally gets photographed with a glamour girl in a night club."

24 June 1953

NEWPORT, RHODE ISLAND. Hugh and Janet (Bouvier) Auchincloss of the Hammersmith Farm and McLean, Virginia, announce the engagement of Mrs.

Kennedy Family Collection. Photographer unknown.

Bobby, Jean, and Teddy, c. 1945.

Auchincloss's daughter, Jacqueline Lee Bouvier, to Senator John F. Kennedy. A mutual friend, newspaperman Charles Bartlett, introduced the two at a dinner party that he and his wife, Martha, gave at their Georgetown home in Washington, D.C.

Born 28 July 1929 in East Hampton, New York, Jacqueline Bouvier attended Miss Porter's School in Farmington, Connecticut, Vassar College, and the Sorbonne in Paris; she graduated from George Washington University. She is of French descent on her father's side. Her mother is divorced from John Vernou Bouvier III, a stockbroker. Her sister Lee is married to Michael Canfield. Jackie recently quit her job at the Washington *Times-Herald* where she wrote the column "Inquiring Camera Girl."

26-28 June 1953
HYANNIS PORT, MASSACHUSETTS. On their first weekend as an engaged couple, Jacqueline Bouvier (without a ring) and John Kennedy sail, play tennis, and enjoy other activities at the Kennedy home.

7 July 1953
WASHINGTON, D.C. Senator John F. Kennedy introduces a bill providing for federal regulation of futures contracts on wool in order to prevent unfair practices in trading prices.

14 July 1953
WASHINGTON, D.C. Senator John F. Kennedy is admitted to George Washington University Hospital following another bout with malaria.

18 July 1953
WASHINGTON, D.C. A controversial report associating the loss of American troops in Korea with Allied trade with Communist China is released by the Senate Permanent Subcommittee on Investigations, headed by Senator Joseph McCarthy. The document, primarily prepared by Assistant Counsel Robert F. Kennedy, also charges that Allied trade with Communist China in the first quarter of 1953 increased twelvefold over that during the same period in 1952.

20 July 1953
WORCESTER, MASSACHUSETTS. On behalf of the Joseph P. Kennedy, Jr. Foundation, Jean Ann Kennedy and Jacqueline Bouvier make a gift of $150,000 to Assumption College. The gift, presented at the Sheraton Hotel, is to aid in the reconstruction of the college, which was devastated recently by a tornado. (The school had no tornado extension insurance.) With this gift, the Foundation has awarded a total of $5.26 million since 1946.

27 July 1953
WASHINGTON, D.C. Speaker of the House Joseph William Martin, Jr., appoints Joseph P. Kennedy to the Commission on Organization of the Executive Branch of the Government (Second Hoover Commission).

SOUTH KOREA. After three years and one month of fighting, the Korean War ends.

29 July 1953
WASHINGTON, D.C. Senator John Kennedy co-sponsors legislation to aid the American shipbuilding industry.

31 July 1953
WASHINGTON, D.C. After six and a half months of serving as assistant counsel to the Senate Permanent Subcommittee on Investigations, Robert F. Kennedy resigns.

7 August 1953
BOSTON. With his marriage to Jacqueline Bouvier sixteen days away, Senator John F. Kennedy returns here by plane from France, where he engaged in discussions about the political situation in Indochina.

16 August 1953
BOSTON. Edward E. "Doc" Moore dies at the age of 76. A personal secretary and close friend of Joseph P. Kennedy and the late John Francis Fitzgerald, he also served as secretary to Boston mayors James M. Curley and Andrew J. Peters. He leaves his wife Mary (Murphy). Edward Moore Kennedy is his namesake.

10 September 1953
NEWPORT, RHODE ISLAND. A bachelor dinner is held at the Clambake Club for Senator John F. Kennedy two days before his wedding.

11 September 1953
NEWPORT, RHODE ISLAND. Hugh and Janet Auchincloss host a dinner, followed by music and dancing, for the Kennedy-Bouvier wedding party at the Clambake Club.

12 September 1953
NEWPORT, RHODE ISLAND. Jacqueline Lee Bouvier, 24, weds Senator John Fitzgerald Kennedy, 36, in St. Mary's Church. The 11 A.M. nuptial mass is conducted by Archbishop Richard J. Cushing of Boston. Before the mass, a special blessing from Pope Pius XII is read: "Holy Father on occasion of marriage cordially imparts Hon. John F. Kennedy and Mrs. Kennedy his pater-

nal apostolic blessing in pledging enduring Christian happiness in married life."

Jacqueline Bouvier is given in marriage by her stepfather, Hugh D. Auchincloss, because her own father, John V. Bouvier III, falls ill and is unable to attend. She wears a gown of ivory silk taffeta with a portrait neckline, tight-fitting bodice, and a floor-length bouffant skirt terminates in a long train.

The wedding party consists of twelve bridal attendants and fourteen ushers. The bride's sister, Lee Canfield, is matron of honor, and her half-sister, Nina Auchincloss, is maid of honor. Robert F. Kennedy is his brother's best man. The ushers include Edward M. Kennedy, Joseph Gargan, Torbert MacDonald, LeMoyne Billings, and Paul "Red" Fay, Jr.

Among the 750 invited guests attending are Rhode Island governor Dennis J. Roberts, Senators Theodore F. Green (R.I.), John O. Pastore (R.I.), and Leverett Saltonstall (Mass.), former governor of Massachusetts Paul Dever, Representatives Joseph Martin and Thomas P. O'Neill (Mass.), movie actress Marion Davies, Senator Eugene J. McCarthy, Arthur Krock, Alfred Vanderbilt, and Don José de Lequercia, the Spanish ambassador.

Outside, close to two thousand people crowd around the little church located on Spring Street. The bride and groom are showered with rice, cheers, and congratulations as they leave the church after the ceremony. A luncheon reception follows for 1,300 guests at Hammersmith Farm, the 75-acre estate belonging to the bride's stepfather and mother. In the evening, the bride and groom fly to New York in a private plane piloted by Robert E. Wood to spend their wedding night.

14 September 1953
NEW YORK. After spending their first two days of married life in New York, John and Jacqueline Kennedy leave for a honeymoon in Acapulco, Mexico.

29 September 1953
WASHINGTON, D.C. At 10:00 A.M. in the Cabinet Room of the White House, the commissioners of the Second Hoover Commission take the oath of office administered by U.S. Supreme Court Justice Harold H. Burton. Among the eleven commissioners sworn in is Joseph P. Kennedy. Herbert Hoover is elected chairman. President Dwight Eisenhower attends the ceremony and extends his wishes for the commission's success.

October 1953
WASHINGTON, D.C. Robert F. Kennedy begins work for the Commission on Organization of the Execu-

John Fitzgerald Kennedy Library. Photographer unknown.

John F. Kennedy runs for Congress.

tive Branch of the Government (the Second Hoover Commission) as an assistant to his father, Commissioner Joseph P. Kennedy.

25 October 1953
CAMBRIDGE, MASSACHUSETTS. Rose Kennedy speaks about her experiences in England during the time her husband was ambassador to Great Britain at a meeting of the Christ Child Society held at the Harvard Club.

2 December 1953
BOSTON. Delivering the keynote speech at the annual convocation of Northeastern University at Symphony Hall, Senator John F. Kennedy calls for public support of politicians who vote according to their convictions rather than those who "forsake principles for flattery and friendship."

3 December 1953
BOSTON. In an address delivered to the delegates of the Massachusetts State Council Convention at the Hotel Bradford, Senator John F. Kennedy says that the Eisenhower administration functions to serve the needs of big business rather than those of the entire country.

4 December 1953
MONTREAL, CANADA. In a speech given at the University of Montreal, Senator John F. Kennedy says that minor squabbles between the United States and Canada will not diminish the friendship between the two countries. "I speak for the great majority of American people when I say to you that the United States highly values her fraternal friendship and associations with Canadians," Kennedy says.

6 December 1953
NEW YORK. Appearing as a guest on "Time's Man of the Year Review," a television special, Senator John F. Kennedy says that his choice for that title in 1953 is the late Senator Robert A. Taft of Ohio.

10 December 1953
CHATTANOOGA, TENNESSEE. In a bold move, Senator John F. Kennedy uses a meeting here as a forum for censuring the South for its "unfair competitive practices." Speaking at a Rotary Club session, the Senator attacks economic and business practices in the region. He criticizes Tennessee's policy of inviting new industries to open "tax-free factories by issuing federally tax-exempt municipal revenue bonds." Many in the audience

John Fitzgerald Kennedy Library. Photographer unknown.

John F. Kennedy shortly after election to Congress.

are employed in businesses that have participated in the region's economic programs.

15 December 1953

BOSTON.   A statement is released in which John F. Kennedy reports on his first year in office as United States senator. Referring primarily to attempts to revive the industrial strength of New England, he declares: "I feel my efforts were fairly successful, not just in terms of legislation enacted, but also in...clarifying issues and waging battles which, even if on the losing side, needed to be waged."

10 January 1954

BOSTON.   An exclusive article written by Senator John F. Kennedy appears in today's edition of the *Boston Post.* "I am a Democrat—both by inheritance and convictions," he writes. "The Democratic Party is not the party of any one group, but of all groups. In our party may be found members of all races—all religions—all walks of life—all income groups in all parts of the country."

12 January 1954

WASHINGTON, D.C.   A delegation of CIO textile workers from Massachusetts and Rhode Island calls on Senator Kennedy to ask his support in helping them obtain legislation and federal action to relieve the unemployment crisis in New England's textile industry.

13 January 1954

WASHINGTON, D.C.   In a radio news conference, Senator John F. Kennedy criticizes President Eisenhower's reference to Massachusetts' asking for special privileges in obtaining defense contracts. Kennedy denies the charge, saying, "We are asking for recognition that this situation is a serious national problem."

14 January 1954

WASHINGTON, D.C.   Although the St. Lawrence Seaway would be of "no direct economic benefit to the economy of Massachusetts," and "the initial investment, even though repaid, will come in part from Massachusetts tax revenues," Senator Kennedy tells the Senate he favors a bill providing for participation in its construction. Pointing out that the project is in the national interest and that he has sought the support of senators from other regions of the country for projects that would benefit New England, Kennedy says, "To those in my state and elsewhere who oppose our participation in the construction of this project for national security merely because the economic benefits go elsewhere, I would say that it has been this arbitrary refusal of many New Englanders to recognize the legitimate needs and aspirations of other sections which has contributed to the neglect of, and even opposition to, the needs of our own region by the representatives of other areas." The Senator notes that, in six votes during the past twenty years,

John Fitzgerald Kennedy Library. Photographer unknown.

"Honey Fitz," Rose, John, Mary Hannon Fitzgerald, and Joseph P. Kennedy, following
both of their victories in the June 1946 Democratic Congressional Primary.

not one Massachusetts congressman voted for the measure due to pressure from port interests in Boston.

17 January 1954
WASHINGTON, D.C. A son, Robert Francis, Jr., is born to Ethel (Skakel) and Robert Kennedy. He is their third child and second son.

21 January 1954
NEW YORK. In an address to the Cathedral Club in Brooklyn, Senator John F. Kennedy questions the effects of a policy for American security that emphasizes atomic power as set forth by the Eisenhower administration. Saying that this new approach has "momentous implications for all Americans," Kennedy asks if atomic weapons would be useful in fighting the ideological infiltration of communism, and if the new policy's success is predicated on Congress's surrender of its war-powers prerogative.

23 January 1954
BOSTON. At the annual Jefferson-Jackson Day banquet at the Hotel Sheraton Plaza, former governor James M. Curley criticizes Senator John Kennedy's support of the St. Lawrence Seaway legislation before 1,200 Democrats. Without directly mentioning Kennedy's name,

Curley makes reference to "some misguided men in the U.S. Senate who voted for the St. Lawrence Seaway." Later, Senator Kennedy tells the gathering why the bill is advantageous and then introduces the main speaker, Governor G. Mennen Williams of Michigan.

29 January 1954
WASHINGTON, D.C. President Eisenhower's refusal to recommend raising the minimum wage from 75¢ to $1 per hour is assailed by Senator John F. Kennedy. "Even $1 an hour or $40 a week," he says, "does not provide a family with the minimum budget required in any part of the country under present prices, according to the Bureau of Labor Statistics."

30 January 1954
WASHINGTON, D.C. Senator John F. Kennedy voices strong opposition to the proposed Bricker amendment, which would restrict presidential powers in world affairs by requiring congressional approval of executive agreements. Kennedy says that the constitutional amendment, proposed by Senator John W. Bricker (Republican, Ohio) and hotly debated over the past few days on Capitol Hill, has "potentially dangerous implications."

9 February 1954

WASHINGTON, D.C. The Senate passes a bill, introduced last July by Senator Kennedy and two colleagues, that would regulate trading in wool futures under the Commodity Exchange Act. Senator Kennedy says he is hopeful that the House will act quickly on the bill.

12 February 1954

PALM BEACH, FLORIDA. Rose and Joe Kennedy announce the engagement of their daughter Patricia to actor Peter Lawford. An only child, Peter was born in London on 7 September 1923 to May (Bunny) and Sir Sydney Lawford. Peter's father served as a general in World War I. Peter Lawford has already appeared in over thirty movies, including *Mrs. Miniver*, *The White Cliffs of Dover*, *The Canterville Ghost*, *The Picture of Dorian Gray*, *Good News*, *Easter Parade*, and *Royal Wedding*.

14 February 1954

WASHINGTON, D.C. Appearing on the NBC television show "Meet the Press," Senator John F. Kennedy voices the opinion that New England has been bypassed for federal aid in developing hydroelectric projects. The government, he says, should assist the region.

16 February 1954

WASHINGTON, D.C. Speaking before the National Legislative Council of the American Federation of Labor, Senator Kennedy proposes a National Conference on Migrating Industry to "alert the public and our government officials to the economic instability and depressed standards caused by runaway plants."

WASHINGTON, D.C. Robert F. Kennedy goes back to work for the Senate Permanent Subcommittee on Investigations as its minority counsel. He had resigned from the subcommittee in July 1953.

19 February 1954

WASHINGTON, D.C. Herbert Hoover, chairman of the Commission on Organization of the Executive Branch of the Government, accepts Counsel Robert Kennedy's letter of resignation. "I realize," Hoover writes, "that there is little to do until the Task Forces have reported and that a restless soul like you wants to work."

12 March 1954

WASHINGTON, D.C. Congressman Kenneth B. Keating, the Republican representative of New York interviews Senator John Kennedy on the Indochina crisis

for broadcast on the Rochester television station WHAM. Kennedy says that the people of Indochina want their independence and that France will never regain control of the area. He predicts that the eventual fall of Indochina to the Communists will be dangerous to the rest of Southeast Asia and to the world.

16 March 1954

EVERETT, MASSACHUSETTS. Addressing a dinner meeting of the Friendly Sons of St. Patrick at the Parlin Junior High School, Senator John F. Kennedy praises Ireland's struggle for freedom through the centuries. This effort, he says, should serve as an inspiration for free nations resisting communism.

18 March 1954

NEW YORK. Following the revelation that Puerto Rican nationalists planned to assassinate notable officials who live here or are in town on United Nations business, police assign bodyguards to certain dignitaries. Among those who are assigned special guards are Ambassador Henry Cabot Lodge, Jr., Representative Adam Clayton Powell, Jr., and Senator John F. Kennedy.

21 March 1954

WASHINGTON, D.C. Interviewed on "Capitol Memo," a Gannett News Service radio program, Senator John F. Kennedy says he favors revision but not repeal of the Taft-Hartley labor law. He blames New England for losing industry to the South because it failed to take advantage of federal funds to develop natural resources.

3 April 1954

BOISE, IDAHO. In town to address a state Jackson-Jefferson Day dinner, Senator John F. Kennedy says that he supports the selection of Boston attorney Samuel P. Sears as counsel for the inquiry by the Senate Permanent Subcommittee on Investigation into the confrontation between Senator Joseph McCarthy and the Army.

6 April 1954

WASHINGTON, D.C. In an address to the Senate, John F. Kennedy says that defending Southeast Asia from the spread of communism is futile unless the Vietnamese and other colonial peoples recognize that France and the nations that support her want to halt Soviet aggression, not maintain French colonialism in the area. Kennedy charges that unless the French relinquish control of the area, the people of Indochina will distance themselves from efforts to repel the Communists. Supplying troops and materials to Indochina will be dangerous, and there will be no hope of victory.

20 April 1954

CHICAGO. Addressing Democrats at a Jackson-Jefferson Day fund-raising dinner, Senator John F. Kennedy says that although weakening of French control in Indochina will prompt the Eisenhower administration to send American support to the area, the country has been kept in the dark about the crisis. "It is my belief that the American people should be told the truth about the situation in the Far East," Kennedy says. "This has not been done." The Senator further says that "if Secretary Dulles' and Vice-President Nixon's words are to be taken at their face value, we are about to enter the jungle and do battle with the tiger."

21 April 1954

WASHINGTON, D.C. Senator John F. Kennedy wires police in Beverly, Massachusetts, that he has found an Irish setter. He has traced the dog to Beverly from information on its license tag. Later the wife of George Cabot, the son of Kennedy's former political opponent Henry Cabot Lodge, Jr., calls Kennedy to say that the dog belongs to her husband. They arrange a meeting, and Senator Kennedy returns the dog.

24 April 1954

NEW YORK. Patricia Kennedy, 19, and actor Peter Lawford, 30, are married in the Church of St. Thomas More. The marriage is performed by the Rev. John C. Cavanaugh, the former president of Notre Dame University and a friend of the Kennedy family. It is the third Kennedy wedding in eleven months.

The bride wears a white satin gown. Her sister Jean is maid of honor, and the bridegroom's friend Robert Neal, Jr., is best man. Following the ceremony, a small reception is given at the Plaza Hotel. At both the church and the hotel, throngs of excited New Yorkers greet the wedding party.

28 April 1954

CHICAGO. A son, Robert Sargent III, is born to Eunice (Kennedy) and R. Sargent Shriver, Jr., at Presbyterian Hospital. He is the couple's first child.

5 May 1954

WASHINGTON, D.C. Senator John F. Kennedy joins other members of Congress in supporting a resolution introduced in the Senate to provide for the inclusion of the words "under God" in the Pledge of Allegiance to the American flag. "I feel that in these difficult times we can and should avow our dependence on Almighty God," he says, "a dependence which the founders of this country recognized and acknowledged in the framing of the Con-

stitution." With the proposed change, the Pledge of Allegiance would read: "I pledge allegiance to the flag of the United States of America and to the Republic for which it stands, one nation, under God, indivisible, with liberty and justice for all."

9 May 1954

WASHINGTON, D.C. In a television interview, Senator John F. Kennedy says that intervention of United States military forces in Indochina would be futile. He declares that unless the people there are prepared to repel Communist aggression, "Indochina is lost."

NEW YORK. *The Three Keys to Success* by Baron William Maxwell Aitken Beaverbrook, with an introduction by Joseph P. Kennedy, is published by Duell, Sloan & Pearce. The 108-page book had been previously published abroad as *Don't Trust to Luck*.

11 May 1954

NEW YORK. Francis Cardinal Spellman confers on Rose Kennedy the Catholic Youth Organization Club of Champions Award. The gold medal is presented for her outstanding contributions to youth at a board-of-directors dinner of the association. She is the first woman to receive the award.

14 May 1954

MALDEN, MASSACHUSETTS. Speaking at a local Veterans of Foreign Wars meeting at Beebe Junior High School, Senator John F. Kennedy declares that cuts in defense funds will weaken the American armed forces. He urges economic support to maintain a superior military machine. At the meeting, Kennedy's college roommate, Torbert H. Macdonald, is installed as commander of the post.

28 May 1954

CHICAGO. Prior to speaking at a meeting of the Chicago Executives' Club, Senator John Kennedy tells reporters that within the next few weeks President Eisenhower will have to decide whether or not to ask Congress to authorize the sending of United States military forces to Indochina. He says the nation "is now paying more than 80 percent of the cost of the largely French-directed war.

30 May 1954

FALL RIVER, MASSACHUSETTS. At a Knights of Columbus meeting, John F. Kennedy is initiated as a fourth-degree member. In his speech, he says that "the rapid advance of Communism is without parallel in history."

11 June 1954

WASHINGTON, D.C. The Export-Import Bank bill favored by the Eisenhower administration is assailed in the Senate by Senator John F. Kennedy. The bill would expand the lending authority of Eximbank (as it is called), which is chartered to finance trade with all countries except Russia. Kennedy says there already exists lending authority of over a billion dollars that is not being used.

WASHINGTON, D.C. A dispute breaks out between Assistant Counsel to the Minority Robert F. Kennedy and Chief Counsel Roy Cohn at the end of a hearing on the Army by the Senate Permanent Subcommittee on Investigations. Afterward, Kennedy and Cohn exchange angry words.

17 June 1954

WASHINGTON, D.C. An amendment, sponsored by Senator John F. Kennedy, to a bill providing new military funds is defeated in the Senate. President Eisenhower's administration requested cutting the twenty-division Army the following year to seventeen divisions; Kennedy proposed to reduce it to nineteen divisions.

21 June 1954

WASHINGTON, D.C. With Representative Harrison A. Williams, Jr. (Democrat, N.J.), Senator John F. Kennedy introduces the Trade Adjustment Act of 1954, a bill designed to assist individuals and companies in the face of the "economic hardships resulting from foreign import competition." The bill provides for such assistance as vocational programs, supplemental unemployment benefits, and loans from the Small Business Administration.

19 July 1954

WASHINGTON, D.C. Legislation to tighten government control on lobbyists is proposed by Senator John F. Kennedy. He suggests that Congress revise the current lobby law and require lobbyists to register with the attorney general and state their expenditures.

4 August 1954

WORCESTER, MASSACHUSETTS. At an annual convention of the Massachusetts Federation of Labor, Senator John F. Kennedy deplores the unemployment situation in New England and scores the Eisenhower administration's labor policies, which he blames for the receipt of fewer defense contracts in the region. Kennedy submits an eight-point federal program designed to bring economic relief to New England. Among the actions, the program provides for raising the minimum wage, amending the Taft-Hartley Act, improving unemployment benefits, strengthening the Walsh-Healy Act, and reducing power costs in New England.

17 August 1954

WASHINGTON, D.C. Suffering from a World War II back injury, Senator John F. Kennedy announces that he will undergo special surgery when Congress adjourns. For the past month, he has been walking with the aid of crutches.

21 August 1954

WASHINGTON, D.C. Vice-President Richard M. Nixon appoints Senator John F. Kennedy to the Senate Foreign Relations Committee, which is investigating the International Technical Assistance program and related foreign-aid programs. Says Kennedy, "I have long regarded our Point 4 program to be one of the keystones of this nation's foreign policy...."

29 August 1954

PORTLAND, MAINE. Senator John F. Kennedy makes a television appearance on WCSH-TV with Democratic senatorial candidate Professor Paul Fullam who is trying to win the senate seat of Margaret Chase Smith (Republican). The Republicans had announced that Vice-President Richard M. Nixon would campaign on behalf of Senator Smith.

20 September 1954

PARIS. The Legion of Honor and the Croix de Guerre are awarded posthumously to Lt. Joseph P. Kennedy, Jr., at the French Foreign Ministry. The awards are presented by French Air Secretary Diomede Catroux to Joseph and Rose Kennedy.

6 October 1954

WASHINGTON, D.C. A statement is filed by Senator John F. Kennedy with the Interstate Commerce Commission urging it to approve the lowering of rail rates for shipping iron ore from Boston to Midwestern cities. It is, he says, in the national interest to encourage ports to expand their facilities. He further states that this will result in the construction of appropriate facilities by a New England railroad, and that, because federal policy has resulted in the equalization of ocean cargo rates, it is only fair for the Port of Boston to enjoy rates comparable to the Port of Baltimore.

7 October 1954

BOSTON. In a campaign effort, Senator John F.

Kennedy appears on a program on WNAC-TV with State Treasurer Foster Furcolo, the Democratic nominee for senator, and Representative Robert F. Murphy, the Democratic nominee for governor. Prior to the 15-minute television broadcast, Kennedy clashes with Furcolo over the latter's request that the Senator assail the record of his opponent, Senator Leverett Saltonstall, instead of discussing the economic conditions in Massachusetts. Kennedy reportedly changes the closing of his script from "I wish you both and the Democratic ticket every success in November" to "I wish you, Bob Murphy, and the entire Democratic ticket every success in November," thus avoiding a direct endorsement of Furcolo. It is believed that Kennedy and Fucolo had been feuding for some years.

10 October 1954

NEW YORK. Senator John F. Kennedy speaks at a rally on behalf of a friend, Anthony B. Akers, who is a Democratic candidate for Congress in the Seventeenth Congressional District. Akers had also been in PT-boat service during World War II.

11 October 1954

NEW YORK. Senator John F. Kennedy is admitted to the Hospital for Special Surgery-Cornell Medical Center at 321 East 42nd Street in Manhattan. Kennedy undergoes X ray and other preliminary medical examinations. Barring any obstacles, he will have an operation to repair a ruptured disk in his spine at some future date.

BOSTON. Francis X. Morrissey, secretary to John F. Kennedy, tells the press that the Senator "definitely will not give Furcolo a personal endorsement." The remark causes an immediate brouhaha among Democratic party regulars in Massachusetts.

In the evening, Robert F. Kennedy reads a statement, prepared by John F. Kennedy from his hospital bed in New York. Says the younger Kennedy: "In view of conflicting statements regarding the Senator's position, I am authorized to say my brother stands by his original statement which he made on a TV program that he is a Democrat and supports the entire Democratic ticket."

18 October 1954

WASHINGTON, D.C. Comptroller General of the United States Lindsay C. Warren receives a memorandum from John F. Kennedy regarding a fishery law that the Senator sponsored. Kennedy asks Warren to authorize the government to increase its spending on fishery products.

21 October 1954

NEW YORK. Major spinal surgery is performed on Senator John F. Kennedy at the Hospital for Special Surgery to correct an injury suffered during his Navy service in World War II. Convalescence from the operation prevents Kennedy from participating in the upcoming vote condemning Joseph McCarthy in the Senate, the Democratic campaign for the Massachusetts election, and other political events during the next few months. A group of physicians, headed by Dr. Philip Wilson, performs a double-fusion operation on Kennedy's spine.

28 October 1954

NEW YORK. Eunice (Kennedy) Shriver reports the loss of a diamond-studded platinum pin valued at almost $30,000. She discovered it was missing five days earlier after leaving a charity function at the Waldorf-Astoria. A reward is offered.

1 November 1954

NEW YORK. The diamond pin lost by Eunice Shriver is anonymously returned by mail, wrapped in tissue paper, with a news article reporting its loss and a note saying, "Give the reward to the Lighthouse." (The Lighthouse is a New York organization that provides aid to the blind.)

3 November 1954

NEW YORK. The $1,000 reward for the return of Eunice Shriver's lost jewel is given to the Lighthouse. The money is paid by the American Universal Insurance Company.

24 November 1954

BOSTON. It is announced that Senator John F. Kennedy, convalescing from a spinal operation, will not return to the office until "about three or four months from now."

2 December 1954

WASHINGTON, D.C. The Senate votes 67 to 22 to condemn Senator Joseph R. McCarthy (Republican, Wisconsin) for abuses stemming from his investigation of alleged Communist influences. Conspicuously absent from the vote is Senator John F. Kennedy, who is recuperating from his recent spinal operation.

21 December 1954

NEW YORK. Senator John F. Kennedy is discharged from the Hospital for Special Surgery. He leaves on a stretcher, accompanied by his wife, Jacqueline, and a nurse. They are taken by ambulance to LaGuardia Airport, where they board a plane for Florida.

MIAMI. At Miami Airport, Senator Kennedy and his party are met and taken to the home of Joseph P. Kennedy in Palm Beach. John Kennedy intends to convalesce and spend the holidays with his family.

5 January 1955
WASHINGTON, D.C. The Eighty-fourth Congress begins its first session. A Democratic majority dominates the Senate. Robert F. Kennedy becomes chief counsel and staff director of the Senate Permanent Subcommittee on Investigations.

8 January 1955
TULSA, OKLAHOMA. Robert F. Kennedy is named as one of America's "ten outstanding young men of 1954" in a Junior Chamber of Commerce survey. He is cited for his "outstanding work in halting trade of United States allies with Red China."

24 January 1955
WASHINGTON, D.C. The appointment of Robert F. Kennedy as chief counsel and staff director of the Senate Permanent Subcommittee on Investigations is confirmed by the seven-member subcommittee under the chairmanship of Senator John L. McLellan (Democrat, Ark.). The subcommittee had been headed by Senator Joseph R. McCarthy in 1953 and 1954, with Roy Cohn as chief counsel.

10 February 1955
NEW YORK. Senator John F. Kennedy is readmitted to the Hospital for Special Surgery for further surgery.

11 February 1955
NEW YORK. Surgeons at the Hospital for Special Surgery remove a metal plate from Senator John F. Kennedy's spine. It is Kennedy's second operation in less than four months.

22 February 1955
BOSTON. Henry S. Fitzgerald dies at the age of 80 of a coronary thrombosis and bronchopneumonia. The uncle of Rose Kennedy, he was the brother of the late John "Honey Fitz" Fitzgerald. He dies at his home at 41 Lyndhurst, Dorchester.

25 February 1955
NEW YORK. Senator John F. Kennedy is released

from the Hospital for Special Surgery and leaves for his parents' home in Palm Beach, Florida.

29 March 1955
SANTA MONICA, CALIFORNIA. A son, Christopher, is born to Patricia (Kennedy) and Peter Lawford at St. John's Hospital. He is the couple's first child.

28 April 1955
NEW YORK. After a routine checkup at the Hospital for Special Surgery, Senator John F. Kennedy departs for Palm Beach, Florida.

4 May 1955
WASHINGTON, D.C. Following passage of the Eisenhower administration's reciprocal trade bill, the Senate rejects a proposal made by Senators John F. Kennedy and Hubert H. Humphrey (Democrat, Minn.) for federal aid to businesses and regions injured by imports.

23 May 1955
WASHINGTON, D.C. After a recuperation of seven months at his parents' home in Palm Beach (during which he wrote *Profiles in Courage*), Senator John F. Kennedy resumes his Senate duties. He arrives by plane with his wife and his sister Jean. The party is greeted at National Airport by Jacqueline Kennedy's mother, Mrs. Hugh Auchincloss, and Ethel Kennedy. They are driven to Capitol Hill by two aides, Theodore J. Reardon, Jr., and Theodore Sorenson.

Senator Kennedy holds a news conference at his office and answers questions on a range of subjects, including international affairs, President Eisenhower's popularity, Russia, his own upcoming public appearances, senatorial work, and personal plans. On Kennedy's desk is a giant basket of fruit with a card saying "Welcome home, Dick Nixon."

24 May 1955
WASHINGTON, D.C. Just after 4:00 P.M., two congressional pages swing open the doors to the Senate chamber and John F. Kennedy enters, accompanied by Majority Leader Lyndon B. Johnson (Democrat, Tex.) and President Pro Tempore Walter George (Democrat, Ga.). Kennedy's colleagues stand and give him a round of applause. Minority Leader William F. Knowland (Republican, Cal.), who had held the floor when Kennedy walked in, extends a "very warm and cordial welcome-back to the Senate of our good friend, Jack Kennedy."

Eunice, Jose, Sr., unidentified prelate, Rose, John, "Honey Fitz," Teddy, c. 1946.

Shortly afterward, roll call is taken, and the senators vote on President Eisenhower's veto of the 8.6 percent postal pay-raise bill. Senator Kennedy votes to override the presidential veto, but the two-thirds majority needed is not there, and the motion fails. Among the visitors watching the proceedings in the gallery are Jacqueline Kennedy, his sisters Patricia and Jean, and his brother Robert and sister-in-law, Ethel Kennedy.

25 May 1955
WASHINGTON, D.C. Senator John F. Kennedy is the lone Democrat to vote for President Eisenhower's national highway plan. It is rejected by the Senate.

27 May 1955
NEW YORK. Senator John F. Kennedy enters the Hospital for Special Surgery, now at 535 East 70th Street, for routine therapy over the Memorial Day weekend.

3 June 1955
WORCESTER, MASSACHUSETTS. At the thirty-eighth annual graduation at Assumption College, Senator John F. Kennedy delivers the commencement address and receives an honorary degree. In his speech, he says that although the totalitarian system of communism has room for churches, "there is no room for God" since "the claim of the State must be total and no other loyalty and no other philosophy of life can be tolerated." He urges the graduates to "stimulate a revival of our religious faith, to renew the battle against weary indifference and inertia." Senator Kennedy is awarded an honorary Doctor of Laws degree.

6 June 1955
WASHINGTON, D.C. Senator John F. Kennedy asks for and gets Senate approval of a budget of a half-million dollars to fund projects of the National Institute of Health in Bethesda, Maryland. His interest in this area began when when he was a patient at the Hospital for Special Surgery in New York. A physician there told him that his research on a federal medical project had been halted for lack of funds. Kennedy wrote to the National Institute of Health and found that fund shortages stopped a number of projects. The half-million dollars approved by the Senate today will enable the resumption of many research projects.

WASHINGTON, D.C. Robert F. Kennedy is admitted to practice before the Supreme Court of the United States.

10 June 1955
HYANNIS PORT, MASSACHUSETTS. At the Kennedy family home, some four hundred state legislators, state house officials, and members of Congress gather at Senator John F. Kennedy's request for the purpose of building "a closer relationship between state and federal elected officials for the benefit of Massachusetts." The guests, who are greeted by Senator and Mrs. Kennedy, dine, play golf and softball, and participate in other recreational activities. Both Democrats and Republicans attend the nonpartisan outing, but high-ranking officials from the GOP, including Governor Christian Herter, declined to come.

15 June 1955
WASHINGTON, D.C. A son, David Anthony, is born to Robert and Ethel (Skakel) Kennedy. He is their fourth child and third son.

23 June 1955
WASHINGTON, D.C. The last meeting of the Second Hoover Commission is held, and Joseph Kennedy's duties as commissioner are ended.

26 June 1955
WASHINGTON, D.C. Senator John F. Kennedy announces his proposal for the establishment of a commission on immigration and naturalization policy to review the McCarran-Walter Immigration Act. He will introduce the bill tomorrow. The commission, which will suggest revisions in the statutes, is to be patterned after the Hoover Commission on Government Reorganization.

29 June 1955
WASHINGTON, D.C. Senator John F. Kennedy, chairman of the Senate's Reorganization Subcommittee, introduces ten bills that provide for implementation of Hoover Commission recommendations.

3 July 1955
BOSTON. Senator John F. Kennedy is admitted to New England Baptist Hospital for X rays and a medical examination.

10 July 1955
BOSTON. After a week at New England Baptist Hospital, Senator John F. Kennedy is released and leaves for Washington, D.C.

15 July 1955
NEW YORK. Senator John F. Kennedy enters the Hospital for Special Surgery for checkup tests and therapy.

17 July 1955
WASHINGTON, D.C. Senator Kennedy urges the Senate Banking and Currency Committee to repeal the Silver Purchase Act. He is cosponsor of a bill for the repeal of the 19 June 1934 law that provides a government market for silver. Kennedy claims that the act results in manufacturers and the public paying higher prices for silver. This has subsequently caused problems and unemployment in the silver-processing and jewelry industries in New England.

20 July 1955
NEW YORK. After five days at the Hospital for Special Surgery, Senator John F. Kennedy is released.

27 July 1955
WASHINGTON, D.C. To begin a tour of areas of the Soviet Union that Westerners have seldom seen, Robert F. Kennedy leaves by plane for Tehran. There he will meet Supreme Court Justice William O. Douglas, who will travel with him. Kennedy is on a leave of absence without pay from his position as chief counsel of the Senate Investigations Subcommittee.

1 August 1955
WASHINGTON, D.C. In a letter to Lewis L. Strauss, chairman of the Atomic Energy Commission, Senator John F. Kennedy urges that the AEC give special consideration to using New England as the site for some nonmilitary atomic power projects. He asks that a proposed atomic energy library and AEC regional office be

built in New England, and that the Yankee Electric Company participate with the AEC in constructing an atomic power reactor in western Massachusetts.

BAKU, USSR. William O. Douglas and Robert F. Kennedy begin a tour of Russian collective farms, factories, and schools. Other cities they plan to visit include Ashkhabad, Bokhara, Samarkand, and Tashkent.

19 September 1955
CASTLE GANDOLFO, ITALY. Pope Pius XII receives Senator John F. Kennedy in a private audience at the papal summer residence. They briefly discuss Communist domination of Poland and other conditions in that country.

20 September 1955
ROME. In a meeting with high-ranking Italian officials and U.S. Ambassador Clare Boothe Luce, Senator John F. Kennedy discusses the need for liberalizing the quota and procedures for Italian immigration to the United States. At the conference are Italy's Minister of Foreign Affairs Gaetano Martino and the head of the Immigration Section of the Italian Foreign Office, Luciano Marcia.

22 September 1955
WARSAW. Senator and Mrs. John F. Kennedy arrive here by plane. They will observe conditions in the country over the next several days.

23 September 1955
NEW YORK. Following a tour behind the Iron Curtain, Robert F. Kennedy arrives here with his wife, Ethel, on the *Isle de France*.

WASHINGTON, D.C. Robert Kennedy makes a surprise visit to his Capitol Hill Office. Later he leaves for Hyannis Port.

9 October 1955
BOSTON. The *Boston Sunday Post* publishes an article by Senator John F. Kennedy on his firsthand observations of Poland. The Senator reports on his perceptions of crowded apartment conditions, the high cost of goods, the Warsaw ghetto where the Nazis confined Jews during the occupation, control of the press by the government, and government attempts to subvert the church.

11 October 1955
NEW YORK. Arriving by ship, John and Jacqueline Bouvier Kennedy return from their trip to Europe.

13 October 1955
TIVERTON, RHODE ISLAND. Speaking at a meeting of the Fall River (Massachusetts) Chapter of the National Association of Cost Accountants, Senator John F. Kennedy calls for the government to provide a program of flood-disaster insurance. Declaring that New England is a major flood area, he says the region should "demand her fair share of federal flood control expenditures."

16 October 1955
BROOKLINE, MASSACHUSETTS. In a speech delivered to members of the brotherhood of Temple Emeth, Robert F. Kennedy warns of Russia's insincerity and urges caution on the part of the United States.

17 October 1955
NEW YORK. Addressing a dinner meeting of the Albert Einstein College of Medicine at Yeshiva University, Senator John F. Kennedy calls for increased government aid in financing medical research. The shortage of doctors is a national problem that Congress cannot ignore, Kennedy says. He continues, "Of course we must spend a significant part of our national wealth in the development of new and more destructive weapons. But we must also broaden our counterattack on the diseases and maladies that attack all mankind."

23 October 1955
BOSTON. Speaking before an audience of 500 in a meeting sponsored by the Polish-American Citizens' Club of South Boston, Senator Kennedy says that Poland is still under the "iron control of Russia." Although the USSR has indicated that it might ease its grip on Poland, Kennedy declares that "when the Polish people are free to talk with visitors, when they can freely visit Western countries, when the Voice of America is no longer jammed, when free elections are held and a free press permitted, then it will be possible to say there has been a genuine change in the policy of the Communists." The club presents Senator Kennedy with a citation for his efforts in helping the Polish people.

28 October 1955
WEYMOUTH, MASSACHUSETTS. Addressing 2,500 U.S. Navy and Marine Corps "weekend warriors" and an additional 2,500 spectators at a military inspection and review at the South Weymouth Naval Air Station, Senator John F. Kennedy discusses various international issues. He says that although some believe the hydrogen bomb has made the necessity for large military forces in the United States obsolete, the country cannot

relax its efforts. If recent events in the Middle East continue, war is inevitable. It is only the great power of the United States that has kept the Soviet Union from conquering other nations of the free world, he concludes.

29 October 1955

BOSTON.   Speaking at a dinner for alumni of the Boston College School of Business Administration, Senator John F. Kennedy outlines a five-point program to stimulate the economy of Massachusetts, particularly in distressed areas. He calls for letting surplus labor bidders for defense contracts match the low bids of others; for equalizing the rail freight rates in New England to those of other areas; for developing low-cost atomic power in New England; for expanding programs to aid business; and for federal action to end below-minimum wages in certain areas of the country enabling businesses to compete unfairly with those in other regions.

4 November 1955

WILLIAMSTOWN, MASSACHUSETTS.   James MacGregor Burns proposes a Democratic ticket for next year's election consisting of Adlai E. Stevenson for president and John F. Kennedy for vice-president. Burns, a professor at Williams College and the former Massachusetts chairman of Americans for Democratic Action (ADA), says, "In my judgment [the ticket] would be unbeatable."

6 November 1955

CHICAGO.   A daughter, Maria Owings, is born to Eunice (Kennedy) and Robert Sargent Shriver, Jr. She is their second child and first daughter.

BOSTON.   Speaking at a fiftieth anniversary banquet of the Massachusetts Grand Lodge of the Order of the Sons of Italy at the Hotel Bradford, Senator John F. Kennedy calls for repeal of U.S. immigration laws and maintenance of the Refugee Act to aid Italy in its recovery plan and to further world peace. Kennedy declares that "the strongest weapon we have in our struggle to prevent the ancient states of Europe from falling into the hands of the enemy is the picture of the United States as a place to which millions of their countrymen have gone and prospered."

9 November 1955

WASHINGTON, D.C.   At a hearing before the Senate Banking and Currency Committee on disaster-risk insurance legislation, Senator Kennedy urges formation of a federal flood-insurance program. He cites damages suffered in recent floods and says that private insurance cov-

ers virtually no part of the losses. Kennedy is co-sponsor, with Senator Leverett Saltonstall, of a federal flood-insurance bill that will be introduced in the next sesison of Congress.

11 November 1955

BOSTON.   Addressing 500 delegates at the sixth annual United Cerebral Palsy Convention, Senator John F. Kennedy reveals that the National Institute of Neurological Diseases and Blindness, under federal auspices, plans "an all-out research attack" on cerebral palsy. "Any nation which can spend $2.5 billion for research and development of military weapons and equipment," he says, "can afford to invest more of its national wealth in broadening the base of medical knowledge and making discoveries which will give the world healthier, more useful lives."

13 November 1955

BOSTON.   At the Statler Hotel, Senator John F. Kennedy joins 1,200 people in paying tribute to Anthony Farina of Newton, Massachusetts, who has been selected "Italian Man of the Year."

15 November 1955

WORCESTER, MASSACHUSETTS.   Speaking before a group of Holy Cross students, Senator John F. Kennedy charges that France has "severely weakened" NATO by withdrawing troops and sending them to North Africa. The French have "never met their NATO commitments," he says.

WORCESTER, MASSACHUSETTS.   At an annual convention of the Massachusetts Farm Bureau Federation, Senator John F. Kennedy speaks on farm issues, describing "what should not go into next year's farm platforms" at the national political conventions. He says that he opposes Adlai Stevenson's recommendation of a return to fixed 90-percent-of-parity farm price supports.

17 November 1955

HOLYOKE, MASSACHUSETTS.   Speaking on next year's elections, Senator John F. Kennedy says that Massachusetts governor Christian A. Herter could be a candidate for the Republican presidential nomination. Although he doubts that President Eisenhower will run again, if he does, Kennedy says, he would be elected, "swamping even Adlai Stevenson worse than before."

BEVERLY, MASSACHUSETTS.   Senator John F. Kennedy offers a three-point program to revitalize the New England economy to an audience of 600 at an intercity Rotary Club meeting. Kennedy charges that the region's distress is caused by Republican "favors" to the South, which has received many defense contracts and tax exemptions.

SALEM, MASSACHUSETTS. Senator Kennedy tells 2,100 workers at an annual North Shore United Church canvass at the local armory that Communists fear religion.

20 November 1955
WASHINGTON, D.C. Senator John F. Kennedy calls for a revision of American immigration policies. Urging that the weak and discriminatory McCarron-Walter Act be dropped, Kennedy asks for congressional enactment of the Lehman Bill, of which he is cosponsor.

27 November 1955
WASHINGTON, D.C. In a Radio Free Europe broadcast sent behind the Iron Curtain, Senator John F. Kennedy describes tensions in Poland and charges that Communist claims of reducing tensions there are lies. Remarking on his recent visit to Poland with his wife, Kennedy says that "carloads of secret police followed us constantly, preventing any opportunity to speak to the average Polish citizen." He points out that "there is no home building. New construction is centered on monuments, theaters, and stadiums in an effort to break up family life." The strongest antiregime forces preventing complete Communist domination of Poland, he says, are the Church and the peasantry. "The impressions I brought with me from Poland were sad and grim," Senator Kennedy says. He adds that it is important for the American people to continue to support the efforts of Radio Free Europe.

WASHINGTON, D.C. Announcement is made by Senator John F. Kennedy that he plans to investigate legislation on lobbies. He says that defects of the Lobbying Act must be remedied, and that he has sent out questionnaires to registered lobbyists and organizations.

4 December 1955
LIBERTYVILLE, ILLINOIS. Senator John F. Kennedy confers with Adlai E. Stevenson at the latter's home.

8 December 1955
BOSTON. A Congressional Town Meeting at the Hotel Sheraton Plaza, Senator John F. Kennedy joins Representatives Thomas P. O'Neill, Jr., Torbert H. MacDonald, John W. McCormack, Donald Nicholson, and Lawrence Curtis in a question-and-answer session before 800 businessmen. Kennedy expresses concern for federal school aid to needy areas but says wealthier states like Massachusetts should be excluded.

12 December 1955
WASHINGTON, D.C. Senator John F. Kennedy announces that the Senate Government Operations Subcommittee, which he heads, will in the next few months hold hearings on proposals to ease the burdens of the president. The subcommittee will consider recommendations of the Hoover Commission on Government Reorganization, of which Joseph P. Kennedy was a member.

1 January 1956
BOSTON. The *Boston Globe* begins serializing Senator Kennedy's *Profiles in Courage*.

2 January 1956
NEW YORK. *Profiles in Courage* by John F. Kennedy is published by Harper & Brothers. The 266-page hardcover book contains a foreword by historian Allan Nevins and a dedication "to my wife." The book, a series of stories about American statesmen, the obstacles they faced, and the special valor they demonstrated despite personal consequences, was written by Kennedy between October of 1954, when he was operated on for a spine injury incurred during World War II, and May of 1955, when he returned to his Senate duties in Washington, D.C.

9 January 1956
BOSTON. On behalf of the Boston City Council, Gabriel F. Piemonte announces that an order has been given to the school department requesting that Senator John F. Kennedy's *Profiles in Courage* be taught in history courses in city schools.

13 January 1956
WASHINGTON, D.C. Joseph P. Kennedy is among those named by President Eisenhower to the Board of Consultants on Foreign Intelligence Activities. The purpose of the group is to watch over foreign activities of appropriate United States agencies, including the CIA, and to submit independent evaluations to the Chief Executive at least twice a year.

25 January 1956
WASHINGTON, D.C. Senator John F. Kennedy assails the Harris-Fulbright bill before the Senate. The legislation provides for exempting producers of natural gas from rates established by the Federal Power Commission. Kennedy charges this would result in higher gas rates in New England.

26 January 1956

WORCESTER, MASSACHUSETTS. Former Massachusetts governor Paul A. Dever says that the state delegation would unanimously choose Senator Kennedy for the vice-presidential nomination at the Democratic National Convention if Kennedy decides to run.

WASHINGTON, D.C. The Democratic party should develop a strong platform on foreign policy, Senator Kennedy tells the National Women's Democratic Club. Discussing possible foreign crises, Kennedy says that the party platform should include a good neighbor policy and a plan to beef up American military forces.

3 February 1956

BOSTON. Hearings are held in the Federal Building by Senator John F. Kennedy on a proposed Senate bill that he is cosponsoring which will provide aid to areas with chronic labor surpluses, unemployment, and loss of industry. The bill would set up an independent federal agency to administer loans, channel government contracts, and give other assistance to revitalize distressed areas and to relocate industry to communities hard hit by unemployment.

In the audience are representatives of state and municipal governments, unions, and industry. Among those who praise the bill are Governor Christian A. Herter and John Callahan, president of the Massachusetts Federation of Labor.

4 February 1956

BOSTON. Supporters pass out "Elect U.S. Sen. Kennedy Vice-President" badges at a Jefferson-Jackson Day banquet. The badges bear photographs of John Kennedy.

6 February 1956

WASHINGTON, D.C. The Senate passes the Harris-Fulbright bill and sends it to President Eisenhower. Senator John F. Kennedy had opposed the bill, which provides for the exemption from federal price controls by national gas producers, in a Senate debate on 25 January 1956.

7 February 1956

NEW YORK. Senator John F. Kennedy urges support of school integration and cites contradictions in the foreign policy of the Eisenhower administration in a speech before the New York Young Democratic Club. The Senator advocates abiding by the recent Supreme Court decision forbidding segregation in public schools. He also points out that Secretary of Defense Charles Wilson asked Congress to reduce the Air Force budget at the

very time when Secretary of State John Foster Dulles claimed the United States was on the verge of war.

9 February 1956

BOSTON. Archbishop Richard J. Cushing announces that the Lt. Joseph P. Kennedy, Jr. Foundation has given $1,178,000, the largest single donation, to the expansion program of the archdiocese of Boston. The beneficiaries will include the Kennedy Memorial Hospital, St. Colletta School, the Boys' Guidance Center, and the Boarding and Day School.

19 February 1956

WASHINGTON, D.C. In a filmed television interview, Senator John F. Kennedy says he believes that Adlai Stevenson will win the Democratic nomination for president, and if he does, a Southerner will be selected as a running mate. He doubts very much that he will receive the Democratic vice-presidential nomination.

23 February 1956

WASHINGTON, D.C. At a luncheon of the Women's National Press Club, Senator Kennedy speaks on the integrity of United States senators and urges that laws governing lobbying be made stronger.

25 February 1956

MANCHESTER, NEW HAMPSHIRE. Senator John F. Kennedy begins a one-day campaign tour for state Democrats and the national Democratic party ticket.

26 February 1956

PURCHASE, NEW YORK. On behalf of the Lt. Joseph P. Kennedy, Jr. Foundation, Rose Kennedy presents a check for $300,000 to the chairman of the Manhattanville College Development Fund for construction of a dormitory and a building for physical education classes at Manhattanville College of the Sacred Heart.

29 February 1956

WASHINGTON, D.C. Following a train collision the day before in Swampscott, Massachusetts, in which thirteen people died, Senator John F. Kennedy asks the Senate to conduct an investigation of the New Haven and Boston & Maine railroads and to provide recommendations on safety precautions for the future. He charges that the railroads "have been taken over by interests with financial ambitions more highly developed than their concern for their passengers or the area they serve.

4 March 1956
WASHINGTON, D.C. Appearing on NBC-TV's "Youth Wants to Know," Senator John F. Kennedy says that the Democrats can wrest the presidency from Dwight Eisenhower in November's election if the party has a "good candidate" and puts forth "strong arguments."

6 March 1956
WASHINGTON, D.C. Senator John F. Kennedy tells the Senate that he opposes farm price supports fixed at 90 percent of parity. "To those of my colleagues who call upon me to support the 90 percent program, despite its shortcomings, as a means of stabilizing farm income during the current farm recession," he says, "I can only point to the decline in farm prices and income which took place during the operation of that program, a decline which has been intensified by the ever-present threat posed by the huge surpluses acquired by the government under that program."

8 March 1956
WASHINGTON, D.C. At a press conference, Senator John F. Kennedy officially announces his support of Adlai E. Stevenson for the Democratic presidential nomination. He tells reporters that he will "exert every effort for his nomination" and that he "wouldn't have announced for Stevenson as early as this if I didn't have confidence that he would be nominated and had a good chance of being elected." The Senator had already said that he would time his announcement to best serve Stevenson in the Tuesday New Hampshire primary, the nation's first primary election.

WASHINGTON, D.C. The Senate approves the Eisenhower administration's flexible farm price-supports plan. Senator John F. Kennedy is one of thirteen Democrats who votes for flexible supports rather than 90 percent-of-parity price supports.

10 March 1956
WASHINGTON, D.C. Senator John L. McLellan (Democrat, Ark.) is elected to head a special committee that will investigate the improper or illegal influence of campaign contributions, among other pressures, on members of the Senate and other employees of the federal government. This bipartisan committee of eight members, including Senator John F. Kennedy, had been authorized by the Senate on 22 February 1956.

11 March 1956
PURCHASE, NEW YORK. A ground-breaking ceremony is held at Manhattanville College of the Sacred Heart, where Rose Kennedy dedicates the Physical Education Building to the memory of her daughter, Kathleen, Lady Hartington. In a 2,000-word speech, Rose Kennedy says of her late daughter, "I think it is very fitting to have her memorial in the form of a recreational center because as a very little girl she was always interested in athletic sports." As a student at the Convent of the Sacred Heart in Darien, Connecticut, twenty years earlier, "she asked her father and me to give a tennis court" to the school. On 27 February 1956, the Lt. Joseph P. Kennedy, Jr. Foundation had presented the grant of $300,000 to Manhattanville College that helped to fund the building.

13 March 1956
WASHINGTON, D.C. A resolution is introduced in the Senate urging England to consult the people of Cyprus, a British colony, regarding their "future political status." Cypriot guerrillas have adopted a violent course in their fight for sovereignty. Senator John F. Kennedy is among the eighteen senators, Democrat and Republican, who sponsor the resolution.

17 March 1956
CHICAGO. Senator John F. Kennedy urges that the United States should "speak out boldly for freedom of all people" at a St. Patrick's Day meeting of the Irish Fellowship of Chicago. That, he says, would strengthen and clarify the whole struggle of the free world against the Communists.

18 March 1956
WASHINGTON, D.C. A three-man subcommittee is named by Senator John Sparkman (Democrat, Ala.), chairman of the Senate Small Business Committee, to investigate complaints of small daytime broadcasters that restrictions on broadcasting hours prohibit them from providing adequate community services. Appointed to the subcommittee are Senators John F. Kennedy, (who is also named chairman of the group), Andrew Schoeppel (Republican, Kan.), and Wayne Morse (Democrat, Ore.).

25 March 1956
BOSTON. In a speech given before 1,500 people attending a one hundred thirty-fifth anniversary celebration of Greek independence at John Hancock Hall, Senator John F. Kennedy says that the United States should recognize the desire of the people of Cyprus to be politically affiliated with Greece.

14 April 1956
LOS ANGELES. At a Democratic party dinner,

held in honor of Southern California congressmen and legislators, Senator John F. Kennedy accuses the Republicans of being decades behind the Democrats. "We are moving ahead," he says. "We will be glad to drag them along with us into the late '50s and the '60s if it will help the cause."

15 April 1956

WASHINGTON, D.C. President Eisenhower vetoes the Agricultural Act of 1956 sent to him by the Senate on 11 April. Senator John F. Kennedy is one of four Democrats who voted against the farm bill.

17 April 1956

WASHINGTON, D.C. Following President Eisenhower's veto of the farm bill, Senator Kennedy releases a statement saying, in part, "I wholeheartedly support the action taken by the President in his veto on the farm bill. As it passed the Congress, this bill would have meant artificially higher food and clothing prices for Massachusetts consumers, artificially higher feed prices for Massachusetts dairy and poultry farmers, and unnecessarily higher cotton prices for Massachusetts textile mills....I am convinced, moreover, that in the long run the President's action will prove to be in the best interest of all the nation and all of its farmers, as well as our consumers and industries."

20 April 1956

SOUTH BEND, INDIANA. Students at the University of Notre Dame and St. Mary's College hold a mock Democratic National Convention, with 2,000 "delegates" turning out. Adlai E. Stevenson receives the nomination for president; Senator John F. Kennedy the nomination for vice-president.

21 April 1956

MINNEAPOLIS, MINNESOTA. Filling in for Senator Estes Kefauver (Democrat, Tenn.), who has a prior engagement, Senator John F. Kennedy makes the principal address at a Jefferson-Jackson Day banquet sponsored by the Democratic Farmer-Labor party.

24 April 1956

WASHINGTON, D.C. Senator John F. Kennedy files a bill, cosponsored with Senators Saltonstall (Republican, Mass.), Payne (Republican, Me.), and Smith (Republican, Me.) to establish a fisheries division in the Interior Department. He also files a bill, cosponsored with Senators Humphrey (Democrat, Minn.), Martin (Republican, Iowa), and Smith (Republican, Me.), to provide for transfer of surplus government property to state defense agencies.

28 April 1956

WASHINGTON, D.C. Senator John F. Kennedy is appointed to the board of an advisory committee on small business formed by the Democratic National Committee to help the party create and maintain an effective policy in preserving small business in the American economy.

4 May 1956

HYANNIS PORT, MASSACHUSETTS. Announcement is made by Joseph and Rose Kennedy of the engagement of their daughter Jean Ann to Stephen Smith. Born 24 September 1927 to Julia and John Smith, Stephen graduated from Poly Prep Country Day School in 1944 and from Georgetown University in 1948. He served as a lieutenant in the Air Force, and is now an executive with Cleary Brothers, Inc., a transportation company founded by his grandfather.

19 May 1956

NEW YORK. Jean Ann Kennedy, 28, marries Stephen Edward Smith, 28, at St. Patrick's Cathedral. The ceremony is performed by Francis Cardinal Spellman. The bride, dressed in a champagne satin gown with a chapel-length train and a short empire jacket, is escorted to the altar by her father. Eunice Shriver is her sister's matron of honor, and Philip Smith, brother of the bridegroom, is the best man.

29 May 1956

WASHINGTON, D.C. Speaking before the Senate, two changes are requested by Senator John F. Kennedy in a pending bill on highways. First, he urges the Senate to let the House approve a method of allocating funds to states according to their needs instead of using its present plan, called the Gore formula [named after its sponsor Senator Albert Gore (Democrat, Tenn.)]. He also asks that the Senate adopt the Davis-Bacon prevailing wage provision, which the Senate Public Works Committee has rejected. Under the Davis-Bacon provision, the secretary of labor would establish pay scales according to prevailing rates in a region.

30 May 1956

DARTMOUTH, MASSACHUSETTS. A clambake and testimonial dinner sponsored by a committee of Fall River and New Bedford citizens in honor of Senator John F. Kennedy is held at Lincoln Park. Some 1,800 people attend, including Senators Henry M. Jackson (Democrat, Wash.), George A. Smathers (Democrat, Fla.), John O. Pastore (Republican, R.I.), and Albert Gore (Democrat, Tenn.); singer Morton Downey; former Notre Dame president, the Rev. John J. Cavanaugh;

Peter Lawford; and Representative Torbert MacDonald. A giant cake is presented to Senator Kennedy in honor of his thirty-ninth birthday.

1 June 1956

WASHINGTON, D.C. Referring to the United States as the "volunteer fire department for the world," Senator John F. Kennedy tells the American Friends of Vietnam that whenever ideological conflict breaks out, "our firemen rush in, wheeling up all their heavy equipment and resorting to every known method of containing and extinguishing the blaze."

2 June 1956

KANSAS CITY, MISSOURI. At a Rockhurst College Day dinner, Senator John F. Kennedy urges that the United States speak out to its allies and the world against colonialism and not take a neutral stand, as Secretary of State John Foster Dulles has. "We have permitted the reputation of the United States as a friend of oppressed people to be hitched to the chariot of the conqueror," Kennedy declares, "because we have believed we could have it both ways." He says that even though a policy against colonialism will dissatisfy America's allies, "it will displease even more the Soviets who have hypocritically assumed the role of freedom's defender."

NEW YORK. The *Saturday Evening Post* publishes an article entitled "Take the Academics Out of Politics" by Senator John F. Kennedy. He cites a lack of congressional appointments of students to the United States military academies and asserts that many of those who are appointed lack the qualities needed to protect the country's future. To correct these problems, Kennedy suggests the establishment of a commission to improve methods of choosing new appointees, a revision of the quota system so that a member of Congress who does not fill his or her appointments for one year can carry them over to the next, and the providing of facilities that will enable members of Congress to select highly qualified candidates.

10 June 1956

SPRINGFIELD, MASSACHUSETTS. Senator John F. Kennedy receives an honorary Doctor of Laws degree at the seventieth annual commencement of Springfield College. In an address to the graduating class, the Senator speaks of "new opportunities to college graduates through the development of atomic energy."

12 June 1956

ROME. At Vatican City, Joseph P. Kennedy has a private audience with Pope Pius XII.

13 June 1956

BOSTON. Senator John F. Kennedy delivers the commencement speech at the eightieth graduation exercises of Boston College. He is also awarded an honorary Doctor of Laws degree.

14 June 1956

CAMBRIDGE, MASSACHUSETTS. At the three hundred fifth commencement at Harvard, Senator John F. Kennedy receives an honorary Doctor of Laws degree, becoming one of the youngest alumni to be so honored. Later, in an address to 15,000 at an annual meeting of the Harvard Alumni Association, Kennedy says that intellectuals and politicians have traditionally distrusted each other, but that the time has come for them "to put aside those horrible weapons of internecine warfare, the barbed thrust, the acid pen, and, most sinister of all, the rhetorical blast."

On this day Edward M. Kennedy graduates from Harvard College with a Bachelor of Arts degree. (Edward Kennedy attended Harvard in 1950-1951 and 1953-1956, but he is formally considered a 1954 graduate.)

17 June 1956

BOSTON. Senator John F. Kennedy is awarded an honorary Doctor of Laws degree from Northeastern University, his fourth honorary degree in the past eight days.

23 June 1956

SOUTH BEND, INDIANA. The Rev. Theodore M. Hesburgh, president of the University of Notre Dame, announces that Joseph P. Kennedy has endowed the Lord Beaverbrook chair in honor of the British cabinet minister and newspaper owner.

25 June 1956

ATLANTIC CITY, NEW JERSEY. At the Governors' Conference, a drive is mounted by Governors Abraham Ribicoff (Connecticut) and Dennis Roberts (Rhode Island) to obtain support for John F. Kennedy as the Democratic vice-presidential nominee. Ribicoff has staunchly supported Kennedy, recommending him for the nomination at the Massachusetts Democratic State Convention earlier this month and pushing his cause in a letter to Adlai Stevenson.

26 June 1956

WASHINGTON, D.C. A bill is introduced by Senators John Kennedy and Lister Hill (Democrat, Ala.) that would provide over $150 million in assistance to senior citizens over a six-year period. Among the bill's features

Rose, John, and Cardinal Cushing, c. 1946.

are matching grants for projects sponsored by states and nonprofit associations for the elderly.

30 June 1956

WASHINGTON, D.C. Senator John F. Kennedy announces that he favors a resolution urging the President to adopt a policy rejecting discrimination against Americans by foreign governments. Under the resolution, federal agencies would not replace qualified diplomats or other representatives who are rejected by another country because of their race, creed, or religion.

1 July 1956

WASHINGTON, D.C. Appearing as part of a panel on CBS-TV's "Face the Nation," Senator Kennedy says "I am not a candidate for vice-president and I doubt if I will be nominated for vice-president." But, he adds, he would be honored and "of course...would accept" if nominated.

Kennedy gives four reasons for believing he will not receive the nomination: he is Catholic; at 39 he might be considered too young; a Southerner might be sought to balance the ticket; and his vote in favor of a flexible price-support program for agricultural commodities was unpopular. On the issue of religion, however, he says that he hopes "that no one would vote for a Catholic for vice-president because he was a Catholic or vote against him because he was a Catholic."

8 July 1956

WASHINGTON, D.C. Representative John W. Mc-Cormack of Massachusetts, a Catholic, is also a possible running mate for Adlai Stevenson. The Stevenson forces believe a Catholic should be nominated as the Democratic candidate for vice-president, and McCormack's name is mentioned along with Kennedy's.

12 July 1956

FALL RIVER, MASSACHUSETTS. Ex-city councilor Edward P. Grace forms a "Kennedy for Vice-President Committee" comprised of three dozen prominent Democrats. Grace announces that members will canvass all Massachusetts delegates and attempt to gain support from national Democratic Convention delegates.

13 July 1956

BURLINGTON, VERMONT. On the campaign trail, Adlai Stevenson says at a news conference that John F. Kennedy would make an "excellent candidate" for the vice-presidential spot on the ticket. He declines to name any other possibilities for the number-two spot.

19 July 1956

FALL RIVER, MASSACHUSETTS. At the Hotel Mellen, members and supporters of the "Kennedy for Vice-President Committee" gather for a strategy meeting. Letters urging Kennedy's nomination are to be sent to all delegates and alternates to the Democratic National Convention. The Massachusetts delegates have already received letters stating, in part, that "the Kennedy for Vice-President Committee feels that the chance of a Democratic victory would be greatly enhanced if Senator Kennedy received the nomination....The committee believes that Senator Kennedy's outstanding record in the House and Senate, his character, principles and talent, entitle him to your thoughtful consideration."

WASHINGTON, D.C. Senator John F. Kennedy introduces a resolution on his own behalf and that of other New England senators, urging the Senate to end discriminatory rail rates to and from New England. He asks that a rate schedule proposed by ten Northeastern railroads become immediately effective.

Senator Kennedy accepts the vice-presidency of the Arthritis and Rheumatism Foundation's Massachusetts chapter.

22 July 1956

HOLLYWOOD, CALIFORNIA. Senator John F. Kennedy narrates a 20-minute film on the history of the Democratic party, to be shown at the party's national convention. Following a script he himself had edited, Kennedy traces the administrations from Thomas Jefferson onward. Directing the film is MGM's Dore Schary.

8 August 1956

BARTOW, FLORIDA. Senator Spessard L. Holland (Democrat, Fla.) says at a press conference that a Stevenson-Kennedy ticket would have a good chance of defeating the Republican candidates.

9 August 1956

NARRAGANSETT, RHODE ISLAND. Senator John F. Kennedy lunches with Governor Dennis J. Roberts, who supports his candidacy for the vice-presidential spot.

SPRINGFIELD, MASSACHUSETTS. Senator Kennedy addresses a convention of the American Federation of Labor.

HARTFORD, CONNECTICUT. Late in the afternoon on the same day, Senator Kennedy confers with Connecticut governor Abraham Ribicoff, who also supports Kennedy for the number-two spot on the Democratic ticket.

12 August 1956

CHICAGO. Prior to the opening of the Democratic National Convention, a drive to help John Kennedy win the party's vice-presidential nomination is launched. A group of approximately fifty supporters, including congressmen and governors as well as delegates, holds an organizational meeting.

NEW YORK. For his book *Profiles in Courage*, Senator John F. Kennedy is named winner of the Christopher Award by a private organization that recognizes individuals who "elevate standards of morality." Winners receive a bronze plaque inscribed "Better to light one candle than to curse the darkness."

13 August 1956

CHICAGO. The first of three "unity" breakfasts, at which delegates to the Democratic National Convention meet each other and exchange ideas, is held at the Palmer House Hotel with Senator John F. Kennedy as host. Over four hundred people attend. The New England delegates, virtually all of whom are present, pledge support to Kennedy, who still has not declared that he is a candidate for the vice-presidential nomination. Kennedy joins with them, saying, "I'd like to invite every one of you to breakfast every morning." Later he and Representative Torbert MacDonald visit different state delegations at various hotels to obtain support.

Kennedy Family Collection. Morgan Studio.

Jacqueline Bouvier and her father, 25 July, 1947.

14 August 1956

CHICAGO. The movement to secure the vice-presidential nomination for Senator John F. Kennedy picks up momentum as delegates from across the country pledge support. Offers of support have previously come in from delegates from California, New Jersey, Connecticut, Rhode Island, Illinois, Louisiana, Mississippi, Florida, Georgia, and Oregon. The race for the party's number-two slot is now led by Senators Kennedy, Kefauver, and Humphrey.

16 August 1956

CHICAGO. Adlai E. Stevenson wins the Democratic party's nomination for president on the first ballot. By a wide margin, he defeats the other contenders, who include Governor Averill Harriman (N.Y.) and Senators Lyndon Johnson (Tex.) and Stuart Symington (Mo.). Senator Kennedy delivers Stevenson's nomination speech. Instead of naming his running mate, Stevenson leaves the choice to the delegates so that the nominee "may join me before the nation not as one man's selection but as one chosen."

17 August 1956

CHICAGO. The first ballot of the Democratic party's vice-presidential nomination is cast. Estes Kefauver leads, but he falls short of the needed majority.

On the second ballot, it looks at one point as if Senator John F. Kennedy will get the nomination, but after Senator Albert Gore (Tenn.) withdraws from the race in favor of his colleague from Tennessee, Estes Kefauver, Kefauver gains the necessary votes and defeats Kennedy for the nomination. Although Kennedy has lost the party's number-two spot, he emerges a national figure.

23 August 1956

NEWPORT, RHODE ISLAND. Jacqueline Kennedy, due to give birth to her first child in October, goes into labor prematurely at Newport Hospital. The unnamed baby girl is stillborn. Her husband Jack is on a cruise in the Mediterranean with his brother Teddy.

25 August 1956

SANTA MONICA, CALIFORNIA. A daughter, Sydney Maleia, is born to Patricia Kennedy and Peter Lawford at St. John's Hospital. She is their second child and first daughter. She is named for her deceased grandfather, Lt. Gen. Sir Sydney Lawford.

1 September 1956

NEWPORT, RHODE ISLAND. In an interview with Edward B. Simmons of the New Bedford *Standard Times*, Senator John F. Kennedy says that even though his vote for the flexible farm parity program supported by the Republicans may have cost him the Democratic nomination for vice-president, he would not change his vote if he could. The interview is conducted at the home of his wife's mother and stepfather, Janet and Hugh Auchincloss.

7 September 1956

BOSTON. At a special academic convocation at Lowell Technological Institute, an honorary Doctor of Science degree is conferred upon Senator John F. Kennedy. A citation accompanying the degree praises the Senator as a "statesman, philanthropist, public servant, inspiration to his own and future generations."

9 September 1956

BOSTON. A daughter, Mary Courtney, is born to Ethel (Skakel) and Robert Kennedy. She is their fifth child and second daughter.

12 September 1956

WASHINGTON, D.C. The Senate Select Committee on Improper Activities in the Labor and Management Field begins an investigation of labor racketeering. Robert F. Kennedy is chief counsel to the Senate Permanent Subcommittee.

13 September 1956

BOSTON. At New England Baptist Hospital, Joseph P. Kennedy, 68, undergoes a prostatectomy (excision of the prostate gland). Kennedy recently returned from Paris, where he was treated at the American Hospital and advised to return to Boston for the operation.

14 September 1956

CHARLOTTESVILLE, VIRGINIA. Classes begin at the University of Virginia School of Law, where Edward M. Kennedy, 24, enters his first year.

21 September 1956

WASHINGTON, D.C. It is announced that Robert F. Kennedy will take a leave of absence from the Senate Permanent Subcommittee on Investigations to join Adlai Stevenson's campaign staff as a special assistant. Robert Kennedy believes that the experience will be valuable if his brother John runs for president in the future.

LOS ANGELES. In an address to a thousand people at a World Affairs Council luncheon, Senator John F. Kennedy says that the threat to peace in Cyprus, French North Africa, Suez, and other areas is an outgrowth of "the revolt against colonialism and the determination of people to control their national destinies." Presidents since World War II have not properly perceived this, he says, and the Eisenhower administration wrongly construes foreign policy to be only a matter of opposing the Communists. Kennedy urges both Democrats and Republicans to address genuine foreign issues and to approach such issues without partisan distortion and without tailoring policies simply to get votes.

10 October 1956

SEATTLE, WASHINGTON, Adlai E. Stevenson names Joseph P. Kennedy an honorary co-chairman of Stevenson's National Business Council, an organization of prominent businessmen and financial leaders who support Stevenson's candidacy for president. The council's purpose, Stevenson says, is to make his views on the economy more available to industry.

24 October 1956

FORT WORTH, TEXAS. Lee Harvey Oswald, a 17-year-old high school dropout, enlists in the U.S. Marines. Born in New Orleans on 18 October 1939, two months after his father died, he was placed in an orphanage as a baby. His mother claimed him a year later, and in the years following he attended schools in Texas, Louisiana, and New York. In New York, a psychiatrist determined that Oswald was emotionally disturbed after he underwent psychiatric observation at an institution for juvenile delinquents. In 1954, he returned with his mother to New Orleans and enrolled in school, but at 16 he dropped out to join the Marines. Refused because of his age, he worked at various jobs until he was old enough to enlist.

25 October 1956

PHILADELPHIA. Despite the predictions of pollsters and Republicans, Adlai E. Stevenson will become president, Senator Kennedy says at a Democratic Committee fund-raising dinner. In response to Republican claims that theirs is the party of the future, Kennedy states that the Democrats "are the party of the future, and the future belongs to us."

3 November 1956

WORCESTER, MASSACHUSETTS. Outside Worcester City Hall, Senator John F. Kennedy begins a homestretch statewide tour for Democratic candidates by endorsing Foster Furcolo for governor before a crowd of 3,000. Other appearances planned for the next day include speeches in Lawrence, Waltham, Quincy, Brockton, Middleboro, and Lowell.

6 November 1956

THE UNITED STATES. President Dwight D. Eisenhower and Vice-President Richard M. Nixon are re-elected to a second term of office.

10 November 1956

WASHINGTON, D.C. The alumni association of the Catholic University of America presents its Cardinal Gibbons Medal to Senator John F. Kennedy at a ceremony at the Statler Hotel. The award is presented annually to a person who has "rendered distinguished service to country, church or the Catholic University."

25 November 1956

BOSTON. The recent riots in Poland and revolution in Hungary are historical milestones that may mark the beginning of the end of the Communist system, Senator John F. Kennedy says in a speech to the sixth annual communion breakfast of the Telephone Workers' Guild for Nazareth at the Hotel Bradford. He continues, "The inability of the Russians in ten years to indoctrinate the young people of Hungary and Poland in Communistic philosophy convinces the rest of the world of the weakness of their system. The balance of power has shifted against the Russians."

6 December 1956

WASHINGTON, D.C. Senator John F. Kennedy calls for unity in the Democratic party. Indicating a difference of opinion over whether the Democrats should present their legislative program before President Eisenhower announces his, Kennedy urges party members to "expend our efforts on a forward-looking legislative record under our present leadership" and "on strengthening party unity rather than arousing dissension."

11 December 1956

WASHINGTON, D.C. In an effort to revitalize the languishing New England fishing industry, Senator John F. Kennedy urges President Eisenhower to establish voluntary agreements with the governments of Canada and Iceland that each nation would impose "self-restraint" on fish exports. Likening the proposed arrangement to the understanding with Japan on that country's cotton exports to the United States, Kennedy expresses his belief that New England's economic distress should not be overlooked at the expense of pleasing our allies. "If we must aid nations friendly to us," he says, "and I certainly believe that we should, let us recognize that this is a burden to be borne by the nation as a whole, not by a very small segment of it, and one which is particularly ill-prepared to do so at this time."

Kennedy Family Collection. Morgan Studio.

Jacqueline Kennedy, far right, at Hialeah Racetrack, 1955.

12 December 1956

MIAMI BEACH, FLORIDA. At the thirty-eighth annual convention of the American Farm Bureau Federation, Senator Kennedy declares that there is little more than a "symbolic" difference between fixed price-support programs and flexible price-support programs. He says it is dangerous for candidates to think that by promising financial aid to farmers they can obtain the farm vote, because no farmer's vote is for sale.

18 December 1956

WASHINGTON, D.C. The Democratic National Committee's proposed twenty-person council to form party policy in the next presidential term is discarded after invited party leaders refuse to join. Senator John F. Kennedy was among those who received invitations on 5 December 1956. Others invited included Eleanor Roosevelt, former president Harry S. Truman, Senate Majority Leader Lyndon B. Johnson, and Adlai E. Stevenson.

28 December 1956

BOSTON. Former mayor James M. Curley, seriously

ill at City Hospital, receives a telegram from Senator John F. Kennedy, who is in Palm Beach, Florida. The telegram expresses "sincere hope that your recovery will be quick and that you will actually follow your often repeated statement 'to live to be 125.'"

3 January 1957

WASHINGTON, D.C. The Eighty-fifth Congress opens. Senator John F. Kennedy is a member of the Foreign Relations Committee and the Labor and Public Welfare Committee.

8 January 1957

WASHINGTON, D.C. Senator John F. Kennedy is appointed to the Senate Foreign Relations Committee by the Democratic Steering Committee. In accepting this prestigious position, his first major committee post, Kennedy resigns from the Government Operations Committee but retains membership on the Labor and Public Welfare Committee.

Kennedy has been chosen for the Foreign Relations spot by the fourteen-member steering committee over Senator Estes Kefauver, even though Kefauver, who has seniority over Kennedy, has requested the position. Senate Majority Leader Lyndon B. Johnson announces the appointment.

20 January 1957
WASHINGTON, D.C.   President Dwight D. Eisenhower and Vice-President Richard M. Nixon are sworn into office for a second term.

22 February 1957
SOUTH BEND, INDIANA.   The Patriotism Award of the University of Notre Dame is presented to Senator John F. Kennedy. The award was established in 1954 to honor "the outstanding patriot of the year who exemplifies the American ideals of justice, personal integrity and service to the country." The university's graduating seniors have elected the recipient.

26 February 1957
WASHINGTON, D.C.   Senate hearings on labor racketeering open. The goal of Robert F. Kennedy, chief counsel of the Senate Select Committee on Improper Activities in the Labor or Management Field, is to expose racketeering in the International Brotherhood of Teamsters, of which James Hoffa of Detroit is vice-president. The committee, headed by Senator John L. McLellan, is popularly called the "Rackets Committee."

1 March 1957
NEW YORK.   The Secondary Education Board presents its annual book awards at its thirty-first annual conference at the Statler Hotel. Among the ten books chosen is John F. Kennedy's *Profiles in Courage.*

11 March 1957
NEW YORK.   *Life* magazine publishes a cover story on Senator John F. Kennedy.

3 April 1957
WASHINGTON, D.C.   A personal investigation into corruption in the Teamster's Union is launched by Robert F. Kennedy, counsel for the Senate Rackets Investigating Committee. He will travel to several cities to conduct his probe.

5 April 1957
WASHINGTON, D.C.   In an interview with Arlene Francis on the "Home" television show, Jacqueline Kennedy reveals that her husband "usually reads about seven newspapers at the breakfast table and then runs out the door" of their Georgetown home. Asked about her cooking skills, Mrs. Kennedy responds, "Fairly good,

but nothing fantastic." Film clips of the family are also shown.

27 April 1957
VILLANOVA, PENNSYLVANIA.   An honorary Doctor of Laws degree is conferred upon Senator John F. Kennedy by Villanova University at a convocation held to dedicate a new building. Chief Justice of the United States Earl Warren, a featured speaker, is among those who receive honorary degrees.

30 April 1957
WASHINGTON, D.C.   Five "outstanding" senators of the past are selected after almost two years of study by a special five-man Senate committee headed by John Kennedy. With help from a survey taken among senators and historians, the committee names John C. Calhoun of South Carolina, Henry Clay of Kentucky, Robert M. LaFollette of Wisconsin, Robert A. Taft of Ohio, and Daniel Webster of Massachusetts. Pictures of these exceptional senators will be placed in a Senate reception area.

2 May 1957
WASHINGTON, D.C.   Senator Kennedy calls on the Eisenhower administration to impose stronger federal restrictions on woolen textile imports.

6 May 1957
NEW YORK.   The Pulitzer Prize for biography is awarded to Senator John F. Kennedy for his book *Profiles in Courage.* Grayson Kirk, the president of Columbia University, announces the 1957 Pulitzer awards.

NEW YORK.   In a speech at the Overseas Press Club, Senator John F. Kennedy calls for more U.S. aid to Poland in hopes that the new Communist regime under Wladyslaw Gomulka can become more independent of the Soviet Union.

7 May 1957
APPLETON, WISCONSIN.   Robert F. Kennedy attends the funeral of the late Senator Joseph McCarthy.

BOSTON.   Senator John F. Kennedy presents the $500 he won with the Pulitzer Prize to the United Negro College Fund.

17 May 1957
OMAHA, NEBRASKA.   Senator John F. Kennedy urges the Democratic party to "move ahead with the same spirit of foresight and progress and imagination that

149

has moved us in the past" in a speech delivered at a Jefferson-Jackson Day dinner. He cautions against the party following the Republicans by "blurring the issues or trimming our sails."

27 May 1957
PITTSBURGH.   A pretaped interview with Senator Kennedy is broadcast over radio station KDKA, in which Kennedy says that a Catholic would not be discriminated against in the next presidential election because of his religion. "The people today are more interested in a man's talent and ability than his religious convictions," he says. Kennedy denies that he will be a candidate in 1960.

28 May 1957
BOSTON.   The B'Nai Brith Sports Lodge Football Award is presented to Senator John F. Kennedy at its fifth annual dinner at the Sheraton-Plaza Hotel. The award is made in recognition of the Senator's efforts to help arrange a game between Boston College and the U.S. Naval Academy on the day in September when Boston College's new Chestnut Hill stadium is to be dedicated.

4 June 1957
ATLANTIC CITY, NEW JERSEY. John F. Kennedy assails employers for aiding labor racketeering before the New Jersey Federation of Labor. He says that some employers collaborate with labor racketeers to drive competition out of business and build monopolies.

5 June 1957
WASHINGTON, D.C.   Senator Kennedy introduces a bill providing for foreign wives and children to join their husbands and/or fathers who are in the United States.

7 June 1957
LITTLE ROCK, ARKANSAS.   In a speech before the Arkansas Bar Association, Senator John F. Kennedy denies that he will be a candidate for president in the next election.

13 June 1957
WORCESTER, MASSACHUSETTS.   At commencement exercises of Assumption College, Robert F. Kennedy receives an honorary degree.

15 June 1957
ROCKLAND, MAINE.   A quick, comprehensive, long-term settlement is needed in the Middle East, Senator Kennedy says in an address at an annual Jefferson-Jackson Day dinner. Kennedy believes that the United States should take the lead in helping to achieve an agreement that would include disarmament and permit ships from all countries to pass through the Suez Canal. Also speaking before the group is Governor Edmund Muskie of Maine.

27 June 1957
WASHINGTON, D.C.   An immigration bill is introduced in Congress by Senator John F. Kennedy. It provides for admissioninto the United States over the next two years of up to 150,000 additional aliens from countries that have already reached their immigration quotas.

28 June 1957
NEW YORK.   A son, Stephen Edward Jr., is born to Jean (Kennedy) and Stephen Edward Smith. He is the couple's first child.

2 July 1957
WASHINGTON, D.C.   The United States should support negotiations for the independence of the French North African colony of Algeria, Senator John F. Kennedy says in a Senate speech. Charging that the United States is "failing to meet the challenge of imperialism," he calls on Congress to ask President Eisenhower to act. Kennedy's proposal was criticized by Secretary of State John Foster Dulles even before it was delivered.

7 July 1957
ALGERIA.   French Minister Robert Lacoste criticizes Senator John F. Kennedy for his condemnation of France's policy in Algeria. Lacoste says that if French military troops leave the country, the United States and Russia will compete for superiority in North Africa.

August 1957
NEW YORK.   An extensive article by Eleanor Harris on the life of Senator John F. Kennedy appears in *McCall's* magazine under the title "The Senator Is in a Hurry." In discussing how Jack Kennedy got into politics, Ms. Harris quotes the Senator's father as saying "I got Jack into politics—I was the one. I told him Joe was dead and that it was therefore his responsibility to run for Congress. He didn't want to. He felt he didn't have the ability and he still feels that way. But I told him he had to." On the family mission in politics, Eleanor Harris quotes the Senator as saying, "If I died my brother Bob would want to be a Senator and if anything happened to him, my brother Teddy would run for us."

2 August 1957
NEW YORK. John Vernou Bouvier III, the father of Jacqueline Kennedy, dies of cancer at the age of 66. He is divorced from Jacqueline's mother, the former Janet Lee, who is now married to Hugh Auchincloss. Bouvier also leaves another daughter, Lee Canfield.

20-21 August 1957
WASHINGTON, D.C. James R. Hoffa, a Midwestern vice-president of the Teamsters Union, is questioned at hearings of the Senate Rackets Committee by Counsel Robert F. Kennedy.

21 August 1957
WASHINGTON, D.C. A bill is introduced by Senator John F. Kennedy that would provide more financial aid to Communist satellites, excluding North Korea and Red China, if such aid will help these countries to achieve economic or political independence from the Soviet Union and thus improve their relations with the United States.

4 September 1957
DETROIT, MICHIGAN. Robert F. Kennedy, chief counsel of the Senate Rackets Investigating Committee, arrives to look into certain affairs of Jimmy Hoffa as part of his investigation of corruption in the Teamsters Union.

12 September 1957
JAPAN. The Marine Air Group unit of which Lee Harvey Oswald is a member is transferred here.

14 September 1957
CHARLOTTESVILLE, VIRGINIA. Edward M. Kennedy begins his second year of study at the University of Virginia School of Law.

19 September 1957
NEW YORK. Suffering from the grippe, Senator John F. Kennedy is treated at New York Hospital-Cornell Medical Center.

NEW ROCHELLE, NEW YORK. Senator Kennedy receives an honorary Doctor of Laws degree from the Rev. Brother William Barnes, the president of Iona College, at a special convocation. Jean (Kennedy) Smith accepts the award for her brother, who is ill with the grippe and cannot attend.

22 September 1957
HYDE PARK, NEW YORK. The Joseph P. Kennedy, Jr. Memorial School on Hale Street is dedicated at a ceremony attended by 5,000 people. Archbishop Richard J. Cushing of Boston delivers an address in which he says many people in the nation would like to see Senator John F. Kennedy run for president. Joseph P. Kennedy is present at the ceremony.

24 September 1957
WASHINGTON, D.C. On the first of five days of hearings before the Senate Select Committee, Counsel Robert F. Kennedy charges that Jimmy Hoffa was elected a delegate to the Teamsters Union convention under conditions that violated the union's constitution.

15 October 1957
CHICAGO. In an address to members of the Inland Daily Press Association, Robert Kennedy urges federal action to stop union improprieties.

24 October 1957
BOSTON. Labor racketeers use trusteeships over local unions to stay in power, and they must be "curbed" for the good of labor, industry, and the nation, says Senator John F. Kennedy in an address to 2,000 attendees of an annual luncheon of the Association Industries of Massachusetts. Pointing out that there is no federal law to safeguard union members, he says that Congress should "pass legislation helping to implement the principles of union democracy." He calls for a law that would give union members a voice in the direction of their welfare and pension funds, that would mandate their consent for any large or unusual expenditure of dues, that would prevent arbitrary exclusion of workers from membership, and that would protect those who object to questionable union policies.

28 October 1957
PURCHASE, NEW YORK. The Kennedy Gymnasium at Manhattanville College, a million-dollar structure largely funded by the Lt. Joseph P. Kennedy, Jr. Foundation in memory of Kathleen, Lady Hartington, is formally dedicated.

November 1957
NEW YORK. *Fortune* magazine lists Joseph P. Kennedy as one of the sixteen richest people in the United States. In a piece entitled "America's Biggest Fortunes," it categorizes individual wealth by amount and ranks individual fortunes within each range. Only J. Paul Getty appears in the top category of $700 million to $1 billion; seven names appear in the $400 million to $700 million range; eight names, including that of Joseph P.

151

United Press International. Bettmann Newsphotos.

John and Jacqueline Kennedy on their wedding day, 12 September, 1953.

Kennedy, appear in the $200 million to $400 million range.

4 November 1957

BOSTON.   A dedication ceremony is held at the Catholic Boys Guidance Center for the Joseph P. Kennedy, Jr. Memorial Gymnasium. Among those attending are Joseph P. Kennedy and Archbishop Richard J. Cushing.

15 November 1957

BOSTON.   A maroon, leather-bound photo album with gold lettering that is to be presented to John F. Kennedy the next day at a dinner in honor of both Representative John W. McCormack and Kennedy is stolen from a parked car. The album, which contains photos of Senator Kennedy taken at the 1956 Democratic National Convention in Chicago, was a personal gift from State Senator John Powers of South Boston. A reward with "no questions asked" is offered for the return of the album.

16 November 1957

BOSTON.   The testimonial dinner to honor Senator John F. Kennedy and Representative John W. McCormack turns into a giant "Kennedy for President" banquet. In what is probably the largest turnout of Democrats in Massachusetts history to date, 6,000 party members attend the $5-a-plate tribute at the Commonwealth Armory. But instead of honoring the two political leaders, the dinner takes a Kennedy-for-president-in-1960 turn. Says McCormack to the cheering audience, "This is the time when we need leadership like that of Franklin D. Roosevelt and Harry S. Truman. I am confident we will win in 1960. And on our ticket will be the name of that courageous young man, Senator Kennedy.

Senator Kennedy tells the wildly enthusiastic audience, "This is a great Democratic dinner. This indicates a Democratic victory in 1958, and further, a Democratic victory in 1958 indicates we are going to capture the country in 1960."

17 November 1957

NEW YORK.   Senator John F. Kennedy urges a study and revision of U.S. immigration policy. "Our immigration laws have devolved into such a tangled mess," he says, "that nobody quite knows what they are."

18 November 1957

DAYTONA BEACH, FLORIDA.   Gerrymandering, labor racketeering, and Adlai Stevenson's recent appointment as policy adviser on NATO affairs are the subjects of an address made by John F. Kennedy to the

Florida League of Municipalities. He says that seats in Congress and state legislatures are improperly balanced with regard to urban and rural population and political representation. City residents are discriminated against, he says, because congressional districts, and particularly state legislatures, are weighted against growing urban populations. Kennedy also calls on federal, state, and local governments to fight labor racketeering, and he praises President Eisenhower's appointment of Adlai Stevenson as an adviser on NATO.

24 November 1957

BOSTON.   John F. Kennedy is made a Grand Officer of the Italian Republic at a dinner at the Sheraton Plaza Hotel, attended by 1,000 Italian-Americans. But the ceremony turns into a "Kennedy for President" rally as Mayor John B. Hynes, Governor Dennis J. Roberts of Rhode Island, and others pledge support to help Kennedy get to the White House in the next election.

27 November 1957

NEW YORK.   A daughter, Caroline Bouvier, is born to Jacqueline (Bouvier) and John F. Kennedy at the New York Lying-In Hospital-Cornell Medical Center. Born at 8:15 A.M. , she is the first surviving child of Jacqueline, 27, and John Kennedy, 40. The baby weighs 7 pounds, 2 ounces and is delivered by Caesarean section.

2 December 1957

NEW YORK.   *Time* magazine publishes a cover story on Senator John F. Kennedy.

1 January 1958

NEW YORK.   The goals of the Joseph P. Kennedy, Jr. Foundation now focus on the problems of mental retardation. The foundation's two objectives are "to seek the prevention of mental retardation by identifying its causes and to improve the means which society deals with its citizens who are already retarded."

6 January 1958

WASHINGTON, D.C.   As the new session of Congress gets under way, Senator John F. Kennedy and his family have a new residence, a three-story house at 3307 N Street, N.W., in Georgetown. They had previously rented a house at 2808 P St., N.W. Senator Kennedy moves in today; his wife and baby daughter will follow in a few days.

12 January 1958

BOSTON.   "Tonight the national interest is in perhaps greater peril than it has been at any time in the twentieth century," Senator Kennedy says at the sixtieth anniversary banquet of the Père Marquette Council of the Knights of Columbus at the National Guard Armory in Dorchester. Kennedy warns that the United States has "no real defense" against Soviet missile attacks and that the country is in danger of falling behind the Russians in overall land, sea, and air military capability.

16 January 1958

BOSTON.　At a banquet celebrating Printing and Publishing Week at the Hotel Sheraton Plaza, Robert F. Kennedy warns that unless loopholes in the labor law are corrected, corruption will continue in labor unions.

31 January 1958

CAPE CANAVERAL, FLORIDA.　The first U.S. satellite, Explorer I, is launched into orbit by the Army.

6 February 1958

WASHINGTON, D.C.　Senator John F. Kennedy introduces a bill providing for improved benefits to the unemployed. The legislation calls for increasing the level of benefit payments and extending the benefit period, among other changes in the unemployment compensation program. The bill is cosponsored by Senator Pat McNamara (Democrat, Mich.).

7 February 1958

LYNN, MASSACHUSETTS. Senator John F. Kennedy speaks on economic competition with Russia, fuel imports, and rail rates in an address to 150 members of the Lions, Kiwanis, Exchange, and Rotary Clubs at the Hotel Edison. While a balance of weapons exists between Russia and the United States, he says, the question is whether "a free nation could compete with a nation that has unrestricted control of its manpower." He warns that Russia's economic strength might attract countries to communism: "Underdeveloped nations may be tempted by Russia's forty-year leap from backwardness to a position where it appears to be a leader." Kennedy also urges New England congressmen to combat attempts to restrict imports of fuel oils, adding that New England industry will benefit greatly if the ICC ends discrimination in rail rates at a hearing next month.

8 February 1958

MALDEN, MASSACHUSETTS.　Representative Torbert H. MacDonald, John F. Kennedy's roommate at Harvard, is praised by Senator Kennedy for his work in the Eighth Congressional District at a dinner honoring the new congressman. Others at MacDonald's tribute in-

clude Professor Archibald Cox of Harvard Law School and Representative Thomas P. O'Neill, Jr.

11 February 1958

WASHINGTON, D.C.　Tunisia has been neglected by United Nations and United States economic programs, charges Senator John F. Kennedy. This has given the Communists "every opportunity to pose as champions of freedom." He calls for the United States to ask NATO "to assert jurisdiction over North Africa where the French Arab struggle is becoming more explosive." Kennedy is chairman of the Africa subcommittee of the Senate Foreign Relations Committee.

15 February 1958

NEW YORK.　An honorary degree is presented to Senator John F. Kennedy at an annual luncheon of Fordham University Law School. In an address, Kennedy scores the attorneys representing union officials at Senate subcommittee hearings on labor racketeering and asks, "What happened to the legal shepherds of the flock who came to our hearing as defenders of the wolves who had despoiled the sheep?"

22 February 1958

SOUTH BEND, INDIANA.　The annual Patriotism Award of the senior class of the University of Notre Dame is bestowed upon Senate investigator Robert F. Kennedy. The citation accompanying the award salutes Kennedy "for the quiet and courageous integrity of your action against negative and malicious elements in our society...." In his acceptance speech, Robert Kennedy warns that unless certain "dangerous changes in American life" are reversed by toughness and moral idealism, "disaster is our destiny." (His brother John had won the award the year before.)

27 February 1958

WASHINGTON, D.C.　A son, Michael LeMoyne, is born to Ethel (Skakel) and Robert Kennedy. Their sixth child and fourth son, he is named for LeMoyne Billings.

28 February 1958

CHICAGO.　On behalf of her brother, Senator John F. Kennedy, Eunice Shriver accepts the "Man of the Year" award from the *Polish Daily News*. Eunice Shriver reads a speech prepared by the Senator urging strengthened ties through expanded trade between the United States and Poland.

1 March 1958

LOS ANGELES, CALIFORNIA.　Senator John F.

Kennedy Family Collection. Photographer unknown.

Ethel and Robert F. Kennedy with children Bobby, Jr., Kathleen, and Joe II, 1955.

Kennedy delivers the keynote speech at a Democratic fund-raising dinner held in memory of Franklin D. Roosevelt. He criticizes pending "right-to-work" legislation, adding that those who favor it opposed increases in the minimum wage.

6 March 1958

BALTIMORE, MARYLAND. Broadcasting on a higher intellectual level is urged by Senator John F. Kennedy in a speech to radio and television executives attending a Westinghouse programming conference. "We should not underestimate the American people. We must not sell their intelligence short," Kennedy says.

7 March 1958

WASHINGTON, D.C. Senator John F. Kennedy releases a statement demanding action from the government to combat rising unemployment. Kennedy calls for "action on a range of programs," including "school and hospital construction, urban renewal and slum clearance, and road construction."

8 March 1958

NEW YORK. The *Saturday Evening Post* publishes an article entitled "Of Stevenson, Truman and Kennedy" by Eleanor Roosevelt. Of the young senator she writes, "During the lively contest for the vice-presidential nomination between Senator Estes Kefauver and Senator John Kennedy, a friend of Senator Kennedy came to me with a request for support. I replied I did not feel I could do so because Senator Kennedy had avoided taking a position during the controversy over Senator Joseph McCarthy's methods of investigation. Senator Kennedy was in the hospital when the Senate condemned Senator McCarthy and, of course, could not record his position. But later, when he returned to the Senate, reporters asked him how he would have voted and he failed to express an opinion on McCarthyism."

10 March 1958

QUINCY, MASSACHUSETTS. While praising New England's industrial strength in a speech before 400 members of the Quincy Chamber of Commerce at the

155

Neighborhood Club, John F. Kennedy says that the regional economy "is aggravated by a lack of raw materials." He calls for an end to discriminatory freight rates in New England, low-cost atomic power, equalizing compensation benefits to unemployed persons across the country, and tax benefits for small businesses.

11 March 1958

WASHINGTON, D.C. Senator Kennedy introduces legislation to curb racketeering in labor unions and to prevent financial underhandedness by union leaders.

16 March 1958

EVERETT, MASSACHUSETTS. Introduced as "the next president of the United States," Senator John F. Kennedy delivers a speech to 500 cheering people at the annual St. Patrick's Day banquet of the Friendly Sons of St. Patrick at the Parlin Junior High School. He predicts that while the present recession is serious, there will be improvement "at least by the end of the summer." He adds, "In April, if the economy has not taken an upturn, I believe there will be a tax cut."

17 March 1958

HOLYOKE, MASSACHUSETTS. Five thousand people cheer Senator Kennedy as he is presented an award as "Outstanding American of Irish-Catholic Descent." Then he and Mrs. Kennedy join the St. Patrick's Day parade, riding in the back of their convertible. Mrs. Kennedy wears a green ribbon in her hair and a green scarf; the Senator wears a green tie borrowed from a stranger at Kennedy's hotel.

SOUTH BOSTON. In drizzly, cold weather, Senator and Mrs. John F. Kennedy ride in another St. Patrick's Day parade in this part of town.

20 March 1958

WASHINGTON, D.C. A constitutional amendment that would radically change the electoral college system is opposed by Senator John F. Kennedy in a speech to the Senate. The amendment, proposed by Senators Price Daniel (Democrat, Tex.) and Estes Kefauver (Democrat, Tenn.), calls for terminating the system under which a majority of votes in a state gives a presidential candidate the state's entire electoral vote. It would provide, instead, for different areas within a state to have independent electoral votes. Kennedy assails the measure, which has already been given favorable review by the Senate Judiciary Committee, claiming that it will give

rural voters overrepresentation, make it more likely that a candidate could be elected with less than a majority of the popular vote, and encourage splinter political parties.

21 March 1958

BOSTON. Senator John Kennedy is released from New England Baptist Hospital after spending three days there for a "slight cold" and a routine checkup. The cold, he believes, is the result of riding in two St. Patrick's Day parades on the 17th.

BOSTON. In the evening, at an annual dinner of the Harvard Club of Boston, Senator John F. Kennedy warns that Soviet aid to underdeveloped countries is a greater threat to the United States than their military might. He calls for giving aid to India, enlarging the International Development Fund, and revising U.S. foreign policy to include more economic aid in general.

22 March 1958

DES MOINES, IOWA. Assailing President Eisenhower for failing to control the recession, Senator John F. Kennedy calls for "the kind of leadership demonstrated by Franklin Roosevelt." Speaking at a Jefferson-Jackson Day fund-raising dinner, Kennedy says, "What is needed in America today is not so much confidence in the economy but confidence in our leadership."

23 March 1958

WAKEFIELD, MASSACHUSETTS. Senator John F. Kennedy tells the 929ers Club of the Wakefield First Congregational Church that American businessmen can assist the United States in its competition with Russia by investing in areas where the Soviet Union is making great efforts to exert its influence, such as the Middle East, Asia, and Africa.

BOSTON. Speaking on human rights before the Freedom House, Senator Kennedy calls for an end to discrimination in employment and an end to segregation. He says that the "denial of equal opportunity penalizes us all."

25 March 1958

WASHINGTON, D.C. In a speech to the Senate, Senator John F. Kennedy proposes a "free world Marshall Plan" to assist India in developing its economy. "Should India fall prey to internal disorder or disillusionment among either its masses or leaders and become absorbed in the Communist system," he warns, "the free world would suffer an incalculable blow."

29 March 1958
INDIANAPOLIS, INDIANA.   At a Jefferson-Jackson Day fund-raising dinner, Senator Kennedy urges the Democrats to assume a leadership role and calls for legislation to aid the unemployed and to raise the standard of living for the aged and the handicapped.

30 March 1958
WASHINGTON, D.C.   Appearing on the CBS television program "Face the Nation," Senator John F. Kennedy says that at present he is concentrating only on being re-elected to the Senate, not running for president; that the Democrats will win across the country in the November elections; that Congress should wait until March statistics on business and unemployment are available before deciding to approve a tax cut; and that he is a liberal.

WASHINGTON, D.C.   Responding to Eleanor Roosevelt's recent allegation in the *Saturday Evening Post* that he had equivocated about McCarthyism, Senator Kennedy declares he has frequently expressed approval of the Senate's censure of Senator McCarthy.

8 April 1958
WASHINGTON, D.C.   In a letter to Assistant Secretary of Defense Perkins McGuire, Senator Kennedy complains that the Defense Department has not channeled contracts to Massachusetts "in sufficient volume to relieve the serious economic plight."

BOSTON.   Speaking before 600 doctors attending a dinner of the Tufts Medical Alumni Association, Special Counsel Robert F. Kennedy of the Senate Rackets Committee says that the influence of organized crime in America is more widespread than ever before. Teamsters Union president Jimmy Hoffa is even dealing with the Communists, he declares, and he urges legislative action.

10 April 1958
MIAMI, FLORIDA.   While poking around in the engine of his car, Senator Kennedy catches two fingers in the gears. He is treated at North Shore Hospital and released.

14 April 1958
CONCORD, NEW HAMPSHIRE.   Speaking before 1,000 persons at a Rotary Club meeting at the State Armory, Senator John Kennedy declares that the American people must be prepared for the struggle against communism. "There are disturbing signs," he says, "that we

as a nation are intellectually and emotionally unprepared for the long test of endurance we face."

19 April 1958
BOSTON.   Archbishop Richard J. Cushing presents the 1958 Lantern Award of the Massachusetts Council of the Knights of Columbus to Robert F. Kennedy at the group's annual Patriots' Day dinner. The award is given for outstanding patriotism, and Robert Kennedy is cited for his work as chief counsel to the Select Committee on Improper Activities in the Labor or Management Field.

20 April 1958
WATERTOWN, MASSACHUSETTS.   Senator John F. Kennedy predicts "decades of conflict" between the United States and Russia in a speech before 6,700 teenagers of the Newton Deanery, Catholic Youth Organization, at the East Junior High School.

1 May 1958
HAVERHILL, MASSACHUSETTS.   Senator John F. Kennedy tells 1,000 guests at a Chamber of Commerce dinner that the absence of an effective economic program is responsible for the recession and that "there is increased sentiment in Congress" for a tax cut.

WASHINGTON, D.C.   Three bills are introduced by Senator Kennedy: one to penalize employers seeking to bribe union officials, another to enable lawful strikers to vote in plant elections, and a third to enable the National Labor Relations Board to certify construction unions without a union election.

3 May 1958
WALLINGFORD, CONNECTICUT.   On Alumni Day at the Choate School, Senator John F. Kennedy is awarded the school's first Alumni Seal Prize for being "Choate Man of the Year." This new award is presented to recognize a Choate graduate who within his trade or profession has "shown outstanding leadership and who has made a significant contribution to the life of his community or his country...thereby reflecting credit on the school, on the Choate family, and on himself." Senator Kennedy (Choate, 1935) accepts the award in the school's chapel before 450 alumni as faculty and students listen in the speech room over a broadcasting system.

4 May 1958
WASHINGTON, D.C.   Senator Kenneth B. Keating (Republican, N.Y.) conducts an interview with John

Kennedy Family Collection. United Press International.

Robert and Senator John F. Kennedy at the McClellan Committee hearings, 2 February 1957.

Kennedy for later broadcast over New York television stations. Kennedy predicts that a tax cut "might be quite likely" if the economy does not improve by the end of the month.

14 May 1958
ATLANTIC CITY, NEW JERSEY.   Senator John F. Kennedy tells delegates to a convention of the Amalgamated Clothing Workers Union that legislation excessively restrictive to unions should not be hastily passed "simply because a few bad apples have been found in the barrel." He says that when people in other jobs commit illegal acts, their businesses or professions are not condemned as a whole.

18 May 1958
MIAMI, FLORIDA.   At the Governors' Conference, Governor Abraham Ribicoff (Democrat, Conn.) advocates the election of Senator John F. Kennedy for president in 1960.

23 May 1958
WASHINGTON, D.C.   Senator Kennedy's amend-

ment authorizing the president to give economic aid to Communist satellite countries if it will strengthen their ties to the United States is approved by the Senate Foreign Relations Committee. North Korea and the People's Republic of China are excluded from such aid.

8 June 1958
MEDFORD, MASSACHUSETTS.   Robert F. Kennedy receives an honorary Doctor of Laws degree from Tufts University.

NORTHAMPTON, MASSACHUSETTS.   At the graduation exercises of Smith College, Senator John F. Kennedy delivers the commencement address. He discusses his belief that providing economic aid to Communist satellite nations will lessen their dependence on the Soviet Union and gradually bring them more freedom.

9 June 1958
CHARLOTTESVILLE, VIRGINIA.   Edward M. Kennedy completes his second year at the University of Virginia School of Law.

21 June 1958

WASHINGTON, D.C. Asked on a local television show if he will run for president in the next election, Senator Kennedy says that he is now only concentrating on the next "major hurdle." "Right now I have an opponent and I'm going to have to do a lot of work for Massachusetts," he explains.

23 June 1958

NEW YORK. *Newsweek* Magazine publishes a cover story on Senator John F. Kennedy.

27 June 1958

WASHINGTON, D.C. John Fox, publisher of the defunct Boston *Post*, testifies before the Special House Subcommittee on Legislative Oversight during hearings on the activities of textile executive Bernard Goldfine. In response to a question about his association with Joseph P. Kennedy, Fox admits that his paper endorsed John F. Kennedy for senator in 1952 after Fox received a large business loan from the elder Kennedy. Fox explains that he bought the newspaper to oust Communists from the White House. He had supported Senator Henry Cabot Lodge, Jr., for re-election in 1952 until he decided Lodge was "soft on Communists." Disillusioned with Lodge, Fox switched his support to John F. Kennedy. It was only after the election, Fox claims, that Kennedy's father gave him the loan.

HARTFORD, CONNECTICUT. The revolt in Lebanon has moved the United States to the "brink of war," Senator John F. Kennedy declares in a keynote speech to the Democratic State Convention. He says that United States policy must be clarified to the American people. "The American people have no clear and consistent understanding of why we are there, what we are going to do, or what we hope to accomplish."

14 August 1958

WASHINGTON, D.C. Senator John F. Kennedy sparks a heated Senate debate when he alleges that a slowdown in U.S. missile development and resulting Russian missile superiority will, in the coming years, create for the United States "a peril more deadly than any wartime danger we have ever known."

9 September 1958

MASSACHUSETTS. John F. Kennedy, running unopposed on the ballot, wins the Democratic primary for senator from Massachusetts. The election results are: Kennedy, 389,921 votes; all others, 17; blanks 110,934 (total votes cast, 500,872).

10 September 1958

ATLANTIC CITY, NEW JERSEY. Senator John F. Kennedy praises delegates at the first constitutional convention of the American Bakery and Confectionery Workers International Union of the AFL-CIO, which has been newly formed to purge the old union of corruption and racketeering. "This is the most important labor meeting I have attended in my twelve years in Congress," he says.

11 September 1958

MIAMI BEACH, FLORIDA. A "Magna Carta" that would provide for fairer recognition of urban areas in elections and for more equitable distribution of public funds is proposed by Senator John F. Kennedy to 500 mayors and municipal representatives attending a meeting of the U.S. Conference of Mayors.

12 September 1958

OMAHA, NEBRASKA. At a Midwest Democratic Conference held to develop campaign issues at the Sheraton-Fontennelle Hotel, Senator John F. Kennedy declares that the crisis over Chinese bombardment of Quemoy and Matsu in the Formosan Strait is an issue. He says that both military and political judgments mandate a policy different from the "vague and inconsistent" action of the Eisenhower administration.

13 September 1958

SAN FRANCISCO. The Eisenhower administration's foreign policy is assailed as "indecisive" by Senator Kennedy in an address at a dinner honoring Representative Claire Engle (Democrat, Cal.), who is running for a seat in the U.S. Senate.

16 September 1958

TULSA, OKLAHOMA. At a dinner held in his honor, Senator John F. Kennedy declares the Formosan islands of Quemoy and Matsu not worth the United States risking a third world war. "The American people," he says, "do not want to be involved in an armed conflict over these islands that are not important to the defense of Formosa—islands that are not defensible." Quemoy and Matsu have been bombarded by the Communist Chinese. The U.S. Seventh fleet has convoyed Nationalist Chinese ships, and mainland Chinese charge that the United States has violated their territorial waters.

19 September 1958

CHARLOTTESVILLE, VIRGINIA. Edward M. Kennedy begins his third year at the University of Virginia School of Law.

21 September 1958

BRONXVILLE, NEW YORK. Harry and Virginia (Stead) Bennett announce the engagement of their daughter Virginia Joan to Ted Kennedy. Joan was born 9 September 1936 and graduated last June from the Manhattanville College of the Sacred Heart in Purchase, New York. In 1954 she made her debut at the Gotham Ball in New York. While a student, she has worked in television commercials.

7 October 1958

NEW BEDFORD, MASSACHUSETTS. Senator John F. Kennedy announces that he will introduce a bill to provide funds to revitalize the U.S. fishing industry in the next session of Congress.

TAUNTON, MASSACHUSETTS. Senator Kennedy says in a speech that in the next Congress he will support enactment of the Hill-Burton Act for the construction of hospitals and hospital facilities.

2 November 1958

JAPAN. Lee Harvey Oswald's Marine unit is transferred to the United States.

4 November 1958

MASSACHUSETTS. By nearly three-quarters of a million votes—the largest margin in the history of the Commonwealth—John F. Kennedy is re-elected to a second term in the United States Senate. The election results are: Kennedy (Democrat), 1,362,926; Vincent J. Celeste (Republican), 488,318; Lawrence Gilfedder (Socialist Labor), 5,457; Mark R. Shaw (Prohibition),5,335; all others, 5; blanks, 90,814 (total votes cast, 1,952,855). Edward M. Kennedy served as his brother's campaign manager.

SANTA MONICA, CALIFORNIA. A daughter, Victoria Frances, is born to Patricia (Kennedy) and Peter Lawford at St. John's Hospital. She is their third child and second daughter. The baby is named in honor of her uncle John's election victory in Massachusetts on the day she is born and after family friend Francis (Frank) Sinatra.

10 November 1958

KETCHIKAN, ALASKA. On the first day of a brief tour of this territory—Alaska will become a state on 3 January 1959, less than two months from now—Senator John F. Kennedy campaigns for Democratic senatorial candidates Ernest Gruening and E. L. Bartlett for the upcoming election on 25 November.

BOSTON. In a speech given to members of the National Association of Citizens' Crime Commissions at the Statler Hilton, Robert F. Kennedy says that the labor movement is full of gangsters in high positions and urges the public to demand that legislation to remove them be passed.

11 November 1958

JUNEAU and ANCHORAGE, ALASKA. Senator John F. Kennedy continues to stump for Democratic candidates running for what will be state offices for the first time.

14 November 1958

SANTA MONICA, CALIFORNIA. Senator John Kennedy is named godfather of his niece Victoria Frances Lawford at her christening.

23 November 1958

NEW YORK. Referring to the United States' position of neutrality on Algeria, Senator John F. Kennedy says, "I do not think we have always recognized the moral principles of self-determination for those still under foreign control." Speaking at a dinner at the Waldorf-Astoria Hotel held by the Jewish Theological Seminary of America in honor of Senator Herbert H. Lehman (Democrat, N.Y.), Kennedy assails American policy, recalling the words of Dante: "The hottest places in hell are reserved for those who, in a time of great moral crisis, maintain their neutrality."

29 November 1958

BRONXVILLE, NEW YORK. Virginia Joan Bennett, 22, and Edward Moore Kennedy, 26, are married in St. Joseph's Church. Francis Cardinal Spellman celebrates the nuptial mass. The groom's eldest brother, John F. Kennedy, is best man.

7 December 1958

WASHINGTON, D.C. On the local television show "College News Conference," Eleanor Roosevelt criticizes Senator John F. Kennedy's qualifications as a presidential candidate. In a reference to Kennedy's failure to speak out against Senator Joseph R. McCarthy, she says that Kennedy understands courage but "does not have the independence to have it." She praises Senator Hubert H. Humphrey as a man who could be an excellent president.

15 December 1958

SAN JUAN, PUERTO RICO. Speaking at a Democratic dinner, Senator John F. Kennedy says that the

United States must not take Latin America for granted and that the area is essential to American security. He proposes a program to improve relations that includes new farm loans, revision of tariff duties, more funds made available from the Development Loan Fund, and the stabilization of commodity markets.

16 December 1958
ST. THOMAS, VIRGIN ISLANDS. At a Jefferson-Jackson Day dinner, Senator John F. Kennedy praises the political stability of the Virgin Islands and says it should be represented by a delegate in Washington, D.C.

30 December 1958
BOSTON. After being confined for five days at New England Baptist Hospital for a virus infection, Senator John F. Kennedy is released.

31 December 1958
NEW YORK. The Joseph P. Kennedy, Jr. Foundation commits a grant of $500,000 to the New Bedford (Massachusetts) Building Fund.

3 January 1959
WASHINGTON, D.C. John F. Kennedy, 41, is sworn in for his second term of office as senator from Massachusetts as the Eighty-sixth Congress opens. Senator Kennedy is a member of the Foreign Relations, Labor and Public Welfare, and Joint Economic committees. The Republican senator from Massachusetts is Leverett Saltonstall.

10 February 1959
WASHINGTON, D.C. The Senate Select Committee on Improper Activities in the Labor or Management Field opens hearings on alleged racketeering in the juke-box industry.

10 March 1959
WASHINGTON, D.C. At a private session of the Senate Rackets Committee, Robert F. Kennedy tells of a threatening phone call he received: "Lay off or we'll throw acid in your kids' faces!" He does not ask for protection, however.

11 April 1959
APPLETON, WISCONSIN. Senator John F. Kennedy winds up a political tour begun in the state two days earlier to gauge reaction to his presidential candidacy. Among the other cities he visits are Milwaukee and Madison.

29 April 1959
WASHINGTON, D.C. President Dwight D. Eisenhower criticizes Senator Kennedy's labor reform bill as having "definite weaknesses." Later in the day, Kennedy defends the bill.

15 May 1959
MIAMI BEACH, FLORIDA. At a convention of the International Ladies Garment Workers Union, Senator John F. Kennedy says that his labor reform bill is designed to prevent Jimmy Hoffa types from rising to top positions in unions.

28 May 1959
NEW YORK. Baudouin I, king of Belgium, presents Joseph P. Kennedy with the Grand Cross Order of Leopold II of Belgium at the Waldorf-Astoria Hotel.

8 June 1959
BOSTON. At Boston College graduation ceremonies, held at the Boston Garden, the school's president, the Very Rev. Joseph R. N. Maxwell, S.J., announces that the Lt. Joseph P. Kennedy, Jr. Foundation has earlier today contributed $150,000 to Boston College.

9 June 1959
WASHINGTON, D.C. Chicago racketeer Momo Salvatore "Sam" Giancana appears before the Senate Select Committee but avoids testifying by invoking the Fifth Amendment.

15 June 1959
CHARLOTTESVILLE, VIRGINIA. Edward M. Kennedy graduates from the University of Virginia School of Law with a Bachelor of Laws degree.

24 June 1959
FORT DEVENS, MASSACHUSETTS. His military obligations complete, Edward M. Kennedy receives an honorable discharge from the United States Army Reserve.

2 July 1959
WASHINGTON, D.C. In a speech before the Senate, John F. Kennedy contradicts President Eisenhower's statement that he does not have the power to convene a board to facilitate settlement of a steel industry strike, and urges him to do so. Eisenhower had made the remark after United Steelworkers' president David McDonald proposed that the President create a fact-finding board.

United Press International.

Pat Lawford, Senator John F. Kennedy, and Peter Lawford in Los Angeles, May 1959.

3 July 1959

HONOLULU, HAWAII.   Senator John F. Kennedy begins a brief tour of the future fiftieth state to stump for Democratic candidates in Hawaii's first election as a state, to be held on 28 July 1959. Accompanying the Senator are Jean (Kennedy) Smith and her husband, Stephen.

5 July 1959

HONOLULU, HAWAII.   Senator Kennedy ends a successful campaign tour of Hawaii and Maui for Democrats in the upcoming election and returns to Washington for a Senate vote and hearing. His speech at the Kaiulani Hotel in Honolulu was televised throughout the islands.

13 July 1959

SPRING LAKE, NEW JERSEY.   In a speech before 1,500 guests at an Essex County Governors' Day picnic at the Homestead Country Club, Senator John F. Kennedy says that the U.S. Lawn Tennis Association should move its major tournament away from the West Side Tennis Club in Forest Hills, New York, because of the club's discriminatory policies. It allegedly does not admit Jews or blacks, and recently turned down Dr. Ralph Bunche and his son for membership.

17 July 1959

WASHINGTON, D.C.   A journalist from the Hearst Headline Service reports that Senator Hubert Humphrey (Democrat, Minn.) confirmed today that Kennedy's staff tried to lure away one of his staff members with an offer of $20,000 per annum. Humphrey has complained that he "simply can't compete in the money field" with Kennedy. Senator Kennedy denies any knowledge of the attempted raid.

22 July 1959
NEW YORK. A prerecorded "Jack Paar Show" on which Robert F. Kennedy is a guest is aired tonight over NBC-TV. On the show, Kennedy levels harsh accusations against Teamsters president Jimmy Hoffa and asks viewers to urge their congressmen to support labor-reform legislation. Something strange happens during the telecast, however. The audio portion of the show goes dead four times within a single minute while Kennedy names the labor racketeers associated with Hoffa. Portions of New York, New England, and other areas are affected.

23 July 1959
WASHINGTON, D.C. The Senate defeats a bill to remove the loyalty oath that students must sign in requesting federal loans. The bill, originally introduced by Senator John F. Kennedy, provided for a repeal of the requirement that students seeking government loans swear that they have never been connected with the Communist party and/or any other subversive organization.

BOSTON. A telephone company official suggests the possibility of electrical storms originating in the Midwest as a cause for the breaks in sound on the "Jack Paar Show" that occurred while Robert Kennedy was speaking.

2 August 1959
WASHINGTON, D.C. Senator John F. Kennedy issues a statement assailing a substitute labor bill proposed by Representatives Robert P. Griffin (Republican, Mich.) and Phil M. Landrum (Democrat, Ga.) that has won President Eisenhower's support.

4 August 1959
SEASIDE, OREGON. On the last day of a three-day political tour of the state, Senator John F. Kennedy addresses a state AFL-CIO convention. He says that his labor reform bill is intended to strike at racketeers without penalizing honest union members. He also urges an increase in the minimum wage and improved health and social security benefits to the elderly.

8 August 1959
WASHINGTON, D.C. Before film cameras and microphones, Representative John Brademas (Democrat,

Ind.) interviews Senator John F. Kennedy on the substitute labor bill sponsored by Representatives Robert Griffin and Phil Landrum. Senator Kennedy criticizes the bill in the interview, which is to be broadcast over radio and television stations in Indiana.

17 August 1959
EL TORO, CALIFORNIA. Lee Harvey Oswald applies for a hardship discharge from the U.S. Marines. Oswald claims that his mother is ill and he must support her. He is not due for discharge until December.

29 August 1959
BOSTON. A son, Timothy Perry, is born to Eunice (Kennedy) and R. Sargent Shriver, Jr. He is their third child and second son.

30 August 1959
GROTON, CONNECTICUT. Addressing the New England Associated Press News Executive Association, Governor Abraham Ribicoff says that New England's presidential convention delegates will be a "nucleus" of support for John Kennedy in helping him win the Democratic nomination for president.

1 September 1959
WASHINGTON, D.C. During a filmed television program conducted by Senator George Smathers (Democrat, Fla.) for broadcast to stations in Florida, Senator John F. Kennedy says that Teamsters Union president James R. Hoffa wants to "dominate everything that moves in this country." Hoffa will use his influence in the next election, Kennedy warns, to try to defeat certain members of Cogress.

6 September 1959
WASHINGTON, D.C. Senators Joseph S. Clark (Democrat, Pa.) and Hugh Scott (Republican, Pa.) interview John F. Kennedy on film for broadcast over Pennsylvania radio and television stations. Kennedy promises that he will announce whether or not he will be a candidate for president by December or January. It does not matter to him where the Democratic National Convention will be held, he says. He challenges other Democratic aspirants to the presidency to enter the primaries, where voters have the opportunity to express themselves, and not to let the party leaders choose a candidate.

8 September 1959
WASHINGTON, D.C. A daughter, Mary Kerry, is born to Ethel (Skakel) and Robert Kennedy. She is their seventh child and third daughter.

10 September 1959

WASHINGTON, D.C. Robert F. Kennedy resigns as chief counsel of the Senate Select Committee on Improper Activities in the Labor or Management Field. Although John Kennedy has not officially declared his candidacy for president, it is expected that Robert will become campaign manager in his brother's bid for the nomination.

11 September 1959

SAN FRANCISCO. The hundreds of delegates to the AFL-CIO Building and Construction Trade Department's annual convention give Senator John F. Kennedy a hearty welcome in his first public speech since Congress passed his labor-management reform bill.

EL TORO, CALIFORNIA. Lee Harvey Oswald is discharged from the United States Marines.

15 September 1959

COLUMBUS, OHIO. John F. Kennedy arrives here to make some public speeches and to confer with Governor Michael V. DiSalle about the state's delegates to the next Democratic National Convention. With his appearances here, he commences a series of speeches throughout the state.

17 September 1959

OXFORD, OHIO. At Miami University, Senator John F. Kennedy describes his personal observations of Soviet premier Nikita Khruschev.

DAYTON, OHIO. Speaking before the Montgomery County Bar Association, Senator Kennedy blasts the small number of unsavory labor lawyers who serve corrupt union leaders. He admonishes bar associations to take action against them.

18 September 1959

AKRON, OHIO. Addressing the Ohio League of Municipalities, Senator John F. Kennedy criticizes President Eisenhower's veto of public housing legislation.

20 September 1959

NEW ORLEANS, LOUISIANA. Lee Harvey Oswald sails for LeHavre, France, aboard the *Marion Lykes.*

22 September 1959

WASHINGTON, D.C. Stephen Smith, who manages Senator Kennedy's speaking invitations, announces that the Senator and his brothers and sisters will pur-

chase a twin-engine Convair. The jet plane will be used mostly to transport Kennedy to and from speaking engagements around the country.

24 September 1959

MADISON, WISCONSIN. Senator John F. Kennedy kicks off a four-day political tour of the state at a breakfast with local labor leaders. He explains the labor reform bill recently passed by Congress.

WASHINGTON, D.C. Senator Kennedy's office issues a statement in which the Senator proposes that hearings be held on the national steel strike before Congress reconvenes. Kennedy, chairman of the Senate Labor Subcommittee, offers this recommendation in response to a letter from Arthur J. Goldberg, counsel for the United Steelworkers of America. Goldberg charges that President Eisenhower has misinterpreted provisions of the Taft-Hartley Act by attempting to obtain an injunction to end the eighty-day walkout.

27 September 1959

RHINELANDER, WISCONSIN. Although country living has its advantages, young people cannot be expected to work on farms when cities offer higher wages, Senator Kennedy declares in a luncheon speech here.

2 October 1959

INDIANAPOLIS, INDIANA. At a fund-raising dinner for Mayor Boswell, Senator John F. Kennedy says that because both sides are so far apart, negotiation cannot settle the conflict between the United States and Russia. In this new era of peace between the two nations, Americans must "sacrifice to protect and extend the world frontiers of peace," Kennedy cautions. This speech launches a thirteen-day political tour through the Midwest.

9 October 1959

FAYETTE CITY, PENNSYLVANIA. In a speech given at a dinner of the Washington County Democratic Club, John F. Kennedy declares that President Eisenhower mishandled the situation by favoring management in the United Steelworkers strike.

BOSTON. Addressing over 1,600 delegates and guests at the second convention of the Massachusetts Labor Council AFL-CIO at the Statler-Hilton Hotel, Senator Kennedy says that in the next session of Congress he will introduce legislation to raise the minimum wage and increase the national minimum unemployment compensation. He also says that, although he can live with it, the new Landrum-Griffin labor bill is "the most unfortunate piece of legislation since the Taft-Hartley Bill in 1947." After Kennedy's speech, union president William J. Belanger introduces a resolution asking him to run for president of the United States. The crowd roars its response. Sidestepping a direct announcement but hinting at one, Kennedy says, "I want to tell you how much I appreciate this, but must quote an old proverb." Paraphrasing Ecclesiastes, he says, "There is a time to sow and a time to reap, a time to live and a time to die, a time to fish and a time to cut bait. I believe this is the time to fish and January, 1960, the time to cut bait."

10 October 1959
HELSINKI, FINLAND. Lee Harvey Oswald arrives here from London. He will apply for a visa to travel to Russia.

11 October 1959
NEW ROCHELLE, NEW YORK. In a speech before the Westchester Democrats at the Glen Island Casino, Senator John F. Kennedy blames the Eisenhower administration for the "deterioration" of American influence around the world and calls for more federal funding for the educational system.

12 October 1959
ATLANTIC CITY, NEW JERSEY. Praising the United Auto Workers as a "basic bulwark of the liberal progressive movement," Senator John F. Kennedy addresses delegates to the union's convention in an attempt to gain their support for his possible presidential candidacy. Speaking of his labor record in Congress and his legislative efforts for labor reform, he says, "I come to you as a friend of labor. I have never apologized for that friendship and I don't intend to start today." Two other Democratic presidential aspirants, Senators Hubert Humphrey of Minnesota and Stuart Symington of Missouri, are scheduled to address the delegates later this week.

14 October 1959
HELSINKI, FINLAND. After a two-day wait, Lee Harvey Oswald receives a visa to enter the Soviet Union.

16 October 1959
MOSCOW. Lee Harvey Oswald arrives here by train from Helsinki, Finland, with a six-day visa. He intends to apply for citizenship.

BOSTON. Edward M. Kennedy's admission to the Massachusetts bar is certified in papers filed in State Supreme Court. His local address is 122 Bowdoin Street on the edge of the neighborhood called Beacon Hill. (This is the same address John Kennedy uses.) He explains his reason for entering the legal profession thus: "Service in public life can best be accomplished by an understanding of the legal process, its procedures, functions, and limitations. My ambition lies in the public service of this state."

18 October 1959
MILWAUKEE, WISCONSIN. The United States faces a dilemma in dealing with countries that are Soviet satellites, declares Senator Kennedy at a dinner honoring Democratic congressman Clement Zablocki of Wisconsin. World peace is necessary for such countries to keep what freedom they have. "No matter how bitter some feelings are...freedom behind the Iron Curtain and world peace are actually inextricably linked," Kennedy says.

20 October 1959
PORTLAND, OREGON. In the coming decades, Africa will be experiencing an industrial, political, and social revolution, claims Senator Kennedy in an address at Portland State College. Having been a catalyst to many changes, he continues, the United States cannot afford to sit by and watch.

21 October 1959
MOSCOW. Denied Russian citizenship and ordered out of the country, Lee Harvey Oswald attempts to kill himself by cutting his wrists. He is rushed to a hospital.

24 October 1959
BLOOMINGTON, ILLINOIS. Senator John F. Kennedy's three-day political tour through nine Illinois cities begins with a speech here.

SPRINGFIELD, ILLINOIS. Senator Kennedy sketches out a national farm program in an address to the Midwest Farm Conference of the Illinois Farmers Union.

JOLIET, ILLINOIS. In the evening, Senator Kennedy attends a local Democratic reception.

25 October 1959
ROCKFORD, ILLINOIS. Senator John F. Kennedy tells a meeting of Democratic county leaders that the United States is too conservative. The government and the public, he says, must be willing to accept new ideas.

26 October 1959
QUINCY, ILLINOIS. Senator John F. Kennedy addresses students and faculty at Quincy College.

United Press International.

Teddy, John and Bobby in Washington, D.C., March 1958.

PEORIA, ILLINOIS. Actions to help the nation's senior citizens are outlined in a speech given by Senator Kennedy at a Democratic rally. Among the programs he calls for are vocational training, a medical and dental care program, and the expansion of federal employment services.

DECATUR, ILLINOIS. Senator Kennedy concludes his tour of the state with a news conference here.

30 October 1959
OAKLAND, CALIFORNIA. Senator John F.

Kennedy arrives here to begin a four-day tour of the state. He speaks on the loyalty oath at Mills College.

31 October 1959
MOSCOW. Lee Harvey Oswald goes to the American Embassy and renounces his U.S. citizenship to a consular official.

2 November 1959
LOS ANGELES. Senator John F. Kennedy tells 2,000 students and faculty at U.C.L.A. that he opposes the conducting of nuclear tests by the United States. Lat-

er at a Jefferson-Jackson Day dinner held on the campus, both Senator Kennedy and Governor Edmund "Pat" Brown address an audience of 1,100. Brown is a possible "favorite son" candidate for the Democratic presidential nomination. In his speech, Kennedy says that the country is "in danger of losing our will to fight, to sacrifice, and to endure."

14 November 1959
MILWAUKEE, WISCONSIN. Addressing delegates to a convention of the state Democratic party, Senator John F. Kennedy says that a new administration is necessary to implement programs that will enable the United States to catch up to the Soviet Union.

15 November 1959
AUGUSTA, MAINE. At a banquet of the state Democratic party, Senator Kennedy declares that "the cause of freedom around the world" can best be served by a Democratic administration.

19 November 1959
INDEPENDENCE, MISSOURI. At the Harry S. Truman Library, Senator John F. Kennedy chats with former president Truman and tours the facilities. The Senator shows much interest in a replica of Truman's office when he was president. Kennedy had contributed nearly $30,000 to the library's construction.

KANSAS CITY, KANSAS. Addressing a Democratic banquet, Senator John F. Kennedy enumerates a number of areas in which Russia is ahead of the United States: education, military force, foreign trade, and science. He also notes that the Soviet Union beat the United States into space and that it has successfully disseminated communism in Indochina, the Middle East, and other areas around the world.

22 November 1959
BOSTON. At the 1959 annual dinner of the Greater Boston Association for Retarded Children at the Sherry Biltmore Hotel, Eunice Kennedy Shriver speaks on research in the field of retardation. She accepts a plaque given in recognition of the Kennedys' outstanding contribution to this work on behalf of the family.

28 November 1959
DENVER, COLORADO. At a Democratic dinner, Senator John F. Kennedy says it would be poor policy for the United States to contribute public funds for birth-control programs in other countries.

29 November 1959
CHEYENNE, WYOMING. At a press conference,

Senator John F. Kennedy says that the Taft-Hartley law should be revised to give the president alternative courses of action to avert labor disputes that threaten the nation's health and welfare.

30 November 1959
DENVER, COLORADO. The problems, the financing, and the future of American cities are a priority issue in the campaign for the 1960 election, Senator John F. Kennedy tells 1,100 delegates to an annual congress of the American Municipal Association. He says that party platforms have touched only lightly on the problems of cities.

5 December 1959
CAMBRIDGE, MASSACHUSETTS. A 15-page pamphlet entitled "Worse Than Futile" and containing an introduction by Senator John F. Kennedy is published by the *Harvard Crimson,* the daily student paper. In his introduction, Kennedy calls the "loyalty oath" of the National Defense Education Act "unworkable." He and Senator Clark (Democrat, Pa.) intend to push for repeal of the provision, he says. The pamphlet is distributed to faculty and students at some 1,000 colleges in the United States.

8 December 1959
BOSTON. In a statement issued to members of the Senate Select Committee on National Water Resources, which is holding hearings at the Federal Building, Senator John F. Kennedy makes a few recommendations. He urges the establishment of a cabinet-level agency to develop policy on resources and conservation, a crash program to develop an economical process for converting salt water into fresh water, a flood-insurance program, and a study of water pollution.

10 December 1959
PITTSBURGH, PENNSYLVANIA. In a closed luncheon at the Penn Sheraton Hotel with Governor David Lawrence among other Democratic leaders, John F. Kennedy warns that if he wins a number of presidential primaries next year and is rejected by the party because of his religion, it could damage the party. This is his last apperance in a twenty-one state political tour.

11 December 1959
SILVER SPRINGS, MARYLAND. In a speech before the Montgomery County Democratic Club, Senator John F. Kennedy claims that the Eisenhower administration has been passive and indecisive ever since the President took office in 1953.

17 December 1959

WASHINGTON, D.C. United Press International carries the news that Senator John F. Kennedy is sending letters dated 28 December 1959 to influential Democratic leaders and supporters stating that he will officially announce his candidacy for president on 2 January 1960. He is also inviting them to contribute ideas on issues for a Democratic platform. An excerpt from the letter reads: "Having visited all fifty states over the past several years and having talked to many political leaders, I believe I can win the nomination, and, most importantly, the election."

31 December 1959

NEW YORK. The Joseph P. Kennedy, Jr. Foundation commits a grant of $500,000 to the New Bedford (Massachusetts) Building Fund.

PRESIDENTIAL CANDIDATE 1960-1961

2 January 1960

WASHINGTON, D.C. "I am announcing today my candidacy for the Presidency of the United States." So declares Senator John F. Kennedy in a formal statement of his political intentions at a press conference held in the caucus room of the Senate Office Building. Before news reporters and enthusiastic supporters, Kennedy talks about how an executive leader can bring a "more vital life to society." He will enter the New Hampshire primary in March, he says, adding that under no conditions will he accept the party's nomination for vice-president. "I have developed an image of America," he says "as fulfilling a noble and historic role as the defender of freedom in a time of peril, and of the American people as confident, courageous, and persevering. It is with this image that I begin my campaign."

14 January 1960

WASHINGTON, D.C. In an address at the National Press Club, Senator John F. Kennedy calls President Eisenhower a "weak" leader. If elected president, he says, he would use the full powers of the office as strong presidents of the past have done.

7 February 1960

ALBUQUERQUE, NEW MEXICO. In a speech before the Western Conference, John Kennedy stresses the importance of candidates entering presidential primaries. If he loses in the latter, he says, he will withdraw from the race.

27 February 1960

BRONXVILLE, NEW YORK. A daughter, Kara Anne, is born to Joan (Bennett) and Edward Kennedy. She is their first child.

5 March 1960

MANCHESTER, NEW HAMPSHIRE. With the nation's first primary in New Hampshire to be held in three days, John F. Kennedy begins a political tour with a speech at St. Anselm's College. Later in the day, he will speak at a Democratic dinner in Nashua. His itinerary also includes an address tomorrow at Dartmouth College in Hanover and another the following day at the University of New Hampshire in Durham.

8 March 1960

NEW HAMPSHIRE. Senator John F. Kennedy wins his first victory in the state's Democratic presidential primary. He receives 43,372 votes, or 85.2 percent of the total vote.

9 March 1960

MAUSTON, WISCONSIN. With the second presidential primary coming up in Wisconsin next month, John Kennedy begins his political campaign with a speech in this small city. Over the next few weeks, he will speak in LaCrosse, Stevens Point, Appleton, Shawano, Madison, Cornell, Superior, Racine, Delavan, Milwaukee, Marinette, Manitowac, Dodgeville, and Beloit.

5 April 1960

WISCONSIN. John F. Kennedy wins the Wisconsin Democratic presidential primary, defeating Senator Hubert Humphrey of Minnesota by more than 100,000 votes. Kennedy receives 476,024 votes, or 56.5 percent of the total; Humphrey polls 366,753 votes.

11 April 1960

CHARLESTON, WEST VIRGINIA. Having completed brief tours through Indiana (7-8 April) and

Arizona (9 April), John F. Kennedy hits the campaign trail in West Virginia. The primary is to be held in two weeks. After a speech here, Kennedy will campaign throughout the state until 8 May, speaking in Beckley, Morgantown, Clarksburg, Fairmount, Wheeling, Bethany, Mount Hope, Huntington, Logan, Williamsburg, Glenwood Park, Mullens, Amherstdale, Hinton, Athens, Bluefield, St. Albans, South Charleston, Parkersburg, Weirton, Welch, White Sulphur Springs, Alderson, Ronceverte, Lewisburg, and Elkins. (Between these appearances, he will appear in Oregon, Indiana, and Nebraska.)

12 April 1960

ILLINOIS. Senator John F. Kennedy wins this state's Democratic presidential primary. With 34,332 votes, or 64.6 percent of the total, he defeats Adlai E. Stevenson (8,029 votes), Stuart Symington (5,744 votes), Hubert Humphrey (4,283 votes), and Lyndon B. Johnson (442 votes).

18 April 1960

FAIRMONT, WEST VIRGINIA. In a campaign speech, Senator John F. Kennedy attacks the issue of religion. "If religion is a valid issue in the presidential campaign," he says, "I shouldn't have served in the Senate and I shouldn't have been accepted by the United States Navy."

19 April 1960

WHEELING, WEST VIRGINIA. After previously refusing to debate Senator Hubert Humphrey, Senator Kennedy agrees to do so before West Virginia's Democratic presidential primary.

21 April 1960

WASHINGTON, D.C. At a conference of the American Society of Newspaper Editors, Senators John Kennedy and Hubert Humphrey both condemn making religion an issue in the presidential campaign. "I am not the Catholic candidate for president," Kennedy says. "I happen to believe that I can serve my nation as president and I also happen to have been born Catholic." Senator Humphrey declares, "I would not want to receive the vote of any American because my opponent or opponents worship in a particular church, whatever that church may be."

26 April 1960

MASSACHUSETTS. Senator John F. Kennedy wins the state's write-in Democratic presidential primary. Receiving 91,607 votes, or 92.4 percent of the total,

Kennedy overpowers the other candidates—Stevenson (4,684 votes), Humphrey (794 votes), Nixon (646 votes), Symington (443 votes), and Johnson (268 votes).

PENNSYLVANIA. Senator John F. Kennedy wins the state's Democratic presidential primary. Receiving 183,073 votes, or 71.3 percent of the total, he defeats Stevenson (29,660 votes), Nixon (15,136 votes), Humphrey (13,860 votes), Symington (6,791 votes), Johnson (2,918 votes), and Nelson A. Rockefeller (1,078 votes).

3 May 1960

INDIANA. Senator John F. Kennedy wins the state's Democratic presidential primary with 353,832 votes, or 81 percent of the total.

4 May 1960

CHARLESTON, WEST VIRGINIA. In a debate carried live on television throughout the state six days before the presidential primary, Senators John F. Kennedy and Hubert H. Humphrey face each other on such issues as a national fair trade law and increased income tax exemptions.

10 May 1960

WEST VIRGINIA. In a state where Catholics comprise little more than 5 percent of the population and Kennedy's Catholicism had become a political issue, Senator John F. Kennedy wins an upset victory over Senator Hubert Humphrey. The victory suggests that Kennedy's religion may not be as difficult an obstacle to overcome as had been thought. Kennedy receives 236,510 votes, or 60.8 percent of the total; Humphrey polls 152,187 votes, or 39.2 percent of the total. With this defeat, Senator Humphrey announces his withdrawal from the race.

NEBRASKA. Senator John F. Kennedy wins the state's Democratic presidential primary. He receives 80,408 votes, or 88.7 percent of the total, against Symington (4,083 votes), Humphrey (3,202 votes), Stevenson (1,368 votes), and Johnson (962 votes).

17 May 1960

MARYLAND. Senator John F. Kennedy makes a strong showing in capturing the state's Democratic presidential primary. He receives 201,769 votes, or 70.3 percent of the total, while Senator Wayne I. Morse of Oregon receives 49,420 votes. Begun six days earlier, his political campaign included speeches in Chestertown, Rockville, Hagerstown, Frederick, Baltimore, Elkton, Easton, College Park, Salisbury, and Cambridge.

20 May 1960

OREGON. Senator John F. Kennedy amasses greater strength as a candidate. In this state's primary, he polls 146,332 votes, or 51 percent of the total, against Morse (91,715 votes), Humphrey (16,319 votes), Symington (12,496 votes), Johnson (11,101 votes), and Stevenson (7,924 write-in votes).

25 May 1960

NEW YORK. The National Father's Day Committee names Robert F. Kennedy "Father of the Year" for 1960. He has four boys and three girls.

14 June 1960

WASHINGTON, D.C. In a major address delivered on the Senate floor, "A Time of Decision—Where Do We Go from Here?," John Kennedy declares that the next president should include Red China in nuclear test ban negotiations at Geneva.

16 June 1960

NEW YORK. During a guest apperance on the "Jack Paar Show," Senator John F. Kennedy says that he does not believe he has enough convention votes to win the Democratic presidential nomination on the first ballot.

18 June 1960

ABERDEEN, SOUTH DAKOTA. John F. Kennedy begins a two-day campaign tour through South Dakota, Colorado, and North Dakota with a speech given at a Democratic dinner here.

22 June 1960

NEW YORK. Addressing members of the state Liberal party, John F. Kennedy says that although Southern delegates to the Democratic National Convention will support Senator Lyndon B. Johnson, he expects to win the nomination without their votes.

2 July 1960

INDEPENDENCE, MISSOURI. Former president Harry S. Truman announces on national television that he has decided not to attend the Democratic National Convention as a delegate. The convention, he says, is a "prearranged affair" that is "controlled" by Kennedy's backers, and the delegates have "no opportunity for a democratic choice." Truman warns that in these troubled times the president should be "someone with the greatest possible maturity and experience," and he calls on Kennedy to put aside personal ambition and withdraw from the race.

4 July 1960

NEW YORK. In a nationwide telecast, Senator Kennedy responds to former president Harry Truman's charges of a rigged convention made two days earlier. Kennedy promises an open convention, and he cites a number of respected political leaders who succeeded before reaching the age of 44.

5 July 1960

WASHINGTON, D.C. With the Democratic National Convention only days away, Senator Lyndon B. Johnson of Texas, the Senate Majority Leader, formally enters the race for the party's presidential nomination.

9 July 1960

LOS ANGELES. A large, cheering crowd greets Senator John F. Kennedy at the airport upon his arrival for the Democratic National Convention.

11 July 1960

LOS ANGELES. The Democratic National Convention opens at the Los Angeles Memorial Sports Arena in the evening.

12 July 1960

LOS ANGELES. Lyndon Johnson and John Kennedy debate each other over such issues as agricultural policies, civil rights, and international peace on a nationally televised program. It is Johnson's final attempt to stop Kennedy's mounting delegate count.

13 July 1960

LOS ANGELES. John F. Kennedy wins the presidential nomination of the Democratic party on the first ballot. The tabulation is as follows:

CANDIDATE	VOTES (Needed to win, 761)
Kennedy (Massachusetts)	806
Johnson (Texas)	409
Symington (Missouri)	86
Stevenson (Illinois)	79.5
Meyner (New Jersey)	43
Humphrey (Minnesota)	41.5
Smathers (Florida)	30
Barnett (Mississippi)	23
Loveless (Iowa)	1.5
Brown (California)	.5
Rosellini (Washington)	.5
Faubus (Alabama)	.5

14 July 1960
LOS ANGELES. Senator Lyndon B. Johnson of Texas is chosen vice-presidential nominee by acclamation of the convention.

15 July 1960
LOS ANGELES. In accepting the presidential nomination of the Democratic party for president of the United States, John F. Kennedy says, "But the New Frontier of which I speak is not a set of promises—it is a set of challenges. It sums up not what I intend to *offer* the American people, but what I intend to *ask* of them."

17 July 1960
BOSTON. Some 13,000 people are on hand to cheer Senator John F. Kennedy as he arrives at Logan Airport following his presidential nomination in Los Angeles. Kennedy's plane carries numerous family members and campaign workers.

19 July 1960
NEW YORK. *Look* magazine publishes an article entitled "The Kennedys: Family Political Machine." The article reveals in words and pictures how family members worked in Kennedy's presidential campaign.

28 July 1960
CHICAGO. Three days after its opening, the Republican National Convention ends with Vice-President Richard M. Nixon nominated for president on the first ballot and Senator Henry Cabot Lodge, Jr., unanimously nominated as his running mate.

NEW YORK. The three television networks offer Vice-President Richard M. Nixon and Senator John F. Kennedy, the Republican and Democratic presidential candidates, free television exposure in prime time if they will meet in person-to-person debate.

HYANNIS PORT, MASSACHUSETTS. His presidential campaign lagging, Democratic candidate John F. Kennedy quickly accepts the networks' offer to debate his Republican opponent on television.

31 July 1960
CHICAGO. Presidential candidate Richard M. Nixon accepts the networks' proposal to debate his Democratic opponent on television.

2 August 1960
HYDE PARK, NEW YORK. Eleanor Roosevelt announces her endorsement of the Kennedy-Johnson ticket.

3 September 1960
BOSTON. After a two-month vacation in Europe, Joseph P. Kennedy returns to the country with his niece, Ann Gargan. His wife Rose plans to return next week.

SAN FRANCISCO. John F. Kennedy speaks at a kick-off rally to launch a ten-day political campaign through the Western and Midwestern United States. During this period, he will make major appearances in Alaska, Michigan, Idaho, Washington, Oregon, California, and Texas, delivering forty speeches in more than thirty cities.

4 September 1960
BOSTON. A son, William Kennedy, is born to Jean (Kennedy) and Stephen Edward Smith at St. Elizabeth's Hospital. He is their second child and second son.

12 September 1960
HOUSTON, TEXAS. A nation in which religion is clearly estranged from politics is the theme of a speech given by John F. Kennedy before the Greater Houston Ministerial Association at the Rice Hotel. "I believe in an America," the Senator says, "where the separation of church and state are absolute...[an America] that is officially neither Catholic, Protestant, nor Jewish...where no public official either requests or accepts instructions on public policy from the Pope, the National Council of Churches, or any other ecclesiastical source...where all men and all churches are created equal." He says that if he becomes president, he will make decisions "with what my conscience tells me to be the national interest and without regard to outside religious pressures or dictates."

22 September 1960
SIOUX FALLS, SOUTH DAKOTA. Speaking at the National Plowing Contest, Senator John F. Kennedy pledges a farm program that will provide "full parity of income for the American farmer." He also campaigns in Fort Dodge and Mitchell.

26 September 1960
NEW YORK. In an address before the General Assembly of the United Nations, Prime Minister Fidel Castro assails the United States for its policies toward Cuba and blasts the American presidential candidates. When he calls John Kennedy an "illiterate and ignorant millionaire," General Assembly president Boland cuts him off.

CHICAGO. The first of four nationally televised one-hour "debates" between presidential contenders Richard M. Nixon and John F. Kennedy is held in a local televi-

United Press International.

John and Jacqueline Kennedy take a cruise on the *Marlin* in Nantucket Sound, 19 July 1960.

sion studio. While debates have been political tradition in the United States since the time of Lincoln and Douglas, this is the first presidential debate in history to be broadcast on national television.

Kennedy and Nixon stand at lecterns several yards apart, with moderator Howard K. Smith seated between them. A panel of newsmen and television cameras face them. The first session is on domestic issues, and each candidate has approximately 8 minutes for opening remarks. After taking correspondents' questions, the candidates may make 3-minute closing statements.

Speaking first, Kennedy declares that freedom around the world depends on the strength of American society. But the country is not as strong as it should be, and he is not satisfied with its progress. He cites poor economic growth, failure to fully develop natural resources, and other causes as reasons why the country is at a standstill. In his opening statement, Nixon agrees that the country needs to move ahead but argues that America has not, under the Eisenhower administration, been standing still. He rebuts Kennedy's points, itemizing progress made during Eisenhower's term. After answering ques-

tions on issues such as their political experience, farm questions, and reducing the federal debt, Nixon and Kennedy make their summations. Nixon says that Kennedy would rely too much on the federal government; Kennedy says that society has much to do to meet its needs and to insure freedom. Approximately 60 million people watch the program.

27 September 1960
CLEVELAND, OHIO.   The 1960 elections are both historically important and the start of a new era, declares Senator Kennedy at a steer roast attended by 5,000 people. He says that the country cannot withstand another term of divided government under a Republican administration. He also speaks in Painesville, Lorraine, Mansfield, Akron, and Canton.

7 October 1960
WASHINGTON, D.C.   Richard Nixon and John Kennedy face off in the second nationally televised presidential debate. The 1-hour program, moderated by

Frank McGee of NBC News, has a new format. First one candidate answers a question by a member of the panel of reporters, then the other responds to his opponent's answer. The order of question and response is then reversed. Reporters may ask questions on any issue.

Responding to questions, the two candidates criticize each other on issues such as civil rights and foreign policy. Nixon is asked to state his intentions on civil rights if he becomes president. He answers that government contracts should be disbursed without regard to race, creed, or color, that the federal government should assist school districts that want to integrate, and that the president's leadership will serve to help the situation. Kennedy points out that Nixon failed to say what he would do and how he would provide fair employment.

They also clash over policy on the question of Quemoy and Matsu, two islands in the Formosa Strait near mainland China that are threatened by Chinese Communists. Kennedy says it would be "unwise" to be dragged into a conflict that could lead to a world war over two islands that are not strategically defensible. Nixon says they should be defended under all circumstances, not because "these two little pieces of real estate" are important, but because of the principle involved. If Chinese Nationalist sympathizers are forced off these islands, he says, the Communists will not be satisfied with these two tiny islands, and a "chain reaction" of conquest will begin.

10 October 1960

NEW YORK. Robert F. Kennedy is the subject of a cover story in *Time* magazine entitled "The Kennedy Strategy: Campaign Manager Bobby Kennedy."

11 October 1960

CHICAGO. Sargent Shriver, Jr., resigns as president of the city's board of education in order to spend more time on Kennedy's campaign.

13 October 1960

NEW YORK and LOS ANGELES. The third debate between presidential candidates Richard Nixon and John Kennedy is held. This time Kennedy is in a Manhattan television studio and Nixon is in a Hollywood studio. They face each other on television monitors. Answering questions posed by reporters, they discuss issues such as United States policy on Quemoy and Matsu and Berlin, disarmament, the nation's budget, and an oil-depletion allowance.

14 October 1960

ANN ARBOR, MICHIGAN. Following the debate, some 10,000 students, who have been waiting for Kennedy, shout his name in greeting as the Senator ascends the steps of the student union at the University of Michigan at 2:00 A.M. In an extemporaneous speech, he asks the large crowd of students how many would be willing to devote years to service in Africa, Asia, or Latin America—his first reference to a peace corps. The audience cheers, and Kennedy declares that efforts to contribute must be greater than in the past.

19 October 1960

NEW YORK. Vice-President Richard M. Nixon releases a white paper, a list of Kennedy's campaign statements criticizing the Eisenhower administration, the Republicans, and Nixon himself. Responding to each allegation, Nixon sets the record straight.

21 October 1960

NEW YORK. Senator John F. Kennedy rebuts each of the points in Vice-President Nixon's white paper.

NEW YORK. The fourth of the "great debates" between Vice-President Nixon and Senator Kennedy takes place. The format for this debate is the same as that of the first, except that each candidate has 4½ minutes for his closing. The hour-long program is broadcast over network radio and television; Quincy Howe, of ABC News, moderates.

Nixon is the first to speak. One issue—how peace can be kept without surrender and how freedom can be extended without war—stands above all others, he says. The nation's military strength must be increased so that it can destroy the war-making capability of any other country. He states that the nation's economy must grow, and that the right foreign policy must be formulated. Senator Kennedy addresses the question of Quemoy and Matsu, then discusses why America's prestige has suffered and why its relative strength is not growing. In closing, Kennedy says that he is running for president because the country has stood still under the Republicans and he sees a great opportunity to make it move forward under the proper leadership. Nixon concludes by saying that the country is not standing still but that it must extend freedom. This means a stronger military, a forward-moving economy, and further progress in civil rights.

26 October 1960

ATLANTA, GEORGIA. John Kennedy calls Coretta Scott King to say that he will do all he can to help her husband, Dr. Martin Luther King, Jr., who has been arrested and jailed. Richard Nixon makes no comment on the King imprisonment.

MICHIGAN. Kennedy campaigns throughout the day, addressing crowds in Mount Clemens, Warren, Rosedale, Hamtramck, and Detroit.

27 October 1960

REIDSVILLE, GEORGIA. Civil-rights leader Martin Luther King, Jr., is released from Georgia State Prison on $2,200 bond. It is reported that Robert Kennedy had called and appealed to DeKalb County judge J. Oscar Mitchell to free King.

2 November 1960

SAN FRANCISCO. Senator John F. Kennedy delivers a speech at the Cow Palace on foreign policy. Declaring that "we can push a button to start the next war—but there is no pushbutton magic to bring a just and lasting peace," he says that the United States has been deficient in seeking peace in three vital areas: in disarmament planning, in the diplomatic and foreign service, and in technical assistance to underdeveloped nations. He outlines methods for resolving these problems, including "a Peace Corps of talented young men willing and able to serve their country...for three years as an alternative to peacetime selective service....We cannot discontinue training our young men as soldiers of war," he says, "but we also need them as 'ambassadors of peace.'"

NEW YORK. Over the CBS television network, Henry Fonda interviews Jacqueline Kennedy in Washington, D.C., and John Kennedy in Los Angeles in a program sponsored by Citizens for Kennedy-Johnson. Movies and pictures of the Kennedy family are shown.

6 November 1960

THE UNITED STATES. With the presidential election two days away, two million pamphlets describing Senator Kennedy's intervention to secure the release from prison of civil-rights leader Dr. Martin Luther King, Jr., are distributed to black churches.

THE NORTHEAST. Throughout the day, John Kennedy addresses crowds in eight cities in Connecticut, New York, New Jersey, and Maine.

7 November 1960

BOSTON. The presidential campaign of Senator John Kennedy winds up with a rally after a final whirlwind tour through New England. Earlier in the day, Kennedy spoke in Providence, Rhode Island; Springfield, Massachusetts; Hartford, Connecticut; and Manchester, New Hampshire. Thousands greet him here as he makes his way by motorcade to the Boston Garden, where he addresses some 22,000 screaming, chanting, roaring fans.

8 November 1960

THE UNITED STATES. John Fitzgerald Kennedy is elected president of the United States. He wins by the smallest plurality—under 115,000 popular votes—since Benjamin Harrison defeated Grover Cleveland by fewer than 100,000 votes in the election of 1888. The results of the election are as follows:

CANDIDATE	ELECTORAL VOTES*	POPULAR VOTE
John F. Kennedy (Democrat)	303	34,221,344
Richard M. Nixon (Republican)	219	34,106,671
Eric Hass (Socialist Labor)	—	47,522

9 November 1960

LOS ANGELES. In the morning, Vice-President Richard M. Nixon concedes the election to John F. Kennedy.

HYANNIS PORT, MASSACHUSETTS. In the living room of Joseph P. Kennedy's home, President-elect John F. Kennedy, his wife, his parents, and his brothers and sisters and their spouses pose for photographs. Shortly afterward, the family leaves for the Hyannis Port Armory, where, in a nationally televised speech, Kennedy acknowledges his victory. With him is his father, who had not appeared with him at all in public during the campaign. Making light of the momentous days ahead, President-elect Kennedy says: "So now my wife and I prepare for a new administration and a new baby."

25 November 1960

WASHINGTON, D.C. A son, John Fitzgerald, Jr., is born to Jacqueline (Bouvier) and President-elect John F. Kennedy. He is their second child and first son, and the eighteenth grandchild of Joseph and Rose Kennedy. Born at Georgetown University Hospital, he is delivered by Caesarean section. The baby had not been expected until mid-December.

3 December 1960

WASHINGTON, D.C. John F. Kennedy, Jr., is taken out of the incubator where he had been placed after his birth nine days ago due to a lung problem.

---

* Harry F. Byrd, Democrat, Virginia, received electoral votes from six unpledged electors in Alabama and eight in Mississippi, plus one vote from a "faithless" elector from Oklahoma, for a total of fifteen. In victory, Kennedy is the first Roman Catholic elected president, the youngest—at 43—elected to the office, and the first president born in the twentieth century.

6 December 1960

LEOPOLDVILLE, THE CONGO. Representing his brother's new administration, Edward Kennedy arrives here with members of the Senate Foreign Affairs Relations Committee to study the chaotic conditions in this country. The Republic of the Congo's provisional constitution was signed on 19 May 1960.

WASHINGTON, D.C. President-elect John F. Kennedy confers with President Eisenhower at the White House. They discuss political issues and the transition to the new administration.

13 December 1960

WASHINGTON, D.C. In a conversation with business leaders at the White House, President Eisenhower attributes John Kennedy's slim presidential victory to the black vote he obtained by "a couple of phone calls." This is an apparent reference to Robert Kennedy's telephone call in October to a judge in DeKalb County, Georgia, to obtain the release of civil-rights leader Martin Luther King, Jr., from the Georgia State Prison.

15 December 1960

WEST PALM BEACH, FLORIDA. Secret Service agents arrest Richard Paul Pavlick, 73, on charges that he planned to kill President-elect John Kennedy. Pavlick had previously been treated in a mental hospital.

16 December 1960

WASHINGTON, D.C. An announcement is made by President-elect Kennedy that he has appointed his brother Robert as attorney general of the United States. This immediately sparks criticism, anger, and charges of nepotism. Many feel that Robert, 35, does not have sufficient legal experience for such an important job.

19 December 1960

THE UNITED STATES. In each state capital, members of the Electoral College assemble to formally elect John F. Kennedy and Lyndon B. Johnson president and vice-president.

22 December 1960

WASHINGTON, D.C. President-elect John F. Kennedy resigns from the United States Senate, where he had served since 3 January 1953.

27 December 1960

BOSTON. Benjamin Atwood Smith II is appointed by Governor Foster Furcolo to fill the Senate seat vacated by President-elect John F. Kennedy. Kennedy had sug-gested that Smith, who had been his roommate at Harvard and who had served in the Navy during World War II, succeed him. Previously Smith had been mayor of Gloucester, Massachusetts.

31 December 1960

WASHINGTON, D.C. The Joseph P. Kennedy, Jr. Foundation commits a grant of $500,000 to the Massachusetts General Hospital for research in the field of mental retardation.

2 January 1961

WASHINGTON, D.C. The United States, under President Dwight Eisenhower, breaks diplomatic relations with Cuba.

6 January 1961

WASHINGTON, D.C. The vote of the Electoral College, which officially elects John F. Kennedy president and Lyndon B. Johnson vice-president, is counted by Congress.

9 January 1961

BOSTON. As he leaves to assume his official duties, President-elect John F. Kennedy delivers a farewell address to the Massachusetts legislature: "For of those to whom much is given, much is required. And when at some future date the high court of history sits in judgment on each one of us—recording whether in our brief span of service we fulfilled our responsibilities to the state—our success or failure, in whatever office we may hold, will be measured by the answers to four questions: First, were we truly men of courage...secondly, were we truly men of judgment...third, were we truly men of integrity...finally, were we truly men of dedication? Courage, judgment, integrity, dedication...these are the qualities which, with God's help, this son of Massachusetts hopes will characterize our Government's conduct in the four stormy years that lie ahead. Humbly, I ask His help in this undertaking. But aware that on earth His will is worked by man, I ask for your help and your prayers, as I embark on this new and solemn journey."

17 Janaury 1961

WASHINGTON, D.C. After two terms in office, President Dwight D. Eisenhower speaks to the country and bids farewell.

President John Fitzgerald Kennedy on 1 November 1962.

FOUR

CAMELOT

1961 · 1964

THE FIRST YEAR
1961-1962

20 January 1961

WASHINGTON, D.C. "I, John Fitzgerald Kennedy, do solemnly swear, that I will faithfully execute the office of the President of the United States, and will to the best of my ability, preserve, protect and defend the Constitution of the United States, so help me God." With these words, John F. Kennedy, 43, takes the oath of office from Chief Justice Earl Warren and becomes the thirty-fifth president of the United States. Lyndon Baines Johnson, 51, is sworn in as vice-president.

The ceremony, beginning at 12:22 P.M. , takes place on a freezing winter day; several inches of snow fell the night before, but the streets have been cleared by the Army. Robert Frost reads his poem "In the Clearing." Richard Cardinal Cushing delivers the invocation.

The changing of the guard begins as President Kennedy declares in his inaugural address, "Let the word go forth from this time and place, to friend and foe alike, that the torch has been passed to a new generation of Americans...." He pledges to defend freedom: "We shall pay any price, bear any burden, meet any hardship, support any friend, oppose any foe, in order to assure the survival and success of liberty"; work for peace: "To those nations who make themselves our adversary we offer not a pledge but a request...that both sides begin anew the quest for peace, before the dark power of destruction unleashed by science engulf all humanity in planned or accidental self-destruction"; and cooperate in space exploration, medical research, and culture: "Let both sides seek to invoke the wonders of science...eradicate disease...encourage the arts...."

He tells the nation that the energy they bring to defending freedom will light the country, "and the glow from that fire can truly light the world." He concludes, "And so, my fellow Americans, ask not what your country can do for you. Ask what you can do for your country."

21 January 1961

WASHINGTON, D.C. As the day begins, President Kennedy continues to make the rounds of the inaugural balls. At 2:00 A.M. , he arrives at the home of columnist Joseph W. Alsop for a private party, then retires to the White House at 3:40 A.M. At 8:52 A.M. , he arrives in his office for his first day of work as chief executive.

His first meeting is at 9:00 A.M. with appointments secretary Kenneth O'Donnell (they visit various offices on the first floor), followed by meetings with Brig. Gen. Andrew J. Goodpastor; Andrew Hatcher; former president Harry S. Truman. Chicago mayor Richard Daley and his wife and children; Theodore Sorenson (special counsel to the president); Myer Feldman (deputy assistant to the special counsel); William J. Hopkins (executive clerk of the White House); Dr. Janet J. Travell (his personal physician); John Bailey (chairman of the Democratic National Committee); and Ralph Dugan and Lawrence O'Brien (special assistants to the president). The President signs his first executive order, no. 10914, providing for more and better surplus food to be distributed to needy families.

At 1:20 P.M. at the Mayflower Hotel, President Kennedy addresses the Democratic National Committee. He expresses appreciation for everyone's support during the campaign, singling out Senator Henry M. Jackson.

Cabinet members are sworn in at a ceremony in the East Room of the White House at 4:00 P.M. Taking office are: Dean Rusk (New York), secretary of state; C. Douglas Dillon (New Jersey), secretary of the treasury; Robert S. McNamara (Michigan), secretary of defense; Robert F. Kennedy (Massachusetts), attorney general; J. Edward Day (California), postmaster general; Stewart L. Udall (Arizona), secretary of the interior; Orville L. Freeman (Michigan), secretary of agriculture; Luther H. Hodges (North Carolina), secretary of commerce; Arthur J. Goldberg (Illinois), secretary of labor; Abraham A. Ribicoff (Connecticut), secretary of health, education, and welfare; and Adlai E. Stevenson (Illinois), ambassador to the United Nations.

WASHINGTON, D.C. President John F. Kennedy responds to a message received yesterday from Premier Nikita S. Khruschev and President Leonid I. Brezhnev of the USSR congratulating him on his inauguration. He expresses hope that through joint efforts, the Soviet Union and the United States "shall succeed in achieving a fundamental improvement in relations...and a normalization of the whole international situation" and be able to "remove existing suspicion and distrust and cultivate seeds of friendship and practical cooperation between our peoples." President Kennedy tells the Soviet leaders that "we are ready and anxious to cooperate with all who are prepared to join in genuine dedication to the assurance of a peaceful and a more fruitful life for all mankind."

22 January 1961

WASHINGTON, D.C. On his first Sunday in office, President Kennedy attends mass at Holy Trinity

John and Jacqueline Kennedy at a news conference, following the Senator's upset victory over Hubert Humphrey in the West Virginia Democratic presidential primary, 11 May 1960.

United Press International.

Church, 3514 O Street, N.W., with his brother Ted and Paul "Red" Fay, who will soon be confirmed as under secretary of the Navy. Later he meets at the White House with poet Robert Frost, and entertains Franklin Roosevelt, Jr., and his wife at dinner.

23 January 1961

WASHINGTON, D.C. Today is President Kennedy's first full day of business in the White House. A morning meeting takes place with Dean Rusk; Robert McNamara; McGeorge Bundy (special assistant to the president for National Security Affairs);, General Lyman L. Lemnitzer (chairman of the Joint Chiefs of Staff); Paul Nitze (Department of Defense); Chester Bowles (under secretary of state); and Jeffrey Parsons (Department of State). Governor Stephen McNichols of Colorado presents Kennedy with a fishing license later in the day.

WASHINGTON, D.C. Attorney General Robert F. Kennedy launches a major federal probe into organized crime.

24 January 1961

WASHINGTON, D.C. In the morning, President Kennedy meets with Vice-President Johnson and attends the first Legislative Leaders' meeting of his administration. Present with him and Vice-President Johnson are Speaker of the House Sam Rayburn (Texas); Representative Carl Albert (Oklahoma); Representative John W. McCormack (Massachusetts); Senator Hubert H. Humphrey (Minnesota); Senator George A. Smathers (Florida); and Senator Mike Mansfield (Montana). President Kennedy also meets with the Food-for-Peace Task Force, including its director, George McGovern, and Murray Lincoln and James Symington, and issues an executive order (no. 10915) amending previous execu-

United Press International.

Eunice Shriver, Pat Lawford, and Ethel Kennedy follow election returns in the presidential election, at Hyannis Port, 8 November 1960.

tive orders to describe further the responsibilities of the director of the Food-for-Peace program. In a memorandum to federal agencies on the director's duties, he writes, "American agricultural abundance offers a great opportunity for the United States to promote the interests of peace in a significant way and to play an important role in helping to provide a more adequate diet for peoples around the world."

25 January 1961
WASHINGTON, D.C. President Kennedy meets with the Joint Chiefs of Staff. They are the following: General Lyman Lemnitzer, chairman; General George Decker, U.S. Army; General Thomas White, U.S. Air Force; General David M. Sharp, commandant of the Marine Corps; and Admiral Arleigh A. Burke, chief of Naval Operations.

At 6:00 P.M. , John Kennedy holds his first presidential news conference, which is televised live from the State Department Auditorium. He announces that the U.S. government "has decided to increase substantially its contribution towards relieving the famine in the Congo" and that Capt. Freeman P. Olmstead and Capt. John R. McKone, the RP-47 fliers who survived after their plane was shot down by Russia over the Barents Sea on 1 July 1960, "have been released by the Soviet government and are now enroute to the United States."

26 January 1961
WASHINGTON, D.C. The Kennedy administration's first cabinet meeting is held. In addition to President Kennedy, Vice-President Johnson, and members of the cabinet, Walter W. Heller, chairman of the Council of Economic Advisers, David E. Bell, director of the Bureau of the Budget, Frederick Dutton, special assistant to the President, and Ted Sorenson also attend.

At 2:30 P.M. , the President and McGeorge Bundy leave the White House for the Central Intelligence Agency at 2430 E Street, N.W. CIA director Allen W. Dulles greets them and, at a meeting in the second floor conference room with Robert McNamara, Walt Whitman Rostow (Bundy's assistant), General C. P. Cabell (deputy director of the CIA), and other officials in attendance, briefs President Kennedy on CIA operations and on "trouble spots" around the world.

27 January 1961
ANDREWS AIR FORCE BASE, MARYLAND. President Kennedy welcomes Air Force captains John McKone and Freeman Olmstead, who had been detained by Soviet authorities since 1 July 1960 after their RB-47 aircraft was shot down. The two flyers and their families are later received at the White House by President and Mrs. Kennedy, Vice-President Johnson, Senator Kenneth Keating (New York), and others.

NEW YORK. *Time* magazine publishes a cover story entitled "The Inauguration of John Fitzgerald Kennedy."

28 January 1961

WASHINGTON, D.C. President and Mrs. Kennedy attend a private dinner party at the residence of Senator and Mrs. John Sherman Cooper at 2900 N Street, N.W. Among the guests are Adlai Stevenson, Ambassador Averell Harriman, David K. Bruce, newspaper publisher Philip Graham, and Joseph Alsop.

29 January 1961

WASHINGTON, D.C. Chief Justice Earl Warren swears in fifteen presidential appointees in the East Room of the White House. Among the new appointees are Byron White (deputy attorney general); Walter Heller, Kermit Gordon, and James Tobin (Council of Economic Advisers); Cyrus Vance (general counsel of the Defense Department); Paul Nitze (assistant secretary of defense); and George Docking (director of the Import-Export Bank). President Kennedy tells them that their "extremely important" work is "vital to the success of this administration and...the country."

30 January 1961

WASHINGTON, D.C. Ten days after taking office, President Kennedy delivers his first State of the Union message to Congress. He says that he speaks "in an hour of national peril and national opportunity," then describes measures he will propose to Congress to improve the "disturbing" state of the economy: (1) help for the unemployed and needy; (2) legislation to provide health care for the elderly under Social Security; (3) increased support for an efficient educational system; and (4) an effective attack on organized crime and juvenile delinquency. But the "greatest challenge" today, he says, is that posed by "the world that lies beyond the Cold War." The country must strengthen its military defenses, he says, and he promises to ask Congress for programs to "assist the economic, educational, and social development of other countries." He will also ask for increased United States support of the United Nations. "Life in 1961 will not be easy," he says. "Wishing will not solve the world's problems....The hopes of all mankind" rest upon all people who share "our hopes for freedom and the future."

31 January 1961

NEW YORK. The "Today" show on NBC-TV airs an interview of President Kennedy by Dave Garroway, had been taped on 28 January in the White House's Broadcast Room. The occasion is the celebration of the one hundred fiftieth anniversary of the Massachusetts General Hospital, on whose board of overseers the President has served since 1947.

February 1961

PLEASANTVILLE, NEW YORK. *Reader's Digest* reruns John Hersey's article on Lt. John Kennedy and the PT-109 incident. The article, condensed from the original version in *The New Yorker*, first appeared in the *Digest* in its August 1944 issue.

1 February 1961

WASHINGTON, D.C. Starting in the morning, President Kennedy meets first with William McChesney Martin, chairman of the Board of Governors of the Federal Reserve System, then with the Council of Economic Advisers, and finally with the National Security Council. At the National Security Council meeting are Vice-President Johnson; Robert McNamara; Dean Rusk; C. Douglas Dillon; Lyman Lemnitzer; David Bell; McGeorge Bundy; Allen W. Dulles; Jerome Weisner; James Lay, Jr.; General Chester V. Clifton; Paul Nitze; Chester Bowles; Robert Amory of the CIA; George McGhee; Edward R. Murrow; and Frank Ellis, director designate of the Office of Civil and Defense Mobilization.

In a televised press conference at the State Department at 4:00 P.M. , the President announces that "the restrictions recently imposed on travel abroad of dependents of service personnel will be lifted as soon as the necessary detailed arrangements can be made" and that "five pilot projects for food stamp distribution...in areas of maximum chronic unemployment" are about to be set up.

2 February 1961

WASHINGTON, D.C. President Kennedy sends a special message to Congress in which he proposes measures "both to alleviate the distress arising from unsatisfactory performance of the economy and to stimulate economic recovery and growth." He submits a program that includes furthering the "complementary effectiveness of debt management and monetary policy"; lowering maximum interest rates on loans insured by the Federal Housing Administration; extending the duration of unemployment insurance benefits; expanding job counseling and placement services in economically depressed areas; expediting implementation of food-stamp programs for poor families in certain depressed areas; recommending to Congress improvements in the Old-Age, Survivors, and Disability Insurance Program; and urging Congress to increase the minimum wage.

3 February 1961

WASHINGTON, D.C. A bound copy of speeches, remarks, and statements he made as senator from Massachusetts between 1 August and 7 November 1960 is presented to President Kennedy by Senator Ralph W. Yarborough of Texas. The President releases a statement following a meeting with Secretary of HEW Abraham Ribicoff in which he announces various federal efforts to help Cuban refugees in southern Florida. In the evening, the President and Paul Fay see the movie *Spartacus* at the Warner Theater at 13th and E streets, N.W.

6 February 1961

BOSTON. Edward M. Kennedy, 29, begins work as an assistant district attorney for Suffolk County (encompassing Boston, Chelsea, Revere, and the town of Winthrop). He serves under District Attorney Garrett H. Byrne.

WASHINGTON, D.C. President Kennedy sends a special message to Congress in which he offers proposals to "cure" the deficit in the country's international balance of payments and to "check the outflow of gold."

7 February 1961

WASHINGTON, D.C. President Kennedy attends a reception in honor of Speaker of the House Sam Rayburn at the home of Representative Clark W. Thompson at 3301 Massachusetts Avenue, N.W.

8 February 1961

WASHINGTON, D.C. During a press conference at the State Department Building, President Kennedy announces that he has directed the surgeon general to establish a Child Health Center within the Public Health Service.

9 February 1961

WASHINGTON, D.C. At a prayer breakfast sponsored by the International Council on Leadership at the Mayflower Hotel, President Kennedy pays a brief tribute to religious freedom and religious conviction. He says that every American president "in his own way has placed special trust in God. Those who were strongest intellectually were also strongest spiritually." The President sends to Congress a special message for improving the health-care system in the United States. He proposes an increase in health insurance benefits under Social Security; federal grants for construction of nursing homes and nursing homeservices; a program of federal aid to help medical and dental schools build new facilities and provide scholarships for students; and provisions for additional federal funds to help handicapped and needy children and to expand medical research.

11 February 1961

WASHINGTON, D.C. President Kennedy attends the swearing-in of Robert C. Weaver as administrator of the Housing and Home Finance Agency. "There are," the President says, "according to our latest Census Bureau figures, over 25 million Americans who live in substandard housing. It is the ambition of this administration to try to provide decent housing for all American families, and Mr. Weaver's responsibility will be to lead this important national effort." Later in the day, the President leaves by helicopter for Glen Ora, his estate in Middleburg, Virginia, to join his wife and children for the rest of the weekend.

13 February 1961

WASHINGTON, D.C. At the Sheraton Park Hotel, President Kennedy delivers an address before the National Industrial Conference Board. He says that government and business must ally themselves in "three areas of common concern: economic growth, plant modernization, and price stability."

14 February 1961

WASHINGTON, D.C. Prime Minister Viggo Kampmann of Denmark is honored at a White House luncheon. Later, in the Cabinet Room, members of the Mexico-United States Interparliamentary Group present a silver tray to President Kennedy as a token of friendship from Governor Juan Gil Preciado of the state of Jalisco.

15 February 1961

WASHINGTON, D.C. At a news conference, President Kennedy warns the Soviet Union against interfering with the United Nations peacekeeping efforts in the Congo. (Premier Patrice Lumumba had been slain on 12 February.) "I would conceive it to be the duty of the United States," he says, "and indeed, all members of the United Nations, to defend the charter of the United Nations by opposing any attempt by any government to intervene unilaterally in the Congo." The President also announces that today the United States has recognized the new government of El Salvador. He also announces various efforts being made by his administration to alleviate "the very serious problem of unemployment."

16 February 1961

GERMANTOWN, MARYLAND. President Kennedy is briefed on matters of importance at the Atomic

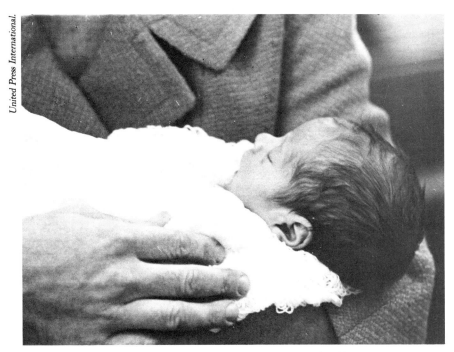

Thirteen-day old John F. Kennedy, Jr., is christened at Georgetown
University Hospital Chapel, 8 December 1960.

Energy Commission. He is with AEC chairman Dr. Glenn T. Seaborg, McGeorge Bundy, Dr. Jerome Weisner, and Brig. Gen. Chester Clifton. Throughout the morning various officials join the group for briefings on reactor development, weapons, research biology, and international affairs.

The President signs executive order number 10918, creating the President's Advisory Committee on Labor-Management Policy which, he says, will advise him "with respect to policies...that will promote free and responsible collective bargaining, industrial peace, sound wage and price policies, higher standards of living, and increased productivity."

The President also sends a bill to Congress asking for a special feed-grain program for 1961 that would alleviate "the accumulation of a burdensome and dangerous surplus" of "commodities for which there is no adequate outlet." In the evening, he and Mrs. Kennedy, with Senator and Mrs. John Sherman Cooper, see the movie *The World of Apu* at the Dupont Theater.

17 February 1961
WASHINGTON, D.C. President Kennedy meets with the foreign minister of the Federal Republic of Ger-

many, Dr. Heinrich von Brentan, to discuss matters of mutual concern, including the North Atlantic Alliance and the international payments situation.

20 February 1961
WASHINGTON, D.C. President Kennedy sends a draft of the Distressed Area Redevelopment bill to Speaker of the House Sam Rayburn. He also sends to the Speaker and to Lyndon Johnson, who, as vice-president, is president of the Senate, a bill to amend the Social Security Act and give "needed impetus" to the administration's economic recovery program. The President meets informally with Prime Minister John Diefenbaker of Canada to review defense and security matters, the United Nations, and cooperation on economic matters.

The President also sends to Congress a special message on education that describes the administration's goals of setting "a new standard of excellence in education and the availability of such excellence to all who are willing and able to pursue it." He recommends legislation to assist in building new classrooms, residential housing, libraries, and other facilities, and to help establish scholarships and low-interest rate loans for students in higher education.

United Press International.

Seated underneath a portrait of Dolly Madison, wife of the fourth U.S. President, First Lady Jacqueline Kennedy appears before a television camera in the White House to tape a salute to the National Gallery for the TV program, *Accent.*

21 February 1961

WASHINGTON, D.C. President Kennedy presents the Medal of Freedom to NATO Secretary General Paul Henri Spaak. At the Health, Education, and Welfare Department Auditorium, the President addresses delegates to the Youth Fitness Conference. "We do not want in the United States a nation of spectators," he says. "We want a nation of participants in the vigorous life."

22 February 1961

CHEVY CHASE, MARYLAND. President Kennedy plays nine holes of golf with Paul "Red" Fay and senators George Smathers and Stuart Symington at the Chevy Chase Country Club.

23 February 1961

WASHINGTON, D.C. President Kennedy sends to

Congress a special message on conservation and the development of natural resources in the United States. "Wise investment in a resource program today," he says, "will return vast dividends tomorrow, and failures to act now may be opportunities lost forever." The program offers proposals for forest lands, electric power, water, saltwater conservation, water- and air-pollution control, and national parks and seashore areas. The President also meets with Representative Adam Clayton Powell, chairman of the House Committee on Education and Labor; FBI Director J. Edgar Hoover and Attorney General Robert Kennedy; and the Joint Chiefs of Staff.

24 February 1961
WASHINGTON, D.C. President Kennedy and Prime Minister Robert Gorden Menzies of Australia meet to discuss peace efforts, the UN, the situation in the Congo, and other international matters.

WASHINGTON, D.C. A task force, headed by R. Sargent Shriver, Jr., submits a report on the establishment of a Peace Corps to President Kennedy, along with a recommendation that the project be undertaken.

26 February 1961
THE UNITED STATES. The CBS television network broadcasts a tribute entitled "Robert Frost: American Poet." The program includes a taped segment of President Kennedy paying homage to Frost. Kennedy says that he invited the poet to speak at inauguration because Frost could remind those in government "that we are dealing with life, the hopes and fears of millions of people, and also to tell us that our own deep convictions must be the ultimate guide to all of our actions."

28 February 1961
WASHINGTON, D.C. President Kennedy sends a special message to Congress urging additional authorization to complete the interstate highway system, which is currently imperiled by a lack of funds.

In the evening, representatives of the Theater Guild and the American Repertory Company visit President Kennedy. Among those present are Helen Hayes, June Havoc, and producer Lawrence Langer.

1 March 1961
WASHINGTON, D.C. President Kennedy signs executive order 10924 directing the State Department to establish and administer a Peace Corps on a temporary pilot basis. He sends a special message to Congress stating that the corps will consist of a trained group of American men and women sent overseas by the United States government or by private organizations to help foreign countries meet their needs for skilled manpower. Kennedy also urges Congress to consider a permanent Peace Corps. The temporary group, he says, "will be a source of information and experience to aid us in formulating more effective plans for permanent organizations."

Kennedy also signs a joint resolution to commemorate the one hundredth anniversary of the first inauguration of Abraham Lincoln.

3 March 1961
WASHINGTON, D.C. President Kennedy dedicates the National Wildlife Federation Building at 1412 Sixteenth Street, N.W. In his message, he recalls that the National Wildlife Federation was formed twenty-five years ago to protect the nation's natural resources, and says that "our future greatness and strength depend upon the continued abundant use of our natural resources."

President Kennedy meets with Prime Minister Keith J. Holyoake of New Zealand to discuss efforts to raise the living standards in poor nations, the situation in Laos, defense measures and the importance of SEATO and ANZUS, and the threat posed by the Chinese Communist regime.

4 March 1961
WASHINGTON, D.C. R. Sargent Shriver, Jr., is appointed head of the Peace Corps by President Kennedy. Shriver has played a significant role in its organization.

7 March 1961
WASHINGTON, D.C. President Kennedy issues executive order 10925, dated 6 March, establishing the President's Committee on Equal Employment Opportunity. The order provides for government agencies and those who do business with them to grant "equal access to employment" to all Americans, regardless of color or belief.

8 March 1961
WASHINGTON, D.C. President Kennedy meets with the president of the Republic of Ghana, Dr. Kwame Nkrumah, to discuss cooperation among African countries in working for peace and the role of the United Nations on the continent.

9 March 1961
WASHINGTON, D.C. President Kennedy sends a special message on housing and community development to Congress. He recommends legislation that would improve housing for the elderly and for low income families thereby helping to revitalize urban and metropolitan areas. In letters to Vice-President Johnson, the president of the Senate, and to Sam Rayburn, Speaker of the House,

Prince Philip, Jacqueline Kennedy, Queen Elizabeth, and President Kennedy following a dinner
at Buckingham Palace, 5 June 1961.

United Press International.

Kennedy endorses former president Eisenhower's earlier message to the House and Senate urging legislation to expand the site of the proposed National Culture Center. The President says that the center is "the most significant cultural undertaking in the history of this city and has enormous importance to the cultural life of the nation as a whole."

10-12 March 1961
NEW YORK.   Touring a few dozen blocks by foot in some troubled East Side neighborhoods, Attorney General Robert Kennedy talks with local youths.

12 March 1961
MIDDLEBURG, VIRGINIA.   At Huntlands farm, Vice-President Johnson presents a pony to Caroline Kennedy.

13 March 1961
WASHINGTON, D.C.   At a White House reception for Latin American diplomats and congressional leaders, President Kennedy announces his plan for an Alliance for Progress—a 10-year program to encourage freedom and raise the standard of living in nations south of the United States. The plan proposes development of long-range plans and technical training programs, provision for educational opportunities in North America for Latin American teachers, and channels through which to supply food during emergencies. "And so I say to the men and women of the Americas," he declares, "to the *campesino* in the fields, to the *obrero* in the cities, to the *estudiante* in the schools—prepare your mind and heart for the task ahead. Call forth your strengths and let each devote his energies to the betterment of all, so that your children and our children in this hemisphere can find an ever richer and freer life."

14 March 1961

WASHINGTON, D.C. President Kennedy sends a message to Congress urging it to appropriate the $600 million it has previously authorized for the Inter-American Fund for Social Progress. He says the funds are needed now to relieve hunger and poverty and to aid areas in Chile struck by natural disasters. The President meets with His Highness, the Aga Khan.

BOSTON. Eunice (Kennedy) Shriver undergoes an appendectomy at St. Elizabeth's Hospital in Brighton.

15 March 1961

WASHINGTON, D.C. Prince Stanislaus Radziwill and his wife, Jacqueline (Bouvier) Kennedy's sister Lee, are guests of honor at a White House dinner. Among more than fifty guests are Robert and Ethel Kennedy, the Aga Khan, Ambassador Kenneth Galbraith, Vice-President Johnson, Hugh and Janet Auchincloss, Sargent Shriver, and Jean and Stephen Smith.

16 March 1961

WASHINGTON, D.C. President Kennedy sends a message to Congress outlining the problems of the American farmer and suggesting actions to deal with surpluses, inadequate distribution, and other farm problems. At the Department of State Auditorium, the President attends a ceremony celebrating the centennial of Italian unification and delivers a brief address.

17 March 1961

WASHINGATON, D.C. The ambassador of Ireland, Thomas J. Kiernan, presents a shamrock and the Kennedy coat of arms to the President. In a letter to Secretary Abraham Ribicoff concerning exiled Cuban scholars and professionals in the United States, the President says that "immediate action" should be taken to open up opportunities for these people in teaching, medicine, and other fields. "I want to make unmistakably clear," he declares, "that we believe in a free Cuba."

18 March 1961

WASHINGTON, D.C. In the evening, President Kennedy briefly visits a birthday party for Chief Justice Earl Warren at the Metropolitan Club, then attends an annual dinner of the Radio-TV Correspondents Association at the Statler Hotel.

19 March 1961

WASHINGTON, D.C. As he has done on most Sundays since his inauguration, President Kennedy attends mass at the Holy Trinity Catholic Church, 3514 O Street, N.W. As always, he is greeted upon arrival by the pastor, Father Martin Casey.

21 March 1961

WASHINGTON, D.C. President Kennedy attends a legislative leaders' meeting with Vice-President Johnson, Speaker Sam Rayburn, Senators Hubert Humphrey and Mike Mansfield, and others. He then speaks before a meeting of the President's Advisory Committee on Labor-Management in the Cabinet Room. He receives winners of the National Civil Service League Awards before meeting with Robert McNamara, Chester Bowles, McGeorge Bundy, Allen Dulles, and others to discuss the situation in Laos. Later, he attends the ceremony at which Edward R. Murrow is sworn in as director of the U.S. Information Agency (USIA), meets with Professor Paul Samuelson of the Massachusetts Institute of Technology and Dr. Walter Heller, and attends a coffee hour for members of Congress.

22 March 1961

WASHINGTON, D.C. John F. Kennedy signs his first two bills. One appoints former president Dwight D. Eisenhower to the active list as an Army general with his previous rank, the other provides for an emergency feed-grain program. The Senate confirms President Kennedy's nomination of R. Sargent Shriver, Jr., as director of the Peace Corps.

23 March 1961

WASHINGTON, D.C. President Kennedy states at a news conference that the United States supports "a neutral and independent Laos" and warns that outside Communists must stop supporting rebel factions in Laos and that attacks by the rebels must stop before negotiations can begin. "The security of all Southeast Asia will be endangered if Laos loses its neutral independence," he says. "Its own safety runs with the safety of us all." The President has just ordered additional military aid to Laos and has sent armed American forces to areas near the border.

24 March 1961

WASHINGTON, D.C. President Kennedy signs the Temporary Extended Unemployment Compensation Act of 1961 to "immediately provide economic help for some 700,000 jobless workers and their families whose rights to receive regular unemployment insurance benefits under state law are exhausted." The bill also provides benefit payments to an additional 2½ million workers who are expected to exhaust their benefits within the next year. A ceremony restoring General Eisenhower's

Mrs. Nikita Khrushchev, President Kennedy, Austrian President Adolf Schaerf, Chairman Khrushchev, and Jacqueline Kennedy in Vienna, June 1961.

five-star rank takes place. The President sends to Congress a special message on the budget for fiscal 1962.

In outlining the principles underlying the actions of his administration, President Kennedy says, "It is my determined purpose to be a prudent steward of the public fund — to obtain a dollar's worth of results for every dollar we spend."

NEW YORK. At a New York *Herald Tribune* Youth Forum meeting, Peace Corps director R. Sargent Shriver, Jr., delivers an address entitled "The Peace Corps Speaks for Itself." Shriver says that Peace Corps volunteers are "skilled workers, young in years, mature in judgment...ready to go and work anywhere in the world at the discretion of the President of the United States" to teach languages, fight disease, improve farm methods, and serve in local governments as clerks and administrators.

25 March 1961
ANDREWS AIR FORCE BASE, MARYLAND. President Kennedy departs by plane for West Palm Beach, en route to Key West for a meeting with Prime Minister Harold Macmillan of Britain. Among those traveling with him are Pierre Salinger, C. Douglas Dillon, McGeorge Bundy, Foy Kohler, Charles Bohlen, and LeMoyne Billings.

26 March 1961
KEY WEST, FLORIDA. John Kennedy and Harold

CAMELOT 1961 – 1964

Macmillan exchange views on the situation in Laos, expressing support for a recent British note to the Russian government calling for an end to warfare and for the initiation of steps to make Laos a neutral country. Attending the conference with the President at the Boca Chica Naval Air Station are McGeorge Bundy, Foy Kohler, Charles Bohlen, Christian Chapman, and Brig. Gen. Paul Fontana.

27 March 1961

WASHINGTON, D.C. President Kennedy meets with the Soviet Foreign Affairs minister, Andrei A. Gromyko, and Russian ambassador, Mikahail A. Menshikov.

Jacqueline Kennedy lunches with Edith Galt Wilson, 88, the second wife of Woodrow Wilson. The widow of the country's twenty-eighth president (1913-1921) tells the First Lady that President Wilson used the same desk that Kennedy is now using. The desk, a gift from Queen Victoria to Rutherford B. Hayes in 1880, is called the "Resolute" because it is made from timbers from the H.M.S. *Resolute,* a British ship that became icebound and was abandoned in May 1854. It was later found, and the timbers recovered, by an American whaling ship.

28 March 1961

WASHINGTON, D.C. In a special message to Congress, President Kennedy requests appropriations for a defense build-up that would result in the largest armamentarium in peacetime history. The budget would expand Polaris missile systems, strengthen warning systems, and increase conventional defense weapons and forces. "No single question of policy," he declares, "has concerned me more...than the adequacy of our present and planned military forces to accomplish our major national security objectives."

29 March 1961

WASHINGTON, D.C. President Kennedy meets with the prime minister of Peru, Pedro G. Beltran, then attends a White House luncheon in honor of the prime minister of Sweden, Tage Erlander. He signs a bill "to authorize certain beach erosion control on the shore of San Diego, California," sends legislation to Congress for housing and urban improvement, and announces that "we have offered a million tons of wheat to Brazil for sale for local currencies to be used in Brazilian economic and social development." The President also signs execu-

President Charles De Gaulle and Mme. Yvonne De Gaulle with President and Mrs. Kennedy at the American Embassy in Paris, 1 June 1961, where the Kennedys give a luncheon in honor of the French leader and his wife.

United Press International.

United Press International.

At the Louis X Theater in Versailles, France, the De Gaulles and the Kennedys stand as the French and American national anthems are played.

tive order number 10931, establishing the President's Council on Youth Fitness.

30 March 1961
WEST PALM BEACH, FLORIDA. At the Palm Beach Country Club, President Kennedy, Joseph P. Kennedy, and Peter Lawford play nine holes of golf. In the evening, the President sees the movie *One-Eyed Jacks*, starring Marlon Brando and Karl Malden.

31 March 1961
WEST PALM BEACH, FLORIDA. Bing Crosby and Chris Dunphy play eleven holes of golf in two hours with President Kennedy and his father at the Palm Beach Country Club. At 5:00 P.M. , John Kennedy drives his father home. In the evening, President Kennedy at-

tends Good Friday mass at St. Ann's Catholic Church.

2 April 1961
WEST PALM BEACH, FLORIDA. At the elder Kennedy's home, John and Jacqueline Kennedy see the movie *All in a Night's Work*, a comedy starring Dean Martin, Shirley MacLaine, and Cliff Robertson.

3 April 1961
WEST PALM BEACH, FLORIDA. John Kennedy and Peter Lawford walk along the beach from Joseph P. Kennedy's home to that of Earl T. Smith. Later in the afternoon, Joseph Kennedy and sports magnate Carrol Rosenbloom join John Kennedy and Earl Smith for nine holes of golf at the Palm Beach Country Club. In the evening, the President and his family see *Posse from Hell*, a western starring Audie Murphy and Zora Lampert.

Jacqueline Kennedy at the Piedmont Foxhounds races in Upperville, Virginia, 25 March 1961.

BRAZIL. President Kennedy extends his greetings to the people of Brazil and the country's president, Janio Quadros, in a radio broadcast. Kennedy presents his interviewer with a copy of Abraham Lincoln's Gettysburg Address, which he inscribes for President Quadros.

4 April 1961

WEST PALM BEACH, FLORIDA. After playing eight holes of golf with his father, Peter Lawford, and Stephen Smith, John Kennedy leaves for Washington by plane. Joseph Kennedy sees his son off at the West Palm Beach Airport.

WASHINGTON, D.C. President Kennedy returns to the White House, arriving by helicopter from Andrews Air Force Base. Late in the afternoon he addresses delegates to the Conference on Foreign Policy briefing at the State Department.

5 April 1961

WASHINGTON, D.C. Prime Minister Harold Macmillan of Great Britain and President Kennedy be-

gin the first of three days of discussions on Western policy strategies regarding the North Atlantic Alliance, the United Nations, the Soviet Union, Laos, Vietnam, a nuclear test ban, and other problems. Other officials at the White House meetings include (for the U.S.) Secretary of State Dean Rusk, U.S. Ambassador to Great Britain David K. Bruce, Under Secretary of State George Ball, Foy Kohler, Dean Acheson, McGeorge Bundy, Averill Harriman, Walter Heller, Robert McNamara, and C. Douglas Dillon; and (for Britain) Secretary of State for Foreign Affairs the Earl of Home, Ambassador to the United States Sir Harold Caccia, Secretary of the Cabinet Sir Norman Brooks, Permanent Under Secretary of Foreign Affairs Sir Frederick Millar, and Prime Minister Macmillan's private secretary, P. F. de Zulveta.

6 April 1961

WASHINGTON, D.C. In his first news conference as attorney general, Robert F. Kennedy announces that he has asked Congress to pass tougher laws to combat racketeering, that the Justice Department will not investigate the John Birch Society, and that he has formed a group to study problems faced in federal courts by poor defendants in criminal cases. He also expresses his belief that business trade associations should develop codes of ethics to fight the rampant corruption in management.

President Kennedy continues his discussions with Prime Minister Harold Macmillan aboard the presidential yacht *Honey Fitz*, which he has named for his grandfather, John Francis Fitzgerald.

7 April 1961

WASHINGTON, D.C. President Kennedy receives a gold season's pass to the American League's baseball games. Those present at the brief ceremony include Joseph Cronin, president of the American League, General Elwood Quesada, president of the Washington Senators, and Ed Dougherty, the Senators' general manager.

8 April 1961

WASHINGTON, D.C. President Kennedy and Prime Minister Macmillan conclude their discussions. The two leaders now summarize their meeting at a press conference in the Rose Garden, reaffirming the alliance between their two countries and expressing delight that their own personal friendship has developed. Later, the President meets with Helen Keller and officials of Lions International.

9 April 1961

MIDDLEBURG, VIRGINIA. Jacqueline Kennedy goes riding at the residence of Paul Font while her husband watches.

191

President Kennedy rides in a motorcade through the streets of Paris, June 1961.

Kennedy Family Collection. Photographer unknown.

10 April 1961

WASHINGTON, D.C.   President Kennedy delivers an address before a meeting of the NATO chiefs of staff at the State Department. He speaks of strengthening conventional forces, continuing effective nuclear capability, and creating a "close understanding between political leaders and senior military officers" in shaping NATO policy. Among those in attendance are Louis Earl Mountbatten of England and General Lyman Lemnitzer.

Back at the White House, at 12:25 P.M. President Kennedy receives Judy Garland and her husband, Sid Luft, for a five-minute meeting.

In the afternoon, President Kennedy opens the sixty-first baseball season of the Washington Senators by throwing out the first ball. Hatless and coatless, with this construction, sounds like his temperature is in the high 40s. The president fires the ball past the Senators and into the glove of a member of the opposing team. His second throw lands in the home-team pitcher's glove. (The tradition of the president opening the baseball season began in 1910 with William Howard Taft.)

11 April 1961

WASHINGTON, D.C.   The first meeting of the President's Committee on Equal Employment Opportunity is held in the Cabinet Room of the White House. President Kennedy speaks briefly, expressing his hopes the committee's work will "permanently" remove from government and from all government contractors any trace of discrimination because of race, creed, color, or place of national origin. Later he meets with General Lauris Norstad, Supreme Allied Commander in Europe.

12 April 1961

WASHINGTON, D.C. Two days of talks begin at the White House between Chancellor Konrad Adenauer of West Germany and President Kennedy. Accompanying the German leader are Foreign Minister Heinrich von Brentano, Ambassador Wilhelm Grewe, and others. The discussions center on the Berlin problem, nuclear test bans, NATO, and other international problems.

MOSCOW. Russia announces that Soviet cosmonaut Yuri Gagarin has completed one orbit of the earth in space in 1 hour and 48 minutes.

WASHINGTON, D.C. President Kennedy issues a public statement congratulating this "outstanding technical accomplishment." To Premier Nikita Khruschev of the Soveit Union he says that the American people share with Soviet citizens "their satisfaction for the safe space flight of the astronaut in man's first venture into space."

At a press conference in the late afternoon, President Kennedy answers a reporter's question regarding possible attempts to dispose of the Castro regime by saying that "there will not be, under any conditions, an intervention in Cuba by the United States armed forces. This government will do everything it possibly can...to make sure that there are no Americans involved in any actions inside Cuba."

14 April 1961

WASHINGTON, D.C. At the Pan American Union Building, President Kennedy addresses the Protocolary Session of the Council of the Organization of American States. The meeting, he says, should serve to encourage all the free nations of the Western hemisphere to set deadlines for planning national economic development.

15 April 1961

WASHINGTON, D.C. President Kennedy addresses a group of African ambassadors, members of the United States Congress, and federal officials assembled for African Freedom Day.

17 April 1961

BAY OF PIGS, CUBA. Over 1,200 anti-Castro Cuban exiles land on the southern coast of the island in an attempt to overthrow the regime of Premier Fidel Castro. Combat-trained by the United States, they are operating under the direction of the American government. The invasion is quickly smashed by Cuba's military forces. The rebels had expected support from insurgents on the island and from United States aircraft. When neither materializes, the raiders are captured and put in prison.

WASHINGTON, D.C. Throughout the day, President Kennedy receives credentials from and meets with newly appointed foreign ambassadors from the Republic of Dahomey, Nigeria, Upper Volta, and Indonesia. A White House luncheon is given in honor of the Prime Minister Constantine Caramanlis of Greece.

18 April 1961

WASHINGTON, D.C. Premier Nikita Khruschev sends President Kennedy a message in which he accuses the United States of supporting the military invasion of the Bay of Pigs. He warns that if "aggression" continues toward Cuba, his country will provide "all necessary assistance" in halting any attack. President Kennedy answers the Soviet leader, promising that the United States "intends no military intervention in Cuba" but that it would oppose armed support from any outside forces.

19 April 1961

LONDON. An interview, videotaped last month, in which President Kennedy answers questions about the meaning of the "New Frontier," the recession, and social welfare programs is broadcast.

WASHINGTON, D.C. President Kennedy presents the Gold Medal Awards of the National Geographic Society to Jacques-Yves Cousteau. The President says, "I can imagine his satisfaction in having opened up the ocean floor to man and to science." Later, President Kennedy meets with Dr. José Miro Cardona, head of an anti-Castro Revolutionary Council, and others, to discuss the Cuban situation.

20 April 1961

WASHINGTON, D.C. At the Statler Hilton Hotel, the President speaks to the American Society of Newspaper Editors about the Bay of Pigs debacle. While the United States has made it clear in the past that it would not intervene in the struggle in Cuba, he says, it would not fail in meeting its primary obligation, the security of America, in the face of outside Communist penetration.

Kennedy draws three lessons from the incident: "That the forces of Communism are not to be underestimated," that the United States and other free nations in the hemisphere "must take an even closer and more realistic look at the menace of external Communist intervention and domination in Cuba," and that "we face a relentless struggle in every corner of the globe that goes far beyond the clash of armies or even nuclear armaments." The security of a country may be lost without a single missile being fired or a border being crossed. But, Kennedy says, the nation will "profit from this lesson"

John Fitzgerald Kennedy Library. Photographer unknown.

John and Jacqueline Kennedy at the Orange Bowl in Miami, 29 December 1962, where the President delivers a speech before the Cuban Invasion Brigade and others.

and will reexamine its tactics to ensure its security. "Let me then make clear as the President of the United States," he says, "that I am determined upon our system's survival and success, regardless of the cost and regardless of the peril!"

21 April 1961

WASHINGTON, D.C. At a press conference, President Kennedy announces the first project of the Peace Corps. The organization will send surveyors, geologists, and civil engineers to Tanganyika to help the country's technicians map and build roads.

22 April 1961

CAMP DAVID, MARYLAND. After President Kennedy and former president Eisenhower have lunch together, Kennedy inspects the camp's lower shelter area and then some of its installations. On the return trip to the White House, the helicopter flies over the Gettysburg battlegrounds.

24 April 1963

WASHINGTON, D.C. President Kennedy meets with President Sukarno of Indonesia at the White House in the first of two days of discussions on Laos, the Indonesian Eight-Year Development Plan, and disarmament. A message is sent to Congress by the President requesting funds for modernizing outdated airports. A draft of a bill that would "provide penalties for threats against the successors to the Presidency" and Secret Service protection for them is also sent to Congress. The current law provides protection only for the president-elect and the vice-president.

25 April 1961

WASHINGTON, D.C. President Kennedy signs a bill amending the Aeronautics and Space Act of 1958. The bill, he says, "is a key step toward moving the United States into its proper place in the space race." In an address to the annual meeting of the National Academy of Sciences, the President says that the country needs scientists to help it move forward and solve its problems.

27 April 1961

WASHINGTON, D.C. President Kennedy sends special messages providing for the reorganization of the Securities and Exchange Commission and the Federal Communications Commission to Congress. He also sends another special message on ethics in government and the actions he will take to prohibit government employees from using their offices for personal gain.

NEW YORK. In the evening, the President addresses the Newspaper Publishers Association's Bureau of Advertising at the Waldorf-Astoria Hotel. He speaks of the relationship between government and the press, and asks that all publishers and reporters consider the dangers facing the United States and "heed the duty of self-restraint which that danger imposes upon us all."

28 April 1961

NEW YORK. In separate meetings at the Waldorf-Astoria, President Kennedy visits with former president Herbert Hoover and General Douglas MacArthur. Later, in the presidential suite, he meets with Dag Hammarskjold and Adlai Stevenson.

CHICAGO. This evening, President Kennedy addresses a fund-raising dinner of the Cook County Democratic Party at the McCormick Place Exposition Center. He speaks of Communist infiltration and the dangers faced by the United States. "We live in a hazardous and dangerous time," he says. "I do not think it's possible to overstate it."

30 April 1961

MINSK, USSR. Lee Harvey Oswald marries a young Russian woman, Marina Prusakova. Oswald is still a United States citizen.

1 May 1961

WASHINGTON, D.C. President Kennedy speaks before a Joint Conference of Regional Commissioners

John F. Kennedy, Jr., Empress Farah of Iran, Jacqueline Kennedy, and Marconi, the Kennedy pony, on the grounds of the White House, 12 April 1962.

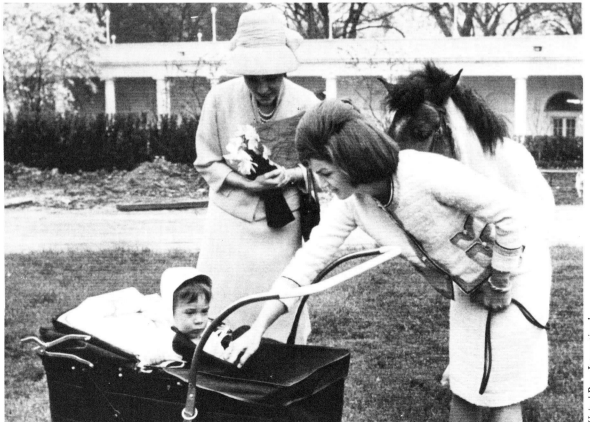

United Press International.

Prime Minister Harold Macmillan and President Kennedy at Andrews Air Force Base, Maryland, 27 April 1962.

and District Directors of the Internal Revenue Services at the Internal Revenue Building. Back at the White House, he signs the Area Redevelopment Act, which provides federal aid for depressed areas that meet eligibility criteria set forth by the Labor Department. The President says this "will help make it possible for thousands of Americans who want to work, to work."

3 May 1961
WASHINGTON, D.C. At George Washington University, an honorary Doctor of Laws degree is conferred upon President Kennedy by Dr. Thomas Henry Carroll, the school's new president, who takes office during this ceremony. It is the twentieth honorary degree Kennedy has received, and his first as president. The White House sends a reorganization plan for the Civil Aeronautics Board to Congress. That night, a White House dinner honors the president of Tunisia, Habib Bourgiba, and his wife. (President and Mrs. Kennedy had greeted them at National Airport at noon.) Bourgiba, whose country opposes a French naval air base in Tunisia, is to address Congress and confer with the President on the right of countries to maintain autonomy and independence.

5 May 1961
CAPE CANAVERAL, FLORIDA. Navy Commander Alan B. Shepard, Jr., makes a 15-minute suborbital flight and becomes America's first astronaut. At 9:54 A.M., he is picked up from the Atlantic Ocean 300 miles from the launch site by helicopter and flown to the recovery vessel, the *Lake Champlain.*

President Kennedy, who watched Commander Shepard's launch from Cape Canaveral on television, calls the astronaut by radio telephone on the recovery ship to congratulate him.

WASHINGTON, D.C. President Kennedy signs the Minimum Wage Bill (the Fair Labor Standards Amendments of 1961). The bill increases the lowest legal pay from $1 to $1.25 by 1963 for workers already covered by law, and extends legal minimum pay to workers whose jobs have not previously been covered by law.

The President meets with Dr. José Miro Cardona, chairman of the Cuban Revolutionary Council. At a press conference, the President announces that he has asked Vice-President Johnson to undertake a special task-finding mission to Asia, and that he considers this "an extremely important assignment."

6 May 1961
ATHENS, GEORGIA. Attorney General Robert F. Kennedy delivers the commencement address at graduation exercises of the University of Georgia Law School. He says that discrimination extends throughout the United States, not just through the South, and promises that the Justice Department will take action to insure compliance with civil-rights laws.

WASHINGTON, D.C. Stephen E. Smith is made an unpaid assistant to the Special Operations Center, a new organization that will function to assimilate information on world crises, recommend responses to the President, and monitor the implementation of any action taken.

Soviet premier Nikita Khruschev congratulates President Kennedy on Alan B. Shepard's suborbital space flight.

7 May 1961
BERRYVILLE, VIRGINIA. President Kennedy joins a luncheon attended by over 125 people at the residence of Senator Harry Byrd.

8 May 1961
WASHINGTON, D.C. At a ceremony in the White House Rose Garden, Commander Alan B. Shepard, Jr., receives the Distinguished Service Medal of the National

Aeronautics and Space Administration from President Kennedy. At the Sheraton Park Hotel, the President introduces Commander Shepard and delivers an address to the annual meeting of the National Association of Broadcasters. At a meeting in the Cabinet Room, the governors of Alabama, Kentucky, Maryland, North Carolina, Pennsylvania, Tennessee, Virginia, and West Virginia confer with President Kennedy on economic problems in Appalachia. The President signs into law a bill providing aid to families with dependent children in certain cases where there is an unemployed parent who has been the principal earner.

9 May 1961

WASHINGTON, D.C.   A plan for reorganizing the Federal Trade Commission is sent to Congress by President Kennedy.

10 May 1961

WASHINGTON, D.C.   Over 1,000 foreign students attending college in the area are guests at a reception hosted by President and Mrs. Kennedy at the White

---

Robert Kennedy, Pat Lawford, daughter Sydney and son Christopher, in Los Angeles, June 1962.

Photographer unknown.

House. Frank Jamieson of the Navy League presents President Kennedy with an old medal commemorating the fiftieth anniversary of Naval aviation.

11 May 1961

WASHINGTON, D.C.   President Kennedy issues executive order 10940, which establishes a Committee on Juvenile Delinquency and Youth Crime. "Measures must be taken to reach deeply into the experiences of everyday life in deprived families and local communities," the President says. "We must undertake a program integrating specific remedies into a total attack upon the prevention and control of youth offenses."

WEST PALM BEACH, FLORIDA.   Accompanied by his friends Charles Spaulding and Chris Dunphy, President Kennedy arrives here for a few days of golf and relaxation. He stays at the residence of Charles B. Wrightsman in Palm Beach.

WASHINGTON, D.C.   Attorney General Robert F. Kennedy is appointed the chairman of the President's Committee on Juvenile Delinquency and Youth Crime.

14 May 1961

BIRMINGHAM, ALABAMA.   A bus carrying white and black Freedom Riders arrives here from Anniston, Alabama, where some of them had been beaten by whites. The passengers, members of the Congress of Racial Equality (CORE), are testing local discrimination laws in the South. When they arrive in Birmingham, a mob of whites attacks them, dragging them into back streets and alleyways and beating them with pipes and fists. Police are noticeably absent.

ANNISTON, ALABAMA.   A second busload of Freedom Riders arrives here to a waiting group of angry whites who hurl rocks and break bus windows. The bus takes off, with whites in pursuit. When a flat tire forces the bus to stop, whites firebomb it.

15 May 1961

WASHINGTON, D.C.   Attorney General Robert F. Kennedy telephones Alabama officials and demands that CORE members traveling in the South be given police protection.

16 May 1961

WASHINGTON, D.C.   President Kennedy announces the second Peace Corps project. Sixty-four volunteers trained in farming and construction will go to Colombia to help small rural communities develop their own economic resources and educational facilities. The

President also meets with Dr. Walter Hallstein, president of the European Economic Community.

OTTAWA, CANADA. President Kennedy makes his first state visit to a foreign country. Prime Minister John George Diefenbaker and other Canadian officials greet President and Mrs. Kennedy at the RCAF Station in Uplands with a 21-gun salute by a 100-man honor guard. On the grounds of Government House, the Kennedys participate in a tree-planting ceremony, and later the two are the guests of honor at a state dinner.

17 May 1961

OTTAWA, CANADA. President Kennedy discusses international issues such as disarmament, Laos, and the United Nations with Canadian prime minister John Diefenbaker. The two also confer on issues involving Canada and the United States. At Confederation Hall, the President addresses the Canadian Parliament on the friendship between the U.S. and Canada, aiding less developed nations of the world, and on America's NATO policy. He says that the United States will provide Polaris atomic-missile submarines to NATO for the defense of Europe. We are faced, he continues, with the task "of finding a widened range of common enterprises between ourselves and those who live under Communist rule. For, in the end, we live on one planet and we are part of one human family."

HAVANA, CUBA. Premier Fidel Castro proposes to exchange the prisoners taken in the Bay of Pigs invasion for 500 American tractors.

18 May 1961

WASHINGTON, D.C. The President and Jacqueline Kennedy return to the White House from Canada. The President joins over fifty members of the House of Representatives at a congressional coffee hour from 6:10 P.M. to 7:00 P.M.

19 May 1961

WASHINGTON, D.C. President Kennedy signs legislation to provide for seventy-three additional circuit and district judges. "I want for our courts," he says, "individuals with...the rare inner quality to know when to temper justice with mercy, and the intellectual capacity to protect and illuminate the Constitution."

20 May 1961

WASHINGTON, D.C. President Kennedy signs an additional amendment to the 1938 Agricultural Act. He also calls upon "the governor and other responsible state officials in Alabama, as well as the mayors of Birming-

ham and Montgomery, to exercise their lawful authority to prevent any further outbreaks of violence [against members of CORE].

MONTGOMERY, ALABAMA. The Freedom Riders are again attacked by hundreds of armed whites as they enter this city by bus. The police are slow to intervene. Attorney General Robert F. Kennedy orders some four hundred U.S. marshals into the city to protect the Freedom Riders.

21 May 1961

MONTGOMERY, ALABAMA. In a tense confrontation, U.S. marshals hold back some 1,000 whites as a large group of blacks assemble at the First Baptist Church. Civil-rights leader Martin Luther King, Jr., one of the meeting's leaders, telephones Robert Kennedy to tell him of the potential danger to the group.

22 May 1961

WASHINGTON, D.C. In the late afternoon, President Kennedy meets briefly with Eleanor Roosevelt in his office. Then he goes to the Cabinet Room, where he announces to the National Advisory Council that 300 teaching assistants will be sent to the Philippines as the third Peace Corps project.

24 May 1961

WASHINGTON, D.C. Lyndon Johnson returns to the White House from a fact-finding mission to Vietnam, Laos, Formosa, the Philippines, and India. President Kennedy welcomes him back in a brief ceremony held in the Rose Garden. The President and Mrs. Kennedy give a luncheon in honor of Prince Rainier III and Princess Grace of Monaco.

25 May 1961

WASHINGTON, D.C. President Kennedy delivers a special address to Congress on urgent national needs. Although the State of the Union address is customarily an annual event, he points out "this tradition has been broken in extraordinary times" and that "these are extraordinary times." Kennedy announces the legislation he will be sending to Congress: a new Manpower Development and Training program to train or retrain workers; a request for $1.885 billion in military assistance during the next fiscal year for national defense and to help other free nations maintain their independence; and a measure to establish a strengthened Disarmament Agency.

With respect to space exploration, he says, "I believe that this nation should commit itself to achieving the goal, before this decade is out, of landing man on the

John Fitzgerald Kennedy Library. photographer unknown.

Three generations of Kennedys, in Hyannis Port, 8 September 1962.

moon and returning him safely to the earth. No single space project in this period will be more impressive to mankind, or more important for the long-range exploration of space—and none will be so difficult or expensive to produce."

27 May 1961

WASHINGTON, D.C. President Kennedy signs a bill providing for aid to Latin American countries, which, he hopes, will build "a hemisphere in which all people from the top down to the bottom of the globe share in hopes for a better life." The National Democratic Committee gives a fund-raising dinner at the National

Guard Armory in honor of Kennedy's forty-fourth birthday, his first birthday as president. (The President's birthday is not for two days.) Morton Downey sings the national anthem and Jerry Lewis entertains. Several people speak, including former president Harry S. Truman, Sam Rayburn, and Vice-President Lyndon Johnson. President Kennedy himself delivers an address in which he discusses his forthcoming meetings in Europe. "And I shall tell the world," he says, "that here in this country American men and women are calling forth all the great resources and untapped power of this country, providing strength for that faith in the freedom of man which will be the silent guest of every conference table."

John Fitzgerald Kennedy Library. Photographer unknown.

At the funeral of Eleanor Roosevelt in Hyde Park, New York on 10 November 1962 President Kennedy with former Presidents Harry Truman and Dwight Eisenhower. Vice-President Lyndon Johnson stands behind Truman.

28 May 1961
HYANNIS PORT, MASSACHUSETTS.   President Kennedy attends mass at St. Xavier's Church and then spends the rest of the day at his father's home.

29 May 1961
BOSTON.   A dinner party in honor of President Kennedy's birthday is given at the Commonwealth Armory. The distinguished guests include Governor John Volpe, Mayor John Collins, Robert Frost, and Richard Cardinal Cushing. Dr. Frederick Good, the obstetrician who delivered the President forty-four years ago, is also there. Kennedy quips, "I have been informed that with this dinner I am now responsible as the leader of the Democratic Party for a debt of one million dollars. Now did anybody ever get a birthday present like that?"

30 May 1961
HYANNIS PORT, MASSACHUSETTS.   The President takes a cruise aboard the *Marlin* with his fa-ther, his cousin Ann Gargan, LeMoyne Billings, and Pat Burke.

President Kennedy sends to Congress legislation that would establish the Peace Corps on a permanent basis. The Peace Corps Act "provides for a Peace Corps to help the peoples of interested countries and areas in meeting their needs for skilled manpower."

NEW YORK.   In Suite 28-A at the Waldorf-Astoria, President Kennedy and Prime Minister David Ben-Gurion of Israel, who recently returned from an official visit to Canada, discuss world and Middle East problems. The President then attends a dinner given by the American Cancer Foundation. Brief speeches are made by James Roosevelt, Bob Hope, and Mayor Robert F. Wagner, of New York. Eleanor Roosevelt presents the Humanitarian Service awards, and President Kennedy delivers a brief address. At 10:00 P.M. , President and Mrs. Kennedy depart on Air Force One from Idlewild Airport for a state visit to France.

31 May 1961

PARIS. Air Force One lands at Orly Field at 10:30 A.M. President Charles de Gaulle, Prime Minister Debre, and other French dignitaries greet President and Mrs. Kennedy. De Gaulle and Kennedy exchange welcoming remarks, then drive to Quai d'Orsay. Madame de Gaulle and Jacqueline Kennedy follow in another car. After luncheon and a diplomatic reception, President Kennedy lights the flame at a wreath-laying ceremony at the Arch of Triumph, and, after a moment of silence, a band plays the "Marseilles." In the evening, President and Mrs. Kennedy are honored at the Elyseé Palace.

1 June 1961

PARIS. President Kennedy visits the American Embassy and then goes to the Elyseé Palace for a meeting with President de Gaulle. Kennedy and his wife then proceed to the Hotel de Ville (City Hall) where the President addresses members of the Bureau of the Municipal Council and other dignitaries. At the American Embassy, the Kennedys give a luncheon in honor of President and Madame de Gaulle. The two leaders again continue talks, after which they drive to the NATO Headquarters Building where President Kennedy speaks to the North Atlantic Council of NATO. At the Versailles Palace in the evening, another dinner honors the American President and his wife. The evening is capped off when the guests attend a performance of the ballet *Rendezvous* at the Louis XI Theater.

2 June 1961

PARIS. In the morning, President Kennedy goes to SHAPE Headquarters, where he is greeted by General Lauris Norstad and speaks briefly. At the Elyseé Palace, Kennedy and de Gaulle continue their discussions. The French press gives a luncheon in honor of President and Mrs. Kennedy at the Palais de Chaillot, after which President Kennedy speaks and then takes questions from the press.

3 June 1961

PARIS. President and Mrs. Kennedy complete their visit here. Jacqueline Kennedy has been wildly popular with the Parisians. During their visit, over a million people crowded the streets of Paris to see the glamorous couple. Thee Kennedys depart from Orly Field at 9:00 A.M.

VIENNA. At Schwechat Airport, President and Mrs. Kennedy are greeted by the President of Austria, Adolf Sharf, Chancellor Alons Gorbach, and other dignitaries. At 12:45 P.M. at the American Embassy, the first of two days of meetings on international issues between President Kennedy and Soviet Premier Nikita Khruschev be-

gins. Those with the President include Dean Rusk, McGeorge Bundy, Charles Bohlen, and Foy Kohler. With Khruschev are Foreign Minister Andrei Gromyko, Mikahail Menshikov, the Soviet ambassador to the United States, and Anatoliy Dobrynin, chief of the American Countries Division of Soviet Foreign Affairs. Later, the two leaders confer alone (with interpreters). In the evening, President Scharf gives a dinner in honor of the two leaders and their wives at the Schonbrunn Palace.

4 June 1961

VIENNA. Discussions continue at the Soviet Embassy between President Kennedy and Premier Khruschev on disarmament, Germany, Laos, and nuclear testing. They fail to agree on certain problems, but at the conclusion of the talks they issue a joint statement that they will "maintain contact on all questions of interest to the two countries and for the whole world."

CARACAS, VENEZUELA. Acting as President Kennedy's emissary to the Alliance for Progress, Adlai E. Stevenson confers with President Romulo Betancourt. This is the first of several discussions he will have with Latin American leaders on the plan.

LONDON. At 8:20 P.M. , the President and Mrs. Kennedy arrive at London Airport North and are greeted by Prime Minister Macmillan, Ambassador David Bruce, and several British dignitaries. The Kennedys then go to the home of Jacqueline Kennedy's sister, Princess Lee Radziwill, where they spend the night.

5 June 1961

LONDON. In the morning, President Kennedy visits the American Embassy, where he speaks briefly, recalling his own work there for a "few months before the outbreak of World War II....I know this square on which this new building is ranged as well as I do my own street at home."

At Westminster Cathedral in the afternoon, the President and Mrs. Kennedy attend the christening of Anna Christina Radziwill, the daughter of Prince and Princess Radziwill. A reception follows at the Radziwill residence, where guests include the Duke and Duchess of Devonshire, Randolph Churchill, Lady Elizabeth Cavendish, Hugh and Lady Antonia Fraser, and Douglas Fairbanks. The Kennedys later attend a dinner given by Queen Elizabeth and Prince Philip at Buckingham Palace. The guests at dinner include Louis Earl Mountbatten, Prime Minister Harold Macmillan, David Ormsby-Gore, and other British dignitaries.

At 11:40 P.M. , the presidential party leaves England for the United States.

John Fitzgerald Kennedy Library. Photographer unknown.

At the White House, composer Richard Adler, Judy Garland, JFK, Carol Burnett and Danny Kaye.

6 June 1961
WASHINGTON, D.C. President Kennedy reports on his trip to Europe over national television and radio. "I found General de Gaulle far more interested in our frankly stating our position," he says, "than in [our] appearing to agree with him when we do not." Of his meetings with Nikita Khruschev he says, "We have wholly different views of right and wrong...where the world is and where it is going."

7 June 1961
ANNAPOLIS, MARYLAND. President Kennedy delivers the commencement address at graduation exercises of the United States Naval Academy. He says that devoting oneself to a life of military service is the greatest contribution a man can make, but that such dedication is a test of will. "When there is a visible enemy to fight,"

the President declares, "the tide of patriotism in this country runs strong. But where there is a long, slow struggle, with no immediate visible foe, when you watch your contemporaries indulging the urge for material gain and comfort and personal advancement, your choice will seem hard."

CHICAGO. R. Sargent Shriver, Jr., delivers the commencement address at graduation exercises of DePaul University. The Peace Corps director asks that employers give temporary leave to young people interested in participating in the project.

8 June 1961
WASHINGTON, D.C. President Kennedy meets with President Abbe Fulbert Youlou of the Republic of

the Congo to discuss economic and hydroelectric development in the Congo. On the same day, White House Press Secretary Pierre Salinger announces that President Kennedy has been suffering from back pains after injuring himself in tree-planting ceremonies in Ottawa last month. To alleviate his discomfort, the President's personal physician, Dr. Janet Travell, has prescribed novocaine shots and swimming in a warm pool.

PALM BEACH, FLORIDA. President Kennedy arrives to spend the next few days at Charles Wrightsman's estate, where he will be able to swim in a heated pool.

12 June 1961
WASHINGTON, D.C. President Kennedy returns to the White House, where he begins two days of discussions with Amintore Fanfani, the president of Italy, on defense, disarmament, and other international problems. The White House sends special messages to Congress on reorganizations of the Federal Home Loan Bank Board and of maritime functions.

16 June 1961
WASHINGTON, D.C. In an address to the National Conference on International Economic and Social Development at the Shoreham Hotel, President Kennedy asks for public backing of his foreign aid program in order to forestall Communist subversion.

MIDDLEBURG, VIRGINIA. President and Mrs. Kennedy arrive here in the evening to spend the next few days. The President continues to suffer from back pain.

22 June 1961
WASHINGTON, D.C. Following two days of meetings between President Kennedy and Prime Minister Hayato Ikeda of Japan, a joint statement is released announcing the establishment of a United States-Japan Committee on Trade and Economic Affairs "to strengthen the partnership between the two countries." Other committees will broaden educational, scientific, and cultural cooperation between the United States and Japan. The President's appointments for today are all canceled because he is ill with a virus.

26 June 1961
WASHINGTON, D.C. Members of the Russian press, including Premier Khruschev's son-in-law, Aleksei I. Adzhubei, who works for *Izvestia*, meet with President Kennedy. Kennedy also sends to Congress the draft of a bill that would provide funds to expedite and expand research on converting salt water, to fresh water and meets

with William O. Douglas, associate justice of the Supreme Court.

29 June 1961
WASHINGTON, D.C. President Kennedy sends draft legislation to Congress proposing "a strengthened and enlarged disarmament agency to make an intensified effort to develop acceptable political and technical alternatives to the present arms race." He signs the Highway Act of 1961 to provide funds for completion of a "vital national system of interstate and defense highways."

30 June 1961
WASHINGTON, D.C. President Kennedy signs into law the Social Security Amendments of 1961 which, he says, "represent an additional step toward eliminating many of the hardships resulting from old age, disability, or the death of the family wage-earner." He meets with Soviet Deputy Foreign Minister Valerian Zorin and other Russian diplomats, and signs the Housing Act of 1961, which establishes various programs to improve cities and housing.

HYANNIS PORT, MASSACHUSETTS. In the evening, John and Jacqueline Kennedy arrive with their children at the home of his parents to spend the Fourth of July weekend.

1 July 1961
HYANNIS PORT, MASSACHUSETTS. On board his father's boat, the *Marlin*, President Kennedy begins the holiday weekend by sailing with his father, Ted and Joan Kennedy, his cousin Ann Gargan, and school chum LeMoyne Billings. They leave at noon and anchor off Sanford Island. President Kennedy also issues a statement congratulating the Colombo Plan for economic development in Southeast Asia "on its first decade of dedicated service to the noble cause of a better life for the peoples of Asia," and a tribute to ten years of economic cooperation between Pakistan and the United States.

2 July 1961
SANTA MONICA, CALIFORNIA. A daughter, Robin Elizabeth, is born to Patricia (Kennedy) and Peter Lawford at St. John's Hospital. She is their fourth child and third daughter.

HYANNIS PORT, MASSACHUSETTS. President and Mrs. Kennedy attend services at St. Francis Xavier's Church in the morning. They go out on the *Marlin* at noon, then sail on the *Vicura* at 2 that afternoon. Ann Gargan and LeMoyne Billings joins them on both cruises. Kennedy accompanies them on the first outing only.

Commenting on the suicide of Ernest Hemingway early today, President Kennedy says, "Few Americans have had a greater impact on the emotions and attitudes of the American people" than the author of *The Old Man and the Sea, A Farewell to Arms, The Sun Also Rises,* and *For Whom the Bell Tolls.*

3 July 1961

WASHINGTON, D.C. Reorganization plans requested by the Kennedy administration for the Civil Aeronautics Board, the independent federal agency that regulates the civil air transport industry, go into effect.

HYANNIS PORT, MASSACHUSETTS. John and Jacqueline Kennedy, Joe Kennedy, Robert Kennedy, Ted and Joan Kennedy, Eunice (Kennedy) Shriver, Ann Gargan, and Ted Sorenson and his wife take a cruise on the *Marlin.* They drop anchor at Lewis Bay. President Kennedy announces that he has ordered the Attorney General to seek an injunction against a maritime strike "under the national emergency provisions of the Taft-Hartley Act."

4 July 1961

HYANNIS PORT, MASSACHUSETTS. President Kennedy, his father, and LeMoyne Billings cruise on the *Marlin* and anchor off Lewis Bay.

In a letter to Soviet leaders Nikita Khruschev and Leonid Brezhnev who had sent Independence Day greetings, PresidentKennedy states that he is confident that "we can, in our time, reach that peaceful goal which all peoples so ardently desire."

5 July 1961

WASHINGTON, D.C. At Simón Bolívar Plaza at 18th Street and Virginia Avenue, N.W., President Kennedy participates in the one-hundred-fiftieth anniversary celebration of Venezuelan independence. He delivers a speech and places a wreath at a statue of Simón Bolívar, the father of Venezuelan independence. Back at the White House, he keeps appointments with McGeorge Bundy, General Maxwell Taylor, Walt Whitman Rostow, C. Douglas Dillon, and Timothy J. Reardon.

6 July 1961

WASHINGTON, D.C. In the morning, President Kennedy meets with officials from the Office of Civil and Defense Mobilization, and presents a $1,000 bond to winners of the Elks Youth Leadership Awards. Later he meets with members of the Business Advisory Council and the executive board of the United Steel Workers of America.

7 July 1961

WASHINGTON, D.C. President Kennedy holds a Cabinet meeting, then meets with members of the Economic Mission from the Federation of Nigeria. He also signs a bill that provides for raising the ceiling on loans to war veterans from $13,500 to $15,000. Late in the afternoon, he departs for Hyannis Port.

9 July 1961

WASHINGTON, D.C. Reorganization plans requested by the Kennedy administration go into effect for the Federal Trade Commission, the independent government agency promoting fair compensation in interstate commerce by preventing unfair business practices.

10 July 1961

WASHINGTON, D.C. President Kennedy addresses the Citizens Committee for International Development, a group formed by business and educational leaders to support the administration's foreign aid program. Its chairman is Warren Lee Pierson of Trans World Airlines.

11 July 1961

WASHINGTON, D.C. In the morning, President Kennedy breakfasts with legislative leaders Lyndon Johnson, John McCormack, and Carl Albert, along with Theodore Sorenson, Kenneth O'Donnell, Lawrence O'Brien, and Pierre Salinger, then participates with the Board of Directors of the Tennessee Valley Authority and congressmen from TVA areas in a ceremony honoring the one hundredth birthday of the late Senator George W. Norris. At noon he and Mrs. Kennedy welcome President Mohammed Ayub Khan of Pakistan at Andrews Air Force Base. The two presidents, with members of their staffs, later confer at the White House.

MOUNT VERNON, VIRGINIA. A state dinner is held in honor of President Mohammed Ayub Khan at Mount Vernon, the home of George Washington. Some one hundred thirty-five guests sail on four yachts down the Potomac to the celebration. Presidents Kennedy and Ayub leave from the Naval Weapons Plant on the *Honey Fitz,* Jacqueline Kennedy and the begum of Pakistan, sail on board the *Sequoia,* and the rest of the party sails on the *Patrick J* and the *Guardian.* In a toast to Ayub Khan, President Kennedy says, "We recognize in you a leader...who recognizes that the independence of his own

Make way for one more: Ted Kennedy, center, is elected to the Senate, 1962.

John Fitzgerald Kennedy Library.

country is not enough, that there is a link which binds your country and ours all the way across the globe."

12 July 1961

WASHINGTON, D.C. President Kennedy presents guns brought to him by Paul Doan of the Winchester Company as a gift to President Ayub of Pakistan. In the afternoon, Kennedy meets with a group of representatives from the National Association for the Advancement of Colored People (NAACP) who are taking a tour of the White House. The group, which includes Roy Wilkins and Medgar Evers, discusses civil rights legislation with the President.

13 July 1961

WASHINGTON, D.C. In the Rose Garden at the White House, President Kennedy addresses some 1,850 American Field Service students from fifty countries. These foreign students have been living and studying in the United States over the past year and will soon be re-

turning home. He tells them, "I hope that you go from here not merely as a friend but understanding our faults and our assets, but most of all understanding what we're trying to do, and what we're trying to be—and that we recognize that we have in this country great unfinished business."

For the remainder of the morning President Kennedy discusses the international situation, including Berlin and Laos, with President Ayub of Pakistan. In the afternoon, Kennedy attends meetings of the Senate Foreign Affairs Relations Committee and the National Security Council, and in the evening he and Mrs. Kennedy attend a dinner given in their honor by President Ayub Khan and Begum Nasir Akhtar Aurangzeb at the Mayflower Hotel.

14 July 1961

WASHINGTON, D.C. President Kennedy meets with Dr. Celso Furtado, director of the Development Agency for Northeast Brazil (SUDENE), and later issues a statement saying the United States will dispatch economists and technicians to Brazil to participate with SUDENE in reconstructing the economy of the depressed northeast area. President Kennedy also declares the third week in July Captive Nations Week in accordance with a motion passed by Congress two years ago.

Later he and Mrs. Kennedy helicopter to Andrews Air Force Base where they leave by plane for a weekend in Hyannis Port.

15 July 1961
HYANNIS PORT, MASSACHUSETTS. President Kennedy transmits to Vice-President Lyndon B. Johnson, as president of the Senate, and Sam Rayburn, Speaker of the House, a draft bill to restore to District of Columbia residents "the basic right to local self-government through the elective process, a right enjoyed by all other American citizens." (At this time, D.C. residents are not allowed to vote in national elections.)

17 July 1961
WASHINGTON, D.C. President Kennedy speaks at swearing-in ceremonies for deLeseps S. Morrison as United States Representative on the Council of the Organization of American States and Robert Woodward as Assistant Secretary of State for Inter-American Affairs. He also meets with Prime Minister Julius Nyerere of Tanganyika on plans to develop the economy of that nation. Tanganyika became autonomous, after being a United Nations trust territory, on 1 May 1961. Later, he meets with the Senate Foreign Relations Committee and various Cabinet members.

18 July 1961
WASHINGTON, D.C. At noon, the newly appointed ambassador from Sierra Leone, Dr. Richard Edmund Kelfa-Caulker, presents his credentials to President Kennedy. Later, the President meets with representatives of small business associations and with the Joint Chiefs of Staff. He also sends to Congress a draft bill "to authorize cooperative arrangements for research relating to maternal and child health services and crippled children's services."

19 July 1961
WASHINGTON, D.C. At a press conference at the State Department, President Kennedy urges American school boards, administrators, and teachers to develop and stress physical fitness programs for their students. He recommends that schools adopt three recommendations of the National Council on Youth Fitness: "First, to identify the physically underdeveloped pupil and work with

him to improve his physical capacity....Two, provide a minimum of 15 minutes of vigorous activity every day for all of our school students, boys and girls alike....Three, use valid fitness tests to determine pupils' physical abilities and to evaluate their progress."

In the evening, President Kennedy and C. Douglas Dillon, Senator Stuart Symington, Clark Clifford, William Walton, and others cruise on the *Honey Fitz* on the Potomac River in the vicinity of Fort Belvoir.

20 July 1961
WASHINGTON, D.C. President Kennedy calls Air Force Captain Virgil Ivan "Gus" Grissom aboard the *Randolph* by radio-phone to congratulate him on his earlier orbital space flight and safe return to earth. President Kennedy watched the launch from Cape Canaveral on television.

President Kennedy signs H.R. 6441, an amendment to the Federal Water Pollution Control Act, that provides for more effective water pollution control. The law, he says, "affords a more comprehensive and precise definition of the Federal government's role in controlling the pollution of our country's rivers and streams."

He lunches with General Douglas MacArthur, Vice-President Johnson, Attorney General Robert F. Kennedy, and a number of senators and representatives.

21 July 1961
WASHINGTON, D.C. In the morning, President Kennedy confers with U.S. Ambassador to the Republic of China Everett F. Drumright and meets with the Special Ad Hoc Panel on Nuclear Testing. In the afternoon, the President signs H.R. 6874, a bill authorizing the National Aeronautics and Space Administration. He also meets with a group of NATO parliamentarians representing Belgium, Canada, Denmark, France, Germany, Greece, Italy, the Netherlands, Norway, the United Kingdom, and the United States. Later, he and Mrs. Kennedy, R. Sargent Shriver, Jr., and others leave for Hyannis Port.

22 July 1961
WHITE HORSE, YUKON TERRITORY. Prime Minister John G. Diefenbaker of Canada calls President Kennedy in Hyannis Port on a new broadband microwave communications system that crosses Canada and links Alaska to the continental United States. He says to the President, "I am very pleased at this opportunity to welcome you again on behalf of the people of Canada. This is a great occasion."

HYANNIS PORT, MASSACHUSETTS. President

Kennedy, Jacqueline and Caroline Kennedy, and Jean and Stephen Smith cruise on Oyster Bay aboard the *Tarpon.* Mrs. Kennedy goes water skiing. A few hours later, President Kennedy swims at the beach with his wife and daughter.

25 July 1961
WASHINGTON, D.C. In the morning, President Kennedy attends a legislative leaders' breakfast and has brief meetings with Senator Hubert Humphrey, C. Douglas Dillon, Under-Secretary of State for Economic Affairs George Ball, Dave Powers, Pierre Salinger, Senator Claiborne Pell of Rhode Island, and Kenneth O'Donnell. At 1:00 P.M. , he attends a luncheon in honor of Abubakar Tafawa Balewa of Nigeria, after which he meets with Sir Balewa and other government officials of the Federation of Nigeria.

At 10:00 P.M. , President Kennedy addresses the nation on television and radio on the Berlin crisis. "We cannot and will not permit the Communists to drive us out of Berlin," he says, "for the fulfillment of our pledge to that city is essential to the morale and security of Western Germany, to the unity of Western Europe, and to the faith of the entire Free World." He indicates that the next day he will ask Congress to increase the current year's defense budget by $3,247,000,000 to increase the size of the Army from 875,000 to 1 million, and to increase the Navy and the Air Force by 29,000 and 63,000 men, respectively.

26 July 1961
WASHINGTON, D.C. President Kennedy presents the Distinguished Service Medal to Admiral Arleigh A. Burke in a ceremony in the Rose Garden.

27 July 1961
WASHINGTON, D.C. In the morning, President Kennedy meets with Representative Gerald R. Ford, Jr., of Michigan and concludes talks with Prime Minister Balewa of Nigeria. A joint statement released afterward says, "The President and the Prime Minister reaffirmed their support for the principle of self-determination for dependent peoples and their unalterable opposition to racial discrimination under any name or in any guise." It continues, "The President reiterated the desire of the United States Government to assist Nigeria in its social and economic development."

President Kennedy sends a telegram of congratulations to Riccardo Cassin and other members of the Italian team "who have achieved such a splendid mountaineering feat on Mount McKinley" in Alaska. In the afternoon, President Kennedy attends a meeting of the

Joint Chiefs of Staff, and later attends a state dinner in his honor given at the Mayflower Hotel by the Prime Minister Balewa of Nigeria.

28 July 1961
WASHINGTON, D.C. A meeting is held on Southeast Asia and the upcoming visit to the United States by Vice-President Chen Cheng. President Kennedy attends, along with Deputy Under-Secretary of State for Political Affairs U. Alexis Johnson, Acting Director of the Office of Chinese Affairs Robert Rinden, Assistant Secretary of State for Far Eastern Affairs Walter P. McConaughy, and several others. Later in the afternoon, President Kennedy leaves by helicopter from the south grounds of the White House for Andrews Air Force Base where he takes a plane for Otis Air Force Base in Massachusetts.

HYANNIS PORT, MASSACHUSETTS. Jacqueline Kennedy is joined by her husband at a dinner celebrating her thirty-second birthday.

29 July 1961
WASHINGTON, D.C. President Kennedy calls Air Force Captain Virgil Ivan ("Gus") Grissom aboard the *Randolph* by radio-phone to congratulate him on his earlier orbital space flight and safe return to earth. President Kennedy watched the launch from Cape Canaveral on television.

President Kennedy signs H.R. 6441, an amendment to the Federal Water Pollution Control Act, that provides for more effective water pollution control. The law, he says, "affords a more comprehensive and precise definition of the Federal government's role is controlling the pollution of our country's rivers and streams."

30 July 1961
HYANNIS PORT, MASSACHUSETTS. President and Mrs. Kennedy attend services at St. Francis Xavier Church in the morning and sail on the *Marlin* in the afternoon with Patricia Lawford and her daughter Sydney, Eunice Shriver, the President's valet, George Thomas, and Secret Service Agent James Rowley. On separate trips later, President Kennedy rides with his children in a golf cart to the beach and to a store.

31 July 1961
WASHINGTON, D.C. A state luncheon is given in the East Room at the White House by President Kennedy in honor of Chen Cheng, vice-president of the Republic of China. Later, Kennedy meets with Mayor Richard Daley of Chicago, with Governor David Lawrence of Pennsylvania, and with Senator Jacob Javits of

New York. Adviser John F. McCloy reports to Kennedy on his recent meeting with Premier Khruschev and their discussions on the Berlin crisis and disarmament.

1 August 1961

WASHINGTON, D.C.   Following a legislative leaders' breakfast at 8:45 A.M. , President Kennedy, Vice-President Johnson, Dean Rusk, George Ball, and other U.S. officials confer with Vice-President Chen Cheng of the Republic of China and other Chinese leaders. At 11:34 A.M. , the President meets privately with Vice-President Johnson, and at 11:41 A.M. , with McGeorge Bundy, General Maxwell Taylor, and General Chester V. Clifton. President Kennedy signs a resolution passed by Congress permitting him to call into service up to 250,000 reserves and to extend the tours of duty of reserve units. The authority for these actions expires on 1 July 1962.

In the afternoon, he speaks at a ceremony marking the fifteenth anniversary of the Fulbright Act. He says, "As a result of this program, which permits this exchange of representatives, scholars, students, educators, and artists from our country to countries around the world and from their countries to our country...over 50,000 people have been permitted to come to a greater understanding of the benefits of our culture and civilization, and the culture and the civilization of other countries." He then congratulates Senator James W. Fulbright.

2 August 1961

WASHINGTON, D.C.   In the morning, President Kennedy confers with C. Douglas Dillon, who will the next day lead an American delegation to the Punta del Este Conference of the Inter-American Economic and Social Council at Montevideo. The President says, "I consider this conference to be the most important international conference which has been held since this administration assumed responsibility on January 20th." Kennedy also meets with McGeorge Bundy, Walter W. Heller, and Senator Hubert H. Humphrey. In the afternoon, he meets with a special delegation from Guatemala and with Secretary of State for the Presidency Bahi Ladgham of Tunisia on French occupation of its naval base near Bizerte.

Following several days of conferences, Vice-President Cheng of the Republic of China and President Kennedy issue a joint statement that confirms "the intention of the United States Government to continue its military aid program to the Republic of China (Taiwan) and to provide substantial assistance to the Republic of China in support of its economic development program designed to achieve accelerated social and economic progress for the welfare of the people of free China." In the evening,

Vice-President Cheng gives a dinner in honor of President Kennedy at the Mayflower Hotel.

3 August 1961

WASHINGTON, D.C.   The newly appointed ambassador from Nepal, M. P. Koirala, presents his credentials to President Kennedy in a meeting attended by Angier Biddle Duke and Armin H. Meyer, deputy assistant secretary of state for Near Eastern and South Asian Affairs. Later, President Kennedy meets with Senator Russell Long, Ambassador Adlai Stevenson, and Alphonse Donahue, who presents him with an original Lincoln letter.

4 August 1961

WASHINGTON, D.C.   Following a Cabinet meeting in the morning, President Kennedy confers with Governor Grant Sawyer of Nevada and with Secretary of Labor Arthur J. Goldberg and members of the AFL-CIO Executive Committee, including George Meany. In the afternoon, he meets with the Ambassador from Thailand, Visutr Arthayukti, and with Senator Robert Kerr of Oklahoma. Later, he leaves for Hyannis Port where a message of congratulations he sent to Admiral Alfred C. Richmond on the one hundred seventy-first birthday of the Coast Guard is released to the press.

5 August 1961

PUNTA DEL ESTE, URUGUAY.   At the Inter-American Economics and Social Conference, Robert A. Conrads, Assistant Secretary General of the Conference, reads a message sent by President Kennedy. The President pledges that "the United States will allocate more than one billion dollars in development assistance to Latin America" during the first year of the Alliance for Progress.

5-7 August 1961

ABIDJAN, IVORY COAST.   Attorney General Robert F. Kennedy represents the United States at the country's independence day celebration.

7 August 1961

WASHINGTON, D.C.   At a ceremony attended by Vice-President Johnson, Senator Benjamin A. Smith II of Massachusetts, members of the Senate Interior Committee and House Insular Affairs Committee, Representative Thomas P. O'Neill, Jr., of Massachusetts, and others, President Kennedy signs H.R. 5.857, An Act to Provide for the Establishment of Cape Cod National Seashore Park. He says, "This act makes it possible for the people of the United States through their Government to acquire and preserve the natural and historic values of a portion of Cape Cod for the inspiration and enjoyment of people all over the United States." Throughout the day, the President has meetings with Representative James Roosevelt and Franklin D. Roosevelt, Jr., Senators Vance Hartke (Indiana), George A. Smathers (Florida), and Pat McNamara (Michigan), and Dr. B. C. Roy, a former physician to Mahatma Ghandi

8 August 1961
WASHINGTON, D.C. Following a legislative leaders' breakfast, President Kennedy signs S. 1643, the Agricultural Act of 1961, at a ceremony attended by Secretary of Agriculture Orville L. Freeman, National Farmers Union President James Patton, National Association of Wheat Growers' President Carl Bruns, and others. President Kennedy says the act "is a major step toward a sound agricultural economy and a better life for the farmers of this country. It is designed to improve farm income, expand the markets for agricultural products, reduce our stocks of grains and wheat, and relieve our taxpayers of carrying some of the cost of carrying these stocks." Later, he attends a meeting of the National Security Council, whose members include Glenn T. Seaborg, Byron White, Allen W. Dulles, David E. Bell, and Roswell L. Gilpatric.

9 August 1961
WASHINGTON, D.C. At a ceremony in the Rose Garden, President Kennedy presents a trophy to Charles Thompson, Sr., the winner of the power boat race in the 1960 President's Cup Regatta. In the evening, he has dinner at the home of Senator John Sherman Cooper at 1900 N Street, N.W.

10 August 1961
WASHINGTON, D.C. At a news conference held in the State Department Auditorium, President Kennedy expresses hope that Great Britain will be admitted as a full member in the European Common Market. He also announces that in view of a report from the special panel on nuclear testing, which has convinced him that "without an inspection system of the kind proposed by the United States and the United Kingdom at Geneva, no country in the world can ever be sure that a nation with a closed society is not conducting nuclear tests," he is "asking Ambassador Dean to return to Geneva on August 24 in an effort to ascertain whether the Soviet Union is now prepared to bring a safeguarded test ban agreement into being."

The White House also announces an agreement between President Kennedy and Vice-President Johnson on procedures in case of the disability of the president. The statement says that "under the arrangement...the Vice-President agrees to serve as Acting President 'after such consultation as seems appropriate to him under the circumstances,'" and that while neither the Constitution nor any law prescribes any procedure of consultation, "the President and Vice-President felt, as a matter of wisdom and sound judgment, that the Vice-President would wish to have the support of the Cabinet...as well as legal advice from the Attorney General...."

11 August 1961
WASHINGTON, D.C. The White House releases a letter from President Kennedy to Basil Williams, president of the Seneca Nation of Indians. President Kennedy writes that after reviewing the issue of the Kinzua Dam on the Allegheny River, he has "concluded that it is not possible" to halt its construction. Later, he leaves for Otis Air Force Base in Massachusetts.

12 August 1961
WASHINGTON, D.C. Plans for the reorganization of the Federal Maritime Commission, which include terminating the Federal Maritime Board, are put into effect. On 12 June 1961, President Kennedy had sent a bill to Congress asking for reorganization of the Commission. (The President's father, Joseph P. Kennedy, had been chairman of the Commission from April 1937 through February 1938.) Also implemented are reorganization plans for the Federal Home Loan Bank Board.

13 August 1961
EAST BERLIN, GERMANY. The "Berlin Wall" is erected, closing the border between East Berlin and West Berlin. Since the beginning of the month, thousands of East Berliners have escaped to West Berlin.

HYANNIS PORT, MASSACHUSETTS. After attending services at St. Francis Xavier Church, President and Mrs. Kennedy, with their daughter Caroline and other members of the Kennedy clan, take a cruise on the *Marlin*, dropping anchor at Great Island.

14 August 1961
WASHINGTON, D.C. President Kennedy requests Congress to appropriate $73.2 million for the transport and storage of wheat and medical supplies for civil defense. He also sends a message to Sir Winston Churchill paying tribute to the former British leader on the twentieth anniversary of the Atlantic Charter.

15 August 1961
WASHINGTON, D.C. With White House aides Kenneth O'Donnell, Dave Powers, and Timothy J. Reardon, President Kennedy attends an All Saints' Day

United Press International.

Lt. Col. John H. Glenn, Jr. and President Kennedy examine the Mercury space capsule in which the astronaut circled the earth three times. Vice-President Lyndon Johnson is on the right. At Cape Canaveral on 23 February 1962.

mass at St. Matthew's Cathedral. Later, he delivers an address before the Foreign Policy Briefing Conference at the State Department Auditorium.

16 August 1961

WASHINGTON, D.C. At a meeting with Representative Samuel S. Stratton of New York, President Kennedy autographs a baseball for the Baseball Hall of Fame. During the day, he meets with Brig. Gen. Chester V. Clifton, Secretary of Health, Education, and Welfare Abraham Ribicoff, and Walter Reuther of the United Auto Workers Union.

17 August 1961

WASHINGTON, D.C. On the occasion of the twenty-fifth anniversary of the first unemployment insurance fund, President Kennedy sends a letter to Secretary of Labor Arthur J. Goldberg praising the fund for helping "ease the financial burden of many millions of workers who lost their jobs through no fault of their own."

PUNTA DEL ESTE, URUGUAY. The charter of the Alliance for Progress is signed at the Inter-American Economics and Social Conference.

19 August 1961

WEST BERLIN, GERMANY. In an address to the city's Parliament, Vice-President Lyndon Johnson affirms President Kennedy's commitment that the United States will defend West Berlin's freedom.

WASHINGTON, D.C. Secretary of the Treasury C. Douglas Dillon, who attended the Inter-American Economics and Social Conference at Punta del Este, Uruguay, arrives at the White House at 8:00 P.M. President Kennedy, along with Mr. and Mrs. Dean Rusk and Mrs. Dillon, welcomes him back. A reception for Dillon in the Blue Room is attended by the President and numerous congressmen and government officials.

20 August 1961

WASHINGTON, D.C. After attending services at St. Matthew's Cathedral, President Kennedy leaves the White House by helicopter with Tazewell Shepard, Pierre Salinger, and domestic staff member Providencia Paredes for Andrews Air Force Base. There they board a plane for Otis Air Force Base in Massachusetts.

HYANNIS PORT, MASSACHUSETTS. At noon,

President Kennedy, along with Jacqueline and Caroline, designer Oleg Cassini, and Robin Butler, leaves for a cruise on the *Marlin*.

21 August 1961

WASHINGTON, D.C. At 5:30 P.M. at the White House,President Kennedy meets with Vice-President Johnson, Secretary of State Dean Rusk, General Lucius Clay, McGeorge Bundy, and Charles Bohlen. At 6:40 P.M., he meets with Secretary of the Treasury Dillon, Henry Fowler, Lawrence O'Brien, and Joseph Barr.

22 August 1961

WASHINGTON, D.C. In the morning, President Kennedy attends a legislative leaders' breakfast, then greets a group of Fulbright teachers from sixteen countries who are on a White House tour. From 11:45 A.M. to 12:40 P.M., he meets with Treasury Secretary Dillon and Democratic members of the House Ways and Means Committee, including Chairman Wilbur D. Mills. After a swim and lunch, President Kennedy participates in a recording for the United Community Campaign. At 4:00 P.M. , he greets handicapped children who are attending a concert given by the symphony orchestra of the Brevard Music Camp of North Carolina on the South Lawn of the White House. He tells them that "this is the first in a series of concerts here at the White House, by students of music, by younger people for younger people—and we hope that we will have many during the coming months and years." In the evening, he briefly attends a reception of the Democratic National Committee at the Mayflower Hotel, and later cruises down the Potomac River on the *Honey Fitz* with John Sherman Cooper, Charles Bartlett, C. Douglas Dillon, Joseph Alsop, and others.

23 August 1961

WASHINGTON, D.C. At 10:30 A.M. , President Kennedy welcomes Mrs. Jack Sprayberry of Rome, Georgia, who is the one-millionth visitor to the White House in 1961. Later, he meets with a delegation from the National Association of Intergroup Relations Officials, whose president is George Culberson, executive director of the Pittsburgh Commission on Human Relations.

24 August 1961

WASHINGTON, D.C. Following meetings with Representative Adam Clayton Powell and Vice-President Johnson, President Kennedy meets with the heads of the Department of Commerce, the Committee for Economic Development, the National Association of Manuafacturers, and the U.S. Chamber of Commerce.

In response to yesterday's Soviet note making certain charges against the United States and its allies, the Kennedy administration releases a statement declaring that "the United States must serve a solemn warning to the Soviet Union that any interference by the Soviet Government or its East German regime with free access to West Berlin would be an aggressive act for the consequences of which the Soviet Government would bear full responsibility."

28 August 1961

WASHINGTON, D.C. A White House celebration is held for the first Peace Corps volunteers to be sent abroad. President Kennedy tells them, "You will be the personification of a special group of young Americans, and if you can impress them with your commitment to freedom, to the advancement of the interests of people everywhere, to your pride in your country and its best traditions and what it stands for, the influence may be far-reaching and will go far beyond the immediate day-to-day tasks that you may do in the months that are ahead." Members of the group will leave for Tanganyika and Ghana to teach in secondary schools.

29 August 1961

WASHINGTON, D.C. President Kennedy meets with a group of Asian newspaper directors and editors representing publications from Japan, Hong Kong, the Philippines, Malaya, India, and Pakistan. Ambassador Berhanu Dinke of Ethiopia presents Kennedy with a gift from Emperor Haile Selassie, a Bible translated from Geez into English.

The President issues a Labor Day statement in which he encourages the labor force to learn modern skills and declares, "In setting the goal of our society at the realization of human dignity, we reach for the highest of stars and seek the outer limit of human capability. In this, now as always the new world for the spirit, the labor of free men is both the reward and the way."

30 August 1961

WASHINGTON, D.C. At a press conference, President Kennedy announces the appointment of General Lucius Clay as his "personal representative in Berlin, with the rank of Ambassador."

WASHINGTON,D.C. The Kennedy administration releases a statement harshly criticizing Russia's decision to resume nuclear weapons testing. The move, the statement says, presents a hazard to all people by increasing the dangers of nuclear fallout and of thermonuclear holocaust. The statement concludes, "The termination

President and Mrs. Kennedy with John, Jr., and
Caroline in Palm Beach on Easter Sunday of 1962.

of the moratorium on nuclear testing by the Soviet unilateral decision leaves the United States under the necessity of deciding what its own national interests require." At a press conference held at the State Department auditorium, President Kennedy announces his appointment of General Lucius Clay as his personal representative to Berlin.

31 August 1961
WASHINGTON, D.C. At a ceremony held to introduce a Workmen's Compensation commemorative stamp on the occasion of the fiftieth anniversary of the first Workmen's Compensation law tomorrow, President Kennedy speaks about the need for the United States to meet the problem of medical care for older citizens.

1 September 1961
WASHINGTON, D.C. President Kennedy sends a letter to Senator Pat McNamara, chairman of the Senate Special Committee on Aging, in which he declares that "the proposal to provide health insurance for the aged under Social Security is one of the most important measures I have advocated."

SIBERIA. After almost three years of complying with a nuclear test ban, the Soviet Union breaks its moratorium and begins a sixty-day series of tests with more than forty nuclear weapons.

2 September 1961
WASHINGTON, D.C. President Kennedy signs the Minimum Wage bill. In a statement issued later, the President says that "while the new minimums of $1.15 per hour for workers presently covered by the law and of $1.00 per hour for those newly covered are admittedly inadequate to provide the full material well-being that this great nation is capable of giving to its citizens, they still provide for millions of workers a chance to enjoy a greater share of our nation's general economic progress. The legislation," he continues, "is one of the most important domestic accomplishments so far of this administration."

WASHINGTON, D.C., and LONDON. The Russian embassies in these two cities receive a joint message from President Kennedy and Prime Minister Harold Macmillan. Addressed to Premier Nikita S. Khruschev, the message asks that the Soviet Union join with the United States and Great Britain in agreeing not to conduct fallout-producing nuclear testing in the atmosphere. They also urge that the Soviets meet with the United States and England in Geneva no later than 9 September to sign an agreement prohibiting such testing.

4 September 1961
HYANNIS PORT, MASSACHUSETTS. President Kennedy signs the Foreign Assistance Act of 1961. The bill authorizes $4,253,500,000 in foreign aid for the following year, and $1,500,000,000 for each fiscal year through 1966. The act also gives the President authority, when he considers it in the national interest, to make development loan commitments through 30 June 1966. In a statement issued after the signing, President Kennedy says that with this legislation, "a decade of development begins"; the bill "will assist the under-developed countries of the world to take the critical steps essential to economic and social progress."

5 September 1961
HYANNIS PORT, MASSACHUSETTS. In a statement released here, President Kennedy urges school administrators to implement physical fitness programs. General Hershey had earlier reported that of six million men who took military physicals, one million were rejected for physical reasons that could have been prevented. President Kennedy says that "young Americans must be made fit to serve our nation in its hour of need—fit to face the future with confidence and strength."

WASHINGTON, D.C. As the Soviet Union continues nuclear tests, President Kennedy announces, "I have today ordered the resumption of nuclear tests in the laboratory and underground, with no fallout....We have no other choice in fulfillment of the United States Government to its own citizens and to the security of other free nations." President Kennedy signs an amendment to the 1958 Federal Aviation Act making the hijacking of an airplane punishable by imprisonment or death. He also signs a bill granting an additional $20 million for the Small Business Administration. This bill provides financial assistance to prospective and established owners of small businesses.

6 September 1961

WASHINGTON, D.C. On the occasion of the Jewish High Holy Days, President Kennedy issues a statement in which he says, "I am happy to extend to millions of our fellow citizens of the Jewish faith, now celebrating Rosh Hashanah, my warm greetings and every good wish for the New Year." President Kennedy signs bills provid-

Three-year-old Caroline Kennedy gives her new baby brother John, Jr., a kiss in his sleep, in Washington, D.C., 1962.

United Press International.

ing funds to treat hog cholera (a contagious and often fatal disease of swine) and to provide fissionable materials to international atomic energy organizations. Members of the Joint Committee for Reenactment of Lincoln's Inauguration and the D.C. Centennial Committee present Kennedy with a gold medallion.

In a letter to them, President Kennedy asks leaders of the steel industry not to increase their prices in the months ahead. Kennedy also releases a statement praising various Southern cities for integrating their public schools. He calls such peaceful integration "a dramatic demonstration of the progress that the United States is making in improving the position of Negroes in our society."

7 September 1961

WASHINGTON, D.C. In a special message, President Kennedy urges Congress to take action in the current session on an agreement his administration has concluded with France, providing for the introduction of defensive nuclear weapons into France's military armaments. The newly appointed ambassador from Ceylon, William Gopallawa, presents his credentials to President Kennedy. Others with whom the President meets during the day include Assistant Secretary of State for Near Eastern Affairs Phillips Talbot, U.S. Ambassador to Tunisia Walter N. Walmsley, Luther Hodges, members of the National Export Expansion Committee of the Department of Commerce, *Time* magazine writer Hugh Sidey, Dean Rusk, Robert F. Kennedy, Edward R. Murrow, and Dean Acheson.

8 September 1961

WASHINGTON, D.C. President Kennedy expresses regret to the nation that the House has held over until next year a bill that would provide compensation to World War II veterans.

9 September 1961

MOSCOW. Premier Khruschev sends letters to President Kennedy and Prime Minister Harold Macmillan rejecting their 3 September proposal to ban fallout-producing nuclear testing in the atmosphere.

HYANNIS PORT, MASSACHUSETTS. In a joint statement issued here, President Kennedy and Prime Minister Macmillan "note with deepest regret" that their proposal to stop nuclear testing has not been accepted by the Soviet Union. At 12:25 P.M. , President Kennedy takes a leisurely ride on the Kennedy family's property in a golf cart and later goes boating with his father, Ann Gargan, sports magnate Carroll Rosenbloom, and others.

12 September 1961

BROOKLINE, MASSACHUSETTS. The house where President John F. Kennedy was born is marked with a commemorative plaque by the Town of Brookline. The text on the plaque reads:

> Birthplace of John F. Kennedy 35th President of the United States Born on May 19, 1917, on this site 83 Beals St., Brookline, Mass.

WASHINGTON, D.C. Representatives and alternates of the United States delegation to the United Nations are sworn in at the White House. President Kennedy tells the delegates that they face a different, more intense situation "with the admission into the United Nations of new countries with all their problems and all their hopes." Later, after greeting them at Andrews Air Force Base, the President confers with President Sukarno of Indonesia and President Modibo Keita of Mali and their aides at the White House. At 5:40 P.M., over fifty members of Congress join President Kennedy and Vice-President Johnson at a coffee hour.

13 September 1961

WASHINGTON, D.C. The President signs three bills that had been requested by Attorney General Robert F. Kennedy: S. 1653, which prohibits interstate transportation in aid of racketeering; S. 1656, which prohibits betting over the telephone; and S. 1657, which makes the commercial transportation of wagering paraphernalia illegal. The President holds separate meetings with President Keita of Mali and President Sukarno of Indonesia and their assistants, then gives a luncheon in honor of the two leaders.

14 September 1961

WASHINGTON, D.C. President Kennedy arrives in his office at 9:30 A.M. and meets with Senators Sam Ervin, Jr., and B. Everett Jordan of North Carolina several minutes later. At 11:00 A.M., he holds a cabinet meeting, and throughout the day he confers with Robert F. Kennedy, U.S. ambassadors Maurice M. Bernbaum (Ecuador) and Robert F. Woodward (Chile), and Ambassador Mohieddine Fekini of Libya, among others. At 5:30 P.M. at the South Portico, he bids farewell to President Keita of Mali, who is taking a helicopter to Andrews Air Force Base, and then attends a congressional coffee hour.

15 September 1961

WASHINGTON, D.C. President Kennedy confers with General Lucius Clay, who is leaving for Berlin, and General Maxwell Taylor, then meets with former Brazilian president Juscelino Kubitschek. The newly appointed ambassador from Portugal, Pedro Theotonio Pereira presents his credentials to the President. A luncheon is held at the White House in honor of the foreign ministers of Western nations who are attending the Quadripartite Meeting, including Hervé Alphand of France, Heinrich von Brentano of Germany, and the Earl of Home of Great Britain.

Following the detonation of atomic bombs at an underground site in Nevada, President Kennedy announces that the United States has resumed nuclear testing. He points out that the explosion produced no fallout, unlike the nuclear tests in the atmosphere conducted by the Soviet Union. Late in the afternoon, President and Mrs. Kennedy leave for Hyannis Port for the weekend.

18 September 1961

WASHINGTON, D.C. President Kennedy awards the President's Cup to Bill Muncey of Seattle, who won the President's Cup Regatta over the weekend. At 10:00 A.M., Kennedy attends a luncheon at the White House for a group of twenty Kentucky publishers.

President Kennedy expresses "shock and loss" over the death of Dag Hammarskjold, who was killed earlier in the day in a plane crash in Northern Rhodesia. "It is tragic and ironic," he says in a statement, "that his death came during a mission he was undertaking in order to bring about a cease-fire in Katanga." Kennedy urges UN members to "build the United Nations into the effective instrument for peace which was Dag Hammarskjold's great ambition."

19 September 1961

WASHINGTON, D.C. Robert F. Kennedy resigns from the Washington Club because of its alleged policy of excluding blacks from membership.

President Kennedy signs a bill (S. 1368) that amends the Shipping Act of 1916 by providing for the licensing of independent ocean freighters. A "salute to the President" plaque is presented to the President on behalf of the Boy Scouts of Everett, Washington. President Kennedy meets with the Senate Preparedness Investigating Subcommittee of the Committee on Armed Services, then with various aides. From 11:42 A.M. to 11:52 A.M., he meets with Sioux chief Johnson Holy Rock of the Pine Ridge Reservation in South Dakota, Public Housing Commissioner Marie McGuire, and others. He congratulates them for working out the first public housing aid for Indian families. At 4:00 P.M., he attends a Joint Chiefs of Staff meeting, and at 8:00 P.M., he and Mrs. Kennedy join a state dinner in honor of President Don Manuel Prado and Mrs. Prado of Peru, whom they had earlier greeted at the airport.

20 September 1961

WASHINGTON, D.C. Following a 9:00 A.M. congressional coffee hour, President Kennedy, Ambassadors Angier Biddle Duke and James Loeb, Robert woodward, and Donald Barnes, interpreter, meet with President Prado of Peru and his aides. The President then signs a bill (H.R. 8102) to extend the Federal Airport Act. In a speech broadcast on behalf of the United Campaign, he urges Americans to help homeless children, the elderly, the sick, and the handicapped with their contributions.

21 September 1961

WASHINGTON, D.C. In the morning, President Kennedy meets with Miss USA, Jo Ann Odum, the chairman of the board of the United States Steel Corporation, Roger M. Blough, and the newly appointed Ambassador from India, Braj Kumar Nehru, among others. He lunches with movie director Otto Preminger and the cast of *Advise and Consent*, which features Peter Lawford and many other stars.

In the afternoon, President Kennedy winds up three days of discussions with President Prado of Peru, and both leaders issue a joint statement affirming their "adherence to the principles of the Alliance for Progress." Kennedy signs the Act of 1961 (H.R. 8666), also known as the Fulbright-Hays Act, which is intended to strengthen foreign relations by promoting mutual understanding among peoples around the world through educational and cultural activities. He then meets with more than fifty members of the Business Council, and, at 8:00 P.M., with Mrs. Kennedy attends a dinner given in their honor by President Prado at the Peruvian Embassy.

22 September 1961

WASHINGTON, D.C. President Kennedy signs the Peace Corps Act, which permanently establishes the organization and appropriates $40 million for its first year of operation. "With the enactment of this legislation," he says, "an avenue is provided by which Americans can serve their country in the cause of world peace and understanding and simultaneously assist other nations toward their legitimate goals of freedom and opportunity...."

He also signs a bill (H.R. 7916) expanding a program to develop economical processes of converting salt water to fresh, the Juvenile Delinquency and Youth Offenses Control Act of 1961, which is intended to deter juvenile delinquency, and the Health, Education, and Welfare Department Appropriation bill, among others.

The Interstate Commerce Commission approves regulations, requested by Attorney General Robert F. Kennedy, that ban segregation in interstate bus travel and in terminals. Interstate bus stations will hereafter be required to post notices stating that segregation is prohibited, and interstate buses will not be able to use stations where discrimination is allowed.

23 September 1961

WASHINGTON, D.C. On President Kennedy's instructions, Secretary of Defense Robert S. McNamara and General Maxwell D. Taylor leave for Saigon to tour South Vietnam and evaluate the war between Viet Cong guerrillas and military forces commanded by the government of President Ngo Dinh Diem. The conflict seems to grow progressively worse as American troops observing there become involved in combat and Buddhist demonstrations and fiery suicides attract world attention.

25 September 1961

NEW YORK. President Kennedy delivers a moving address before the General Assembly of the United Nations. "We meet in an hour of grief and challenge," he begins. "Dag Hammarskjold is dead." He speaks of varous problems faced by the UN: its leadership ("however difficult it may be to fill Mr. Hammarskjold's place, it can better be filled by one man rather than three"); on disarmament ("a treaty assuring the end of nuclear tests of all kinds"); on the use of outer space ("extending the United Nations Charter to the limits of man's explorations in the universe, reserving outer space for peaceful use"); on colonialism; and on threats to peace, as in South Vietnam, Laos, and West Berlin. President Kennedy urges all nations to persevere in the pursuit of peace. "Together we shall save our planet," he says, "or together we shall perish in its flames. Save it we can—and save it we must—and then shall we earn the eternal thanks of mankind and, as peacemakers, the eternal blessing of God."

27 September 1961

NEWPORT, RHODE ISLAND. Speaking at the Pringle Auditorium of the Naval War College, President Kennedy announces the appointment of John McCone to succeed Allen Dulles as director of the Central Intelligence Agency. Following his remarks, Kennedy returns to Hammersmith Farm, where he goes sailing on the *Honey Fitz* with his wife and the designer Oleg Cassini.

30 September 1961

WASHINGTON, D.C. President Kennedy signs legislation authorizing funds for the Atomic Energy Commission, for public works programs, and for foreign aid.

2 October 1961

ROME. Pope John XXIII receives Rose Kennedy at a private audience at the Vatican.

3 October 1961

WASHINGTON, D.C. After meetings with Foreign Minister Thanet Khoman and Ambassador Visutr Arthayukti of Thailand, and with close aides, President Kennedy attends the swearing-in ceremony of Fowler Hamilton as administrator for the Agency for International Development. At 12:45 P.M. , he leaves for the Statler-Hilton Hotel where he is met by *Washington Post* publisher Phillip Graham and J. R. Wiggins. After a luncheon celebrating the publication of *The Adams Papers: Diary and Autobiography of John Adams,* President Kennedy talks about Adams's times, an "extraordinary golden age in our history which produced so many men of exceptional talent."

4 October 1961

WASHINGTON, D.C. President Kennedy signs a bill creating the Woodrow Wilson Commission, which will formulate plans to construct a permanent memorial to the twenty-eighth president in the capital area; legislation restricting the recruitment of Mexican farm laborers under certain conditions; an act to amend the 1916 Shipping Act permitting ocean carriers to charge dual rates depending upon the service offered; and a bill to increase the scope of the Fugitive Felon Law. As previously arranged, Kennedy authorizes the United States to instruct French representatives in the use of nuclear power. He also establishes a commission to study the financing of presidential campaigns with an eye toward providing a federal share in the costs.

In the evening, a White House dinner honors El Ferik Ibrahim Abboud, president of the Supreme Council for the Armed Forces and prime minister of the Republic of Sudan. In his toast to his American hosts, President Abboud says, "President Kennedy has opened a New Frontier in foreign policy which bespeaks the very highest order of courage on his part, and on the part of your great nation."

5 October 1961

WASHINGTON, D.C. Following a full morning of meetings, including a conference with President Abboud of Sudan, President Kennedy lunches with network television board chairmen William Paley of CBS, Robert Sarnoff of NBC, Leonard Goldenson of ABC, and LeRoy Collins of the National Association of Broadcasters, and Edward R. Murrow.

The President signs the Community Health Services and Facilities Act which authorizes federal aid for the construction of health research facilities as well as grants to develop less costly out-of-hospital care for the elderly and the chronically ill. Kennedy sends a message of con-

gratulations to Chiang Kai-shek on China's National Day, which this year is also the fiftieth anniversary of the Chinese Revolution.

6 October 1961

WASHINGTON, D.C. A White House luncheon is held for nineteen New Jersey newspaper publishers. President Kennedy then meets with President Abboud of Sudan, and they issue a joint statement summarizing their discussions. With Dean Rusk, Foy Kohler, Charles Bohlen, McGeorge Bundy, Theodore Sorenson, and an interpreter, President Kennedy meets with Soviet Minister of Foreign Affairs Andrei Gromyko, Soviet Ambassador Mikahail A. Menshikov, Soviet Deputy Foreign Minister Vladimir Semenov, and an interpreter. They discuss Berlin, Laos, and other international situations.

In the evening, President Kennedy attends a dinner given in his honor by President Abboud at the Mayflower Hotel.

9 October 1961

NEWPORT, RHODE ISLAND. Aboard the *Honey Fitz,* President Kennedy, Jacqueline and Caroline Kennedy, Janet and Hugh Auchincloss, Senator Claiborne Pell and his wife, and Charles Bartlett observe exercises of the submarine *Corsair.*

DALLAS, TEXAS. At 3:45 P.M. CST, President Kennedy arrives at Love Field and proceeds to Baylor Memorial Hospital where he visits with the ailing Sam Rayburn in Room 729. At 4:35 P.M., he leaves the hospital for Love Field and his flight back to the capital.

11 October 1961

WASHINGTON, D.C. At a press conference at the State Department auditorium, President Kennedy announces that he has asked General Maxwell Taylor "to go to Saigon...and discuss with the President and American officials on the spot ways we can perhaps better assist the government of Vietnam" in meeting threats to its independence. He concludes by saying that he is going "to appoint a panel of outstanding scientists, doctors, and others to prescribe a program of action in the field of mental retardation."

12 October 1961

CHAPEL HILL, NORTH CAROLINA. President Kennedy and a large party arrive at the Raleigh-Durham Airport, where they are greeted by Governor Terry Sanford and others. Kennedy officially opens the North Carolina Trade Fair at Charlotte, and the presidential party then leaves for the University of North Carolina at Chapel Hill, 17 miles away.

Caroline Kennedy leads the way for her father, who is also her doll-carrier, in Washington, D.C.

At 11:00 A.M. , the University Day program at the school begins. President Kennedy delivers an address in which he says that "peace and freedom do not come cheap, and we are destined, all of us here today, to live out most if not all of our lives in uncertainty and challenge and peril." After receiving an honorary degree from the University of North Carolina, President Kennedy and his party and several North Carolina congressmen leave for the Raleigh-Durham Airport where they all board a plane for Fort Bragg.

FORT BRAGG, NORTH CAROLINA. President Kennedy inspects the Eighty-second Airborne Division, speaks to the troops, and observes a demonstration of military techniques. Prior to his visit, he had sent a telegram authorizing the green beret as part of the Special Forces uniform.

13 October 1961

WASHINGTON, D.C. In the morning, President Kennedy speaks briefly with executives from the American Trucking Association and attends a National Security Council meeting. Later, he lunches with a group of more than twenty Missouri newspaper publishers. He issues a statement urging Americans to support UNICEF. At 4:30 P.M. , he leaves the White House to spend the weekend in Hyannis Port.

16 October 1961

WASHINGTON, D.C. A White House luncheon is held in honor of President Urho Kekkonen of Finland and his wife, whom President and Mrs. Kennedy had earlier met at Andrews Air Force Base. Following the luncheon, President Kennedy and his aides confer with President Kekkonen and high-ranking Finnish officials, who express their government's desire to remain neutral in world politics. At 5:00 P.M. , President Kennedy meets with civil-rights leader Martin Luther King, Jr., who proposes that the President issue another "emancipation proclamation."

Following several weeks of discussions with the management of the Louisville and Nashville, the Southern, and the Illinois Central railroads, Attorney General Robert F. Kennedy announces that these lines have agreed to ban discrimination at their depots.

17 October 1961

WASHINGTON, D.C. The President's morning and early afternoon schedule includes meetings with Senator Joseph Clark of Pennsylvania, Chief Minister Benedicto Kiwanuka of Uganda, and Senator Robert S. Kerr and Governor Howard Edmondson of Oklahoma. His Royal Highness Prince Khampan, the newly appointed Laotian ambassador, presents his credentials. The President then meets with representatives of the National Football Foundation and Hall of Fame. A White House statement is released urging that the Soviet Union not proceed with the testing of a 50-megaton nuclear bomb.

In the afternoon, Kennedy confers with the Foreign Intelligence Advisory Board and President Kekkonen of Finland. In the evening, he and Mrs. Kennedy attend part of a concert by the National Symphony Orchestra at Constitution Hall.

18 October 1961

WASHINGTON, D.C. President Kennedy meets with members of the panel on mental retardation, chaired by Dr. Leonard Mayo. Kennedy and United States officials also meet with President William U. S. Tubman of Liberia and his aides. They exchange views on international problems and reaffirm the friendship of the two nations. President Kennedy expresses a desire to provide American economic assistance to Liberia, including a long-term loan for the Mount Coffee hydroelectric project. A White House luncheon is then held in honor of President Tubman.

24 October 1961
WASHINGTON, D.C. President Kennedy sends a message of congratulations to Walter P. Marshall, president of the Western Union Telegraph Company in Omaha, Nebraska, on the occasion of the transcontinental telegraph centennial. The President had received copies of historic messages received by President Lincoln one hundred years ago today over a line linking the cities along the original route. President Kennedy also sends a letter to President Ngo Dinh Diem on the sixth anniversary of the Republic of Vietnam. Expressing sorrow for the suffering and death in that country, President Kennedy declares that "the United States is determined to help Vietnam preserve its independence...."

25 October 1961
WASHINGTON, D.C. With Under-Secretary of State George Ball, Deputy Assistant Secretary of State for European Affairs William Tyler, Richard Goodwin, and Arthur Schlesinger, Jr., assisting him, President Kennedy confers with Dr. Cheddi B. Jagan, premier of British Guiana. Later, President Kennedy meets with poet Carl Sandburg and Secretary of the Interior Stewart Udall; Charles B. Shuman, president of the American Farm Bureau Federation; Chester Bowles; and John McCone.

26 October 1961
WASHINGTON, D.C. In a morning cabinet meeting, President Kennedy speaks on the current outlook for the 1962 and 1963 federal budgets. Newly appointed ambassadors Dr. Louis Mars of Haiti and Sir David Ormsby-Gore of England present their credentials to President Kennedy.

27 October 1961
WASHINGTON, D.C. In the morning, President Kennedy meets with Mayor Robert F. Wagner of New York and Robert Moses, president of the New York World's Fair and with officials of the Export-Import Bank. Directors of the National Recreation Association present the President with their award for Outstanding Reporting in the Field of Physical Recreation (magazine category). President Kennedy and Vice-President Johnson lunch with nineteen Texas newspaper publishers. In the evening, President and Mrs. Kennedy leave the White House with Eunice Shriver, Gore Vidal, William Walton, and Alice Longworth for the National Guard Armory where they attend the International Horse Show.

28 October 1961
WASHINGTON, D.C. President Kennedy designates "Thursday, the twenty-third day of November of this year, as a day of national thanksgiving." Instead of the traditional fourth Thursday of November, this date is chosen to call attention to "the plight of those in many parts of the world to whom hunger is no stranger and the plight of those millions who live without the blessings of liberty and freedom."

WASHINGTON, D.C. President Kennedy names his sister Eunice Shriver as an unpaid consultant to the Panel on Mental Retardation.

29 October 1961
FORT SMITH, ARKANSAS. President Kennedy makes a brief speech and greets a group of twenty-five invalids and retarded children.

BIG CEDAR, OKLAHOMA. President Kennedy participates in a dedication ceremony opening the Cuachita National Forest Road. In his remarks he says, "We open this north-south highway, but in a larger sense, this meeting contributes to the education and well-being, in a sense, of the President of the United States. There is nothing more valuable than for any occupant of that high office than to leave that city once in a while and come and see this country, and to see what a great asset we have, in these difficult times.

POTEAU, OKLAHOMA. At 3:00 P.M., President Kennedy arrives at Ker-Mac, Senator Robert S. Kerr's ranch, to spend the night. Governor Edmondson of Oklahoma, Senator Monroney, and the Kerr family greet him there.

1 November 1961
WASHINGTON, D.C. A White House dinner is held in honor of former president Harry S. Truman and his wife, Bess. The Trumans spend the night at the Executive Mansion.

2 November 1961
WASHINGTON, D.C. President Kennedy signs the Delaware River Basin Compact, which establishes a commission comprised of representatives from the federal governemt and four states, Delaware, New Jersey, New York, and Pennsylvania, to devise and supervise water resource programs for the Delaware River Valley. At a National Security Council meeting later, joined by Harry Truman, President Kennedy announces to reporters that pursuant to nuclear testing by the Soviet Union, the United States will "proceed in developing nuclear weapons" without testing them in the atmosphere.

NEW YORK. Mayor Robert F. Wagner greets President Kennedy and his party at LaGuardia Airport. Kennedy issues a statement announcing his support for Mayor Wagner's re-election. Later, the President arrives at the Carlyle Hotel.

TRENTON, NEW JERSEY. At the War Memorial Building, President Kennedy participates in a political rally and endorses former county judge Richard Joseph Hughes for governor of New Jersey.

3 November 1961
WASHINGTON, D.C. President Kennedy greets President Leopold Sedar Senghor of the Republic of Senegal at Washington National Airport. The two leaders go by helicopter to the White House, where they discuss American economic aid to Senegal. After a luncheon in honor of President Senghor, Kennedy listens as General Maxwell Taylor reports on his trip to South Vietnam, Thailand, Hong Kong, and the Philippines.

WASHINGTON, D.C. The White House Historical Association, a nonprofit organization chartered to enrich public appreciation of the presidential residence, is incorporated. The association resulted from a suggestion by Jacqueline Kennedy, who wanted to restore the White House and its interior furnishings.

6 November 1961
QUONSET POINT NAVAL AIR STATION, RHODE ISLAND. President Kennedy greets Prime Minister Jawaharlal Nehru of India, his daughter Indira, and Ambassador Braj Kumar Nehru. They leave on the *Honey Fitz* for a luncheon at Hammersmith Farm.

7 November 1961
WASHINGTON, D.C. At 10:00 A.M. , President Kennedy, Ambassador to India John Kennedy Galbraith, and Phillips Talbot confer with Prime Minister Nehru of India, Ambassador Braj K. Nehru, and the foreign secretary in the Ministry of External Affairs on India, M. J. Desri. The President addresses by amplified telephone hookup the first regional White House conference being held in Chicago. In the evening, a dinner is held at the White House in honor of Prime Minister Nehru.

9 November 1961
WASHINGTON, D.C. Following a cabinet meeting, President Kennedy confers with the Commission on Campaign Financing, the chairman of which is Alex Heard, dean of the University of North Carolina at Chapel Hill. At 3:00 P.M. , President Kennedy begins a final round of discussions with Prime Minister Nehru. Over

the past days, the two leaders have conferred on developments in Berlin and Southeast Asia, nuclear testing, and disarmament. In the evening, Prime Minister Nehru entertains the Kennedys at the Indian Embassy.

10 November 1961
WASHINGTON, D.C. The reliability of the Labor department's statistics has called questionable, and President Kennedy announces the appointment of a committee to review data-measuring procedures used to gather statistics on employment and unemployment. Kennedy also presents the American Legion Merchant Marine Achievement Award to Solen B. Turman, president of Lykes Brothers Steamship Company, a major dry cargo concern.

11 November 1961
ARLINGTON, VIRGINIA. At a Veterans' Day ceremony at Arlington National Cemetery, President Kennedy places a wreath at the Tomb of the Unknown Soldier. In his address, he sounds a warning that the United States is "prepared in the final extreme to fight" for peace: "Let no nation confuse our perserverance and patience with fear of war or unwillingness to meet our responsibilities," he says.

12 November 1961
KANSAS CITY, MISSOURI. At the opening meeting of the Centennial Convocation of Land-Grant Colleges and State Universities, a film is shown in which President Kennedy praises land-grant schools.

CAMP DAVID, MARYLAND. President and Mrs. Kennedy spend the day here.

13 November 1961
NEW YORK. In an address to the Economic Club, Attorney General Robert F. Kennedy speaks on how antitrust laws promote competition in business and protect the public.

WASHINGTON, D.C. In a noon ceremony in the Rose Garden, Rabbi Maurice N. Eisendrath, president of the Union of American Hebrew Congregations, presents a Torah to President Kennedy. In a brief speech, Kennedy thanks the Union's board of trustees and tells them that their presence here "symbolizes the happy relations which exist between all religious groups, and must continue to exist in this country if we are to be worthy of our heritage."

At 8:00 P.M. , President and Mrs. Kennedy give a dinner in honor of Luis Munoz Marin, governor of Puerto Rico, and his wife. Among those attending are Hugh and

United Press International.

Attorney General, Robert F. Kennedy at the University of South Carolina, Columbia, April 1963.

Janet Auchincloss, Samuel Barber, Harry Belafonte, Leonard Bernstein, Henry Ford II, Alice Roosevelt Longworth, Gian Carlo Menotti, Eugene Ormandy, Adam Clayton Powell, and Leopold Stokowski. Following the dinner, the renowned Spanish cellist Pablo Casals, who now lives in Santurce, Puerto Rico, gives a concert in the East Room of the White House. Casals had vowed never to play in the White House again after the United States recognized the Spanish dictator Generalissimo Francisco Franco. (In 1904 when he was 28, Casals had performed in the Executive Mansion for Theodore Roosevelt. Alice Roosevelt Longworth, Roosevelt's daughter, who was present then is also present for Casals's performance tonight.) In introducing the famed cellist, President Kennedy says that Pablo Casals has demonstrated in his own life that "an artist must be a free man."

14 November 1961

WASHINGTON, D.C. President Kennedy addresses the board of trustees and advisory committee of the National Cultural Center. He reaffirms their goal of building a performing arts facility and says that creating a great cultural center in the nation's Capital is a most important national responsibility.

After a White House luncheon in honor of General Chung Lee Park of Korea, President Kennedy and Chairman Park meet to discuss the current situation in Korea and the Far East. (On 16 May 1961, an army coup had ousted the government of Prime Minister John M. Chang, and General Park took over as chairman of the military junta.) They reaffirm friendly relations between their two countries and discuss other world problems, such as mutual defense. President Kennedy pledges continued American economic aid to Korea.

15 November 1961

WASHINGTON, D.C. President Kennedy announces the establishment of a Presidential Committee on Youth Employment. The panel of academicians and government officials will study the bleak employment situation of the nation's youths and will recommend improvements.

16 November 1961

WASHINGTON, D.C.   Upon the death of Sam Rayburn, 79, President Kennedy's office releases a statement in which he praises the late Speaker of the House of Representatives as "a strong defender of the constitutional responsibilities of Congress."

SEATTLE, WASHINGTON.   Speaking on the one-hundredth anniversary program of the University of Washington, President Kennedy declares that the United States cannot: "compete with our adversaries in tactics of terror,...tell different stories to different audiences, foreign and domestic,...abandon the slow processes of consulting with our allies,...or abandon or control" the United Nations. He says that the country's citizens must remain calm in the wake of problems and crises throughout the world. Later, President Kennedy attends a dinner at the Olympic Hotel in honor of Senator Warren G. Magnuson of Washington.

17 November 1961

PHOENIX, ARIZONA.   At the Westward Ho Hotel, President Kennedy attends a dinner in honor of Senator Carl Hayden of Arizona and addresses the audience.

BONHAM, TEXAS.   President Kennedy attends funeral services at the First Baptist Church for the late Sam Rayburn. The President joins the Rayburn family in the offices of Reverend Jack Carson and then attends the burial at Willow Wild Cemetery. The ceremonies over, Kennedy leaves for the Bonham Golf Course where he boards a helicopter for Perrin Air Force Base.

LOS ANGELES.   Governor Edmund G. Brown of California greets President Kennedy and his party at the airport. At the Los Angeles Country Club, they are met by Mayor Samuel Yorty and a number of city officials. President Kennedy then proceeds to the Beverly Hills Hotel, where Conrad Hilton escorts him to his suite. At 6:15 P.M. , President Kennedy attends the first of two receptions in the hotel, and at 7:30 P.M. he leaves for the Hollywood Palladium where the Southern California Democratic Committee is giving a dinner in his honor. Frank Sinatra, Nat "King" Cole, and other entertainers perform. At 10:00 P.M. , Governor Brown introduces the President, who delivers an address.

19 November 1961

SANTA MONICA, CALIFORNIA.   President Kennedy lunches at the home of Peter Lawford at 625 Pacific Coast Highway. Actress Angie Dickinson and film director Billy Wilder are among the guests.

20 November 1961

WASHINGTON, D.C.   President Kennedy begins an exchange of views with Chancellor Konrad Adenauer of the Federal Republic of Germany and a number of German government officials on Berlin, NATO, the European Economic Committee, and other international situations.

21 November 1961

WASHINGTON, D.C.   Meetings continue between Chancellor Adenauer and President Kennedy. A White House luncheon honors the German leader.

22 November 1961

WASHINGTON, D.C.   The Rev. Theodore M. Hesburgh, president of the University of Notre Dame, presents the Laetare Medal to President Kennedy at the White House. The medal, awarded every year since 1883, is "the greatest honor Notre Dame can bestow upon a Catholic layman in the United States." Rev. Hesburgh salutes President Kennedy for "the calm determination and imaginative courage of your statesmanship in the age of prolonged and ever-increasing danger...."

23 November 1961

HYANNIS PORT, MASSACHUSETTS.   On a Thanksgiving Day hiatus from official duties, President Kennedy is joined at the Kennedy Memorial Skating Rink by Jacqueline, Eunice and Pat, and Ted and his wife, Joan.

24 November 1961

HYANNIS PORT, MASSACHUSETTS.   At his father's home, President Kennedy discusses increases in the size of American military forces with Secretary of Defense Robert S. McNamara, General Lyman Lemnitzer, McGeorge Bundy, Luther Hodges, and others.

25 November 1961

HYANNIS PORT, MASSACHUSETTS.   *Izvestia* journalist Aleksei I. Adzhubei, son-in-law of Premier Nikita Khruschev of the USSR, interviews President Kennedy on Soviet-American relations, communism, Berlin, NATO, nuclear testing, and other international problems. Adzhubei tells the President that Kennedy's election last year "was met with great hope by public opinion" in Russia.

28 November 1961

MOSCOW.   Aleksei I. Adzhubei's interview with President Kennedy appears in *Izvestia* in its entirety.

WASHINGTON, D.C. At the CIA Building, President Kennedy presents the National Security Award to Allen W. Dulles, who will retire as director of the CIA tomorrow.

29 November 1961

WASHINGTON, D.C. In the morning, President Kennedy gives a press conference, then attends two ceremonies, one for the swearing-in of John McCone as CIA director, the other for the Rockefeller Public Service Awards. In the afternoon, the President participates in a brief film for the Medical Progress dinner of the New York Hospital–Cornell Medical Center, meets with the Monetary Policy Group, and speaks before the Inter-American Economic and Social Council of the Pan-American Union.

30 November 1961

WASHINGTON, D.C. Directors of the Amateur Athletic Union present their AAU Life Membership Plaque to President Kennedy. Following that, the President meets with a group of Army commanders, including General Bruce C. Clarke, commander in chief of the U.S. Army in Europe, and James F. Collins, commander in chief of the Pacific Army. Later Kennedy confers with the Atomic Energy Commission, chaired by Dr. Glenn Seaborg.

1 December 1961

WASHINGTON, D.C. President Kennedy attends the swearing-in ceremony for Brooks Hays, his new special assistant, and presents the Enrico Fermi Award to Dr. Hans Bethe before the Atomic Energy Commission. This presentation is followed by a White House luncheon for more than twenty Minnesota newspaper publishers and editors.

2 December 1961

WASHINGTON, D.C. At Philadelphia Municipal Stadium, President Kennedy attends the Army-Navy football game. He sits on Army's side during the first half and on Navy's during the second half.

5 December 1961

NEW YORK. At the Waldorf-Astoria Hotel, President Kennedy attends the National Football Foundation Hall of Fame Awards. After accepting a Gold Medal for helping to advance amateur football in America, he addresses the audience.

6 December 1961

NEW YORK. The National Association of Manufacturers gives a reception at the Waldorf-Astoria Hotel in honor of President Kennedy. In a lengthy speech, Kennedy discusses the balance of payments and balance of trade.

WEST PALM BEACH, FLORIDA. President Kennedy arrives at his father's home, where he will spend the next few days.

7 December 1961

MIAMI, FLORIDA. At the Deauville Hotel, President Kennedy addresses the delegates of the Young Democrats of America. At noon, the President speaks before delegates to the national convention of the AFL-CIO, declaring that a vigorous foreign trade program will result in expanded employment for Americans.

11 December 1961

WASHINGTON, D.C. President Kennedy accepts the resignation of Secretary of the Navy John B. Connally. Connally, whose resignation becomes effective in nine days, intends to run for governor of Texas.

14 December 1961

WASHINGTON, D.C. The Commission on the Status of Women is established by President Kennedy. Declaring that "women should not be considered a marginal group to be employed periodically only to be denied opportunity to satisfy their needs and aspirations," he says that the purpose of the Commission will be to further the rights of women so that they may "make the best use of their talents and function constructively, both through legislation and through necessary supportive services by private or public agencies." Following the breaking of a cease-fire between government and Katangese forces in the Republic of the Congo, President Kennedy urges Prime Minister Cyrille Adoula and Moise Tshombe of the Katanga province to restore civil order.

15 December 1961

WASHINGTON, D.C. President Kennedy responds to a letter from President Ngo Dinh Diem requesting aid. Kennedy writes, "We are prepared to help the Republic of Vietnam to protect its people and to preserve its independence. We shall promptly increase our assistance to your defense effort...."

Kennedy meets with assistants in the morning, and at 11:55 A.M., leaves the White House by helicopter for Andrews Air Force Base where he and Mrs. Kennedy, along with a group of government officials, board a plane for Puerto Rico.

SAN JUAN, PUERTO RICO. At 4:15 P.M., President Kennedy and his party arrive at International Airport. They are greeted by Governor Luis Munoz Marin and various Puerto Rican political leaders and government officials. In a brief speech, President Kennedy says that "Puerto Rico serves as an admirable bridge between Latin America and North America....It is most important and appropriate as we start this journey to two great countries, Venezuela and Colombia, that we should come here first." President and Mrs. Kennedy then ride in a motorcade to the governor's mansion for a formal dinner at 7:00 P.M.

16 December 1961

CARACAS, VENEZUELA. At 9:00 A.M., the presidential party arrives at Maiquetia Airport, where they are greeted by President Romulo Betancourt, numerous government officials, and thousands of Venezuelans. After a brief speech, President Kennedy is praised by President Betancourt for fulfilling the special promise he made in his inauguration address to help "our sister republics south of our borders...in casting off the chains of poverty." The party leaves by motorcade for Caracas and on to LaCarlota Airport.

EL FRIO, VENEZUELA. At 11:25 A.M., President Kennedy participates in a ribbon-cutting ceremony, inaugurating a planned Alliance for Progress housing project at the newly renamed Aldea Alianza.

LA MORITA, VENEZUELA. President Kennedy delivers an address at this resettlement project where, under the Agrarian Reform Program, families will receive title to their land today. Kennedy pledges economic security to the people of Latin America. Jacqueline Kennedy speaks to the crowd in Spanish, about the rights of all people in this hemisphere to a fair-paying job and a decent education and lifestyle.

MARACAY, VENEZUELA. Mrs. Kennedy arrives here for a 1:30 P.M. lunch at the Hotel Maracay.

CARACAS, VENEZUELA. Following a visit to the American Embassy, the presidential party arrives at the home of President Betancourt where the two discuss the Alliance for Progress, the development of Venezuelan industry development loans, the Guri Hydroelectric Dam, and other concerns. A dinner and reception for three hundred people follow.

17 December 1961

CARACAS, VENEZUELA. At the Pantheon at 7:50 A.M., President Kennedy places a wreath on the tomb of the legendary statesman Simón Bolivar. He and

Mrs. Kennedy then go to Miraflores Palace where they celebrate the signing of a $10 million loan to capitalize a new Venezuelan savings and loan system.

BOGOTÁ, COLOMBIA. President Albertas Camargo greets President and Mrs. Kennedy at El Dorado Airport. After an address by President Kennedy, they leave by motorcade for Techo, a suburb of Bogotá, with half a million Colombians lining the streets and cheering the American leader and his wife. At Techo, President Kennedy participates in ceremonies dedicating housing and school projects. Here he reaffirms the "energy and will" of the United States to improve the welfare of the people of Latin America and says that "those of us who love freedom realize that a man is not really free if he doesn't have a roof over his head, or if he cannot educate his children, or if he cannot find work, or if he cannot find security in his old age." In the evening, a state dinner is held at the San Carlos Palace in honor of President and Mrs. Kennedy.

18 December 1961

PALM BEACH, FLORIDA. After leaving Bogotá and stopping at Ramey Air Force Base in Puerto Rico for refueling, President and Mrs. Kennedy arrive at Palm Beach International Airport, where they are met by Joseph P. Kennedy.

19 December 1961

PALM BEACH, FLORIDA. Joseph Kennedy says goodbye to his son when the President's plane leaves from Palm Beach International Airport at 9:15 A.M. Later, while playing golf, the elder Kennedy becomes ill and is brought home. His symptoms worsen, and he is rushed by ambulance to St. Mary's Hospital in West Palm Beach where physicians diagnose his condition as a massive stroke.

WASHINGTON, D.C. Arriving at the White House at 11:25 A.M., President Kennedy confers with General Maxwell Taylor, Major General Chester V. Clifton, the National Security Council, and others throughout the day. When he is later informed of his father's stroke, he departs by air for Palm Beach at 5:42 P.M.

20 December 1961

PALM BEACH, FLORIDA. In the morning, President and Mrs. Kennedy visit Joseph P. Kennedy at St. Mary's Hospital and then attend services at St. Edward's Church. In the afternoon, they visit the President's father again and are joined by Robert and Ethel Kennedy.

21 December 1961

BERMUDA, BRITISH WEST INDIES. President Kennedy arrives with over twenty aides and government officials to meet with Prime Minister Harold Macmillan and his staff to discuss various world issues, including atmospheric testing of nuclear weapons, the Congo, and the Berlin problem. The party is met at Kindley Air Force Base by Sir Julian Gascoigne, governor general of Bermuda, and Prime Minister Macmillan. The conference takes place later at Government House.

22 December 1961

BERMUDA, BRITISH WEST INDIES. President Kennedy, Prime Minister Macmillan, and their staffs confer throughout the day. The American aides include Dean Rusk, McGeorge Bundy, and Dr. Glen Seaborg; the British representatives include Lord Home, Sir Evelyn Shuckburg, and Ambassador Ormsby-Gore. At 5:30 P.M., President Kennedy and his party leave from Kindley Air Force Base.

WEST PALM BEACH, FLORIDA. Jacqueline Kennedy meets the President at West Palm Beach Airport, and they proceed to St. Mary's Hospital to visit Joe Kennedy.

24 December 1961

PALM BEACH, FLORIDA. After attending mass at St. Edward's Church, President Kennedy greets President Arturo Frondizi of Argentina at the airport. They confer for a couple of hours, and at 6:40 P.M. , President Kennedy returns to St. Mary's Hospital to visit his father.

25 December 1961

MINSK, USSR. The Russian government notifies Lee and Marina Oswald that their application to emigrate to the United States has been approved.

26 December 1961

NEW YORK. President Kennedy confers with President Arturo Frondizi of Argentina over breakfast at the Carlyle Hotel and pledges United States support for Argentina's economic development. President Kennedy also signs the Disarmament bill, which establishes the Arms Control and Disarmament Agency, the first full-fledged organization dedicated to reducing the production and testing of nuclear weapons. He also signs legislation providing for permanent establishment of the Alien Orphan Act.

BOSTON. A son, Edward Moore, Jr., is born to Joan (Bennett) and Edward M. Kennedy. He is their second child and first son.

27 December 1961

PALM BEACH, FLORIDA. President and Mrs. Kennedy take a cruise abroad the *Honey Fitz* with their daughter, Caroline, Prince and Princess Radziwill Cassini, and others.

30 December 1961

BUENOS AIRES, ARGENTINA. The Argentine Public Opinion Research Institute names Jacqueline Kennedy "International Woman of the Year."

31 December 1961

PALM BEACH, FLORIDA. President Kennedy sends a New Year's greeting to Soviet leaders Nikita Khruschev and Leonid Brezhnev, wishing them and the Soviet people a prosperous New Year and saying, "It is my earnest hope that the coming year will strengthen the foundations of world peace and will bring an improvement in the relations between our countries, upon which so much depends." President and Mrs. Kennedy spend New Year's Eve at the home of Charles K. Wrightsman.

THE SECOND YEAR
1962-1963

3 January 1962

PALM BEACH, FLORIDA. In the early afternoon, President Kennedy takes a cruise aboard the *Honey Fitz* with his wife, Vice-President Johnson, Prince and Princess Radziwill, Robert McNamara, Roswell Gilpatric, and LeMoyne Billings. In the evening, he and his wife and children visit his father at St. Mary's Hospital.

PALM BEACH, FLORIDA. President Kennedy instructs that the size of the U.S. Army be increased from fourteen to sixteen divisions.

5 January 1962

NEW YORK. In a *Time* magazine cover story, President John F. Kennedy is named *Time*'s "Man of the Year" for 1961.

COLUMBUS, OHIO. At the Buckeye Building, President Kennedy attends a birthday dinner and Demo-

United Press International.

Expecting babies in the summer of 1963, three members of the Kennedy clan:
Joan Kennedy, Jacqueline Kennedy, and Ethel Kennedy.

cratic fund-raising event for Governor Michael DiSalle. The President discusses some of the achievements of his administration and mentions some unattained goals, such as a health care program for the nation's elderly.

8 January 1962
WASHINGTON, D.C.   With George Ball, Foy Kohler, and Walter Heller, President Kennedy meets with Vice-Chancellor Ludwig Erhard of Germany and the minister of the German Embassy, George von Lilienfeld, to discuss financial aid to Germany.

9 January 1962
WASHINGTON, D.C.   Following a legislative leaders' breakfast, cabinet meeting, and conferences with various aides in the morning, President Kennedy greets the Vienna Boys' Choir, who sing "Haec Dies" and Zoltan Kodaly's "Angels and the Shepherds."

10 January 1962
WASHINGTON, D.C.   Two newly appointed ambassadors Neftali Ponce Miranda of Ecuador and Jules Mbah of Gabon present their credentials to the President. Later, Kennedy confers with U.S. Ambassador to Yugoslavia George Kennan.

11 January 1962
WASHINGTON, D.C.   President John F. Kennedy delivers his annual State of the Union address before a joint session of the Eighty-seventh Congress. Calling attention to the importance of cooperation between the Chief Executive and Congress, he begins, "Members of

the Congress, the Constitution makes us not rivals for power, but partners for progress. We are all trustees for the American people, custodians of the American heritage. It is my task to *report* the State of the Union—to *improve* it is the task of us all...our overriding obligation in the months ahead is to fulfill the world's hopes by fulfilling our own faith...."

After presenting his programs for strengthening the economy, supporting civil rights, and other issues of national concern, the President speaks of the future of the United Nations as a world peace-keeping organization ("Our instrument and hope is the United Nations, and I see little merit in the impatience of those who would abandon this imperfect world instrument because they dislike our imperfect world...."); the need to provide additional funds for the Alliance for Progress program; the need to find a peaceful resolution to the Berlin situation; and the need for a wholly new American trade policy.

"Few generations in all history," he concludes, "had been granted the role of being the great defender of freedom in its maximum hour of danger. This is our good fortune....For it is the fate of this generation—of you in the Congress, and me as President—to live with a struggle we did not start, in a world we did not make....And while no nation has ever faced such a challenge, no nation has ever been so ready to seize the burden and the glory of freedom."

15 January 1962
WASHINGTON, D.C.   At a press conference in the State Department Auditorium, President Kennedy notes the dwindling number of college graduates in the physi-

cal sciences and announces that he has asked the Science Advisory Committee and the Federal Council for Science and Technology to review studies and recommend "specific measures that can be taken within and without the Government to develop the necessary and well-qualified scientists and engineers and technicians to meet our society's complex needs—governmental, educational, and industrial." Arriving back at the White House, the President videotapes a statement in the Monroe Cabinet Room for his wife's television tour of the Executive Mansion, to be broadcast next month.

16 January 1962

WASHINGTON, D.C. President Kennedy informs Congress that he has "approved a plan for the reorganization of the Department of the Army. This plan was recommended by the Secretary of the Army after a detailed study and approved by the Secretary of the Defense."

17 January 1962

WASHINGTON, D.C. President Kennedy meets with members of the Committee on Traffic Safety, which is chaired by William R. Hearst, Jr. He tells them that he hopes they will take the lead in bringing about traffic safety measures that will "improve traffic conditions which are resulting every year in some 38,000 deaths, 1½ million serious injuries and billions of dollars of property loss."

At a ceremony before the Task Force on Employee-Management Relations in the Federal Service, President Kennedy signs executive orders to "define and provide a legal base for the rights of Federal employees and employee organizations to participate in improving personnel policies and working conditions not specifically fixed by the Congress."

18 January 1962

WASHINGTON, D.C. President Kennedy submits to Congress a balanced budget for fiscal 1963 (1 July 1962–30 June 1963). Noting that it is the first complete budget of his administration, the President estimates expenditures to total $92.5 billion (an increase of $3.4 billion over the present fiscal year) and receipts to total $93 billion. Budget expenditures are requested for defense, international affairs and finance, space research and technology, agriculture, natural resources, housing development, health, labor, and welfare, education, veterans' benefits, and general government.

Members of the American Booksellers Association present President Kennedy with books for the White House library. At 8:00 P.M. , the President and Mrs. Kennedy give a dinner party for the composer Igor Stravinsky and his wife.

19 January 1962

WASHINGTON, D.C. At the Sheraton Park Hotel, President Kennedy speaks before Secretary of the Treasury Douglas Dillon, Under-Secretary of State Henry B. Fowler, and others at the opening of the 1962 U.S. savings bond campaign.

NEW YORK. At a luncheon meeting at the Waldorf-Astoria Hotel, President Kennedy discusses various international issues with Acting Secretary-General of the United Nations U Thant of Burma and Ambassador Adlai E. Stevenson.

In the evening, the President and Charles Spaulding attend a performance of the Broadway show "How to Succeed in Business Without Really Trying."

20 January 1962

WASHINGTON, D.C. President and Mrs. Kennedy attend a dinner at the National Guard Armory in honor of the first anniversary of the President's inauguration. Entertainment is provided by Rosemary Clooney, Lee Remick, and Danny Thomas. In a speech, President Kennedy says that "the role of the Democratic Party, the reason it has outlived the Federal Party, the Whig Party, and now holds responsibility in the executive branch and the House and the Senate, after this long history, has been because it has believed in moving out, in moving ahead, in starting on new areas, and bringing new programs here and abroad."

22 January 1962

WASHINGTON, D.C. President Kennedy sends to Congress a message presenting his first Economic Report. The report reviews economic conditions and current trends in 1961 and presents the administration's economic program and legislative recommendations for 1962.

The President also announces that the United States will make available $25 million in emergency credit to the Dominican Republic, following the overthrow of General Rafael Trujillo Molina.

23 January 1962

WASHINGTON, D.C. At the Agriculture Department auditorium, President Kennedy addresses the National Conference on Milk and Nutrition. He speaks of the drop in milk consumption, saying, "I have long been convinced that milk is an important aid to good health. This has led me to direct that milk be served at every White House meal from now on—and I expect that all of us will benefit from it."

25 January 1962

WASHINGTON, D.C. President Kennedy meets with members of the National Grange, receives the new ambassador of the Syrian Arab Republic, Omar Abou Riche, greets two celebrated Pakistani squash players, meets with members of the National Newspapers Association, and confers with General Lauris Norstad, Supreme Allied Commander in Europe. In the evening, he leaves with his wife and children to visit his convalescing father in Palm Beach.

30 January 1962

WASHINGTON, D.C. In a special message to Congress, President Kennedy transmits Reorganization Plan No. 1 of 1962, in which he recommends "the establishment in the executive branch of a new Department of Urban Affairs and Housing, of Cabinet rank." He lunches with Premier Khruschev's daughter and her husband, journalist Aleksei I. Adzhubei (they discuss world crises confronting the United States and Russia), and dines with Mrs. Kennedy at the residence of Franklin D. Roosevelt, Jr., at 5188 Palisades Lane, N.W.

31 January 1962

WASHINGTON, D.C. President Kennedy submits to Congress a special farm message presenting strict government controls of agricultural production designed to raise the income of farmers and reduce surpluses. In introducing his plans, Kennedy says, "Abundance, Balance, Conservation, Development—these are our common-sense goals, as common sense as A, B, C. D. The program that follows—an A B C D farm program for the 60s—is designed to meet those goals." President Kennedy takes "pleasure in welcoming" Aleksei and Rada Adzhubei to his press conference—"We're glad to have them here to observe an ancient American"—and announces that he has appointed a commission to review American stockpiling of strategic materials which now exceed the country's requirements.

1 February 1962

WASHINGTON, D.C. In a special message to Congress, President Kennedy transmits recommendations for new public welfare programs "to meet our current needs." In the Rose Garden, Kennedy welcomes Secretary of State Dean Rusk and members of the American delegation back from the Inter-American (Punta del Este) Conference, and tells them that "as a result of this meeting,....I think Communism has been isolated in this hemisphere and I think the hemisphere can move on towards progress."

WASHINGTON, D.C. Attorney General Robert F. Kennedy and his wife, Ethel, begin a month-long goodwill tour to the Far East, where Kennedy plans to meet with Prime Minister Hayato Ikeda of Japan, among other leaders. Altogether they will visit over a dozen countries. Robert Kennedy will also serve as an intermediary between Indonesia and the Netherlands in their dispute over Netherlands New Guinea.

2 February 1962

WASHINGTON, D.C. The American Heart Association presents its "Heart of the Year Award" to President Kennedy. The President also confers with U.S. Ambassador to Nato Thomas Finletter, and greets a group of women who are to be sworn in as Army nurses.

3 February 1962

WASHINGTON, D.C. President Kennedy orders an embargo virtually cutting off all United States trade with Cuba. For "humanitarian" reasons, "certain foodstuffs, medicines, and medical supplies...would be excepted from this embargo."

4 February 1962

MIDDLEBURG, VIRGINIA. At Glen Ora, the Kennedys, the Franklin D. Roosevelts, and the Charles Bartletts take a walk on the estate grounds and look at the cattle. Later, the President takes Franklin Roosevelt, Jr., for a 5-minute drive in a 1962 Mark 10 Jaguar.

JAPAN. As Robert Kennedy addresses students at Waseda University, the meeting is disrupted by a group of Leftist youths.

5 February 1962

WASHINGTON, D.C. Following a luncheon in his honor attended by over thirty congressmen and dignitaries, Prime Minister Adoula of the Republic of the Congo meets with President Kennedy to confer about what can be done to prevent the province of Katanga from seceding.

6 February 1962

WASHINGTON, D.C. The typewriter of former President Woodrow Wilson is presented to President Kennedy. The President notes that Wilson "typed his Fourteen Points and other messages" on it. In a reference to a White House historical collection, he also jokes that his "wife has collected everything and this is my...[laughter]...this is the only thing I have produced...." In a special message to Congress, President Kennedy asks that it appropriate funds for his educational program. "No task before our nation," he begins "is more important than expanding and improving the educational opportunities of all our people." He outlines various forms of assistance for elementary, secondary, and higher education and concludes with an historical reference—one he is to use in other speeches—that conveys the urgency of the problems he is addressing: " 'If a nation,' wrote Thomas Jefferson in 1816, 'expects to be ignorant and free, in a state of civilization, it expects what never was and never will be.' That statement is even truer today than it was 146 years ago."

7 February 1962

WASHINGTON, D.C. At a press conference, President Kennedy responds to Francis Cardinal Spellman's charge that the President's proposed education program will mean the demise of the parochial school system because being deprived of federal subsidies will render private schools unable to compete with public schools. President Kennedy answers that unless a change of ruling is made by the Supreme Court, religious schools should not receive aid from the federal government.

President Kennedy also sends to Congress his Communications Satellite Act, a bill that "provides for the establishment, ownership, operation, and regulation of a commercial communications satellite system." At a press conference, the President announces that in view of Russia's breaking the nuclear moratorium last fall, "we are making necessary preparations for testing...."

That evening, children of foreign dignitaries attend an opera at the White House. Jacqueline Kennedy serves as their hostess.

8 February 1962

WASHINGTON, D.C. The White House releases a statement declaring that it is the view of both the United States and British governments that "the existing state of nuclear development, in which the recent massive Soviet tests are an important factor, would justify the West in making such further series of nuclear tests as may be necessary for purely military reasons." A book of caricatures of President Kennedy is presented to him by members of the Association of American Editorial Cartoonists.

10 February 1962

BOSTON. Edward M. Kennedy leaves for a tour of various European and Middle Eastern countries.

12 February 1962

WASHINGTON, D.C. President Kennedy confers with the Commission on the Status of Women, chaired by Eleanor Roosevelt. In greeting them he says, "We have established this Commission for two reasons....One

Jean Kennedy Smith with sons William, left, and Stephen, Jr., in New York, 1963.

is for my own self-protection (every two or three weeks Mrs. May Craig asks me what am I doing for women!); the other reason is because...one-third of our working force are women." Later, President Kennedy meets with Mrs. Roosevelt alone.

JAKARTA, INDONESIA. President Sukarno welcomes Robert and Ethel Kennedy. Indonesia is currently suffering from inflation; it is also embroiled with the Netherlands in an altercation over Netherlands New Guinea.

13 February 1962

WASHINGTON, D.C. President Kennedy greets His Majesty Saud Ibn Abd Al-Aziz Al Saud, the King of Saudi Arabia, at Andrews Air Force Base. After the two leaders confer, a state dinner is given at the White House in honor of King Saud. Saudi Arabia is currently involved in a conflict with the United Arab Republic.

14 February 1962

WASHINGTON, D.C. At a press conference, President Kennedy announces that with regard to the whereabouts of U-2 pilot Francis Gary Powers, "I can state at this time only that he's in this country, that he has seen his father and mother, and that his wife is with him. He is undergoing important interviews by appropriate officials of this government." Powers had been released from prison in the Soviet Union four days earlier in exchange for Russian spy Rudolf Abel.

THE UNITED STATES. A 60-minute taped TV program entitled "A Tour of the White House with Mrs. John F. Kennedy" is broadcast simultaneously over the CBS and NBC television networks. In the show, the First Lady takes CBS's Charles Collingwood through the Executive Mansion, describing the purpose and historical background of the different rooms, including details about their furnishings. They walk through the Reception Room, the State Dining Room, the Red Room, Blue Room, Green Room, and the Lincoln Room, examining such items as wallpaper, silverware, china, sofas, portraits, and a clock. President Kennedy makes a brief appearance near the end of the show. He compliments his wife's efforts, saying, "I think it makes the White House really a stronger panorama of our great story." Over forty-five million Americans watch the telecast.

15 February 1962
WASHINGTON, D.C. President Kennedy meets with the Organziation of American States Task Force, and confers with officials of the World Council of Churches and the National Council of the Churches in Christ in the U.S.A. It is a cold day, and Kennedy sends pots of coffee to students protesting outside the White House against United States plans to resume nuclear testing.

19 February 1962
WASHINGTON, D.C. President Kennedy signs legislation to establish in Indiana the Lincoln Boyhood National Memorial. He confers with directors of the National Conference of Christians and Jews on the 1962 Brotherhood Award, and later he meets with the Brazilian minister of Labor, Andre Franco Montoro.

BANGKOK, THAILAND. President Sarit Thanarat confers with U.S. Attorney General Robert F. Kennedy. Thailand is threatened by an influx of Communist guerrillas from Laos.

20 February 1962
WASHINGTON, D.C. A federal pay reform program is submitted to Congress by President Kennedy. At 4:10 P.M., the President calls Lt. Col. John H. Glenn, Jr., of the United States Marines, who had earlier splashed

down safely from his triple orbit of the earth, aboard the *Noa* in the Atlantic Ocean near the Bahamas. President and Mrs. Kennedy give a dinner at 8:00 P.M. in honor of Vice-President Johnson, Chief Justice of the Supreme Court Earl Warren, and Speaker of the House John McCormack.

21 February 1962
WASHINGTON, D.C. President Kennedy receives a message from Soviet Premier Nikita S. Khruschev urging that Russia and the United States unite their scientists and astronauts and cooperate in space research and exploration. Khruschev also sends congratulations on John Glenn's flight, a feat already accomplished by two Soviet cosmonauts. President Kennedy responds that a joint Soviet-U.S. space program is something he has long wanted.

ROME, ITALY. Pope John XXIII receives Robert and Ethel Kennedy in a private audience.

22 February 1962
WEST BERLIN, GERMANY. Addressing a crowd of 100,000 at the city hall, Robert Kennedy expresses support for West Germany against Soviet invasion. He says that a Russian assault on the city would "be the same as an attack on Chicago, New York, London, or Paris."

23 February 1962
CAPE CANAVERAL, FLORIDA. President Kennedy presents NASA's distinguished service medals to Dr. Robert R. Gilruth, director of the Manned Spacecraft Center, and Lt. Col. John H. Glenn, Jr.

WEST BERLIN, GERMANY. Robert and Edward Kennedy, each on a separate trip abroad, meet as their tours coincide.

24 February 1962
BONN, WEST GERMANY. Chancellor Konrad Adenauer meets with Robert F. Kennedy. West Germany continues to grow apart from Communist East Germany as the Cold War continues.

25 February 1962
PALM BEACH, FLORIDA. President Kennedy cruises on the *Honey Fitz* with his father and other family members.

THE HAGUE, THE NETHERLANDS. Queen Juliana meets with Robert F. Kennedy.

26 February 1962

WASHINGTON, D.C. The President holds a reception in his White House office for astronauts John Glenn, Alan Shepard, Virgil Grissom, Scott Carpenter, and Donald Slayton. Afterward, Col. John Glenn is the star of a parade to the Capitol.

On the occasion of the Voice of America's twentieth anniversary, President Kennedy later delivers an address at the Health, Education, and Welfare Building in which he says, "We compete with other means of communications, of those who are our adversaries who tell only the good stories. But the things that go bad in America, you must tell that also, and we hope that the bad and the good is sifted together by people of judgment and discretion and taste and discrimination, that they will realize what we are trying to do here." President Kennedy also sends to Congress a bill to continue and expand the Peace Corps program.

27 February 1962

PARIS. President Charles de Gaulle confers with Robert F. Kennedy. France is fighting in an Algerian civil war.

WASHINGTON, D.C. In a message to Congress, President Kennedy asks for passage of legislation providing for "two urgent needs—health insurance for the aged and assistance to education for the health professionals."

28 February 1962

WASHINGTON, D.C. President Kennedy proclaims March as Red Cross Month. The Minute Man Hall of Fame Citation is awarded to President Kennedy by officials of the Reserve Officers' Association of the United States. Following their four-week international goodwill tour, Attorney General Robert F. Kennedy and his wife visit President Kennedy at his White House offices. Vice-President Lyndon Johnson and Dean Rusk are also present.

1 March 1962

WASHINGTON, D.C. President Kennedy sends a special conservation message to Congress. "We depend on our natural resources," he says, "to sustain us—but in turn their continued availability must depend on our using them prudently, improving them wisely, and, where possible, restoring them promptly. We must reaffirm our dedication to the sound practices of conservation which can be defined as the wise use of our natural environment....Our deep spiritual confidence that this nation will survive on the perils of today—which may well be with us for decades to come—compels us to invest in our nation's future, to consider and meet our obligations to our children and the numberless generations that will follow."

The President also addresses members of the American Legion at the White House. He speaks of the burden of the United States in maintaining "the cause of freedom around the globe....What really counts is not the immediate act of courage or of valor, but those who bear the struggle day in and day out—not the sunshine patriots, but those who are willing to stand for a long period of time." The President's conservation program addresses national concerns such as outdoor recreational lands, water resources, public lands, soil, timber growth, minerals, and power.

2 March 1962

WASHINGTON, D.C. On a radio and television broadcast from his White House office, President Kennedy addresses the nation on nuclear testing and disarmament. "Until mankind has banished both war and its instruments of destruction," he says, "the United States must maintain an effective quantity and quality of nuclear weapons, so deployed and protected as to be capable of surviving any surprise attack and devastating the attacker." Because "the Soviet Union [in September] callously broke its moratorium with a two month series of more than forty nuclear tests..., I have today authorized the Atomic Energy Commission and the Department of Defense to conduct a series of nuclear tests." He adds that the United States will offer plans for a major "breakthrough to peace...to halt the promotion of fissionable materials...to destroy the warheads and the delivery systems that threaten man's existence...to reserve outer space for peaceful use...to reduce all armed forces...[and] to halt permanently the testing of all nuclear weapons, in every environment: in the air, in outer space, underground, and under water."

6 March 1962

WASHINGTON, D.C. The White House releases President Kennedy's message to Premier Khruschev concerning the Geneva disarmament negotiations that are to begin on 14 March. "Our object now must be to make real progress toward disarmament," he states, "and not to engage in sterile exchanges of propaganda."

7 March 1962

WASHINGTON, D.C. At a press conference, President Kennedy is asked to comment on Brazil's seizure of an American-owned telephone company in Rio Grande do Sul. The President responds, "I can think of nothing more unwise than to attempt to pass a resolution at this time which puts us in a position not of disagreement with a governor of a state, who is not particularly our friend, but, instead, really, with the whole Brazilian nation which is vital and which is a key and with which we must have the closest relations." In a message to Premier Khruschev, President Kennedy proposes that the Soviet Union and the United States undertake joint projects in the exploration of outer space.

8 March 1962
WASHINGTON, D.C. Jacqueline Kennedy leaves for an unofficial trip to India and Pakistan via Rome.

9 March 1962
PALM BEACH, FLORIDA. President Kennedy and his children visit with his father at his home.

10 March 1962
MIAMI BEACH, FLORIDA. At the Fountainbleau Hotel, President Kennedy speaks at a Democratic fund-raising dinner in honor of Senator George A. Smathers. He says, "I believe the New Frontier can be captured here in Florida as almost no other State of the Union....I prophesy in the next ten years that this State is going to have the greatest period of development of any State in the United States...."

11 March 1962
ROME. Jacqueline Kennedy and Lee Radziwill arrive for a tour of Italy.

13 March 1962
WASHINGTON, D.C. President Kennedy sends a special foreign aid message to Congress, saying that the new policy "aims at strengthening the political and economic independence of developing countries." A White House luncheon honors President Ahmadou Ahidjo of the Republic of Cameroon, with whom President Kennedy later confers. At 5:30 P.M., a reception is given in honor of the Alliance for Progress's first anniversary. In an address, the President says that the "Alliance for Progress is more than a doctrine of development—a blueprint of economic advance. Rather it is an expression of the noblest goals of our society. It says that want and despair need not be the lot of free men."

14 March 1962
BOSTON. After serving for over thirteen months as an assistant district attorney for Suffolk County, Edward M. Kennedy resigns and announces that he will run for the United States Senate from Massachusetts. The seat

he will seek is his brother's old seat, which is currently occupied on an interim basis by Benjamin A. Smith II.

WASHINGTON, D.C. Asked at a press conference about "the announcement this morning of a new Democratic candidate for the Senate in Massachusetts, a young man I believe you are familiar with," President Kennedy responds, "This is a judgment for the people of Massachusetts. I will not take part in that campaign except I will go to vote in the primary in September. But my brother is carrying this campaign on his own and will conduct it that way."

15 March 1962
BOSTON. Rose Kennedy undergoes surgery for a pelvic hernia at St. Elizabeth's Hospital.

WASHINGTON, D.C. President Kennedy signs the Manpower Development and Training Act of 1962, saying that it will make possible "the training of the hundreds of thousands of workers who are denied employment because they do not possess the skills required by our constantly changing economy." The bill provides unemployed workers with up to fifty-two weeks of training and an allowance for family support while learning new skills. The President also sends a message to Congress proposing legislation that will enable American consumers to exercise their rights "to safety," "to be informed" against fraudulent advertising, "to choose...a variety of products and services at competitive prices," and "to be heard" with respect to having a voice in the formulation of government policy.

20 March 1962
WASHINGTON, D.C. President Kennedy signs the Welfare and Pension Plans Disclosure Act, which, he says, "will give the more than forty-four million workers covered by welfare and pension plans greater assurance of accurate and full disclosures of plan operations." The President also signs an executive order "providing for the administration of the Ryukyu Islands." He welcomes President Sylvanus Olympic of Togo at Washington National Airport and confers with him later at the White House. The West African republic of Togo is embroiled in a conflict with Ghana, whose president wants the two countries to merge.

21 March 1962
WASHINGTON, D.C. President Kennedy announces this morning at a press conference that he has received a reply from Nikita Krushchev to his 7 March letter on joint U.S.-Soviet space projects. The reply, he says,

"indicates that there are a number of areas of common interest." He adds that "the United States is deeply committed to making all possible efforts to carry forward the exploration and use of space in a spirit of cooperation and for the benefit of all mankind." When asked to comment on demonstrations by mobilized reservists who want to be released, President Kennedy says that they "are doing a very important job" which is necessary for the national security. But, he adds, "there is always inequity in life. Some men are killed in a war and some men are wounded, and some men never leave the country, and some men are stationed in the Antarctic and some are stationed in San Francisco....Life is unfair."

21 March 1962
PAKISTAN.   Jacqueline Kennedy and Lee Radziwill, whose trip is heavily covered by the press, begin a six-day vacation.

22 March 1962
WASHINGTON, D.C.   President Kennedy confers with Ali Bengelloun, the Ambassador to Morocco. He then meets with Marian Anderson and with Ethel Kennedy, then lunches with, director of the FBI. J. Edgar Hoover.

23 March 1962
BERKELEY, CALIFORNIA.   At an anniversary ceremony in Memorial Stadium at the University of California at Berkeley, President Kennedy declares that "this emerging world is incompatible with the Communist world order. It will irresistibly burst the bonds of the Communist organization and the Communist ideology." America must shape policies," he says, "to speed progress toward a more flexible order." He dramatizes the urgency of this task with an anecdote he is to use again and again: "I am reminded of the story of the great French Marshal Lyautey, who once asked his gardener to plant a tree. The gardener objected that the tree was slow-growing and would not reach maturity for a hundred years. The Marshal replied, 'In that case, there is no time to lose, plant it this afternoon.' " "We have no time to lose," the President says. "Let us plant our trees this afternoon." Following the speech, Kennedy receives an honorary Doctor of Laws Degree.

VANDENBURG AIR FORCE BASE, CALIFORNIA.   President Kennedy observes the firing of an Atlas missile and inspects a Minuteman missile.

PALM SPRINGS, CALIFORNIA.   President Kennedy spends the evening at the residence of Bing Crosby.

24 March 1962
PALM SPRINGS, CALIFORNIA.   President Kennedy meets with his predecessor, Dwight D. Eisenhower.

26 March 1962
WASHINGTON, D.C.   In a special ceremony at the White House, President Kennedy presents a Congressional Medal to Robert Frost. In bestowing the award, the President good-naturedly says that he supposes the poet "is disappointed that this was not a more controversial decision by the Congress, but instead was a unanimous one."

LONDON.   Jacqueline Kennedy concludes her trip to Italy, India, and Pakistan with a visit here.

29 March 1962
WASHINGTON, D.C.   President Kennedy is asked at a press conference whether, if he had it to do all over again, he would work for the presidency and whether he would recommend the job to others. "Well," responds the President, "the answer is—to the first 'yes' and the second is 'no!' I don't recommend it to others at least for awhile."

30 March 1962
WASHINGTON, D.C.   President Kennedy announces that he has appointed Byron White as Associate Justice of the Supreme Court. The former deputy attorney general of the United States replaces Associate Justice Charles Evans Whittaker who retires on 1 April.

31 MARCH 1962
PITTSBURGH, PENNSYLVANIA.   The United Steelworkers' Union ratifies a new two-year contract with steel producers, providing for a wage freeze and a small increase in benefits. President Kennedy had warned the steel industry in a letter of 6 September 1961 that inflationary wages and prices would be harmful to the economy.

3 April 1962
WASHINGTON, D.C.   President Kennedy greets President Joao Goulart of Brazil at Andrews Air Force Base and confers with him later at the White House.

4 April 1962
WASHINGTON, D.C.   President Kennedy and President Joao Goulart of Brazil conclude two days of meetings. A joint communique states that the two leaders have reaffirmed "the traditional friendship between Brazil and the United States [that] has grown through the

President Kennedy at a military reception, 2 May 1963.

years" as well as the "dedication of their countries to the InterAmerican system and to the values of human dignity, liberty, and progress on which that system is based."

5 April 1962

WASHINGTON, D.C. In a special message to Congress, President Kennedy presents a detailed plan for revising the federal transportation system and urges Congress to consider the recommendations "at the earliest practicable date."

7 April 1962

HAVANA, CUBA. A military court sentences the Cuban rebels who invaded the Bay of Pigs to prison terms of thirty years and annuls their Cuban citizenship.

9 April 1962

WASHINGTON, D.C. At the Statler Hilton Hotel, President Kennedy delivers a speech before the Children's Bureau on its fiftieth anniversary. Noting that this "is an appropriate occasion for us to recall the accomplishments of the Bureau," the President says that "it is also a more appropriate occasion for us to rededicate ourselves to making the life of every child as fruitful and productive as it possibly can be, and lay the groundwork for a useful and happy adult life." President Kennedy also proclaims the week of 9 April 1962 as Voluntary Overseas Aid Week.

President Kennedy throws out the first ball at the season-opening game of the Washington Senators. Pitching for the home team is Bennie Daniels, the first black ever to open a baseball season in the city. The team wins its first game in the recently finished District of Columbia Stadium, defeating the Detroit Tigers 4 to 1.

10 April 1962

WASHINGTON, D.C. Composer Meredith Wilson, who wrote "The Music Man", receives the Brother of the Year Award from President Kennedy. Roger M. Blough, chairman of the United States Steel Corporation, pays a personal visit to the White House to inform President Kennedy that the company is increasing its prices by $6 a ton.

11 April 1962

WASHINGTON, D.C. At a press conference, a visibly upset President Kennedy assails the increase in steel prices by U.S. Steel and other major producers. He says that in view of the "grave crises in Berlin and Southeast Asia" and other efforts being made to achieve economic recovery in the United States, the increase is "a wholly unjustifiable and irresponsible defiance of the public interest." "Some time ago," he says, "I asked each American to consider what he would do for his country and I asked the steel companies. In the last twenty-four hours we had their answer." Kennedy calls for the increase to be withdrawn. (Eleven days earlier the Steelworkers' union had approved an agreement with steel manufacturers which did not provide for wage increases."

At 8:00 P.M. , a dinner at the White House in honors His Imperial Majesty the Shah of Iran and Empress Farah. President Kennedy had greeted them on their arrival at Washington National Airport.

12 April 1962

WASHINGTON, D.C. Attorney General Robert F. Kennedy announces that the major steel companies will be investigated for violating antitrust laws.

WASHINGTON, D.C. President Kennedy confers with Dr. Walter Hallstein, president of the Commission of the European Common Market, and with General Lucius Clay, who he says is no longer required as a full-time representative in Berlin.

13 April 1963

WASHINGTON, D.C. Following three days of discussions between President Kennedy and Shah Mohammed Riza Pahlevi of Iran, the White House releases a joint statement that says, in part, "Their talks included a review of political and military situations in the world, a discussion of the progress which Iran is making in economic and social advancement; a review of defense ar-

rangements in which the two countries are associated; and aspects of United States economic and military aid programs in Iran."

OCEANA, VIRGINIA. President Kennedy visits the naval air station here.

NORFOLK, VIRGINIA. The President boards and inspects the submarines *Thomas Edison* and *Northampton*. He makes an overnight cruise on the *Northampton* and observes naval exercises.

THE UNITED STATES. A number of major steel producers, including Bethlehem Steel, U.S. Steel, and Inland Steel, retract their price increases.

14 April 1962

ONSLOW BEACH, NORTH CAROLINA. At Camp Lejune, President Kennedy visits Point Bluejay, andPoint Whiskey (where he observes a squad demonstration), Risely Pier (where he witnesses special-purpose exercises with the Shah of Iran), and Bogus Field (where he observes more special-purpose exercises).

CHERRY POINT, NORTH CAROLINA. President Kennedy observes a combat-readiness demonstration at the marine air station.

THE UNITED STATES. Singer Jimmy Dean's Columbia recording "P.T. 109" hits the Top 40. Written by Marijohn Wilkin and Fred Burch and published by Cedarwood Publishing Company on 15 December 1961, the song recounts John Kennedy's famous World War II experience:

> In forty-three they put to sea Thirteen men and Kennedy Aboard the P.T.109 to fight the brazen enemy And off the isle of Olasana in the strait beyond Naru A Jap destroyer in the night cut the 109 in two. Smoke and fire upon the sea Ev'rywhere they looked was the enemy The heathen gods of old Japan Thought they had the best of a mighty good man. Now who would guess, who could possibly know that the same man named Kennedy: Would be the leader of the nation, be the one to take command The P.T. 109 was gone But Kennedy lived to fight again.*

16 April 1962

WASHINGTON, D.C. Byron Raymond White, the first person to be appointed to the United States Supreme Court by President Kennedy, is sworn in. Kennedy attends the ceremony at the Supreme Court.

---

* Copyright 1961. Cedarwood Publishing Company, Inc.

17 April 1962

WASHINGTON, D.C. Officials of the Civil War Centennial Commission presents its medallion to President Kennedy. Dr. Alan Nevins, chairman, and Senator Ralph Yarborough of Texas are among the commission members present. The 1961 volume of *Public Papers of the President* is presented to President Kennedy.

18 April 1962

WASHINGTON, D.C. At a morning press conference, President Kennedy announces that the United States has today "tabled at Geneva an outline of basic provisions of a treaty on general and complete disarmament in a peaceful world"; that with respect to last week's decision of steel companies to retract their price increases, the "administration harbors no ill will against any individual, any industry, corporation, or segment of the American economy...when a mistake has been retracted and the public interest preserved, nothing is to be gained from further public recrimination"; "that upon learning that a private first class faced a courtmartial for writing a letter critical" of Kennedy's calling reservists to service, he has asked the Army to cancel the trial; and "that Mrs. Eisenhower has agreed to serve as honorary co-chairman, with Mrs. Kennedy. of the National Cultural Center." In the afternoon, President Kennedy makes a film with Eleanor Roosevelt for the National Educational Television's *Prospects of Mankind* series and another on freedom bonds. Following a National Security Council meeting, President Kennedy and his family leave for a ten-day Easter vacation in Florida.

PALM BEACH, FLORIDA. President and Mrs. Kennedy arrive for a ten-day vacation at the President's parents' home.

21 April 1962

PALM BEACH, FLORIDA. Pressing a golden telegraphic key in Florida, President Kennedy opens the Century 21 Exposition in Seattle, Washington. Speaking over the telephone to an audience at the fairgrounds stadium, the President says, "By closing this key, may we open an era of peace and understanding among all mankind."

25 April 1962

CHRISTMAS ISLAND, PACIFIC OCEAN. Under President Kennedy's orders, the United States resumes nuclear tests in the atmosphere.

27 April 1962

WASHINGTON, D.C. At a White House ceremony, President Kennedy welcomes a group of descendants of Civil War veterans who had received the Congressional Medal of Honor. The President later meets with Prime Minister Harold Macmillan of Great Britain to discuss disarmament, nuclear test control, and NATO. In the evening, Prime Minister Macmillan gives a dinner in honor of President Kennedy at the British Embassy.

29 April 1962

WASHINGTON, D.C. Forty-nine Nobel Prize winners, including Dr. Ralph J. Bunche (Peace), Dr. Joseph Erlanger (Medicine and Physiology), Dr. Linus Pauling (Chemistry), Lester Pearson (Peace), and Dr. Harold Urey (Chemistry), attend a dinner at the White House in their honor. Also present are prominent persons from the arts, letters, and sciences, including James Baldwin, Col. John Glenn, Mrs. Ernest Hemingway, Frederic March, and Lionel Trilling. In welcoming the group, President Kennedy says, "I think this is the most extraordinary collection of talent, of human knowledge, that has ever been gathered together at the White House, with the possible exception of when Thomas Jefferson dined alone."

1 May 1962

WASHINGTON, D.C. President Kennedy signs the Educational Television Act of 1962, which, he says "will provide vitally needed Federal support for the construction of educational television stations while assuring at the same time, state and local operation." The President meets with officials from the American Medical Association and with members of the Labor-Management Advisory Committee.

3 May 1962

WASHINGTON, D.C. Attorney General Robert F. Kennedy announces that the business affairs of Billy Sol Estes have been under the scrutiny of the Justice Department. Since Estes's arrest in March, scandal has touched many public figures, including Secretary of Agriculture Orville L. Freeman.

WASHINGTON, D.C. President Kennedy meets with Gherman Stepanovich Titov, the Russian cosmonaut who, in August of 1961, orbited the earth seventeen times aboard *Vostok II*. Also present are Lt. Col. John Glenn, Jr., and the Soviet ambassador, Anatoliy F. Dobrynin. Following a White House luncheon for Chancellor Alfons Gorbach, President Kennedy confers with the Austrian leader. They reaffirm the friendship between their two countries and discuss possible Austrian membership in the European Economic Community and association with Euratom.

4 May 1962

NEW ORLEANS, LOUISIANA. At a dedication ceremony for the opening of the Nashville Avenue Wharf and Dockside Building, President Kennedy is introduced by Louisiana Representative Hale Boggs, and delivers a speech on foreign trade policy. He says, "Those who preach the doctrine of the inevitability of the class struggle and of the Communist success, should realize that in the last few years the great effort which has been made to unify economically the countries of the Free World, offers far greater promise than the sterile and broken promises of the Communist system." At City Hall Plaza, the key to the city and the International Order of Merit are bestowed upon the President. Here Kennedy speaks on education: "All of those of you who are now in school and college must realize that the brightest future lies before those who work, those who grapple with the future, those who recognize what changes are coming."

ELGIN AIR FORCE BASE, FLORIDA. President Kennedy observes a flying exhibition here.

8 May 1962

ATLANTIC CITY, NEW JERSEY. At Convention Hall, President Kennedy addresses the United Auto Workers of America. The President says that the administration cannot intervene in every labor dispute but that it is his responsibility as chief executive to promote the public welfare and, consequently, he can suggest guidelines.

GROTON, CONNECTICUT. Jacqueline Kennedy christens the *Lafayette,* a 7,000-ton nuclear-powered submarine.

9 May 1962

WASHINGTON, D.C. President Kennedy confers with Prime Minister Einar H. Gerhardsen of Norway. In February, Norway had signed a fishing agreement with the Soviet Union and is now considering association with the European Economic Community. In toasting the Norwegian leader at a White House luncheon in his honor, President Kennedy quips, "It is almost 'sad' that there are so few issues which are causing intense controversy between Norway and the United States—an unaccustomed feeling as I welcomed the Prime Minister here. We searched all morning in an attempt to find something that would cause 'alarm' in both capitals."

11 May 1962

WASHINGTON, D.C. In presenting the Lifesaving Awards of the American Automobile Association, Presi-

dent Kennedy pins medals on the five young school safety-patrol recipients. Following a meeting with Prime Minister Gerhardsen of Norway, a joint statement is released saying that the two leaders pledged support to the United Nations and the NATO alliance and reviewed European economic and political developments. President Kennedy meets with André Malraux, the French Minister of Cultural Affairs.

12 May 1962

MILWAUKEE, WISCONSIN. President Kennedy delivers an address to the Jefferson-Jackson Day dinner crowd at the Milwaukee Arena.

15 May 1962

WASHINGTON, D.C. President Kennedy expresses regret over the decision of President Diosdado Macapagal of the Philippines to cancel his visit to the United States the following month. Macapagal is upset by the failure of Congress to pass a Philippines war reparations bill, and, Kennedy notes, a new bill has been introduced in Congress. President Kennedy also announces that he has ordered American troops into Thailand "because of recent attacks in Laos by Communist forces, and the subsequent movement of Communist military units toward the border of Thailand." He declares that "a threat to Thailand is of grave concern to the United States." President Kennedy also sends to the Speaker of the House Speaker and Senate President a draft of a senior citizens bill.

WASHINGTON, D.C. President Kennedy receives a message from Senator John Tower of Texas urging him to seek the resignation of cabinet member Orville L. Freeman. In the wake of the Billy Sol Estes scandal, Secretary of Agriculture Freeman has been assailed by Republicans after it was learned that a grain-storage company owned by Estes had received $7 million from the government.

17 May 1962

WASHINGTON, D.C. President Kennedy delivers an address on trade policy at the Sheraton Park Hotel. Speaking of a trade alliance between the United States and Europe, he declares that "now the time has come for a new chapter in American trade policy—a chapter that symbolizes our great new aspirations for greater growth at home, greater progress around the world, and above all, the emergence of a greater Atlantic partnership."

18 May 1962

NEW YORK. President Kennedy visits his father,

Joseph P. Kennedy, who is a patient at Horizon House. The elder Kennedy is undergoing a program of therapy at the institute to help him redevelop his motor functions.

19 May 1962

NEW YORK. At a dedication ceremony for a cooperative housing project sponsored by the International Ladies' Garment Workers Union, and before an audience that includes union representatives, Governor Nelson Rockefeller, Mayor Robert F. Wagner, and Eleanor Roosevelt, President Kennedy speaks of the great opportunity that the labor force has to strengthen the country. After this, the President visits his father at Horizon House, then attends a reception at the Four Seasons restaurant with almost 400 guests.

In the evening, President Kennedy, who will turn 45 in ten days, attends a birthday salute at Madison Square Garden. He thanks the many celebrities present, including Ella Fitzgerald, Peggy Lee, Jimmy Durante (who, he remarks, is the godfather of one of his sister's children), and Marilyn Monroe, who sings "Happy Birthday" to the President. ("I can now retire from politics....") Proceeds of the fund-raising event go to the Democratic party.

20 May 1962

NEW YORK. At Madison Square Garden, President Kennedy addresses a senior citizens rally in support of his program to provide federal health insurance (Medicare) for the elderly. He says that "the AMA is doing very well in its efforts to stop" the bill and adds that Congress "should pass this legislation as soon as possible." The rally is attended by some 20,000 people, mostly senior citizens, and the President's speech is nationally televised.

21 May 1962

NEW YORK. The American Medical Association, strongly opposed to the administration-backed King-Anderson, or Medicare, bill, sponsors a telecast from Madison Square Garden defending private medicine and assailing Medicare. There is no audience.

22 May 1962

WASHINGTON, D.C. President Felix Houphouet-Boigny of the Ivory Coast meets with President Kennedy. The Ivory Coast, a pro-Western African nation, receives substantial economic aid from France. The National Academy of Television Arts and Sciences presents a Special Trustee Emmy award to Jacqueline Kennedy for her televised tour of the White House in February.

23 May 1962

WASHINGTON, D.C. On the South Lawn of the White House, President Kennedy welcomes state directors of the Selective Service System. He tells the group, "Unless you and those who work with you were able to maintain the confidence of the Governors and the people of the various States in the equity of this system, I cannot imagine anything that would be more destructive to the common welfare."

24 May 1962

WASHINGTON, D.C. President Kennedy attends the laying of the cornerstone for the new Rayburn House Office Building. He says "No monument, no memorial, no statue would please" the late Speaker of the House "half so much, I believe, as to have his name preserved here in this fashion on Capitol Hill." President Kennedy offers congratulations by phone to Lt. Comdr. M. Scott Carpenter, who had earlier become the second American in orbit when he circled the earth three times, aboard the *Intrepid*. The President watched the launch from Cape Canaveral on television.

25 May 1962

WASHINGTON, D.C. President Kennedy addresses delegates of the White House Conference on Conservation. He talks of finding methods for the desalinization of water, of bringing "water to bear on the deserts surrounding the Mediterranean and the Indian Sea," of "getting food from the ocean depths," and of finding "new uses for minerals."

29 May 1962

MIDDLEBURG, VIRGINIA. After a day of work at the White House, President Kennedy arrives at his Glen Ora estate where, with his family, he celebrates his forty-fifth birthday. Arriving with him by helicopter are Robert and Ethel Kennedy, Jean (Kennedy) Smith, Sargent and Eunice Shriver, LeMoyne Billings, and Cap. Tazewell Shepard.

31 May 1962

WASHINGTON, D.C. As the President's Committee on Juvenile Delinquency and Youth Crime presents its first report to President Kennedy, he announces the commencement of Mobilization for Youth, the first project of the Juvenile Delinquency and Youth Offenses Control Act of 1961. The program will provide job opportunities, educational assistance, and other services in an attempt to correct or prevent delinquency. With a budget of $12,600,000, the project will be undertaken in New York City.

Ethel Kennedy carries newborn son Christopher George to his christening in Hyannis Port, 19 July 1963.

1 June 1962

MOSCOW, USSR. Lee and Marina Oswald leave for the United States.

2 June 1962

SANTA CLARA, CALIFORNIA. At graduation ceremonies of the University of Santa Clara, Eunice (Kennedy) Shriver makes the commencement address and is awarded an honorary Doctor of Letters degree.

5 June 1962

WASHINGTON, D.C. President Kennedy greets astronaut Scott Carpenter and his family in the East Room of the White House. Later, he confers with His Beatitude Archbishop Makarios, president of Cyprus.

6 June 1962

WEST POINT, NEW YORK. President Kennedy delivers the commencement address at the graduation exercises of the United States Military Academy. He speaks of the military and nonmilitary challenges the graduates will face in the future, but declares that "above all, you will have a responsibility to deter war as well as to fight it. For the basic problems facing the world today are not susceptible of a final military solution." Following his speech, the President is made an honorary member of the West Point class of 1962.

NEW YORK. President Kennedy and President Makarios of Cyprus conclude their discussions. They confer on international issues and American economic aid to the small Mediterranean country, which gained full independence on 16 August 1960.

9 June 1962

SPRINGFIELD, MASSACHUSETTS. At the Massachusetts Democratic convention, Ted Kennedy wins the delegates' endorsement on the first ballot. He will run for the senatorial nomination in the state Democratic primary to be held in September.

10 June 1962

NEW YORK. President Kennedy, with Peter Lawford, visits Joseph P. Kennedy at Horizon House.

11 June 1962

NEW HAVEN, CONNECTICUT. At the Yale University graduation exercises, President Kennedy receives an honorary Doctor of Laws degree. The President then delivers the commencement address. "Let me begin," he says, "by expressing my appreciation for the very deep honor that you have conferred upon me....It might be said now that I have the best of both worlds, a Harvard education and a Yale degree." He speaks on "myths" perceived by the public: "that government is big and bad," that federal fiscal integrity is measured by inaccurate administrative budgets, and that unfavorable turns in the economy are due to a lack of public confidence in the administration. To attack contemporary problems, he declares, the nation cannot be bound by traditional labels, trite slogans of the past, but must keep pace with actual change: "What is at stake in our economic decisions today is not some grand warfare of rival ideologies which will sweep the country with passion but the practical management of a modern economy."

12 June 1962

WASHINGTON, D.C. President Roberto F. Chiari of Panama begins two days of discussions with President Kennedy to discuss Panamanian dissatisfaction with certain provisions of the Treaty on the Canal Zone. Following the formation of a coalition government in Laos under Prince Souvanna Phouma, President Kennedy sends a message to Soviet Premier Krushchev in which he declares, "If together we can help in the establishment of an independent and neutral Laos, securely sustained in this status through time, this accomplishment will surely have a significant and positive effect far beyond the borders of Laos." In the evening, the President and Mrs. Kennedy, with Mr. and Mrs. David Ormsby-Gore, attend a performance of *Irma La Douce* at the National Theater.

13 June 1962
NEW YORK. Having lived in the Soviet Union since 1959, Lee Harvey Oswald returns to the United States with his wife, Marina, and their daughter. While in Russia, he had worked in a radio factory.

14 June 1962
NEW YORK. Lee Harvey Oswald leaves by plane with his wife and daughter for Dallas, Texas.

15 June 1962
WASHINGTON, D.C. President Kennedy confers with John R. Marshall, deputy prime minister of New Zealand, on England's possible entry into the European Common Market.

19 June 1962
WASHINGTON, D.C. Prime Minister Robert Gordon Menzies of Australia and President Kennedy confer on the situation in Southeast Asia, the effects on Australian-American trade if England should join the European economic community, and possible solutions to the problems that might arise.

21 June 1962
WASHINGTON, D.C. President Kennedy greets students from the graduating class of Glen Lake (Michigan) High School in the Rose Garden. He tells them, "All the people you read about in your history books— Lincoln, the Adamses, Monroe, the Wilsons, Roosevelt, Truman, Eisenhower, and all the others all lived here and all participated in making this country greater."

25 June 1962
WASHINGTON, D.C. A White House luncheon is held in honor of President-elect Guillermo Leon Valencia of Colombia. Valencia will take the oath of office in August.

26 June 1962
WASHINGTON, D.C. Vice-President Emmanuel Palaez of the Philippines meets with President Kennedy. The anti-Communist Philippine government is pursuing closer relations with independent Asian countries.

FORT WORTH, TEXAS. The FBI conducts its first interview with Lee Harvey Oswald, who returned to the United States from Russia on 13 June. They question the possibility that he is a Soviet agent.

27 June 1962
WASHINGTON, D.C. President Kennedy attends the opening of an exhibition of Franklin D. Roosevelt's naval prints at the National Archives. The President remarks, "Our naval history is one of the most exciting threads that runs throughout the long history of our country and the combination of the Navy and the Maritime and the extraordinary men who served and who gave it life and thrust and thesis deserves to be recorded.

28 June 1962
WASHINGTON, D.C. President Kennedy signs the Migration and Refugee Assistance Act, saying that with the legislation, "the American people will be assured that this Government's leadership will be maintained in the great humanitarian endeavor of helping the world's stateless and homeless people." In a ceremony in the White House Conference Room, copies of the new *White House Guide Book* are presented to President and Mrs. Kennedy. The publication, with a foreword by Jacqueline Kennedy, was prepared by the National Geographic Society and the White House Historical Association.

29 June 1962
MEXICO CITY. President and Mrs. Kennedy begin a three-day diplomatic visit to Mexico. They are greeted by President Adolfo López Mateos at Mexico City International Airport. The two leaders confer at Los Piños, the residence of President Mateos, and then leave for the National Palace where a luncheon is given for President and Mrs. Kennedy. In his speech, the President recalls Abraham Lincoln's instruction to his secretary of state to tell the Mexicans how much he respected their love of civil liberty. "Today, one hundred years later," President Kennedy says, "that deep respect remains in the hearts of the people and the President of the United States....We now dream the same dream of opportunity in the future. And our two continuing revolutions have now been joined as one, one great effort, one great continent, in one great *Alianza para el Progreso. Viva Mexico!*" At the Municipal Palace, President Kennedy receives the key to Mexico City.

239

30 June 1962

MEXICO CITY. At Independence Monument, President Kennedy participates in a wreath-laying ceremony. The President then takes an automobile tour of the United Independencia Housing Project and delivers a speech. He then confers with President Mateos at Los Piños, and attends an Independence Day celebration held by the American Society of Mexico. President Kennedy says he thinks it is appropriate to celebrate the Fourth of July here "because the people who wrote the Declaration of Independence from the beginning recognized...that they were not merely advancing a theory of government for the people of the United States, but for the people around the world."

1 July 1962

MEXICO CITY. At the Monument to the Revolution of 1910, President Kennedy lays wreaths at the tombs of the heroes of the Mexican Revolution buried there.

WASHINGTON, D.C. Back at the White House, President Kennedy signs a bill to increase the public debt and another to revise the 1949 Export Control Act.

3 July 1962

WASHINGTON, D.C. The French government issues a proclamation recognizing the independence of Algeria, which President Kennedy immediately acknowledges. "I am proud," he says, "that it falls to me as the President of the people of the United States to voice on their behalf the profound satisfaction we feel that the cause of freedom of choice among peoples has again triumphed."

4 July 1962

PHILADELPHIA, PENNSYLVANIA. At an Independence Day celebration at Independence Hall, President Kennedy delivers an address on the importance of the Declaration of Independence to contemporary Americans. "To read it today," he says, "is to hear a trumpet call. For that Declaration unleashed not merely a revolution against the British, but a revolution in human affairs. Its authors were highly conscious of its worldwide implications." The President challenges Americans now to "be ready for a Declaration of Interdependence...to discuss with a united Europe the ways and means of forming a concrete Atlantic partnership...to throw off the yoke of poverty...balance our world-wide trade...[and] deter any aggression...[in order] to achieve a world of law and free choice."

5 July 1962

WASHINGTON, D.C. At a press conference at the State Department Auditorium, President Kennedy urges "strong support for the Senate effort" to pass a bill providing medical care for the aged under Social Security.

6 July 1962

WASHINGTON, D.C. In a statement released following the death earlier today of Nobel laureate, author William Faulkner, President Kennedy comments, "Since Henry James, no writer has left behind such a vast and enduring monument to the strength of American literature....From this world he sought to illuminate the restless searching of all men. And his insight spoke to the hearts of all who listened."

7 July 1962

HYANNIS PORT, MASSACHUSETTS. President Kennedy and his family visit his father, Joseph P. Kennedy, who has just been released from the Institute of Physical Medicine and Rehabilitation in New York. The former ambassador has undergone months of therapy to improve his speech and movement, which were impaired by his stroke in December of 1961.

9 July 1962

ANDREWS AIR FORCE BASE, MARYLAND. President Kennedy greets troops from the One Hundred Thirty-Second Tactical Control Group on their return from Germany. American military forces sent to Germany in 1961 because of violent demonstrations when the Berlin wall went up have now been ordered home.

10 July 1962

WASHINGTON, D.C. President Kennedy attends the All-Star baseball game at D.C. Stadium. He throws out the first ball to American League catcher Earl Battey.

11 July 1962

WASHINGTON, D.C. On the South Lawn, President Kennedy addresses over 2,000 students from Africa, Western Europe, Asia, Australia, and elsewhere. He speaks about the responsibilities that the United States has to the world after a long tradition of isolation and welcomes the students, particularly those from Great Britain: "Your forebears as you know burned our White House, and it is a pleasure to welcome you here on this peaceful occasion." He closes by quoting the German statesman Otto von Bismarck with a remark he is to repeat in many of his speeches: "[von Bismarck] once said that one-third of the students of German universities broke down from overwork, another third broke down from dissipation, and the other third ruled Germany. I don't know which third we have here today, but I'm confident that some future President of the United States will welcome you as either President or perhaps even better, the wife of a President, to the White House, and you'll be able to say to him, 'I have been here before.'"

12 July 1962
WASHINGTON, D.C. Abraham Ribicoff resigns as secretary of Health, Education, and Welfare.

16 July 1962
NEW YORK. *Sports Illustrated* publishes "The Vigor We Need," an article on physical fitness in America by President John F. Kennedy.

17 July 1962
WASHINGTON, D.C. The Senate kills the King-Anderson (Medicare) bill that President Kennedy had supported. This legislation, fought by the American Medical Association, would have provided a system of health insurance for the aged through Social Security. After the defeat, President Kennedy goes on television to express hope that in November Americans "will return...a Congress that will support a program like Medical Care for the Aged."

21 July 1962
HYANNIS PORT, MASSACHUSETTS. President Kennedy goes sailing with Jacqueline, Ethel Kennedy, John Glenn and his family, LeMoyne Billings, and Sir David Ormsby-Gore, the British ambassador to the United States.

23 July 1962
HYANNIS PORT, MASSACHUSETTS. In the morning, President Kennedy, his mother, Rose, Robert Kennedy, and David Ormsby-Gore travel by helicopter to Otis Air Force Base where they take a plane to the nation's capital.

WASHINGTON, D.C. A White House luncheon is held in honor of President Carlos Julio Arosemena Monroy of Ecuador and his wife. Rose Kennedy is her son's official hostess in Jacqueline Kennedy's absence. President Kennedy's press conference today is telecast to Europe by the Telstar communications satellite. Later, the President confers with President Arosemena.

24 July 1962
WASHINGTON, D.C. President Kennedy and President Arosemena conclude two days of meetings that included discussions about the need for change in Ecuador's economic and social structure. The country's economy is still depressed, and the government has been troubled by leftist actions.

25 July 1962
WASHINGTON, D.C. President Kennedy signs into law the Public Welfare Amendments of 1962. This legislation stresses provisions for family rehabilitation and training for useful work. In a previous message to Congress, President Kennedy called for such a "new public welfare program."

26 July 1962
WASHINGTON, D.C. President Kennedy welcomes William Neely, this year's one-millionth visitor to the White House.

27 July 1962
WASHINGTON, D.C. President Kennedy meets with Prince Souvanna Phouma of Laos. At a White House luncheon held in honor of the Prince, President Kennedy says, "If we can succeed in Laos, it makes the future brighter. If our common efforts and the commitments in Laos fail, then the future not only of Laos but of a good deal of the rest of the world becomes darker."

31 July 1962
WASHINGTON, D.C. President Kennedy meets with the Brazilian ambassador, Roberto de Oliveira Campos, and a group of Brazilian students who are invited to ask any questions they have. Anthony J. Celebrezze becomes the secretary of Health, Education, and Welfare. Appointed by President Kennedy to succeed Abraham Ribicoff, who resigned 12 July, Celebrezze is the administration's first cabinet replacement. President Kennedy and Prince Souvanna Phouma announce in a joint statement that President Kennedy has "confirmed the determination of the United States to work actively in supporting the independence and neutrality of Laos."

1 August 1962
WASHINGTON, D.C. President Kennedy signs into law the Foreign Assistance Act of 1962 which, he says, "provides military assistance to countries which are on the rim of the Communist world and under direct attack" and "provides economic assistance to those governments which are under attack from widespread misery

and social discontent which are exploited by our adversaries...." Questioned at a press conference about the tragic results of using the drug thalidomide, President Kennedy calls for stronger laws to protect consumers against harmful or worthless drugs. He also reports that the United States is reviewing plans for monitoring a nuclear test-ban treaty with the hope that "an internationally supervised system of detection and verification for underground testing" can be implemented.

2 August 1962

WASHINGTON, D.C. President Kennedy announces that he has asked the Agriculture Department to continue the food-stamp program for another year and to expand it to a number of other states.

6 August 1962

WASHINGTON, D.C. The National High School Symphony Orchestra from the National Music Camp of Interlochen, Michigan, gives a concert on the South Lawn. President Kennedy greets the orchestra members as well as some 1,200 handicapped children and others in the audience. In a brief speech, he says, "I know that there is some feeling...that the arts are developed in solitude, that they are developed by inspiration and by sudden fits of genius. But the fact of the matter is that success comes in music or in the arts like success comes in every other form of human endeavor—by hard work, by discipline, over a long period of time."

7 August 1962

WASHINGTON, D.C. President Kennedy presents the President's Distinguished Civilian Service Awards at a ceremony in the Rose Garden. Among the recipients is Dr. Frances A. Kelsey of the Food and Drug Administration, whose refusal to approve thalidomide for use in the United States prevented widespread birth deformities in the country. (Originally thought to be a safe and effective sedative, thalidomide had been more widely used in Europe.)

8 August 1962

NEW YORK. Jacqueline and Caroline Kennedy leave for Ravello, Italy, to begin a twenty-three-day vacation.

10 August 1962

WASHINGTON, D.C. President Kennedy signs a bill authorizing over $48 billion for defense in fiscal 1963.

BRUNSWICK, MAINE. President Kennedy makes a brief speech at the Festival for Charity at the U.S. Naval Air Station.

JOHNS ISLAND, MAINE. President Kennedy arrives at the residence of Gene Tunney for a weekend vacation.

11 August 1962

JOHNS ISLAND, MAINE. With senators Edmund Muskie and Benjamin Smith II, Under-Secretary of the Navy Paul Fay, Jr., Assistant Treasury Secretary James Reed, and Charles Spaulding, President Kennedy spends the day cruising Maine waters in four different Coast Guard ships. Later, Pat (Kennedy) and Peter Lawford join the President as guests at the Gene Tunney home.

12 August 1962

BOOTHBAY HARBOR, MAINE. President Kennedy issues a message of congratulations to Russia following the launch of Soviet cosmonauts into orbit around the earth.

13 August 1962

WASHINGTON, D.C. President Kennedy signs the Work Hours Standards Act of 1962. This law, he says, replaces the series of eight-hour laws dating back to 1892 which "permitted work up to 56 hours a week—seven days of eight hours—with no overtime compensation...and establishes a 40-hour workweek standard— long prevalent in private industry." In the evening, the President delivers a national radio and television address on the American economy.

15 August 1962

WASHINGTON, D.C. NAVY YARD. At Pier 2 of the Navy Yard Annex, President Kennedy inspects the U.S. Coast Guard Academy training barque *Eagle*. An honor guard is given on the deck. Later, at the White House the President greets delegates from the American Indian Chicago Conference.

16 August 1962

WASHINGTON, D.C. President Kennedy signs bills authorizing the secretary of the Interior to construct, operate, and maintain the Frying Pan (Arkansas) Reclamation Project, which "includes hydroelectric power, municipal and industrial water supply, flood control, irrigation, recreational opportunities, and fish and wildlife preservation and enhancement," and the Mann Creek (Idaho) Federal Reclamation Project "to conserve spring run-off...and thereby provide a more reliable source of irrigation water." Later, he meets with Gen. Douglas MacArthur and makes a film in support of the senatorial and gubernatorial campaigns of Joseph S. Clark and Richardson Dilwirth of Pennsylvania.

17 August 1962

PIERRE, SOUTH DAKOTA.   At the dedication of the Oahe Dam, the world's largest rolled-earth dam, President Kennedy opens a two-day nonpolitical visit to conservation centers in the western United States. Begun in 1948, the project is expected to be completed in two years.

PUEBLO, COLORADO.   At the Pueblo Public School stadium, President Kennedy speaks on the Frying Pan (Arkansas) Project that he authorized yesterday.

CASTLE AIR FORCE BASE, CALIFORNIA. President Kennedy visits here and is accorded full military honors.

18 August 1962

YOSEMITE NATIONAL PARK, CALIFORNIA. John F. Kennedy is the first American president to visit here since Theodore Roosevelt.

LOS BANOS, CALIFORNIA.   President Kennedy attends groundbreaking ceremonies for the San Luis Dam. In a speech, he notes that on this brief trip he has observed how well Americans can work together. It would be disastrous, he says, for citizens in one part of a state not to share what they have with citizens in other parts. "Progress represents the combined will of the American people," he says.

FRESNO, CALIFORNIA.   At the Fresno City Airport, President Kennedy speaks briefly.

22 August 1962

WASHINGTON, D.C.   At a press conference, President Kennedy announces that two American nuclear-powered submarines, the *Skate* and the *Sea Dragon,* "have completed an historic rendezvous under the polar ice pack, and then surfaced together through a small opening in the ice at the North Pole."

27 August 1962

BOSTON.   A television debate takes place between Edward M. Kennedy and Edward J. McCormack, Jr., candidates for the Democratic nomination for senator from Massachusetts. They will face each other in the Democratic primary on 18 September.

28 August 1962

WASHINGTON, D.C.   On the south Lawn, President Kennedy bids farewell to a group of college students who participated in a summer political internship program. "This tree behind me," he says, "was planted by Andrew Jackson. The balcony was built by Harry Truman and the tree over there was planted by John Adams. So I think that just visiting this historic house and these grounds does bring you in more intimate contact with American history." He urges the students to seek a career in government saying, "A great American educator asked a century ago, at the time of the Kansas-Missouri struggle, 'Would you have counted him a friend of ancient Greece who quietly discussed the theory of patriotism on that hot summer day through those hopeless and immortal hours Leonidas and the 300 stood at Thermopylae for liberty? Would you count anyone a friend of freedom who stands aside today?' So I hope that you come in and join us because the water is not too cold."

WASHINGTON, D.C.   Following two strokes in recent months, Felix Frankfurter, 79, retires as associate justice of the Supreme Court. In a letter to him, President Kennedy expresses "respectful gratitude for the character, courage, learning and judicial dedication" with which Frankfurter has served the country over the previous twenty-three years.

29 August 1962

WASHINGTON, D.C.   President Kennedy welcomes to the White House more than 110 representatives of the Junior Red Cross from over forty countries. He then meets with His Beatitude Paul Boutros Meouchi, patriarch of Lebanon's Maronite church. At a press conference, the President announces his nomination of Arthur J. Goldberg to succeed Felix Frankfurter as associate justice of the Supreme Court.

30 August 1962

WASHINGTON, D.C.   President Kennedy signs a bill to pay the Philippines $73 million in war damages. The failure of Congress to pass an earlier reparations bill had caused some disaccord with the government of President Diosdado Macapagal.

31 August 1962

WASHINGTON, D.C.   President Kennedy signs the Communications Satellite Act of 1962, the purpose of which is "to establish a commercial communications system utilizing space satellites which will serve our needs and those of other countries...to be accomplished through the joint efforts of private individuals and concerns, and agencies of the Federal Government."

NEWPORT, RHODE ISLAND.   President Kennedy greets Jacqueline and Caroline Kennedy at the Quonset Naval Air Station on their return from a three-week vacation in Italy. The family then goes to Hammersmith Farm on Ocean Boulevard where they will spend the Labor Day weekend.

1 September 1962
NEWPORT, RHODE ISLAND. President Kennedy inspects the *Joseph P. Kennedy, Jr.* at the Naval base.

3 September 1962
NEWPORT, RHODE ISLAND. Speaking on his second Labor Day as president, Kennedy announces the convening of "an international conference devoted to the role of human skills in creating rapid economic progress for the developing countries." He says the conference is "a milestone in the formulation of economic development." In a message to American youths, he declares, "My urgent message to you is, 'Return to school.' For thousands of you, the decision you make this September about returning to school may mean the difference between possible hardship and unemployment or a fruitful life as a productive member of our society."

5 September 1962
MASSACHUSETTS. Edward M. Kennedy and Edward J. McCormack, Jr., face each other in their second and final televised "Teddie-Eddie" debate.

7 September 1962
WASHINGTON, D.C. President Kennedy asks Congress for the authority to call 150,000 reserves to active duty. The request is made in view of possible action in response to the Soviets supplying missiles and other equipment to Cuba. Although the President is empowered to order up a million reserves in a national emergency, declaring an emergency would cause unnecessary panic. A draft proposal that would permit the President to order units in the Ready Reserves to active duty goes to Congress. In an accompanying letter, Kennedy says that "this renewed authorization is necessary to permit prompt and effective responses...to challenges which may be presented in any part of the free world."

10 September 1962
WASHINGTON, D.C. President Kennedy confers with Dwight D. Eisenhower, who has just returned from a tour of Western Europe. They first meet alone, then with Dean Rusk, Robert McNamara, and Gen. Marshall Carter.

11 September 1962
HUNTSVILLE, ALABAMA. President Kennedy addresses 470 troops from thirteen foreign nations under-

going training at the Redstone Army Airfield. "This kind of joint community effort," he says, "would have been regarded as impossible two decades ago." At Building 4705, President Kennedy examines the Saturn C-1 and F-1 engines that will be used for moon landings. Dr. Werner Von Braun, director of the Marshall Space Flight Center, provides background on the advanced Saturn rocket.

CAPE CANAVERAL, FLORIDA. President Kennedy talks with astronaut Walter Schirra on the Mercury-Atlas-8 Mission at Mercury-Atlas Launch Complex no. 14. The President then visits other Gemini and Saturn projects. At the Manned Space-Craft Center, President Kennedy speaks briefly to the staff. "I don't think that we can exaggerate the great advantage which the Soviet Union secured in the fifties by being first in space," he says, "but...I believe that we are on the rise...."

12 September 1962
HOUSTON, TEXAS. President Kennedy speaks about the country's space efforts in an address at Rice University. Of the nation's commitment to solve the mysteries of space, he says, "We set sail on this new sea because there is new knowledge to be gained, and new rights to be won, and they must be won and used for the progress of all people....Space can be explored and mastered without feeding the fires of war, without repeating the mistakes that man has made in extending his writ around this globe of ours." He also affirms that America will put a man on the moon and return him safely to earth "before the end of this decade."

ST. LOUIS, MISSOURI. President Kennedy gives a brief speech to some 10,000 employees of the McDonnell Aircraft Corporation at Lambert Field.

13 September 1962
WASHINGTON, D.C. President Kennedy signs a bill to establish the Point Reyes National Seashore in California. At a press conference, the President announces that "if at any time the Communist buildup in Cuba were to endanger or interfere with our security in any way...then this country will do whatever must be done to protect its own security and that of its allies." He also pledges protection, and, if necessary, "extra legislation and force," to enable blacks to vote. The Senate approves President Kennedy's 7 September request for the authority to call up reserves to active duty.

14 September 1962
WASHINGTON, D.C. President Kennedy signs into law a bill to provide $900 million for public works

President Kennedy and his wife watch the royal Highland Regiment, 13 November 1963, in one of their last White House photos together.

projects in economically depressed areas. He says that the Public Works Acceleration Act "is a significant milestone in our efforts to strengthen the economy and provide a greater measure of economic security to the unemployed." He extends best wishes to Jewish Americans on the occasion of Rosh Hashanah and the Jewish High Holy Days. "This is a time," Kennedy says, "for a personal and spiritual inventory and for reflection on goals and achievements. It calls for a reaffirmation of the willingness to sacrifice that there may be righteousness for all mankind."

NEWPORT, RHODE ISLAND. President and Mrs. Kennedy attend the America's Cup dinner, given by Ambassador and Lady Beale of Australia.

15 September 1962
NEWPORT, RHODE ISLAND. On board the *Joseph P. Kennedy, Jr.,* President Kennedy receives a

model of a destroyer. In thanking the captain and others aboard, he says, "The *Kennedy* means a good deal to all of us. My sister took part at the commissioning. My father and mother attended it. It was built in Fall River, Massachusetts. My brother Robert served on it as a seaman in the Caribbean in 1944 and 1945. My father and mother have visited it on several occasions when it was stationed in the Mediterranean. It was, of course, as you know, named after my brother who had a distinguished combat record in the Second World War....We realize that whatever may come for this country and for the Navy, that the U.S.S. *Joseph P. Kennedy, Jr.,* will be playing an important and forward part."

18 September 1962
BOSTON. President Kennedy arrives here with his wife from Newport, Rhode Island, to vote in the Massachusetts primary at the police station at 80 Joy Street. After voting, they immediately return to Newport.

MASSACHUSETTS. Edward M. Kennedy wins a special Democratic primary for senator from Massachusetts by a margin of 311,900 votes. The election results are: Edward M. Kennedy of Boston, 559,303 votes; Edward J. McCormack of Boston, 247,403; all others, 26; blanks, 28,607 (total votes cast, 835,239).

19 September 1962

WASHINGTON, D.C. President Kennedy confers with President Gregoire Kavibanda of Rwanda on relations between the United States and Rwanda, which became independent on 1 July, and some of the problems facing the new Rwandan government.

20 September 1962

WASHINGTON, D.C. President Kennedy signs a bill to establish the Delaware River and Bay Authority "for the development of the area bordering on the Delaware River and Bay." In an address before a joint session of the Governors of the World Bank and the International Monetary Fund at the Sheraton-Park Hotel, Kennedy appeals to other nations to share the economic burden of foreign aid carried by the United States. This nation, he says, has assumed a "disproportionate share of the costs of defending the free world and fostering social and economic progress in the less developed parts of the world." The President meets with the Advisory Committee on Banking and the Comptroller of the Currency, then tapes a number of messages, including one on the Emancipation Proclamation and one for the Air Force Day Association.

HARRISBURG, PENNSYLVANIA. President Kennedy speaks at a Democratic fund-raising dinner. "I will introduce myself," he begins, "I am Teddy Kennedy's brother, and I'm glad to be here tonight."

21 September 1962

COLUMBUS, OHIO. President Kennedy addresses the Ohio State Democratic Convention in Veterans' Memorial Hall by telephone from Rhode Island.

22 September 1962

NEWPORT, RHODE ISLAND. President and Jacqueline Kennedy watch the America's Cup Races from a vantage point aboard the *Joseph P. Kennedy, Jr.*

WASHINGTON, D.C. At a ceremony at the Lincoln Memorial commemorating the centennial of the Emancipation Proclamation, a tape made by President Kennedy two days ago is played. "Like the proclamation we celebrate," he says, "this observance must be regarded not as an end, but a beginning. The best commemoration lies not in what we say today, but in what we do in the days and months ahead to complete the work begun by Abraham Lincoln a century ago."

23 September 1962

NEW YORK. Many celebrities, including Jacqueline Kennedy, attend the concert of the New York Philharmonic Orchestra which opens Philharmonic Hall. The hall is the first to be completed of a half-dozen units that will comprise the Lincoln Center for the Performing Arts.

24 September 1962

NEWPORT, RHODE ISLAND. President Mohammed Ayub Khan of Pakistan is the guest of President and Mrs. Kennedy at Hammersmith Farm. After a luncheon in his honor, the two leaders confer informally on the world situation and on matters of mutual concern to the United States and Pakistan.

25 September 1962

WASHINGTON, D.C. Military artist Kenneth P. Riley presents his painting of the Battle of Bunker Hill, "The Whites of Their Eyes," to President Kennedy. At 10:20 P.M. , Kennedy enters the presidential box at the National Theater to join his wife and mother for the second act of the play *Mr. President.*

27 September 1962

WASHINGTON, D.C. At the Department of State Auditorium, President Kennedy opens a two-day White House Conference on Narcotics and Drug Abuse, a subject he says, "needs great, urgent, public attention." Attorney General Robert F. Kennedy is chairman of the conference. Later, the President signs the Food and Agriculture Act of 1962, saying that it is "an important step forward in our program to increase farm income while reducing costs to the Government of the farm program and holding the accumulation of farm surpluses."

WHEELING, WEST VIRGINIA. President Kennedy speaks at a Democratic public rally at Wheeling Stadium.

28 September 1962

WASHINGTON, D.C. President Kennedy signs a bill to establish a national seashore on Padre Island in the Gulf of Mexico off the Texas coast.

29 September 1962

WASHINGTON, D.C. President Kennedy confers

with Attorney General Robert F. Kennedy and other government officials about the trouble developing in Mississippi over the attendance of a black veteran, James H. Meredith, Jr., at the University of Mississippi, a school which heretofore has refused entry to black students. They authorize the presence of federal marshals on the scene.

30 September 1962

WASHINGTON, D.C. President Kennedy meets with England's foreign secretary, the Earl of Home, to discuss Cuba, Berlin, and the Congo.

In the evening, President Kennedy delivers a 10-minute national radio and television address denouncing local violence over the enrollment of James Meredith at the University of Mississippi in Oxford. U.S. marshals and federal troops have been brought in to suppress the rioting, which has left two men dead. Kennedy appeals to residents of Mississippi not to disobey the federal court order to integrate, saying, "Americans are free in short, to disagree with the law, but not to disobey it. It lies in your courage to accept those laws with which you disagree as well as those with which you agree."

1 October 1962

WASHINGTON, D.C. President Kennedy attends the swearing in of Arthur J. Goldberg as associate justice of the Supreme Court. Later, at the White House, the President bestows the Distinguished Service Medal on General Lyman L. Lemnitzer, who retired the day before as the chairman of the Joint Chiefs of Staff. Kennedy speaks at the swearing-in ceremony of Lemnitzer's successor, General Maxwell D. Taylor.

Attorney General Robert F. Kennedy charges that Governor Ross R. Barnett of Mississippi, who had initially opposed the matriculation of James H. Meredith, Jr., at the University of Mississippi, has failed to maintain order after promising that Meredith's presence on campus would be peaceful. According to Kennedy, local police were ordered to leave as soon as violence broke out.

2 October 1962

WASHINGTON, D.C. President Kennedy signs the United Nations Loan bill, saying that it will "permit the United States to lend up to $100 million to the United Nations in order to help it meet the financial crisis it faces," which "is largely the result of the failure of some members of the organization to pay their share of the costs of the peace-keeping machinery in the Middle East and in the Congo." At a White House luncheon honoring the foreign ministers of several Latin American coun-

tries, the President speaks on actions that will prevent communism from spreading from Cuba to its neighbors.

3 October 1962

WASHINGTON, D.C. President Kennedy offers congratulations to Commander Walter M. Shirra, Jr., who orbited the earth six times earlier in the day aboard the vessel *Kearsarge* in the Pacific Ocean.

WASHINGTON, D.C. President Kennedy approves a bill authorizing the President to call to active duty 150,000 members of the National Reserves for not more than twelve months.

4 October 1962

WASHINGTON, D.C. For the first time since he becoming president, Kennedy cancels all appointments and meetings because he has a cold. He does, however, sign official documents.

5 October 1962

WASHINGTON, D.C. President Kennedy meets with Mayor Willy Brandt of West Berlin on the Berlin crisis. Next, he confers with Crown Prince Faisal of Saudi Arabia on relations between the United States and Saudi Arabia and on the Saudi conflict with the United Arab Republic.

ERLANGER, KENTUCKY. President Kennedy delivers an address at the Greater Cincinnati Airport to begin a three-day campaign tour in support of various Democratic office-seekers.

CINCINNATI, OHIO. Kennedy speaks at Fountain Square.

DETROIT, MICHIGAN. At Metropolitan Airport, Kennedy speaks on behalf of Michigan Democrats.

6 October 1962

DETROIT, MICHIGAN. President Kennedy opens a day of campaigning by speaking at a Democratic rally outside the Sheraton Cadillac Hotel.

FLINT, MICHIGAN. Reviewing the record in Congress of Michigan Republicans, President Kennedy urges residents to "register and vote, and vote Democratic!"

MUSKEGON, MICHIGAN. The President continues his campaign tour for state Democrats in a speech at the Muskegon County Airport.

ST. PAUL, MINNESOTA. At a local event, the Bean Feed, President Kennedy speaks on behalf of Minnesota Democrats. He is accompanied by Senators Hubert Humphrey and Eugene McCarthy.

9 October 1962
DALLAS, TEXAS. Lee Harvey Oswald rents post office box number 2915 in the Oak Cliff Station annex.

10 October 1962
WASHINGTON, D.C. President Kennedy signs the Drug Labeling Bill which, he says, "will help give the American consumer protection from unsafe and ineffective drugs," then addresses a group of United States attorneys in the Rose Garden. After greeting President Sékou Touré of Guinea at Washington National Airport, he confers with him at the White House on American financial assistance to the country.

BALTIMORE, MARYLAND. At the Fifth Regiment Armory, President Kennedy campaigns for Maryland Democrats running for Congress. In a speech there, he urges the election of Democratic candidates to the House and Senate who support medical care for the elderly, the minimum wage, and other programs of his administration. "All the political cheers, all the political speeches," he declares, "don't mean anything unless in the final analysis a party functions."

11 October 1962
WASHINGTON, D.C. President Kennedy signs the Postal Service and Federal Employees Salary Act of 1962 to increase postage rates as of 7 January 1963 and to reform federal salary systems. He also signs the Trade Expansion Act, which grants the authority to adjust tariffs.

12 October 1962
NEWARK, NEW JERSEY. At a Columbus Day rally at City Hall, President Kennedy lists the Americans of Italian extraction who are governors or who serve in the United States Congress.

NEW YORK. From a reviewing stand at 64th Street and Fifth Avenue, President Kennedy and Mayor Robert F. Wagner watch a Columbus Day parade.

ALIQUIPPA, PENNSYLVANIA. President Kennedy urges election of state Democrats at a rally held in a municipal parking lot.

PITTSBURGH, PENNSYLVANIA. The President continues campaigning for Pennsylvania Democrats

by speaking at a rally held in the Fitzgerald Field House at the University of Pittsburgh.

13 October 1962
PENNSYLVANIA. President Kennedy campaigns for Pennsylvania Democrats at rallies in McKeesport, Monessen, and Washington.

INDIANAPOLIS, INDIANA. The President urges election of Indiana Democrats in a speech at Indianapolis Airport.

LOUISVILLE, KENTUCKY. President Kennedy speaks at a Democratic rally at the Freedom Hall Coliseum at the State Fairgrounds.

14 October 1962
NIAGARA FALLS, NEW YORK. President Kennedy delivers a brief speech at Municipal Airport.

BUFFALO, NEW YORK. President Kennedy speaks at a Pulaski Day Parade and declares that "we must strengthen the economic and cultural ties that bind Poland to the West."

15 October 1962
WASHINGTON, D.C. Ahmed Ben Bella, recently inaugurated as prime minister of Algeria, meets with President Kennedy. They discuss problems confronting the new Algerian government and their countries' foreign policies.

16 October 1962
WASHINGTON, D.C. Aerial photos taken by an American U-2 reconnaissance plane flying over Cuba two days ago are shown to President Kennedy. Photo analysts see evidence of Soviet missile buildup at bases in San Cristobal.

WASHINGTON, D.C. President Kennedy signs the Revenue Act of 1962, which, he says, "will provide added stimulus to investments in machinery and equipment, and give American firms tax treatment which compares favorably with their competitors in world markets." He also signs a bill revising a previous requirement that anyone applying for a student loan must sign an affidavit declaring that "he does not believe in, belong to, or support any organization which believes in or teaches the overthrow of the United States Government by force or by an illegal method." A substitute provision makes it illegal to apply if one is or has been a member of the Communist party. The President meets with Crown Prince Hasan

President Kennedy and son, John, Jr., leaving Arlington National Cemetery, 11 November 1963.

al-Rida al-Sanusi of Libya to discuss relations between the United States and Libya and to exchange views on the current world situation.

17 October 1962
WASHINGTON, D.C. President Kennedy signs a bill to establish the National Institute of Child Health and Human Development, which, he says, "will encourage imaginative research into the complex processes of human development from conception to old age."

CONNECTICUT. In the late afternoon and evening, President Kennedy delivers speeches at Democratic rallies at the Bridgeport Municipal Airport, Waterbury, and New Haven.

18 October 1962
WASHINGTON, D.C. President Kennedy meets with Eisaku Sato, the Japanese international trade minister. He confers with Minister of Foreign Affairs Andrei Gromyko of the USSR on the Berlin and Cuban situations. The Russian diplomat says that Soviet equipment is being sent to Cuba for defensive purposes only.

19 October 1962
CLEVELAND, OHIO. At Public Square, President Kennedy urges residents to re-elect Governor Michael V. DiSalle, Senators Stephen Young and Frank Lausche, and other Ohio Democrats.

SPRINGFIELD, ILLINOIS. John Kennedy visits Lincoln's tomb, then continues his one day on the stump by delivering a speech at the State Fairgrounds, in which he supports the re-election of Governor Otto Kerner and Senator Paul Douglas.

CHICAGO, ILLINOIS. In the company of Mayor Richard Daley and Governor Otto Kerner at McCormick Place, President Kennedy asks state residents to elect Illinois Democrats in the upcoming election.

21 October 1962
WASHINGTON, D.C. President Kennedy confers all day with advisers on the arms crisis in Cuba.

22 October 1962
WASHINGTON, D.C. From the Oval Office in the White House, at 7:00 P.M. President Kennedy apprises the nation over radio and television of the military build-up in Cuba. He reports that "within the past week, unmistakable evidence has established the fact that a series of offensive missile sites is now in preparation on that imprisoned island. The purpose of these bases can be none other than to provide a nuclear strike capability against the Western Hemisphere. [As a result]...a strict quarantine on all offensive military equipment [has been ordered]....All ships of any kind bound for Cuba from whatever nation or port will, if found to contain cargoes of offensive weapons, be turned back." The President also announces that he has "directed the continued and increased close surveillance of Cuba and its military buildup....It shall be the policy of this nation to regard any nuclear missile launched from Cuba against any nation in the Western Hemisphere as an attack by the Soviet Union on the United States, requiring a full retaliatory response upon the Soviet Union."

The President calls for "an immediate meeting of the Organ of Consultation under the Organization of American States to consider this threat to hemispheric security" and asks "that an emergency meeting of the Security Council be convoked without delay to take action against this latest Soviet threat to world peace." Kennedy calls upon Chairman Krushchev "to halt and eliminate this clandestine, reckless, and provocative threat to world peace and to stable relations between our two nations."

23 October 1962

NEW YORK. Demonstrators begin peace strikes to protest the American quarantine of Cuba. Similar strikes take place in Chicago and other cities in the United States and Europe. Some demonstrations support President Kennedy's actions, however.

The United Nations Security Council holds an emergency meeting. Heated debate ensues between U.S. Ambassador to the United Nations Adlai E. Stevenson and Mario Garcia-Inchaustegui of Cuba and Valerian Zoron of Russia.

MOSCOW. Russia calls the United States blockade of Cuba "provocative," and repeats its earlier assertion that the arms buildup in Cuba is merely defensive. Russia rejects the American demand that ships bound for Cuba be inspected by the Navy and declares that America is "taking a step" toward "unleashing a thermonuclear world war."

HAVANA, CUBA. Premier Fidel Castro defends the arms buildup in Cuba and harshly criticizes American actions against his country. In a special session, the Organization of American States votes to support the United States blockade of Cuba.

WASHINGTON, D.C. President Kennedy signs "Proclamation 3504: Interdiction of the Delivery of Offensive Weapons to Cuba," to prohibit the shipment to Cuba of: "suface-to-surface missiles; bomber aircraft; bombs, air-to-surface rockets and guided missiles; warheads for any of the above weapons; mechanical or electronic equipment to support or operate the above items; and any other classes of material hereafter designated by the Secretary of Defense for the purpose of effectuating this proclamation." The proclamation also states that "any vessel or craft which may be proceeding toward Cuba may be intercepted and may be directed to identify itself, its cargo, equipment and stores...and submit to visit and search." The proclamation becomes effective "at 2:00 P.M. Greenwich Time, October 24, 1962."

27 October 1962

WASHINGTON, D.C. In a reply to Chairman Khruschev's letter of 26 October, President Kennedy says that before the Khruschev's proposals for resolving the crisis may be acted upon, work must first "cease on offensive missile bases in Cuba and for all weapons systems in Cuba capable of offensive use to be rendered inoperable." The President reviews his understanding of Khruschev's proposals: Russia will agree to remove weapons from Cuba under United Nations supervision, and the United States will agree to lift the quarantine and give assurances against an invasion of Cuba.

28 October 1962

MOSCOW. Chairman Khruschev announces that the Soviet government has ordered a halt to the building of bases in Cuba. Its offensive weapons are to be dismantled and returned to Russia. The Soviets are, he says, prepared to have United Nations representatives verify the dismantling.

WASHINGTON, D.C. President Kennedy accepts the Soviet government's offer as "an important and constructive contribution to peace."

29 October 1962

WASHINGTON, D.C. The establishment of the Foreign Commerce Section, a special unit in the Justice Department's Anti-Trust Division, is announced by Attorney General Robert F. Kennedy. The section will handle foreign antitrust cases.

30 October 1962

HAVANA, CUBA. Secretary-General of the United Nations U Thant meets with Premier Fidel Castro to discuss UN observation of the dismantling of missile installations in Cuba. Castro outlines his government's position, but no agreement is reached.

31 October 1962

WASHINGTON, D.C. President Kennedy addresses the graduating class of the FBI National Academy at the departmental auditorium. He says that FBI director J. Edgar Hoover is "one of the most distinguished public servants who have occupied positions of high responsibility in the long history of this republic." He tells the graduates that their work "permits us to meet our responsibilities as a nation."

1 November 1962

HAVANA, CUBA. Premier Castro announces that he will not permit the UN to inspect the dismantling of missile bases.

WASHINGTON, D.C. President Kennedy appears in a campaign film urging Americans to vote in the 6 November election.

2 November 1962

WASHINGTON, D.C. On a three-minute radio and

television broadcast, President Kennedy reports that "the Soviet missile bases in Cuba are being dismantled, their missiles and related equipment being crated, and the fixed installations at these sites are being destroyed."

3 November 1962

WASHINGTON, D.C. An Election Day message from President Kennedy is broadcast over radio and television. The President says, "People all over the world who desire freedom look to the United States. The best evidence that we can give of how strongly we believe in freedom is by voting on Tuesday, November 6th, for the candidate and the Party of our choice...."

4 November 1962

ATOKA, VIRGINIA. President Kennedy, Jacqueline Kennedy, and Lee Radziwill visit Rattlesnake Farm, a plot of land recently acquired by the Kennedys. They inspect the area where a new house is to be built.

5 November 1962

BOSTON. President Kennedy visits his maternal grandmother, Mary (Hannon) Fitzgerald, at her home at 3 Rundle Park. His uncle, Thomas F. Fitzgerald lives there as well.

6 November 1962

MASSACHUSETTS. In a special election, Edward M. Kennedy is elected to the Senate seat held by his brother John from January of 1953 through December of 1960 and filled by Benjamin Smith II since his brother's resignation. The election results are: Edward M. Kennedy (Democrat), 1,162,611 votes; George C. Lodge (Republican), 877,669; Lawrence Gilfedder (Socialist Labor), 5,330; H. Stuart Hughes (Independent), 50,013; Mark R. Shaw (Prohibition), 1,439; all others, 23; blanks, 46,966 (total votes cast, 2,144,051). Two years remain in Ted Kennedy's term of office.

President Kennedy votes today at the Sixth Precinct Station at 80 Joy Street in Boston.

WASHINGTON, D.C. Congress is not in session, and therefore Senator-elect Edward M. Kennedy will not be sworn in until early next year.

7 November 1962

WASHINGTON, D.C. President Kennedy issues a proclamation declaring "Thursday, the twenty-second day of November this year, as a day of national thanksgiving." "It is fitting that we observe this year our own day of thanksgiving," he says.

Following the death earlier today of Eleanor Roosevelt, 78, President Kennedy issues a statement saying that "one of the great ladies in the history of this country has passed from the scene. Her loss will be deeply felt by all those who admired her tireless idealism or benefited from her good works and counsel. Since the day I entered this office, she has been both an inspiration and a friend....Our condolences go to all members of her family, whose grief at the death of this extraordinary woman can be tempered by the knowledge that her memory and spirit will long endure among those who labor for great causes around the world." He also issues an executive order mandating U.S. flags on government and military property to fly at half-staff.

10 November 1962

HYDE PARK, NEW YORK. President and Mrs. Kennedy attend funeral services for Eleanor Roosevelt at St. James's Church. They then ride in a procession to the Roosevelt estate's rose garden for Mrs. Roosevelt's burial alongside the grave of her late husband, Franklin Delano Roosevelt.

13 November 1962

WASHINGTON, D.C. President and Mrs. Kennedy attend the opening of the Bolshoi Ballet at the Capitol Theater. They are greeted at their seats by impressario Sol Hurok, and during intermission, they go backstage to meet the Bolshoi's prima ballerina and premier danseur.

15 November 1962

WASHINGTON, D.C. President Kennedy concludes two days of meetings with Dr. Konrad Adenauer, chancellor of West Germany. Their discussions include "the events relating to Cuba and their effect both on the general situation and the problems of special interest to the two countries," Berlin, NATO, and other international problems.

17 November 1962

WASHINGTON, D.C. A preliminary report on the feasibility of a domestic Peace Corps is presented by Attorney General Robert F. Kennedy. The group assigned to make the study, of which Robert F. Kennedy is chairman, recommends the formation of a volunteer corps of adults of all ages to serve in the United States.

CHANTILLY, VIRGINIA. President Kennedy participates in the dedication of Dulles International Airport, speaking after Najeeb Halaby, administrator of the Federal Aviation Agency, and Dwight D. Eisenhower.

President Eisenhower had named the airport after John Foster Dulles in 1959.

20 November 1962

WASHINGTON, D.C. President Kennedy sends a message of condolence to Mrs. Niels Bohr, whose Nobel laureate husband died two days earlier. The President writes, "His great achievements in the quantum theory of the atom have been basic to modern advances in physical science." Kennedy also signs an executive order prohibiting discrimination in federal housing. At a press conference, the President announces that following a message from Chairman Krushchev "that all of the IL-28 bombers now in Cuba will be withdrawn in thirty days," he has ordered the Naval quarantine of Cuba lifted. He adds that "the evidence to date indicates that all known offensive missile sites in Cuba have been dismantled."

22 November 1962

HYANNIS PORT, MASSACHUSETTS. President and Mrs. Kennedy and their children spend Thanksgiving Day with members of the Kennedy family at the Kennedy compound. The family, with patriarch Joseph P. Kennedy, has a holiday dinner at 7:00 P.M.

23 November 1962

HYANNIS PORT, MASSACHUSETTS. In the morning, the Executive Committee of the National Security Council meets with President Kennedy to discuss the Cuban situation. The committee, comprised of a dozen high-ranking officials, including Dean Rusk, Robert McNamara, McGeorge Bundy, John McCloy, and Robert Kennedy, was formed the previous month in the wake of the crisis. The President spends the afternoon visiting the different homes of Robert and Ted Kennedy and his father. (Ted lives in Squaw Island, not Hyannis Port.)

26 November 1962

PORT STEWART, GEORGIA. President Kennedy reviews the First Armored Division, observes troops in training, and receives a Top Secret briefing in the War Room.

HOMESTEAD AIR FORCE BASE, FLORIDA. The President inspects a Static Aircraft Display and presents unit citations to two reconnaissance units, one which originally photographed the missile sites in Cuba, and the other of which followed up with confirming shots. He says, "The work of these two units has contributed as much to the security of the United States as any units in our history, and any group of men in our history."

KEY WEST, FLORIDA. Following a tour of the Boca Chica Naval Air Station, President Kennedy presents unit citations to Navy and Marine light photographic squadrons. The President later visits the naval base and boards the submarine *Chopper.*

27 November 1962

WASHINGTON, D.C. President Kennedy begins two days of discussions with Dr. Abdiraschid Ali Schermarche, the prime minister of Somalia, on international problems and the economic development of Somalia. He meets with Foreign Minister Paul-Henri Spaak of Belgium to discuss the Congo-Katanga situation. The President later meets with a group of scientists to commemorate the experiment in which University of Chicago physicist Enrico Fermi unleashed the first nuclear chain reaction twenty years earlier. Many of the scientists in the group had worked with the late Dr. Fermi.

28 November 1962

WASHINGTON, D.C. In a thirteen-minute visit, President Kennedy receives entertainers Judy Garland, Danny Kaye, Carol Burnett, and composer Richard Adler.

29 November 1962

WASHINGTON, D.C. A two-hour fund-raising benefit for the National Cultural Center is broadcast by closed-circuit television to seventy-five American and Canadian cities. Many celebrities, including Robert Frost, Van Cliburn, and Pablo Casals, attend the event at the National Guard Armory. President Kennedy delivers an address in which he says, "Art and the encouragement of art is political in the most profound sense, not as a weapon in the struggle, but as an instrument of understanding of the futility of struggle between those who share man's faith."

30 November 1962

WASHINGTON, D.C. President Kennedy meets with President Ramon Villeda Morales of Honduras to discuss the Cuban situation and future measures to safeguard peace in the Western hemisphere.

1 December 1962

PHILADLELPHIA, PENNSYLVANIA. President Kennedy attends the Army-Navy football game at Municipal Stadium. In keeping with tradition, Kennedy sits on the Navy side during the first half and on the Army side during the second half. Navy defeats Army, 34-14.

3 December 1962

WASHINGTON, D.C. At a White House ceremo-

United Press International.

The First Family greeting well-wishers after a performance of the Black Watch, November 1963.

ny, President Kennedy presents the 1962 Enrico Fermi Award to Dr. Edward Teller for his contributions to thermonuclear research. The award carries a $50,000 prize.

6 December 1962

WASHINGTON, D.C. In the morning, President Kennedy presents the 1962 Rockefeller Public Service Awards. In the evening, the first awards dinner of the Joseph P. Kennedy, Jr. Foundation is held at the Statler-Hilton Hotel. Among the guests at the banquet are Rose Kennedy, Edward Kennedy, Eunice (Kennedy) Shriver, Vice-President Lyndon Johnson, Judy Garland, and Burt Lancaster. President Kennedy delivers a speech.

7 December 1962

OFFUTT AIR FORCE BASE, NEBRASKA. In the first leg of a nonpolitical trip to the West, President Kennedy presents a plaque to the commanding officer of the Strategic Air Command for its contributions during the Cuban crisis and for maintaining the peace and security of the United States.

SANTA FE, NEW MEXICO. At the Municipal Airport, the President speaks to a crowd that includes Senator Clinton Anderson, Governor-elect Jack Campbell, and others.

LOS ALAMOS, NEW MEXICO. The President is briefed on Project River at the Los Alamos Scientific Laboratories. At the high-school football stadium, he speaks of "the will and the courage and the power of the people of the United States of America" and the country's efforts around the world regarding "containment of the Communist empire."

ALBUQUERQUE, NEW MEXICO. President Kennedy makes brief speeches at the Kirkland Air Force Base and the Commercial Terminal Airport. He later attends a Top Secret briefing at the Sandia Corporation, a government contractor with security clearance, and the Atomic Energy Commission.

8 December 1962

ALBUQUERQUE, NEW MEXICO. President Kennedy sends a message of congratulations to President Julius K. Nyerere "on the establishment of the Republic of Tanganyika."

INDIAN SPRINGS AIR FORCE BASE, NEVADA. The President arrives for a brief visit and tour of the base.

ROVER MISSILE SITE TEST AREA, NEVADA. The President arrives here by helicopter for a tour and briefing.

PALM DESERT, CALIFORNIA. President Kennedy and Kenneth O'Donnell spend the rest of the day at Bing Crosby's home.

12 December 1962

WASHINGTON, D.C. President Kennedy concludes two days of meetings with President Jorge Alessandri Rodriguez of Chile. Their discussions included the Alliance for Progress and the economic development of Chile. A Christmas party for the White House staff is held in the East Room at 6:00 P.M. The President and his wife arrive at the party late, and still later, arrive with Robert and Ethel (Skakel) Kennedy, Eunice (Kennedy) and Sargent Shriver, and others at the Capitol Theater to see a performance of the American Ballet Theater.

13 December 1962

WASHINGTON, D.C. President and Mrs.

253

Kennedy, Eunice (Kennedy) Shriver, and Ambassador Kenneth Galbraith attend an 8:30 P.M. performance of the play *A Shot in the Dark* at the National Theater.

14 December 1962

NEW YORK. President Kennedy participates with Mayor Robert F. Wagner, Robert Moses, and others in ground-breaking ceremonies for the New York World's Fair in Flushing Meadow Park. At the site of the United States Pavilion, the President says, in a brief speech, that the fair will show people around the world what America has accomplished through freedom. "So we begin today with this ceremony," he declares. "We'll begin again in April of 1964, and we'll show what we've done in the past, and even more important, what America is going to be in the future."

In the evening, the President delivers an address before a dinner of the Economic Club at the Waldorf-Astoria Hotel; he discusses his proposed tax-reduction legislation for 1963. "It is increasingly clear," he says, "that no matter what party is in power, so long as our national security needs keep rising, an economy hampered by restrictive tax rates will never produce enough revenue to balance our budget just as it will never produce enough jobs or enough profits." Following the speech, the President answers questions on taxes, trade, foreign aid, and monetary policies.

15 December 1962

THE UNITED STATES. A good-natured spoof of the White House's celebrated occupants and their families reaches the number one spot on the national chart of top-selling LPs. Featuring Vaughn Meader and containing material "adapted from real life" by Earle Doud, Bob Booker, and George Foster, the album is called *The First Family*. (The album stays on the charts for three months and sells more than 5 million copies.)

16 December 1962

WASHINGTON, D.C. An interview between President Kennedy and reporters from the three TV networks is taped for television and radio broadcast tomorrow evening. William Lawrence of the American Broadcasting Company asks Kennedy if, after two years in office, he finds the presidency to be what he originally expected it to be. "I would say that the problems are more difficult than I had imagined them to be," responds President Kennedy. He speaks of the difficulty of arriving at policy based on the different opinions of those who counsel and legislate. "It is much easier to make speeches than it is to finally make the judgments, because unfortunately your advisers are frequently divided. If you take the wrong

course, and on occasion I have, the President bears the burden of the responsibility quite rightly. The advisers may move on to new advice."

17 December 1962

WASHINGTON, D.C. In the morning, President Kennedy welcomes to the White House the Pennsylvania State football team and meets with the Executive Committee of the National Security Council. At 5:15 P.M., he arrives at the Ellipse to participate in the annual Christmas tree–lighting ceremony. He says that Christmas "is the day when all of us dedicate our thoughts to others; when all are reminded that mercy and compassion are the enduring virtues...when we remind ourselves that man can and must live in peace with his neighbors...." The switch that lights the nation's Christmas tree, he continues, "was first pressed by President Coolidge in 1923 and succeedingly by President Hoover, Vice-President Curtis, by President Truman, by President Eisenhower, by Vice-President Johnson. I am delighted to be in that illustrious company and we therefore light the tree."

BRASÍLIA, BRAZIL. Attorney General Robert F. Kennedy meets with President Joao Goulart to discuss Brazilian economic problems.

18 December 1962

NASSAU, THE BAHAMAS. President Kennedy and Prime Minister Harold Macmillan begin four days of meetings to discuss East-West relations following the Cuban crisis, a nuclear test-ban treaty with Russia, Berlin, the Congo, and advanced nuclear weapons systems.

NEW YORK. An article by President Kennedy entitled "The Arts in America" appears in this week's issue of *Look* magazine.

21 December 1962

NASSAU, THE BAHAMAS. Following meetings between President Kennedy and Prime Minister Macmillan, a joint statement, the "Nassau agreement," sets forth the agreement the two leaders have reached on nuclear defense systems. President Kennedy has cancelled plans for production of the Skybolt missile in the United States, and the United States will supply Polaris missiles, minus warheads, for British submarines as an alternative-weapons system.

HAVANA, CUBA. Attorney James Donovan negotiates an agreement with Premier Fidel Castro for the release of rebel Cubans imprisoned following the Bay of

Pigs invasion. The final arrangement provides for Cuba to release 1,113 prisoners in exchange for over $50 million in vital supplies such as medicines. A cash proviso of nearly $3 million is also included for wounded prisoners previously released by the Cubans.

PALM BEACH, FLORIDA. President Kennedy and his family visit his parents. They spend the night at the Capton Michael Paul residence at 601 North Country Road.

23 December 1962
WASHINGTON, D.C. A group that includes Attorney General Robert F. Kennedy privately raises the cash to effect the release of Cuban prisoners as per the agreement negotiated two days earlier.

HAVANA, CUBA. Premier Castro begins releasing the prisoners captured in last April's invasion of the country, and all the prisoners will be freed by tomorrow. Castro has also agreed to permit relatives of the prisoners to emigrate to the United States.

25 December 1962
PALM BEACH, FLORIDA. After attending services at St. Anne's Church and cruising on the *Honey Fitz,* the President and Mrs. Kennedy give a Christmas party for their Secret Service agents and the White House press and their families.

27 December 1962
PALM BEACH, FLORIDA. President Kennedy confers in the morning with Foreign Minister Golda Meier of Israel. Later he meets with a Cuban exile group.

MIAMI, FLORIDA. Over 900 relatives of the Bay of Pigs invasion forces arrive here from Havana.

28 December 1962
PALM BEACH, FLORIDA. President Kennedy issues a proclamation declaring that "the Emancipation Proclamation expresses our nation's policy, founded on justice and morality, and that it is therefore fitting and proper to commemorate the centennial of the historic Emancipation Proclamation throughout the year 1963."

29 December 1962
MIAMI, FLORIDA. At the Orange Bowl, President Kennedy delivers an address before members of the 2506th Cuban Invasion Brigade, their relatives, and thousands of others. After the presentation of the bri-

gade's flag, he says: "Castro and his fellow dictators...may imprison bodies but they do not imprison spirits, they may destroy the exercise of liberty but they cannot eliminate the determination to be free....The Cuban people were promised by the revolution political liberty, social justice, intellectual freedom, land for *compesinos,* and an end to economic exploitation. They have received a police state....I can assure you that it is the strongest wish of the people of this country, as well as the people of this hemisphere, that Cuba shall one day be free again...."

30 December 1962
PALM BEACH, FLORIDA. President Kennedy sends New Year's greetings to Soviet leaders Nikita Krushchev and Leonid Brezhnev. "The American people look forward to the coming year with the deepest desire that the cause of peace be advanced," he writes. "For our part, I assure you that no opportunity will be missed to promote world peace and understanding among all peoples."

31 December 1962
PALM BEACH, FLORIDA. At the Charles Wrightsman estate, President and Mrs. Kennedy attend a New Year's Eve party. Other guests include Prince and Princess Radziwill, Pat (Kennedy) and Peter Lawford, Ambassador and Lady Ormsby-Gore, Leland Hayward, George Plimpton, Eunice (Kennedy) and Sargent Shriver, and Douglas Fairbanks, Jr.

THE FINAL YEAR
1963

January 1963
WASHINGTON, D.C. A critique by President Kennedy of the four volumes of *The Adams Papers: Diary and Autobiography of John Adams* appears in the January issue of the *The American Historical Review.*

NEW YORK. Richard Whalen's lengthy article entitled "Joseph P. Kennedy: A Portrait of the Founder" appears in this month's issue of *Fortune* magazine. The article asserts that the Kennedy family is now worth approximately $300 million.

1 January 1963
MIAMI, FLORIDA. President Kennedy, Senator Mike Mansfield, and Adm. Bedloe W. Anderson, Jr., attend the Orange Bowl football game between the University of Alabama and the University of Oklahoma.

2 January 1963
LANTANA, FLORIDA. President and Jacqueline Kennedy attend a luncheon at the Vanderbilt estate, hosted by Harold Vanderbilt. They travel to and from the residence on the *Honey Fitz* with Lee Radziwill and others.

4 January 1963
OKLAHOMA CITY, OKLAHOMA. President Kennedy and Vice-President Johnson attend the funeral of the late Senator Robert Kerr at the First Baptist Church and his burial at the Rose Hill Cemetery.

8 January 1963
PALM BEACH, FLORIDA. President John Kennedy, Vice-President Lyndon Johnson, and Peter Lawford go for a cruise on the *Honey Fitz*.

WASHINGTON, D.C. After a three-week stay in Florida, the President and Mrs. Kennedy return to the capital. In the evening, with 1,300 other important guests, they attend the first showing in America of Leonardo da Vinci's *Mona Lisa* at the National Gallery of Art. In a brief address at the West Statuary Hall, the President says of the legendary painting, "We citizens of nations unborn at the time of its creation are among the inheritors and protectors of the ideals which gave it birth. For this painting is not only one of the towering achievements of the skill and vision of art, but its creator embodied the central purpose of our civilization."

9 January 1963
WASHINGTON, D.C. In the White House, President Kennedy attends the swearing-in ceremony of Kathryn Granahan as Treasurer of the United States and then presents the Distinguished Service Medal to Gen. Lauris Norstad.

WESTON, MASSACHUSETTS. At commencement exercises of Regis College, Eunice (Kennedy) Shriver receives an honorary Doctor of Laws degree.

10 January 1963
WASHINGTON, D.C. President Kennedy confers with Dr. Juan E. Bosch, the President-elect of the Dominican Republic.

14 January 1963
WASHINGTON, D.C. President Kennedy delivers the State of the Union Message to Congress. He says, "We need to strengthen our nation by investing in our youth...by safeguarding its health...by protecting the basic rights of its citizens...by making the best and most economical use of its resources and facilities." He calls for a tax reduction and reviews the role of the United States in the worldwide situation. "My friends," he says, "I close on a note of hope. We are not lulled by the momentary calm of the sea or the somewhat clearer skies above. We know the turbulence that lies below, and the storms that are beyond the horizon this year. But now the winds of change appear to be blowing more strongly than ever....With thanks to Almighty God for seeing us through a perilous passage, we ask His help anew in guiding the 'Good Ship Union.' "

16 January 1963
WASHINGTON, D.C. President Kennedy begins two days of meetings with Prime Minister Amintore Fanfani of Italy to discuss NATO, the political and economic situation in Europe, disarmament, and nuclear testing.

17 January 1963
WASHINGTON, D.C. President Kennedy presents to Congress the federal budget for fiscal 1964. The administrative budget expenditures are estimated at $98.8 billion, an increase of $4.5 billion over 1963; administrative budget receipts are estimated at $86.9 billion in 1964, an increase of $1.4 billion over 1963.

WASHINGTON, D.C. Attorney General Robert F. Kennedy appears before the Supreme Court to argue against the constitutionality of Georgia's county-unit voting system. The system, opposed by the federal government, assigns different numbers to different counties, and the candidate receiving the most votes in a particular county receives the number assigned to that unit. In certain state primaries, the system can be used to give rural areas greater influence.

18 January 1963
WASHINGTON, D.C. Among the other fund-raising affairs celebrating the second anniversary of Presi-

John F. Kennedy Library.

President and Mrs. Kennedy arrive at Houston Airport, 22 November 1963.

dent Kennedy's inauguration, President and Mrs. Kennedy attend a $1,000-a-plate dinner at the International Inn and a Second Anniversary Salute, with Kirk Douglas and Gene Kelly as emcees.

21 January 1963
WASHINGTON, D.C. President Kennedy issues a statement which says that "the end of secession announced by the provincial regime in Katanga...today is warmly welcomed by the United States and all who are concerned with the future of the Congo." His Economic Report is transmitted to Congress. In the evening, President and Mrs. Kennedy give a White House dinner in honor of Vice-President Lyndon Johnson and Chief Justice of the Supreme Court Earl Warren. More than 150

senators, representatives, Supreme Court justices, and dignitaries attend.

24 January 1963
WASHINGTON, D.C. President Kennedy sends to Congress a message on tax reduction and tax reform.

29 January 1963
WASHINGTON, D.C. Following the death today of Robert Frost, 88, President Kennedy issues a statement in which he says of the late winner of four Pulitzer prizes, "He was the great American poet of our time....His death impoverishes us all." The President sends to Congress a special message on education, calling for more federal aid to improve the quality of instruction,

to increase the number of educational facilities, and to provide opportunities and incentives for students to complete their education.

31 January 1963

WASHINGTON, D.C. President Kennedy sends to Congress a special farm message proposing new government programs for feed grains, cotton, milk, food stamps, and Food for Peace. The American Democratic Legacy Award of the Anti-Defamation League of B'nai Brith is presented to President Kennedy at an anniversary dinner of the League at the Sheraton-Park Hotel. Screenwriter Dore Shary is chairman of the event.

5 February 1963

WASHINGTON, D.C. President Kennedy sends Congress a major program to help fight mental illness and mental retardation. In the interest of mental health, he recommends federal aid "for the construction of comprehensive community health centers," improvement in "the quality of care in existing state mental institutions," and "an expansion of clinical, laboratory, and field research in mental illness and mental health." To combat mental retardation, he sets prevention and community services as goals. "We as a nation," he declares, "have long neglected the mentally ill and the mentally retarded. This neglect must end if our nation is to live up to its own standards of compassion and dignity and achieve the maximum use of its manpower."

7 February 1963

WASHINGTON, D.C. President Kennedy attends the annual Presidential Prayer Breakfast at the Mayflower Hotel. In a speech he says, "These breakfasts are dedicated to prayer and all of us believe in and need prayer." Among the guests are Vice-President Lyndon Johnson, Chief Justice Earl Warren, and the Rev. Billy Graham. The President also sends to Congress a special health message. He presents a program to provide federal aid for medical, dental, and nursing education, and for construction of hospitals, nursing homes, and mental health facilities. He also recommends stricter federal control over the food, cosmetic, and drug industries.

9 February 1963

NEW YORK. The President and Mrs. Kennedy attend a performance of *Beyond the Fringe* at the Golden Theater.

11 February 1963

WASHINGTON, D.C. President Kennedy sends a bill to Congress providing for the creation of a National Academy of Foreign Affairs to "provide our foreign affairs personnel with the fundamental knowledge and understanding which is indispensable to serving our nation effectively in today's complex world."

12 February 1963

WASHINGTON, D.C. The U.S. Commission on Civil Rights presents to President Kennedy a report on civil rights in America over the last century that he requested a year ago. The report was timed to coincide with the birthday today of Abraham Lincoln in the centennial year of the Emancipation Proclamation. At a ceremony, Kennedy says, "In freeing themselves, the Negroes have enlarged the freedoms of all Americans....American Negroes have never succumbed to defeatism but have worked bravely and unceasingly to secure the rights to which as Americans they are entitled."

14 February 1963

WASHINGTON, D.C. In a special message to Congress, President Kennedy proposes a number of legislative measures to help America's youth. The proposals include youth employment opportunities and recommendations for health and physical fitness programs. "To the extent that the nation is called upon to promote and protect the interests of our younger citizens," he declares, "it is an investment certain to bring a high return, not only in basic human values, but in social and economic terms."

18 February 1963

WASHINGTON, D.C. President Kennedy sends the Urban Mass Transportation Act of 1963 to Congress "to establish a long-range program of assistance to urban areas in solving their mass transportation problems." At a ceremony in the Flower Garden at the White House, the President participates in presenting the National Medal of Science to Dr. Theodore von Karman for his contributions to aerodynamics and the development of supersonic aircraft.

19 February 1963

WASHINGTON, D.C. President Kennedy begins two days of meetings with President Romulo Betancourt of Venezuela to discuss the Alliance for Progress, Cuba, and Venezuelan oil exports to the United States.

20 February 1963

WASHINGTON, D.C. President Betancourt and his wife give a dinner in honor of President and Mrs. Kennedy at the Venezuelan Embassy.

21 February 1963

WASHINGTON, D.C.   President Kennedy sends to Congress a special message on the needs of America's senior citizens. He calls for hospital insurance, higher monthly benefits in Social Security insurance, and more high-quality nursing homes, tax benefits, employment opportunities, special housing facilities and loan assistance, and federal assistance to state and local agencies for research and community programs. In his message the President says, "We can continue to move forward...by doing all we can, as a nation and as individuals, to enable our senior citizens to achieve both a better standard of life and a more active, useful and meaningful role in a society that owes them much and can still learn much from them."

22 February 1963

WASHINGTON, D.C.   President Kennedy issues executive order 11085 changing the Medal of Freedom, established on 6 July 1945, to the Presidential Medal of Freedom. The medal will henceforth be given to those who make meritorious contributions to national security, world peace, or cultural endeavors. "In a period when the national government must call upon an increasing portion of the talents and energies of its citizens," he declares, "it is clearly appropriate to provide ways to recognize and reward the work of persons within and without the Government, who contribute significantly to the quality of American life."

25 February 1963

WASHINGTON, D.C.   President Kennedy delivers an address before the American Bankers Association Symposium on Economic Growth, chaired by David Rockefeller, at the Mayflower Hotel. He also answers questions from guests at the symposium. The President meets with King Sri Savang Vatthana of Laos to discuss the political situation in that Asian country and Lao-American relations. Also present is Prime Minister Souvanna Phouma.

26 February 1963

WASHINGTON, D.C.   A White House luncheon is given in honor of the prince of Liège, Albert of Belgium, who is visiting the United States unofficially. The Prince and President Kennedy exchange toasts.

28 February 1963

WASHINGTON, D.C.   President Kennedy sends a special civil-rights message to Congress. He recommends legislation to ensure that blacks can freely exercise their voting rights, federal action to facilitate desegregation in

certain areas, expansion of the responsibilities and extension of the life of the Commission on Civil Rights, and federal action against discrimination in employment and public facilities.

2 March 1963

CHICAGO.   President Kennedy delivers an address at ceremonies dedicating O'Hare International Airport. In referring to the late World War II hero Edward "Butch" O'Hare for whom the airport is named, the President says, "I am proud to be...honoring a great American to whom we owe so much, looking to the past and saluting him, and looking to the future and saluting the city of Chicago."

3 March 1963

WASHINGTON, D.C.   Taking a break from his official duties, President Kennedy visits the Smithsonian Institute's Aeronautics Building with Charles Bartlett, then takes a walk along the reflecting pool at the Lincoln Memorial.

ARLINGTON, VIRGINIA.   President Kennedy and Charles Bartlett tour the Custis-Lee Mansion at Arlington National Cemetery.

4 March 1963

WASHINGTON, D.C.   President Kennedy delivers an address at a fiftieth anniversary dinner of the Department of Labor at the Sheraton-Park Hotel. In praising the program, which was considered revolutionary when it was put forward by former secretary of Labor Frances Perkins, he says, "It gives us some hope that some of the things which may be suggested today, which are not controversial but which may be regarded as controversial ten or twenty years from now, will be accepted as part of ordinary life of Americans. That's what progress is."

5 March 1963

WASHINGTON, D.C.   President Kennedy sends a letter to Congress urging that it "establish a transportation policy consistent with the new demands upon the economy"; he also sends draft legislation outlining a "comprehensive framework of equal competitive opportunity... at the lowest social and economic cost to the nation." In greeting a delegation of the National Congress of American Indians at the White House, the President says that the government wants to make sure that "the American Indians have every chance to develop their lives in the way that best suits their customs and traditions and interests."

7 March 1963

WASHINGTON, D.C. President Kennedy greets delegates of the 1963 New York Herald Tribune World Youth Forum and meets with Tony Boyle, president of the United Mine Workers.

8 March 1963

WASHINGTON, D.C. President Kennedy sends to Congress "proposed legislation to assure effective legal representation for every man whose limited means would otherwise deprive him of an adequate defense against criminal charges." The President also greets Brenda Heaton, the Easter Seal child for the year.

11 March 1963

WASHINGTON, D.C. President Kennedy sends to Congress his first Manpower Report along with proposals to close "the gap between our manpower performance and our objective of the full use of our human resources."

17 March 1963

PALM BEACH, FLORIDA. Aboard the *Honey Fitz*, President Kennedy and Dave Powers observe landing exercises by Marine reserves.

DALLAS, TEXAS. Using the name A. Hidell and a return address of P.O. Box 2915, Lee Harvey Oswald orders a Mannlicher-Carcano 6.5 mm rifle with a telescopic sight from Klein's Sporting Goods Company at 227 W. Washington Street in Chicago. The rifle costs $19.95.

18 March 1963

SAN JOSÉ, COSTA RICA. With the leaders of several Central American countries, President Kennedy participates in a two-day Presidents' Conference, held at the National Theater, to discuss problems in the Western hemisphere. Stating that "the people of Cuba have been forcibly compelled to submit to a new imperialism, more ruthless, more powerful, and more deadly in its pursuit of power than any that this hemisphere has ever known," President Kennedy proposes that hemisphere leaders "build a wall around Cuba—not a wall of mortar or brick or barbed wire, but a wall of dedicated men determined to protect their freedom and their sovereignty."

19 March 1963

SAN JOSÉ, COSTA RICA. The Central American conference concludes with a declaration in which the participating nations agree to strengthen economic cooperation among themselves, work for a stronger Alliance for Progress, and take measures to stop the spread of Communist propaganda and arms from Cuba to Central America. President Kennedy later attends a dedication ceremony at the El Bosque Housing Project, which was built under an Alliance for Progress program. In his speech here, the President says, "These houses, these medical units, these books, are today freeing men and women from centuries of bondage and poverty which has imprisoned their capacity, their happiness, and their future."

22 March 1963

WASHINGTON, D.C. President Kennedy sends telegrams to governors of states that have not yet ratified a constitutional amendment forbidding a poll tax requirement in federal primaries and elections. Congress had approved the proposal in August of 1962. When ratified by the legislatures of three-fourths of the states, it will become the Twenty-fourth Amendment to the Constitution. Twenty-two state legislatures have so far ratified the proposed amendment, and the President notes that "every effort should be made to broaden the base of citizen participation in national and local affairs through the voting process."

26 March 1963

WASHINGTON, D.C. In the Cabinet Room of the White House with members of the Roosevelt family looking on, President Kennedy attends the swearing-in ceremony of Franklin D. Roosevelt, Jr., as under-secretary of Commerce. Later, the President greets Gary Anderson, the world's champion rifle shooter.

29 March 1963

WASHINGTON, D.C. President Kennedy concludes three days of meetings with King Hassan II of Morocco. A joint statement released afterward says that President Kennedy has reaffirmed a previous agreement made by President Dwight Eisenhower that American troops would vacate bases in Morocco by the end of the year and turn them over to the Moroccan government.

30 March 1963

SAN JOSÉ, COSTA RICA. At the University of Costa Rica, President Kennedy delivers a speech "dedicated to democracy." "We are committed," he says, "to four basic principles in this hemisphere in the Alliance for Progress...the right of every nation to govern itself...the right of every individual citizen to political liberty...the right of every citizen to participate in the progress of his nation...[and] the right of every nation to make economic progress with modern technological means."

31 March 1963
GETTYSBURG, PENNSYLVANIA. President Kennedy, Jacqueline Kennedy, and their children tour the Gettysburg Battlefield.

1 April 1963
WASHINGTON, D.C. President and Mrs. Kennedy, with Mr. and Mrs. Goddard Leiberson and Mr. and Mrs. Max Freedman, see *The School for Scandal* at the National Theater.

2 April 1963
WASHINGTON, D.C. In a special message to Congress, President Kennedy sets forth recommendations for aiding foreign countries economically and assisting in their defense against Communist attack. He requests $4.5 billion for the program, which would encourage investment in poor countries by private enterprise. "We have dared to label the Sixties the Decade of Development," he concludes. "But it is not the eloquence of our slogans, but the quality of our endurance which will determine whether this generation of Americans deserves the leadership which history has thrust upon us."

3 April 1963
DALLAS, TEXAS. Lee Harvey Oswald is fired from his job at a photographic company. He had moved to Dallas with his wife and daughter in October 1962.

7 April 1963
SHARPSBURG, MARYLAND. President Kennedy takes his children, Caroline and John, Jr., Ted and Joan Kennedy, and LeMoyne Billings on a tour of the Antietam National Battlefield.

8 April 1963
WASHINGTON, D.C. President Kennedy opens the Washington Senators' baseball season by throwing out the first ball. Guests watching the game from the presidential box include two members of the Boys' Club of Washington, House Speaker John McCormack, Senate Democratic leader Mike Mansfield, Senate Republican leader Everett Dirksen, and Governor Edmund Brown of California. Before 45,000 fans, the Baltimore Orioles shut out the Senators 3-0.

9 April 1963
WASHINGTON, D.C. With the approval of Congress, President Kennedy signs a proclamation making Winston Churchill an honorary U.S. citizen. Churchill watches the Rose Garden ceremony on television at his home in London. Joseph P. Kennedy, former ambassador to England, is among the guests at the ceremony.

10 April 1963
DALLAS, TEXAS. A bullet is fired into the ground-floor window of General Edwin A. Walker's home at 4011 Turtle Creek Boulevard this evening. Walker is a retired Army general and a devout anti-Communist. He is not hurt, and police do not have a suspect. (Later testimony will implicate Lee Harvey Oswald as the person who fired the shot.)

11 April 1963
PALM BEACH, FLORIDA. President Kennedy, Jacqueline, Caroline, and John Jr., begin a seven-day Easter vacation here.

18 April 1963
WASHINGTON, D.C. A White House luncheon honors Princess Beatrix of the Netherlands.

19 April 1963
WASHINGTON, D.C. President Kennedy delivers an address and participates in a question-and-answer period following a luncheon of the American Society of Newspaper Editors at the Statler-Hilton Hotel.

20 April 1963
BOSTON. President Kennedy delivers an address at Boston College at ceremonies commemorating the one-hundredth anniversary of the school. On the way back to Logan International Airport, his motorcade stops at the proposed site of a Kennedy library off Storrow Drive near Soldiers Field Road.

22 April 1963
WASHINGTON, D.C. At a ceremony in the Fish Room (later the Roosevelt Room), President Kennedy pushes a button, activating the clock that marks the one-year countdown until the opening of the New York World's Fair.

23 April 1963
WASHINGTON, D.C. President Kennedy signs into law a bill making permanent the Eleanor Roosevelt Memorial Foundation.

24 April 1963
DALLAS, TEXAS. Lee Harvey Oswald leaves for New Orleans to look for work. His wife and daughter will go to live with Ruth Paine, whom the Oswalds met

at a party in February and whose home is in Irving, a town just west of Dallas.

25 April 1963
MONTGOMERY, ALABAMA. Attorney General Robert F. Kennedy meets with Governor George Wallace to discuss Wallace's refusal to admit two black students to the University of Alabama.

30 April 1963
WASHINGTON, D.C. President Kennedy confers with Grand Duchess Charlotte and Prince Jean, the hereditary grand duke of Luxembourg. Later, a state dinner is given in honor of Her Royal Highness Charlotte.

2 May 1963
BIRMINGHAM, ALABAMA. Under orders from Attorney General Robert F. Kennedy, Assistant Attorney General Burke Marshall arrives to help bring order. Police have arrested many black civil-rights demonstrators, including Martin Luther King, Jr.

4 May 1963
WALLINGFORD, CONNECTICUT. President Kennedy's tape-recorded message is played by LeMoyne Billings at an Alumni Day ceremony at the Choate School, where William Draper's portrait of the President—the only one he ever "sat" for—is also unveiled.

8 May 1963
WASHINGTON, D.C. President Kennedy greets over forty Latin-American air-force chiefs-of-staff who are here to observe American air force installations. He also telephones Harry S. Truman in Kansas City, Missouri, to congratulate him on his seventy-ninth birthday, holds a press conference at the State Department Auditorium, and welcomes a group of foreign students on the South Lawn of the White House.

9 May 1963
WASHINGTON, D.C. President Kennedy greets members of the Association of American Editorial Cartoonists. "I want you to get this...," he begins his remarks to the group. "I deliberately took off about five pounds before this meeting."

ARLINGTON, VIRGINIA. President Kennedy participates in services marking the grave of Ignace Jan Paderewski, the great Polish pianist who died in the United States in 1941.

10 May 1963
HYANNIS PORT, MASSACHUSETTS. President Kennedy and Prime Minister Lester Pearson of Canada begin two days of informal discussions at the President's home on a number of topics, including the North Atlantic Alliance, the development of the Columbia River, and maritime union problems on the St. Lawrence River and the Great Lakes.

12 May 1963
WASHINGTON, D.C. Following civil disturbances in Birmingham, Alabama, at 9:00 P.M. President Kennedy makes a radio and television appeal to residents of the city "to live up to" an agreement reached the previous week. The home of Rev. A. L. King, the brother of Martin Luther, Jr., and the Gaston Motel, which is integrated, have been bombed, and the reaction has been violent. The President announces that he is sending Assistant Attorney General Burke Marshall back to Birmingham to meet with local citizens and that he has federalized the Alabama National Guard to maintain order.

13 May 1963
WASHINGTON, D.C. The expiration of President Kennedy's six-year term on the Board of Overseers of Harvard University is commemorated at a White House dinner for the board that is hosted by the President.

16 May 1963
WASHINGTON, D.C. President Kennedy offers congratulations by phone to Major Leroy Gordon Cooper, Jr., of the Air Force whose space capsule had successfully orbited the earth twenty-two times, aboard the *Kearsarge* in the Pacific Ocean.

18 May 1963
NASHVILLE, TENNESSEE. President Kennedy delivers the keynote address at a ninetieth-anniversary salute to Vanderbilt University. He declares that, as educated citizens, students have certain responsibilities: to use their talents for the benefit of society, to serve the public, to uphold the law.

MUSCLE SHOALS, ALABAMA. At a thirtieth anniversary celebration of the Tennessee Valley Authority, President Kennedy speaks about how the TVA and the national government have helped the country. He is accompanied by Governor George C. Wallace.

HUNTSVILLE, ALABAMA. At the Redstone Army Airfield, President Kennedy addresses an audience

President Kennedy addresses a Chamber of Commerce breakfast, at the Texas Hotel in Fort Worth, 22 November 1963.

of armed forces and space program personnel praising their efforts to put the United States first in space.

21 May 1963

WASHINGTON, D.C. Astronaut L. Gordon Cooper is awarded the NASA Distinguished Service Medal by President Kennedy. "I think one of the things which warmed us the most during this flight," says the President, "was the realization that however extraordinary computers may be, that we are still ahead of them and that man is still the most extraordinary computer of all."

23 May 1963

NEW YORK. The first of three meetings on the subject of opening public accommodations to blacks in the South is held between Attorney General Robert F. Kennedy and Southern leaders.

NEW YORK. At Battery Park, President Kennedy speaks at the dedication of the East Coast Memorial to the Missing at Sea, a monument erected in honor of 4,500 American servicemen killed in World War II in the Western Atlantic. He warns that it may be wrenching for families to come here and read their sons' names. "It is, after all," he says, "against the law of nature for parents to bury their children." And with the perilous international situation today, these people may wonder what significance their loss has. The President says, "I suppose it means that every generation of Americans must be expected to do their part to maintain freedom for their country...that there is no final victory but rather all Americans must be always prepared to play their part in a difficult and dangerous world." In the evening, he attends a birthday fund-raising dinner held in his honor at the Waldorf-Astoria Hotel. The entertainment director of the event is lyricist Alan Jay Lerner, who had collaborated on the musical *Camelot.*

28 May 1963

WASHINGTON, D.C. President Kennedy signs the

Outdoor Recreation Bill, which will "promote the coordination and development of effective outdoor recreation programs."

29 May 1963

WASHINGTON, D.C. The "Father of the Year" Award is presented to President Kennedy. President Kennedy sponsors a luncheon for the governors of nine states to gain their states' cooperation in the federal campaign to guarantee all citizens equal rights. Members of Kennedy's staff at the White House Navy Mess throw a surprise party in honor of his forty-sixth birthday. Later, he celebrates his birthday with a dinner cruise around the Potomac River on the *Sequoia*. His brothers, Robert and Ted, and sisters Jean, Pat, and Eunice, and their spouses are present, as are such friends as Mr. and Mrs. Benjamin Bradlee, William Walton, Senator and Mrs. George Smathers, Mr. and Mrs. Paul Fay, and Mr. and Mrs. David Niven.

30 May 1963

ARLINGTON, VIRGINIA. At the Arlington National Cemetery, President Kennedy places a wreath at the Tomb of the Unknown Soldier.

3 June 1963

WASHINGTON, D.C. President Kennedy begins two days of meetings with President Sarvepalli Radhakrishan of India. Following the death of Pope John XXIII today, President Kennedy issues a statement in which he says that the late pontiff's "wisdom, compassion, and kindly strength have bequeathed humanity a new legacy of purpose and courage for the future."

4 June 1963

WASHINGTON, D.C. At the Departmental auditorium on Constitution Avenue, President Kennedy addresses members of the World Food Congress, a two-day symposium sponsored by the UN to establish policy for helping starving people around the world. He says, "So long as freedom from hunger is only half achieved, so long as two-thirds of the nations have food deficits, no citizen, no nation, can afford to be satisfied. We have the ability, as members of the human race...to eliminate hunger from the face of the earth in our lifetime. We need only the will."

5 June 1963

COLORADO SPRINGS, COLORADO. President Kennedy begins a five-day speaking and observation tour of the Western states by delivering the commencement address at graduation exercises of the U.S. Air Force Academy.

WHITE SANDS, NEW MEXICO. At the Missile Range, the President observes missile demonstrations at launch sites 1 and 2.

EL PASO, TEXAS. At International Airport, Mayor Judson B. Williams presents President Kennedy with a pair of colt .45 revolvers, a Texas Ranger badge, and the keys to the city. In a brief speech, the President says, "And I am glad to leave Washington, D.C. and come to the Pass of the North, El Paso, a part of the Old West, but also a part of the new America. I am proud to be with you. This state and country is going to continue to move forward, and El Paso and Boston will be in the lead." Also at the airport are Vice-President Lyndon B. Johnson and Governor John B. Connally.

6 June 1963

SAN DIEGO, CALIFORNIA. At graduation exercises at San Diego State College, President Kennedy receives an honorary Doctor of Laws degree and delivers the commencement address. He speaks of the responsibility of America to give all its children fair educational opportunities and of the programs needed to provide them. "No country can possibly move ahead," he says, "no free society can possibly be sustained, unless it has an educated citizenry whose qualities of mind and heart permit it to take part in the complicated and increasingly sophisticated decisions that pour not only upon the President and upon the Congress, but upon all the citizens who exercise the ultimate power....There is no greater asset in this country than an educated man or woman."

On the same day, he gives a speech at the Marine Corps Recruiting Depot before 10,000 servicemen and women assembled in Hall Field. He then goes by helicopter to the *Oriskany*, where he observes a weapons demonstration by vessels of the Pacific Fleet, and to the *Kitty Hawk*, where he chats with the crew after a brief speech in which he says, "Control of the seas can mean peace. Control of the seas can mean victory. The United States must control the seas if it is to protect your security and those countries which stretch thousands of miles away that look to you on this ship and the sister ships of the United States Navy." The President spends the night aboard the carrier.

7 June 1963

POINT MUGU, CALIFORNIA. President Kennedy is introduced by Governor Pat Brown and gives a speech at the Naval Air Station.

CHINA LAKE, CALIFORNIA. The President observes a weapons demonstration. Later, he speaks at the Naval Air Facility.

LOS ANGELES. President Kennedy attends a fund-raising dinner at the Beverly Hilton Hotel. After delivering an address, he and comedian Jack Benny go to the Grand Ballroom where graduates of a local high-school present the President with a silver tray.

8 June 1963
LOS ANGELES. The Democratic State Committee Women of California give a breakfast in honor of President Kennedy at the Hollywood Paladium.

HONOLULU, HAWAII. President Kennedy arrives here in the evening and speaks briefly at International Airport. He spends the night at Makalapa Naval Base.

9 June 1963
HONOLULU, HAWAII. At the Arizona Memorial, President Kennedy places a wreath. Later, in an address before the U.S. Conference of Mayors at the Hilton Hawaiian Village Hotel, he calls for actions on the part of cities to stop racism.

10 June 1963
WASHINGTON, D.C. At graduation exercises of the American University held, at the John M. Reeves Athletic Field, President John F. Kennedy receives an honorary Doctor of Laws degree and delivers the commencement address. The topic of this major policy speech is world peace. In today's nuclear age, Kennedy says, it is essential that the United States spend billions each year on weapons to make sure they will never be used. But these "idle stockpiles" are not the true means of assuring peace, the kind of peace that is "the necessary rational end of rational men." It is dangerous and defeatist, he says, to think of world peace or world disarmament as impossible and war as inevitable. Problems are man-made and therefore can be solved by man. But instead of trying to achieve absolute, infinite, and universal peace and good will, he says, "Let us focus on a more practical, more attainable peace based not on a sudden revolution in human nature but on a gradual evolution of human institutions." The President laments that the enormous sums spent on weapons cannot be devoted to fighting poverty, disease, and illiteracy. For while peoples must not be blind to their ideological differences, there are common interests, and "in the final analysis our most basic common link is that we all inhabit this small planet— we all breathe the same air, we all cherish our children's future, we are all mortal." America must not only defend the frontiers of freedom, he says, but pursue the paths of peace. He then announces that the United States, Russia, and England will shortly begin high-level discussions on a comprehensive nuclear test-ban treaty. He also promises that if other countries do not conduct nuclear tests in the atmosphere, the United States will not do so either.

11 June 1963
WASHINGTON, D.C. President Kennedy signs a proclamation commanding the governor of Alabama and anyone else to cease and desist from unlawfully obstructing the enrollment and attendance of black students at the University of Alabama.

At 8:00 P.M., Kennedy delivers a civil-rights message to the nation on television and radio. "Today we are committed to a worldwide struggle to promote and protect the rights of all who wish to be free," he declares. "It ought to be possible, in short, for every American to enjoy the privileges of being American without regard to his race or his color....One hundred years of delay have passed since President Lincoln freed the slaves, yet their heirs, their grandsons, are not fully free....The fires of frustration and discord are burning in every city, North and South, where legal remedies are not at hand....We face, therefore, a moral crisis as a country and as a people. It cannot be met by repressive police action. It cannot be left to increased demonstrations in the streets. It cannot be quieted by token moves or talk. It is a time to act in the Congress, in your state and local legislative body, and, above all, in all of our daily lives."

13 June 1963
WASHINGTON, D.C. President Kennedy speaks at a convention of the National Council of Senior Citizens at the Willard Hotel. Following the defeat of area-development legislation, he issues a statement saying that the defeat "could not have come at a worse time." Because unemployment persists, "this program must not be allowed to die and it is my intention to give the Congress another opportunity to support it." With Harry Truman, he attends a social hour for members of Congress.

14 June 1963
WASHINGTON, D.C. Over 200,000 people participate in a "freedom march" in support of black civil rights. Among others, Attorney General Robert F. Kennedy speaks to the crowd.

17 June 1963
WASHINGTON, D.C. President Kennedy meets with a group of over 230 religious leaders in the East Room of the White House.

19 June 1963
WASHINGTON, D.C. President Kennedy proposes

to Congress that it stay in session this year until it enacts the Civil Rights Act of 1963. The bill would provide voting rights and an end to discrimination in schools, public facilities, and employment. He calls upon every member of Congress to put political pressures aside and look into their hearts, "not in search of charity, for the Negro neither wants nor needs condescension—but for the one plain, proud, and priceless quality that unites us all as Americans: a sense of justice. In this year of the Emancipation Centennial, justice requires us to insure the blessings of liberty for all Americans and their posterity—not merely for reasons of economic efficiency, world diplomacy and domestic tranquility—but, above all, because it is right." Congress, however, will ignores Kennedy's plea and will adjourn on December 30, without voting on the Civil Rights Act.

20 June 1963
CHARLESTON, WEST VIRGINIA. President Kennedy attends a celebration honoring the one hundredth anniversary of West Virginia's admission to the Union. He salutes the state and declares his own gratitude to its citizens. "I would not be where I now am, I would not have some of the responsibilities which I now bear, if it had not been for the people of West Virginia."

22 June 1963
WASHINGTON, D.C. With Robert Kennedy and Bourke Marshall, President Kennedy confers in separate meetings with Roy Wilkins, executive secretary of the NAACP, and Martin Luther King, Jr.

ANDREWS AIR FORCE BASE, MARYLAND. With a group of officials that includes Secretary of State Dean Rusk, President Kennedy embarks on a unity-building visit to five Western European countries.

23 June 1963
BONN, WEST GERMANY. Chancellor Konrad Adenauer and other high-ranking German officials greet the presidential party at Wahn Airport at 9:50 A.M. In a brief speech, the President says that "together we look forward to a new future. Former foes have become faithful friends....Your safety is our safety, your liberty is our liberty, and any attack on your soil is an attack upon our own."

COLOGNE, WEST GERMANY. At the Rathaus, the President signs the Golden Book. Then, before 300,000 West Germans assembled in Rathaus Borplatz, he makes a brief speech hailing the citizens of Cologne "with the old Rhenish saying, "Koelle Alaaf."

BONN, WEST GERMANY. Another enormous and wildly cheering crowd gathers in Market Square to hear the President give a speech. "This city of Bonn," he says, "is the capital of the free world." The President then goes to the American Community Theater where he addresses the American embassy staff. In the evening, President Kennedy attends a dinner given in honor of Chancellor Adenauer at the Palais Schaumburg.

24 June 1963
BONN, WEST GERMANY. President Kennedy, Chancellor Adenauer, and their aides hold discussions on disarmament, NATO, and a European-American alliance at the Palais Schaumburg. At the Villa Hammerschmidt, the President attends a ceremony for the establishment of a German peace corps. He congratulates the country on its commitment to help those in dire need of assistance. "Dante once said that the hottest places in hell are reserved for those who in a period of moral crisis maintain their neutrality," he says. "This is a moral crisis." Later, the President meets with other West German officials, including Mayor Willy Brandt of West Berlin.

25 June 1963
HANAU, WEST GERMANY. President Kennedy addresses American servicemen at Fliegerorst Kaserne and has lunch in the mess hall.

FRANKFURT, WEST GERMANY. At the Rathaus, the President signs the Golden Book. In a brief speech, he says, "The last two days have been among the most heartwarming days that I have spent since I have been in public service." Outside he addresses a large crowd in Roemerberg Square, saying, "Abraham Lincoln, in the dark days before the Civil War in my own country, said, 'I know there is a God. I see a storm coming. If He has a part and a place for me, then I am ready.' No one can tell in the future whether there is a storm coming for all of us, but what we can be sure of is that no matter what happens, we believe in God and we are ready." President Kennedy departs for Paolskirche, where he urges a common defense among the nations of the Atlantic Community and pledges American military aid to defend Europe.

WIESBADEN, WEST GERMANY. President Kennedy confers with Vice-Chancellor Ludwig Erhard and attends a reception in his honor at the Kurhaus.

26 June 1963
WEST BERLIN, GERMANY. At Congress Hall, President Kennedy addresses a trade union meeting of

German labor officials and construction workers. AFL-CIO president George Meany greets him. At Branden-burg Gate and Checkpoint Charlie, President Kennedy attempts to view parts of East Berlin. The President re-turns to the Schoneberger Rathaus where an immense crowd is gathered in the Rudolph Wilde Platz. He deliv-ers a stirring speech on freedom, and the crowd roars with cheers as he declares, "All free men, wherever they may live, are citizens of Berlin, and, therefore, as a free-man, I take pride in the words 'Ich bin ein Berliner' ['I am a Berliner']." The President also speaks at the Free University and at U.S. military headquarters. At Tegel Airport, Chancellor Adenauer and Mayor Brandt bid him goodbye.

DUBLIN, IRELAND. In the evening, President Kennedy arrives in his ancestors' homeland where he is greeted by President Eamon de Valera and Prime Minis-ter Sean F. Lemass.

WASHINGTON, D.C. In the first of a series of ap-pearances, Robert F. Kennedy testifies before the House Committee on the Judiciary regarding the Civil Rights Bill of 1963, which he favors.

27 June 1963
NEW ROSS, IRELAND. At the town from which Patrick Kennedy left for Boston some 115 years earlier, President Kennedy is welcomed in a festive ceremony. At the quay he says, "When my great-grandfather left here to become a cooper in East Boston, he carried nothing with him except two things: a strong religious faith and a strong desire for liberty. I am glad to say that all of his great-grandchildren have valued that inheritance."

DUNGANSTOWN, IRELAND. President Ken-nedy visits the birthplace of his great-grandfather Patrick Kennedy. The home where Patrick Kennedy was born is now part of a farm occupied by Kennedy descendant Mary Ann Ryan and her family. Mary Ryan, born in 1900, is the granddaughter of Patrick Kennedy's brother James, born in 1815. Mary Ryan, her two daughters, Josephine (born 1938) and Mary Ann (born 1940), and several other relatives talk about the family with the President over tea.

WEXFORD, IRELAND. The President places a wreath at the John Barry statue, then delivers a speech before 5,000 at Redmond Place. "There is an impression in Washington," he says, "that there are no Kennedys left in Ireland, that they are all in Washington, so I wonder if there are any Kennedys in this audience. Could you hold up your hand so I can see?" [Pause.] "Well, I am glad to see a few cousins who didn't catch the boat."

28 June 1963
CORK, IRELAND. President Kennedy speaks at City Hall on Ireland's leadership in the struggle for inde-pendence and freedom.

DUBLIN, IRELAND. At Arbour Hall, the Presi-dent lays a wreath at the graves of the countrymen who took part in the 1916 Easter uprising. He then delivers a speech to the Irish Parliament in Leinster House, and re-ceives honorary degrees from the National University of Ireland and the University of Dublin.

29 June 1963
GALWAY, IRELAND. President Kennedy is given the "freedom of the city" at Eyre Square and then speaks briefly.

LIMERICK, IRELAND. The "freedom of the city" is conferred upon President Kennedy by Mayor Frances Condell at the Green Park Race Course. The President speaks again, saying, "This is not the land of my birth, but it is the land for which I hold the greatest affection."

DERBYSHIRE, ENGLAND. At Chatsworth, President Kennedy visits the grave of his sister Kathleen in the family plot of the Cavendish family.

SUSSEX, ENGLAND. Prime Minister and Lady Macmillan give a dinner in honor of President Kennedy at their Birch Grove home.

30 June 1963
MILAN, ITALY. President Kennedy stops over at Villa Serbelloni before his meeting with Italian officials in Rome the next day. Neither the President nor the Ital-ians want Kennedy's visit to detract from today's corona-tion in Rome of Pope Paul VI, which follows the death of Pope John XXIII on 3 June.

1 July 1963
ROME. President Kennedy, Italian President Antonio Segni, and other major Italian leaders meet at the Palaz-zo Quirinale. Later, at the Piazza Venezia, President Kennedy prays at the Tomb of the Unknown Soldier.

2 July 1963
ROME. President Kennedy meets with Pope Paul VI for over half an hour at Vatican City. At the North American College, he is presented with a copy of the *Pa-*

cem in Terris that has been signed by the late Pope John XXIII.

NAPLES, ITALY. At the NATO headquarters here, President Kennedy speaks on Western unity and affirms the NATO pledge that an attack on one member is regarded as an attack on all.

4 July 1963

WASHINGTON, D.C. President Kennedy names thirty-one recipients of the first Presidential Medal of Freedom. Among those honored are singer Marian Anderson, cellist Pablo Casals, jurist Felix Frankfurter, inventor Edwin H. Land, and Governor Luis Muñoz Martin of Puerto Rico.

BOSTON. A son, Christopher George, is born to Ethel (Skakel) and Robert F. Kennedy at St. Elizabeth's Hospital. He is their fifth son and eighth child. The baby is delivered by Caesarean section.

5-7 July 1963

HYANNIS PORT, MASSACHUSETTS. President Kennedy spends the weekend with his family, resting, sailing, and golfing.

8 July 1963

WASHINGTON, D.C. President Kennedy presents the Hubbard Medal to members of an American expedition to Mount Everest. He also confers with Prime Minister Robert G. Menzies of Australia.

15 July 1963

WASHINGTON, D.C. President Kennedy begins two days of discussions with President Julius Nyere of Tanganyika on political developments in Africa and relations between the two countries.

19 July 1963

HYANNIS PORT, MASSACHUSETTS. President and Mrs. Kennedy attend the christening of their nephew Christopher George Kennedy at St. Francis Xavier Church.

NEW ORLEANS, LOUISIANA. Lee Harvey Oswald is fired from his job as a machine-maintenance man at the Reilly Coffee Company.

23 July 1963

WASHINGTON, D.C. President Kennedy sends to Congress legislation for "revising and modernizing our immigration laws."

26 July 1963

WASHINGTON, D.C. In a nationwide television and radio address, President Kennedy announces that on the previous day, "negotiations were concluded in Moscow on a treaty to ban all nuclear tests in the atmosphere, in outer space, and under water." He says the treaty is a step toward peace. "A war today or tomorrow, if it led to nuclear war, would not be like any war in history. A full-scale nuclear exchange, lasting less than sixty minutes, with the weapons now in existence, could wipe out more than 300 million Americans, Europeans, and Russians, as well as untold numbers elsewhere. And the survivors, as Chairman Khruschev warned the Communist Chinese, 'the survivors would envy the dead.' For they would inherit a world so devastated by explosions and poison and fire that today we cannot even conceive of its horrors. So let us try to turn the world away from war."

1 August 1963

ANNAPOLIS, MARYLAND. At the U.S. Naval Academy, President Kennedy addresses a new class of midshipmen. Of service with the Navy, he says, "I can think of no more rewarding a career. You will have a chance in the next ten, twenty, and thirty years to serve the cause of freedom and your country all over the globe, to hold positions of the highest responsibility...."

2 August 1963

WASHINGTON, D.C. President Kennedy addresses delegates of the Girls Nation in the White House Flower Garden. "Last week we had a group of boys from Boys Nation and I said they showed more initiative than the Governors, which got me into a great deal of difficulty. So I will be very careful today and say that you are more beautiful than the Governors." On a serious note, he tells them, "This is a great country and requires a good deal of all of us, so I can imagine nothing more important than for all of you to continue to work in public affairs and be interested in them, not only to bring up a family, but also give part of your time to your community, your state, and your country."

5 August 1963

MOSCOW. A nuclear test-ban treaty prohibiting testing of nuclear weapons in the air and under water, but not underground, is signed by representatives of Russia, England and the United States.

7 August 1963

HYANNIS PORT, MASSACHUSETTS. Feeling

Jacqueline Kennedy at a Washington, D.C. ceremony on 3 December 1963 honoring Clinton J. Hill, the Secret Service agent who jumped into the presidential car in Dallas as shots were ringing out.

labor pains, Jacqueline Kennedy is rushed from her home here by helicopter to the Otis Air Force Base Hospital.

WASHINGTON, D.C. After hearing of his wife's condition, President Kennedy cancels a meeting at the White House with Dr. Neftali Ponce-Miranda, the foreign minister of Ecuador. At 12:15 P.M. , he flies by helicopter to Andrews Air Force Base.

FALMOUTH, MASSACHUSETTS. At 1:15 P.M., a son, Patrick Bouvier, is born over five weeks prematurely to Jacqueline (Bouvier) and President John F. Kennedy. He is their third child and second son.

BOSTON. Suffering with respiratory complications, newborn Patrick Kennedy is transferred in the early evening to Children's Hospital Medical Center where he can receive special treatment. President Kennedy visits him, and spends the night at the Ritz-Carlton Hotel.

8 August 1963
BOSTON. President John F. Kennedy confers with physicians at Children's Hospital about his newborn son's condition.

FALMOUTH, MASSACHUSETTS. The President visits his wife at Otis Air Force Base Hospital.

SQUAW ISLAND, MASSACHUSETTS. The President makes a brief stop at his home here.

BOSTON.   President Kennedy returns to Children's Hospital where, after talking with physicians about his baby's current status, he decides to spend the night.

9 August 1963
BOSTON.   At 4:04 A.M., Patrick Bouvier Kennedy dies of hyaline membrane disease due to prematurity at Children's Hospital. The baby had lived less than thirty-nine hours.

FALMOUTH, MASSACHUSETTS.   At the end of the day, President John F. Kennedy visits his wife at Otis Air Force Base Hospital for the third time.

NEW ORLEANS, LOUISIANA.   Carrying a pro-Castro sign and handing out literature favorable to the Cuban leader, Lee Harvey Oswald gets into a fight with members of an anti-Castro group he had tried to join a few days earlier. The trouble-makers are arrested, and Oswald is held overnight.

10 August 1963
BROOKLINE, MASSACHUSETTS.   Patrick Bouvier Kennedy is buried at the Holyhood Cemetery at 10:45 A.M. President Kennedy, family members, and close friends attend the funeral. The marker at the burial site reads: "Patrick Bouvier Kennedy—August 7, 1963–August 9, 1963."

FALMOUTH, MASSACHUSETTS.   In the evening, the President makes his second visit of the day to his wife at the Otis Air Force Base Hospital.

NEW ORLEANS, LOUISIANA.   At his own request, Lee Harvey Oswald is interviewed in jail by an FBI agent. He gives erroneous information about his past and current activities.

12 August 1963
NEW ORLEANS, LOUISIANA.   Following his arrest three days earlier, Lee Harvey Oswald pleads guilty to disturbing the peace and pays a $10 fine.

17 August 1963
NEW ORLEANS, LOUISIANA.   A reporter for a local radio station interviews Lee Harvey Oswald about his opposition to the Directorio Revolucionario Estudiantil, an anti-Castro organization. Oswald says he is a member of the New Orleans chapter of the Fair Play for Cuba Committee.

27 August 1963
WASHINGTON, D.C.   On the South Lawn of the White House, President Kennedy addresses 5,000 students who participate in a government seminar. In urging the students to pursue a career in government, he cites a quotation he has often used before. The Greeks, he says, defined happiness as "the full use of your powers along lines of excellence," and he can imagine no place where the students could use their powers "more fully along lines more excellent in the 1960s than to be in the service of the United States."

28 August 1963
WASHINGTON, D.C.   A mass civil-rights demonstration in support of equal rights and passage of legislation ending discrimination takes place today. While almost a quarter-million marchers assemble at the Lincoln Memorial, civil-rights leaders, including Martin Luther King, Jr., and Roy Wilkins, meet with President Kennedy at the White House to discuss the President's proposed civil-rights program. Later, the leaders return to the Lincoln Memorial to address the crowd.

Martin Luther King, Jr., delivers a moving and emotionally charged speech in which he accuses America of not honoring its constitutional promise to citizens of color. Warning that there will be no tranquility in America until the Negro is granted equal rights, he urges the people to return to their homes, not with despair, but with the knowledge that the racial situation can and will change. "So even though we face the difficulties of today and tomorrow, I still have a dream....I have a dream that one day this nation will rise up and live out the true meaning of its creed, 'We hold these truths to be self-evident and that all men are created equal.' I have a dream that one day on the red hills of Georgia, sons of former slaves and the sons of former slave owners will be able to sit down together at the table of brotherhood. I have a dream...."

30 August 1963
WASHINGTON, D.C.   A special communications connection, called a "hot line," is established between the president of the United States and the leader of the Soviet Union in case of political and military emergencies.

5 September 1963
WASHINGTON, D.C.   President Kennedy meets with King Mohammed Zaher of Afghanistan to discuss that Asian nation's economic and social progress and relations between the two countries. A dinner is given in honor of King Mohammed and Queen Homaira in the evening.

9 September 1963

WASHINGTON, D.C. NBC newscasters Chet Huntley and David Brinkley conduct a taped television interview with President Kennedy in the morning for broadcast this evening.

10 September 1963

WASHINGTON, D.C. President Kennedy federalizes National Guard troops in Alabama and signs a proclamation restricting Governor George Wallace and all others from taking any action to prevent desegregation. His action, in effect, integrates the public schools in Alabama.

11 September 1963

WASHINGTON, D.C. President Kennedy presents the Congressional Gold Medal to Bob Hope "in recognition of his having rendered outstanding service to the cause of democracies throughout the world." The comedian thanks him, saying, "This is a great thing. There is only one sobering thought—I received this for going outside the country. I think they are trying to tell me something."

13 September 1963

DALLAS, TEXAS. Local papers carry the announcement that President Kennedy will be visiting Texas in November.

14 September 1963

BOSTON. Joseph Kennedy undergoes minor surgery for the removal of a skin lesion at New England Baptist Hospital.

PRINCE EDWARD COUNTY, VIRGINIA. Black children here attend public schools for the first time in four years, largely through the efforts of the Free School Association, which Attorney General Robert F. Kennedy has helped to form.

15 September 1963

BIRMINGHAM, ALABAMA. A bomb explodes in the Sixteenth Street Baptist Church as Sunday school classes are in session. Many children are injured, and four young black girls are killed.

17 September 1963

NEW ORLEANS, LOUISIANA. A tourist card to visit Mexico is issued to Lee Harvey Oswald.

20 September 1963

NEW YORK. With the statement "we meet again in the quest for peace," John F. Kennedy sets the theme of his third address before the United Nations General Assembly. He speaks of building peace, of a joint space exploration by the United States and the Soviet Union, and of programs such as worldwide conservation, food distribution, and common medical research. He says that it is the responsibility of all nations, not just a few, to "improve the conditions of man," and that every nation can use science, technology, and education to move toward this goal. "Never before has man had such capacity to control his own environment, to end thirst and hunger, to conquer poverty and disease, to banish illiteracy and massive human misery. We have the power to make this the best generation of mankind in the history of the world—or to make it the last." The President urges industrialized nations to continue providing development assistance and the UN to "play a larger role in bringing to all men the fruits of modern science and industry." He then suggests various programs which would advance medical knowledge, provide for a system of worldwide satellite communication, and establish food-distribution systems. President Kennedy concludes his address with this exhortation: "My fellow inhabitants of this planet— let us take our stand here in this assembly of nations. And let us see if we, in our own time, can move the world to a just and lasting peace."

23 September 1963

WASHINGTON, D.C. President Kennedy meets with Foreign Minister Attilio Piccione of Italy and Prince Souvanna Phouma, the prime minister of Laos.

IRVING, TEXAS. Ruth Paine brings Marina Oswald and her daughter back from New Orleans to her home. Oswald's wife and daughter had lived at the Paine home briefly in the spring but had joined Oswald in New Orleans when he found a job there. Now pregnant, Marina Oswald has decided to stay with Paine again.

24 September 1963

WASHINGTON, D.C. President Kennedy signs the Health Professions Educational Assistance Act. The bill establishes a three-year program of federal grants to build training facilities in medical and dental schools and to provide student loans.

MILFORD, PENNSYLVANIA. The President begins a five-day trip across the country to encourage conservation of resources. Here he participates in ceremonies dedicating the Pinchot Institute of Conservation Studies.

ASHLAND, WISCONSIN. The President announces that a study will be made of pollution in the Upper Mississippi and Minnesota River in an address given at the county airport.

DULUTH, MINNESOTA. At the University of Minnesota, President Kennedy announces programs to relieve economic distress in a speech before the Conference of Land and People.

25 September 1963

WASHINGTON, D.C. Attorney General Robert F. Kennedy appears before a Senate Committee to report on the federal government's investigation of organized crime.

GRAND FORKS, NORTH DAKOTA. At the University of North Dakota, President Kennedy receives an honorary Doctor of Laws degree. Following the presentation, he delivers an address which begins: "Politics is a somewhat abused profession in the United States...but I would want to say that it has some advantages. It permitted me to go from being a somewhat indifferent lieutenant in the United States Navy to becoming Commander-in-Chief in the short space of fifteen years, and it has also permitted me to become a graduate of this university in 30 seconds, when it takes you four years. So in determining what career you should follow, you might consider this lowly career." In his speech, the President speaks of conserving natural resources, automation, and education. "What we seek to advance, what we seek to develop in all of our colleges and universities," he says, "are educated men and women who can bear the burdens of responsible citizenship, who can make judgments about life as it is, and as it must be, and encourage the people to make those decisions which can bring not only prosperity and security, but happiness to the people of the United States and those who depend upon it."

LARAMIE, WYOMING. In a speech at the University of Wyoming, President Kennedy declares that the primary task in understanding the environment is to "maintain a living balance between man's actions and nature's reactions, for this nation's great resources are as elastic and productive as our ingenuity can make them."

BILLINGS, MONTANA. President Kennedy urges development and protection of resources in an address at the Yellowstone County Fair Grounds.

26 September 1963

GREAT FALLS, MONTANA. In a speech at the high-school stadium, President Kennedy talks of what America can do to develop its resources. He says that he hopes "that we will take this rich country of ours, given to us by God and by nature, and improve it through science and find new uses for our natural resources, to make it possible for us to sustain in this country a steadily increasing standard of living, the highest in the world, and, based on that powerful fortress, to move around the world in the defense of freedom...."

HANFORD, WASHINGTON. Speaking to a crowd outside the city's generating plant, the President declares that science must be used to improve the environment. To meet the growing need for electric power, he recommends "an aggressive program to use our hydro resources to the fullest," developing new methods for using coal, and hastening the "development of low-cost atomic power."

SALT LAKE CITY, UTAH. President Kennedy talks about United States foreign policy in an address given at the Mormon Tabernacle. He recalls the country's traditional isolation until World War II, saying, "The end of isolation consequently meant a wrench with the very lifeblood, the very spine, of the nation....Yet as time passed, we came to see that the end of isolation was not such a terrible error or evil after all. We came to see that it was the inevitable result of growth, the economic growth, the military growth, and the cultural growth of the United States. No nation so powerful and dynamic and rich as our own could hope to live in isolation from other nations, especially at a time when science and technology was making the world so small."

27 September 1963

MEXICO CITY. Lee Harvey Oswald arrives by bus to obtain visas for Russia and Cuba.

TACOMA, WASHINGTON. At Cheney Stadium, President Kennedy urges a national commitment to maximum use of the country's energies and talents in order to exploit its natural resources fully.

TONGUE POINT, OREGON. President Kennedy announces that the Defense Department and the Coast Guard will establish operations here early next year.

28 September 1963

WHISKEYTOWN, CALIFORNIA. President Kennedy participates in dedication ceremonies of the Whiskeytown dam and reservoir.

LAS VEGAS, NEVADA. In his last public address on this trip, President Kennedy says at the Convention

Center here that in the past five days he has reached three major conclusions: that a new campaign should be mounted to preserve the natural environment, that improvements to the educational system should be made to keep children in school, and that every opportunity should be taken to promote peaceful relations around the world.

PALM DESERT, CALIFORNIA. President Kennedy spends the night at the home of Bing Crosby.

1 October 1963
WASHINGTON, D.C. President Kennedy begins two days of meetings with Emperor Haile Selassie I of Ethiopia to discuss African problems and world peace.

MEXICO CITY. Lee Harvey Oswald visits the Soviet Embassy to apply for a visa to travel to Russia. He has also visited the Cuban Consulate to get permission to stop off in Cuba en route.

2 October 1963
GREECE. Following the tragic death of her infant son, Patrick, Jacqueline Kennedy begins a two-week vacation in Greece with her sister Lee Radziwill.

WASHINGTON, D.C. Following President Kennedy's meeting this morning with Secretary of Defense Robert McNamara and Gen. Maxwell Taylor, who recently returned from South Vietnam, the White House issues a statement that "we will adhere to our policy of working with the people and government of South Vietnam to deny this country to Communism and to suppress the externally stimulated and supported insurgency of the Viet Cong as promptly as possible.

3 October 1963
DALLAS, TEXAS. Cuba and the Soviet Union deny Lee Harvey Oswald's visa requests, and he returns to Dallas from Mexico.

HEBER SPRINGS, ARKANSAS. President Kennedy participates in the dedication of the Greers Ferry Dam.

LITTLE ROCK, ARKANSAS. The President talks of the progress of the new South in a speech at the Livestock Exposition Grounds.

4 October 1963
THE AEGEAN SEA. As the guests of Aristotle Onassis, Jacqueline Kennedy and Lee and Stanislas Radziwill, among others, begin an eight-day Aegean cruise aboard the *Christina*.

WASHINGTON, D.C. President Kennedy confers separately with Governor John B. Connally of Texas and Vice-President Lyndon B. Johnson. He cuts off American military and economic aid to Honduras following a coup there and the expulsion of President José Ramon Morales.

WASHINGTON, D.C. Following reports that Lee Harvey Oswald has been in Mexico City, the Central Intelligence Office asks the Office of Naval Intelligence for recent photographs of Oswald in order to identify the ex-Marine.

6 October 1963
ISTANBUL, TURKEY. The *Christina* docks, and Jacqueline Kennedy tours the city.

CAMP DAVID, MARYLAND. President Kennedy drives his children Caroline and John, to church in an electric cart.

7 October 1963
WASHINGTON, D.C. President Kennedy signs the Nuclear Test Ban Treaty, stating, "With our courage and understanding enlarged by this achievement, let us press onward in quest of man's essential desire for peace."

9 October 1963
WASHINGTON, D.C. President Kennedy announces at a press conference that he has approved the sale of surplus American wheat to the Soviet Union. The cargo will be carried in American ships. Leading Republicans and others dispute the decision, saying that the food will help Russia's suffering economy at a critical time.

10 October 1963
WASHINGTON, D.C. The Robert J. Collier Trophy, an aeronautics and space award, is presented by President Kennedy to the seven astronauts—Alan B. Shepard, L. Gordon Cooper, John H. Glenn, Jr., Virgil I. Grissom, Donald K. Slayton, Malcolm Scott Carpenter, and Walter M. Schirra, Jr.—who took part in Project Mercury, the American man-in-space program.

11 October 1963
WASHINGTON, D.C. On the seventy-ninth anniversary of Eleanor Roosevelt's birth, President Kennedy participates in a ceremony at which a commemorative stamp honoring the former first lady is issued.

United Press International.

Jacqueline Kennedy at Barnstable Airport on 29 May 1964,
to appear on a TV program honoring her late husband.

14 October 1963

DALLAS, TEXAS. Lee Harvey Oswald rents an apartment for himself at 1026 North Beckley Avenue under the fictitious name O. H. Lee.

IRVING, TEXAS. Having been told about a possible job opening, family friend Ruth Paine calls the Texas School Book Depository to make an inquiry on Oswald's behalf.

15 October 1963

WASHINGTON, D.C. President Kennedy meets with Prime Minister Sean F. Lemass to discuss economic development in Ireland.

16 October 1963

DALLAS, TEXAS. Lee Harvey Oswald begins work as a shipping clerk at the Texas School Book Depository, located at the intersection of Elm and Houston Streets.

17 October 1963

WASHINGTON, D.C. President Kennedy meets with President Josip Broz Tito of Yugoslavia for an exchange of views. In May, President Kennedy had supported an effort to continue American aid to Yugoslavia after a new charter, adopted a month earlier, established Communist party domination of the country.

19 October 1963

ORONO, MAINE. His administration's effort to improve relations with the Soviet Union and advance peace is the subject of President Kennedy's address at the University of Maine. He is also awarded an honorary Doctor of Laws degree.

BOSTON. President Kennedy attends the Harvard-Columbia football game at Harvard Stadium.

BROOKLINE, MASSACHUSETTS. At Hollyhood Cemetery, President Kennedy visits the grave of his son Patrick, who died two months ago.

United Press International.

Robert F. Kennedy on 20 June 1964 after visiting brother Ted at Cooley Dickinson Hospital following the Senator's plane crash.

United Press International.

International ladies Garment Workers Union president David Dubinsky holds
Robert Kennedy's hand at a union rally in New York.

BOSTON.   In a fund-raising speech given at the Commonwealth Armory, President Kennedy says that while the United States still moves within a dangerous environment, it is more secure than it has been in years. "So I do not look to the future with gloom," he concludes.

BOSTON.   After looking at several possible locations for a presidential library, President Kennedy selects a 12-acre site along the Charles River in Cambridge.

20 October 1963
IRVING, TEXAS.   A second daughter is born to Marina and Lee Harvey Oswald.

22 October 1963
WASHINGTON, D.C.   In an address before the National Academy of Science at Constitution Hall, President Kennedy calls attention to areas that might deserve scientific attention: the conservation of natural resources, use of ocean resources, study of the atmosphere, and control of the effects of scientific experiments. The President meets with President Victor Paz Estenssoro of Bolivia to discuss Latin American concerns and relations between the two countries.

24 October 1963
WASHINGTON, D.C.   President Kennedy signs the

Maternal and Child Health and Mental Retardation Planning Amendments Act of 1963, "to initiate a new program of comprehensive maternity and infant care aimed directly at preventing mental retardation." He refers to the legislation as "an important landmark" in combatting this health hazard: "Although children may be the victims of fate, they will not be victims of our neglect." In a speech before the National Association for Retarded Children, the President says that efforts to fight mental retardation should have a high priority. "We have conquered the atom," he says, "but we have not yet begun to make a major assault upon the mysteries of the human mind." The President writes the preface to *Looking Outward: Years of Crisis at the United Nations* by Adlai E. Stevenson.

DALLAS, TEXAS. After delivering a speech on the United Nations, Adlai E. Stevenson is swatted on the head with a placard, spat on, and verbally abused by hostile anti-United Nations partisans in the crowd.

25 October 1963
DALLAS, TEXAS. Governor John B. Connally, city officials, and prominent businessmen send a message to Adlai Stevenson apologizing for the crowd's behavior after his speech yesterday. A carbon of the apology is forwarded to President Kennedy.

26 October 1963
AMHERST, MASSACHUSETTS. President Kennedy receives an honorary Doctor of Laws degree from Amherst College. In his speech, he praises the late Robert Frost, whose memory is being honored by the school today, and says, "A nation reveals itself not only by the men it produces, but also by the men it honors, the men it remembers." He also declares that artists strengthen society by criticizing it when it does not reach its highest potential. "If art is to nourish the roots of our culture," he says, "society must set the artist free to follow his vision wherever it takes him. We must never forget that art is not a form of propaganda. It is a form of truth." Later, the President participates in ground-breaking ceremonies at the site of the new Robert Frost Memorial Library, named in honor of the famous American poet, who died on 29 January 1963.

30 October 1963
PHILADELPHIA, PENNSYLVANIA. President Kennedy attends a Democratic Committee fund-raising dinner for local politicians at Convention Hall. In a speech, the President reports on his administration's progress in employment, education, housing, public welfare, and civil rights.

31 October 1963
WASHINGTON, D.C. President Kennedy signs the Mental Retardation Facilities and Community Mental Health Centers Construction Act of 1963, "to provide research facilities to determine the cause of retardation, establish university-related diagnostic treatment clinics, and permit the construction of community centers for the care of the retarded." Asked at a news conference how he would appraise his job, the President answers, "Well, I find the work rewarding. Whether I am going to stay and what my intentions are and all of the rest, it seems to me it is still a good many, many months away. But as far as the job of President goes, it is rewarding." In light of "talk that Lyndon Johnson will be dumped next year," a reporter asks if President Kennedy would want Johnson on the ticket and does he expect Johnson to be on the ticket. "Yes," the President responds, "to both of those questions."

1 November 1963
WASHINGTON, D.C. President Kennedy calls a special meeting to discuss actions in response to the military coup in South Vietnam. Following the meeting, the Defense Department sends American vessels to the vicinity of South Vietnam.

Plans for a forthcoming trip to Dallas on 22 November are laid, and a route for President Kennedy's motorcade through downtown Dallas to the Trade Mart is chosen. Two sites for the speech he is to deliver before a luncheon of the Dallas Citizens Council have been considered, but the Dallas Women's Building was rejected when Governor John B. Connally expressed a preference for the Trade Mart.

IRVING, TEXAS. Lee Harvey Oswald makes a weekend visit to his wife Marina and their children at Ruth Paine's home.

2 November 1963
SOUTH VIETNAM. President Ngo Din Diem of South Vietnam is assassinated.

WASHINGTON, D.C. To plan strategy in response to events in South Vietnam, President Kennedy cancels his trip to Chicago where he was to open the Army-Air Force football game.

ATOKA, VIRGINIA. In the evening, the President joins his family at their new home for the weekend.

United Press International.

Robert F. Kennedy campaigning for the New York Senate with sisters Jean Smith and
Pat Lawford. The three stand on a car on Seventh Avenue in New York,
24 September 1964.

4 November 1963
WASHINGTON, D.C. President Kennedy signs a proclamation declaring 28 November Thanksgiving Day this year.

8 November 1963
NEW YORK. President Kennedy receives the Family of Man Award at a dinner of the New York Protestant Council at the Hilton Hotel. In a speech, the President declares that America must not let itself grow tired of carrying out its tasks to relieve world problems, but must continue to persevere and endure. "If we maintain the peace," he says, "we shall in due season reap the kind of world we deserve and deserve the kind of world we will have."

IRVING, TEXAS. Lee Harvey Oswald begins his four-day weekend visit with his wife and children at the home of Ruth Paine.

11 November 1963
ARLINGTON, VIRGINIA. In a customary ritual, President Kennedy lays a wreath at the Tomb of the Unknown Soldier at the Memorial Ampitheater of the Arlington National Cemetery. John Jr. accompanies him to the cemetery.

13 November 1963
WASHINGTON, D.C. The 1963 Christmas Seal Campaign is opened with the presentation to President Kennedy of the first 1963 seals. The national honorary chairman of the campaign, Ann Landers, participates in the ceremony.

14 November 1963
WASHINGTON, D.C. President Kennedy holds his sixty-fourth press conference in the morning. A reporter asks him to appraise the situation in South Vietnam and inquires about the purpose of a meeting attended by Defense Secretary Robert McNamara, Ambassador Henry Cabot Lodge, and others in Honolulu. The President answers that the meeting took place to assess the situation in South Vietnam and to discuss the nature of American policy and aid. He says that it "is our object to bring Americans home, permit the South Vietnamese to maintain themselves as a free and independent country, and permit democratic forces within the country to operate—which they can, of course, much more freely when the assault from the inside, and which is manipulated from the north, is ended."

ELKTON, MARYLAND. In the afternoon, President Kennedy delivers a speech at the ribbon-cutting ceremony opening a new highway from Baltimore, Maryland to Wilmington, Delaware.

15 November 1963
DALLAS, TEXAS. Lee Oswald's usual weekend visit to Irving is cancelled when Marina Oswald tells him that because overnight guests will be attending a birthday party for Ruth Paine's daughter, there will not be enough room for him to stay there.

NEW YORK. In a speech before a convention of the AFL-CIO at the Americana Hotel, President Kennedy asks for labor's support for programs to improve conditions in the United States. Following this, the President addresses a national Catholic Youth Organization convention at the New York Hilton. He tells the young audience that "we expect something of you. And unless in this free country of ours we are able to demonstrate that we are able to make this society work and progress, unless we can hope that from you we are going to get back all of the talents which society has helped develop in you, then, quite obviously, all the hopes of all of us that freedom will not only endure but prevail, of course, will be disappointed."

PALM BEACH, FLORIDA. President Kennedy visits his parents at their home here.

16 November 1963
CAPE CANAVERAL, FLORIDA. President Kennedy is briefed on the Gemini capsule and the Manned Lunar Landing program. Those conferring with him include Gordon Cooper, Virgil Grissom, and Dr. Werner Von Braun. During a helicopter tour, the President observes the Titan II and Merritt Island launch areas. From the deck of the *Observation*, President Kennedy watches a Polaris missile being fired from a submarine.

18 November 1963
DALLAS and IRVING, TEXAS. Lee Harvey Oswald and Marina argue over the fact that he is registered at his boarding house under the false name O. H. Lee.

DALLAS, TEXAS. Local newspapers print the route President Kennedy's motorcade will take when he visits the city in four days.

TAMPA, FLORIDA. President Kennedy speaks on the pending tax-cut bill and the economy in an address before members of the Florida Chamber of Commerce at the Fort Homer Hesterly Armory. A question-and-answer period follows. Later, at the International Inn, the President addresses a United Steel Workers meeting.

MIAMI BEACH, FLORIDA. In an address before some 1,200 delegates to the Inter-American Press Association convention and dinner at the Americana Hotel, President Kennedy declares that the ideals of the Alliance for Progress must be won through social justice, economic welfare, political democracy and stability, and international responsibility. He says that what divides Cuba from other nations of the hemisphere "is the fact that a small band of conspirators has stripped the Cuban people of their freedom." But, he says that "once Cuban sovereignty has been restored, we will extend the hand of friendship and assistance...."

19 November 1963
GETTYSBURG, PENNSYLVANIA. A statement sent by President Kennedy is read at the centennial ceremony in Gettysburg National Military Park on the site where President Abraham Lincoln delivered his famous address ("Fourscore and seven years ago....") and dedicated a portion of the battlefield as a national cemetery. Kennedy's statement says, in part, "From the past man obtains the insights, wisdom, and hope to face with

Following a family dinner at the New York residence of Stephen Smith, senatorial candidate Robert F. Kennedy and wife Ethel are on their way to Democratic headquarters to wait for returns, 3 November 1964.

confidence the uncertainties of the future....On this solemn occasion let us rededicate ourselves to the perpetuation of those ideals of which Lincoln spoke so luminously. As Americans, we can do no less."

20 November 1963
WASHINGTON, D.C.   Following receipt of a report from the U.S. representative to the Geneva Radio Conference on Space Communications, President Kennedy says that the conference, which "allocated frequencies for communications satellites and adopted procedures governing their use," enables the United States to cooperate with foreign governments and businesses in develop-

ing "a single global commercial space communications system." He transmits to Congress an annual report on American participation in the United Nations in 1962. He declares that in 1962, the UN, "like most institutions devised by man...exhibited both accomplishments and shortcomings. But despite noncooperation from some members and wavering support from others, the organization moved significantly toward the goal of a peace system worldwide in scope. The United States will continue to lend vigorous support to the building of that system." The last bill Kennedy signs authorizes medals commemorating the founding of the International Ladies Garment Workers Union's first union health center.

21 November 1963

WASHINGTON, D.C. The President has a light morning schedule at the White House before leaving for Texas. He is making this trip partly because a split in the Democratic party there could hurt him in next year's election. In view of the physical abuse Adlai Stevenson suffered in Texas last month, some aides have advised him not to go, but the President thinks a visit would improve his image there, and he has decided to go anyway. He enters his office at 9:55 A.M., and, a half-hour later, he confers with U.S. Ambassador to Upper Volta Thomas S. Estes and Ambassador to Gabon Charles F. Darlington. At 10:50 A.M., he departs by helicopter for Andrews Air Force Base where he and a party board Air Force One for Texas.

SAN ANTONIO, TEXAS. At Brooks Air Force Base, President Kennedy participates in a dedication ceremony for new research facilities at the Aerospace Medical Center. In an address, he says that research in space medicine has great potential benefit for people on earth and that the United States has the talent and resources to lead the way in this endeavor. "A country as rich and powerful as this," he declares, "which bears so many burdens and responsibilities, which has so many opportunities, should be second to none....The space effort must go on. The conquest of space must and will go ahead....This nation has tossed its cap over the wall of space and we have no choice but to follow it....With the help and support of all Americans, we will climb this wall with safety and with speed—and we shall then explore the wonders on the other side."

HOUSTON, TEXAS. President Kennedy attends a meeting of the League of United Latin American Citizens at the Rice Hotel, followed by a testimonial dinner in honor of Representative Albert Thomas at the Coliseum.

IRVING, TEXAS. In the evening, Lee Harvey Oswald visits his family at the Paine house. He will stay the night, leaving the next morning for his job at the Texas School Book Depository in Dallas.

22 November 1963

FORT WORTH, TEXAS. A brief rally is held in a parking lot in front of the Texas Hotel at 8:45 A.M. (C.S.T.). President Kennedy addresses the enthusiastic crowd, telling them, "What we are trying to do in this country...and around the world...is to build a military structure which will defend the vital interests of the United States." Then he goes inside the hotel where he

speaks at a Chamber of Commerce breakfast. He talks of ways in which the United States works for freedom around the world and how the people of Texas have participated in the maintenance of America's security. "So I am glad to come to this state," he says, "which has played such a significant role in so many efforts of this country...." With the President are Vice-President Lyndon B. Johnson, Governor John B. Connally, and Senator Ralph W. Yarborough. The three men have accompanied him since he arrived in Texas the day before. Following the breakfast, President Kennedy will move on to Dallas and then to Austin for other addresses later in the day.

DALLAS, TEXAS. The Presidential plane lands at Love Field at 11:39 A.M. (C.S.T.). Ten minutes later, a motorcade leaves the airport for a 45-minute ride to downtown Dallas where President Kennedy is to speak at an annual meeting of the Citizens Council at the Trade Mart.

President and Mrs. Kennedy sit in the back seat of an open "bubbletop" limousine. In the front are two Secret Service agents, Roy Kellerman and Bill Geer, the driver. Governor John B. Connally and his wife, Nellie, take seats behind the driver and in front of the Kennedys. Behind the President's 1961 Lincoln Continental is a car of Secret Service agents, followed by the car carrying Vice-President and Mrs. Johnson, then another car of Secret Service agents and the vehicles carrying reporters.

Hordes of Texans along the route cheer President Kennedy. The motorcade reaches downtown Dallas and proceeds on Main Street. It then turns right on Houston Street and makes a sharp left turn onto Elm. While it moves slowly toward a triple underpass, a sniper aims a rifle with a telescopic sight from an upper floor of the Texas School Book Depository at 411 Elm Street. The bright, peaceful day is shattered when, at 12:30 P.M., shots ring out. One bullet strikes President Kennedy at the base of the neck, a little to the right of the spine. Another hits Governor Connally, seated by the right passenger door and facing left, in his back. A third bullet enters the right rear of the President's head, and brain tissue splatters over the car. The President falls over onto his wife. The car accelerates as a secret-service agent from the car behind leaps into the back, then speeds off. In the pandemonium at the scene, a number of witnesses point to the Texas School Book Depository as the source of the gunfire.

12:33 P.M. * Marrion Baker, a Dallas policeman searching the Texas School Book Depository, encounters a man

---

* All times are Central Standard Time.

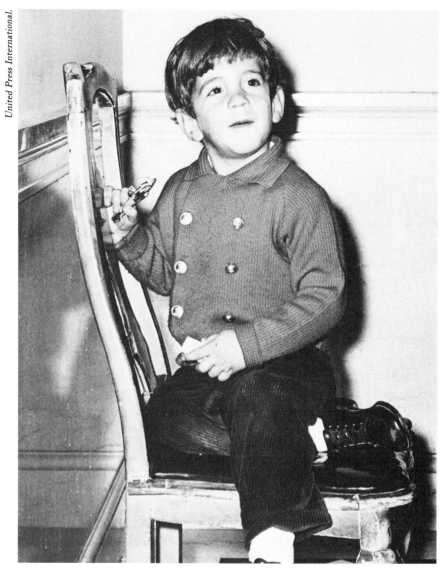

United Press International.

**John F. Kennedy, Jr., at the election night dinner held by
Stephen and Jean Kennedy Smith, 3 November 1964.**

named Lee Harvey Oswald on the second floor. After the building superintendent identifies the empty-handed Oswald as an employee, however, Baker lets him go.

12:39 P.M. Lee Harvey Oswald leaves the Texas School Book Depository.

12:45 P.M. Based on the observations of a witness claiming to have seen a man in the Texas School Book Depository aiming a rifle, a description of a suspect is broadcast by police.

12:55 P.M. Dallas police locate the specific site from which the shots were fired. It is by a window on the southeast corner of the sixth floor of the Texas School Book Depository.

1:00 P.M. President Kennedy is pronounced dead by physicians at Parkland Memorial Hospital. Some fifteen doctors had tried in vain to save him. A Catholic priest and his assistant have administered last rites. Connally's wounds are serious, but not fatal.

Having taken a bus and a taxi and then walking several blocks, Lee Harvey Oswald enters his rooming house at 1026 North Beckley Avenue.

1:04 P.M. Lee Harvey Oswald leaves his rooming house.

1:10 P.M. The stock market plummets, and the New York Stock Exchange is shut down.

1:14 P.M. From a patrol car, Dallas policeman J. D. Tippit sees a man who fits the description of the suspect walking on East 10th Street. Tippit stops, and the man approaches the car. After a few words, Tippit gets out of his car and the man, only a few feet away, opens fire, killing Tippit.

1:30 P.M. The manhunt continues in the city for the assassin of the late President.

1:41 P.M. The cashier of the Texas Theater calls police to inform them that a suspicious-looking man has entered the movie house. She has been alerted by a store manager who had earlier seen the man attempt to hide in his doorway as a police car passed.

1:45 P.M. Police enter the Texas Theater. The suspect is told to stand. He draws a gun but is overcome by the police and arrested.

2:38 P.M. Aboard Air Force One at Love Field, Lyndon B. Johnson takes the oath of office as president of the United States. U.S. District Court Judge Sarah T. Hughes swears in the thirty-sixth president.

2:40 P.M. Air Force One takes off from Love Field with the body of the late President aboard.

ANDREWS AIR FORCE BASE, MARYLAND. At 5:58 P.M. (E.S.T.), Air Force One arrives here. President Lyndon B. Johnson makes a brief statement and departs for the White House by helicopter. President Kennedy's body is taken to Bethesda Naval Medical Center for an autopsy.

DALLAS, TEXAS. At 7:15 P.M. (C.S.T.), Lee Harvey Oswald is arraigned for the murder of Patrolman J. D. Tippit.

23 November 1963

People from every nation mourn the death of President Kennedy, as the shock and sorrow of his passing continue.

WASHINGTON, D.C. President Lyndon Johnson signs a proclamation declaring the late John F. Kennedy "a man of wisdom, strength and peace." He then appoints Monday, 25 November, a day of national mourning. The body of the late President lies in state in the East Room of the White House.

DALLAS, TEXAS. At police headquarters, Lee Harvey Oswald, 24, is questioned and formally charged with the assassination of President John F. Kennedy. Oswald, however, does not admit guilt.

24 November 1963

DALLAS, TEXAS. Authorities lead Lee Harvey Oswald through a basement corridor in police headquarters for transfer to the Dallas County Jail. The proceedings are televised. At 11:20 A.M. , 52-year-old Jack Ruby lurches forward from a crowd of reporters and shoots Oswald in the stomach with a Colt .38. Ruby is subdued by police, and Oswald is rushed to Parkland Memorial Hospital. Doctors frantically operate in an attempt to save him, but he is pronounced dead at 1:06 P.M.

WASHINGTON, D.C. The caisson bearing John Kennedy's coffin is drawn in a procession from the White House to the Capitol. Masses of people line the streets. The casket is carried into the Capitol and placed in the Rotunda where, over the next day, people will pay their last respects to the fallen president.

25 November 1963

ARLINGTON, VIRGINIA. At Arlington National Cemetery, Jacqueline, Robert, and Edward Kennedy light the Eternal Flame and President Kennedy is laid to rest. The Kennedy family is present, except for Joseph P. Kennedy, who watches the proceedings on television at his Hyannis Port home.

26 November 1963

DALLAS, TEXAS. Jack Ruby is indicted for the murder of Lee Harvey Oswald.

WASHINGTON, D.C. The Domestic Names Committee of the United States Board of Geographic Names formally changes the name Cape Canaveral to Cape Kennedy.

29 November 1963

WASHINGTON, D.C. President Johnson issues executive order 11129 changing the name of Cape Canaveral Auxiliary Air Force Station and the Launch Operations Center of the National Aeronautics and Space Administration to the John F. Kennedy Space Center. The President also appoints a commission, under the leadership of Chief Justice of the Supreme Court Earl Warren, to investigate John Kennedy's assassination.

United Press International.

At groundbreaking ceremonies for the John F. Kennedy Center for the Performing Arts in Washington, D.C. on 2 December 1964, Jean Kennedy Smith, Bishop Philip Hannan of Washington, Robert Kennedy, and President Johnson.

The other members of the commission are Representative Gerald R. Ford, of Michigan, former CIA head Allen W. Dulles, former World Bank president John J. McCloy, Representative T. Hale Boggs, Senator Richard B. Russell, and Senator John Sherman Cooper.

4 December 1963
ARLINGTON, VIRGINIA. The bodies of the Kennedys' unnamed baby girl, still-born in 1956, and Patrick Bouvier Kennedy, who died in August of this year, are brought to Washington aboard the *Caroline*, then interred in graves on either side of their father, the girl to the right, the boy to the left, at Arlington National Cemetery.

WASHINGTON, D.C. Attorney General Robert Kennedy returns to work for the first time since his brother's assassination.

6 December 1963

WASHINGTON, D.C. At a ceremony in the White House, President Johnson confers the Presidential Medal of Freedom, created in February by the late President Kennedy, on thirty-one recipients. In awarding a posthumous medal to the late President, the new President says, "John Kennedy is gone. Each of us will know that we are the lesser for his death. But each is somehow larger because he lived." Robert Kennedy accepts the award.

10 December 1963

WASHINGTON, D.C. President Johnson sends legislation to Congress authorizing the Treasury Department to mint half-dollar coins bearing the image of the late President Kennedy. Congressional approval is necessary because the designs of American coins may not be changed more than once in twenty-five years without an act of the legislative body.

20 December 1963

CAPE CANAVERAL, FLORIDA. Carrying out President Johnson's executive order of 29 November 1963, James Webb, administrator of the National Aeronautics and Space Administration, issues an order changing the name of NASA's Launch Operations Center to the John F. Kennedy Space Center.

22 December 1963

WASHINGTON, D.C. A candlelight ceremony at the Lincoln Memorial marks the end of a month of national mourning for the late President Kennedy.

30 December 1963

WASHINGTON, D.C. Congress enacts public law 88-256 directing the United States Mint to manufacture John F. Kennedy 50-cent pieces. With the minting of the Kennedy 50-cent pieces, the Benjamin Franklin half-dollars will be discontinued.

2 January 1964

PHILADELPHIA, PENNSYLVANIA. Mayor James H. Tate signs a bill changing the name of the Philadelphia Municipal Stadium at Broad Street and Pattison Avenue to the John F. Kennedy Stadium. In December, the City Council passed an ordinance providing for the new name.

7 January 1964

CAPE KENNEDY, FLORIDA. Cape Canaveral Air Force Station is renamed Cape Kennedy Air Force Station by the United States Air Force.

10 January 1964

WASHINGTON, D.C. After several hearings, Congress amends the National Cultural Center Act of 1958 by passing the John F. Kennedy Center Act (public law 88-260), which designates the planned performing arts center in the nation's capital as a memorial to the late President Kennedy. On 2 September 1958, President Dwight D. Eisenhower had signed the National Cultural Center Act establishing "a national institution dedicated to the performing arts." Because of Kennedy's great interest in the arts, trustees of the National Cultural Center and associates of the late president thought it would be appropriate to name the center after him. With the stipulation that the center would be the only memorial to President Kennedy in the capital, the Kennedy family agreed.

14 January 1964

WASHINGTON, D.C. Jacqueline Kennedy thanks the American people over national television for their outpouring of condolences. The former first lady made the tape of her first public statement since the assassination in Robert F. Kennedy's Justice Department office.

17-27 January 1964

THE FAR EAST. Sent on the peace mission by President Lyndon B. Johnson, Robert F. Kennedy mediates a six-month cease fire between Indonesia and the Federation of Malaysia, thus bringing this bitter conflict to a temporary halt. Malaysia, consisting of Malaya and the former British territories of Singapore, Sarawak, and Sabah, was established on 16 September 1963. President Sukarno of Indonesia, who claims that the federation was created to maintain Great Britain's economic presence in the region, has opposed it from the start.

23 January 1964

BANGKOK, THAILAND. Robert F. Kennedy announces that he has negotiated a halt to fighting on the border of Indonesia and Malaysia. In mediating this dispute, Kennedy is serving as President Johnson's personal representative.

WASHINGTON, D.C. President Johnson signs into law the John F. Kennedy Center Act, a bill passed by Congress thirty days ago.

27 January 1964

WASHINGTON, D.C. After a thirteen-day tour of the Far East, where he represented President Johnson in talks with the heads of government in the Philippines, Ja-

Robert Kennedy visits losing candidate in the N.Y. mayor election, 15 September 1965.

pan, Indonesia, Thailand, Malaysia, and Korea, Robert Kennedy returns to his duties as attorney general.

3 February 1964
WASHINGTON, D.C. The Warren Commission begins hearings on the Kennedy assassination.

5 February 1964
NEW YORK. With Rose Kennedy at a dinner given by the Joseph P. Kennedy, Jr. Foundation, President Lyn-

don B. Johnson presents awards to those who have made major contributions to the field of mental retardation.

11 February 1964
DENVER, COLORADO, and PHILADELPHIA, PENNSYLVANIA. The first Kennedy half-dollars are struck at mints in these two cities.

17 February 1964
WASHINGTON, D.C. A son, Mark Kennedy, is

Jacqueline Kennedy at a ceremony in Sihanoukville, Cambodia, where a street is named for her late husband. Date unknown.

United Press International.

United Press International.

Caroline Kennedy on horse at Hyde Park in London, Spring 1965.

born to Eunice (Kennedy) and R. Sargent Shriver, Jr. He is their fourth child and third son.

17 February 1964

BOSTON. The Boston *Traveler* runs an interview with Miss Myra Fiske, the headmistress of Nobles and Greenough Lower School/Dexter School when John Kennedy was in the second, third, and fourth grades. "I especially remember him," she recalls, "because he was so eager to help everybody in need, whether it was another boy or a teacher, and I still feel so grateful that he was a part of Dexter School in those days....When Jack was with us—he was always 'Jack' and he always will be—I can truly say that we all held him in great affection."

14 March 1964

DALLAS, TEXAS. The jury in the murder trial of

Jack Ruby arrives at a verdict of guilty and recommends the death sentence.

17 March 1964
SCRANTON, PENNSYLVANIA. Robert Kennedy breaks the ground for the first elementary school in America to be named after the late President Kennedy.

24 March 1964
THE UNITED STATES. The Kennedy half-dollar is put into circulation. The mints ship 26 million coins to the Federal Reserve Banks and branches, which, in turn, fill orders from commercial banks.

9 April 1964
WASHINGTON, D.C. In his maiden address to the Senate, Edward M. Kennedy urges passage of the civil-rights bill. Its enactment was so much his brother's wish, he says, that the "heart and soul" of President Kennedy is in the legislation.

Lord Harlech, Kennedy friend and former British ambassador to the U.S., Queen Elizabeth, John Kennedy, Jr., and Jacqueline Kennedy at a ceremony dedicating a shrine in honor of the late JFK at Runnymede, England, 14 May 1965.

United Press International.

11 April 1964
NORFOLK, VIRGINIA.   Services are held for Gen. Douglas MacArthur, the World War II hero who died six days ago at the age of 83. Many foreign dignitaries are present for the burial at the MacArthur Memorial. Attorney General Robert F. Kennedy, accompanied by his wife Ethel, attends on behalf of President Johnson.

CHATTANOOGA, TENNESSEE.   James R. Hoffa is again in court, accused of tampering with the jury in his 1962 trial for violations of the Taft-Hartley Act. The prosecution cites a witness's report that the Teamsters president threatened to murder Robert Kennedy, but Hoffa denies the charge.

22 April 1964
NEW YORK.   The New York World's Fair officially opens. The theme of the United States pavilion, originally proposed by the late President Kennedy, is "Challenge to Greatness." Kennedy had visited the site when construction began in December of 1962.

26 May 1964
NEW YORK.   Substituting for Robert Kennedy, Rose Kennedy makes the address at dedication ceremonies of several new cottages at the Lt. Joseph P. Kennedy, Jr. Home for Neglected Children in the Bronx.

29 May 1964
THE UNITED STATES.   The United States Postal Service issues a 5-cent memorial stamp honoring the late President John F. Kennedy today, the forty-seventh anniversary of his birth. The stamp bears a portrait of the late president, an illustration of the eternal flame, and a quote from Kennedy's inaugural address, "...and the glow from that fire can truly light the world." Jacqueline Kennedy selected the design from 100 submissions.

1 June 1964
WASHINGTON, D.C.   Joan (Bennett) Kennedy suffers a miscarriage at Georgetown Hospital, where she was admitted four days earlier.

8 June 1964
WASHINGTON, D.C.   R. Sargent Shriver receives an honorary Doctor of Laws degree from Georgetown University.

16 June 1964
ROME.   Ethel (Skakel) Kennedy and her children Kathleen, Joseph III, and Robert, Jr., have an audience with Pope Paul VI at the Vatican.

19 June 1964
SOUTHAMPTON, MASSACHUSETTS.   A plane carrying Edward M. Kennedy and four others to Springfield crashes in poor weather. Two passengers are killed, and Senator Kennedy suffers cracked vertebrae and broken ribs. Kennedy's private plane had been on its way from Washington, D.C., to a Massachusetts Democratic convention.

24 June 1964
NEW YORK.   Robert F. Kennedy, with his wife, Ethel, and children Kathleen, Joe, and Bobby, Jr., leave for a week-long visit to West Germany and Poland.

25 June 1964
FRANKFURT, WEST GERMANY.   The Robert Kennedys begin their tour, which will include stops made by President John Kennedy when he visited the country a year ago.

BONN, WEST GERMANY.   On this first leg of the visit, Robert F. Kennedy meets with representatives of the West German government.

26 June 1964
WEST BERLIN, WEST GERMANY.   At the Schoneberger Rathaus, where President Kennedy delivered a speech a year earlier, Robert F. Kennedy unveils a plaque erected in front of the city hall in honor of his late brother. Before a quarter of a million people, he says, "A man from West Berlin is not free until his brother from East Berlin is free also," and he repeats his brother's words, "Ich bin ein Berliner." Later, Robert Kennedy receives an honorary degree from the Free University of Berlin, where he addresses an audience of a few thousand. He tells them that although President Kennedy is dead, the hope he offered for a better world lives on. "The torch still burns," he declares, "and because it does, there remains for all of us a chance to light up the tomorrows and brighten the future."

27 June 1964
HEIDELBERG, WEST GERMANY.   Robert F. Kennedy calls on West Germany to help the United States fight off communism in South Vietnam in a speech at the University of Heidelberg.

28 June 1964
WARSAW, POLAND.   Continuing on their tour of two European countries, the Robert Kennedys are greeted by large crowds here.

United Press International.

Rose Kennedy, left, and the Duchess of Windsor at the Paris Ball in New York, 29 October 1965.

30 June 1964

CZESTOCHOWA, POLAND. Despite efforts by Poland's Communist government to prevent the meeting, Robert F. Kennedy talks with the leader of Poland's Roman Catholic church, Stefan Cardinal Wyszynski.

CAPE COD, MASSACHUSETTS. Mary Moore, a close friend of Rose Kennedy for over forty years, dies at Cape Cod Hospital after suffering burns earlier in the month in a fire at the Centerville Nursing Home.

1 July 1964

NEW YORK. Robert and Ethel Kennedy and their children return to the United States.

2 July 1964

WASHINGTON, D.C. President Johnson signs the Civil Rights Act of 1964 (PL88-352). In a special message to Congress in June of 1963, President Kennedy had

declared it "imperative" that both houses enact the Civil Rights Act of 1963 in its then-current session.

8 July 1964

WASHINGTON, D.C. At a conference of United States attorneys, President Johnson praises Robert F. Kennedy's outstanding service in seeing to the rights of the underprivileged when they appear in court.

19 July 1964

WASHINGTON, D.C. The Advisory Board on National Parks, Historic Sites, Buildings, and Monuments designates the house where the late John F. Kennedy was born a National Historic Landmark. The house is at 83 Beals Street in Brookline, Massachusetts.

29 July 1964

WASHINGTON, D.C. In his White House office, President Johnson informs Robert F. Kennedy that he has ruled out having any member of his cabinet run with

Jackie Kennedy flanked by U.N. Secretary General U Thant (left), and Francis
Cardinal Spellman at a U.N. reception, 30 January 1967.

him as the vice-presidential candidate on the Democratic
ticket in November. This eliminates Kennedy from the
number-two spot on Johnson's ticket in the upcoming
election.

8 August 1964

BOSTON. Mary Josephine (Hannon) Fitzgerald
dies of a heart attack at the age of 98. The widow of former mayor John Fitzgerald dies at her home at 3 Rundel
Park in Dorchester. At the time of her death, the maternal grandmother of the late President Kennedy does not

know that her grandson has been assassinated. She leaves
two sons, Thomas and John Jr., a daughter, Rose
Kennedy, and numerous grandchildren and great-grandchildren.

10 August 1964

NEW YORK. In an address before members of the
American Bar Association, Attorney General Robert F.
Kennedy announces the formation of the Office of Criminal Justice. This "watchdog" division of the Justice Department will ensure that the rights of the poor are fairly

United Press International.

Pat Lawford, Stephen Smith, Jean Smith, Senator Edward Kennedy, Rose Kennedy, and Joan Kennedy at a fund-raising dinner in New York, 1969.

and legally served in the criminal process, from arrest to rehabilitation.

11 August 1964
BOSTON. The funeral of Mary (Hannon) Fitzgerald takes place at St. Brendan's Church in Dorchester.

Due to the fact that Richard Cardinal Cushing of Boston is on a trip in Peru, another close friend of the Kennedy family, Francis Cardinal Spellman, Archbishop of New York, presides. Over 1,000 persons, including political and religious leaders, jam the church. Later, the body is interred at St. Joseph's Cemetery in West Roxbury.

Senator Edward M. Kennedy

FIVE

THE POLITICAL HEIRS

1964 · PRESENT

ROBERT F. KENNEDY
1964-1968

21 August 1964
NEW YORK. Mayor Robert F. Wagner endorses Robert F. Kennedy as Democratic nominee for the New York U.S. Senate seat.

23 August 1964
NEW YORK. Only a day before the Democratic National Convention, Robert F. Kennedy withdraws as a Massachusetts delegate. He is seriously considering seeking his party's nomination for Kenneth Keating's New York Senate seat. He also announces that he will take up temporary residence in New York City.

24 August 1964
ATLANTIC CITY, NEW JERSEY. The Democratic National Convention opens.

25 August 1964
NEW YORK. At Gracie Mansion, Attorney General Robert F. Kennedy officially declares his candidacy for the Democratic nomination for U.S. senator from New York. This is the first elective office he has sought, and charges have already been made that he is a "carpetbagger," running for an office in one state when he lives and votes in another.

At a news conference on the front lawn of Gracie Mansion, Robert F. Kennedy announces his candidacy for the Democratic senatorial nomination, saying, "I shall devote all my efforts and whatever talents I possess to the state of New York. This I pledge."

27 August 1964
ATLANTIC CITY, NEW JERSEY. On the last day of the Democratic National Convention, which has nominated Lyndon B. Johnson and Hubert H. Humphrey to head the party ticket in November, Robert F. Kennedy is brought onstage to present the film *A Thousand Days* about John F. Kennedy's presidential years. Kennedy gives a brief emotional address in which he evokes the memory of his late brother with a quote from Shakespeare's *Romeo and Juliet:* "When he shall die take him and cut him out into stars and he shall make the face of heaven so fine that all the world will be in love with night and pay no worship to the garish sun."

31 August 1964
NEW YORK. Senator Kenneth Keating, the Republican incumbent, wins the New York State Republican nomination for the U.S. Senate seat by acclamation of the convention.

1 September 1964
NEW YORK. At the New York State Democratic Convention, Robert Kennedy wins the nomination for U.S. senator on the first ballot by a wide margin. Nominated by Mayor Robert F. Wagner of New York, he is chosen over Representative Samuel Stratton of Amsterdam.

3 September 1964
WASHINGTON, D.C. Robert F. Kennedy resigns as attorney general of the United States.

NEW YORK. Stephen E. Smith is named Robert Kennedy's campaign manager.

10 September 1964
MASSACHUSETTS. Edward M. Kennedy, running unopposed in the primary, wins the Democratic nomination for U.S. senator from Massachusetts. The election results are: Kennedy, 608,791 votes; all others, 32; blanks, 142,115 (total votes cast, 750,938).

BOSTON. Mary (Hannon) Fitzgerald, who died last August, leaves an estate estimated at $32,300, according to her will filed in Suffolk Probate Court. Under the terms of the will, her daughter, Rose Kennedy, receives nothing. The will was executed on 25 May 1955.

24 September 1964
WASHINGTON, D.C. The Warren Report, a study of the assassination of the late President Kennedy, is presented to President Lyndon Johnson. The seven-person commission concludes that "on the basis of the evidence" before it, "the shots which killed President Kennedy and wounded Governor Connally were fired by Lee Harvey Oswald" and that Oswald "acted alone."

27 September 1964
WASHINGTON, D.C. The Warren Report on the assassination of President John F. Kennedy is released.

7 October 1964
PALM BEACH, FLORIDA. Today is the fiftieth wedding anniversary of Joe and Rose Kennedy.

Courtesy Joseph P. Kennedy II. Photographer unknown.

Bobby and Joe II, aged 10, horsing around at Hyannis, 1962.

Joe, Sr. and Rose in 1958 at Hickory Hill with their grandchildren (l. to r.) RFK, Jr., Joe II, Maria Schriver, Bobby Schriver, Kathleen, and David.

15 October 1964

BOSTON. Under his instructions, Robert F. Kennedy's name is deleted from the Massachusetts voting list.

16 October 1964

WASHINGTON, D.C. R. Sargent Shriver, Jr., becomes the head of the Office of Economic Opportunity, a government agency established to help relieve poverty in economically distressed areas of America.

20 October 1964

NEW YORK. *The Pursuit of Justice,* a 148-page book by Robert F. Kennedy, is published by Harper & Row.

30 October 1964

NEW YORK. Senatorial candidates Kenneth Keating and Robert Kennedy debate each other on Barry Gray's radio program.

3 November 1964

THE UNITED STATES. Democrats Lyndon B. Johnson and Hubert Humphrey defeat Republicans Barry M. Goldwater and William E. Miller and become president and vice-president. This will be Johnson's first full term as president.

MASSACHUSETTS. Edward Kennedy is elected to his first full term as U.S. senator from Massachusetts. In a landslide victory, he receives nearly 75 percent of the popular vote. With 1,716,907 votes, he defeats Republican candidate Howard Whitmore, Jr., who polls 587,663 votes. Kennedy, hospitalized since his plane crash last June, had been unable to make campaign appearances. Leverett S. Saltonstall (Republican) is the other senator from Massachusetts.

NEW YORK. Robert Kennedy is elected U.S. senator from the state of New York. He defeats incumbent Senator Kenneth B. Keating by a plurality of over a half-million votes. The election results are: Kennedy (Democrat), 3,823,749 votes; Keating (Republican), 3,104,056; Henry Paolucci (Conservative), 212,216; John Emmanuel (Socialist Labor), 7,358; and Richard Garza (Socialist Workers), 4,202. Kennedy's campaign was marked by charges of "carpetbagging," and, in fact, he is ineligible to vote in New York State because he has not been a resident of New York long enough. Jacob Javits (Republican) is the other senator from New York.

17 November 1964

MEXICO CITY. A large housing project named for the late John F. Kennedy is dedicated. Robert Kennedy participates in the ceremony with President Mateos.

22 November 1964

CANADA. Prime Minister Lester B. Pearson announces the naming of Mount Kennedy, the highest unclimbed Canadian mountain, to the House of Commons. This memorial to the late American president had been requested by Pearson, and Dr. Bradford Washburn, director of the Boston Museum of Science, had selected the mountain. Formerly called East Hubbard, Mount Kennedy is in the St. Elias Range in the Yukon Territory, 60° and 20 minutes north, and 138° and 58 minutes, 30 seconds west.

2 December 1964

WASHINGTON, D.C. Ground-breaking for the John F. Kennedy Center for the Performing Arts begins as President Johnson lifts the first shovelful of dirt. Among the guests are Robert and Ethel (Skakel) Kennedy, Edward and Joan (Bennett) Kennedy, Eunice (Kennedy) Shriver, Jean (Kennedy) Smith, Lady Bird Johnson, and Mr. and Mrs. Hubert Humphrey. Congress has authorized $15.5 million toward the construction of the center.

3 December 1964

WASHINGTON, D.C. An honorary Doctor of Laws degree is posthumously bestowed upon the late President Kennedy by Georgetown University.

4 December 1964

INDIANAPOLIS, INDIANA. Bobbs-Merrill Company publishes *Rights for Americans: The Speeches of Robert F. Kennedy*, a 262-page book edited and with a commentary by Thomas Hopkins.

11 December 1964

SYRACUSE, NEW YORK. Senator-elect Robert F. Kennedy continues his tour of upstate New York, meeting with political leaders and voters.

31 December 1964

WASHINGTON, D.C. The Joseph P. Kennedy, Jr. Foundation has committed grants of $1,123,000 to the Stanford University School of Medicine, $1,500,000 to the University of Chicago for laboratories to study mental retardation, and $1,450,000 to the Albert Einstein College of Medicine in New York for the Rose Kennedy Institute for the Study of Mental Retardation.

4 January 1965

WASHINGTON, D.C. As the Eighty-ninth Congress convenes, Robert F. Kennedy, 39, and Edward M. Kennedy, 32, are sworn in as United States senators from New York and Massachusetts, respectively. It is the first time that two brothers will serve simultaneously in the Senate since Theodore and Dwight Foster both sat from 1800 to 1803. (Theodore Foster represented Rhode Island from 1790 to 1803; his brother, Dwight, represented Massachusetts from 1800 to 1803.) In this session, Robert Kennedy will serve on the District of Columbia, Government Operations, and Labor and Public Welfare committees; Edward will serve on the Judiciary and the Labor and Public Welfare committees. Senator Edward Kennedy, who had been seriously injured in a plane crash last June, has kept his promise that he would be present when this Congress opens.

11 January 1965

NEW YORK. A son, Matthew Maxwell Taylor, is born to Ethel (Skakel) Kennedy and Robert Kennedy at Roosevelt Hospital. Their ninth child and sixth son, he is delivered by Caesarean section. The baby is named after family friend Maxwell D. Taylor, American ambassador to South Vietnam.

20 January 1965

WASHINGTON, D.C. Lyndon B. Johnson takes the oath of office as president, and Hubert H. Humphrey is sworn in as vice-president.

5 February 1965

NEW YORK. At the second annual awards dinner of the Joseph P. Kennedy, Jr. Foundation, at the Carlyle Hotel, President Johnson presents achievement awards totaling over $200,000 to six recipients for their promotion of research on mental retardation. At the dinner, Prime Minister Lester B. Pearson of Canada presents the foundation with $70,000 and announces the establishment in Canada of a John F. Kennedy Memorial Fund for Mental Retardation.

Bobby and Ethel relaxing at Hickory Hill with their pet dog and children (l. to r.) Michael, RFK, Jr., David, Kathleen, Courtney, and Joe II. c. 1950's.

Courtesy Joseph P. Kennedy II. Ollie Atkins

10 February 1965

NEW YORK.   Responding to reports that state legislators have been hiring supporters to fill open positions, Senator Robert F. Kennedy sends a letter to Democratic leaders to ask that they award jobs on the basis of merit, not patronage. He recommends that they conduct a talent search to find the best-qualified candidates and questions the number of jobs being offered.

23 February 1965

WASHINGTON, D.C.   Senator Robert F. Kennedy declares that the United States should give military support to the South Vietnamese government to keep the Communists out of the country, but for "not a minute more than is necessary."

25 February 1965

[?]   A deed providing for the donation of the late John F. Kennedy's "papers and other historical materials" to a planned library devoted to his presidency and personal life is signed by Jacqueline Kennedy, Robert F. Kennedy, and Edward M. Kennedy.

22 March 1965

YUKON TERRITORY, CANADA. With the goal of becoming the first man to scale the mountain named in honor of his late brother, Robert Kennedy and a party of seven begin an ascent of Mount Kennedy. They leave from a base camp at 9,000 feet, where they were dropped by a Royal Canadian Air Force helicopter. Another base camp is waiting at 12,000 feet. Mount Kennedy, almost 4 miles inside the Canadian border, is 13,880 feet high.

24 March 1965

YUKON TERRITORY, CANADA. At about 1:00 P.M., Robert Kennedy reaches the top of Mount Kennedy. At the 13,880-foot peak, he plants a family flag and the Canadian flag, then buries a copy of the late President's 20 January 1961 inaugural address, a John F. Kennedy medallion, and the National Geographic emblem. James Whittaker and Barry W. Prather, members of the American team that conquered Mount Everest, reach the summit with him.

5 April 1965

WASHINGTON, D.C. Senator Robert F. Kennedy introduces a bill to amend the statute denying the right to vote to those who fail a literacy test.

9 April 1965

NEW YORK. *Life* magazine publishes Robert Kennedy's "Our Climb Up Mount Kennedy," the Senator's first-person account of the climb he and a small party recently made in Canada.

14 May 1965

RUNNYMEDE, ENGLAND. Queen Elizabeth II dedicates a shrine here honoring the late President John F. Kennedy. Jacqueline Kennedy is present at the ceremony. Runnymede, near London, is the site where King John signed the *Magna Carta* in 1215. The inscription on the monument to Kennedy reads: "This acre of English ground was given to the United States of America by the people of Britain in memory of John F. Kennedy (born 29 May 1917), President of the United States 1961-1963. Died by an assassin's hand on 22 November 1963. Let every nation know whether it wishes us well or ill that we shall pay any price, bear any burden, meet any hardship, support any friend, or oppose any foe in order to assure the survival and success of liberty."

17 May 1965

WEST HANOVER, MASSACHUSETTS. *The Fruitful Bough,* a privately printed book containing rec-

ollections and essays about Joseph Kennedy by friends and family, compiled by Edward M. Kennedy, is in production at the Halliday Lithograph Corporation on Circuit Street.

20 May 1965

WASHINGTON, D.C. The Senate passes a bill co-sponsored by Senators Robert F. Kennedy and Jacob Javits of New York that extends voting rights to those who cannot read or write English but who meet certain academic requirements.

26 May 1965

NEW YORK. Because his political duties require Senator Robert F. Kennedy to remain in Washington, Rose Kennedy reads her son's speech at a dedication ceremony of three new cottages at the Lt. Joseph P. Kennedy, Jr. Home in the Bronx.

29 May 1965

FORT BRAGG, NORTH CAROLINA. The headquarters of the U.S. Army's John F. Kennedy Center for Special Warfare is dedicated in honor of the late president. Robert and Ethel Kennedy and several of their children are present at the ceremony to dedicate John F. Kennedy Hall as command headquarters.

BROOKLINE, MASSACHUSETTS. The house at 83 Beals Street, owned by the Kennedys from 1914 to 1921, is designated a National Historic Landmark. The late President John F. Kennedy was born here, as were his brother Joe and sisters Rosemary and Kathleen. A plaque and certificate are presented at the ceremony.

31 May 1965

SCRANTON, PENNSYLVANIA. The John F. Kennedy Elementary School is dedicated.

1 June 1965

WEST HARTFORD, CONNECTICUT. Rose Kennedy receives an honorary degree from St. Joseph's College at its thirtieth annual commencement exercises. She receives this honor for her outstanding contributions in the area of mental retardation.

16 June 1965

WASHINGTON, D.C. In a Senate debate Robert F. Kennedy favors bill S. 539 requesting cigarette packages to display a warning against the hazards of smoking.

23 June 1965

WASHINGTON, D.C. In his maiden speech before

the Senate, Senator Robert F. Kennedy calls upon the Johnson administration to initiate immediate negotiations with Russia and any other country with nuclear power for a nonproliferation agreement. He asks that all American aid to any country in developing nuclear capability be halted until that country permits international inspection of its reactors.

20 July 1965
BOSTON. A son, Anthony Paul, is born to Eunice (Kennedy) and R. Sargent Shriver, Jr. He is their fifth child and fourth son.

30 July 1965
WASHINGTON, D.C. President Johnson signs into law the medical-care-for-the-aged legislation urged by the late President Kennedy (Medicare PL89-97). Congress had passed the legislation two days ago.

29 August 1965
HYANNIS PORT, MASSACHUSETTS. Riding in a West Barnstable horse show, Kathleen Kennedy, 14, suffers a concussion and internal injuries when her horse, Attorney General, misses a jump and falls on her. She is rushed by police ambulance to Cape Cod Hospital for treatment.

13 September 1965
TORONTO, CANADA. The Canadian Association for Retarded Children awards its first International Award for Distinguished Service in the Field of Mental Retardation to Rose Kennedy. Among the political dignitaries present is Prime Minister Lester B. Pearson.

4 October 1965
NEW YORK. Pope Paul VI delivers an address before the General Assembly of the United Nations. With Jacqueline Kennedy, Senator Robert F. Kennedy attends the speech and a reception held afterward in a delegates room at the UN.

5 October 1965
NEW YORK. *Kennedy*, a study of the late president by his speechwriter and top aide, Theodore C. Sorensen, is published by Harper & Row.

13 October 1965
WASHINGTON, D.C. Robert F. Kennedy proposes before the Senate that Communist China be included in the United Nations Disarmament Committee, to be held in January at Geneva, Switzerland.

21 October 1965
BOSTON. At a legislative committee hearing to consider a bill providing state funding for a Kennedy Memorial Library, Rose Kennedy reveals that John had planned to help establish a library for his papers and records, and thanks the Commonwealth for its support.

23 October 1965
CAPETOWN, SOUTH AFRICA. A national organization of South African students announces that Senator Robert F. Kennedy has consented to participate in the next annual Day of Affirmation in May 1966.

SAIGON, SOUTH VIETNAM. Led by Senator Edward M. Kennedy, members of the Senate Judiciary Subcommittee on Refugees, begin a five-day visit here. The subcommittee is investigating ways to help refugees.

5 November 1965
LOS ANGELES, CALIFORNIA. Senator Robert F. Kennedy calls for the United States and other Western nations to "seek new answers to the problem of the military security of Western Europe" so that adequate defense measures can be taken without Russian objections.

10 November 1965
LIMA, PERU. Robert F. Kennedy and an entourage consisting of his wife and staff members begin a three-week fact-finding tour of Latin America. The Standard Oil Company subsidiary's refusal to renegotiate an existing oil-drilling contract and the consequent postponement of American economic assistance has caused some anti-American sentiment. The trip is unofficial and privately financed.

16 November 1965
SANTIAGO, CHILE. At the University of Santiago, militant Chinese students throw eggs and delay a speech by Senator Robert Kennedy. Many oppose United States support to the junta in the Dominican Republic that began last May.

19 November 1965
BUENOS AIRES, ARGENTINA. Senator Robert Kennedy speaks to student groups on the situation in the Dominican Republic.

26 November 1965
MANAUS, BRAZIL. Starting from the capital of Amazonas, a state in northwest Brazil, Robert F. Kennedy's entourage visits areas along the Amazon River and the Rio Negro.

United Press International.

Bobby with Kathleen (left), and David. c. 1960–61.

30 November 1965

CARACAS, VENEZUELA. Senator Robert F. Kennedy calls for Latin American nations to pursue communications with African and Asian countries more vigorously, particularly since they share common problems.

1 December 1965

NEW YORK. After a twenty-one-day tour of Latin America, Senator Robert F. Kennedy's party returns to the United States.

5 December 1965

WASHINGTON, D.C. Senator Robert F. Kennedy says on "Meet the Press" that American military support alone will not drive the Communists out of South Vietnam, and that perhaps more could be done economically and diplomatically.

31 December 1965

WASHINGTON, D.C. The Joseph P. Kennedy, Jr. Foundation has committee grants of $1,235,000 to the

Albert Einstein College of Medicine, $1,040,000 to Georgetown University, and $960,000 to George Peabody College for the study of ways to improve the methods and techniques for training mentally retarded children.

5 January 1966
[?]   Patricia and Peter Lawford announce their separation.

23 January 1966
MIAMI, FLORIDA.   Rose Kennedy joins Governor Haydon Burns in dedicating the Sunland Training Center for the Mentally Retarded.

31 January 1966
WASHINGTON, D.C.   Following resumption by the United States of bombing in North Vietnam, numerous pro and con speeches are given in Congress. In the Senate, Robert F. Kennedy declares that the United States is "heading straight for disaster" if it believes that bombing will win the war. President Johnson's decision to resume the bombing follows unsuccessful efforts by American representatives to persuade other countries to pressure the North Vietnamese into a negotiated peace. During the thirty-seven days that these efforts were under way, the North Vietnamese increased their terrorist activities against the South Vietnamese and ignored any attempt at a truce. Senator Kennedy expresses regret over this failure and calls for continued efforts toward peace.

1 February 1966
GOODING, IDAHO.   After nearly twelve years of marriage, Patricia (Kennedy) Lawford is granted a divorce from Peter Lawford on the grounds of "grievous mental anguish." She has fulfilled a six-week residency requirement in Idaho by living in Sun Valley. She is granted custody of their children, Christopher, 10, Sydney, 9, Victoria, 7, and Robin, 4, and their father has visitation rights. Patricia is the first Kennedy to be divorced.

NEW YORK.   A spokesman for the Archdiocese of New York announces that Patricia (Kennedy) Lawford, a Roman Catholic, will remain in good standing with the church unless she remarries.

19 February 1966
WASHINGTON, D.C.   In a statement read at a press conference, Senator Robert F. Kennedy suggests a coalition government in South Vietnam as a means of bringing peace to the region. Any negotiated settlement,

he declares, "must accept the fact that there are discontented elements in South Vietnam, Communist and non-Communist" who want to change the country's economic and political system, and this would require participation of the National Liberation Front in a South Vietnamese government. Senator Kennedy's statement is highly criticized by members of Congress and the Johnson administration.

27 February 1966
THE UNITED STATES.   Following up on his controversial statement that an end to the conflict in South Vietnam would require a coalition government that included the Communists, Senator Robert F. Kennedy appears on the "Face the Nation" to amplify his views. Realistically, he says, "in some way or another" the Viet Cong will end up "within the governmental structure of South Vietnam."

28 February 1966
WASHINGTON, D.C.   R. Sargent Shriver, Jr., submits his resignation as director of the Peace Corps in compliance with the organization's five-year maximum on administrative positions. Jack Vaughn succeeds him.

10 April 1966
WASHINGTON, D.C.   *John F. Kennedy: Years of Lightning, Days of Drums,* a documentary on the late president, commissioned by the United States Information Agency, is released worldwide.

27 April 1966
WASHINGTON, D.C.   In an address to the Senate, Robert F. Kennedy declares that the people of South Vietnam must "organize their society and government if they are to wage a successful war." He warns against the United States undertaking any escalation "until some progress has been made toward achieving the stability that is essential for the successful prosecution of our efforts in Vietnam."

1 May 1966
CAMBODIA.   American military forces become involved on combat here.

9 May 1966
WASHINGTON, D.C.   Addressing the Senate on the Alliance for Progress, Senator Robert F. Kennedy declares that the United States should reshape its Latin American policy to support the forces working for peaceful change and to maintain at least some communication with the students of the region.

Courtesy Joseph P. Kennedy II. Photographer unknown.

Bobby with Joe II. c. 1964.

GENEVA, SWITZERLAND.   Senator Edward M. Kennedy meets with representatives of the International Red Cross in an effort to have American prisoners of war in Vietnam exchanged for Viet Cong captives held in South Vietnam.

10 May 1966
WASHINGTON, D.C. Continuing his Senate speech on American policy in Latin America, Senator Robert Kennedy says that the United States should do what it can to help the region "build a better life for its

305

United Press International.

Jacqueline Kennedy leading son, John, Jr., and daughter, Caroline, at JFK International
Airport en route to Argentina for a holiday, 4 April 1966.

people," increase aid to the area, and support social reform.

11 May 1966
CAPETOWN, SOUTH AFRICA. The government of the Republic of South Africa headed by Prime Minister Hendrik F. Verwoerd bans student leader Ian Robertson from participating in activities of the National

Union of South African Students. Robertson had invited Senator Robert F. Kennedy to speak during the annual Day of Affirmation.

27 May 1966
HYANNIS PORT, MASSACHUSETTS. A single-engine World War II plane, ordered as a gift by Joseph Kennedy for his grandchildren, is delivered to the

Kennedy compound. It is placed in the yard of the late John Kennedy's summer home.

4 June 1966
JOHANNESBURG, SOUTH AFRICA. Amid much controversy, Senator Robert F. Kennedy arrives here in response to an invitation from the National Union of South African Students to participate in the Day of Affirmation. His visit has been put off a month by the South African government, whose policy of apartheid Kennedy opposes. Kennedy's party, which consists of his wife, Ethel, and a small coterie of staff members, will travel to four African nations over a two-week period.

6 June 1966
CAPETOWN, SOUTH AFRICA. Before an audience of more than 16,000 at the University of Capetown, Senator Robert F. Kennedy delivers a speech in which he condemns apartheid and praises those who champion human rights. "Each time a man stands up for an ideal," he declares, "or acts to improve the lot of others, or strikes out against injustice, he sends forth a tiny ripple of hope, and crossing each other from a million different centers of energy and daring, those ripples can build a current which can sweep down the mightiest walls of oppression and resistance."

7 June 1966
DURBAN, SOUTH AFRICA. Senator Robert Kennedy speaks on human rights before a large crowd at the University of Natal and, later, addresses another gathering nearby.

8 June 1966
GROUTVILLE, SOUTH AFRICA. Robert Kennedy meets with peace crusader Albert J. Luthuli, whose activities are restricted by policy of the South African government. Chief Luthuli had won the Nobel Prize for Peace in 1960.

9 June 1966
JOHANNESBURG, SOUTH AFRICA. During the day, Robert Kennedy visits Soweto, a poor black quarter of the city. Later, he gives an address at the University of Witwatersand, where he urges that the power of reason be used to end racial discrimination and calls for more open communications between South Africa and other countries.

10 June 1966
DAR ES SALAAM, TANZANIA. In the capital of this federation of Tanganyika and Zanzibar, Senator

Robert F. Kennedy delivers an address in which he declares that whatever form of government the people of South Vietnam vote to have, the United States will abide by their choice.

11 June 1966
MBEYA, TANZANIA. Robert Kennedy travels here to meet with American Peace Corps workers.

14 June 1966
NAIROBI, KENYA. Following a meeting with President Jomo Kenyatta, Robert Kennedy holds a press conference in which he urges American companies in Africa to hire blacks.

15 June 1966
ADDIS ABABA, ETHIOPIA. In an address before African political leaders, Senator Kennedy calls on Third World countries to press nations with nuclear weapons to try harder to reach a nuclear control agreement. He also meets with Emperor Haile Selassie I.

16 June 1966
ATHENS, GREECE. The Kennedy party visits here for two days.

18 June 1966
ROME, ITALY. Robert and Ethel Kennedy stop over for an audience with Pope Paul VI with whom they discuss the situation in Vietnam.

19 June 1966
NEW YORK. The Kennedy party returns to the United States after a fifteen-day trip to Africa, Greece, and Italy. Senator Kennedy answers questions about his trip to South Africa from reporters at JFK International Airport. Asked whether he has plans to run for president in 1968, he says that he does not and will back President Johnson for re-election.

29 June 1966
HANOI, NORTH VIETNAM. American planes begin attacks on this capital city, terminating an American moratorium on the bombing of large cities in Vietnam.

WASHINGTON, D.C. Before a hearing of the Armed Services Committee on the draft, Senator Edward M. Kennedy speaks in favor of a lottery.

4 July 1966
THE JUDEAN HILLS, ISRAEL. The John F.

Kennedy Memorial is dedicated on a hill a few miles west of Jerusalem.

17 July 1966

HYANNIS PORT, MASSACHUSETTS. Joseph P. Kennedy suffers a mild heart attack. His physician, Dr. Robert D. Watt, places him in an oxygen tent and he later improves.

8 August 1966

JACKSON, MISSISSIPPI. In the wake of race riots in several American cities, members of the Southern Christian Leadership Conference gather for their annual meeting. Addressing the convention on its first day and urging stronger federal measures to help the plight of poor black families are Martin Luther King, Jr., and Senator Edward M. Kennedy. The Senator calls for a "major upgrading" of opportunities in education, housing, and employment.

15 August 1966

WASHINGTON, D.C. On the opening day of two weeks of hearings on problems in the cities, Senator Robert Kennedy testifies before the Executive Reorganization Subcommittee of the Senate Government Operations Committee. The most pressing problem of American cities, he says, is the demoralizing condition of blacks in the ghettos, and he calls for federally funded employment programs.

16 August 1966

WASHINGTON, D.C. After meeting with Frank O'Connor, a candidate for the Democratic nomination for governor of New York, Senator Robert F. Kennedy announces that he will not endorse any Democratic candidate now but will support the candidate chosen at the national convention.

6 September 1966

CAPETOWN, SOUTH AFRICA. While seated at his bench during a parliamentary session, Prime Minister Hendrik Verwoerd of South Africa is stabbed to death. Verwoerd had declined to meet with Robert Kennedy during the Senator's trip to South Africa in June.

13 September 1966

MASSACHUSETTS. Former state attorney general Edward J. McCormick defeats Kenneth P. O'Donnell, a close friend and aide to the late President John Kennedy, in the Democratic primary for governor. Senator Edward M. Kennedy had not endorsed a candidate.

24 September 1966

RIGGINS, IDAHO. Ethel Kennedy's brother George Skakel, Jr., 44, and four others are killed when his Cessna 185 crashes into Crooked Creek Canyon. He and a party were going deer-hunting in the mountains in the western part of the state. Skakel leaves his wife, Joan, and their four children, Cathleen, George, Susan, and Mark.

27 September 1966

WASHINGTON, D.C. Senator Edward M. Kennedy is among the politicians to address participants in the Poor People's March, held to call attention to the lack of effective laws to fight poverty. Other speakers include New York Representative Adam Clayton Powell and New York Senator Jacob Javits.

5 October 1966

AUSTIN, TEXAS. The Texas Court of Criminal Appeals overturns the 14 March 1964 conviction of Jack Ruby for the murder of Lee Harvey Oswald. The presiding judge, W. A. Morrison, holds that the introduction in the trial of Ruby's jail-house confession by police sergeant Patrick Dean violated state law. Under Texas law, a murder confession must be given voluntarily and spontaneously, and during the time between Ruby's arrest and his conversation with Dean ("between 10 and 40 minutes") the defendant "had been incarcerated, undressed and interrogated by other officers...." Morrison also holds that "it is abundantly clear...that the trial court reversibly erred in refusing appellant's motion for change of venue." "For the errors pointed out," Morrison concludes, a retrial is ordered "to some county other than Dallas."

12 October 1966

NEW YORK. Senator Robert F. Kennedy accompanies President Lyndon B. Johnson as he campaigns throughout the day for local and state Democrats in the metropolitan area.

17 October 1966

CAMBRIDGE, MASSACHUSETTS. The Graduate School of Public Administration at Harvard University is renamed the John Fitzgerald Kennedy School of Government. The school, founded in 1935, offers advanced courses to those working in or intending to pursue careers in government service. In the evening, Robert F. Kennedy is a guest speaker, and members of the Kennedy family are among the guests at a dinner reception held at the Holyoke Center.

23 October 1966

LOS ANGELES.   Efforts by black leaders to use violence in combatting racial prejudice are assailed by Senator Robert F. Kennedy in an address at the University of Southern California.

31 October 1966

WASHINGTON, D.C.   Negatives, slides, and X rays taken during the autopsy of President Kennedy are donated to the National Archives and Record Service by the Kennedy family. The federal government also places in the Archives the clothing the late President wore when he was shot.

1 November 1966

WASHINGTON, D.C.   The Justice Department places the materials used by the Warren Commission in the National Archives. Included are the gun allegedly used to kill the President, a 6.5 mm Italian carbine with a telescopic sight.

BROOKLINE, MASSACHUSETTS.   The house at 83 Beals Street where John Kennedy was born is repurchased by the Kennedy family for $60,500. The house is purchased from Mr. and Mrs. Louis Pollack. The deed to the house is in the name of Joseph Gargan, Rose Kennedy's nephew.

Jacqueline Kennedy accompanied by John, Jr. and Caroline at a press conference held on horseback 16 June 1967, in Waterford, Ireland.

United Press International/Maurice Sayers.

8 November 1966

NEW YORK. On the eve of the New York gubernatorial election, Senator Robert F. Kennedy joins a gathering that includes Russian poet Yevgeny Yevtushenko, author of the poem "Babi Yar," and others. Nelson Rockefeller is re-elected governor, defeating Democratic candidate Frank O'Connor.

23 November 1966

AUSTIN, TEXAS. In a press conference at the Texas state capitol, Governor John Connally, Jr., affirms his belief in the findings of the Warren Commission, although he does not believe that the bullet that struck him also hit President Kennedy. He says a new investigation of the assassination would not be justified.

9 December 1966

NEW YORK. In a speech at P.S. 305, Senator Robert F. Kennedy announces a program to develop the economically depressed Bedford-Stuyvesant community in Brooklyn. Two newly formed companies, the Bedford-Stuyvesant Renewal and Rehabilitation Corporation and the Bedford-Stuyvesant Restoration Corporation, will carry out these plans.

3 January 1967

DALLAS, TEXAS. Before his second trial for the murder of Lee Harvey Oswald, 55-year-old Jack Ruby dies of cancer at the Parkland Memorial Hospital.

19 January 1967

NEW YORK. In an address before the Columbia Law School Forum, Senator Robert F. Kennedy speaks on improving the administration of criminal justice.

28 January 1967

LONDON. Senator Robert F. Kennedy begins an eight-day trip, primarily to discuss the Vietnam War with political leaders and others in four European countries.

OXFORD, ENGLAND. Robert Kennedy speaks before a student debating organization at Oxford University, then answers questions on Vietnam and other issues.

30 January 1967

WICHITA FALLS, TEXAS. Judge Louis Holland dismisses charges against Jack Ruby for killing Lee Harvey Oswald.

30-31 January 1967

PARIS. Robert Kennedy meets with French political leaders on resolutions to the conflict in Vietnam. On the last day of his trip, he confers with President Charles deGaulle. DeGaulle tells him the Vietnamese should have autonomy in choosing the form of government they want.

2 February 1967

BONN, WEST GERMANY. Senator Robert F. Kennedy meets with Foreign Minister Willy Brandt of West Germany and Chancellor Kurt Georg Kiesinger.

3 February 1967

ROME. Robert Kennedy confers with Italian government officials, including Foreign Minister Amintore Fanfani.

4 February 1967

ROME. Senator Robert F. Kennedy has an audience with Pope Paul VI.

6 February 1967

WASHINGTON, D.C. In a meeting on his trip to Europe, Robert F. Kennedy discusses with President Johnson a report that appears in today's *New York Times* and will appear in the forthcoming issue of *Newsweek* to the effect that while Kennedy was in Paris, the North Vietnamese government had sent him a peace "signal." According to the story, Hanoi indicated that it would come to the negotiation table if the United States would stop bombing North Vietnam. President Johnson accuses Robert Kennedy of leaking Hanoi's offer to the media at what may be a propitious time in the war for the United States, and the Senator denies having even been aware that he had received such a "signal."

8 February 1967

CHICAGO, ILLINOIS. In an address at the University of Chicago, Senator Robert F. Kennedy speaks of the need to revitalize U.S. policy toward Communist China. He declares that a policy must be based on the reality of today's Asia and on honest evaluation of American capacities and interests. "China policy must be formed against the probability that when present convulsions subside," he says, "we will still face a hostile China....Our policy must also rest on the knowledge that we cannot predict the possibility of military expansion....Policy demands finally a conscious and open recognition that we live in the same world and move in the same continent with China....Only when we accept this reality can we work toward our central task—to bring about Chinese acceptance of the fact that it too must live with us and the other nations of the world."

Courtesy Joseph P. Kennedy II. Photographer unknown.

Joe II and Teddy in Latin America. c. 1979-80.

13 February 1967

WASHINGTON, D.C. President Johnson announces that the United States will resume full-scale bombing of North Vietnam.

2 March 1967

WASHINGTON, D.C. A three-step plan to bring about a peace accord in Vietnam is proposed by Senator Robert F. Kennedy in a Senate address. He says that the United States should stop bombing North Vietnam in order to determine the truth of Soviet statements that the North Vietnamese would begin negotiating within a week of such action; that in negotiating a mutual agreement, neither side should "substantially increase the size of the war in South Vietnam by infiltration or reinforcement;" and that North Vietnam and the United States should gradually reduce their forces, which would be replaced by an international peace-keeping force.

Senator Kennedy says it is now clear that bombing North Vietnam will not end the war but may in fact prolong it. Any attempt at peace must include a cessation of United States attacks. "It is not weakness for this great nation to take a generous step toward ending the war," he declares. "It is not bravery to refuse an act which may save thousands of lives with little risks to ourselves....Not escalation, but an effort to achieve negotiation now opens the most hopeful prospect of peace." Following the speech, Secretary of State Dean Rusk says that proposals similar to Kennedy's have already been explored and rejected.

4 March 1967

HANOI, NORTH VIETNAM. The Communist newspaper *Nhan Dan* calls Senator Robert F. Kennedy's three-point plan proposed two days ago "embarrassing" to the United States.

5 March 1967

PALM BEACH, FLORIDA. Joseph P. Kennedy suffers a heart seizure and oxygen is administered.

14 March 1967

ARLINGTON, VIRGINIA. The body of President John F. Kennedy is reinterred in a permanent grave at Arlington National Cemetery. Reinterred with him are the bodies of his two infant children. The three bodies lie in a plot that measures 18 by 30 feet in lot 45, section 30, lying about 20 feet east of the grave where the President was originally buried.

15 March 1967

ARLINGTON, VIRGINIA. A 20-minute service is led by Richard Cardinal Cushing, archbishop of Boston, to bless the permanent resting place of President Kennedy. At the service are Jacqueline Kennedy, President Lyndon Johnson, Robert and Ethel Kennedy, Edward and Joan Kennedy, and the late President's sisters, Patricia, Jean, and Eunice.

17 March 1967

NEW YORK. Senator Robert F. Kennedy tells journalists at a St. Patrick's Day parade that Lyndon B. Johnson, "has been an outstanding president" and that he will support him for re-election in 1968.

24 March 1967

WASHINGTON, D.C. A son, Douglas Harriman, is born to Ethel (Skakel) and Robert Kennedy at Georgetown University Hospital. He is their tenth child and seventh son of the family. Born one month prematurely, he is delivered by Caesarean section. The baby is named after family friends C. Douglas Dillon, former secretary of the Treasury under President Kennedy, and U.S. Ambassador-at-Large W. Averell Harriman, and former governor of New York.

11 April 1967

THE MISSISSIPPI DELTA, MISSISSIPPI. Following hearings into conditions of the poor in the Mississippi Delta, Senator Robert F. Kennedy and other members of the Subcommittee on Employment, Manpower, and Poverty of the Senate Labor and Welfare Committee, including the subcommittee chairman, Joseph S. Clark, Jr., visit a number of impoverished black communities in the Delta, including the Freedom City project, to get a first-hand account of life there. Senator Kennedy enters the homes of the poor, talks to the people, and is touched by their destitution.

20 April 1967

HAIPHONG, NORTH VIETNAM. The United States begins the first bombings of this port city.

25 April 1967

WASHINGTON, D.C. In a Senate debate, Robert F. Kennedy assails the Johnson administration's policy in Vietnam.

1 May 1967

THE UNITED STATES. In the fiftieth year of his birth, the United States Postal Service issues a 13-cent memorial stamp in honor of the late President John F. Kennedy. The design is based on a photograph taken by Jacques Lowe, a White House photographer during the Kennedy administration. The photo had appeared in the book entitled *The Kennedy Years*.

16 May 1967

WASHINGTON, D.C. Senator Robert F. Kennedy introduces a bill that would establish a rehabilitation program for convicted criminals.

17 May 1967

WASHINGTON, D.C. Senator Robert Kennedy co-sponsors a bill that would require cigarette manufacturers to include a warning that cigarettes may be dangerous to one's health in all cigarette advertisements. The warning must also appear on cigarette packages that are to be shipped interstate or outside the United States.

18 May 1967

GREENWICH, CONNECTICUT. Joan Patricia Skakel, Ethel Kennedy's 39-year-old sister-in-law, dies after choking on a piece of meat at a small dinner party at her home. Her husband, George, had been killed in an airplane crash a few months ago.

26 May 1967

WASHINGTON, D.C. Congress authorizes the inclusion of the house where John Kennedy was born, 83 Beals Street in Brookline, Massachusetts, in the National Park System. Previously a National Historic Landmark, the house now becomes a National Historic Site.

27 May 1967

NEWPORT NEWS, VIRGINIA. The *John F. Kennedy*, a 88,000-ton aircraft carrier named in honor of the late president, is launched. Costing $200 million to build, it is the largest conventionally powered ship afloat. Attending the ceremony are Jacqueline, Caroline, and John Kennedy, Jr., and other members of the immediate family. Caroline, 9, christens the vessel by breaking a bottle of champagne against its bow, sending the vessel down the ways into the James River.

6 June 1967

WASHINGTON, D.C. Following the outbreak of war in the Middle East, many senators address the United States policy of neutrality. Senator Robert F. Kennedy declares that a settlement must be negotiated that will guarantee "Israel's right to live, permanent security from invasion for Israel and her neighbors...and international support for the economic development of the entire region."

7 June 1967

WASHINGTON, D.C. President Johnson appoints R. Sargent Shriver, Jr., to a six-person committee charged with examining the problems of Mexican-Americans.

11 June 1967

TAMPA, FLORIDA. Following the fatal shooting of a black teenager by a white police officer during a robbery chase, violence breaks out in the city, with fires and looting.

13 June 1967

CINCINNATI, OHIO. Racial disorder breaks out here, and the National Guard is called in.

19 June 1967

ATLANTA, GEORGIA. A minor police arrest triggers civil disorder among discontented blacks, who throw bottles and rocks, set off firecrackers, and cause other disturbances.

25 June 1967

THE UNITED STATES. The first of four consecutive telecasts on the assassination of President Kennedy begins tonight over the CBS television network.

11 July 1967

WASHINGTON, D.C. Senator Robert F. Kennedy testifies before the Judiciary Committee's Subcommittee on Juvenile Delinquency on the subject of firearms-control legislation.

12 July 1967

NEWARK, NEW JERSEY. Riots erupt here in what is to be nearly a week of violence that leaves twenty-one blacks and two whites dead.

WASHINGTON, D.C. Legislation providing for industrial investment in urban poverty areas is introduced by bill co-sponsors, Senators Robert F. Kennedy and James B. Pearson (Republican, Kansas).

14 July 1967

BOSTON. A son, Patrick Joseph, is born to Joan (Bennett) and Edward M. Kennedy at St. Elizabeth's Hospital. He is their third child and second son, and the twenty-sixth grandchild of Joe and Rose Kennedy.

United Press International.

Teddy Kennedy, surrounded by Arizona State University students after addressing the student body on 22 October 1974.

23 July 1967
DETROIT, MICHIGAN.   Riots break out here in what is to be the most violent expression of racial unrest during the troubled summer of 1967. In one week, there will be 7,200 arrests and $22 million in damages due to looting, fires, and bombings; forty-three people will be killed as a result.

29 July 1967
WASHINGTON, D.C.   In response to racial strife throughout the United States this summer, President Johnson appoints a National Advisory Commission on Civil Disorders to determine the causes of the riots and recommend ways in which such riots can be prevented in the future Governor Otto Kerner is the commission's chairman.

29 August 1967
WASHINGTON, D.C.   Testifying before the Senate Committee on Finance, Senator Robert F. Kennedy urges that welfare benefits and Social Security payments be increased.

3 September 1967
SOUTH VIETNAM.   In the national election held today, Nguyen Van Thieu is elected president and Nguyen Cao Ky, vice-president.

8 September 1967
ROCHESTER, NEW YORK.   Senator Robert F. Kennedy participates in a hearing held here by the Senate Subcommittee on Migratory Labor. The subject of the hearing is to take testimony on four bills: (1) provide for collective bargaining under supervision of National Labor Regulations Board; (2) create a National Advisory Council; (3) regulate child labor on farms; and (4) provide improved ways to recruit farm labor.

26 September 1967
BROOKLINE, MASSACHUSETTS.   The house where John F. Kennedy was born is deeded to the federal government as a gift to the people of the United States from Joseph and Rose Kennedy. Since 1 November 1966 it has been privately owned by Joseph Gargan, a nephew of Rose Kennedy.

4 October 1967
BOSTON.   During the fourth inning of the first game in the World Series between the Boston Red Sox and the St. Louis Cardinals at Fenway Park, Joseph P. Kennedy collapses in his seat. He is moved in a wheelchair to a ramp and given oxygen, then taken from the stadium by his sons Robert and Teddy.

31 October 1967
WASHINGTON, D.C.   Legislation to amend welfare and Social Security statutes is introduced by Senator Robert F. Kennedy.

THE UNITED STATES.   *JFK—The Childhood Years: A Memoir for Television by His Mother* is telecast over CBS. The half-hour special features a tour of the house at 83 Beals Street in Brookline where President Kennedy was born and spent his first four years. Harry Reasoner and Rose Kennedy also discuss her methods in rearing her children.

3 November 1967
CAMBODIA.   Jacqueline Kennedy begins a six-day tour of the country's cities and ancient ruins.

6 November 1967
SIHANOUKVILLE, CAMBODIA.   Jacqueline Kennedy dedicates the Avenue John F. Kennedy.

8 November 1967
CAMBODIA.   On the last day of her visit, Jacqueline Kennedy asks Chief of State Norodom Sihanouk about the status of Douglas Ramsey, an American aide who is a prisoner of the Viet Cong. Sihanouk asks that she have members of Ramsey's family write to him and promises to make inquiries.

18 November 1967
TARRYTOWN, NEW YORK.   In an address at Marymount College, Senator Robert F. Kennedy says that he will not be a candidate for the Democratic presidential nomination in next year's election.

24 November 1967
GARDEN CITY, NEW YORK.   *To Seek a Newer World*, by Robert F. Kennedy, is published by Doubleday and Company. This collection of the Senator's speeches since he served as U.S. attorney general presents his views on such topics as the younger generation, the ghetto, nuclear disarmament, Communist China, and Vietnam. The book runs 233 pages.

26 November 1967
THE UNITED STATES.   Speaking on "Face the Nation" television program, Senator Robert F. Kennedy declares that his brother's administration was making efforts to let the people of South Vietnam choose their own

form of government. But now, he says, the United States is fighting for South Vietnam even though the people there perhaps do not want the war. "We're killing South Vietnamese, we're killing women, we're killing innocent people," he says, "because we don't want the war fought on American soil...."

28 November 1967

NEW YORK. *Look* magazine publishes an article by Robert Kennedy entitled "What We Can Do to End the Agony of Vietnam."

30 November 1967

WASHINGTON, D.C. Senator Eugene McCarthy announces that he will seek the Democratic nomination for the presidency.

7 December 1967

NEW YORK. Senator Robert Kennedy attends the funeral of Francis Cardinal Spellman, 78, at St. Patrick's Cathedral. The Roman Catholic Archbishop of New York, who died five days earlier, was a friend of the Kennedys.

13 December 1967

WASHINGTON, D.C. The Subcommittee on Indian Education of the Committee on Labor and Public Welfare begins hearings on the educational needs of Indians. Senator Robert F. Kennedy opens the hearings.

31 December 1967

THE UNITED STATES. By year's end, there is widespread feeling among Americans that United States military operations in Vietnam should end. Some 475,000 American troops are stationed there, and full-scale bombing of North Vietnam continues.

4 January 1968

SAN FRANCISCO, CALIFORNIA. On a local television program, Senator Robert F. Kennedy declares that the United States should take up the recent offer of Hanoi and stop bombing North Vietnam in order to bring that Communist government to peace talks.

5 January 1968

WASHINGTON, D.C. The National Archives and Records Service releases the contents of an agreement with the Kennedy family regarding the X-rays and slides of the autopsy of the late President Kennedy that were turned over to the Archives. The agreement provides that until 29 October 1971, the materials may be examined only by official government investigators or others

having the consent of the Kennedy family. After that date, the specimens may be examined by recognized experts who are seriously investigating President Kennedy's death.

8 January 1968

NEW YORK. In an address at Manhattan Community College, Senator Robert F. Kennedy says that supporting Eugene McCarthy for president will not further the cause for peace. He will remain neutral in the presidential primaries, he says.

23 January 1968

THE SEA OF JAPAN. A North Korean patrol boat seizes the *Pueblo,* a U.S. Navy intelligence vessel, and takes its crew of eighty-three to a North Korean port.

25 January 1968

BOSTON. Following a recent fact-finding mission to South Vietnam, Senator Edward M. Kennedy describes his observations to members of the World Affairs Council. The people of South Vietnam, he says, are not devoted to the war, and corruption is rampant among government officials, who are not above appropriating American aid for their personal gain.

30-31 January 1968

SOUTH VIETNAM. The Tet offensive begins on the Vietnamese New Year. North Vietnamese troops rush to overtake Saigon and topple the government. In the provinces, local people resist, and bitter fighting ensues.

4 February 1968

PALM BEACH, FLORIDA. Joseph Kennedy suffers a slight spasm of a blood vessel in his brain.

8 February 1968

CHICAGO, ILLINOIS. Senator Robert Kennedy assails the Johnson administration's policy in Vietnam before a Chicago *Sun-Times* book luncheon. He declares that a total military victory in Vietnam is "probably beyond our reach" and that "we must be willing to foresee a settlement which will give the Viet Cong a chance to participate in the political life of the country."

14 February 1968

WASHINGTON, D.C. At a congressional hearing, Senator Robert F. Kennedy brands the failure of the Johnson administration's programs in ghettos across the United States and in Appalachia as unacceptable.

Courtesy Joseph P. Kennedy II. Photographer unknown.

Teddy and Joe II touring India.

18 February 1968
McLEAN, VIRGINIA. At his home here, Senator Robert F. Kennedy meets with advisers and associates on whether he should challenge President Johnson for the Democratic nomination.

1 March 1968
WASHINGTON, D.C. The National Advisory Commission on Civil Disorders releases its study, the Kerner Commission Report, on racial disorders in American cities during the summer of 1967.

7 March 1968
WASHINGTON, D.C. In a speech before the Senate, Robert F. Kennedy assails the Vietnam War, calling the administration's policies "immoral and intolerable" and asking: "Are we like...God...that we can decide, in Washington, D.C., what cities, towns, and hamlets in Vietnam are going to be destroyed?" He supports a motion by Senator J. William Fulbright (Democrat, Arkansas) that the Senate be consulted before any increase in American troops in Vietnam can be authorized.

10 March 1968
DELANO, CALIFORNIA. Senator Robert F. Kennedy attends a rally marking the end of a twenty-day fast on the part of Cesar Chavez, the farm-workers' labor leader. Chavez has been protesting against the practices of grape growers in the region.

12 March 1968
NEW HAMPSHIRE. In the nation's first presidential Democratic primary of 1968, President Lyndon B. Johnson ekes out a victory over Senator Eugene J. McCarthy of Minnesota by less than 5,000 votes. The election results are: Johnson (write-in), 27,520 votes, or 49.6 percent of the total; McCarthy, 23,263 votes, or 41.9 percent; Richard M. Nixon (write-in), 2,532 votes, or 4.6 percent; all others, 2,149 votes, or 3.9 percent. McCarthy's significant showing against President Johnson brings him national attention. When he announced his candidacy on 30 November 1967 he was virtually unknown throughout the United States and considered to have no chance against the President.

13 March 1968
BOSTON. Boston University confers an honorary doctoral degree upon R. Sargent Shriver, Jr., director of the U.S. Office of Economic Opportunity.

15 March 1968
NEW YORK. Robert F. Kennedy decides to become a candidate for the Democratic presidential nomination. He and his aides notify political associates of his decision and obtain their support. He later leaves for his home in Virginia to draft his announcement speech.

GREEN BAY, WISCONSIN. Senator Edward M. Kennedy informs Eugene McCarthy of his brother's decision to seek the Democratic nomination for the presidency.

17 March 1968
MANHATTAN and LAWRENCE, KANSAS. In speeches at Kansas State University and Kansas University, Senator Robert F. Kennedy pledges to change the country's direction.

18 March 1968
MANHATTAN, KANSAS. Senator Robert F. Kennedy assails the Johnson administration's policy in Vietnam in his first campaign speech at Kansas State University's Ahearn Fieldhouse. He also sharply attacks South Vietnam for its corruption and North Vietnam for its torture and terror. While admitting his involvement in formulating U.S. policy in Vietnam during his brother's administration, he declares that "past error is no excuse for its own perpetuation." Kennedy asks that the public support him: "If you will give me your help, if you will give me your hand, I will work for you and we will have a new America."

LAWRENCE, KANSAS. In an afternoon campaign speech at the Phog Allen Fieldhouse of the University of Kansas, Senator Robert F. Kennedy declares that the country is divided over the Vietnam war and by the isolation of the "invisible" poor. He is running, he says, because America needs a new direction now.

21 March 1968
NASHVILLE, TENNESSEE. In a campaign speech made at Vanderbilt University, Senator Robert Kennedy blames the country's policymakers for the dissent and riots in America.

TUSCALOOSA, ALABAMA. Declaring that America is "divided as never before," Senator Robert F. Kennedy asks students at the University of Alabama to help him build a better, united country.

22 March 1968
NEW YORK. *Decisions for a Decade: Policies and Programs for the 1970s* by Senator Edward Kennedy is published by Doubleday and Company. The book criticizes past policies and looks at the problems of the next decade that America must address.

WASHINGTON, D.C. President Johnson announces that he will submit the name of R. Sargent Shriver, Jr., to the Senate for confirmation as U.S. ambassador to France. He also announces that he has appointed Gen. William Westmoreland to replace General Harold K. Johnson in Vietnam in July as the Army Chief of Staff.

ABC Television Network.

Senator Edward Kennedy and his mother, Mrs. Rose Kennedy, recall their memories of the late John F. Kennedy in an ABC television special, "JFK—A Time to Remember," telecast on 21 November 1973.

23 March 1968
CALIFORNIA. Senator Robert F. Kennedy campaigns in Sacramento, San Jose, Stockton, Salinas-Monterey, and Los Angeles.

24 March 1968
LOS ANGELES, CALIFORNIA. In the Watts section, Senator Robert F. Kennedy speaks on the community's problems.

26 March 1968

PORTLAND, OREGON. Senator Robert F. Kennedy addresses a group at Portland State University.

SEATTLE, WASHINGTON. Senator Kennedy delivers a speech at the University of Washington.

PROVO, UTAH. The role of youth in America's future is the theme of a speech given by Senator Kennedy at Brigham Young University.

29 March 1968

ALBUQUERQUE, NEW MEXICO. In an address, Senator Robert F. Kennedy outlines new health-care programs.

30 March 1968

PHOENIX, ARIZONA. Senator Robert F. Kennedy speaks on the state of America in an address before a state Democratic party dinner.

31 March 1968

WASHINGTON, D.C. President Johnson orders a curb on the bombing of North Vietnam.

WASHINGTON, D.C. President Lyndon B. Johnson announces that he will not seek or accept the nomination of the Democratic Party to run for re-election. He also orders a halt to air and naval bombing of North Vietnam and invites leaders of the North Vietnamese government to cooperate in peace negotiations.

1 April 1968

NEW YORK. At the Overseas Press Club, Senator Robert F. Kennedy discusses the meaning of President Johnson's decision not to seek re-election with reporters.

PHILADELPHIA, PENNSYLVANIA. Senator Robert Kennedy tours the suburbs of the city.

2 April 1968

WISCONSIN. Senator Eugene J. McCarthy wins the state's Democratic presidential primary. The election results are: McCarthy, 412,160 votes, or 56.2 percent of the total; Lyndon B. Johnson, 253,696 votes, or 34.6 percent; Robert F. Kennedy (write-in), 46,507 votes, or 6.3 percent; unpledged delegates, 11,861 votes, or 1.6 percent; George C. Wallace, 4,031 votes, or 0.5 percent; Hubert H. Humphrey, 3,605 votes, or 0.5 percent; all others, 1,142 votes, or 0.2 percent.

Richard M. Nixon wins the state's Republican presidential primary with 390,368 votes, or 79.7 percent of the total.

PHILADELPHIA, PENNSYLVANIA. Robert Kennedy declares that the United States will have to negotiate with the North Vietnamese government.

3 April 1968

WASHINGTON, D.C. Senator Robert F. Kennedy speaks on the city's problems at a rally. Later, he meets with Lyndon Johnson to discuss the implications of the President's withdrawal.

4 April 1968

MEMPHIS, TENNESSEE. The Rev. Dr. Martin Luther King, Jr., is assassinated by a sniper as he stands on the balcony of the Lorraine Motel. He was here to support a strike by the city's sanitation workers, who are predominantly black.

THE UNITED STATES. Following the assassination of Martin Luther King, Jr., race riots break out in cities throughout the nation and continue for a full week.

INDIANAPOLIS, INDIANA. Robert Kennedy urges blacks not to take revenge for Dr. King's assassination but to carry out his dream and end the divisions among Americans.

5 April 1968

MEMPHIS, TENNESSEE. Coretta Scott King brings the body of her husband, Martin Luther King, Jr., home to Atlanta, Georgia, in a plane chartered by Senator Robert R. Kennedy.

CLEVELAND, OHIO. Having canceled all campaign engagements, Senator Robert F. Kennedy speaks on racial problems at the City Club.

7 April 1968

WASHINGTON, D.C. In an area hit by racial violence, Robert and Ethel Kennedy attend a memorial service for the late Martin Luther King, Jr.

8 April 1968

MEMPHIS, TENNESSEE. Coretta Scott King leads tens of thousands of blacks in a civil-rights demonstration.

9 April 1968
ATLANTA, GEORGIA. Senator Robert F. Kennedy attends the funeral of Martin Luther King, Jr.

10 April 1968
FORT WAYNE, INDIANA. In an address delivered before the Scottish Rite Banquet, Senator Robert Kennedy says that legislation alone will not stop the dangerous division between whites and blacks in America. Fresh and deeper communication is necessary to remove suspicion and hatred, he says.

11 April 1968
WASHINGTON, D.C. President Lyndon B. Johnson signs into law the 1968 Civil Rights Act which provides for the elimination of racial discrimination in housing in the United States. The legislation will become effective in 1970.

FORT WAYNE, INDIANA. Senator Robert F. Kennedy speaks on measures to reduce poverty at a "Housewives for Kennedy" rally.

LANSING, MICHIGAN. Police spot what they believe to be a sniper on a rooftop near the spot where Senator Robert F. Kennedy is to deliver a campaign speech. Undeterred, Senator Kennedy proceeds with his speech on appropriating funds from federal projects to establish programs to build up poor black communities.

13 April 1968
APPALACHIA, WEST VIRGINIA. Senator Robert F. Kennedy tours the area.

CHARLESTON, WEST VIRGINIA. In a speech, Robert Kennedy declares that the survival of America is more threatened by the injustice and violence that divides it than by any foreign enemy.

15 April 1968
INDIANA. Campaigning in northern cities of the state, Senator Robert F. Kennedy speaks about training the unemployed to fill the nation's labor needs.

17 April 1968
PORTLAND, OREGON. In a speech given before a journalism fraternity, Senator Robert Kennedy says that the image of America has deteriorated abroad and that the United States must honorably end the Vietnam War to reassure the world about its judgment.

18 April 1968
CORVALLIS, OREGON. Senator Robert F. Kennedy calls on the young adults of America to use their talents and skills to shape the country's future in an address at Oregon State University.

19 April 1968
WASHINGTON, D.C. The Senate Foreign Relations Committee confirms the nomination of R. Sargent Shriver, Jr., as ambassador to France.

22 April 1968
KOKOMO, INDIANA. The problems of the elderly are the subject of a speech here by Senator Robert F. Kennedy.

VINCENNES, INDIANA. In an address to a group of businesspeople, Senator Robert Kennedy discusses how private industry can help to cure America's social ills.

EVANSVILLE, INDIANA. Robert Kennedy says that the next administration must reform the tax system and control inflation.

23 April 1968
PENNSYLVANIA. The state's Democratic presidential primary is captured by Eugene J. McCarthy with 428,259 votes, or 71.7 percent of the total. Other challengers, all write-ins, include Robert Kennedy, with 65,430 votes; Hubert Humphrey, with 51,998 votes; George Wallace, with 24,147 votes; Lyndon Johnson, with 21,265 votes; Richard Nixon, with 3,434 votes; and all others, 2,556 votes.
Richard M. Nixon wins the state's write-in Republican presidential primary.

LOGANSPORT, INDIANA. Senator Robert F. Kennedy leaves on the *Wabash Cannonball* for a whistlestop tour of central Indiana.

24 April 1968
BLOOMINGTON, INDIANA. In a speech at the Indiana University campus, Senator Robert Kennedy speaks of the conditions under which the United States should involve itself in the affairs of foreign governments.

26 April 1968
INDIANAPOLIS, INDIANA. Before an audience of medical students at Indiana University Medical Cen-

321

ter, Robert F. Kennedy delivers a speech on health care in America. When the students angrily challenge him, Kennedy chastises them, saying that they are "privileged" to be in medical school while the poor and the blacks are fighting the war for them in Vietnam.

27 April 1968

WASHINGTON, D.C.   Vice-President Hubert H. Humphrey announces that he will seek the Democratic nomination for president.

28 April 1968

VALPARAISO, INDIANA.   Senator Robert F. Kennedy discusses a study made by a citizens' board of inquiry on hunger in America at Valparaiso University.

30 April 1968

MASSACHUSETTS.   Eugene J. McCarthy wins the state's Democratic presidential primary with 122,697 votes, or 49.3 percent of the total. All other write-in challengers are Robert F. Kennedy, with 68,604 votes; Hubert H. Humphrey, with 44,156 votes; Lyndon B. Johnson, with 6,890 votes; Nelson A. Rockefeller, with 2,275 votes; George C. Wallace, with 1,688 votes; and all others, 2,593 votes.

Nelson A. Rockefeller wins the state's write-in Republican presidential primary.

1 May 1968

WEST LAFAYETTE, INDIANA.   The difficulty of getting North Vietnamese and American delegates to peace talks is the subject of Senator Robert F. Kennedy's speech at Purdue University.

2 May 1968

ELKHART, INDIANA.   Senator Robert F. Kennedy delivers an address on the economic problems of America.

4 May 1968

WASHINGTON, D.C.   Senator Robert F. Kennedy suggests a greater role for community associations in this city.

5 May 1968

SOUTH VIETNAM.   North Vietnamese guerrillas attack dozens of villages in the country in an all-out drive.

WASHINGTON, D.C.   Senator Robert F. Kennedy proposes a reorganization plan for the nation's capital.

6 May 1968

INDIANA.   Senator Robert F. Kennedy makes a final tour through the northeast part of the state before tomorrow's primary.

7 May 1968

DISTRICT OF COLUMBIA.   A slate of delegates favoring Robert F. Kennedy wins the district's presidential primary. Kennedy's slate defeats Humphrey's slate, with 57,555 votes, or 62.5 percent of the total vote.

WASHINGTON, D.C.   R. Sargent Shriver, Jr., 52, is sworn in as U.S. ambassador to France, succeeding Charles H. Bohlen. The installment date was to be one week later, but it was moved up when the United States and North Vietnam agreed on Paris as the location for upcoming peace talks.

INDIANA.   Robert F. Kennedy wins the state's Democratic presidential primary with 328,118 votes, or 42.3 percent of the total. He defeats Roger D. Branigin of Indiana, with 238,700 votes, and Eugene J. McCarthy, with 209,695 votes.

8 May 1968

PARIS.   R. Sargent Shriver, Jr., the new ambassador to France, arrives and begins his official duties.

NEW YORK.   Senator Robert F. Kennedy speaks before the Synagogue Council of America.

ATLANTIC CITY, NEW JERSEY.   Senator Robert Kennedy addresses a convention of the United Auto Workers.

10 May 1968

NEBRASKA.   With the primary five days off, Senator Robert F. Kennedy begins a political tour here. His motorcade travels through a half-dozen cities in the southeastern part of the state, and he delivers an address at a dinner in Omaha.

11 May 1968

SOUTH DAKOTA.   Senator Robert F. Kennedy makes a brief tour through the state in preparation for next month's primary.

WASHINGTON, D.C.   Robert Kennedy's office issues a policy statement, entitled "A Program for a Sound Economy," containing proposals for income tax, government spending, wages, and antipoverty programs.

Joe II and the former Sheila Brewster Rauch on their wedding day, 3 February 1979.

Joe II with wife, Sheila, and twin sons, JPK III and Matthew. c. 1980-81.

13 May 1968
OMAHA, NEBRASKA. In a speech at Creighton University, Robert Kennedy speaks of the disproportionate number of blacks fighting the war in Vietnam.

PARIS. Discussions over a peaceful settlement to the war in Vietnam commence between American and North Vietnamese representatives. W. Averell Harriman is the chief delegate for the United States, and Xuan Thuy represents North Vietnam.

14 May 1968
NEBRASKA. Robert F. Kennedy wins the state's Democratic presidential primary. The election results are: Kennedy, 84,102 votes, or 51.7 percent of the total; Eugene J. McCarthy, 50,655 votes; Hubert H. Humphrey (write-in), 12,087 votes; Lyndon B. Johnson, 9,187 votes; Richard M. Nixon (write-in), 2,731 votes; Ronald Reagan (write-in), 1,905 votes; George C. Wallace (write-in), 1,298 votes; all others, 646 votes.

Richard M. Nixon wins the state's Republican presidential primary with 140,336 votes, or 70 percent of the total.

COLUMBUS, OHIO. Senator Robert F. Kennedy delivers a speech entitled "Citizen Control."

15 May 1968
DAVENPORT and DES MOINES, IOWA. Senator Robert F. Kennedy meets with Democratic party members and addresses rallies in both cities on the needs of the farmers.

DETROIT, MICHIGAN. In a speech at John F. Kennedy Square, Senator Robert Kennedy declares that he is going to build on what the Democratic party has accomplished in America.

16 May 1968
WASHINGTON, D.C. While passing a crime-control bill, the Senate votes down Senator Edward M. Kennedy's amendment to prohibit the sale of rifles by mail.

17 May 1968
PORTLAND, OREGON. Senator Robert F. Kennedy speaks on the economic effects of the war in Vietnam before a meeting of the Portland City Club.

18 May 1968
EUGENE, OREGON. The Vietnam War is the subject of an address given by Senator Robert F. Kennedy at the University of Oregon.

WASHINGTON, D.C. Senator Robert Kennedy's office issues "Solutions to the Problems of Welfare," a policy statement outlining proposals for providing jobs and assistance to the poor.

20 May 1968
LOS ANGELES, CALIFORNIA. Senator Robert F. Kennedy discusses the quest for peace in the Middle East. He states that any settlement must recognize the existence of Israel and that the United States must protect Israel against any military imbalance.

26 May 1968
PORTLAND, OREGON. In an address before a local temple, Senator Robert F. Kennedy says the United States must keep defending Israel against aggression.

27 May 1968
ROSEBURG, OREGON. Senator Robert F. Kennedy openly disputes with residents who oppose gun-control legislation. He tells them that such legislation will only serve to "keep guns from criminals and the demented" and that weapons should be kept from people "who have no business with guns or rifles."

28 May 1968
OREGON. Eugene J. McCarthy upsets Robert F. Kennedy in the state's Democratic presidential primary. The election results are: McCarthy, 163,990 votes, or 44 percent of the total; Kennedy, 141,631 votes; Lyndon B. Johnson, 45,174 votes; Hubert H. Humphrey (write-in), 12,421 votes; Ronald Reagan (write-in), 3,082 votes; Richard M. Nixon (write-in), 2,974 votes; Nelson A. Rockefeller (write-in), 2,841 votes; George C. Wallace (write-in), 957 votes.

Richard M. Nixon wins the state's Republican presidential primary.

29 May 1968
COUNTY WEXFORD, IRELAND. The 460-acre John F. Kennedy Memorial Park near Dunganstown and near the home of Kennedy's great-grandfather, who emigrated from Ireland more than a century earlier, is dedicated by President Eamon de Valera. Imprinted on a stone fountain are the stirring words from Kennedy's inaugural speech: "Ask not what your country can do for you...ask what you can do for your country."

LOS ANGELES, CALIFORNIA. Senator Robert F. Kennedy accepts Senator Eugene McCarthy's challenge to a debate. He also says that he will withdraw from the Democratic primaries if he loses the election in California.

CALIFORNIA.   In an effort to draw the suburban vote, Senator Robert F. Kennedy campaigns through several cities in the Central Valley.

OAKLAND, CALIFORNIA.   Senator Robert Kennedy meets with a black caucus group. He also issues a policy statement, "Proposal for a Comprehensive Cities Program."

SAN FRANCISCO, CALIFORNIA.   The Vietnam War is the subject of Senator Kennedy's speech before the Commonwealth Club.

1 June 1968
LOS ANGELES, CALIFORNIA.   Senators Robert F. Kennedy and Eugene McCarthy debate each other on television. The format is similar to that of the forum in which John Kennedy met Richard Nixon in 1960: reporters ask the candidates questions and the candidates may react to their opponent's answers. The issues include Vietnam, the Middle East, and housing for blacks. Because the two men have similar points of view, no clear winner emerges.

3 June 1968
CALIFORNIA.   Senator Robert F. Kennedy makes his final campaign swing before the state primary, appearing in San Francisco, Long Beach, and San Diego.

4 June 1968
MALIBU, CALIFORNIA.   As voters go to the polls for the presidential primary, Robert and Ethel Kennedy and three of their children have an outing on the beach. Robert's son David Kennedy, 12, is caught in a dangerous Pacific undertow, but his father rescues him.

SOUTH DAKOTA.   Robert F. Kennedy wins the state's Democratic presidential primary. With 31,826 votes, or 49.5 percent of the total, he defeats Lyndon B. Johnson, who receives 19,316 votes, or 30 percent, and Eugene McCarthy, who polls 13,145 votes, or 20.4 percent.

NEW JERSEY.   Eugene J. McCarthy wins the state's write-in Democratic presidential primary. The election results are: McCarthy, 9,906 votes, or 36.1 percent of the total; Robert F. Kennedy, 8,603 votes, or 31.3 percent; Hubert H. Humphrey, 5,578 votes, or 20.3 percent; George C. Wallace, 1,399 votes, or 5.1 percent; Richard M. Nixon, 1,364 votes, or 5 percent; all others, 596 votes, or 2.2 percent.

CALIFORNIA.   Robert F. Kennedy wins the state's Democratic presidential primary with 1,472,166 votes, or 46.3 percent of the total. He defeats Eugene J. McCarthy, who polls 1,329,301 votes, or 41.8 percent. Unpledged delegates receive 380,286 votes, or 12.09 percent.

5 June 1968
LOS ANGELES.   Following his 4 June victories in the South Dakota and California Democratic presidential primaries, Senator Robert F. Kennedy addresses his cheering campaign workers in the Embassy Room of the Ambassador Hotel. His talk reflects the happy promise of the occasion. At once both serious and funny, it blends comment on the important issues ahead with humorous banter about personal matters. At about 12:13 A.M. P.D.T.,* he leaves the stage and heads for the Colonial Room where he is to hold a news conference. He leaves by the back exit in order to enter the makeshift press room by way of the hotel pantry. An entourage precedes and follows him—Ethel, his security guards, campaign workers, and others.

Robert Kennedy passes through the swinging doors of the kitchen, stopping en route to shake the hands of workers there. Standing beside a stack of serving trays is a young man brandishing a .22-caliber Iver Johnson revolver. At 12:15 A.M., he steps out and begins shooting at the Senator from a distance of 2 to 4 feet. He fires eight times — most of the shots fired as he is being subdued. Kennedy is hit, and five other people are wounded.

Kennedy collapses on the cement floor. The first bullet has struck him in the head behind the right ear, the second passed through his coat and hit someone next to him. Blood drips from the back of his head. Ethel Kennedy makes her way through the frantic crowd to her wounded husband and kneels beside him. A priest places a rosary in the wounded Senator's hand.

Meanwhile, a number of men, among them Roosevelt "Rosie" Grier, a Los Angeles Rams lineman, Rafer Johnson, winner of the 1960 Olympic decathlon, author George Plimpton, and hotel maitre d' Karl Uecker, swarm over the gunman. As two of them wrestle for his weapon, several bullets are discharged. The other men grab and restrain him. The cursing, screaming crowd threatens to beat him to death, but the men protect him. When word of the shootings reaches Kennedy supporters in the Embassy Room, the room fills with cries and screams.

In the midst of the hysteria, a physician in the hotel rushes to Kennedy's side. Minutes later, police arrive. At 12:30 A.M., the police carry the gunman out, his left index finger broken and his ankle sprained, by his arms and legs. Ten minutes later Robert Kennedy is taken by stretcher to a waiting ambulance. At Central Receiving

---

* All times given are Pacific Daylight Time.

Joe II with twin sons Matthew (top) and JPK III.

Hospital he is given an adrenalin injection, receives heart massage, and is connected to a heart-lung machine. The last rites are administered. He is then taken to Good Samaritan Hospital where neurosurgeons operate for over three and a half hours to remove lead fragments from his brain. As the family gathers in the hospital, a crowd keeps vigil outside.

The anonymous gunman is taken to a police station near the Ambassador Hotel, then transferred to headquarters on North Los Angeles Street. (To prevent a recurrence of the Oswald/Ruby incident, the assailant is transported in a converted pickup truck rather than a police car.) He is short, dark-haired, and appears to be foreign-born. He refuses to identify himself. Among the effects found on his person are four $100 bills and a newspaper article by columnist David Lawrence describing Kennedy's sympathy with Israel's cause. In court at 7:30 A.M., six counts of assault with intent to murder are lodged against the gunman, identified only as "John Doe," and he is then put in a maximum security cell.

The police try to identify the man through ownership of the gun. Their computer search turns up the name Munir Bishari Salameh "Joe" Sirhan. With his brother Adel, he is brought to the jail where the two men identify the suspect as Sirhan Bishara Sirhan.

5 June 1968
LOS ANGELES. At a press conference, Mayor Samuel W. Yorty announces that a search of Sirhan B. Sirhan's home has turned up a notebook in which it is written that Robert Kennedy must be killed by 5 June, the first anniversary of the six-day Arab-Israel War.

WASHINGTON, D.C. In the evening, President Johnson announces on a television broadcast the formation of a commission to study violence in America.

6 June 1968
LOS ANGELES. Senator Robert F. Kennedy, 42, dies at 1:44 A.M., almost twenty-five and a half hours after having been shot. His wife, Ethel, sisters Patricia and Jean, sister-in-law Jacqueline, and brother-in-law Stephen Smith are by his side in Good Samaritan Hospital. Senator Kennedy's three oldest children are in an adjacent room. His death is announced 15 minutes later by Frank Mankiewicz, his press secretary. An autopsy is later performed by a team of hospital and government doctors, presided over by Los Angeles medical examiner, Dr. Thomas Nogucchi.

NEW YORK. At 9:00 P.M., the body of Robert F. Kennedy arrives from Los Angeles at LaGuardia Airport aboard Air Force One.

A crowd, including Senator Jacob Javits and Governor Nelson A. Rockefeller of New York, waits solemnly as the plane lands. In a corner of the airport, members of the Kennedy family also wait. Ethel Kennedy, her son Joseph, Ted Kennedy, Jacqueline Kennedy, and Coretta Scott King leave the plane. The coffin is removed, and Archbishop Terence J. Cook offers a brief prayer. The coffin is then placed in a hearse, and a motorcade led by police brings the body and members of the Kennedy family to St. Patrick's Cathedral on Fifth Avenue. Along the way, thousands gather on the street, watching silently, many weeping. Outside the church, thousands more stand vigil, separated by barricades and police. At around 10 P.M., the coffin is carried into the cathedral, accompanied by the Kennedy family. They leave shortly afterward. Edward Kennedy later returns, and an honor guard comprised of the late senator's friends keeps vigil by the coffin throughout the night.

WASHINGTON, D.C. Congress approves legislation providing Secret Service protection for major presidential candidates. President Johnson signs the bill.

7 June 1968
LOS ANGELES, CALIFORNIA. Sirhan Bishara Sirhan is indicted on a charge of first-degree murder.

NEW YORK. Beginning at 5:30 A.M., the body of Senator Robert F. Kennedy lies in state at St. Patrick's Cathedral. The line of people outside stretches for a mile and a half. Some mourners wait up to seven hours to enter the church and pass the closed African mahogany coffin.

8 June 1968
HYANNIS PORT, MASSACHUSETTS. A requiem mass is celebrated at St. Francis Xavier Church in honor of Robert F. Kennedy.

LONDON, ENGLAND. James Earl Ray, the alleged killer of Martin Luther King, Jr., is arrested at Heathrow Airport.

NEW YORK. The body of Robert F. Kennedy lies in state at St. Patrick's until 5:00 A.M. It is estimated that more than 100,000 people have paid their respects. Just before 10 A.M., a solemn pontifical requiem mass is celebrated at St. Patrick's Cathedral. Over 2,000 people attend, including President Lyndon Johnson, Vice-President Hubert Humphrey, former vice-president Richard Nixon, Governor Nelson Rockefeller, UN Secretary General U Thant, Cary Grant, Averell Harriman, Walter Reuther, Coretta Scott King, Barry Goldwater, Ralph Abernathy, Senator Eugene McCarthy.

Richard Cardinal Cushing, assisted by a representative of Pope Paul IV, says the mass. Archbishop Terence J. Cooke is a principal celebrant. Senator Edward M. Kennedy delivers the eulogy, his voice occasionally breaking: "My brother need not be idealized, nor enlarged beyond what he was in life. He should be remembered simply as a good and decent man, who saw wrong and tried to heal it, saw war and tried to stop it. Those of us who loved him and who take him to his rest today pray that what he was to us, and what he wished for others will someday come to pass for all the world."

The late senator's wife, Ethel, his mother, Rose, Eunice and Jean, Jacqueline, and other family members attend the service. His sons Joseph, Robert, David, and Michael serve as acolytes, along with other Kennedy cousins. Andy Williams sings "The Battle Hymn of the Republic". Following the mass, the coffin is placed in a hearse which proceeds in a motorcade slowly down Fifth Avenue. Tens of thousands of people have lined the sidewalk, many weeping quietly. The funeral procession turns right on 34th Street and proceeds to Pennsylvania Station. The coffin is placed aboard a twenty-one car train that will carry it to Washington, D.C., where it will be taken to Arlington Cemetery for burial near the grave of the late President John F. Kennedy. The train leaves at 1:00 P.M. and travels slowly. On the route, approximately a million mourners have lined up along the tracks and watch silently as the train passes by. Fatal accidents mar the already tragic occasion—two people watching the Kennedy train are killed in Elizabeth, New Jersey, by an express train headed for New York, and one youth is severely burned by a wire in Trenton. The funeral train also carries members of the Kennedy family, public officials, and friends of the late Senator.

ARLINGTON, VIRGINIA. During the evening, Robert F. Kennedy is buried at Arlington National Cemetery in lot 45-A, section 30, part of a parcel of land that was assigned in 1963 in honor of the late President John F. Kennedy. (Robert Kennedy is eligible for burial at Arlington because of his service in the Navy, his cabinet rank as attorney general, and his status as a U.S. senator.) President and Mrs. Johnson join members of the Kennedy family at the service.

9 June 1968
THE UNITED STATES. President Johnson declares this day a national day of mourning for the late Senator Robert F. Kennedy.

11 June 1968
ILLINOIS. Edward Kennedy receives more than 33 percent of the votes in the state's write-in Democratic presidential primary. The election is won, however, by Eugene J. McCarthy with 4,646 votes, followed by Kennedy, with 4,052 votes, and Hubert Humphrey, with 2,059 votes.

WASHINGTON, D.C. After Democratic leaders express interest in his accepting the Democratic nomination for vice-president, Senator Edward Kennedy issues a statement that he would decline any such offer.

12 June 1968
HYANNIS PORT, MASSACHUSETTS. In a taped telecast, Rose Kennedy and Senator Edward Kennedy thank the nation for its condolences.

12 July 1968
CHICAGO. The Joseph P. Kennedy, Jr. Foundation, together with the Chicago Park District, sponsors the first International Special Olympic Games. It is held in Soldiers Field with 1,000 mentally retarded athletes from twenty-six states and Canada participating. The goal of the games is to create opportunities for mentally retarded people to participate in sports training and athletic competition and to demonstrate their capabilities.

26 July 1968
WASHINGTON, D.C. Responding to speculation that he might run as the Democratic nominee for vice-president, Senator Edward M. Kennedy announces that he will not be a candidate under any circumstances.

21 August 1968
WORCESTER, MASSACHUSETTS. In an address before the Chamber of Commerce, Senator Edward M. Kennedy outlines a plan for ending the war in Vietnam. The plan includes an unconditional bombing halt in North Vietnam, negotiation with the North Vietnamese over the mutual withdrawal of troops from South Vietnam, and providing of American aid to help rebuild South Vietnam.

22 August 1968
NEW YORK. *Decisions for a Decade: Policies and Programs for the 1970s* by Senator Edward Kennedy is published by New American Library. The book criticizes past political policies and looks at the problems that America must address in the next decade.

26 August 1968

CHICAGO. On the first day of the Democratic National Convention, a movement to nominate Senator Edward Kennedy as vice-president begins, but Kennedy asks that he not be nominated.

29 August 1968

CHICAGO. The Democratic National Convention closes. Hubert H. Humphrey is nominated for president and Edmund S. Muskie is nominated for vice-president.

On the last day of the Democratic National Convention, a film commemorating the late Robert F. Kennedy is shown. The convention later closes.

7 September 1968

BOSTON. Thomas Acton Fitzgerald, brother of Rose Kennedy, dies at the age of 73 at Massachusetts General Hospital. The cause of death is Naennec's cirrhosis, which he had had for 20 years. Thomas Fitzgerald had married twice, on 7 September 1921 to Marion W. Riordan (who died on 17 February 1925), and on 10 November 1930 to Margaret B. Fitzpatrick. He resided at 251 Tremont Street in Boston when he died.

12 September 1968

ALBANY, NEW YORK. Filling the late Robert F. Kennedy's Senate seat, Representative Charles E. Goodall of Jamestown is sworn in today. Governor Nelson A. Rockefeller had appointed him two days earlier.

23 September 1968

WASHINGTON, D.C. Addressing the Senate for the first time since his brother was slain in June, Senator Edward M. Kennedy speaks out against belated American action in the Nigerian crisis. Currently, the Biafrans are rebelling against the federal government of this West African nation, and the horrible effects of civil war are further compounded by a devastating famine that is killing thousands of people. Senator Kennedy declares that the United States has not acted with a sense of urgency or with adequate compassion for those who are starving.

30 September 1968

WEST HANOVER, MASSACHUSETTS. Compiled by Patricia Kennedy and written by family members and friends, *That Shining Hour* , a privately printed book of essays remembering Robert F. Kennedy, is in production at the Halliday Lithograph Corporation.

20 October 1968

SKORPIOS, GREECE. In a 30-minute traditional Greek Orthodox wedding ceremony, Jacqueline (Bouvier) Kennedy, 39, marries shipping millionaire Aristotle Socrates Onassis, 62. The couple are married on Onassis's private 500-acre island in the Ionian Sea off the west coast of Greece. The ceremony is performed in the Chapel of Panayitsa (the Little Virgin). Among those attending the wedding are Caroline and John Kennedy, Patricia (Kennedy) Lawford, Jean (Kennedy) Smith, Hugh and Janet Auchincloss, and Alexander and Christina Onassis. Officiating at the ceremony is Father Polykarpos Athanassion, a Greek Orthodox priest from Athens.

22 October 1968

SKORPIOS, GREECE. Caroline and John Kennedy, Jr., leave by plane for New York as Aristotle and Jacqueline (Kennedy) Onassis begin their honeymoon aboard the *Christina*.

27 October 1968

RUNNYMEDE, ENGLAND. A bomb explodes at the monument to the late President Kennedy dedicated by Queen Elizabeth II in May 1965. Authorities believe that it was set off in protest against the Vietnam War. (Earlier, a large protest march had taken place in London.)

29 October 1968

WASHINGTON, D.C. A foundation in memory of the late Robert F. Kennedy is established to help carry out the Senator's goals, including solutions to serious national social problems and the promotion of peace. The foundation will attempt to raise $10 million to carry out its plans.

30 October 1968

NEW YORK. "Abraham, Martin and John," a popular song about two presidents and a civil-rights leader who were assassinated, is released. Recorded by Dion on Laurie Records, the Dick Holler composition also refers to "Bobby" (Kennedy).

31 October 1968

NORTH VIETNAM. President Johnson orders a cessation of the bombing here.

12 December 1968

WASHINGTON, D.C. A daughter, Rory Elizabeth Katherine, is born to Ethel (Skakel) Kennedy at Georgetown Medical Center. She is the family's eleventh child and fourth daughter, and she is delivered by Caesarean section. Ethel had been pregnant when her husband was assassinated.

EDWARD M. KENNEDY
1968-PRESENT

3 January 1969
WASHINGTON, D.C. At a Democratic party caucus, Senator Edward Kennedy defeats Senator Russell Long of Louisiana to become assistant Senate majority leader.

7 January 1969
LOS ANGELES. The trial of Sirhan Bishara Sirhan for the murder of Robert F. Kennedy begins.

18 January 1969
WASHINGTON, D.C. The District of Columbia (D.C.) Stadium at 22nd and East Capitol Streets is renamed Robert F. Kennedy Memorial Stadium.

20 January 1969
WASHINGTON, D.C. Richard M. Nixon is inaugurated as the thirty-seventh president of the United States. Spiro T. Agnew is sworn in as vice-president.

NEW YORK. *Thirteen Days: A Memoir of the Cuban Missile Crisis* by Robert Kennedy is posthumously published by W. W. Norton and Company.

4 March 1969
LOS ANGELES, CALIFORNIA. Sirhan B. Sirhan testifies that he decided he had to assassinated Robert Kennedy after watching the Senator participate in an Israeli independence celebration on television.

4 April 1969
MEMPHIS, TENNESSEE. On the first anniversary of the slaying of Dr. Martin Luther King, Jr., Senator Edward M. Kennedy delivers a speech to a crowd of over 8,000 persons after a march held in honor of the murdered civil rights leader.

8 April 1969
ALASKA. The Senate Subcommittee on Indian Education begins a three-day investigative tour of poor areas. Senator Edward Kennedy is chairman of the subcommittee, a position held by his late brother Robert.

11 April 1969
FAIRBANKS, ALASKA. Senator Edward M. Kennedy, with members of the Special Subcommittee on Indian Education, concludes a four-day trip to poor communities in the state to assess schools and health problems. (His brother Robert had planned to tour the area to make his own investigation.) The trip is somewhat marred by the withdrawal of three of the four Republican members of the subcommittee (with the exception of Senator Ted Stevens of Alaska), because they believe that Senator Kennedy is using the trip to gain publicity.

14 April 1969
LOS ANGELES. The film *Robert Kennedy Remembered* wins an Oscar for "best live-action short subject" of 1968.

17 April 1969
LOS ANGELES, CALIFORNIA. Sirhan B. Sirhan is convicted of murder in the first degree for the 5 June 1968 slaying of Robert F. Kennedy.

23 April 1969
LOS ANGELES, CALIFORNIA. The jury in the Sirhan B. Sirhan murder trial recommends death in the gas chamber.

18 May 1969
WASHINGTON, D.C. Senator Edward M. Kennedy sends a letter to the Los Angeles District Attorney asking for mercy in the sentencing of the convicted killer of his late brother, Senator Robert F. Kennedy.

21 May 1969
LOS ANGELES, CALIFORNIA. An appeal of the death sentence of Sirhan B. Sirhan is upheld by Superior Court Judge Herbert W. Walker.

24 May 1969
WASHINGTON, D.C. In a speech before the new Democratic Coalition, Senator Edward M. Kennedy lashes out against the war in Vietnam, calling it "unjustified" and "immoral."

29 May 1969
BROOKLINE, MASSACHUSETTS. On the fifty-second anniversary of John Kennedy's birth, the house where he was born, which has been included in the National Park System, is officially opened to the public. Rose Kennedy has restored the house to the way it looked when her son John was born.

Boston Herald/Peter Southwick.

Caroline Kennedy and cousin Michael Kennedy at Harvard graduation, 5 June 1980.

7 June 1969

WASHINGTON, D.C. A dedication ceremony is held at the renamed Robert F. Kennedy Memorial Stadium. Honored guests are Secretary of the Interior Walter J. Hickel, Under Secretary of the Interior Russell E. Train, Mayor-Commissioner of the District of Columbia Walter E. Washington, and the Honorable Stewart Udall. No members of the Kennedy family are listed on the program.

18 July 1969

CHAPPAQUIDDICK ISLAND, MASSACHU-SETTS. A party held this evening at Lawrence Cottage following the annual Edgartown Regatta is attended by Senator Edward Kennedy, his cousin, attorney Joseph F. Gargan, ex-U.S. Attorney Paul F. Markham, chauffeur John B. Crimmins, state officer Raymond LaRosa, and aides Charles Tretter, Ester Newburgh, Nancy Lyons, Mary Ellen Lyons, Mary Jo Kopechne, Rosemary Keogh, and Suzy Tannenbaum.

Late in the evening, Senator Edward Kennedy leaves the party in his car with 28-year-old Mary Jo Kopechne, who had once worked as a secretary to his brother Robert F. Kennedy. The car plunges off the narrow wooden Dyke Bridge into a tidal pond where it sinks to the bottom. Edward Kennedy escapes, but Miss Kopechne dies.

19 July 1969

EDGARTOWN, MASSACHUSETTS. On Chappaquiddick, a diver recovers the body of Mary Jo Kopechne just minutes before 9 A.M. The police trace ownership of the car they have dredged up to Edward Kennedy. Edgartown police chief Dominick J. Arena returns to the Edgartown police station where Senator Kennedy waits.

331

Caroline Kennedy and brother, John, having a tete-a-tete.

Kennedy gives a statement about events of the previous evening:

"On July 18, 1969, at approximately 11:15 P.M. in Chappaquiddick, Martha's Vineyard, Mass., I was driving my car on Main Street on my way to get the ferry back to Edgartown. I was unfamiliar with the road and turned right on to Dyke Road instead of bearing hard left on Main Street. After proceeding for approximately one-half mile on Dyke Road, I descended a hill and came upon a narrow bridge. The car went off the side of the bridge. There was one passenger with me, one Miss Mary [Kopechne], a former secretary of my brother, Senator Robert Kennedy. The car turned over and sank into the water and landed with the roof resting on the bottom. I attempted to open the door and the window of the car but have no recollection of how I got out of the car. I came to the surface and then repeatedly dove down to the car in an attempt to see if the passenger was still in the car. I was unsuccessful in the attempt. I was exhausted and in a state of shock. I recall walking back to where my friends were eating. There was a car parked in front of the cottage, and I climbed into the back seat. I then asked for someone to bring me back to Edgartown. I remember walking around for a period of time and then going back to my hotel room. When I fully realized what had happened this morning, I immediately contacted the police."

20 July 1969
THE MOON. The late John F. Kennedy's dream of having Americans walking on the moon before the close of the 1960s is fulfilled today, with a landing on the lunar surface by astronauts Neil A. Armstrong and Eugene Aldrin, Jr., of the Apollo II mission. In a special message to Congress on 2 May 1961, President Kennedy had said that he believed the United States "should commit itself to achieving the goal, before this decade is out, of landing a man on the moon and returning him safely to the earth." At 4:18 P.M. E.D.T., the lunar module *Eagle*

lands the two astronauts in the Sea of Tranquility while Air Force Lt. Col. Michael Collins remains in orbit on Apollo II's main spacecraft *Columbia*. At 10:55 P.M. E.D.T., as most of the world watches on television, Neil Armstrong is the first human to walk on the moon. Eighteen minutes later, Eugene "Buzz" Aldrin, Jr., takes his moon walk.

22 July 1969
PLYMOUTH, PENNSYLVANIA. Mary Jo Kopechne's funeral service is held. Senator Edward M. Kennedy arrives by plane to attend the funeral with his wife, Joan, and Ethel (Skakel) Kennedy.

LAKEVILLE, PENNSYLVANIA. Mary Jo Kopechne is buried in a cemetery here.

28 August 1969
HYANNIS PORT, MASSACHUSETTS. Brought to Cape Cod Hospital from her home on Squaw Island by Ethel Kennedy and Jean Smith, Joan (Bennett) Kennedy, 32, suffers a miscarriage. Her husband, Senator Edward Kennedy, was on a camping trip with friends but arrived later at the hospital. It is Joan Kennedy's third miscarriage. The baby had been due in February.

8 November 1969
TAUNTON, MASSACHUSETTS. Speaking at a luncheon of the Federated Junior Clubwomen at the Governor Paul A. Dever School, Rose Kennedy urges members to inspire an interest in helping the mentally retarded in young people.

15 November 1969
HYANNIS PORT, MASSACHUSETTS. Joseph P. Kennedy suffers a mild heart attack and loses consciousness. He is given last rites.

WASHINGTON, D.C. A mass demonstration is held here against the war in Vietnam. Some quarter-of-a-million protestors turn out for the demonstration.

18 November 1969
HYANNIS PORT, MASSACHUSETTS. At the age of 81, Joseph Patrick Kennedy dies of cerebrovascular thrombosis due to arteriosclerosis at 11:05 A.M. in his summer home at the family compound on Cape Cod. He never regained consciousness after his heart attack three days earlier. With him in his second-floor bedroom when he dies are his wife, Rose, his children Eunice, Patricia, Jean, and Edward, his daughters-in-law Jacqueline (Kennedy) Onassis, Ethel (Skakel) Kennedy, and Joan (Bennett) Kennedy, his son-in-law R. Sargent Shriver, Jr., his nephew Joseph Gargan, and his niece, Anne Gargan. Family physician Dr. Robert D. Watt pronounces the patriarch dead. Shortly after his death, Kennedy's body is taken to the Doane, Beal and Ames Funeral Home on West Main Street. In the evening, the Rev. John Cavanaugh, a longtime friend of the Kennedys and chaplain at St. Mary's College in Indiana, celebrates a special mass for family members at St. Francis Xavier Church on South Street.

WASHINGTON, D.C. People across the nation send messages of condolence to the Kennedy family. President Richard M. Nixon issues a statement in which he declares that Joseph Kennedy leaves "a genuinely unique record that involved his entire family in the making of American history. Surely, he felt great satisfaction in his own and in his family's service and accomplishments."

20 November 1969
HYANNIS PORT, MASSACHUSETTS. A requiem mass is celebrated at 9 A.M. for Joseph P. Kennedy at St. Francis Xavier Church. Richard Cardinal Cushing offers the service. The mass is attended only by immediate family and friends. Senator Edward Kennedy delivers a eulogy, and the Kennedy grandchildren participate in the mass. Other family members present include Kennedy's sisters, Mary Loretta Connelly of Florida and Margaret Burke of Brookline. Among the family friends present are former Commissioner of Boston police Joseph Timilty, K. LeMoyne Billings, Judge Francis X. Morrissey, owner of the Baltimore Colts football team, Carroll Rosenblum, and Terence Cardinal Cooke of New York. Well-known singer and Kennedy intimate Morton Downey sings the *Panis Angelicus*. Altogether there are some fifty mourners in the church.

BROOKLINE, MASSACHUSETTS. The body of Joseph P. Kennedy is buried in the family plot at the Holyhood Cemetery.

30 December 1969
ATHENS, GREECE. Rose Kennedy arrives here to spend a New Year's holiday with Aristotle and Jacqueline Onassis.

18 MAY 1970
NEW YORK. At the dedication of the Rose Fitzgerald Kennedy Center for Research in Mental Retardation and Human Development at the Albert Einstein College of Medicine, Rose Kennedy speaks on her

personal experiences of searching for help with her own mentally retarded daughter, Rosemary.

30 May 1970

PURCHASE, NEW YORK. Senator Edward Kennedy delivers the commencement address at Manhattanville College graduation ceremonies.

24 June 1970

DALLAS, TEXAS. At the site of John F. Kennedy's assassination, a roofless rectangular structure is dedicated as a memorial to the late President.

22 July 1970

ADDIS ABABA, ETHIOPIA. Rose Kennedy and Emperor Haile Selassie share a joint birthday celebration at the Imperial Palace. Mrs. Kennedy has taken the Lion of Judah up on a suggestion he made while visiting President Kennedy at the White House that the two, who have back-to-back birthdays, should one day celebrate the occasion together. Rose is 80 today; tomorrow, Haile Selassie turns 78.

15 September 1970

MASSACHUSETTS. Running unopposed, Edward M. Kennedy wins the Democratic primary for senator from Massachusetts. The election results are: Kennedy, 517,443 votes; all others, 116; blanks, 185,546 (total votes cast, 703,105).

3 November 1970

MASSACHUSETTS. Edward M. Kennedy is re-elected to his third term (and second full term) as United States senator despite allegations of wrongdoing at Chappaquiddick. He defeats Republican candidate Josiah A. Spaulding by a plurality of over a half million votes. The election results are: Kennedy, 1,202,856 votes; Spaulding (Republican), 715,978; Lawrence Gilfedder (Socialist Labor), 10,378; Mark R. Shaw (Prohibition), 5,944; all others, 451; blanks, 107,680 (total votes cast, 2,043,287).

31 December 1970

LONDON, ENGLAND. British documents from World War II released after thirty years reveal government antipathy toward Joseph P. Kennedy because of his unpopular belief that the British could not defeat Germany. As Sir Robert Vansittart wrote about the former Ambassador in 1940, "Mr. Kennedy is a very foul specimen of a double-crosser and defeatist."

3 January 1971

WASHINGTON, D.C. As the Ninety-second Congress opens, Edward M. Kennedy begins his third term as U.S. senator from Massachusetts. In this Congress, Senator Kennedy is a member of the Judiciary, Labor and Public Welfare, and Joint Economic committees. He also serves on the Select Committee on Nutrition and Human Needs and the Special Committee on Aging.

21 January 1971

WASHINGTON, D.C. Senator Robert C. Byrd of West Virginia captures the position of Assistant Senate Majority Leader from Senator Edward M. Kennedy, after defeating the incumbent Democratic Whip at a party caucus.

23 January 1971

WASHINGTON, D.C. Senate Majority Leader Mike Mansfield of Montana appoints Senator Edward M. Kennedy to the Democratic Steering Committee.

5 July 1971

HYANNIS PORT, MASSACHUSETTS. David Frost tapes an interview with Rose Kennedy for his television show. In discussing her role as a parent, she says, "I think to be a mother of a child is a thrill and a great vocation; to see a child and think you can form that child's mind and soul—it's overwhelming, and the more children you have, the greater the responsibility.

15 July 1971

BOSTON. Rose Kennedy's niece Ann Gargan, who often helped care for Joe Kennedy when he was ill, is married to Thomas C. King, a native of Ireland. King, divorced, has two sons. The couple are married by a justice of the peace. Rose Kennedy does not attend the ceremony.

10 August 1971

INDIA. Thousands and thousands of East Pakistanis seek refuge here as civil war continues in their country. Senator Edward M. Kennedy, the chairman of the Senate Sub-Committee on Refugees, arrives here to visit refugee camps and talk to Indian and East Pakistani leaders.

12 August 1971

PAKISTAN. The government, under the leadership of General Agha Mohammed Yahya Khan, the country's

Caroline Kennedy with mother, Jacqueline Onassis.

president, cancels Senator Edward M. Kennedy's planned visit to refugee sites in East Pakistan. It cites Kennedy's earlier pro-India statements as the reason.

16 August 1971
NEW DELHI, INDIA. Senator Edward M. Kennedy meets with Prime Minister Indira Gandhi to discuss the refugee situation and India's foreign relations. (On 9 August, India signed a twenty-year treaty of peace and friendship with the Soviet Union.) Later in the day, Senator Kennedy leaves for the United States.

26 August 1971
WASHINGTON, D.C. Senator Edward M. Kennedy announces that he will not be a candidate for the presidency.

8 September 1971
WASHINGTON, D.C. Thirteen years after its conception, the John F. Kennedy Center for the Performing Arts opens to the public. The opening ceremony is celebrated in the Center's Opera House with the world premier of Leonard Bernstein's *Mass* , a work requested by Jacqueline (Kennedy) Onassis. Among the guests are Rose Kennedy, Edward and Joan Kennedy, and the composer Aaron Copland.

16 September 1971
TEL AVIV, ISRAEL. A helicopter carrying Ted and Joan Kennedy to the home of Israeli Defense Minister Moshe Dayan makes a forced landing due to a technical malfunction at a beach near here.

30 October 1971
PUERTA VALLARTA, MEXICO. Peter Lawford, who was divorced from Patricia (Kennedy) Lawford in February of 1966, and with whom he has four children, Christopher, 16, Sydney, 15, Victoria, 12, and Robin, 10, marries Mary Rowan, 21, daughter of comedian Dan Rowan. This is his second marriage.

30 November 1971
ARLINGTON, VIRGINIA. The body of Robert F. Kennedy is moved from lot 45-A, section 30, where it was temporarily interred at Arlington National Cemetery, to a permanent grave in the cemetery.

26-30 December 1971
NORTH VIETNAM. American bombers attack military installations here in reprisal for alleged violations of agreements concerning the bombing halt in 1968.

31 December 1971
WASHINGTON, D.C. With a grant of $1,348,000, the Joseph P. Kennedy, Jr. Foundation establishes the Joseph and Rose Kennedy Institute of Ethics at Georgetown University. The purpose of the Institute shall be the study of applications of ethical principles to scientific and medical purposes.

23 January 1972
MONTEREY PARK, CALIFORNIA. Lady May Lawford, widowed mother of Peter Lawford, dies at the age of 85 in a convalescent home.

United Press International.

Caroline and uncle, Teddy.

14 February 1972
DACCA, BANGLADESH. Senator Edward M. Kennedy arrives here for a two-day visit in the aftermath of a violent civil war that has left hundreds of thousands dead and resulted in the establishment of this independent Bengal nation last December. Several Communist countries recognize the new state, although at this time the United States does not. The Senator observes conditions of the country and meets with its leader, Sheik Mujubur Rahman.

18 February 1972
CALIFORNIA. The state's death penalty is abolished by the California State Supreme Court. As a result of the ruling, Sirhan B. Sirhan will not be executed in the gas chamber.

22 February 1972
ADEN, SOUTHERN YEMEN. The 172 passengers aboard yesterday's hijacked plane are released here. Joseph P. Kennedy II was on the plane that was taken over by armed Palestinian guerrillas. The plane had departed from New Delhi and was headed for Athens when the hijackers took control.

15 June 1972
SACRAMENTO, CALIFORNIA. Following the abolition of the state death penalty, the California Supreme Court upholds the 1969 conviction of Sirhan B. Sirhan for the murder of Senator Robert F. Kennedy but commutes his sentence to life imprisonment.

10 July 1972
MIAMI BEACH, FLORIDA. The Democratic National Convention opens. Despite much interest among delegates in nominating Edward M. Kennedy to a spot on the ticket, the Senator has declared that he will absolutely not accept any nomination.

13 July 1972

MIAMI BEACH, FLORIDA.   Senator George Mc-Govern of South Dakota, an outspoken critic of the Vietnam War, is nominated at the party's presidential candidate with Thomas F. Eagleton of Missouri as his running mate. In the final session, Edward M. Kennedy presents Senator McGovern to the delegates and delivers an address criticizing the Nixon administration.

25 July 1972

WASHINGTON, D.C.   Senator Edward M. Kennedy announces that he has been in communication with North Vietnamese President Ton Duc Thang about a list of Americans taken prisoner by Communist guerrillas in South Vietnam. Lists of American prisoners in North Vietnam have previously been available, but not lists of those in South Vietnam.

8 August 1972

WASHINGTON, D.C.   At a special session, the Democratic National Committee nominates R. Sargent Shriver, Jr., as the party's candidate for vice-president. Senator Thomas Eagleton of Missouri, had withdrawn from the ticket on 31 July after it was disclosed that he had undergone psychiatric treatment in the 1970s for depression, and presidential candidate Senator George McGovern had announced on television his choice of Shriver three days earlier.

16 August 1972

WASHINGTON, D.C.   Former President Lyndon B. Johnson endorses the Democratic ticket of McGovern and Shriver.

7 November 1972

THE UNITED STATES.   President Richard M. Nixon and Vice-President Spiro T. Agnew are re-elected in a landslide victory over Democratic candidates George S. McGovern and R. Sargent Shriver, Jr.

15 November 1972

SAXMUNDHAM, ENGLAND.   Stewart Evans, a police officer in Lowestoft, whose hobby it is to locate wreckage of World War II airplanes, announces that he and co-workers have found the parts of the PB4Y Liberator that exploded on 12 August 1944, killing Lt. Joseph P. Kennedy, Jr., USNR, and Lt. Wilford J. Willy, USN. Evans says he found the fuselage, wing, and engine of the drone buried in a wood.

18 November 1972

WINFIELD, ILLINOIS.   Mary Loretta (Kennedy) Connelly dies of a ruptured abdominal aneurysm at the age of 80. She was the paternal aunt of the late President John F. Kennedy. A resident of 23 W. 220 St. James Ct., Glen Ellyn, she dies at Central DuPage Hospital at 7:30 A.M. She leaves a daughter, Mary Lou.

25 November 1972

ST. AUGUSTINE, FLORIDA.   Mary (Kennedy) Connelly is buried at the San Lorenzo Cemetery.

20 January 1973

WASHINGTON, D.C.   President Nixon and Vice-President Agnew begin their second term of office.

27 January 1973

PARIS.   A four-party agreement to halt fighting in Vietnam is signed here, ending the war. Under its terms, the United States promises to withdraw its troops and North Vietnam pledges to release American prisoners.

2 March 1973

WASHINGTON, D.C.   Palestinian guerrillas who have taken over the Saudi Arabian Embassy demand the release of Sirhan B. Sirhan, but President Nixon announces that he will not arrange for the release. Later in the day, the terrorists kill two Americans and one Belgian envoy.

29 March 1973

SOUTH VIETNAM.   The last remaining American troops leave the country.

1 April 1973

NORTH VIETNAM.   The North Vietnamese government releases nearly 600 American soldiers who have been held as prisoners of war.

20 June 1973

CLAIRFIELD, TENNESSEE.   Accompanied by Secret Service agents, Caroline Kennedy, 15, arrives here to assist a film crew making a documentary on East Tennessee coal miners. She will stay with a local family and spend the summer here.

27 June 1973

WASHINGTON, D.C.   At a Senate select committee hearing on the Watergate scandal, John W. Dean III reveals that President Richard M. Nixon kept an "enemies list." Among the senators listed as political foes is Edward M. Kennedy; among those listed in the business field is former U.S. ambassador to France and Democratic vice-presidential candidate R. Sargent Shriver, Jr.

9 October 1973

WASHINGTON, D.C. Reversing a change made in 1964, the Board on Geographical Names of the Department of the Interior eliminates the name Cape Kennedy and restores that of Cape Canaveral.

16 November 1973

WASHINGTON, D.C. Senator Edward M. Kennedy's office announces that bone cancer in the lower part of his son Edward's right leg has been diagnosed. The leg will have to be amputated. The boy entered Georgetown University Hospital on 13 November 1973 for diagnostic tests which revealed the malignancy.

17 November 1973

WASHINGTON, D.C. Surgeons at Georgetown University Hospital amputate the cancerous lower right leg of 12-year-old Edward Kennedy, Jr. This operation is the only known way to stop the spread of malignant cells to the rest of the body.

WASHINGTON, D.C. Kathleen Kennedy, 22, marries David Townsend, 26. The bride is the eldest child of Ethel (Skakel) and the late Senator Robert F. Kennedy. Kathleen, who will graduate from Harvard in June 1974, worked in 1970 with Alaskan Eskimos in a community action program; in 1968 she helped make adobe bricks and tutored English on a Navajo Indian Reservation in Arizona.

The groom, who is studying for a doctorate in English at Harvard, is a 1969 graduate of Loyola College in Baltimore. His father, Raymond Townsend, is a principal in the Baltimore county schools; his mother, Delores, is a secretary in the Baltimore school district.

1 April 1974

WASHINGTON, D.C. The United States Air Force changes the name of Cape Kennedy Air Force Station back to Cape Canaveral Air Force Station. On 9 October 1973, the Department of the Interior's Board on Geographical Names had restored the cape's historical name.

7 April 1974

BONN, WEST GERMANY. On a tour of Eastern Europe, Senator Edward M. Kennedy meets with Chancellor Willy Brandt to discuss American defenses and other United States involvements in Europe.

8 April 1974

BONN, WEST GERMANY. In a speech to members of the Foreign Policy Association, Senator Edward M. Kennedy calls for the United States and Europe to revitalize their economic and political relationships.

16 April 1974

BELGRADE, YUGOSLAVIA. Senator Edward Kennedy meets with President Josip Broz Tito.

21 April 1974

MOSCOW. In an address on world peace before students and faculty at Moscow State University, Senator Edward M. Kennedy urges disarmament and calls for Russian cooperation with other nations.

22 April 1974

MOSCOW. Senator Edward M. Kennedy confers with General Secretary of the Communist Party Leonid Breshnev on issues of mutual concern.

6 May 1974

BONN, WEST GERMANY. Following a scandal over the employment of an East German spy in his administration, Willy Brandt resigns as chancellor.

31 May 1974

WASHINGTON, D.C. Senator Edward Kennedy's office announces that Joan (Bennett) Kennedy is undergoing treatment for emotional strain at the Silver Hill Foundation, a psychiatric facility in New Canaan, Connecticut.

13 June 1974

CAMBRIDGE, MASSACHUSETTS. Kathleen (Kennedy) Townsend graduates with honors from Harvard College with a Bachelor of Arts degree in American History and Literature. She entered as a freshman in 1969.

21 June 1974

WASHINGTON, D.C. Senator Edward Kennedy's office announces that Joan (Bennett) Kennedy has been readmitted to Silver Hill Hospital for treatment.

9 July 1974

WASHINGTON, D.C. Earl Warren, the former chief justice of the Supreme Court, who also headed the commission that investigated President Kennedy's assassination, dies at the age of 83.

25 July 1974

WASHINGTON, D.C. The Second Air Medal is posthumously awarded to Lt. Joseph P. Kennedy, Jr., USNR. The citation accompanying the medal reads:

Joan Bennett Kennedy with son, Ted, Jr., at a John Fitzgerald Kennedy Library fund-raising event, 4 October 1985.

"For meritorious achievement in aerial flight as Pilot of a United States Naval Patrol Bomber Plane in Anti-Submarine operations in the Bay of Biscay and the Western Approaches to the United Kingdom from October 22, 1943, to June 16, 1944. Completing his fifth mission during this period, Kennedy contributed materially to the success of his squadron. His courage and devotion to duty were in keeping with the highest traditions of the United States Naval Service."

9 August 1974

WASHINGTON, D.C. Facing possible impeachment following the scandal in which White House aides broke into Democratic headquarters at the Watergate, Richard M. Nixon resigns as president of the United States. He is succeeded by Vice-President Gerald R. Ford.

15 August 1974

BOSTON. A group of citizens meets to protest a 21 June ruling by a United States District Court Judge that segregated Boston public schools be integrated by means of busing. When Senator Edward M. Kennedy attempts to address the protesters, they throw food at him and prevent him from speaking.

23 September 1974

BOSTON. Citing family responsibilities, Senator Edward Kennedy announces at a press conference that he will not run for president in the 1976 election. Recent political polls show Kennedy as a leading choice for the presidency, but his decision, he says, is firm and final.

8 October 1974

LA PAZ, BOLIVIA. Dissidents opposed to President Hugo Banzer Suarez's government blow up a statue of the late President Kennedy.

14 November 1974

BROOKLINE, MASSACHUSETTS. Margaret (Kennedy) Burke, paternal aunt of the late President John F. Kennedy, dies at the age of 76. She had married Charles Joseph Burke.

3 January 1975

SANTA MONICA, CALIFORNIA. A divorce is granted to Mary (Rowan) Lawford from Peter Lawford on the grounds of "irreconcilable differences." No alimony is requested.

6 February 1975

CAMBRIDGE, MASSACHUSETTS. Following the release of an environmental-impact report on the planned location of the Kennedy library and museum, the John F. Kennedy Library Corporation announces that it has abandoned plans to build the facilities in Cambridge. The community had opposed the site because of potential traffic and parking problems.

13 February 1975

SAN FRANCISCO. The California Supreme Court denies a request for a new trial of Sirhan B. Sirhan. A lawyer for Sirhan, who is serving a life sentence, charges that evidence in favor of the defendant was not allowed in his trial.

15 March 1975

NEUILLY-SUR-SEINE, FRANCE. Aristotle Onassis, 69, dies of pneumonia at the American Hospital. His daughter, Christina, is with him when he dies; his wife, Jacqueline Onassis, is in New York. This evening, Mrs. Onassis leaves by plane for Paris.

5 June 1975

CONCORD, MASSACHUSETTS. Caroline Kennedy, 17, graduates from Concord Academy. Family members present at her commencement include Jacqueline Onassis and Rose Kennedy.

15 July 1975

WASHINGTON, D.C. A committee to support the Democratic nomination of R. Sargent Shriver, Jr., for president is registered.

8 September 1975

BROOKLINE, MASSACHUSETTS. President Kennedy's birthplace at 83 Beals Street is firebombed. (The fire is confined to the kitchen and hallway.) On the sidewalk in front of the house are the spray-painted words "Bus Teddy." Earlier in the day, phase 2 of the Boston school desegregation program backed by Senator Edward Kennedy went into effect.

20 September 1975

WASHINGTON, D.C. R. Sargent Shriver, Jr., announces that he will seek the Democratic nomination for president.

6 October 1975

LOS ANGELES. A state court releases the report of a panel of weapons experts that investigated the possibility of a second gun being used in Robert Kennedy's assassination. Although the deterioration of three bullets since the shooting made ballistics identification impossible, the panel concludes that the bullets that struck Kennedy were fired from Sirhan's gun.

22 March 1976

WASHINGTON, D.C. Following a poor showing in the primaries, R. Sargent Shriver officially leaves the race for the Democratic presidential nomination. He had entered in the New Hampshire, Vermont, Massachusetts, and Illinois primaries.

17 May 1976

NEW HAVEN, CONNECTICUT. Robert Sargent Shriver III graduates from Yale University with a Bachelor of Arts degree in American Studies.

27 May 1976

BOSTON. Joseph P. Kennedy II graduates from the University of Massachusetts with a Bachelor of Arts degree in Legal Education Services.

25 June 1976

ARLINGTON, VIRGINIA. Peter Lawford, 52, marries Deborah Gould, 25, in a brief ceremony in judge's chambers. This is his third marriage.

14 September 1976

MASSACHUSETTS. Edward M. Kennedy easily

Boston Herald.

Kara Anne Kennedy, eldest child of Edward M. Kennedy.

defeats three challengers to win the Democratic primary for senator from Massachusetts. The election results are: Kennedy, 534,725 votes; Robert Emmett Dinsmore, 117,496; Frederick C. Langone, 59,315; Bernard P. Solomon, 12,399; all others, 53; blanks, 24,828 (total votes cast, 748,816).

17 September 1976

WASHINGTON, D.C.   In the light of new information in connection with the assassinations of President John F. Kennedy and the Rev. Dr. Martin Luther King, Jr., the House of Representatives votes to form a special committee to study the shootings further.

2 November 1976

MASSACHUSETTS.   Edward M. Kennedy is re-elected to the United States Senate for his fourth term. The election results are: Kennedy (Democrat), 1,726,657 votes; Michael S. Robertson (Republican), 722,641; Carol Henderson Evans (Socialist Workers Party), 26,283; H. Graham Lowry (U.S. Labor Party), 15,517; all others, 157; blanks, 103,007 (total votes cast, 2,594,262).

20 November 1976

WASHINGTON, D.C.   Hugh D. Auchincloss, 79, stepfather of Jacqueline (Kennedy) Onassis, dies of emphysema.

4 January 1977

WASHINGTON, D.C.   As the Ninety-fifth Congress opens, Senator Edward M. Kennedy is sworn in and begins his fourth term of office. In this Congress, Senator Kennedy is a member of the Human Resources, Judiciary, and Joint Economic committees, and also serves on the Select Committee on Nutrition and Human Needs.

20 January 1977

WASHINGTON, D.C.   Former Georgia governor Jimmy Carter is inaugurated as the thirty-ninth president of the United States. Walter F. Mondale is sworn in as vice-president.

22 May 1977

WASHINGTON, D.C.   Maria Shriver, 21, graduates from Georgetown University with a Bachelor of Arts degree in Political Science and American Studies from the College of Arts and Sciences. She transferred to Georgetown from Manhattanville College, where she studied from 1973 to 1975.

16 June 1977

CAMBRIDGE, MASSACHUSETTS.   Robert F. Kennedy, Jr., 22, graduates from Harvard University cum laude with a Bachelor of Arts degree.

United Press International/Bettmann Newsphotos.

Jackie, flanked by Caroline and John, arrive at a John Fitzgerald Kennedy Library fund-raising dinner, 4 October 1986.

9 September 1977

BOSTON. Kenneth P. O'Donnell, 53, one of John F. Kennedy's closest aides and his appointments secretary when his administration was cut short, dies of liver disease at Beth Israel Hospital. One of "Kennedy's Irish Mafia," O'Donnell was the coauthor of a bestselling book on the late president, *Johnny, We Hardly Knew Ye: Memories of John Fitzgerald Kennedy.*

1 October 1977

WASHINGTON, D.C. An honorary Doctor of Humane Letters degree is conferred on Rose Kennedy by Georgetown University in Gaston Hall. The citation reads in part: "Faced with the grief—shared by many millions of other parents—of knowing one of her children to be mentally retarded, she chose, unlike so many of her contemporaries, not to hide the fact. Rather she turned this affliction into the occasion for beginning a crusade on behalf of all others similarly afflicted." Following the presentation, Senator Edward M. Kennedy speaks briefly.

3 October 1977

LONDON. Robert F. Kennedy, Jr., enters the London School of Economics for the 1977-1978 session. He registers for the Master of Science program in international relations, but will withdraw after Christmas.

7 November 1977

SANTA FE, NEW MEXICO. A daughter, Meaghan Ann, is born to Kathleen (Kennedy) and David Townsend. Their first child, the baby is born at home.

7 December 1977

WASHINGTON, D.C. In response to a request made under the Freedom of Information Act, the Federal Bureau of Investigation releases 40,000 pages of memoranda, letters, reports, and other materials connected with its investigation into the assassination of President John F. Kennedy.

18 January 1978

WASHINGTON, D.C. A second batch of FBI files—over 58,000 pages—connected with the investigation of the late President Kennedy's assassination is released by the FBI in response to a request made under the Freedom of Information Act. A first batch had been released in 1977.

12 August 1978

ROME, ITALY. Senator Edward M. Kennedy attends the funeral of Pope Paul VI in Vatican City.

6 September 1978

WASHINGTON, D.C.   The House Select Committee on Assassinations opens a series of hearings on the assassinations of John F. Kennedy and Martin Luther King, Jr. Those scheduled to appear in the Kennedy hearings include the former governor of Texas, John B. Connally, and his wife, Nellie; Michael Baden, chief medical examiner of New York; Marina Oswald Porter, Lee Harvey Oswald's remarried widow; and former president Gerald Ford, who had served on the Warren Commission.

21 October 1978

CAMBRIDGE, MASSACHUSETTS.   Dedication ceremonies for a new building at the John F. Kennedy School of Government at Harvard University are held at the John F. Kennedy Memorial Park. Guest speakers include Michael Dukakis, the governor of Massachusetts, and Thomas P. O'Neill, Jr., the Speaker of the House of Representatives. Senator Edward Kennedy delivers an address entitled "A Living Memorial."

16 December 1978

ALBUQUERQUE, NEW MEXICO.   Kathleen (Kennedy) Townsend graduates from the University of New Mexico School of Law with a Doctor of Laws degree.

29 December 1978

WASHINGTON, D.C.   After numerous hearings beginning in September, the Select Committee on Assassinations of the House of Representatives files a summary of its findings and recommendations. It concludes that Lee Harvey Oswald fired three shots at President John F. Kennedy on 22 November 1963 from the sixth floor window of the southeast corner of the Texas School Book Depository Building. The second and third bullets hit the President from behind, the last bullet causing his death. The Committee also finds that acoustical evidence indicates that two people probably shot at President Kennedy—the second gunman's identity is unknown—and that a conspiracy probably existed. Involvement by any agencies of foreign governments is ruled out.

3 February 1979

GLADWYNE, PENNSYLVANIA. Joseph P. Kennedy II, 26, marries Sheila Brewster Rauch, an Epis-

John F. Kennedy, Jr., Mrs. Michael Dukakis, Senator Edward Kennedy, and Jacqueline Kennedy Onassis at dedication ceremonies for the John F. Kennedy Park in Cambridge, Mass. November, 1985.

United Press International/Bettmann Newsphotos.

343

United Press International/Bettmann Newsphotos.

First cousins Joseph P. Kennedy, II, Caroline Kennedy and Sydney Lawford arrive in West Palm Beach
after the death of Joe's younger brother, David.

copalian, at St. John Baptist Vianney Roman Catholic Church. The bride, 29, is the daughter of banker Rudolph Stewart Rauch, Jr., and Frances S. Brewster Rauch.

11 February 1979
BOSTON. Thomas King, the husband of the former Ann Gargan, dies at the age of 55 at Massachusetts General Hospital after a heart attack.

28 March 1979
BOSTON. John Francis Fitzgerald, Jr., dies at the age of 81 at New England Deaconess Hospital after a long illness. He lived in Milton and was a retired executive of the Boston Edison Company. He leaves his wife Catherine (O'Hearn), whom he married on 28 April

1928, three sons, Frederick, John (a pastor), and Robert, and several grandchildren, nieces, and nephews. He was the godfather of the late President Kennedy and last surviving brother of Rose (Fitzgerald) Kennedy.

7 June 1979
CAMBRIDGE, MASSACHUSETTS. Stephen E. Smith, Jr., graduates from Harvard College with a Bachelor of Arts degree.

17 July 1979
WASHINGTON, D.C. The House Select Committee on Assassinations issues its final report on the assassination of President Kennedy. The report concludes that a conspiracy in the killing of President Kennedy is likely, but that there is no direct proof of it.

20 October 1979

BOSTON.   The newly completed John F. Kennedy Library is dedicated at a ceremony attended by several thousand, including President Jimmy Carter, Senator Edward Kennedy, and Joseph P. Kennedy, II, each of whom speaks.

In his address, Joe Kennedy II recalls his father's struggle to improve the circumstances of impoverished migrant farm workers, miners, tenant farmers, Indians, blacks, and Chicanos, as well as those of ordinary working families. He expresses hope that his generation of Americans will summon what Robert F. Kennedy referred to as "moral courage" and use it to "work to bring about the decent and just world he so much wanted to see in his lifetime."

The Boston Pops Orchestra plays Aaron Copland's *Fanfare for the Common Man*. The building in Columbia Point stands on 12 acres next to the University of Massachusetts, overlooking Dorchester Bay. Designed by architect I. M. Pei of New York, the building houses a library, museum, and visual archives.

1 November 1979

NEW HAVEN, CONNECTICUT.   A daughter, Maeve Fahey is born to Kathleen (Kennedy) and David Townsend. She is their second daughter and is born at home.

7 November 1979

BOSTON.   Before a capacity audience at Faneuil Hall, Senator Edward M. Kennedy announces his candidacy for the Democratic nomination for president for the 1980 election. His wife, Joan, from whom he has been separated for two years but who is with him today, says she will actively campaign on his behalf. Also present are Rose Kennedy and Jacqueline (Kennedy) Onassis.

4 January 1980

WASHINGTON, D.C.   After denying requests made in 1978 and 1979 by the House Select Committee on Assassinations to reopen the investigation of President Kennedy's murder, the Justice Department decides to conduct a "limited" probe of the assassination. Part of the investigation will center on sound recordings suggesting the possibility of a second assassin.

26 February 1980

NEW HAMPSHIRE.   Jimmy Carter wins the Democratic presidential primary with 52,692 votes, or 47.1 percent of the total. Edward M. Kennedy receives 41,745 votes, or 37.3 percent of the total. (Lyndon LaRouche of New York gets 2,326 votes, or 2.1 percent.)

4 March 1980

MASSACHUSETTS.   Edward M. Kennedy wins the Democratic presidential primary with 590,393 votes, or 65.1 percent of the total. Jimmy Carter receives 260,401 votes, or 28.7 percent of the total.

VERMONT.   Jimmy Carter wins the Democratic presidential primary with 29,015 votes, or 73.1 percent of the total. Edward M. Kennedy receives 10,135 votes, or 25.5 percent of the total. (Lyndon LaRouche receives 6 votes.)

11 March 1980

ALABAMA.   Jimmy Carter wins the Democratic presidential primary with 193,734 votes, or 81.6 percent of the total. Edward M. Kennedy receives 31,382 votes, or 13.2 percent of the total.

FLORIDA.   Jimmy Carter wins the Democratic presidential primary with 666,321 votes, or 60.7 percent of the total. Edward M. Kennedy receives 254,727 votes, or 23.2 percent of the total.

GEORGIA.   Jimmy Carter wins the Democratic presidential primary with 338,772 votes, or 88 percent of the total. Edward M. Kennedy receives 32,315 votes, or 8.4 percent of the total. (Lyndon LaRouche receives 513 votes.)

16 March 1980

PUERTO RICO.   Jimmy Carter wins the Democratic presidential primary with 449,681 votes, or 51.7 percent of the total. Edward M. Kennedy receives 418,068 votes, or 48 percent of the total.

18 March 1980

ILLINOIS.   Jimmy Carter wins the Democratic presidential primary with 780,787 votes, or 65 percent of the total. Edward M. Kennedy receives 359,875 votes, or 30 percent of the total. (Lyndon LaRouche gets 19,192 votes, or 1.6 percent.)

25 March 1980

CONNECTICUT.   Edward M. Kennedy wins the Democratic presidential primary with 98,662 votes, or 46.9 percent of the total. Jimmy Carter receives 87,207 votes, or 41.5 percent of the total.

NEW YORK.   Edward M. Kennedy wins the Democratic presidential primary with 582,757 votes, or 58.9 percent of the total. Jimmy Carter receives 406,305 votes, or 41.1 percent of the total.

United Press International/Bettmann Newsphotos.

Joe II smiles as he announces he will seek the congressional seat being vacated by House Speaker Thomas "Tip" O'Neill. 4 December 1985.

1 April 1980

KANSAS. Jimmy Carter wins the Democratic presidential primary with 109,807 votes, or 56.6 percent of the total. Edward M. Kennedy receives 61,318 votes, or 31.6 percent of the total.

WISCONSIN. Jimmy Carter wins the Democratic presidential primary with 353,662 votes, or 56.2 percent of the total. Edward M. Kennedy receives 189,520 votes, or 30.1 percent of the total. (Lyndon LaRouche gets 6,896 votes, or 1.1 percent.)

5 April 1980

LOUISIANA. Jimmy Carter wins the Democratic presidential primary with 199,956 votes, or 55.7 percent of the total. Edward M. Kennedy receives 80,797 votes, or 22.5 percent of the total.

22 April 1980

PENNSYLVANIA. Edward M. Kennedy wins the Democratic presidential primary with 736,854 votes, or 45.7 percent of the total. Jimmy Carter receives 732,332 votes, or 45.4 percent of the total.

3 May 1980

TEXAS. Jimmy Carter wins the Democratic presidential primary with 770,390 votes, or 55.9 percent of the total. Edward M. Kennedy receives 314,129 votes, or 22.8 percent of the total.

6 May 1980

DISTRICT OF COLUMBIA. Edward M. Kennedy wins the district's Democratic presidential primary with 39,561 votes, or 61.7 percent of the total. Jimmy Carter receives 23,697 votes, or 36.9 percent of the total. (Lyndon LaRouche gets 892 votes, or 1.4 percent.)

INDIANA. Jimmy Carter wins the Democratic presidential primary with 398,949 votes, or 67.7 percent of the total. Edward M. Kennedy receives 190,492 votes, or 32.3 percent of the total.

NORTH CAROLINA. Jimmy Carter wins the Democratic presidential primary with 516,778 votes, or 70.1 percent of the total. Edward M. Kennedy receives 130,684 votes, or 17.7 percent of the total.

TENNESSEE. Jimmy Carter wins the Democratic presidential primary with 221,658 votes, or 75.2 percent of the total. Edward M. Kennedy receives 53,258 votes, or 18.1 percent of the total. (Lyndon LaRouche gets 925 votes, or 0.3 percent.)

13 May 1980

MARYLAND. Jimmy Carter wins the Democratic presidential primary with 226,528 votes, or 47.5 percent of the total. Edward M. Kennedy receives 181,091 votes, or 38 percent of the total. (Lyndon LaRouche gets 4,388 votes, or 0.9 percent.)

NEBRASKA. Jimmy Carter wins the Democratic presidential primary with 72,120 votes, or 46.9 percent of the total. Edward M. Kennedy receives 57,826 votes, or 37.6 percent of the total. (Lyndon LaRouche gets 1,169 votes, or 0.8 percent.)

20 May 1980

OREGON. Jimmy Carter wins the Democratic presidential primary with 208,693 votes, or 56.7 percent of the total. Edward M. Kennedy receives 114,651 votes, or 31.1 percent of the total.

27 May 1980

ARKANSAS. Jimmy Carter wins the Democratic presidential primary with 269,375 votes, or 60.1 percent of the total. Edward M. Kennedy receives 78,542 votes, or 17.5 percent of the total.

IDAHO. Jimmy Carter wins the Democratic presidential primary with 31,383 votes, or 62.2 percent of the total. Edward M. Kennedy receives 11,087 votes, or 22 percent of the total.

KENTUCKY. Jimmy Carter wins the Democratic presidential primary with 160,819 votes, or 66.9 percent of the total. Edward M. Kennedy receives 55,167 votes, or 23 percent of the total.

Joe II formally kicks off his campaign for 8th Congressional seat as his wife Sheila holds her squirming 5 year old twins, Matthew (left) and JPK III. 1 January 1986.

United Press International/Bettmann Newsphotos.

NEVADA. Jimmy Carter wins the Democratic presidential primary with 25,159 votes, or 37.6 percent of the total. Edward M. Kennedy receives 19,296 votes, or 28.8 percent of the total.

3 June 1980

CALIFORNIA. A slate of delegates favoring Edward M. Kennedy wins the Democratic presidential primary with 1,507,142 votes, or 44.8 percent of the total. Jimmy Carter's slate receives 1,266,276 votes, or 37.6 percent of the total. (The slate pledged to Edmund G. Brown, Jr., the governor of California, receives 135,962 votes, or 4 percent; Lyndon LaRouche's slate receives 71,779 votes, or 2.1 percent.)

NEW MEXICO. Edward M. Kennedy wins the Democratic presidential primary with 73,721 votes, or 46.3 percent of the total. Jimmy Carter receives 66,621 votes, or 41.8 percent of the total. (Lyndon LaRouche gets 4,798 votes, or 3 percent.)

MONTANA. Jimmy Carter wins the Democratic presidential primary with 66,922 votes, or 51.5 percent of the total. Edward M. Kennedy receives 47,671 votes, or 36.7 percent of the total.

OHIO. Jimmy Carter wins the Democratic presidential primary with 605,744 votes, or 51.1 percent of the total. Edward M. Kennedy receives 523,874 votes, or 44.2 percent of the total. (Lyndon LaRouche gets 35,269 votes, or 3 percent.)

RHODE ISLAND. Edward M. Kennedy wins the Democratic presidential primary with 26,179 votes, or 68.3 percent of the total. Jimmy Carter receives 9,907 votes, or 25.8 percent of the total. (Lyndon LaRouche gets 1,160 votes, or 3 percent.)

SOUTH DAKOTA. A slate of delegates favoring Edward M. Kennedy wins the Democratic presidential primary with 33,418 votes, or 48.6 percent of the total. Jimmy Carter's slate receives 31,251 votes, or 45.4 percent of the total.

NEW JERSEY. Edward M. Kennedy wins the Democratic presidential primary with 315,109 votes, or 56.2 percent of the total. Jimmy Carter receives 212,387 votes, or 37.9 percent of the total. (Lyndon LaRouche gets 13,913 votes, or 2.5 percent.)

WEST VIRGINIA. Jimmy Carter wins the Democratic presidential primary with 197,687 votes, or 62.2 percent of the total. Edward M. Kennedy receives 120,247 votes, or 37.8 percent of the total.

5 June 1980

CAMBRIDGE, MASSACHUSETTS. Caroline Kennedy, 22, graduates from Radcliffe College with a Bachelor of Arts degree in Fine Arts.

Michael L. Kennedy, 22, the son of Ethel (Skakel) Kennedy and the late Robert Kennedy, graduates from Harvard College with a Bachelor of Arts in History.

14 June 1980

WASHINGTON, D.C. Mary Courtney Kennedy, 23, daughter of Ethel (Skakel) Kennedy and the late Robert Kennedy, marries Jeffrey Ruhe, 28.

11 August 1980

NEW YORK. Only hours after the thirty-eighth Democratic National Convention opens at Madison Square Garden, Senator Edward M. Kennedy withdraws as a candidate for the party's presidential nomination. Although President Carter had months ago won enough delegates to ensure the nomination, Kennedy had refused to concede. But after losing a last-minute attempt to enable delegates to disregard their pledges on the first ballot, Kennedy drops out of the race.

4 October 1980

BOSTON. Twin sons, Joseph Patrick and Matthew Rauch, are born to Sheila (Rauch) and Joseph P. Kennedy II at Brigham and Women's Hospital. Joseph is born at 9:34 P.M., Matthew at 9:42 P.M. They are the couple's first children.

15 January 1981

WASHINGTON, D.C. Victoria Lawford, 23, graduates from Mount Vernon College with a Bachelor of Arts degree in Arts and Humanities, and Communications.

20 January 1981

WASHINGTON, D.C. A former movie actor and an ex-governor of California, Ronald Wilson Reagan is inaugurated as the fortieth president of the United States. George Bush is sworn in as vice-president.

21 January 1981

BOSTON. Edward and Joan Kennedy announce their decision to divorce.

14 March 1981

NEW YORK. Michael LeMoyne Kennedy, 23, marries Victoria Gifford, 23, at St. Ignatius Loyola Catholic

United Press International/Bettmann Newsphotos.

Caroline Kennedy at brother John F. Kennedy, Jr.'s graduation ceremonies at Brown University, where he received a bachelor's degree in history.

Church. The groom is the son of Ethel (Skakel) Kennedy and the late Senator Robert F. Kennedy. The bride is the daughter of sportscaster and former football star Frank Gifford.

23 May 1981
CAMBRIDGE, MASSACHUSETTS. Joan (Bennett) Kennedy receives a Master of Education degree from Lesley College. She has completed her work on an independent study basis.

24 May 1981
NEW HAVEN, CONNECTICUT. Timothy Perry Shriver graduates from Yale University with a Bachelor of Arts degree. He majored in history.

9 June 1981
NEW HAVEN, CONNECTICUT. Robert Sargent Shriver III graduates from the Yale University School of Law with a Doctor of Laws degree.

24 August 1981
HYANNIS PORT, MASSACHUSETTS. An honorary Doctor of Humane Letters degree is conferred upon Rose Kennedy by Boston College. The award was to have been presented at the school's 18 May 1981 commencement, which Rose Kennedy could not attend because of ill health.

29 October 1981
BOSTON. Joseph P. Kennedy II establishes the Citizens Conservation Corporation to promote energy conservation and savings in low-income multifamily dwellings and to provide energy-conservation education for low-income families and the elderly.

3 April 1982
BLOOMINGTON, INDIANA. Robert F. Kennedy, Jr., 28, marries Emily Ruth Black, 24, in a Catholic-Protestant ceremony at the First Christian Church, 205 East Kirkwood Avenue.

21 May 1982
SOLEDAD, CALIFORNIA. The California State Parole Board revokes Sirhan B. Sirhan's scheduled 1 September 1984 parole hearing. The decision is based on threats made by the accused assassin on the lives of prison officials, Senator Edward Kennedy, and others. Sirhan is in Soledad Prison.

23 May 1982
CHARLOTTESVILLE, VIRGINIA. Robert F. Kennedy, Jr., receives a Doctor of Laws degree from the University of Virginia.

7 June 1982
PROVIDENCE, RHODE ISLAND. Mary Kerry Kennedy graduates from Brown University with a Bachelor of Arts degree. She was a linguistics major. (She entered with and is listed as a member of the class of 1981.)

23 August 1982
NEW YORK. Robert F. Kennedy, Jr., 28, is sworn in as an assistant district attorney for the Borough of Manhattan. He will serve under Manhattan District Attorney Robert Morgenthau at a salary of $20,000 per year.

14 September 1982
MASSACHUSETTS. Unopposed, Senator Edward M. Kennedy wins the Democratic primary for senator from Massachusetts. The election results are: Kennedy, 869,985; all others, 361; blanks, 340,871 (total votes cast, 1,211,217).

2 November 1982
MASSACHUSETTS. Senator Edward M. Kennedy is re-elected to a fifth (and fourth full) term in the U.S. Senate. He receives 1,247,084 votes to Republican challenger Raymond Shamie's 784,602. Howard Katz of the Liberty party receives 18,878 votes.

1 December 1982
BOSTON. Citing family obligations and distress over his recent divorce, Senator Edward Kennedy announces that he will not be a candidate for president in the 1984 election. He does not rule out a future candidacy, however. "I don't think it's any mystery that I would like to be President," he says.

6 December 1982
BARNSTABLE, MASSACHUSETTS. After twenty-three years of marriage, Ted and Joan Kennedy, accompanied by their lawyers, file for divorce under the state's no-fault divorce law in Barnstable Probate Court. "Irretrievable breakdown" is cited as grounds for the divorce, which becomes final in a year.

8 December 1982
NEW YORK. The *New York Law Journal* releases the list of those who passed the New York State Bar exam given in July. Robert F. Kennedy, Jr.'s name is not

on the list. Kennedy began working as an assistant district attorney for the Borough of Manhattan in August.

3 January 1983
WASHINGTON, D.C.   As the Ninety-eighth Congress opens, Senator Edward M. Kennedy, 50, is sworn in and begins his fifth term as U.S. senator from Massachusetts. In this Congress, Senator Kennedy serves on the Armed Services, Judiciary, Labor and Human Resources, and Joint Economic committees.

9 January 1983
CHARLOTTESVILLE, VIRGINIA.   A son, Michael, Jr., is born to Victoria (Gifford) and Michael LeMoyne Kennedy. He is their first child.

29 May 1983
BOSTON.   Christopher Lawford, 28, graduates from the Boston College Law School with a Doctor of Laws degree.

30 May 1983
MEDFORD, MASSACHUSETTS.   At graduation exercises of Tufts University, Senator Edward Kennedy delivers the commencement address and receives an honorary Doctor of Laws degree.

6 June 1983
PROVIDENCE, RHODE ISLAND.   John F. Kennedy, Jr., 22, graduates from Brown University with a Bachelor of Arts degree in History.

24 July 1983
JEFFERSON, WISCONSIN.   The Kennedy family donates $1 million to the St. Coletta School in Jefferson, Wisconsin, in honor of Rose Kennedy's ninety-third birthday.

1 September 1983
DURHAM, NORTH CAROLINA.   William Kennedy Smith graduates from Duke University with a Bachelor of Arts degree in History.

17 September 1983
CENTERVILLE, MASSACHUSETTS.   Sydney Lawford, 27, marries James Peter McKelvey, 28, at Our Lady of Victory Church. The groom is a video and television producer from Boston. A dinner reception follows at the Kennedy compound for more than 400 guests.

26 October 1983
BOSTON.   Joseph P. Kennedy II founds the Citizens Heat and Power Corporation, an organization that will provide energy management services to institutional energy users such as hospitals, schools, and municipal buildings.

22 November 1983
ARLINGTON, VIRGINIA.   The Kennedy family gathers at John Kennedy's grave on the twentieth anniversary of his assassination.

WASHINGTON, D.C.   President Ronald Reagan and other dignitaries attend a service at the Holy Trinity Church to honor President Kennedy. Caroline Kennedy reads from her father's speeches.

17 December 1983
WESTON, MASSACHUSETTS.   A daughter, Rose Katherine, is born to Kathleen (Kennedy) and David Townsend. She is their third daughter and is born at home.

25 April 1984
PALM BEACH, FLORIDA.   David Kennedy, 28, is found dead in Room 107 at the Brazilian Court Hotel. The hotel secretary finds him after receiving a phone call from a "Mrs. Kennedy" who said that he had not arrived in Boston on the flight he was expected to take. The cause of death is not immediately clear, although David's history of drug problems is known. Police find 1.3 grams of cocaine in his wallet. Kennedy had been staying at the posh Brazilian Court while visiting his grandmother, Rose Kennedy, at her estate on Ocean Boulevard.

27 April 1984
BROOKLINE, MASSACHUSETTS.   David Kennedy is buried in the family plot at Holyhood Cemetery.

16 May 1984
PALM BEACH, FLORIDA.   Police arrest and charge David Dorr and Peter Marchant, bellhops at the Brazilian Court Hotel, in connection with the death of David Kennedy. Both had left Florida to vacation with their families in New England for the summer.

NEW YORK.   Stephen E. Smith, Jr., graduates from the Columbia University School of Law with a Doctor of Laws degree.

Courtesy Dennis Reggie.

Kathleen Kennedy Townsend with husband, David, and daughters (l. to r.) Meaghan, Kate, and Maeve.

19 May 1984

PURCHASE, NEW YORK. At graduation exercises at Manhattanville College, Joan (Bennett) Kennedy delivers the commencement address and is awarded an honorary Doctor of Humane Letters degree. The citation accompanying her degree says, "Today we recognize the quiet courage of one who confronted serious illness and personal tragedy, of one who has prevailed against circumstances to emerge victor rather than victim." In her address, Joan Kennedy reflects on her years at Manhattanville, the mores of society then, her life after graduation as the wife of a U.S. senator, and her experience as a candidate for a master's degree years later. "The most important thing I can share with you," she

tells the graduating students, "is the personal knowledge that decisions are not irrevocable, that choices...can be remade. And there is time—time to shape a balance between family and friends, work and career over the course of your entire lives."

20 May 1984

CHARLOTTESVILLE, VIRGINIA. Michael LeMoyne Kennedy receives a Doctor of Laws degree from the University of Virginia School of Law.

24 May 1984

PALM BEACH, FLORIDA. An official autopsy report on the death of David Kennedy released by the

Palm Beach County Prosecutor's office says that young Kennedy died of "drug intoxication from a combination of cocaine and the prescription drugs Demerol and Mellaril." His death is ruled an "accident." The report was signed on 3 May 1984 by Palm Beach Medical Examiner James Benz.

3 June 1984
MIDDLETOWN, CONNECTICUT. Edward Kennedy, 22, graduates from Wesleyan University with a Bachelor of Arts degree in American Studies.

6 July 1984
WASHINGTON, D.C. A daughter, Kyle Frances, is born to Victoria (Gifford) and Michael LeMoyne Kennedy. She is their second child and first daughter.

19 July 1984
SAN FRANCISCO. At the Democratic National Convention held at the Moscone Convention Center, Senator Edward M. Kennedy introduces the party's presidential nominee, Walter F. Mondale, and praises Mondale's choice of Representative Geraldine H. Ferraro of New York as his running mate.

2 September 1984
MOUNT KISCO, NEW YORK. A son, Robert Francis III, is born to Emily (Black) and Robert Francis Kennedy, Jr., at Northern Westchester Hospital. He is their first child.

20 November 1984
WASHINGTON, D.C. The first Robert F. Kennedy Human Rights Award is conferred on the Co-Madres (The Committee of Mothers and Relatives of political prisoners, disappeared and murdered in El Salvador), on the anniversary of his fifty-ninth birthday. Established by the Robert F. Kennedy Memorial Foundation, the award annually honors those who have made a significant contribution to human rights.

27 November 1984
NEW YORK. Robert F. Kennedy is posthumously honored at the African-American Institute's thirtieth anniversary dinner held at the Waldorf-Astoria Hotel. Bishop Desmond Tutu presents the award to Senator Edward Kennedy, who accepts on behalf of the family.

[?]. December 1984
BEQUIA, WEST INDIES. Christopher Lawford, 29, marries Jeanne Olsson, also 29.

22 December 1984
ADDIS ABABA, ETHIOPIA. Senator Edward Kennedy and his children Kara and Ted end their tour that began four days ago of camps set up to provide famine relief. The Kennedys have visited refugee camps in Mekele, Bati, Khartoum, Kassala, and El Obeid.

24 December 1984
LOS ANGELES. Peter Sydney Lawford, 61, dies at Cedars of Sinai Hospital of medullary failure as a consequence of hepato-renal syndrome and cirrhosis. He resided at 1275 N. Havenhurst Drive.

20 January 1985
WASHINGTON, D.C. President Ronald Reagan and Vice-President George Bush begin their second term of office.

28 January 1985
NEW YORK. *People* magazine carries Senator Edward Kennedy's first-person account of his tour of famine-stricken Ethiopia as its cover story. The article appears in diary form, covering the days between 19 December and 26 December 1984. Kennedy donates his fee for the story to charity.

28 March 1985
HEMPSTEAD, NEW YORK. A three-day conference on the presidency of John F. Kennedy begins at Hofstra University, the largest scholarly gathering yet to analyze the record of the Kennedy administration. Speakers include Dave Powers, Walter Heller, Arthur Schlesinger, Jr., and Senator Edward Kennedy.

28 May 1985
NEW YORK. Robert Kennedy, Jr., a 1982 graduate of the University of Virginia Law School, passes his exams and is admitted to the bar of the state of New York.

20 August 1985
BOSTON. Caroline Kennedy becomes a member of the commission established by the state to plan a memorial to the late President John F. Kennedy.

26 August 1985
NEW YORK. Caroline Kennedy, 27, enrolls in Columbia University Law School. She has worked previously at the Metropolitan Museum of Art as a researcher.

3 September 1985
NEW YORK. Maria Shriver, 29, is named coanchor of CBS *Morning News*, a 2-hour network program that

begins daily at 7 A.M. Maria began her broadcasting career in 1977 as a newswriter/producer for KYW-TV in Philadelphia. The next year, she moved to a Baltimore television station, and in 1980, she left to join the presidential campaign of Senator Edward M. Kennedy. After working on special projects for an Atlanta TV station, in September 1981 she joined *PM Magazine* as a national correspondent. Two years later, she became a reporter for the Los Angeles bureau of CBS News.

4 November 1985

CAMBRIDGE, MASSACHUSETTS. Jacqueline (Kennedy) Onassis, along with Caroline and John Jr., attends the dedication of a public park next to Harvard University in honor of the late President Kennedy.

8 December 1985

NEW YORK. The engagement of Timothy Shriver, 26, to Linda Potter, is announced. Ms. Potter, an attorney in the city, is a graduate of the Vanderbilt University Law School.

19 December 1985

BOSTON. Two local television stations broadcast a paid five-minute message in which Senator Edward Kennedy announces that he will not be a candidate for the Democratic nomination for president in 1988. "I know that this decision means that I may never be president," he says, "but the pursuit of the presidency is not my life. Public service is." He also announces that he will seek re-election to the Senate in 1988. Associates say that Kennedy believed he could win the party's nomination but not the popular election.

THE NEW GENERATION
1986-PRESENT

19 January 1986

CAMBRIDGE, MASSACHUSETTS. "My name is Joe Kennedy and I've come home to the city of my ancestors, and the district of my birth, to run for the Congress of the United States." With this declaration, the 33-year-old Joseph P. Kennedy II becomes the first member of the "new generation" of Kennedys to seek public office. He announces his candidacy for the Democratic nomination as representative from Massachusetts's Eighth Congressional District at VFW Post 8818. This is the seat being vacated by House Speaker Thomas P. "Tip" O'Neill at the end of the current term.

In his speech, Joe Kennedy recounts the history of the seat—it had been held by his uncle John F. Kennedy and his great-grandfather John "Honey Fitz" Fitzgerald—and says he views the campaign not as a contest but an "opportunity." He devotes himself to answering three questions: What are his qualifications, where does he stand on important public issues, and what kind of future does he want for America?

Joe recalls the family tradition of politics and public life and the values instilled in him early. The family's good fortune, he says, imposed upon the children "a very special duty to the less fortunate." He reviews his experience with the Community Service Administration, the federal antipoverty agency in Washington, D.C., and with the Citizens Energy Corporation. Nationally, he says, he would reduce the country's deficit by cutting the defense budget, eliminate weapons systems that add nothing to American security, and see to "efficient, cost-conscious management" in government. As for the future, Joe declares that to meet new problems, government must find new ways for inscribing "on its own banner the high purpose and moral conviction for which this country stands—and then liberate the vast, untapped energies of the American people to pursue them."

6 February 1986

MOSCOW. Senator Edward M. Kennedy concludes a visit to the Soviet Union where he met with General Secretary Mikhail S. Gorbachev to discuss arms limitations and the emigration of Jews from Russia, among other issues.

2 March 1986

NEW YORK. The engagement of Caroline Kennedy, 29, to Edwin Arthur Schlossberg, 41, is announced. Schlossberg is a graduate of Birch Wathen, a private school in New York. He has received doctorates from Columbia University in literature and in science, has written or coauthored nine books, and currently owns a firm that designs museum exhibits. He has homes in New York and Chester, Massachusetts. Schlossberg, who is Jewish, is the son of Mae and Alfred Schlossberg, the owner of a textile firm. Caroline Kennedy and her fiance met at a party five years ago.

Courtesy Dennis Reggie.

Kathleen Kennedy Townsend, 1986.

4 March 1986

LOS ANGELES. The Los Angeles Police Commission releases a 1,500-page summary of the investigation into the assassination of Robert F. Kennedy. The abridged report states that police investigation found that Sirhan B. Sirhan fired the shots that killed the Senator, that he acted alone, and that there was no evidence of a conspiracy.

7 April 1986

WASHINGTON, D.C. Ted Kennedy, Jr., is among those honored at a Victory of the Human Spirit benefit sponsored by the National Rehabilitation Hospital. The eldest son of Edward and Joan (Bennett) Kennedy is head of a nonprofit Boston organization, Facing the Challenge, that helps the physically disabled.

26 April 1986

HYANNIS PORT, MASSACHUSETTS. Maria Shriver, 31, marries Arnold Schwarzenegger, 38, five-times Mr. Universe and now a movie actor.

TOWSON, MARYLAND. Kathleen Kennedy Townsend announces that she will seek the Democratic nomination for the Second Congressional District in Maryland.

29 May 1986

TOWSON, MARYLAND. Kathleen Kennedy Townsend announces her candidacy for the Democratic nomination for Congress in Maryland's Second Congressional District at the Towson American Legion Post 22, 125 York Road. Kathleen's husband David and their three children are present, as are her mother, Ethel (Skakel) Kennedy, and Kathleen's parents-in-law, Ray and Delores Townsend. State comptroller Louis Goldstein introduces the young candidate.

Kathleen has served as an Assistant Attorney General of Maryland in the Office of Environmental Programs, where she worked with business and government agencies to solve pollution problems in Baltimore and Harford Counties and to clean up the Chesapeake Bay. Kathleen also worked as a policy analyst in the Governor's Office of Human Resources in Massachusetts, where she helped start a program to help place welfare recipients in jobs, and served on the staff of Governor Michael Dukakis' Anticrime Council, where she directed efforts to secure policy enlistments from college students by offering full scholarships to those who agree to serve as policy officers.

In her announcement speech, Kathleen Kennedy Townsend outlines the themes of her candidacy—economic development, the environment, and education are priority issues.

Following the speech, members of the media individually interview the young candidate, who will campaign door-to-door in the Second District.

THE ACADEMIC EDUCATION OF PRESIDENT JOHN F. KENNEDY

Year	Age	Classes Begin	Grade/Level	School
1918	1			
1919	2			
1920	3			
1921	4			
1922	5	12 September	Kindergarten	Edward Devotion School
1923	6	11 September	1	Edward Devotion School
1924	7	29 September	2	Nobles and Greenough Lower School
1925	8	28 September	3	Nobles and Greenough Lower School
1926	9	29 September	4	Dexter School[1]
1927	10	27 September	5	Riverdale Country School
1928	11	26 September	6	Riverdale Country School
1929	12	25 September	7	Riverdale Country School
1930	13	24 September	8 (second form)	Canterbury School[2]
1931	14	29 September	9 (third form)	Choate School
1932	15	3 October	10 (fourth form)	Choate School
1933	16	2 October	11 (fifth form)	Choate School
1934	17	1 October	12 (sixth form)	Choate School[3]
1935	18	7 October	Freshman	London School of Economics and Political Science[2]
		26 October	Freshman	Princeton University[2]
1936	19	28 September	Freshman	Harvard University
1937	20	27 September	Sophomore	Harvard University
1938	21	26 September	Junior	Harvard University[4]
1939	22	25 September	Senior	Harvard University[5]
1940	23	25 September	Graduate	Stanford University[6]

[1]Formerly called Nobles and Greenough Lower School.

[2]Officially withdraws early due to illness.

[3]Graduates 8 June 1935.

[4]Spends second semester of Junior year abroad.

[5]Graduates 20 June 1940.

[6]Leaves school before end of Autumn Quarter (no official withdrawal is made); goes to South America.

THE KENNEDY POLITICAL DYNASTY

	1885	1890	1895	1900	1905	1910	1915	1920	1925	1930
PATRICK JOSEPH KENNEDY										
JOHN FRANCIS FITZGERALD										
JOSEPH PATRICK KENNEDY										
JOHN FITZGERALD KENNEDY										
ROBERT FRANCIS KENNEDY										
EDWARD MOORE KENNEDY										

PATRICK JOSEPH KENNEDY

Mass. State Rep.: Jan. 6, 1886 – Dec. 31, 1890. • Mass. State Senator: Jan. 6, 1892 – Dec. 31, 1893. • Boston Election Commissioner: Dec. 21, 1899 – Apr. 30, 1902. • Boston Wire Commissioner: 1902 – 1908. • Acting Fire Commissioner: Feb 17, 1905 – Mar. 20, 1905.

JOHN FRANCIS FITZGERALD

Boston Councilman: Jan. 4, 1892 – Jan. 3, 1893. • Mass. State Senator: Jan. 4, 1893 – Dec. 31, 1894. • Mass. Congressman: Mar. 4, 1895 – Mar. 3, 1901. • Mayor of Boston: Jan. 1, 1906 – Dec. 31, 1907; Feb. 7, 1910 – Jan. 31, 1914. • Mass. Congressman: Mar. 4, 1919 – Oct. 23, 1919. • Member, Boston Port Authority: Feb. 12, 1934 – Nov. 17, 1948.

JOSEPH PATRICK KENNEDY

Chairman, Securities and Exchange Commission: July 2, 1934 – Sept. 23, 1935. • Chairman, U.S. Maritime Commission: Apr. 16, 1937 – Feb. 17, 1938. • U.S. Ambassador, Great Britain and N. Ireland: Mar. 8, 1938 – Nov. 30, 1940.

JOHN FITZGERALD KENNEDY

Mass. Congressman: Jan. 3, 1947 – Jan. 3, 1953. • U.S. Senator (Mass.): Jan. 3, 1953 – Dec. 31, 1960. • U.S. President: Jan. 3, 1961 – Nov. 22, 1963.

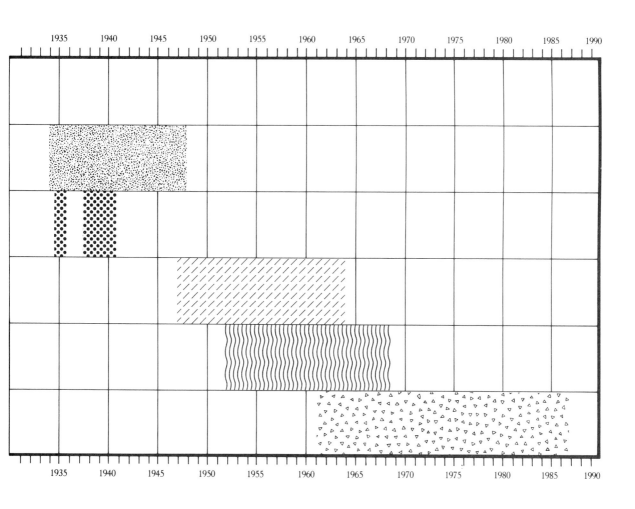

ROBERT FRANCIS KENNEDY

Attorney Advisor, Criminal Div., N.Y.S. Dept. of Justice: Nov. 21, 1951 – Feb. 27, 1952. ● Special Asst. to the Attorney General, Criminal Div., N.Y.S. Dept. of Justice: Feb. 28, 1952 – June 6, 1952. ● Campaign Mgr., J.F.K.'s U.S. Senatorial bid: June 7, 1952 – Nov. 4, 1952. ● Asst. Counsel, State Permanent Subcommittee on Investigations: Jan. 14, 1953 – July 31, 1953. ● Asst. Counsel, Commission on the Reorganization of the Executive Branch (Hoover Commission): Aug. 1953 – Feb. 1954. ● Minority Counsel, Senate Permanent Subcommittee on Investigations: Jan. 5, 1954 – Feb. 25, 1957. ● Chief Counsel and Staff Director, Senate Permanent Subcommittee on Investigations: Jan. 5, 1955 – Feb. 25, 1957. ● Chief Counsel, Senate Select Committee on Improper Activities in Labor or Management Fields: Feb.

26, 1957 – Sept. 10, 1959. ● Campaign Mgr., J.F.K.'s U.S. Presidency bid: Jan. 2, 1960 – Nov. 8, 1960. ● U.S. Attorney General: Jan. 21, 1961 – Sept. 3, 1964. ● U.S. Senator (New York): Jan. 4, 1965 – June 6, 1968.

EDWARD MOORE KENNEDY

Asst. District Attorney (Suffolk County, Mass.): Feb. 6, 1961 – Mar. 14, 1962. ● U.S. Senator (Mass.): Nov. 7, 1962 – .

BIBLIOGRAPHY

Burns, James MacGregor. *Edward Kennedy and the Camelot Legacy.* New York: W. W. Norton, 1976.

Collier, Peter, and David Horowitz. *The Kennedys: An American Drama.* New York: Summit, 1984.

Davis, John H. *The Kennedys: Dynasty and Disaster 1848–1984.* New York: McGraw-Hill, 1984.

Kennedy, Robert F. *To See a Newer World.* New York: Doubleday, 1967.

Kennedy, Rose. *Times to Remember.* New York: Doubleday, 1974.

Koskoff, David. *Joseph P. Kennedy: A Life and Times.* Englewood Cliffs, New Jersey: Prentice-Hall, 1974.

Lieberson, Goddard. *John Fitzgerald Kennedy...As We Remember Him.* New York: Atheneum, 1965.

Martin, Ralph G. *A Hero For Our Time: An Intimate Story of the Kennedy Years.* New York: Macmillan, 1983.

McTaggart, Lynne. *Kathleen Kennedy: Her Life and Times.* New York: Dial, 1983.

Newfield, Jack. *Robert Kennedy, A Memoir.* New York: Dutton, 1969.

O'Donnell, Kenneth P. and David, Powers, with Joe McCarthy. *Johnny, We Hardly Knew Ye.* Boston: Little, Brown, 1972.

Searls, Hank. *The Lost Prince Young Joe, the Forgotten Kennedy.* New York: World Publishing, 1969.

Schlesinger, Arthur M., Jr. *Robert Kennedy and His Times.* Boston: Houghton Mifflin, 1978.

Shepard, Tazewell, Jr. *John F. Kennedy, Man of the Sea.* New York: William Morrow, 1965.

INDEX

* This index is predicated on the John F., Robert F., and Edward M. Kennedy generation and so these qualifiers are meant
to show relationships to them.

THE FITZGERALDS

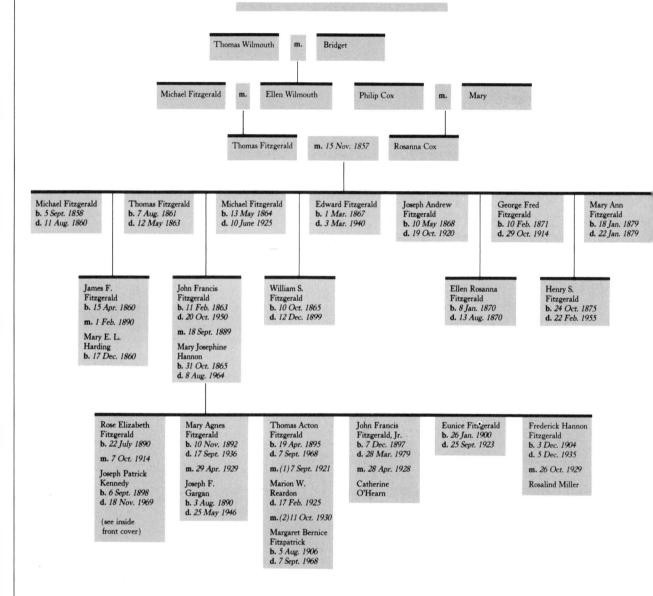

Thomas Wilmouth **m.** Bridget

Michael Fitzgerald **m.** Ellen Wilmouth   Philip Cox **m.** Mary

Thomas Fitzgerald   **m.** *15 Nov. 1857*   Rosanna Cox

Michael Fitzgerald
b. *5 Sept. 1858*
d. *11 Aug. 1860*

Thomas Fitzgerald
b. *7 Aug. 1861*
d. *12 May 1863*

Michael Fitzgerald
b. *13 May 1864*
d. *10 June 1925*

Edward Fitzgerald
b. *1 Mar. 1867*
d. *3 Mar. 1940*

Joseph Andrew
Fitzgerald
b. *10 May 1868*
d. *19 Oct. 1920*

George Fred
Fitzgerald
b. *10 Feb. 1871*
d. *29 Oct. 1914*

Mary Ann
Fitzgerald
b. *18 Jan. 1879*
d. *22 Jan. 1879*

James F.
Fitzgerald
b. *15 Apr. 1860*

m. *1 Feb. 1890*

Mary E. L.
Harding
b. *17 Dec. 1860*

John Francis
Fitzgerald
b. *11 Feb. 1863*
d. *20 Oct. 1950*

m. *18 Sept. 1889*

Mary Josephine
Hannon
b. *31 Oct. 1865*
d. *8 Aug. 1964*

William S.
Fitzgerald
b. *10 Oct. 1865*
d. *12 Dec. 1899*

Ellen Rosanna
Fitzgerald
b. *8 Jan. 1870*
d. *13 Aug. 1870*

Henry S.
Fitzgerald
b. *24 Oct. 1875*
d. *22 Feb. 1955*

Rose Elizabeth
Fitzgerald
b. *22 July 1890*

m. *7 Oct. 1914*

Joseph Patrick
Kennedy
b. *6 Sept. 1898*
d. *18 Nov. 1969*

(see inside
front cover)

Mary Agnes
Fitzgerald
b. *10 Nov. 1892*
d. *17 Sept. 1936*

m. *29 Apr. 1929*

Joseph F.
Gargan
b. *3 Aug. 1890*
d. *25 May 1946*

Thomas Acton
Fitzgerald
b. *19 Apr. 1895*
d. *7 Sept. 1968*

m. *(1) 7 Sept. 1921*

Marion W.
Reardon
d. *17 Feb. 1925*

m. *(2) 11 Oct. 1930*

Margaret Bernice
Fitzpatrick
b. *5 Aug. 1906*
d. *7 Sept. 1968*

John Francis
Fitzgerald, Jr.
b. *7 Dec. 1897*
d. *28 Mar. 1979*

m. *28 Apr. 1928*

Catherine
O'Hearn

Eunice Fitzgerald
b. *26 Jan. 1900*
d. *25 Sept. 1923*

Frederick Hannon
Fitzgerald
b. *3 Dec. 1904*
d. *5 Dec. 1935*

m. *26 Oct. 1929*

Rosalind Miller